The Role of Women in Work and Society in the Ancient Near East

Studies in Ancient Near Eastern Records

General Editor:
Gonzalo Rubio

Editors:
Nicole Brisch, Petra Goedegebuure, Markus Hilgert, Amélie Kuhrt, Peter Machinist, Piotr Michalowski, Cécile Michel, Beate Pongratz-Leisten, D. T. Potts, Kim Ryholt

Volume 13

The Role of Women in Work and Society in the Ancient Near East

Edited by
Brigitte Lion and Cécile Michel

DE GRUYTER

ISBN 978-1-5015-1701-3
e-ISBN (PDF) 978-1-61451-908-9
e-ISBN (EPUB) 978-1-61451-997-3
ISSN 2161-4415

Library of Congress Cataloging-in-Publication Data
A CIP catalog record for this book has been applied for at the Library of Congress.

Bibliographic information published by the Deutsche Nationalbibliothek
The Deutsche Nationalbibliothek lists this publication in the Deutsche Nationalbibliografie; detailed bibliographic data are available on the Internet at http://dnb.dnb.de.

This volume is text- and page-identical with the hardback published in 2016.
Typesetting: Meta Systems Publishing & Printservices GmbH, Wustermark
Printing and binding: CPI books GmbH, Leck
♾ Printed on acid-free paper
Printed in Germany

www.degruyter.com

Foreword

The idea for the conference on *Women in Work and Society* is already ten years old. It was first conceived to be an event open to historians of the classical world, as well as ethnologists. However, historians who specialize in ancient Greece and Rome are much ahead of Assyriologists on the matter of gender studies, and it appeared that it would be interesting to explore the involvement of women in the economy of ancient Mesopotamia.

In January 2012 the French-Japanese project *Le Rôle Economique des Femmes en Mésopotamie Ancienne* (REFEMA, *The Economic Role of Women in Ancient Mesopotamia*) was launched, involving researchers of the team *Histoire et Archéologie de l'Orient Cunéiforme* (HAROC, Archéologies et Sciences de l'Antiquité) in Nanterre and a group of Japanese colleagues from several institutions based in Tokyo, the majority of them belonging to Chuo University.[1] The goal of this project was to use ancient Mesopotamian written sources (3rd–1st millennia BC) to study the various aspects of women as economic agents, both inside and outside the family structure. This program, which lasted three years (2012–2014) was divided into three main themes: the economic role of women in the family, women and external economy, and women and the estate. The four REFEMA workshops, two in France (Nanterre, Carqueiranne) and two in Tokyo, addressed the economic role of women as producers of wealth, both in the private sphere and in large institutions (temples and palaces), as operators in the transmission of estates, and as involved in all types of economic activities, even though they are less attested in this field than men and their transactions often concern smaller quantities.

The conference on *Women in Work and Society* was the closing event of the REFEMA research program. Many colleagues from various countries, including historians, art historians and a historian of law, all specializing in the ancient Near East, were invited to join the small REFEMA team. By gathering colleagues who work on different types of sources, we wanted to look for con-

---

1 The French team was lead by Francis Joannes (University Paris 1 Panthéon-Sorbonne, ArScAn-HAROC) and involved the following Assyriologists: Laura Cousin (University Paris 1 Panthéon-Sorbonne, ArScAn-HAROC), Josué Justel (University of Alcalá, Spain), Bertrand Lafont (CNRS, ArScAn-HAROC), Brigitte Lion (University Lille 3, HALMA), Cécile Michel (CNRS, ArScAn-HAROC) and Gauthier Tolini (ArScAn-HAROC). The Japanese team was conducted by Fumi Karahashi (Chuo University) and involved the following colleagues from Tokyo's various institutions: Eiko Matsushima (Hôsei University), Ichiro Nakata (Ancient Orient Museum, Chuo University), Yoko Watai (Chuo University) and Masamichi Yamada (Chuo University). An issue of the journal *Orient* was edited by Fumi Karahashi with contributions of nine members of this project (Orient 51, 2016).

stants, evolutions, and to show how each society produces its own gender categories. This book, as well as the conference, follows a chronological order, and its chapters cover the three millennia of Mesopotamian history.

Participants to the conference on November 6, 2014, in front of the Maison Archéologie et Ethnologie, Nanterre.

Acknowledgements

The conference, as well as this volume, would not have been possible without the help of the following sponsors to whom we extend our thanks: the laboratory *Archéologies et Sciences de l'Antiquité* (ArScAn) and its team *Histoire et Archéologie de l'Orient Cunéiforme* (HAROC), the institute housing the laboratory *Maison de l'Archéologie et de l'Ethnologie René-Ginouvès* (MAE, Nanterre), the National Center of Scientific Research (CNRS), the Universities of Paris 1 Panthéon – Sorbonne, Paris Ouest Nanterre La Défense and Charles-de-Gaulle Lille 3, the laboratory *Histoire, Archéologie, Littérature des Mondes Anciens* at Lille, the Groupement d'Intérêt Scientifique (GIS) *Institut du Genre*, the *Institut Emilie du Châtelet* within the frame of the Domaine d'Intérêt Majeur in Île-de-France, and last but not least, the *Agence Nationale de la Recherche* and the *Japanese Society for the Promotion of Science*, which have both sponsored the French-Japanese REFEMA research program between January 2012 and December 2014.

We address our warmest thanks to Gonzalo Rubio who accepted this volume for publication within the SANER series, Timothy Leonard who polished the English of all the contributions, the two anonymous referees who read the volume and gave constructive feedback to the authors, John Whitley and Lena Ebert for their work on this volume.

Contents

Foreword — v

Acknowledgements — vii

Brigitte Lion and Cécile Michel
Women and Work in the Ancient Near East: An introduction — 1

Catherine Breniquet
Weaving, Potting, Churning: Women at work during the Uruk period
Evidence from the cylinder seals — **8**

Camille Lecompte
Representation of Women in Mesopotamian Lexical Lists — 29

Fumi Karahashi
Women and Land in the Presargonic Lagaš Corpus — 57

Maria Giovanna Biga
The Role of Women in Work and Society in the Ebla Kingdom (Syria, 24th century BC) — 71

Massimo Maiocchi
Women and Production in Sargonic Adab — 90

Adelheid Otto
Professional Women and Women at Work in Mesopotamia and Syria (3rd and early 2nd millennia BC): The (rare) information from visual images — 112

Bertrand Lafont
Women at Work and Women in Economy and Society during the Neo-Sumerian Period — 149

Agnès Garcia-Ventura
The Sex-Based Division of Work *versus* Intersectionality: Some strategies for engendering the Ur III textile work force — 174

Cécile Michel
Women Work, Men are Professionals in the Old Assyrian Archives — 193

Jerrold S. Cooper
The Job of Sex: The social and economic role of prostitutes in ancient Mesopotamia — 209

Jana Matuszak
"She is not fit for womanhood": The Ideal Housewife According to Sumerian Literary Texts — 228

Ichiro Nakata
Economic Activities of *nadītum*-Women of Šamaš Reflected in the Field Sale Contracts (MHET II/1–6) — 255

Katrien De Graef
Cherchez la femme!
The Economic Role of Women in Old Babylonian Sippar — **270**

Nele Ziegler
Economic Activities of Women According to Mari Texts (18th century BC) — 296

Sophie Démare-Lafont
Women at Work in Mesopotamia: An attempt at a legal perspective — 310

Matteo Vigo
Sources for the Study of the Role of Women in the Hittite Administration — 328

Brigitte Lion
Work and Gender in Nuzi Society — 354

Josué J. Justel
Women in Economic Agreements: Emarite sale contracts (Syria, 13th century BC) — 371

Masamichi Yamada
The *kubuddā'u*-Gift in the Emar Texts — 388

Eiko Matsushima
Women in Elamite Royal Inscriptions: Some observations — 416

Virginie Muller
Women and their Activities in Divinatory Texts — 429

Saana Svärd
Studying Gender: A Case study of female administrators in Neo-Assyrian palaces — 447

Francis Joannès
Historiography on Studies Dedicated to Women and Economy during the Neo-Babylonian Period — 459

Louise Quillien
Invisible Workers: The role of women in textile production during the 1st millennium BC — 473

Yoko Watai
Economic Activities of Women in 1st Millennium Babylonia — 494

Laura Cousin
Beauty Experts: Female perfume-makers in the 1st millennium BC — 512

Julien Monerie
Women and Prebends in Seleucid Uruk — 526

Violaine Sebillotte Cuchet
Women and the Economic History of the Ancient Greek World: Still a challenge for gender studies — 543

Index of professions and activities — 565

Brigitte Lion and Cécile Michel

Women and Work in the Ancient Near East: An introduction

Women have been a subject for historians for more than half a century. In Europe, an important step was the publication in 1990 (in Italy) and 1991 (in France) of the five-volume *L'Histoire des femmes en Occident* (History of Women in the West), under the direction of two French historians, Georges Duby and Michèle Perrot. However, as the title suggests, this important work did not include the Ancient Near East; the first volume, concerning Antiquity, directed by Pauline Schmitt-Pantel, was limited to Greek and Roman history. For Mesopotamian history, following the pioneering work of Jean Bottéro (1965), there have been two *Rencontres Assyriologiques Internationales*, one devoted to women (Durand 1987) and another to sex and gender (Parpola and Whiting 2002), and a great deal of limited historical studies on women and gender, but still few syntheses.[1]

The topic of work has not been much addressed in these studies. Economic history is well-developed in Assyriology, thanks to the hundreds of thousands of tablets recording administrative operations, contracts and letters. Most of these tablets deal with the management of institutions in which numerous workers were employed. Private archives have yielded loans, purchases, and hiring and leasing contracts. Letters, in particular those of merchants, are a great source for the study of local and international trade. However, all these texts were mainly written by men and concern primarily men, even if women could also have been involved in such activities. Despite this extensive documentation, up to now, the history of work in the ancient Near East did not much include the female aspects.[2]

1 See, however, Lesko 1989, and the very important synthesis by Bahrani 2001; for other historiographic overviews, see also Lion 2007, Michel 2015 and Svärd in this volume.

2 See, for example, the synthesis presented by Warburton 2005, and, most recently, the impressive volume by Steinkeller and Hudson 2015 – in which Jursa pays however some attention to tavern-keepers and wet-nurses (2015: 368–369).

Acknowledgements: We address our warmest thanks to Jerry Cooper who kindly corrected the English of this introduction.

Brigitte Lion, Université Lille 3 – UMR HALMA 8164; brigitte.lion@univ-lille3.fr
Cécile Michel, CNRS, Archéologies et Sciences de l'Antiquité, Nanterre; cecile.michel@mae.cnrs.fr

This is perhaps linked to the way the term "work" has been understood for a long time. It has many definitions, but is often quite widely referred to as an activity whose aim is to produce something, and which might be rewarded by a salary. With that meaning, the census in France distinguishes active people from inactive people, and farmers' wives, for example, were not recognized as active until the seventies because they did not earn wages. But even if they do not get out of the house, women have occupations, in particular domestic activities: An "inactive woman," who only performs domestic tasks, works about forty hours a week.[3] These occupations are not always socially recognized, and that is perhaps why they have attracted little attention. However, in Mesopotamian societies, like in many others, women were probably the main producers of everyday goods, and this has been progressively taken into account, even if the written data on that topic is not very abundant. As S. Pollock stated, "While feminists have embraced the concern with what households do, they have also stressed the importance of focusing on household composition, pointing out that the household is almost always a primary locus of women's labor" (Pollock 1999: 24–25).

However, the idea that women have an important role in the household has sometimes been emphasized. In Greek Antiquity, Xenophon (*Oeconomicus*, 7) makes a gender division of labor: women are "adapted" to inside work, and men to outside work. Such a distinction is not "natural," of course, despite Xenophon's presentation of it, and it is far from universal.[4] Some Sumerian literary texts, for example dialogues and proverbs copied during the scribal curriculum, may point to the same conceptions: the qualities expected from a wife were related to her capacity to manage the household, and to be a good domestic administrator who is able to contribute to the family's welfare (Jana Matuszak). This is true in general until the end of the Neo-Babylonian period, during which the activities of a majority of women of urban families are limited to the domestic household (Yoko Watai). Women were also, to a great extent, held responsible for harmony in marriage, in the family, and in the household (Virginie Muller).

Even when women work outside the home, the kind of jobs they take are often considered as a ("natural?") prolongation of their domestic activities, as for example child care, domestic tasks, etc. Nowadays, investigations in France highlight jobs in which there is a huge majority of women, contrasted to jobs from which they are nearly absent. Some examples are given in the following table:[5]

3 Maruani 2004, 176, n. 9, mentioning a study by Annie Fouquet.

4 Even in ancient Greece, there are other opinions, see for example Plato, *Republic*.

5 Source: Ministère du Travail, de l'Emploi, de la Formation Professionnelle et du Dialogue Social, *Dares, Analyses*, décembre 2013, no. 079; the percentages are given for the year 2011.

Tab. 1: Percentages of women in various jobs in France in 2011.

jobs	% of women
child and home assistants	97.7 %
secretaries	97.6 %
domestic employees	94.3 %
healthcare assistants	90.4 %
nurses	87.7 %
construction workers	2.2 – 4 %
car mechanics	2.1 %
drivers of excavators or cranes	1 %

In Mesopotamia, women's production in households sometimes exceeded the family needs and was then integrated into trade networks. Their production was rewarded by silver, but they were not considered professionals (Cécile Michel). Independent persons, such as inn-keepers, seemed to reproduce at a wider scale the tasks of the housekeepers, like preparing beer and food. In the same way, many women worked within the frame of large institutions and received rations in exchange for their work, but it is no surprise to find that, very often, women were employed in the broad sectors of food-processing (as millers: Agnès Garcia-Ventura, Bertrand Lafont) and textiles (especially as weavers: Agnès Garcia-Ventura, Bertrand Lafont, Massimo Maiocchi, Louise Quillien). These same "feminine" tasks are often depicted on cylinder-seals (Adelheid Otto), even though the economic world in general is usually not represented (Catherine Breniquet). The professions linked to these sectors, textile worker and inn-keeper, are also the only female jobs to be mentioned in law collections, together with the wet-nurse (Sophie Démare-Lafont). The case of prostitution is under debate: it has been described as involving an activity that most other women performed only at home, with their husbands (Jerrold Cooper).

Despite this pronounced distribution, only the job of wet nurse can be considered to be exclusive to one sex. All the others are gendered, and each society produces its own conceptions of what is masculine or feminine, even in the field of work. That's why, in different places and at different moments of Mesopotamian history, we also find male textile workers, and male brewers and cooks (Brigitte Lion, Cécile Michel). During the Neo-Babylonian period, men and women alike seem to have produced textiles (Louise Quillien). And we find women in domains which were previously thought mainly masculine, in jobs that require physical strength, like boat haulers and brick transporters (Bertrand Lafont).

A specific context can also reverse the usual tendencies. For example, in time of war, when all men are recruited as soldiers, women have to replace them and take charge of the production centers; this reality was extensively studied in contemporary history for the two World Wars. What was the situation in Mesopotamia when men were enlisted as soldiers? The role of women in production did certainly increase, for example in agricultural exploitation, but it was not always recorded in written records. Outside the context of war, Bertrand Lafont has shown that, according to Neo-Sumerian sources, when servile men escaped, their sisters or wives might be obliged to replace them at work, without any consideration of their gender. And, interestingly, in Garšana, men performing tasks usually assigned to women received the same compensation as women.

Mesopotamia also offers examples of women experiencing a certain degree of confinement, such as royal wives and concubines on the one hand (the best-known examples being Mari and the Neo-Assyrian palaces, see Saana Svärd and Nele Ziegler), and consecrated women on the other, especially the Old Babylonian *nadītums* (see Katrien de Graef and Ichiro Nakata) – without any masculine equivalent in either case. In that context, to avoid contact with too many men, it happened that some women were engaged in professions that were usually rather monopolized by men, especially professions requiring education, like physicians (Maria Giovanna Biga, Nele Ziegler)[6] and scribes (Lion 2011); Camille Lecompte has noticed that the existence of female scribes during the Old Babylonian period had an impact on the contemporaneous lexical lists which give more space to feminine professions. Female metalworkers and seal cutters are also attested in Neo-Assyrian palaces.[7] During the 3rd millennium, female workers seem to be especially numerous on large estates belonging to queens or princesses, in Girsu (Fumi Karahashi) or Garšana (Bertrand Lafont). In Ebla, the queen was also at the head of an estate, but her personnel do not seem to be clearly gender-oriented (Maria Giovanna Biga), and in the Neo-Assyrian period, the *šakintu* who was managing the wealth and household of the queen had both male and female slaves (Saana Svärd). However, in the Hittite kingdom, women of the royal court were active in the management of the palace together with men (Matteo Vigo).

Apart from their occupations and jobs, following one of the main axes of research developed during the REFEMA program, other aspects of the implication of women in economic life have been taken into account, as operators in

---

6 See also the text from Old Babylonian Larsa, TCL 10, 107:26, 1(BARIGA) ŠE *ša a-na* ^{d}*Ki-it-um-li-iz-zi-iz* ^{munus}A-ZU *ad-di-nu*, “1 BARIGA grain which I gave to Littum-lizziz, the female doctor.”
7 SAA 7, 24: rev.5, 15 ^{MUNUS}SIMUG^{MEŠ} ^{MUNUS}GAR-U-U^{MEŠ}, “15 female smiths and stone-borers.”

the transmission of wealth, be it movable goods or real estate. In Old Sumerian Girsu, high-ranking female personal received subsistence land, as well as men (Fumi Karahashi). During the Neo-Sumerian Period, elite women owned their properties and managed them freely (Bertrand Lafont). The situation of consecrated women during the Old Babylonian period is especially well-known: the *nadītums* bought, inherited and received as dowries fields which they then leased (Katrien De Graef, Ichiro Nakata). Documents from Emar show married women controlling property, even if their transactions often concern smaller amounts than those of men (Josué Justel, Masamichi Yamada). In Seleucid Uruk, rich women of the local elite even sold and purchased prebend shares without interference from their male relatives (Julien Monerie).

Some of these examples show that women, as well as men, had full capacity as economic agents. In that case, is gender still an important category? It is, at least, not the only category to take into account: "other socio-culturally constructed categories, such as race, class, and ethnicity, intersect with and transform gender."[8] For our topic, as far as written documentation of historical periods is concerned, ethnicity may sometimes be important (Massimo Maiocchi, Laura Cousin). The status of people (slave or free, religious or lay persons), the milieu in which they are born and live (city or countryside, private household or institutional organization, nuclear family or larger family unit), and their age also matter (Francis Joannès, Yoko Watai). Class is probably one of the most visible criteria: women who developed the same agency as men are, very often, members of elite groups (Violaine Sébillotte Cuchet), distinguished by prestigious religious offices, by wealth, by high-ranking positions in administration or at court (Saana Svärd), or by family links with the rulers (Maria Giovanna Biga, Eiko Matsushima, Adelheid Otto). In the workplace, the question of hierarchies was important: female workers were supervised by male or women overseers, while, in queens' households, female stewards could supervise male workers (Saana Svärd); at the lowest scale, gender was perhaps not always an important category. All this shows that it is necessary to cross-check the data, and to be conscious that gender may be only one among many factors, and not always the most important (Agnès Garcia-Ventura on intersectionality).

***

Creations myths like *Enki and Nimah* (Lambert 2013: 330–345) or *Atra-hasīs* (Lambert and Millard 1969; Foster 2005: 227–280) attest that the gods created

8 Pollock 1999: 24–25. See also Díaz-Andreu 2005.

humankind to discharge themselves from the burden of labor. The Neo-Assyrian version of *Atra-hasīs* insists on the fact that men and women were created at the same time and in the same manner. The conclusion is that men and women alike were created to work. But this aspect, inscribed in the destiny of both men and women from the beginning, seemed to us not to have been taken enough into consideration when it comes to women. We hope that this volume will be a significant contribution to the study of the role of women in work and society.

Bibliography

Bahrani, Zainab. 2001. *Women of Babylon. Gender and representation in Mesopotamia*, London and New York: Routledge.

Bottéro, Jean. 1965. La femme dans la Mésopotamie ancienne. Pp. 158–223 in *Histoire mondiale de la femme*, ed. Pierre Grimal, Paris: Nouvelle librairie de France.

Díaz-Andreu, Margarita. 2005. Gender Identity. Pp. 13–42 in *The Archaeology of Identity. Approaches to gender, age, status, ethnicity and religion*, eds. Margarita Díaz-Andreu, Sam Lucy, Stasa Babic, and David Edwards, London and New York: Routledge.

Durand, Jean-Marie (ed.). 1987. *La femme dans le Proche-Orient antique. XXXIIIe Rencontre assyriologique international (Paris, 7–10 juillet 1986)*, Paris: Éditions Recherche sur les Civilisations.

Foster, Benjamin. 2005. *Before the Muses. An Anthology of Akkadian Literature*, Bethesda: CDL Press.

Jursa, Michael 2015. Labor in Babylonia in the First Millenium BC. Pp. 345–396 in Steinkeller and Hudson 2015. *Western Asia*, Atlanta: Scholars Press.

Lambert, Wilfred G. 2013. *Babylonian Creation Myths*. Mesopotamian Civilizations 16, Winona Lake: Einsebrauns.

Lambert, Wilfred G. and Alan R. Millard. 1969. *Atra-ḫasīs, The Babylonian Story of the Flood*, Oxford: Oxford University Press.

Lesko, Barbara S. (ed.). 1989. *Women's Earliest Records from Ancient Egypt and Western Asia. Proceedings of the Conference on Women in the Ancient Near East, Brown University, Providence, Rhode Island November 5–7, 1987*. Brown Judaic Studies 166, Atlanta: Scholars Press.

Lion, Brigitte. 2007. La notion de genre en assyriologie. Pp. 51–64 in *Problèmes du genre en Grèce ancienne*, eds. Violaine Sébillotte Cuchet and Nathalie Ernoult. Histoire ancienne et médiévale 90, Paris: Publications de la Sorbonne.

Lion, Brigitte. 2011. Literacy and gender. Pp. 90–112 in *Oxford Handbook of Cuneiform Culture*, eds. Karen Radner and Eleanor Robson, Oxford: Oxford University Press.

Maruani, Margaret. 2004. Travail et genre: les tribulations de la variable sexe. Pp. 171–187 in *Quand les femmes s'en mêlent. Genre et pouvoir*, eds. Christine Bard, Christian Baudelot, and Janine Mossuz-Lavau, Paris: La Martinière.

Michel, Cécile. 2015. Quelle place occupent les femmes dans les sources cunéiformes de la pratique ? *Les Nouvelles de l'Archéologie* 140, Juin 2015, 46–50, http://nda.revues.org/3019.

Parpola, Simo and Robert M. Whiting (eds.). 2002. *Sex and Gender in the Ancient Near East. Proceedings of the XLVIIe Rencontre assyriologique internationale, Helsinki*, Helsinki: The Neo-Assyrian Text Corpus Project.

Pollock, Susan. 1999. *Ancient Mesopotamia. The Eden that Never Was*, Cambridge: Cambridge University Press.

Schmitt-Pantel, Pauline (ed.). 1991. *Histoire des femmes en Occident. I – L'Antiquité*, Paris: Plon.

Steinkeller, Piotr and Michael Hudson (eds.). 2015. *Labor in the Ancient World*, Dresden: ISLET (Institute for the Study of Long-term Economic Trends).

Warburton, David. 2005. Working. Pp. 185–198 in Daniel C. Snell, *A Companion to the Ancient Near East*, Oxford: Blackwell.

Catherine Breniquet

Weaving, Potting, Churning: Women at work during the Uruk period

Evidence from the cylinder seals

Over the last few decades, contemporary history has set the agenda for understanding past societies, focusing on new goals such as ethnicity or gender. All chronological periods of history are concerned. Especially field research concerning women has been active since World War II in English-speaking countries. Some propaganda posters showing women replacing men in factories have begun to be studied as art history documents. In fact, since women were associated with production with World War I, and got voting rights in the first half of the 20th century, they have become more visible in society. However, their economic role has been major since Antiquity. Even if a perfect consensus hasn't already come out among scholars, this new research theme brought new light to the social or economic role of women in ancient societies.

In the field of the Near Eastern studies, we are very much indebted to the pioneering work of Julia Asher-Greve for opening the door to these modern approaches since the 70s.[1] Specifically using texts, archaeology and visual arts, she was able to emphasize both the role of women in society and their representation in the ancient Near East. Many specialized conferences and publications followed suit.[2] However, if gender studies are the domain English-language research, French scholars focus much more on the social and economic roles of women in the ancient Near East, following in some ways M. Stol (1995). This seems to be a wise position as many ancient societies didn't have such a dualistic, male/female, view of themselves. Many other paradigms such as age, ethnic origin, social status or rank, could be key for understanding these societies.

The global approach of this conference is particularly suitable for collaborations between historians and archaeologists. Within this framework, we chose to explore the economic role of women in the Uruk period, as seen from

1 Asher-Greve 1985. For a complete bibliographical survey, see Asher-Greve 2013.
2 Bahrani 2001. Parpola and Whiting 2002.

Catherine Breniquet, Université Blaise-Pascal Clermont 2;
catherine.breniquet@univ-bcpclermont.fr

the cylinder seals. It is well known that our main iconographic source comes from cylinder seals for the ancient Near East. Especially those from the Uruk period offer the richest diversity of themes as they show people at work, but also cultic activities or mythological scenes. This is not the case for the later periods of Mesopotamian history.

The general chronology of the Uruk period is still a matter of scientific controversy depending on the stratigraphy and the relative chronology between sites, the acceptance of a late phase of the Ubaid culture (i.e. Ubaid 5 found at Tell el'Oueili), the new calibrated dates coming from recently excavated sites in Greater Mesopotamia, etc. Generally speaking, the Uruk period covers a large part of the 4th millennium BC, from 3700 (4200 for some scholars[3]) to 2900 BC (frequently referred to as Jemdet-Nasr period). We would like to discuss several points here, such as the way women are depicted, the many tasks they perform and the economic interpretation we can make of them. As we shall see, conclusions are not so easy to bring out.

1 The Uruk period

The Uruk period was named after the German excavations of the eponymous site in southern Mesopotamia, which have taken place since the 20s. This period is known to be the first historical period of Mesopotamian history, as writing appeared there for the first time. As we know, this first writing used pictographic signs, and the cuneiform system came about later.

As the first historical period, the Uruk period deals with the origins of the Sumerian civilization. Since the 70s, archaeology has made considerable efforts to shed light on the prehistory of Mesopotamia. Despite the problems brought about by the natural setting of sites in the alluvial plain, which made exploration difficult, if not impossible,[4] and the aridity of archaeological records, it is now admitted that the Uruk period is deeply rooted in the previous one, the Ubaid.[5] From at least 5000 BC, the increasing complexity of that society brought up the emergence of complex "chiefdoms", probably organized on kinship and "conical clans".[6] The most impressive evidence is the erection of monumental architectural edifices on several sites, probably built by the *corvée*

3 Wright and Rupley 2001.
4 Sanlaville 1989; Pournelle 2007.
5 Huot 2005.
6 Adams 1966.

workers by the request of the chiefs.[7] Other proof could be found in the development of craft production performed by specialists, especially for ceramics, which tend to be made with new tools such as the slow wheel, and began to be less decorated. These products were probably stored in central places and redistributed to sustain the power of the chiefs. The pre- and proto-literate periods in southern Mesopotamia (i.e. the Uruk period and the Early Dynastic) are the final steps of this evolution. They end violently and suddenly with the conquest of the area by Sargon of Agade around 2340 BC, who federated by force for the first time the independent cities of the south.

The Uruk period is characterized by the first emergence of the urban way of life which was theorized by the great anthropologist V. Gordon Childe in the 1920s.[8] He had a very limited knowledge of the Mesopotamian archaeology, as the excavations at Uruk had just started at that time. Childe identified the "urban" civilization by different criteria mixed together, such as archaeology (the increasing size of the site, the appearance of monumental architecture, the existence of long-distance exchanges), history (the appearance of the first written records, the payment of taxes and tributes, the appearance of exact sciences), economy (the development of crafts, the mass-produced objects such as beveled-rim bowls), and visual arts with the appearance of the first narrative scenes with realistic representations on cylinder seals and sculptures in the round. This general theory had been criticized for being too evolutionist and too linked with the emergence of the pristine states, and was improved many times.[9] However, it still gives the general frame of the understanding of the Uruk period: a new political order, the improving economic role of the main cities (and of their colonies in greater Mesopotamia), the development of crafts and exchanges. Recent studies focus on the development of administration and bureaucracy, and linked together the three main innovations of the period: writing, the cylinder-seal, and the use of a complex system of tokens for recording.[10]

Visual art depictions often represent people involved in different tasks supposed to be "daily" or cultic life. Among them, men and especially a personage called the "King-Priest", who seems to be at the highest social position, are easy to recognize as they are involved in gardening, war and the cult. Most of the iconographic studies discuss the position and activities of this "King-Priest". They connect the scenes with the economic and social transformations

---

7 Forest 1996: 205–210.

8 Childe 1950.

9 Butterlin 2003, for an overview.

10 Pittman 1994; Glassner 2000.

of the period, especially with the emergence of hierarchies and the increasing demand for manufactured goods. It is easy to observe two points. First, the very materialistic or positivist point of view of most of the archaeological studies, which emphasizes the economic dimension of the Uruk period, more or less always connected with the origins of the State. Second, until recently, social archaeology has paid little attention to women. However, women are depicted in the sculpture in the round (the stone face of the Lady of Uruk, for instance, which could be the depiction of the Goddess Inanna) or on cylinder seals, on which the scenes seem to be less official. We shall concentrate on both cylinder seals and women.

2 Cylinder seals

Cylinder seals first appear during the Uruk period. They are among the most important instruments used for recording economic practices in the ancient Near East. Cylinder seals were made from various stones, ordinary or semi-precious ones, with different degrees of hardness, although some may have been made of organic materials such as wood, bone or ivory. For the Uruk period, we have no direct information about seal cutters, workshops or seal owners.[11]

It is often assumed that that cylinder seals replaced the older stamp seals which were previously in use. They are supposed to be more efficient in terms of administrative business as they were rolled over *bullae* containing tokens or tablets. However, in southern Mesopotamia, seals and sealings are very few from the Ubaid period, and no prehistoric impressions with the imprint of a seal have ever been found. We must conclude that this interpretation is too limited. The shape of the object, a cylinder, is probably the main parameter of its agency,[12] replaying the engraved scenes it portrays without a beginning or an end. Although we find true depictions of what is missing in the archaeological records, the world they show is not the real world. This world is an ideal one probably embedded in a cyclic conception of the time. In other words, we can document daily life from these depictions, but we have to keep in mind that they should not be considered to be documents which convey an immediate meaning. A specific approach is therefore needed.

11 Dittmann 2012, for an essay of interpretation.
12 Porada 1993.

Indeed, all the seals are not the same. For the Uruk period, they fall into two main categories, probably linked with specific owners and/or uses. They may reflect different people, offices or dependent domains under the control of the central authority of each city. Unfortunately, all of them, or impressions of them on *bullae* or early tablets are much more numerous than the objects themselves (sometimes with different versions of the same scene), which come from secondary contexts. In Uruk, for instance, when out of use, tablets are reused as filling material for pits, foundations,[13] etc. The largest cylinder seals, often finely incised, depict official scenes with the King-Priest. The other cylinder seals are smaller, more roughly carved or drilled with a specific tool (the "*bouterolle*"). These small seals have a more schematic, sometimes geometric, design than the others do. According to Brandes (1979), they may have been slightly earlier, but the stratigraphy of Uruk remains a matter of discussion. The depictions of women at work we are looking for are found on these small cylinder seals or their imprints. They date from the end of the late fourth into the early third millennium BC.

The Mesopotamian glyptic has been studied until the 21th century, but syntheses remain scarce. Some of them, focusing on early periods, should be mentioned, as they set the general framework of this study. The pioneering work of Pierre Amiet, which deals with the early glyptic of Mesopotamia and Susa (from the first seals to the Akkad period), tries to organize a catalogue of the main scenes and understanding them.[14] R. Boehmer and M. Brandes published the specific data in their studies of the first cylinder seals from Uruk.[15] These three books set the *status quaestionnis*. They present the excavations, contexts, cylinders and impressions. They also try to recognize, classify and interpret the engraved scenes on the cylinders. They provide invaluable information on the matter. However, the identification of the scenes remains a difficult task due to the size of the objects, the schematization of the depictions and often the complex organization of the scenes, mixing several themes and registers together. Last in date, E. Rova's synthesis of the Urukian cylinder seals collects all the occurrences, seals and impressions, and gives an accurate catalogue with new data from the most recent excavations in Greater Mesopotamia.[16] She also tried to organize the catalogue according to a statistical basis which allows the application of factorial analysis on the iconographic material.

---

13 Englund 1998: 34–42.
14 Amiet 1972, 1981.
15 Boehmer 1965; Brandes 1979.
16 Rova 1994.

According to her work, 969 seals or impressions are recorded for the Uruk period, which come from the main sites of the south of Mesopotamia and from Syria, Turkey, Iran, Egypt, etc. We can use this catalogue as a good representation of the archaeological situation, although it is always possible to add some more occurrences from the latest excavations. Rova's catalogue will be used here as a kind of database and will give us a global statistic estimation. Among her collection of one thousand seals or impressions, two thirds have depictions of human beings, both male and female. But things are not so clear.

3 Women on cylinder seals

The first question that arises is how to recognize the women, as most of the depictions are very schematic. J. Asher-Greve previously – and partially – solved this problem.[17] On the basis of sculpture in the round and on some human-shaped seals, she proposed to identify women through several iconographic details (Fig. 1a):

- Their clothes: a long dress, perhaps a single fabric wrapped around the body, and covering a shoulder supposedly the left one (as it is shown on the upper register of the Uruk vase).[18] However, clothing doesn't seem to be generalized as the seal from the Metropolitan Museum of New York (Fig. 1b), unfortunately without context, depicts a nude woman!
- Their long hair held back with a headband, or left free on the shoulders as on the MET seal. Due to this peculiar detail, these women are referred to as "pig-tailed". We shall come back later to this interpretation.
- Their attitude, often depicted as squatting, with a knee up, or in the so-called "worshipper's" kneeling attitude. They can sit on a kind of "platform" (which can be a mud brick platform, a reed mat or wooden furniture, as details are too schematic to reach a conclusion). Although some of them are standing up, too, and walking. Arms are more or less always bent, projected in front of them, with hands raised.

We face a quite different problem for identifying men. Except for the so-called "King-Priest" highly recognizable with his beard, skirt and attitudes of power (fighting with "enemies", travelling in a boat, feeding animals and offering goods to a woman who could be the goddess),[19] men are usually very roughly

17 Asher-Greve 1985: 13.
18 Lindemeyer *et al.* 1993: Taf. 39.
19 Amiet 1981: nos. 609, 651, 655, 656, 659, 661, 662, 1614, 1669.

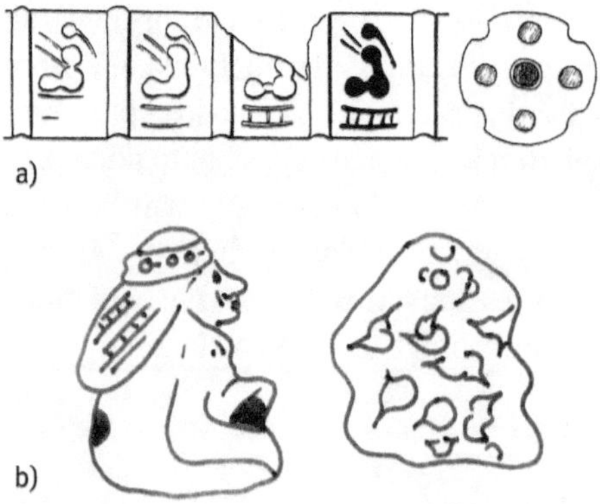

Fig. 1: Pig-tailed women. a) Cylinder seal (Susa, after Rova 1994: nb 438). b) Stone-Stamp Seal in the form of a seated female (top and reverse), Rhodochrosite, Late Uruk-Jemdet Nasr period, 1.5 x 2.3 x 3 cm, Southern Mesopotamia. Metropolitan Museum of New York, Credit Line: Gift of Martin and Sarah Cherkasky, 1988. Accession Number: 1988.380.1. Drawing of the author.

designed, depicted without headdress or clothes. Usually their identification is based on the actions they perform: fishing in the marshes, tending herds in the steppe, gardening with tools, filling storerooms, and manipulating weapons.[20] These scenes probably refer to the official activities of the elite but the identity of the figures is unclear. Mixed scenes with women are rare.

4 Potting or churning?

J. Asher-Greve, following many other scholars, proposed to identify women when involved in several tasks such as crafts (pottery; textile work: spinning or weaving), farming (gardening; tending animals) and religious acts (gestures of worship).[21] From time to time, different activities are mixed in the same image. We shall start with these categories, although this taxonomy is probably incorrect in the details. We suggest here that there is less variety in these scenes than is usually assumed. But first of all, on the basis of these characteristics put together, we can identify without a doubt a hundred representations of women in our basic catalogue. However, most of the depictions are schematic, showing a “naked” ungendered personage. Using the general depiction of

20 Amiet 1981: nos. 203, 267, 268, 280, 618, 1615.
21 Asher-Greve 1985: 11–13.

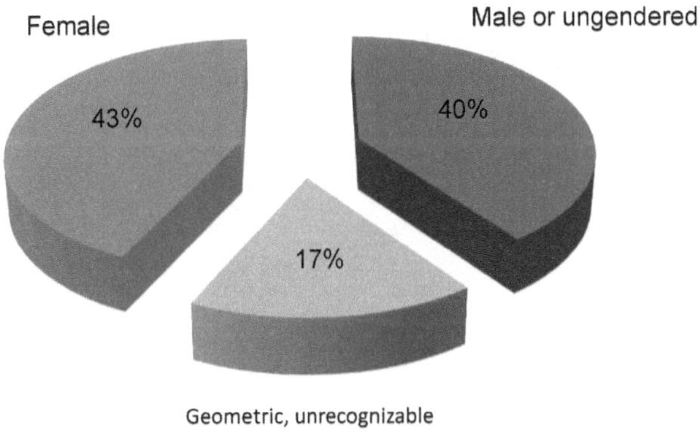

Fig. 2: Statistics about depictions.

the attitude or the activity performed, we can add 68 more seals or impressions from the Rova's catalogue. We obtain there the following table (Fig. 2). It is easy to notice that women represent only a part (less than 50 %) of two thirds of the occurrences from Rova's catalogue. Surprisingly, the other parts are men and ungendered people who could be men or women or both, and geometric or unrecognizable scenes for us, making true statistics difficult.

The professional craftsmanship starts during the Uruk period[22]. The first written records refer to important movements of manufactured objects (exchange, storage, rations, or offering)[23] suggesting that craft production had increased greatly from the Ubaid period. However, these early records remain elusive on many points such as the origin of goods, the craftsmen, their gender, the organization of the production, etc. With this economic paradigm in mind, numerous glyptic art historians proposed to identify women at work, making pottery or handling pots in some scenes.[24] It is true that most of the depictions show a woman in front of a schematic pot, with two handles or a spout (Fig. 3b, d, e, f). Sometimes the pot is reduced to a simple dot or triangle (Fig. 3a, c). None of these depictions could be linked without doubt with pottery making and even the so-called pottery kilns (with their dome-shaped structure) are debatable (Fig. 3h).[25]

During the Uruk period, pottery making starts to be a "professional" work, with specific tools like the potter's wheel which appears more or less at the

22 Stein 1996; Stein and Blackmann 1993.

23 Englund 1998: 44.

24 Amiet 1981: 77–78.

25 Amiet 1981: 102. D'Anna, Desbat and Garcia 2003, 32 for parallels.

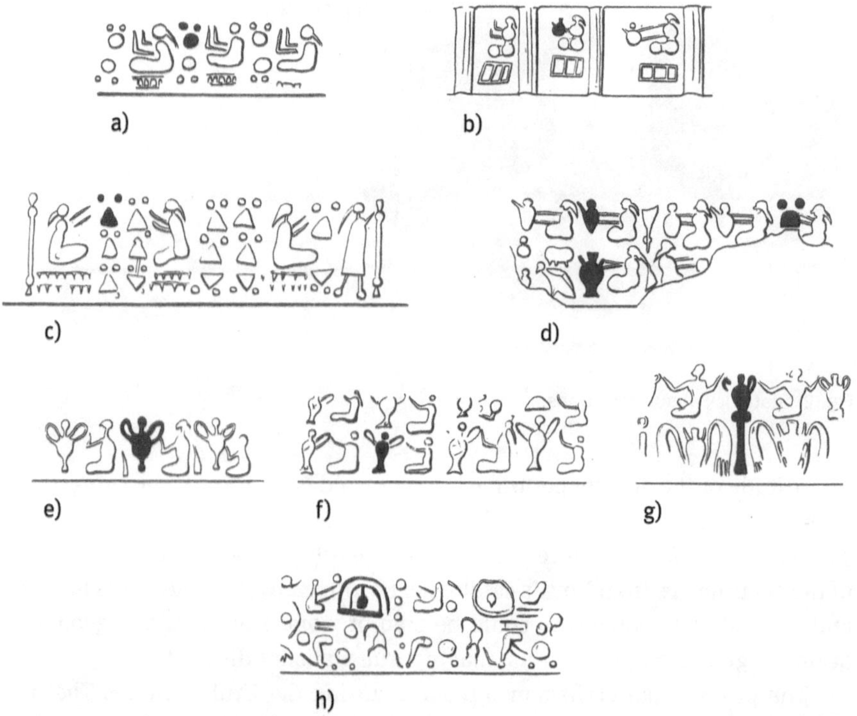

Fig. 3: Potting? a) Habuba Kabira. After Rova 1994: no. 51; b) Telloh. After Rova 1994: no. 798; c) Susa. After Rova 1994: no. 434; d) Susa. After Rova 1994: no. 431; e) Susa. After Amiet 1981: no. 291; f) Unknown provenience. After Amiet 1981: no. 339; g) Susa. After Rova 1994: no. 342; h) Tell Agrab. After Rova 1994: no. 949.

end of the Uruk period.[26] We would suggest identifying this tool on some cylinder-seals where the "pot" (already finished in most cases) is located on the top of an elongated stand which could be the wheel itself (Fig. 3g).[27] However it is not possible to identify women in these scenes, the images themselves can be read both ways, male and female. The depictions are too vague and it is impossible to conclude if the activity is ungendered or if potting starts to be performed by men as a professional activity.

Except for those seals, we suggest using other interpretations: the women could be involved in some activities where pots are required such as brewing beer or churning butter. Women sometimes appear two-by-two, on either side

26 Nissen 1989; Forest 1996: 120.
27 D'Anna, Desbat and Garcia 2003: 13–22 for parallels.

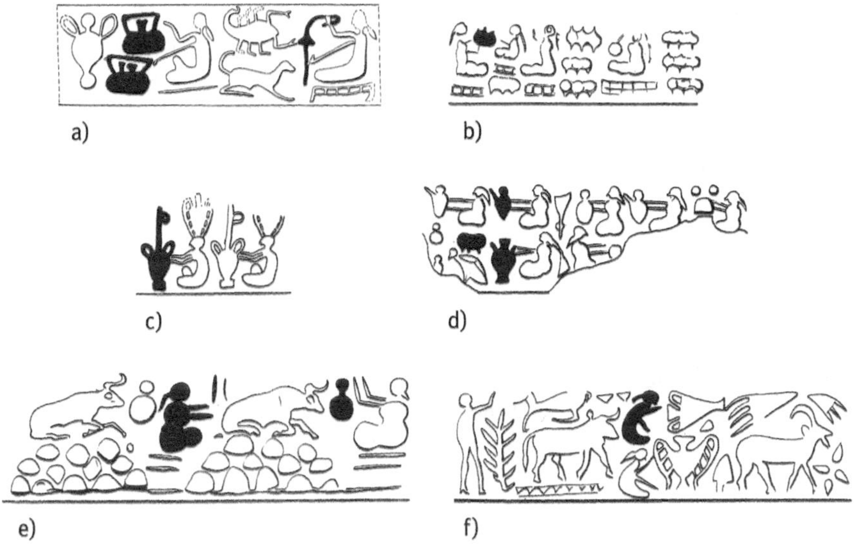

Fig. 4: Churning and farming? a) Choga Mish. After Rova 1994: no. 80; b) Telloh. After Rova 1994: no. 796; c) Choga Mish. After Rova 1994: no. 85; d) Susa. After Rova 1994: no. 431; e) Unknown provenience. After Amiet 1981: no. 312; f) Çatal Hüyük. After Amiet 1981: no. 314

of the pot, maneuvering it. Sometimes, the pot seems to be held by a small stand (Fig. 3e). For us, following Potts in his parallel with contemporary pictograms,[28] these scenes probably refer to churning, and not potting. We know from ethnographic evidence that churns have different forms (quite different from the ones we know in our country): clay pots, wooden pots, skin,[29] etc. They need to be shaken by hand to transform the milk. The churns shown on the Urukian glyptic are double-handed, handled in alternation by two women (Fig. 4a).

Churns appear too as an elongated "bottle" with a kind of spout (Fig. 3e, f), as found in the contemporary archaeological sites.[30] It is not clear if the spout was used to pour liquids or if it was a gripping device as some were upside down or without an opening. Churns can be made also of goat-skin, probably suspended from a wooden tripod which is not depicted due probably to the small size of the seals (Fig. 4b). These churns are suggested by a circular

---

28 Potts 1997: 143–146. Also Englund 1998: 95–98. Vessels in lexical lists seem to be containers for dairy products. Just after vessels, we find cheeses.

29 Bazin and Bromberger 1991; Gouin 1996; Mahias 2010.

30 Breniquet 2014b.

hole, drilled in the stone, with some elongated prolongations made with a cutting tool. Some cylinder seals represent farming or care for animals: women with cattle, apparently outside (Fig. 4e, f). They might be shown milking, the first step of dairy production.

5 Textile work

The textile work is the easier task to recognize,[31] but its depiction on cylinder seals does not shed light on the all technical details.[32] It involves people spinning (Fig. 5a, b) or warping or weaving (Fig. 5c, d, e, f). Tools (spindle whorls and horizontal loom) are sometimes depicted in a realistic manner, sometimes in close association with a spinning animal, a spider, but very often the details are scarce (Fig. 4a, 5f).[33]

Of course they are a simplification as textile work involves many other tasks, from the gathering of the raw material (flax or wool at the Uruk period) to the final embellishment of the fabric. Some of these other steps could be found in different iconographic categories. For instance, some scenes have been interpreted as gardening activities. They depict women walking or standing up holding "flowers" (Fig. 5b, g) close in shape to those depicted on the lower register of the Uruk vase, interpreted as flax.[34] It is honestly impossible to identify without doubt the plants depicted, as they are too schematic. But we should keep in mind that some scenes that are difficult to read could be related to textile fiber processing. Flax and wool were the main weaving materials in the Uruk period, probably connected with different uses (daily life, prestige or religious fabrics)[35]. From this point of view, the depiction of one or two people working together using sticks (?) could correspond to the "airing" of the wool (Fig. 5h).[36]

We suggest that on some more schematic engravings more textile tasks such a spinning with a short distaff and a suspended spindle (Fig. 5a, b), or weaving with different kinds of loom (vertical loom, horizontal loom: Fig. 5c, d, e, f), can be identified. Women involved in these activities are squatting, sitting or standing, alone or two by two. They perform both spinning and weav-

31 Barber 1991: 84.

32 Breniquet 2008: 320–322.

33 Please note that we show only a selection here. For more details, see Breniquet 2008.

34 Crawford 1985; Breniquet 2008: 272–274.

35 Breniquet 2014a.

36 Michel 2014: 239.

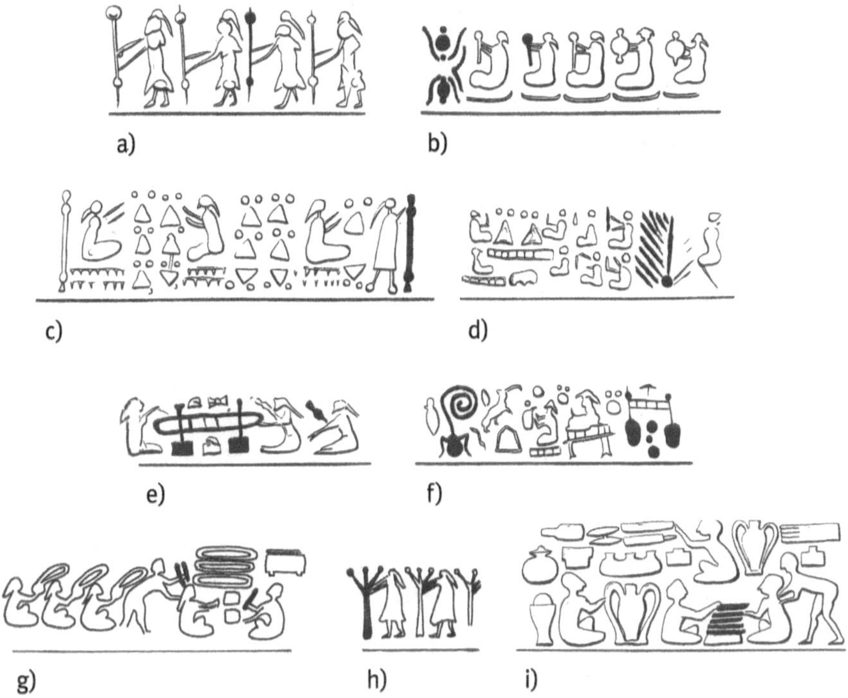

Fig. 5: Textile work: weaving and other tasks. a) Jemdet-Nasr. Spinning. After Amiet 1981: no. 306; b) Susa. Spinning. After Rova 1994: no. 430; c) Susa. Weaving on vertical loom? After Amiet 1981: no. 330; d) Tell Brak. Weaving? After Rova 1994: no. 905; e) Choga Mish. Weaving on horitontal loom. After Amiet 1981: no. 319; f) Ur. Weaving. After Rova 1994: no. 891; g) Ur. Weaving. After Rova 1994: no. 320; h) Susa. Flax processing? After Rova 1994: no. 419; i) Susa. Airing the wool with sticks? After Rova 1994: no. 337.

ing, which is often said to be a feminine task. Details on the location, whether outside or inside, are tiny if not absent. These two main steps of the textile work were probably chosen by the seal cutter because they are relevant of the entire *chaîne opératoire*. Visually speaking they are easy to read. The look of symmetry in the arrangement of the scenes makes it hard to determine how many people were really involved in the different parts of the activity.

6 Women at work

In order to interpret the scenes, the most common paradigm used by scholars is the depiction of daily life and economic activities. Pictures are used for the immediate details they convey. What is unclear or undeveloped in the texts would be clarified by art. We totally agree with the idea that weaving, pottery making and churning were economic necessities in which women were certainly involved in the Uruk period. These three basic activities of weaving, potting and churning were probably the basic "daily" tasks of any Sumerian woman (with household maintenance and care for babies): the production of food, textile and artifacts for the family. We can therefore infer that women were involved in economic production.

However, we are skeptical about an univocal interpretation of iconography. We would suggest a more cautious approach. We suggest first interpreting the "squatting woman" as an iconographic stereotype for "working woman", and not as a realistic depiction of a specific task. This stereotype could be used and adapted to any economic activity mentioned above. But we can try to go further.

An iconographic detail could give the beginning of an explanation. As many ethnographical examples show, women at work with the activities concerned here do not have a pig-tail. On the posters or war paintings from the 20th century, women working in factories have their hair in a net or a kerchief, for reasons of safety and cleanliness.[37] On the contrary, women from the ancient times or from traditional contexts have their hair undone, in order not to "compromise" what they are doing, especially weaving, by uncontrolled knots.[38] This fact shows us a more "symbolic" world where daily activities are embedded in a complex system where craft activities are thought of in terms of creation and not only as economic facts.

We know, from other periods (especially from classical Antiquity[39]) that the depiction of women can be used to convey social ideas in a different way. Their economic role as the good spouse weaving to clothe her family and to participate to the economy of the *oikos* can be emphasized, as well as the image of women designed by men in a men's world (their father's, their husband's, their brothers', etc.): beautiful, elegant in attitude but kept at home, without a role in society, entirely devoted to her husband and children. That is to say, women are depicted according to a masculine perspective.

A preliminary conclusion can be drawn here: most of our cylinder seals involving women at work combine two activities: weaving and spinning (Fig. 6a), churning (rather than potting or even brewing beer as already mentioned) and textile work (« weaving » in a general sense) (Fig. 6b), gardening

37 http://en.wikipedia.org/wiki/Ruby_Loftus_Screwing_a_Breech_Ring.
38 Breniquet 2008: 350–353 for a short synthesis on the matter; for an example in Berber context: Bourdieu 1980: 409.
39 Lissarrague 1991.

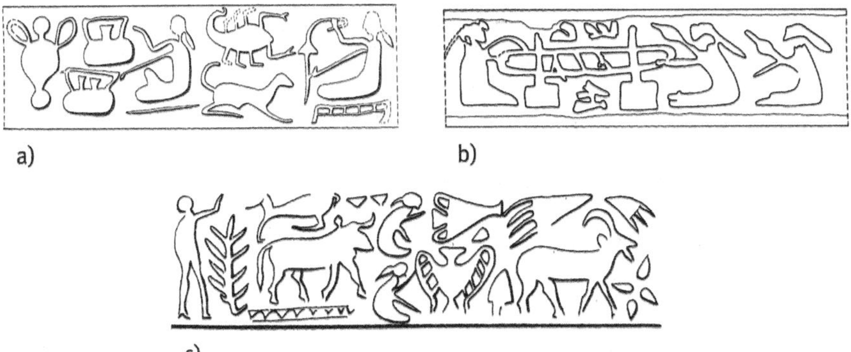

a) b) c)

Fig. 6: Two activities together. a) Choga Mish. Churning and spinning. After Rova 1994: no. 8; b) Choga Mish. Weaving and spinning. After Amiet 1981: no. 319; c) Çatal Hüyük. Male and female tasks? After Amiet 1981: no. 314.

(?) (Fig. 6c). As art has its own language, we can hardly imagine that the graphic organization of the figures has no meaning. Several tracks are emerging and need to be discussed within the framework of historical and ethnographical parameters. These activities can be male and female tasks, but they can also illustrate only feminine tasks in a cyclical organization of labor throughout the year in which daily or gender activities occur. However, it is not possible – in our cylinder seals' iconography – to oppose women at weaving with men at war.

From Mediterranean ethnographic comparisons, in the Berber world for instance, weaving is often thought as the female counterpart of ploughing. This doesn't appear clearly in our documentation as most of the depictions are ungendered (or without any counterpart). Men and women don't appear together at work. However, the association between weaving and ploughing exists later, during the Early Dynastic period.[40] We suggest that the iconographic norms are not fully set up during the Uruk period. During the proto-dynastic period, this iconography changes a little, with the introduction of other steps of the *chaîne opératoire*[41], showing men as craftsmen[42] with new tools and new combinations of weaving and other activities.

Going back to the women at work, due to the agrarian foundations of the Uruk civilization, we wonder too if these feminine activities are not part of a

40 Breniquet 2008: 359–361.

41 Breniquet 2008: 322–324.

42 They are usually forgotten by feminist studies! Barber 1994.

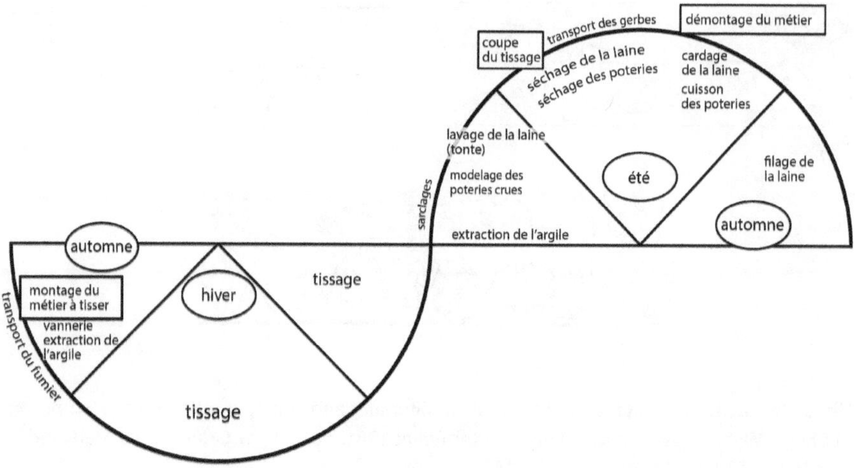

Fig. 7: The cyclical organization of the year. After Bourdieu 1980: 409, redrawn by Sidsel Frisch, *Centre for Textile Research*, Copenhagen.

more general organization of labor involving the entire year. This organization is probably linked with a cyclical perception of time in which the craft activities take place, and involves the seasons throughout the year (Fig. 7):

- In the house during the winter for weaving,
- Outside for spring activities such as potting, churning or spinning (and more generally wool or fiber processing).

Most of the scenes combining two steps of the weaving's *chaîne opératoire*, such as spinning and weaving, could suggest a complete process of creation too: a beginning and an end. Moreover, such an articulation could have been chosen as a metaphor for human life. Moreover, we must observe that the first act of "production" done by women, i.e. giving birth, is not shown, suggesting that this iconography is not fully "gendered" or that the scenes do not have an immediate meaning. All these observations and hypotheses drive us far from daily life and the economic world.

7 Who are the pig-tailed women?

Many scholars use these pictures as a documentary source on economy.[43] This interpretation is probably based on a positivist and confident idea concerning

43 Amiet 1981: 101–105.

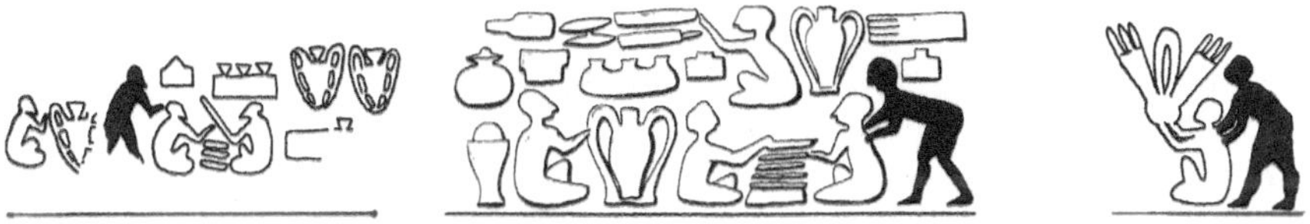

a) b) c)

Fig. 8: The advisers. a) Susa. After Rova 1994: no. 108; b) Susa. After Rova 1994: no. 337; c) Susa. After Rova 1994: no. 115.

the first urban civilization. What is depicted would be real life, and everyone could have an access to the images. From that point of view, the pigtailed women could be ordinary "citizens" i.e. ordinary "inhabitants" of the main Mesopotamian cities of that time, weaving in the domestic sphere, for the *oikos*. But it is easy to notice that what is shown is very selective. Moreover, the first city-states of Mesopotamia are ranked societies, with a strong hierarchy. In this configuration, people from the bottom level of the society could hardly be depicted. Even if we accept the economic behavior of ancient people, and we fully accept the idea that an economic thought had existed in Mesopotamia, it is difficult to imagine such a close and direct link between economy and iconography ...

An explanation more closely related to the economic world, but based on the Ur III situation, interprets these women as female workers engaged in the production of textiles.[44] The most documented task is probably the one related to weaving, but for later periods (mainly Ur III). Female workers and their children were employed in huge factories for basic tasks, such as spinning. Weaving on complex looms was performed by master weavers, mostly men, perhaps teaching as "advisers". On some of our cylinder seals "advisers" are depicted (Fig. 8), always ungendered. This detail could provide the proof that huge factories began during the Uruk period and that their organization required skilled and trained workers. However, the emergence of these factories didn't take place during the Uruk period. Their emergence is linked with two historical facts: war, which brought huge number of prisoners who must be occupied, and the impoverishment of a large part of the urban population which no longer had access to the land and was obliged to work to live.[45] They received rations in oil, barley and wool which are recorded in cuneiform Ur III texts.

44 Waetzold 1972.
45 Gelb 1965, 1972, 1973.

We would suggest a less sophisticated explanation for the Uruk cylinder seals' iconography: the image of a mother teaching her daughters.[46]

In comparison with other similar cultural organization (pristine states like the Inca Empire, also based on kinship), we know that at least weaving and potting can be performed by women who also belong to the upper level of a society.[47] Fabric or pottery were among the major economic products of the State and all the women were certainly among the first workers to be exploited, both ordinary people and women from dominant lineages. The role of crafts needs to be understood within the framework of the theoretical comments of Karl Polanyi or Timothy Earle and Terence D'Altroy on "primitive" economies.[48] Wealth was based on staple finance coming from agriculture, husbandry and handicrafts. It needed important means of transportation and storage. Ordinary people and elite women from high families were involved in the production's system (in Ebla, even women from the royal court wove for instance.[49]) However, they probably do not play the same role. While ordinary people could be involved in tasks that did not require specific tools or specialized knowledge (making yarn for the authority as tribute for instance), specialized handicraft could be performed by women of high lineages, weaving or potting for their kin. Depending on the rank of the recipients, these crafts were probably distributed during social ceremonies to ordinary people, dignitaries, soldiers, or officials, as they conveyed a high identity value. These fabrics no doubt conformed to strict production standards. The archaic texts of Uruk use ideograms which designate fabrics and also seem to refer to measurements.[50] This well-known mechanism is the consequence of the evolution of local chiefdoms in a typical case of a "pristine" state, probably deeply rooted in the local evolution of Ubaidian chiefdoms. The link between a society's elite and handicraft is in any case embedded in the manipulation of the environment which accompanied the emergence and development of chiefdoms, early cities and states. With the respect to this interpretation, the images on our Urukian cylinder seals could be prestige iconography too.

Considering that the images show both daily and ritual activities, we can also postulate that the women involved in these tasks could also be cloistered women, that is, members of the **arua** institution, who could be high born wom-

---

46 Breniquet 2008: 331–335: such a scene, mother teaching her daughters, is depicted in Peruvian iconography for instance.

47 Murra 1962.

48 D'Altroy and Earle 1985. See also Cleuziou 1994 and 1999.

49 Biga 2010: 168.

50 Englund 1998

en weaving for the temple at the beginning of the institution, as well as slaves.[51] It is not clear whether the **arua** existed from the Uruk period or started in the 3rd millennium BC, when an official workshop is recorded.[52] The **arua** could have been involved in the production of fine textiles such as curtains for the temple or clothes for the priests and perhaps also beverages like beer or secondary milk products.

***

Historical disciplines focus their investigations on tangible, material remains, such as records and artifacts (generally speaking), often trying to link them in a common approach. However, material and iconographic data can also be understood as true documents that reveal what was in the mind of their creators and users. Iconography is a way to understand this cultural construct and to give access to the ancient imagination. In other words, despite the material dimension of cylinder seals and the veracity of the images they carry out, iconography is probably much more closely linked with mental than with material world.

Of course, we can use it as a perfect and transparent documentary source showing women at work. But in order not to oversimplify the role of iconography in ancient societies, we ought to keep in mind that this iconography can be read in different ways. We are here far from historical explanations. What is depicted is not the economic world of textile workshops or domestic units. We are probably within the symbolic world. All these scenes are parts of more complex system-like series, as they appear to be often combined in linear, but not logical, compositions showing primary symbolic aspects of the world. They act as graphic metaphors to express different ideas such as human existence, the cycle of time, which are both probably linked with agriculture. What is shown on cylinder seals remains probably very far beyond our control, and only gives little real information about the organization of labor and the economy.

Bibliography

Adams, Robert McC. 1966. *The Evolution of Urban Society.* Chicago: Aldine.

Amiet, Pierre. 1972. *Glyptique susienne, des origines à l'époque des Perses Achéménides. Cachets, sceaux-cylindres et empreintes antiques découverts à Suse de 1913 à 1967.* Paris: Geuthner.

51 Gelb 1972. The status of the **arua** people seem diversified, from free to slave. It is tempting to compare the Sumerian **arua** with the Peruvian *akla*: Breniquet 2008: 214–216.

52 Charvat 1997.

Amiet, Pierre. 1981. *La glyptique mésopotamienne archaïque*, deuxième édition revue et corrigée avec un supplément. Paris: CNRS éditions.
Asher-Greve, Julia. 1985. *Frauen in altsumerischer Zeit*. Malibu: Undena Publications.
Asher-Greve, Julia. 2013. Women and Agency: a Survey from Late Uruk to the End of Ur III. Pp. 359–377 in *The Sumerian World*, ed. Harriet Crawford. New York, London: Routledge.
Bahrani, Zainab. 2001. *Women of Babylon: Gender and Representation in Mesopotamia*. New York, London: Routledge.
Barber, Elizabeth. 1991. *Prehistoric Textiles. The Development of Cloth in the Neolithic and Bronze Ages, with Special Reference to the Aegean*, Princeton: Princeton University Press.
Barber, Elizabeth. 1994. *Women's Work. The First 20 000 Years. Women, Cloth and Society in Early Times*. New York, London: W. W. Norton & Company.
Bazin, Marcel and Christian Bromberger. 1991. Churns and Churning. *Encyclopaedia Iranica* V-5: 551–557.
Biga, Maria-Giovanna. 2010. Textiles in the Administrative Texts of the Royal Archives of Ebla (Syria, 24th Century BC) with Particular Emphasis on Coloured Textiles. Pp. 146–172 in *Textile Terminologies in the Ancient Near East and Mediterranean from the Third to the First Millennia BC*, eds. Cécile Michel and Marie-Louise Nosch. Oxford: Oxbow Books.
Boehmer, Rainer Michael. 1965. *Die Entwicklung der Glyptik wahrend der Akkad-Zeit*. Mainz: Philipp von Zabern.
Bourdieu, Pierre. 1980. *Le sens pratique*. Paris: éd. de Minuit.
Brandes, Mark. 1979. *Siegelabrollungen aus den archaischen Bauschichten in Uruk-Warka*. Wiesbaden: Franz Steiner Verlag.
Breniquet, Catherine. 2008. *Essai sur le tissage en Mésopotamie, des premières communautés sédentaires au milieu du IIIe millénaire avant J.-C.* Paris: de Boccard.
Breniquet, Catherine. 2014a. Archaeology of Wool in Early Mesopotamia. Pp. 52–78 in *Wool Economy in the Ancient Near East and the Aegean, from the Beginnings of Sheep Husbandry to Institutional Textile Industry*, eds. Catherine Breniquet and Cécile Michel. Oxford: Oxbow Books.
Breniquet, Catherine. 2014b. Tüllengefäß (Tülle, Tüllekanne), *RlA* 14–1/2: 154–156.
Butterlin, Pascal. 2003. *Les temps proto-urbains de Mésopotamie: Contacts et acculturation à l'époque d'Uruk au Moyen-Orient*, Paris: CNRS éditions.
Charvat, Petr. 1997. *On People, Signs and States. Spotlights on Sumerian Society, c. 3500–2500 B.C.* Prague: the Oriental Institute, Academy of Sciences of the Czech Republic.
Childe, Vere Gordon. 1950. Urban Revolution, *Town Planning Review* 21: 3–17.
Cleuziou, Serge. 1994. Un jour l'Etat viendra: sous les lunettes molles de l'archéologue. *La Pensée* 294–95: 27–45.
Cleuziou, Serge. 1999. Transitions vers l'État au Proche et Moyen Orient: éléments pour une étude comparatiste. Pp. 245–266 in *La production du social. Autour de Maurice Godelier*, dir. Philippe Descola, Jacques Hamel, and Pierre Lemonnier. Paris: Fayard.
Crawford, Harriett. 1985. A Note on the Vegetation on the Uruk Vase. *Bulletin on Sumerian Agriculture* 2: 72–76.
D'Altroy, Terence and Timothy Earle. 1985. Staple Finance, Wealth Finance, and Storage in the Inka Political Economy. *Current Anthropology* 26: 187–206.
D'Anna, André, Armand Desbat, and Dominique Garcia. 2003. *La céramique: la poterie du Néolihtique aux temps modernes*. Paris: Errance.
Dittmann, Reinhard. 2012. Multiple Sealed Hollow Balls. A Fresh Look at the Uruk System Almost Thirty Years Later. Pp. 69–89 in *Stories of Long Ago: Festschrift für Michael D.*

Roaf, eds. Heather D. Baker, Kai B. Kaniuth, and Adelheid Otto. AOAT 397. Münster: Ugarit-Verlag.
Englund, Robert K. 1998. The Texts from the Late Uruk Period. Pp. 15–233 in Josef Bauer, Robert K. Englund, and Manfred Krebernik, *Mesopotamien Späturuk-Zeit und frühdynastische Zeit*. OBO 160/1. Freiburg: Universitätsverlag, and Göttingen: Vandenhoeck & Ruprecht.
Forest, Jean-Daniel. 1996. *Mésopotamie. L'apparition de l'État, VIIe–IIIe millénaires*. Paris: Paris-Méditerranée.
Gelb, Ignace. 1965. The Ancient Mesopotamian Ration System, *JNES* 24: 230–243.
Gelb, Ignace. 1972. The *Arua* Institution, *RA* 66: 1–32.
Gelb, Ignace. 1973. Prisoners of War in Early Mesopotamia, *JNES* 32: 70–98.
Glassner, Jean-Jacques. 2000. *Ecrire à Sumer: l'invention du cunéiforme*. Paris: Seuil.
Gouin, Philippe. 1996. L'outre ou la jarre ? Le beurre et les barattes dans l'Orient ancien. *Techniques et culture* 28: 153–192.
Huot, Jean-Louis. 2005. Vers l'apparition de l'État en Mésopotamie. Bilan des recherches récentes, *Annales. Histoire, Sciences Sociales* 5: 953–973.
Lindemeyer, Elke *et al.* 1993. *Uruk – Kleinfunde III*. AUWE 9. Deutsches Archäologisches Institut, Abteilung Baghdad, Mainz am Rhein: Philipp von Zabern.
Lissarrague, François. 1991. Femmes au figuré. Pp. 159–251 in *Histoire des femmes en Occident, 1, L'Antiquité*. Pauline Schmitt Pantel dir. Paris: Plon.
Mahias, Marie-Claude. 2010. Les mots et les actes. Baratter. *Techniques & Culture* 54–55: 165–181.
Michel, Cécile. 2014. Wool Trade in Upper Mesopotamia and Syria According to the Old Babylonian and Old Assyrian Texts. Pp. 232–255 in *Wool Economy in the Ancient Near East and the Aegean, from the Beginnings of Sheep Husbandry to Institutional Textile Industry*, eds. Catherine Breniquet and Cécile Michel. Oxford: Oxbow Books.
Murra, John. 1962. Cloth and its Function in the Inca State. *American Anthropologist* 64: 710–728.
Nissen, Hans. 1989. The 'Ubaid Period in the Context of the Early History of the Ancient Near East. Pp. 245–256 in *Upon This Foundation – The 'Ubaid Reconsidered*, eds. Elizabeth Henrickson and Ingolf Thuesen. Copenhagen: Museum Tusculanum Press.
Parpola, Simo and Robert M. Whiting (eds.). 2002. *Sex and Gender in the Ancient Near East. Proceedings of the 47th Rencontre Assyriologique Internationale, Helsinki, July 2–6, 2001*, Helsinki: The Neo-Assyrian Text Corpus Project, University of Helsinki.
Pittmann, Holly. 1994. Towards an Understanding of the Role of Glyptic Imagery in the Administrative Systems of Proto-Literate Greater Mesopotamia. Pp. 177–203 in *Archives before Writing: Proceedings of the International Colloquium, Oriolo Romano, October 23–25, 1991*, eds. Piera Ferioli, Enrica Fiandra, Gian Giacomo Fissore, and Marcella Frangipane. Rome: Ministerio per i bene culturali e ambientali.
Porada, Edith. 1993. Why Cylinder Seals? Engraved Cylindrical Seal Stones of the Ancient Near East, Fourth to First Millennium B.C. *The Art Bulletin*, 75: 563–582.
Potts, Daniel T. 1997. *Mesopotamian Civilization: the Material Foundations*, London: Athlone Press.
Pournelle, Jennifer R. 2007. KLM to Corona: A Bird's-Eye View of Cultural Ecology and Early Mesopotamian Urbanization. Pp. 29–62 in *Settlement and Society. Essays Dedicated to Robert McCormick Adams*, ed. Elizabeth C. Stone. Los Angeles: Costen Institute of Archaeology, University of California, and Chicago: The Oriental Institute of the University of Chicago.

Rova, Elena. 1994. *Ricerce sui sigilli a cylindro vicino-orientali del periodo di Uruk/Jemdet Nasr*. Istituto per l'Oriente. Roma: C. A. Nallino.

Sanlaville, Paul. 1989. Considérations sur l'évolution de la Basse Mésopotamie au cours des derniers millénaires. Paléorient 15: 5–27.

Stein, Gil. 1996. Producers, Patrons, and Prestige: Crafts Specialists and Emergent Elites in Mesopotamia from 5500–3100 B.C. Pp. 25–38 in *Craft Specialization and Social Evolution: in Memory of V. Gordon Childe*, ed. Bernard Wailes. Philadelphia: University Museum of Archaeology and Anthropology, University of Pennsylvania.

Stein, Gil and Jeremy Blackman. 1993. The Organizational Context of Specialized Craft Production in Early Mesopotamian States. *Research in Economic Anthropology* 14: 29–59.

Stol, Marten. 1995. Women in Mesopotamia. *JESHO* 38: 123–144

Waetzoldt, Harmut. 1972. *Untersuchungen zur Neusumerischeen Textilindustrie*. Roma: Centro per la Antichita e la Storia dell'Arte del Vincino Oriente.

Wright, Henry T. and Eric S. A. Rupley. 2001. Calibrated Radiocarbon Age Determination of Uruk Related Materials. Pp. 85–122 in *Uruk Mesopotamia and its Neighbors: Cross-cultural Interactions in the Era of State Formation*, ed. Michael S. Rothman. Santa Fe: School of American Research Press.

Camille Lecompte

Representation of Women in Mesopotamian Lexical Lists

The Mesopotamian lexical lists are a series of school texts which were used as glossaries and training exercises by pupils for their education.[1] These lists, which existed from the advent of the invention of writing until the end of the use of cuneiform script, refer to several aspects of Mesopotamia's material culture and, to a lesser extent, its society. In this respect, the lists of professions and personal names[2] offer valuable evidence of Mesopotamia's social organization, although women are generally not very well represented in these texts, which did not intend to give an exhaustive description of society, even for professions assigned to men.[3] As is well-known, a wide variety of lists was created over time, dealing with several different topics. The professional lists considered here aim to record occupations but, since they were created for educational purposes, only contain a limited sample of the Mesopotamian social categories. The first lists, known as Archaic/Early Dynastic *Lu₂* and *Officials* respectively, created at the end of the 4th millennium, consist merely of an unilingual enumeration of titles. This presentation changed over time and, at the beginning of the 2nd millennium, an Akkadian translation was additionally provided for some entries of the occupation lists. This presentation was later retained in the so-called canonical series, widely attested during the 1st millennium. In turn, the content of these lists experienced such a remarkable evolution, that two traditions can be distinguished, one from the 4th and 3rd millennia on the one hand, and the other from the 2nd and 1st millennia on the

1 On the lexical lists, see now Veldhuis (2014a), with bibliography; Cavigneaux (1980–1983); Civil (1976).

2 The present article relies on the edition of the lists of professions found in MSL 12, as well as a more recent score edition, notably prepared by J. Taylor, available on the website DCCLT, which also suggests translation for most of the entries. For the sake of convenience, lists of personal names which are known from the ED period are not dealt with.

3 It is relevant to keep in mind that Sumerian is a gender-neutral language, since the lists from the third millennium were written in this language.

Acknowledgements: I wish to express my gratitude to A. J. Edmonds for having accepted to correct my English. Furthermore, G. Nicolet and A. Cavigneaux provided me with some valuable suggestions, for which I thank them.

Camille Lecompte, CNRS, Archéologies et Sciences de l'Antiquité;
camille.lecompte@mae.cnrs.fr

other. As pointed out by N. Veldhuis, "the history of research into Mesopotamian lexical texts may be roughly divided into two approaches: the dictionary approach, and the cultural history approach."[4] The former focuses upon the contribution of the lexical lists to the understanding of Sumerian and Akkadian, while the latter analyses their intellectual background. Both approaches, which shed different light on the lexical texts, will be used here, first in order to find out the professional terms relating to women, second to understand why they were chosen and how they were integrated within the organizational framework of the lists.

1 Invisible women in the earliest school texts

During the Late Uruk period, the lists of professions,[5] still not fully understood as of yet, refer to many officials who are not well documented in the administrative records. The analysis of these lists is somewhat impeded by philological uncertainties, a limited understanding of the signs, as well as by the nature of the archaic writing which was not "language oriented."[6] Notwithstanding these difficulties, two lexical entries from the relevant lists may refer to women:

Archaic Lu_2	52.	DAM
	68.	NINKUM[7]

Both terms, though their meaning seems clear, are not unproblematic. NINKUM, which D. Charpin interprets as a priestess of Enki from Eridu,[8] is seemingly never attested in the administrative documents from the Late Uruk period. Regarding the word DAM, "spouse", which can also refer to a man, the uncertainty comes from different publications' transliteration as DAM of signs

4 Veldhuis (2014a: 16, see also Veldhuis 1997: 2–5).

5 The lists Archaic Lu_2 and Officials have been edited in ATU 3, p. 69–86 and 86–89 respectively. For the ED manuscripts of those lists, see MSL 12, p. 4–12 (*Lu_2 A*) and the edition offered by Pettinato in MEE 3, p. 176–185 (*Officials*).

6 Englund (1998: 79), see also Damerow, Englund and Nissen (1993: 30): "The various tablets from the earliest phases of writing therefore bear closer resemblance to such modern documents as punched cards, dockets, clearing checks, balance sheets or many other formalized data carriers than to independently and freely composed manuscripts in the modern sense."

7 ATU 3, p. 78 and 80.

8 Charpin (1986: 389–390), Huber Vulliet and Sallaberger (2003–2005: 632).

that are both sparsely attested and highly variable in form.[9] Interestingly, the term DAM is to be found in the later Early Dynastic manuscripts of the same list as DAM ME, which might show that it was interpreted at that time as denoting a member of the cultic personnel, with the sign ME for **išib.**

The lists belonging to the Lu_2 categories and attested during the Early Dynastic Period[10] provide more evidence of the role of women and display more items relating to feminine designations. Thus, in the so-called ED Lu_2 List E,[11] feminine designations can be classified according to their professional branches as follows:

- priestesses: **lukur,**[12] **ereš-dingir,**[13] **nu-gig** (?), **amalu**, maybe **dam-dingir**[14]
- role in the family, nurses and mid-wives: nursemaid **emeda,**[15] "nurse of god" **emeda^{da}-dingir,**[16] child-bearing mother **munus ama-gan**, midwife **ša$_3$-zu,**[17] midwife **nu-gig,**[18] widow **nu-mu-kuš**[19]
- only one term seems to relate to an administrative profession: **munus agrig**, "female steward"

---

9 While in CUSAS 1, 155. 00205. DAM EN_a BU_a as well as in ACTPC 92, 00305. DAM SAL E_{2b} have the same shape as in the lexical list, a more "modern" variant occurs in ATU 6, pl. 89 VAT 15288. 00203. DAM TUG_{2a} GU, which, however, might be another sign, such as NIN. The first attestation might merely refer to the wife of a person, but the second seems to be a personal name.

10 ED Lu_2 B-E are edited in MSL 12, p. 13–21; on ED Lu_2 C and D, see also Taylor (2003).

11 Edited in MSL 12; MEE 3, p. 27–46 and Veldhuis (2014b: 144–145); on the website DCCLT a score transliteration is also available, provided with a translation of individual entries.

12 On the **lukur**, an occupation nevertheless attested in ED Lagaš texts: see Asher-Greve (1985: 157).

13 Steinkeller (1999: 120–121 and 128). For the attestations in ED Lagaš texts, see Asher-Greve (1985: 157).

14 See Steinkeller (1999: 122–123): this function as a "wife of a god" is a peculiar feature of Ebla; see also Huber Vulliet and Sallaberger (2003–2005: 627) with bibliography.

15 Civil (2011: 283–284).

16 Seemingly only attested in the manuscript from Gasur, the texts from Abū Ṣalābīḫ showing SAL.AN GIŠGAL.

17 On **emeda**, and **ša$_3$-zu**, see Stol (2000: 171 and 181). In the Fāra texts, **ša$_3$-zu** also refers to a category of personnel under the supervision of the **gala-mah**, Visicato (1995: 105–109), see also Civil (2011: 284).

18 As shown by Stol (2000: 116, 173 and 186–188) and Civil (2011: 281–283), **nu-gig** not only refers to a type of priestess but to a woman involved in childbirth. Furthermore, during the Fāra period, the **nu-gig** belongs to the personnel receiving rations, see Visicato (1995: 105–109); for the ED IIIb texts, see the contribution of Karahashi in this volume. Attestations of the **nu-gig** in the ED Lagaš documentation are also to be found in Asher-Greve (1985: 158).

19 On **nu-mu-(un)-kuš**, see Cavigneaux and Al-Rawi (1993: 111).

- low status or worker: **geme$_2$**, "servant", **geme$_2$ lunga$_3$** "female brewer", **munus sag-rig$_9$**
- prostitute: **geme$_2$-karkid$_x$$^{kar\text{-}kid}$$_3$**[20]

Tab. 1: Some feminine designations in the ED Lu$_2$ List E.[21]

49	**agrig**	(Male) steward 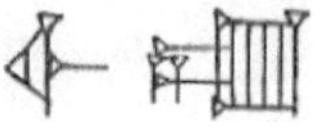	71	**nu-A$_2$**	Unknown 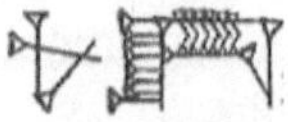
50	**munus agrig**	Female counterpart of the former 	72	**emeda^{da} dingir** /SAL AN URU×MIN	**emeda^{da} dingir, occurring** in the manuscript HSS 10, 22, is featured by the sign DA, which is similar to A$_2$. The latter, mentioned in earlier versions, does not seem to display any connection with the former 
51	**lukur**	Shares the sign MUNUS 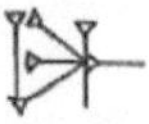	72a	**ereš dingir**	Shares the sign DINGIR 
52	**šita**	Priest Sign similar to MUNUS, priest like the former 	73	**dam dingir**	Shares the same sign DINGIR; DAM and NIN (**ereš**) are similar 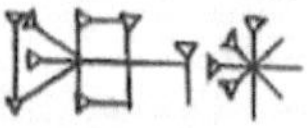
53	**geme$_2$**	Shares the sign MUNUS 	74	**amalu** (AMA ^{d}INANNA)	Shares the sign DINGIR, might also be attracted by the reference of a priestess 

20 The term **geme$_2$-kar-kid**, see Cooper (2006–2008: 13), is well attested during the third millennium and notably occurs in the Fāra documentation: see, for instance, Visicato (1995: 107). Later, during the Ur III period, the term is still in use: see, for instance, in Iri-sagrig, see Owen (2013: 435).

21 Signs are taken from the copy by Meek of HSS 10, 222.

Tab. 1 (continued)

54	**arad$_2$**	Male servant. Shares with the former the sign KUR. Masculine slave. 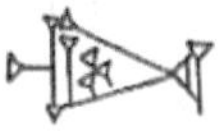	75	**lu$_2$/nu dingir**	Shares the sign DINGIR. Masculine. 
55	**geme$_2$ lunga$_3$**	Term consisting of / **geme$_2$** = 53 			
56	**sag-rig$_9$**	Type of personnel, if of low status, probably arranged here because of the pair of **geme$_2$** and **arad$_2$**			
57	**munus sag-rig$_9$**	Female counterpart of the former			

Interestingly, this list focuses on some aspects of the role of women that are also present in the later professional lists, especially on the designations of priestesses and on involvement within the family sphere. It shows that, as early as the 3rd millennium, women were reflected in some professions and occupations. Moreover, the position of the women in society may be reflected by several of those professional and familial terms, which tally with designations relating to women in the administrative records, although the documentary evidence also includes further feminine occupations.[22]

The organization of the items and their order seem, in many instances, to follow graphical criteria which determine the creation of acrographic and graphic sections, most prominently in three instances (49–57, 71–75 and 135–137).

It must also be noted that the succession between the three following terms, ED Lu$_2$ E 135–137: **nu-gig** (priestess or midwife) – **nu-mu-kuš** (widow) – **nunuz-gig** (= **nu-siki**, orphan), relies, on the one hand, upon the sign NU and, on the other, upon the sign GIG (cf. Veldhuis 2014b: 245). As suggested above, in the sections 49–57 and 71–75, thematic features also explain the associations

22 For an overview of the occupations ascribed to women in the ED documentation, see Asher-Greve (1985: 145–168). Note the absence, for example, of the **ki-siki**, weaver.

of some terms: the categories of personnel designated as **geme$_2$**, **arad$_2$**, and **sag-rig$_9$** are indeed close to one another; the like for the succession of priestesses' occupations, notably **ereš-dingir** – **dam-dingir** – **amalu** which are followed by **lu$_2$-dingir**. In another instance, two terms succeed each other according to a thematic principle: **emeda** and **munus ama-gan**, entries 193 and 194 in the list, both refer to birth or care for children.

Another list, commonly called the Cultic Personnel List,[23] also refers to a number of feminine professions or designations and represents another valuable piece of evidence of the type of relevant occupations paid attention to in these scholarly documents. Although several occupations mentioned in this list seem to occur only scarcely in the cuneiform documents, most of the terms, if not all, can be identified with the personnel of different shrines whose function is unfortunately not clear. The following priestesses and feminine related terms are to be noted:

Tab. 2: Priestesses in the ED Cultic Personnel List.

Text	Term	Type of priestess (place)	Observations
SF 57:obv. i 3. IAS 46:obv. i 3.	**nunuz$_x$-zi Nanna** **^{nu}[nunuz$_x$]^{nuz} Nanna**	Priestess of Nanna (Ur)	Attested for instance in archaic Ur[24]
SF 57:obv. i 4. IAS 46:obv. i 4.	**nunuz$_x$-zi Utu** **^{nu}[nunuz$_x$]^{nuz} U[tu?]**	Priestess of Utu (Larsa?)	Occurs in the Uruk period texts[25]
SF 57:obv. i 5. IAS 46:obv. i 5.	**[mur]ub$_2$ Unug** **murub$_2$ U[nu]g**	Priestess of Enki?[26] (Uruk)	Occurs in the Uruk period texts[27]
SF 57:obv. i 6. IAS 46:obv. i 6.	SALDU$_{10}$ GIŠGAL SAL DU$_{10}$ GIŠGAL	Unclear	Occurs in the archaic texts from Ur.[28]

23 Krebernik (1998: 341 and 362) with bibliography; see also Lecompte (2013b: 154–156). This list is here merely called the Cultic Personnel List.
24 See for instance Steinkeller (1999: 121–122), Westenholz (1989: 541–544 and 2012: 295–297), Marchesi (2004: 170, fn. 109). More recently, Lecompte (2013a: 160) with bibliography.
25 CUSAS 1, 098, R0106. See Lecompte (2013b: 156).
26 According to the Diri list, more precisely in the Old Babylonian Diri Oxford, 400. SAL.LAGAR: *e-nu-um ša ^{d}en-ki* (MSL XV, p. 45). See also Renger (1967: 115) for further mentions and readings of the SAL.LAGAR according to Diri IV. However, since this function is here connected to the town Uruk, it may have been devoted to another divinity.
27 See Lecompte (2013b: 155 n. 66 for the references).
28 UET 2, PN 311, p. 32.

Tab. 2 (continued)

Text	Term	Type of priestess (place)	Observations
SF 57:obv. i 7. IAS 46:obv. i 7.	SAL EN GIŠGAL <SAL> EN GIŠGAL	Unclear	Another term consisting of the sign GIŠGAL. This might occur in Uruk documents.[29]
SF 57:obv. vi 18. IAS 48:obv. v 5′.	**engar $^{nu-nuz}$nunuz$_x$-zi Utu** **engar $^{n[u?]-nu[z!]}$ ⸢nunuz$_x$⸣-zi ⸢Utu⸣**	Unclear	The addition of the term **engar** seems somewhat puzzling.
SF 57:obv. vii 12.	**^{nu}nunuz$_x$ (?)-** MUŠ×PA**(lahšu)**[30]	Incantation priestess?	This term does not seem to occur in other documents and is exclusively lexical in the extant documentation.
SF 57:rev. iii 5. IAS 46:obv. ix 4′.	**nunuz$_x$-zi** PAP **Nanna** **$^{nu-nuz}$nunuz$_x$-z[i]** PAP **$^{d⸢}$Nanna⸣**	Unclear	The addition of PAP seems to refer to a peculiar feature which is unclear to me here.
SF 57:rev. iii 6. IAS 46:obv. ix 5′.	SAL PAP DU$_{10}$ GIŠGAL ⸢SAL⸣ PAP DU$_{10}$ GIŠGAL	Unclear	

The entries relating to priestesses are thus mainly gathered in the beginning of the list (3–7), following two relatively unknown designations, NIG$_2$ EN and ME UNKEN, and all share the sign SAL for woman, which determines the group and is arranged in IAS 46 in the first position. Within this cluster, the two first entries consist of **nunuz$_x$-zi** priestesses, followed by the **murub$_2$** priestess who is somewhat isolated and by a pair of terms including the sign GIŠGAL: it appears therefore that these five very entries sharing the sign SAL are classified according to a graphic codification. Similarly, the term **engar $^{nu-nuz}$nunuz$_x$-zi Utu** is to be found along with three other entries consisting of the sign APIN (= **engar**), while the last two occupations in the table above might be arranged according to the here enigmatic sign PAP.

29 Unpublished text available on the CDLI website: IM 046107 = P002862. See Lecompte (2013b: 155)

30 Krebernik (1998: 279) points out a reading **lahšum** for the sign registered as LAK442, according to the Ebla sign list. The term therefore likely refers to a priestess "whispering, murmuring prayers", CAD L: 40.

2 Women in the Old-Babylonian Lu$_2$ lists

Among the numerous lists known from the Old Babylonian **e$_2$-dub-ba**, one of the main lists dealing with professions is Proto-Lu$_2$,[31] which represents a forerunner to the later canonical Lu$_2$ = *ša* series and gives many insights into the Mesopotamian social organization,[32] although it also contains many entries which are not related to professions.[33] On the other hand, the "Old Babylonian Lu$_2$ series" – here abbreviated as OB Lu$_2$ –, whose initial line is **lu$_2$-azlag$_2$** = *ašlāku*,[34] designates a group of bilingual tablets, which has "a wider anthropological outlook" than the former and "contains mostly terms for psychological qualities."[35] While the former refers in many instances to feminine occupations or to terms relating to women, the latter only provides scarce evidence.

2.1 Categories of feminine designations

Similar to the lists from earlier periods, cultic personnel and terms for priestesses are one of the main categories of feminine occupations represented in

31 Edition in MSL 12, p. 23–73 and on the website DCCLT; another exemplar is published by Taylor (2001). See Cavigneaux (1980–1983: 628–629), Taylor (2001) and Veldhuis (2014a: 159–162) for an overview.

32 However, since the only available edition so far is MSL 12, which has been thoroughly revised and provided with a commentary by J. Taylor in his unpublished PhD thesis, the following discussion will be restrained to general considerations. The exemplar also published by J. Taylor (2001), which includes many new entries and displays an order slightly different than in the published lists, demonstrates the need for a revision and, indeed, a new edition for the sake of the understanding of Proto-Lu$_2$. An updated edition is also available on the website DCCLT, which is provided with an exhaustive score transliteration.

33 Furthermore, as pointed out by J. Taylor (2001: 209), Proto-Lu$_2$ also "has a wider remit and contains numerous extensive digressions, generally because of having a sign in common with" the designations of humans. See also Veldhuis (2014a: 160–162).

34 Edition in MSL 12, p. 149–219 and on the website DCCLT. For an overview, see Cavigneaux (1980–1983: 629) and Veldhuis (2014a: 162–166).

35 MSL 12, p. 151. According to Cavigneaux (1980–1983: 629), **lu$_2$ azlag$_2$** = *ašlāku*, might also have been "utile surtout pour la lecture des textes littéraires." Proto-Lu$_2$, however, also refers to designations relating to the quality or the physical conditions of women, Proto-Lu$_2$ entry number 543, **munus u$_2$-hub$_2$**, "deaf", according to the Akkadian translation as *sukkuku* in other lexical lists, see CAD S: 362; Gantzert (2008: 141); see also Cavigneaux (in press) for the interpretation of **u$_2$-hub$_2$**/*sukkuku* as a function, notably attested in Mari, as pointed out by Charpin (1993–1994: 22). **munus giš$_3$-nu-ba$_9$-ra$_2$**, probably bearing a sexual connotation, seems also to be connected with the following entry, **guruš i$_3$-zu**.

Proto-Lu_2. Notably the following section, which has already received attention from other scholars,[36] consists of several types of priestesses (see Tab. 3).

The cultic titles refer, in this section, to the head priestesses of several institutions, geographically and chronologically scattered, and do not describe a general hierarchy which would prevail as a unique template for the Sumerian cultic personnel. For instance, the terms **egi$_2$-zi** and **ereš-dingir** were in use during the Ur III period and designated high priestesses of several divinities, while the Proto-Lu_2 list quotes them as generic titles. In contrast, four so-called **en**, *ēnum*, priests and priestesses are distinguished according to the logogram representing them and the divinities to which the occupation was assigned. Interestingly, some of these terms occur only scarcely in the documentation or may be considered to be rare forms, such as the logograms for the *ēnum* priest(ess), which is generally merely written by means of the sign EN. The term **murub$_2$** (SAL.LAGAR), which seems to be exclusively lexical during the Ur III and Old Babylonian periods, is provided with an Akkadian commentary which focuses on the feminine intimate parts, *qinnatum*, "anus", *ḫurdatum*, "vulva", *šuḫḫū*, "buttocks",[37] and probably *pingum*, "knob", and might be an indication that this title needed an explanation in this period. The succession of the *ēnum* priestesses (**zirru**, **nunuzzi**, etc.) and the **murub$_2$** seems to have been influenced by the Early Dynastic Cultic Personnel List.[38] Furthermore, the association between such priestesses is also common to a version of the Diri list, which may point out the existence of a kind of intertextuality.[39]

Another section worthy of note, Proto-Lu_2 257–265, deals with **lukur** priestesses, Akkadian *nadītum*.[40] The term **lukur** is encountered four times alone therein: three entries are provided, in only one of the available manuscripts, with the Akkadian correspondences *nadītum*, which is to be expected here,

36 Renger (1967) relied partly in his study of Old Babylonian priests and priestesses on this excerpt. See also Charpin (1986).

37 Note also the presence of "female genitals" and intimate parts in the Emar Lu_2 list, according to the new edition of Gantzert (2008: 138).

38 It is well known that some of the Uruk and ED lexical lists were still copied during the OB period, see Taylor (2008) and Veldhuis (2010). As pointed out by J. Taylor (2008: 205), the ED Lu_2 A played a role in elementary scribal education and may have influenced scribes. Although there is no evidence for the Cultic Personnel List being copied during the Old Babylonian period, the succession of some of its entries could also have been taken during the creation of Proto-Lu_2.

39 Interestingly, the entries 241–242, **engiz** and **ensi** respectively, are also found in the same section of the "Oxford" Diri, namely 393–394, which confirms that those designations for priestesses and priests were considered to form a consistent group.

40 See also Stol (2000: 172) and Barberon (2012: 207–208), for their role as midwives or as taking care of children.

Tab. 3: Priestesses in the Proto-Lu_2 list.

Entry	Term	Translation and Akkadian equivalency	Parallels in the Cultic Personnel List	Parallels in Diri "Oxford"[41]
230	**egi$_2$-zi**	high priestess *igiṣītum*[42]		
231	**egi$_2$-zi an-na**	priestess of An[43]		
232	**ereš-dingir**	high priestess *ēntum/ugbabtum*[44]		
232.a	NIN-**^{d}nin-urta**	priestess of Ninurta, ereš?[45]		
233	**zirru**	priestess of Nanna[46]	SF 57. I.3.	398
234	**nunuzzi**	priestess of Utu[47]	SF 57. I.4.	399
235	**ukurrim**	priest of Inanna[48]		396
236	**šennu**	priest of Nanše[49]		397
237	**murub$_2$**$^{pi\text{-}in\text{-}ku}$	priestesses of Ea/Enki[50]	SF 57. I.5.	400
238	**murub$_2$**$^{qí\text{-}na\text{-}tum}$			
239	**murub$_2$**$^{ḫu\text{-}ur\text{-}da\text{-}tum}$			
240	**murub$_2$**$^{šu\text{-}úḫ\text{-}ḫu}$			

41 See also Huber Vulliet (2014: 376), who focuses on the similarities between Proto-Lu_2, OB Diri Oxford, Diri IV 55–58, UET 6/2, 390 1–4 and Antagal G 14–16. I thank the author for having provided me with a copy of her unpublished PhD dissertation, which deals extensively with the cultic personnel from the Neo-Sumerian period.

42 The term **egi$_{(2)}$/igi-zi** is very common during the Ur III period, and sources seem to show that this function was assigned to the cult of Ninurta or Iškur, see Steinkeller (2005) and Huber Vulliet and Sallaberger (2003–2005: 627).

43 It seems that this cultic occupation is scarcely attested during the Ur III period; according to M. Sigrist (1984: 163), in the Old Babylonian archive of the Ninurta's temple, the **egi$_2$-zi-an-na** receives a ration and seems to have a high-ranking position, as is proven by the Išbi-Erra's year name relating to the choice of his daughter for this function.

44 Renger (1967: 134–149). During the Ur III period, this title was notably applied to the priestess of the goddess Ba-U_2, Yuhong (2011). See also Steinkeller (1999: 128), Huber Vulliet and Sallaberger (2003–2005: 627) and Huber Vulliet (2014: 99–103).

45 On this term: see for the 3rd millennium and the Ur III period Such-Gutierrez (2003: 147 and 163) and Huber Vulliet (2014: 99–100); for the Old Babylonian period: Sigrist (1984: 163).

46 This term is well known, see for instance Renger (1967: 118–121) and above; Huber Vulliet (2014: 161–165) for the Neo-Sumerian period.

47 Renger (1967: 122–123).

48 Renger (1967: 117–118).

49 Rarely mentioned, see Cavigneaux (1991), Steinkeller (1999: 119) and Huber Vulliet (2014: 376–377).

50 Renger (1967: 115). According to Charpin (1986: 380): "on ne possède que des attestations lexicales de ce titre qui est susceptible de plusieurs lectures (emeš, emezi, múrub, usuh)." As suggested above, this title may have been in use only during archaic times, but remained seemingly later exclusively in the lexical list as a relic of a former tradition, as shown in the Cultic Personnel List.

qadištum, another type of priestess in theory represented by the Sumerian term **nu-gig**, and *batultum*, "nubile girl". The list also contains the **lukur-gal**,[51] probably to be interpreted as "chief **lukur**", the **lukur ^{d}Nin-urta**, who is a member of the Nippur cultic personnel during the OB period,[52] and the **ama-lukur-ra**, who seems to be merely mentioned there.[53] Other cultic-related occupations are encountered, such as **munus kisal-luh**, "courtyard sweeper" and **munus ensi**, "dream interpreter".[54]

Feminine occupations in the Proto-Lu$_2$ list can also consist of terms being merely considered as the counterpart of a masculine profession, such as **munus ra-gaba**, "female rider", following **ra-gaba**. Also, a coherent section, namely Proto-lu$_2$ 705–716, contains several relevant terms for women. As noticed by J. Taylor, "this MUNUS-section has many variants among the exemplars bearing a version of it", including notably terms not present in the Nippur manuscripts and relating to "sexual behaviour".[55] The professions encountered can be classified as follows:

- professions relating to cooking and food preparation: **munus i$_3$-sur**, "oil-presser", mainly lexical but to be compared with the Ur III **geme$_2$ i$_3$-sur**;[56] **munus muhaldim**, "cook", **munus lu$_2$-lunga**, "brewer", both also scarcely mentioned in Akkadian administrative documents;[57]
- artisans and workers: **munus lu$_2$-ur$_3$-ra** (polisher?),[58] **munus šu-i** (barber),[59] **munus bar-šu-gal$_2$** (hairdresser, cosmetic producer?),[60] which are scantily mentioned apart from the lexical lists;

51 Though seemingly rather lexical during the OB period (CAD L, p. 240 under *lukurgallu*), this occupation is scarcely mentioned in the Ur III documents, in turn, mainly from Umma, recording the delivery as regular offerings by the **e$_2$ lukur-gal** of cereals for Šara (see for instance SAT 2, 45, 48 and 55). See Huber Vulliet (2014: 111, 264, 267), who also gleaned attestations from Nippur.

52 Sigrist (1984: 153).

53 Renger (1967: 158), with reference to Harris (1963: 141–142).

54 On earlier attestations of this profession in other documents than lexical lists, see Asher-Greve (1987: 30–32). See also Heimpel (1998). According to Charpin (1986: 382–387), **ensi** is a "clairvoyant", who not only interprets dreams, but also uses other, non-technical means of divination and was complementary with **maš$_2$-šu-gid$_2$-gid$_2$** (diviner).

55 Taylor (2001: 226).

56 CAD Ṣ: 62 refers to one example of *ṣāḫittu*; as for the Ur III period texts, see for instance the index of the Iri-sagrig texts: Nisaba 15/1, p. 434.

57 CAD N: 313. CAD S: 306.

58 Compare with OB Lu$_2$ (**lu$_2$ azlag$_2$** = *ašlāku*) A 19. 152: [**lu$_2$**]-**ur$_3$-ra**: *ma-⸢ar⸣-ra-qú-um*, CAD M/1: 285.

59 CAD G: 16.

60 Taylor (2001: 226) for the discussion of the term.

- specialists and women having a specific knowledge: **munus dub-sar**, "female scribe",[61] **munus a-zu**, "female physician";
- prostitutes or terms concerning sexual behaviour: **munus suhur-la$_2$**,[62] **munus ke-ze$_2$-er-ak**,[63] **munus ga-an-za-za** (?);[64] a subsection of four entries (Proto-Lu$_2$ 713–717) consists of the term **kar-kid**;[65]
- sorceress: **munus uš$_7$-zu**[66] and exorcist: **munus ka-pirig**.

Those occupations are therefore unequally representative of the social position of women and do not systematically correspond to professions which were ascribed to them according to the documentation, as proven by the polisher, **munus lu$_2$-ur$_3$-ra**, the female rider, **munus ra-gaba**, and the female doorkeeper, **munus i$_3$-du$_8$**, all being rarely mentioned.[67] By contrast, a number of female scribes are mentioned in the cuneiform documentation, such as in Old Babylonian Sippar.[68]

In the Proto-Lu$_2$ list, especially in the section 303–308, women are also represented according to their position and role within the family:

- **e$_2$-gi$_4$-a**, Akkadian *kallatum*, is repeated twice: the term, though generally interpreted as "bride", corresponds to "a specific status within a *royal* household"[69] or, as recently pointed out by M. Stol, to the "betrothed or married woman until the first child is born."[70]
- **nin$_9$**, "sister", **dumu-munus** "daughter", **ama**, "mother;" a whole section of Proto-Lu$_2$ (319–343) consists more specifically of the latter, though some

---

61 Lion (2011: 98–101). CAD Ṭ: 150–151.

62 Taylor (2001: 226) and CAD K: 314 (*kezertu*). On the *kezertum* in Kiš during the Old Babylonian period, who were involved in the cult of Ištar, see more recently Barberon (2012: 56–58).

63 CAD K: 314–315; Renger (1967: 188) includes the *kezertum* among the priestesses and reminds that this term is associated with the *kisalluḫatum* and *sekertum*.

64 See the discussion offered by Taylor (2001: 226–227).

65 In the Nippur manuscripts: **kar-kid** – **kar-kid-mu-gub** – **kar-kid-šuhub$_2$-si** – **kar-kid-gi-te-te** – **kar-a-[kid?]**.

66 See Klein – Sefati (2002: 571–574), with references to the incantations mentioning the "mother sorceress," **ama uš$_7$-zu**.

67 Interestingly, this occupation also occurs in a lentil-shaped school tablet from Mari, which belongs to school texts currently undertaken by G. Nicolet for edition. As the author kindly suggested to me, the relevant lentil associates the doorkeeper, a female doorkeeper, and an apprentice, **dumu i$_3$-du$_8$**. This lentil has a more didactic purpose than the Proto-Lu$_2$ list.

68 Lion (2011: 99–100) points also out that "at the beginning of the second millennium BC, there are many more attestations of women scribes."

69 Michalowski (1975: 718); on the interpretation of *kallatum*, see Ziegler (1999: 45–46 and 215) with bibliography.

70 Stol 2012: 133.

of the relevant entries are apparently unrelated with the meaning of mother, such as **amalu** (AMA.^{d}INANNA), a kind of priestess; note also the term for "wife of a (young) man," **dam guruš**.
- midwife: similarly to the Early Dynastic lists, the **emeda** is mentioned in three succeeding entries, Proto-Lu_2 385–387.

The OB Lu_2 list provides a complementary piece of evidence, albeit much more limited. Unlike Proto-Lu_2, no section is to be found which gathers together feminine occupations or titles of priestesses, while terms relating to women generally follow a masculine counterpart. According to the nature of the list, a disease is mentioned: **munus lu_2-giš-gi-sag-$keš_2$** refers to the Akkadian *naqimtum*, therefore identical with a seemingly mysterious complaint in *Ludlul*.[71] The only professional designation to be found is seemingly **munus lu_2-kaš-$kurun_2$**, Akkadian *sābītum*, "beer merchant". Note also the presence of an ecstatic, **munus lu_2-gub-ba**, Akkadian *muḫḫūtum* and of the less clear **munus lu_2-$tilla_2$**, "the one who is going?"

2.2 Organization of the entries relating to women in Proto-Lu_2

The arrangement of the entries relating to women in Proto-Lu_2 can follow several criteria, in the spirit of this list, which, as is reminded by Cavigneaux,[72] not only relies on a thematic organization, but also follows a graphical and semantic classification.

As a first example, two groups of priestesses, gathered respectively in subsections of Proto-Lu_2, 230–240 and 257–267, will here be considered. As to the first case, three smaller units relying on a succession of a key-sign can be distinguished (see Tab. 4).

The logograms and terms for those priestesses are classified according to their first and most meaningful sign, successively NIN (with the values **egi_2**, also represented by **egi** = $ŠE_3$, **ereš** and NIN), EN and SAL. As to the second subsection – Proto-Lu_2 257–267 –, the common sign which renders consistency to the section is SAL, present in the logogram of LUKUR (SAL+ME), in **munus** (Proto-Lu_2 261 and by phonetic analogy **^{nu}nunus**, the **eme-sal** writing for the

71 CAD N: 335–336.

72 Cavigneaux (1980–1983: 628–629) suggests that Proto-Lu_2 is in that respect similar to Proto-Izi, which was associated with it. See also Veldhuis (2014a: 159–162).

Tab. 4: Subsections in the Proto-Lu$_2$ list.

Entries	Common sign	Terms
230	NIN	**egi$_2$-zi**
231		**egi$_2$-zi an-na**
232		**ereš-dingir**
232.a		NIN-^{d}**nin-urta**
233	EN	**zirru**
234		**nunuzzi**
235		**ukurrim**
236		**šennu**
237	SAL	**murub$_2$**$^{pí-in-ku}$
238		**murub$_2$**$^{qí-na-tum}$
239		**murub$_2$**$^{bu-ur-da-tum}$
240		**murub$_2$**$^{šu-ú\text{ḫ}-bu}$

latter is attracted) and in **munus dub-za-la$_2$**. This means of classification has of course an implication for the meaning of Proto-Lu$_2$ 237–252 which was held by D. Charpin to refer to the priesthood of the god Enki in Eridu.[73] It is therefore possible that the entries referring to these types of priestesses and priests, who, according to the whole Mesopotamian documentation, are not exclusively tied with Enki and Eridu,[74] are also arranged according to a graphic order and to the stream of the older tradition from the Cultic Personnel List. Similarly, in the aforementioned section studied by D. Charpin, the succession of **engiz**, temple cook, and **ensi**, dream interpreter (Proto-Lu$_2$ 241–242), relies on their graphical similarities, since both are respectively written EN.ME.GI and EN.ME.LI, therefore sharing the sign EN with the entries referring to *ēnum*-like priestesses.[75] Note also that the association of **enkum** and **ninkum** is probably bequeathed from the archaic Lu$_2$ list, entries 67–68.[76]

73 Charpin 1986: 379–396.

74 Among the terms of the aforementioned section given attention by D. Charpin, it is striking to observe that **engiz** and **ensi** are attested as early as in the archaic texts from Ur (UET 2, p. 15 Occupation 9 and PN 296, p. 32) without apparent connection to Enki; likewise, **ensi** and **abgal** are also connected with Nanše, Enki's daughter. Huber Vulliet (2014: 376, 412) also observes that such titles as **ensi**, **engiz** and **abgal$_2$** belong to the personnel of Nanše.

75 Such a graphical principle is also true for **abgal** and **abrig** (Proto-Lu$_2$ 247–248). On the frequent association between **engiz** and **ensi** in the lexical as well as administrative documents, see also Huber Vulliet (2014: 417–418) with bibliography.

76 On their association in the documentation, see Charpin (1986: 389–393). Note that, according to the author, **enkum** and **ninkum** are also associated in several Sumerian literary works and hymns, in which they are connected to the divinities Enki, Nanše, Ninmah.

Nevertheless, the Proto-Lu_2 list also demonstrates a global thematic organization which relies upon sections dealing with specific professions or terms and therefore distinguishes coherent groups. As is reinforced by D. Charpin, the group considered above belongs to a broader section of the list dealing with priesthood. Likewise, the analysis of the Proto-Lu_2 manuscript published by J. Taylor shows that its content consists of the succession of several separate topics: singers and noise, finance, childbirth, etc. It is therefore not unexpected that some feminine occupations, notably the priestesses, are gathered in a same group. Similarly, Proto-Lu_2 705–716,[77] a group mainly relating to women, consists of three parts: the first, which is the most significant, relies upon the sign SAL, the second, consisting only of two entries, relies upon the term **lukur**, which nevertheless also contains SAL, and the last deals with prostitutes designated as **kar-kid**, which is probably attracted by two other similar entries of the first group, **munus suhur-la$_2$** and **munus ke-ze$_2$-er-ak.**[78] As pointed out by J. Taylor,[79] Proto-Lu_2 746–750, also contains a section concerning childbirth and fecundity: **u$_3$-tu**, "woman able to give birth," **u$_3$-nu-tu**, "barren woman," **la-ra-ah**, "woman suffering a difficult childbirth," **zum**, "womb."

On the other hand, as noted above, feminine designations are to be found associated with a masculine profession of which they are the counterpart. This is the case for **lu$_2$-ur$_3$-ra/munus-lu$_2$-ur$_3$-ra, uš$_7$-zu/munus-uš$_7$-zu, u$_2$-zuh/munus-u$_2$-zuh** ("ritually impure person"), **i$_3$-sur/munus-i$_3$-sur**, etc. When sections are devoted to feminine professions, their coherency seems notably to result from common signs like SAL or NIN. Since the Proto-Lu_2 list apparently relies upon several kinds of classification,[80] mainly using a thematic organization but also giving attention to graphic feature, and using pairs and triads, entries relating to women are logically scattered and arranged in sections which do not focus upon their respective gender.

---

77 In the manuscript published by Taylor (2001), iii 16′–36′, though the entries 32′–36′ do not seem to be exclusively concerned with women.

78 Taylor (2001: 226) suggests that **munus suhur-la$_2$** = *kezertum* might refer to a prostitute. However, within the MUNUS section, the progression from one entry to the other is not fully clear but may also rely upon coherent groups of professions: thus, Proto-lu_2 705–708c concern professions of several economic sectors, Proto-Lu_2 708e–709 are connected with prostitution.

79 Taylor (2001: 215, 218 and 229).

80 Cavigneaux (1983: 628–629) shows that the Proto-Lu_2 list includes many digressions which are attracted to the main topic of a section by semantic or graphical similarities.

3 Women in the canonical series Lu_2 = *ša*

Though based on the Old Babylonian Proto-Lu_2 list, the canonical Lu_2 = *ša* list,[81] well documented during the first millennium, displays some deep changes and presents an Akkadian translation for each Sumerian term. Female professions assume a much more significant role, since several social and economic categories, some of them already present in the Old Babylonian forerunners, are represented and provide more realistic insights into their role.[82]

3.1 Categories of women

3.1.1 Priestesses

More or less the same designations as in the OB forerunner are encountered, albeit not in the same order; **ereš-dingir-ra** = *ēntum/ugbabtum*, **lukur** = *nadītum/šugītum*, **egi-zi** = *igiṣitum* are, for instance, stable (respectively Lu_2 I, Excerpt I, 19, Lu2 IV, 22 and 18). Some entries were added, most notably **nu-gig** = *qadištum*, **nu-bar** = *kulmašītum* (respectively Lu_2 I, Excerpt I: 196–197).

3.1.2 High position and court titles

The canonical series contain notably three common terms relating to the queen: **gašan** = *šarratum*, **ereš** = *šarratum* and **egi** = *rubātum*. Note also the mention of **munus** $\mathbf{ga_2}$**-**$\mathbf{ga_2}$ = *muṣappirtum*, "lady's attendant", which is merely lexical and seemingly scarcely attested respectively Lu_2 I:43, 42 II iii, 16 and I, Excerpt II, 15).

---

81 Edition in MSL 12, p. 85–147. In the present article, the versions of the Lu_2 from the Middle Babylonian period are only cursorily dealt with. However, a scan of the lists from Emar, which were reedited by Gantzert (2008), seems to show that women were not very well represented. Note the presence of the following terms: **lukur**, the generic name for mother **ama**, references to female genitals, the nurse **emeda, nu-gig, munus-geštin** (woman producing wine?), female physician, female scribe, prostitutes; see also Gantzert (2011 Chapter 4: 63).

82 It is worth recalling that Akkadian, unlike Sumerian, marks gender.

3.1.3. Musicians and mourners

While the Proto-Lu$_2$ list only refers to the terms **munus u$_3$-li-li**, "mourner," and **munus eš$_3$-ta-la$_2$**,[83] the canonical series contains a whole section of female musicians:[84]

Tab. 5: Musicians in the canonical Lu$_2$ list.

Tablet III: ii.			
16	SAL **u$_2$-li-li**	*za-am-me-er-tu*	"singer"
17	SAL **u$_2$-še$_3$-la$_2$**	*za-am-me-er-tu*	"singer"
18	SAL $^{na-ar}$**nar**	*na-ar-tu*	"musician"
19	SAL $^{na-[ar]}$**[na]r-ra**	*na-ar-tu*	"musician"
20	[SAL NAR]-BALAG	*te-gi-tu*	"player of the *tigi*"
21	SAL **eš$_3$-ta-lu$_2$**	*eš-ta-l[i-tu]*	"musician"

The designations for the female musicians used in this section of the Lu$_2$ list are of course well-known terms which are commonly in use, such as in the Old Babylonian archives from Mari[85] as well as from other cities.[86]

3.1.4 Textile occupations

Unlike Proto-Lu$_2$, a few entries of the canonical series concern professions related to textiles, which indeed are to be expected from women in such a context:

83 Respectively in the manuscript published by Taylor (2001: 217), iii 25 and Proto-Lu$_2$ 586. The Proto-Lu$_2$ list refers of course to many musicians (Taylor 2001: 216 and Shehata 2009: 15–17), but only the two aforementioned are featured as women. Since female musicians are known, for instance, during the Neo-Sumerian period (Pruzsinszky 2007: 344–345), one would have expected their occurrence in Proto-Lu$_2$.

84 For the sake of convenience, translations of the relevant occupations follow Ziegler (2007).

85 Ziegler (2007) has extensively dealt with musicians in Mari. Accordingly, the *aštalû* and *aštalītum* referred to musicians less experienced than the *nārū*: "il s'agissait peut-être des musiciens qui n'étaient pas encore assez formés pour enseigner, mais qui exerçaient déjà leur métier," as suggested by Ziegler (2007: 17). As for the *nārum/nārtum*, Ziegler (2007: 17) considers the term referring on the one hand to any professional musician and, on the other, to "musiciens-instrumentistes." By contrast, *zammerum/zammertum* refers to the "chanteurs specialisés."

86 Shehata (2009) has collected the occupations related to music in the texts from the beginning of the second millennium in Babylonia. According to her results, some of designations recorded in the Lu$_2$ list also occur in other contexts. The *tigiātum* (both written in Sumerian, **munus tigi**, and in Akkadian, *ti-gi-a-tum*) "*tigi* players" are also mentioned in Nippur (Shehata

Tab. 6: Feminine professions involved in textile production in the canonical Lu_2 list.

Tablet I.			
17.	SAL **al-nu-nu**	*ṭa-me-tum*	"spinner"
Tablet III: ii.			
15	SAL **tug_2-tug_2-bal**	*ḫab-bi-iš-tu*	"worker"
14′	[SAL **siki $peš_5$**]-**ak-a**	*na-pi-eš-tu*	"female wool plucker"
15′	[SAL **ga-rig_2**]-**ak-a**	*ḫa-le-eš-tu*	"wool comber"

The Sumerian terms used here, though they correspond to concrete parts of the work on wool, such as proven by the Neo-Sumerian documentation, occur, however, only rarely in relation to women.[87] Their Akkadian counterparts seem also not to be frequently mentioned, although women are expected to have taken part in such work on wool.[88] Interestingly, this section relating to textile concerns processes taking place in the first stages of the treatment of the wool, plucking, *napāšum*, and combing, *ḫalāṣum*, succeeding one another.[89]

2009: 29 n. 132 and 176), Malgium (Shehata 2009: 41), Larsa (Shehata 2009: 42), Isin (Shehata 2009: 156) and Sippar (Shehata 2009: 191), note also the presence of the *wakil tigiātim* in OB Nippur and Sippar (Shehata 2009: 40). The *eštalītum* and *zammertum* are, according to Shehata (2009: 13), not attested during the OB period with the exception of Mari.

87 The terms mentioned in this section of the "canonical" Lu_2 can be compared with the Neo-Sumerian terminology, which was extensively studied by Waetzoldt (1972). As noticed by Waetzoldt (1972: 121, n. 357), NU.NU in **munus al-nu-nu** can be compared with the Neo-Sumerian term U.NU, although no woman seems to be designated in this way. In the Neo-Sumerian documentation, **tug_2-tug_2-bal** is seemingly unattested, but it may be compared with a type of textile occurring in Old Akkadian documents, **tug_2 bal**, translated as "linen," see for instance Maiocchi (2009: 251), though the relationship between both terms is unclear. The terms **sig_2 $peš_5$** and GA-ZUM, **ga-rig_2**, are regularly attested in the Ur III texts (Waetzoldt 1972: 115–119), but not in the same sign set as in the lexical list nor associated with the sign MUNUS. Nevertheless, feminine personnel designated as **$geme_2$** are assigned work consisting of plucking and combing wool: **$geme_2$ 1-e u_4-1-a 15 gin_2 i_3-$peš_x$**(ŠU-$PEŠ_5$)**-e ^{giš}ga-rig_2 i_3-ba-ak-ke_4** (Waetzoldt 1972: 116).

88 The terms *nāpištu*, *ḫabbištu*, and *ḫāliṣtu* are, according to CAD N: 304 and CAD Ḫ: 14 and 43 respectively, only lexical. By contrast, *ṭāmītum* occurs also in the cuneiform documentation and is represented by a syllabic writing.

89 See above and Waetzoldt (1972: 112–119).

3.1.5 Interpreters of dreams and signs

Tab. 7: Female interpreters in the canonical Lu$_2$ list.

Tablet I. Excerpt II.			
19	SAL IGI.ŠID-**e$_{11}$-e-de$_3$**	*mu-še-[li]-tum*	"necromancer"
Tablet II: iii.			
24′	[SAL **en]si**	*ša-il-tu*	"female diviner"
25′	**[m]ur-ra-aš**	*ša-il-tu*	"female diviner"
26′	**[l]u$_2$-ma**[90]	*ša-il-tu*	"female diviner"
Tablet III: iv.			
53	**ama-lul-la**	*za-ab-ba-[tu]*	"ecstatic"
Tablet IV.			
119	SAL **al-e$_3$-de$_3$**	*maḫ-ḫu-tu*	"ecstatic"
121	SAL **ni$_2$-su-ub**	*za-ab-ba-[tu]*	"ecstatic"

Those terms refer to well-known practices and match the documentary evidence, although the feminine designations are, for some of these examples, only lexically attested. For instance, necromancy, which has notably been evidenced by I. Finkel, was practised, but the only evidence of a "female necromancer" is taken from the Lu$_2$ list.[91] As for the dream interpreter, Oppenheim noticed that "women function as interpreters of dreams",[92] the goddess Nanše being one of the most ancient examples of use of the term **munus ensi** in the Cylinder A of Gudea.[93] The Sumerian terms following SAL **ensi**, which nevertheless refer to a female diviner, were considered by Oppenheim to be an explanation of the former.[94] Ecstatic women, called in Akkadian *muḫḫūtum* and *zabbatum*, are also mentioned in other documents apart from the lexical lists.

90 This term has been diversely interpreted by Oppenheim (1956: 223) as **lu$_2$-<gidim>-ma**, see also CAD Š/1: 110. In the so-called HAR-ra XXV tablet, HAR-gud B (MSL 12, p. 226–227), one also finds the entry: 148. **lu$_2$-gidim-ma**: *šá e-ṭim-mu*: *man-za-[zu]-ú*.

91 Finkel (1983–1984: 1), who gathered the evidence, only refers to the entry of the Lu$_2$ list about a female necromancer.

92 See above and Charpin (1986: 382–386).

93 Oppenheim (1956: 221). Veldhuis (2004: 26–29).

94 Oppenheim (1956: 223).

3.1.6 Sorceresses

Tab. 8: Sorceresses in the canonical Lu_2 list.

Tablet I. Excerpt II.			
18	SAL **uh_2-zu**	*kaš-šap-tum*	"sorceress"
Tablet III: ii.			
8	[SAL ...]	*mu-pi-iš-[tu]*	"sorceress"
b4′	[SAL ...]-SAR	*mu-piš-tu*	"sorceress"

The presence of sorceresses, also recorded in Proto-Lu_2, contrasts with the few occurrences seemingly referring to the sorcerer,[95] this situation is reminiscent of the observations of Klein and Sefati: "Nearly all cultures and civilizations throughout the ages ascribed to women a major role in witchcraft and ancient Mesopotamia was not an exception."[96] This is, for example, also true in the case of the *Maqlû* series, the incantation of which, as noticed by the scholars in question, are mainly directed against sorceresses.

3.1.7 Terms relating to prostitution and sexual behaviour

Unlike the Proto-Lu_2 list, the **kar-kid** is mentioned only once in the canonical series. Nevertheless, the list also contains three terms following each other and probably denoting a related meaning: *anzaliltu*, "pimp," *tibûtu*, meaning unknown, and *najāktu*, "promiscuous."[97] By contrast, the list also refers to nubile girl, **ki-sikil-tur**/*batultum* and **ki-sikil**/*ardatum*.[98]

3.1.8 Women as nurses and midwives – women in the family

The role of women in the family, as well as those employed by families is also evidenced through the mention of nurses and midwives: two entries form a small coherent group, **munus $ša_3$-zu**/*šabšūtum* and **munus en-nu-un**/*tārī-*

95 In the lexical lists the main reference to a sorcerer seems to be OB Lu_2 A 299, see also CAD K: 292.

96 Klein – Sefati (2002: 569).

97 Tablet III: ii 26–30, with *najāktu* being repeated.

98 On terms referring to virginity, see Cooper (2002).

tum;[99] further in the list are also encountered **um-me-ga-la$_2$**/*mušēniqtum* and **ama-e-he-a$_2$-e$_3$**/*murabbītum*. A number of terms in the list concern kinship, such as **e$_2$-gi$_4$-a**/*kallatum*, **munus ušbar$_3$**/*emētum*, mother-in-law and **dam-gal**/*ḫīratum*, "wife of equal status with the husband."[100]

3.2 Place of the entries relating to women

The organization of the canonical Lu$_2$ list and the place of women generally follow a thematic classification which proves to be more systematic than in Proto-Lu$_2$.[101] For instance, the female musicians are collected within a coherent subsection, which is included in a broader group focusing more generally on women and on terms consisting of the sign SAL. Likewise, female dream interpreters, **munus ensi**, and ecstatic women are included in sections related to diviners and ecstatic people respectively. Thus, the subsection containing **munus ensi** also refers to several Sumerian designations for *bārû* diviners, such as **a-zu** or **maš-šu-gid$_2$-gid$_2$**, as well as to the male diviner, **ensi**, who precedes his female counterpart. The female ecstatic also follows the male ecstatic and is therefore arranged according to the succession, already observable in Proto-Lu$_2$, of a male and female designation of the same profession. High priestesses belonging to the type of the **ereš** as well as the terms **nu-gig** and **nu-bar** which, in all likelihood referred to specific feminine occupations,[102] are associated within a group of cultic personnel also consisting of **gudu$_4$**, "anointed" and of **nu-eš$_3$**, a dignitary. Two sections from the Tablets I (15–32) and III (ii 6–20′) of the canonical Lu$_2$ list feature designations displaying the sign MUNUS or relating to women. The inner organization of the former, which is included in a broader group also referring to prostitutes, **kar-kid**, does not

99 Tablet I, Excerpt II: 20–21.
100 CAD Ḫ: p. 197.
101 Cavigneaux (1980–1983: 629): "elle est devenue une liste plus strictement thématique, éliminant les digressions de la version ancienne qui ne s'appliquent pas aux êtres humains et à leurs fonctions." Note that, for instance, terms relating to technical musical terminology, which are mentioned by Veldhuis (2014a: 161), are no longer present in the canonical list.
102 The terms **nu-gig** and **nu-bar** have been granted much attention in Assyriological literature, see, for instance, Renger (1967: 179–180 and 185) and more recently Cavigneaux and Al-Rawi (1995: 193–194) and Zgoll (1997). Interestingly, as demonstrated by Barberon (2012: 140), the type of priestess **nu-bar**/*kulmašītum* merged with the **lukur**/*nadītum*, during the time of the First Dynasty of Babylon in Sippar. A. Cavigneaux, in a personal communication, suggests that both **nu-gig** and **nu-bar** are occupations related with feminine sicknesses, intimacy, and taboo, and are therefore set apart, as shown by the etymology of both, **nu-gig** referring to impurity.

always seem clear since the succession of some of the entries is not apparently based on consistent professions nor similar signs, as in the following excerpt, in which unrelated professions are set together:

Tab. 9: Example of a section from the canonical Lu_2 list.

Tab I/II			
15	SAL **ga_2-ga_2**	*mu-ṣap-pir-tum*	"lady's attendant"
16	SAL **sag-rig_7-ga**	*šar-ra-[ak]-tum*	type of personnel
17	SAL **al-nu-nu**	*ṭa-me-tum*	"spinner"
18	SAL **uh_2-zu**	*kaš-šap-tum*	"sorceress"
19	SAL IGI.ŠID-**e_{11}-e-de_3**	*mu-še-[li]-tum*	"necromancer"
20	SAL **$ša_3$-zu**	*[š]ab-su-tum*	"midwife"
21	SAL **en-nu-un**	*ta-ri-tum*	"nursemaid"
22	SAL **[dam-dam]**	*i-ki-šu*	"brother-in-law?"[103]

***

The representation of women in the lexical lists from Mesopotamia shows some continuity and changes in the course of their successive stages:

a) In all the lists considered here, feminine occupations and designations relating to women refer primarily to priestesses and to the cultic personnel of the shrines. Some general designations for workers of a low status as well as prostitutes are also encountered in the lists from all periods. On the other hand, the representation of women in the lists experiences a noticeable evolution in the course of its long history. The lexical texts from the 3rd millennium only focus on priestesses, servants and prostitutes. By contrast, the Proto-Lu_2 list from the beginning of the 2nd millennium pays more attention to other professions and designations, as is proven by the presence of artisans and cook, albeit in a very limited way. The canonical series of the Lu_2 list still gives more insights into the social, economic and ritual status of the women by adding some professions relating to textile, a whole group focusing on the musical activities of women as well as a number of terms for omen interpreters. That women were better represented in the latter texts can be explained as the result of both lists gathering relevant entries which were only scattered in the 3rd millennium forerunners.

103 CAD I and J: 49: "person of undetermined status," compare with SAA 16, p. 183: "brother-in-law."

b) The professions and designations relating to women in the lexical lists seem only partly representative of their real position within society. For instance, few professions belonging to the textile industry are recorded therein. Similarly, few entries, such as **munus i_3-sur, munus muḫaldim** or **munus lu_2-lunga** concern the preparation of food. Other professional terms are seemingly merely lexical, either because they correspond to occupations not otherwise encountered in the documentary evidence, or because they refer to a real position of women which is, however, never mentioned in other texts, such as the female necromancer, *mušēlītum*, or the textile workers *nāpištum* or *ḫabbištum*. Lists from the 3rd millennium, by contrast, seem to refer to designations also in use in the administrative records. The lexical lists also reflect some of the branches and sectors which were ascribed to women in common representations, such as the sorceress, *kaššaptum*.
c) Feminine entries are generally classified and arranged within the lists either in coherent professional clusters or according to a graphical order. For example, several priestesses are classified in the Old Babylonian Proto-Lu_2 list within a section dealing with cultic personnel. Likewise, female musicians are gathered in a coherent subsection of the canonical series Lu_2. On the other hand, designations relating to women are also put in sections sharing the sign SAL, but without other apparent common points of reference. Feminine occupations also happen to merely follow a masculine designation.

By comparison, masculine occupations are more present in the lexical lists, which record an array of professions mostly assigned to men. For instance, in the Proto-lu_2 list, the hierarchy of administrators, notably responsible for groups of people, is represented by quite a number of Sumerian terms, such as **nu-$banda_3$, ugula** or **$ša_3$-tam**. Soldiers and military officers are also encountered: soldier **aga_3-us_2**, general **$šakkan_6$**, etc. Professions involved in agriculture (**engar, sa_{12}-du_5**) or husbandry (**sipa, $ša_3$-gu_4**) are also specifically masculine designations. However, the entries relating to men in Proto-lu_2 are more or less similar to the feminine designations: priests (especially 205–265), lamentation-priests (**gala**), singers (**nar**), professions in charge of food preparation or cooking (several kinds of cook **muhaldim**, brewer **lu_2-lunga**, butcher **gir_2-la_2**, but also cupbearer **sagi**), barbers and hairdressers (**šu-i, kinda**), workers (**guruš, $arad_2$**), role in the family (**a-a, ad-da** both for father, **pa_4-bil_2-ga**, ancestor, **šeš**, brother). Artisans as well as professions involved in textile industry are also scarce and are generally identical to their feminine counterparts. Note, for instance, the presence of **lu_2-uš-bar**, *išparu*, weaver, in the canonical Lu_2 series.

Accordingly, on a more theoretical level of interpretation, potentially following perspectives offered by other scholars,[104] the place of women in the lexical lists can be connected with several kinds of factors. Firstly, the rise of women scribes during the Old Babylonian period and the education of girls in the Sumerian **e$_2$-dub-ba** may explain the fact that attention to feminine professions played a more important role in the contemporaneous lists.[105] However, the lexical texts do not strive to provide a precise description of the social position of women,[106] but are to be held to be the result of the reflections of scholars in organizing their knowledge and creating "a community of graduates."[107] The increase of feminine entries therefore reflects the new organization of lexical lists during the Old Babylonian period, which led the scribes to include many more terms than in their archaic forerunners. Similarly, the canonical Lu$_2$ = *ša* list shows that the process of collecting professional designations was more systematic and accordingly paid attention to feminine occupations. The lists, lastly, may also reflect the evolution of the Mesopotamian conceptions regarding women,[108] as proven by the rise of the sorceress over the course of time and the significant role of priestesses.[109]

---

104 More particularly, Veldhuis (1997: 137–146) with consideration to the background theories of Goody and Bourdieu; Gantzert (2011, notably Chapter 4) with attention given to Foucault's work.

105 The implication of the presence of girls within the Old Babylonian school is notably pointed out by Lion (2011: 100).

106 It is, however, striking that the women recorded in the ED Cultic Personnel List are probably high priestesses belonging to the *élite*, therefore from the same social level as the women represented in the statuary and art from the ED period, see Asher-Greve (1985: 170) who refers to the "oberste Gesellschaftsschicht, die uns hauptsächlich in repräsentativer und kultischer Funktion faßbar ist."

107 Veldhuis (1997: 143).

108 The position of women within the family as witnessed by the lists can be compared with the representation expressed in Sumerian literature, see Kramer (1987).

109 Asher-Greve (2002: 16) has distinguished five subgroups of functions ascribed to women in Mesopotamia: 1. Family women. 2. Classes of priestesses and cult personnel. 3. Concubines, secondary wives, slave women as secondary wives and mothers. 4. Slave women, women in low status occupations. 5. Prostitutes, tavern keepers, seductresses, witches and magicians, foreign women. Lexical lists are thus consistent with these observations.

Bibliography

Asher-Greve, Julia. 1985. *Frauen in altsumerischer Zeit.* Bibliotheca Mesopotamica, 18. Malibu: Undena Publications.

Asher-Greve, Julia. 1987. The Oldest Female Oneiromancer. Pp. 27–32 in Durand 1987.

Asher-Greve, Julia. 2002. Decisive Sex, Essential Gender. Pp. 1–10 in Parpola and Whiting 2002.

Barberon, Lucile. 2012: *Les religieuses et le culte de Marduk dans le royaume de Babylone.* Mémoires de NABU 14. Paris: SEPOA.

Cavigneaux, Antoine. 1980–1983. Lexikalische Listen. *RlA* VI–8: 609–641.

Cavigneaux, Antoine. 1991. Ur-Nanše et Ur-Ningirsu, prêtres de Nanše. *RA* 85: 63–66.

Cavigneaux, Antoine. in print. Le sceau d'Aman-Aštar et les portes de Sumer. In *Mille et une empreintes. Un Alsacien en Orient. Mélanges en l'honneur du 65ᵉ anniversaire de D. Beyer*, ed. Pascal Butterlin Turnhout: Brepols.

Cavigneaux, Antoine and Farouk N. H. al-Rawi. 1993. Gilgameš et taureau de ciel (ŠUL.MÈ.KAM). *RA* 87: 97–130.

Cavigneaux, Antoine and Farouk N. H. al-Rawi. 1995. Textes Magiques de Teil Haddad (Textes de Teil Haddad II). Troisième partie. *ZA* 85: 169–220.

Charpin, Dominique. 1986. *Le clergé d'Ur au siècle d'Hammurabi (XIXᵉ–XVIIIᵉ av. J.-C.).* Genève-Paris: Droz.

Charpin, Dominique. 1993–1994. Review of CAD S. *AfO* 40–41: 1–23.

Civil, Miguel. 1969. *The Series lú = ša and Related Texts.* MSL 12. Rome: Pontificium Institutum Biblicum.

Civil, Miguel. 1976. Lexicography. Pp. 123–157 in *Sumerological Studies in Honor of Thorkild Jacobsen on his Seventieth Birthday June 7, 1974*, ed. Stephen J. Lieberman. AS 20. Chicago: The University of Chicago Press.

Civil, Miguel. 2011. The Law Collection of Ur-Namma. Pp. 221–286 in *Cuneiform Royal Inscriptions and Related Texts in the Schøyen Collection*, ed. Andrew R. George. CUSAS 17. Bethesda, Maryland: CDL Press.

Cooper, Jerrold. 2002. Virginity in Ancient Mesopotamia. Pp. 91–112 in Parpola and Whiting 2002.

Cooper, Jerrold. 2006–2008. Prostitution, *RlA* XI/1: 13–21.

Damerow, Peter, Robert K. Englund, and Hans J. Nissen. 1993. *Archaic Bookkeeping.Early Writing and Techniques of Economic Administration in the Ancient Near East.* Chicago and London: The University of Chicago Press.

Durand, Jean-Marie (ed.). 1987. *La Femme dans le Proche-Orient antique. XXXIIIᵉ Rencontre Assyriologique Internationale (Paris, 7–10 juillet 1986).* Paris: ERC.

Englund, Robert K. and Hans J. Nissen. 1993. *Die lexikalischen Listen der archaischen Texte aus Uruk.* ATU 3. Berlin: Gebr. Mann.

Englund, Robert K. 1998. Texts from the Late Uruk Period. Pp. 13–233 in *Mesopotamien. Späturuk-Zeit und Frühdynastische Zeit. Annäherungen 1*, eds. Pascal Attinger and Markus Wäfler. OBO 160/1. Fribourg: Universitätsverlag and Göttingen: Vandenhoeck & Ruprecht.

Finkel, Irving L. 1983–1984. Necromancy in Ancient Mesopotamia. *AfO* 29–30: 1–17.

Gantzert, Merijn. 2008. *The Emar lexical Texts. Part 2. Composite Edition.* Maastricht: Uitg. Boekenplan.

Gantzert, Merijn. 2011. *The Emar lexical Texts. Part 4. Theoretical Interpretations.* Maastricht: Uitg. Boekenplan.

Harris, Rivkah. 1963. The Organization and Administration of the Cloister in Ancient Babylonia. *JESHO* 6: 121–157.

Heimpel, Wolfgang. 1998. A female dream interpreter. *NABU* 1998/3 77: 77.

Huber Vulliet, Fabienne and Walther Sallaberger. 2003–2005. Priester. A. I. Mesopotamien, RlA X/8: 617–640.

Huber Vulliet, Fabienne. 2014. *Le personnel cultuel à l'époque néo-sumérienne (ca. 2160–2003 avt. J.-C.)*. Ph.D. thesis, Université de Genève.

Klein, Jacob and Yitschak Sefati. 2002. The Role of Women in Mesopotamian Witchcraft. Pp. 569–587 in Parpola and Whiting 2002.

Kramer, Samuel N. 1987. The Woman in Ancient Sumer: Gleanings from Sumerian Literature. Pp. 107–112 in Durand 1987.

Krebernik, Manfred. 1998. Die Texte aus Fāra und Tell Abū Ṣalābīḫ. Pp. 237–427 in *Mesopotamien. Späturuk-Zeit und Frühdynastische Zeit. Annäherungen 1*, eds. Pascal Attinger and Markus Wäfler. OBO 160/1. Fribourg: Universitätsverlag and Göttingen: Vandenhoeck & Ruprecht.

Lecompte, Camille. 2013a. *Archaic Texts and Fragments from Ur*. Nisaba 25. Messina: Dipartimento di Civiltà antiche e moderne dell'Università degli Studi di Messina.

Lecompte, Camille. 2013b. Temps, mémoire et évolution des cultures aux époques archaïques: écriture du passé et listes lexicales. Pp. 143–158 in *Time and History in the Ancient Near East. Proceedings of the 56th Rencontre Assyriologique Internationale at Barcelona*, eds. Lluis Feliu Winona Lake: Eisenbrauns.

Lion. Brigitte. 2011. Literacy and Gender. Pp. 90–112 in *The Oxford Handbook of Cuneiform Culture*, eds. Karen Radner and Eleanor Robson. Oxford: Oxford University Press.

Maiocchi, Massimo. 2009. *Classical Sargonic Tablets Chiefly from Adab in the Cornell University Collections*. CUSAS 13. Bethesda: CDL Press.

Marchesi, Gianni. 2004. Who Was Buried in the Royal Tombs of Ur? The Epigraphic and Textual Data. *OrNS* 73: 153–197.

Michalowski, Piotr. 1975. The Bride of Simanum. *JAOS* 95: 716–719.

Oppenheim, A. Leo. 1956. *The Interpretation of Dreams in the Ancient Near East*. TAPS 46/3. Philadelphia: American Philosophical Society.

Owen, David I. 2013. *Cuneiform Texts Primarily from Iri-Sag̃rig /* Āl-Šarrākī *and the History of the Ur III Period. Volume I Commentary and Indexes*. Nisaba 15/1. Bethesda: CDL Press.

Parpola, Simo, and R. M. Whiting. (eds.). 2002. *Sex and Gender in the Ancient Near East. Proceedings of the XLVIIe Rencontre Assyriologique Internationale, Helsinki*. Helsinki: The Neo-Assyrian Text Corpus Project

Pruzsinszky, Regine. 2007. Beobachtungen zu den Ur III-zeitlichen königlichen Sängern und Sängerinnen. Pp. 329–352 in *Festschrift für Hermann Hunger zum 65. Geburtstag gewidmet von seinen Feunden, Kollegen und Schülern*, ed. Markus Köhbach. WZKM 97.

Renger, Johannes. 1967. Untersuchungen zum Priestertum in der altbabylonischen Zeit. 1. Teil. *ZA* 58: 109–188.

Shehata, Dahlia. 2009. *Musiker und ihr vokales Repertoire. Untersuchungen zu Inhalt und Organisation von Musikerberufen und Liedgattungen in altbabylonischer Zeit*. Göttinger Beiträge zum Alten Orient, vol. 3. Göttingen: Universitätsverlag Göttingen.

Sigrist, Marcel. 1984. *Les* sattukku *dans l'Ešumeša durant la période d'Isin-Larsa*. Bibliotheca Mesopotamica 11. Malibu: Undena Publications.

Steinkeller, Piotr. 1999. On Rulers, Priests and Sacred Marriage: Tracing the Evolution of Early Sumerian Kingship. Pp. 103–137 in *Priests and Officials in the Ancient Near East*, ed. Kazuko Watanabe. Heidelberg: Universitätsverlag C. Winter.

Steinkeller, Piotr. 2005. The Priestess égi-zi and Related Matters. Pp. 301–310 in *An Experienced Scribe who Neglects Nothing. Ancient Near Eastern Studies in Honor of Jacob Klein*, ed. Yitschak Sefati Bethesda: CDLI Press.

Stol, Marten. 2000. *Birth in Babylonia and the Bible*. CM 14. Groningen: Styx Publications.

Stol, Marten. 2012. Payment of the Old Babylonian Brideprice. Pp. 131–167. In *Looking at the Ancient Near East and the Bible through the Same Eyes. Minha LeAhron: A Tribute to Aaron Skaist*, eds. Kathleen Abraham and Joseph Fleishman. Bethesda: CDL Press.

Such-Gutierrez, Marcos. 2003. *Beiträge zum Pantheon von Nippur im 3. Jahrtausend*. Materiali per il vocabolario sumerico 9. Rome: Università degli studi di Roma la Sapienza.

Taylor, Jon. 2001. A New OB Proto-Lu – Proto-Izi Combination Tablet. *OrNS* 70: 209–234.

Taylor, Jon. 2003 Collations to ED Lu C and D. *CDLB* 2003/3.

Taylor, Jon. 2008 Lexicographical Study of the Already-Ancient in Antiquity. Pp. 203–210 in *Proceedings of the 51st Rencontre Assyriologique Internationale Held at The Oriental Institute of the University of Chicago July 18–22, 2005*, ed. Robert D. Biggs et al. SAOC 62. Chicago: University of Chicago Press.

Veldhuis, Niek C. 1997. *Elementary Education at Nippur. The Lists of Trees and Wooden Objects*. Ph.D. Dissertation, University of Groningen.

Veldhuis, Niek C. 2004. *Religion, Literature, and Scholarship: the Sumerian Composition Nanše and the Birds, with a Catalogue of Sumerian Bird Names*. CM 22. Leiden-Boston: Brill-Styx.

Veldhuis, Niek C. 2010. Guardians of Tradition: Early Dynastic Lexical Texts in Old Babylonian Copies. Pp. 379–400 in *Your Praise is Sweet. A Memorial Volume for Jeremy Black from Students, Colleagues and Friends*, ed. Heather D. Baker. London: British Institute for the Study of Iraq.

Veldhuis, Niek C. 2014a. *History of the Cuneiform Lexical Tradition*. Guide to the Mesopotamian Textual Record 6. Ugarit Verlag: Münster.

Veldhuis, Niek C. 2014b. The Early Dynastic Kish Tradition. Pp. 241–259 in *He Has Opened Nisaba's House of Learning. Studies in Honor of Åke Waldemar Sjöberg on the Occasion of His 89th Birthday on August 1st 2013*, ed. Leonhard Sassmannshausen. CM 46. Leiden/Boston: Brill/Styx.

Visicato, Giuseppe. 1995. *The Bureaucracy of Šuruppak. Administratives Centres, Central Offices, Intermediate Structures and Hierarchies in the Economic Documentation of Fara*. ALASPAM 10. Münster: Ugarit Verlag.

Waetzoldt, Hartmut. 1972. *Untersuchungen zur neusumerischen Textilindustrie*. Studi economici e tecnologici I. Rome: Istituto per l'Oriente. Centro per le antichità e la storia dell'arte del vicino oriente.

Westenholz, Johann Goodnick. 1989. Enḫeduanna, En-Priestess, Hen of Nanna, Spouse of Nanna. Pp. 539–556 in *DUMU-E_2-DUB-BA-A. Studies in Honor of Åke W. Sjöberg*, ed. Hermann Behrens OPSKNF 11. Philadelphia: University Museum.

Westenholz, Johann Goodnick. 2012. EN-Priestess: Pawn or Power Mogul. Pp. 201–312 in *Organization, Representation and Symbols of Power in the Ancient Near East. Proceedings of the 54th Rencontre Assyriologique Internationale at Würzburg*, ed. Gernot Wilhelm. Winona Lake, Indiana: Eisenbrauns.

Yuhong, Wu. 2011. 19 Years' Finance of the Household of Geme-Lamma, the High Priestess of Baba in Girsu of Ur III (Š 31–AS 1 = 2065–2046 B.C.). *JAC* 26: 1–39.

Zgoll, Annette. 1997. Inana als nugig. *ZA* 87: 181–195.

Ziegler, Nele. 1999. *Le Harem de Zimrî-Lim*. Florigelium marianum 4. Mémoires de NABU 5. Paris: SEPOA.

Ziegler, Nele. 2007. *Les Musiciens et la musique d'après les archives de Mari*. Florigelium Marianum 9. Mémoires de NABU 10. Paris: SEPOA.

Websites

DCCLT: http://oracc.museum.upenn.edu/dcclt/corpus
CDLI: http://cdli.ucla.edu/

Fumi Karahashi

Women and Land in the Presargonic Lagaš Corpus

The Presargonic (ED IIIb) city-state of Lagaš, or more precisely one of its district centers, Girsu, has yielded some 1800 texts (Foxvog 2011: 59, with n. 2). The majority of the documents are administrative records from an institution called E_2-mi_2[1] "the House of the Woman" (i.e., of the Queen)[2] and later E_2-^{d}Ba-ba_6 "the House of the Goddess Baba."[3] The institution dates to a period of over 20 years in the reigns of the last three rulers of Lagaš (Enentarzi, Lugalanda, and Urukagina), and was presided over by their wives (Dimtur, Baranamtara, and Sasa). The change of name of the institution was probably related to Urukagina's Reform, in which he claimed that land and services previously appropriated by the ruling circle were returned to the goddess Baba. In practice, however, the E_2-^{d}Ba-ba_6 seems to have continued to control them under Urukagina and his wife even more than the E_2-mi_2 had previously done (Maekawa 1973–74: 136; Steinkeller 1999: 298).

In the corpus, women are mentioned as holding arable land. The size of Dimtur's subsistence land (**šuku**) amounted to 210 **iku** in E (year) 4 (Nik 1, 42 = AWEL 42) and 378 **iku** in E5 (VS 14, 188 = AWL 8).[4] Sasa's land was more than twice as large as that of Dimtur (Steinkeller 1999: 295). Besides these high-ranking women, other women are also mentioned in land allotment documents as holders of subsistence and/or leased land. They were mostly from the elite, female members of the ruling families and wives of high officials, or female royal household servants called **ar_3-tu munus**, with the exception of "one **kar-kid_3** ("prostitute?")."[5] This paper examines what kind of land and how much

1 Its reading: **e_2-munus** (CDLI), **e_2-munus** "house of the Lady" (Beld 2002; 5, with n. 3); **e_2-mi_2** (Marchesi 2011: 195, n. 15; Bartash 2014); **e_2**-MI_2 (Prentice 2010).

2 "[M]unus frequently refers to the consort of the ruler ... and may be translated 'queen'" (Beld 2002: 77, n. 70).

3 On the reading of the goddess' name, see most recently Rubio 2010: 35–39.

4 For **u_2-rum Dim_3-tur** and **šuku Dim_3-tur**, see Yamamoto 1981: 109, n. 3.

5 See Cooper's article in this volume.

Acknowledgements: I thank Frederick W. Knobloch for helpful discussion and comments. All flaws and errors are of course mine alone.

Fumi Karahashi, Chuo University, Tokyo; fumi.karahashi@gmail.com

these women received. It attempts to understand the relationship between women and landholding from the perspectives of kinship and labor.

1 Texts and people

In the organization of arable land by the E_2-mi_2, Deimel (1931: 80–81) recognized three categories of land. The first category, **gan_2 nig_2-en-na**, literally "Herrenland," was "the field under the direct control of the ruler" (Yamamoto 1979: 85), and its crop was used to run the E_2-mi_2 and other institutions (Maeda 1984: 33). The other two categories, **gan_2 šuku** "Arbeitlos-Land" and **gan_2 apin-la_2** "Pachland," are often translated into English as "subsistence land" and "leased land" respectively. The former was given "to the leading members of the E_2-mi_2 in order to provide a livelihood for its members," while the latter was rented to "members of the E_2-mi_2 as well as to people belonging to other organizations" (Maeda 1984: 33). Tenants were supposed to pay rent in silver and barley representing one third to one half of the yield (Nakahara 1961; Maekawa 1977). The total number of texts dealing with **gan_2 šuku** and **gan_2 apin-la_2** is about fifty.[6] Of these, this paper focuses on the following eleven texts in which women occur as landholders:

L1 VS 14, 156 (AWL 6) (**mu-ne-šum$_2$**); RTC 75 (**mu-gid$_2$**)
L4 VS 14, 72 (AWL 5) (**mu-gid$_2$**)
UL1 VS 25, 70 (**mu-ne-šum$_2$-mu**); HSS 3, 40 (AWAS 39) (**mu-gid$_2$**)
UL2 DP 583 (**mu-ne-šum$_2$**); VS 25, 93 (**mu-ne-šum$_2$**)
UL3 DP 580 (**mu-gid$_2$**)
UL4 DP 587 (**mu-gid$_2$**); DP 592 (**mu-gid$_2$**); TSA 7 (**gid$_2$**)

The verb utilized in each text, either **šum$_2$** "give" or **gid$_2$** "measure," is indicated in parentheses. In one agricultural cycle, both **šum$_2$**-tablets and **gid$_2$**-tablets were produced, as implied by the situation in L1 and UL1. In the latter case, VS 25, 70 (**mu-ne-šum$_2$-mu**) listed 88 individuals and groups, while HSS 3, 40 (**mu-gid$_2$**) listed 79 individuals.[7] In these two texts there are in total some 120

6 By courtesy of Camille Lecompte.

7 In VS 25, 70 occupational groups such as carpenters (**nagar**), leatherworkers (**ašgab**), and fullers (**azlag$_3$**) were collectively recorded with the total area given to them, while in HSS 3, 40 the names of its members are individually listed: for example, a collective entry for carpenters in VS 25, 70 (obv. iv 10–12: 5 **iku gan_2** FN_1 / 5 **iku gan_2** FN_2 / **nagar**) partly corresponds to the individual entries recorded in two separate blocks in HSS 3, 40 (obv. v 9–12: 1 **iku gan_2**

individuals and occupational groups, with 47 individuals present in both texts. There might have been, however, additional documents relevant to land allotment in UL1 that are not extant and therefore more individuals holding subsistence and/or leased land in that year.[8]

A total of fifteen women, named and unnamed, are attested in the aforementioned eleven texts. They are listed below by name in alphabetical order with the two unnamed ones at the bottom:

Bara$_2$-a-ra$_2$-nu$_2$: wife of Lugal-mu-da-kuš$_2$
E$_2$-mete: female servant (**ar$_3$-tu munus**)
Gan-ki
Geme$_2$-šu-ga-lam-ma: midwife (**nu-gig**)
Geme$_2$-ub$_5$-ku$_3$-ga: mother of Baranamtara (**ama munus**)
Ki-tuš-lu$_2$: sister of Baranamtara (**nin munus**), wife of the chief scribe Il$_2$
Ku$_3$-ge-pa$_3$: sister of Lugalanda (**nin ensi$_2$-ka**), wife of the scribe Du-du
Nin-e$_2$-muš$_3$-še$_3$: sister of Baranamtara (**nin munus**)
Nin-nig$_2$-mu: **kar-kid$_3$**
Nin-u$_3$-ma: female servant (**ar$_3$-tu munus**)
Nin-uru-da-kuš$_2$: female servant (**ar$_3$-tu munus**)
Šeš-a-mu: female servant (**ar$_3$-tu munus**)
No name: mother of Sasa (**ama munus**)
No name: wife of the chief administrator Šubur

Table 1 summarizes the information as to the recipient name, the land type and area she received, and her family relationship or occupation.

šuku PN$_1$ / 2 **iku gan$_2$ šuku** PN$_2$ / 1 **iku gan$_2$ šuku** PN$_3$ / **nagar-me**, and obv. vi 4–6: 1 **iku gan$_2$ šuku** PN$_4$ / 1 **iku gan$_2$ šuku** PN$_5$ / **nagar-me**).

8 On the fact that the names of subsistence-land holders and the individuals occurring in Type I lists (**lu$_2$-šuku-dab$_5$-ba**) do not completely coincide, see Prentice 2010: 73–74.

Tab. 1: Women and land in the Presargonic Lagaš corpus.

Text (Date)	Name of Recipient	Land Type	Area (iku)	Family Relation / Occupation
VS 14, 156 (L1)	No name	Unspecified	12	**dam Šubur nu-banda$_3$**
RTC 75 (L1)	Bara$_2$-a-ra$_2$-nu$_2$*	**gan$_2$ apin-la$_2$**	9	**dam Lugal-mu-da-kuš$_2$**
VS 14, 72 (L4)	Geme$_2$-ub$_5$-ku$_3$-ga	**šuku**	36	**ama munus****
	Nin-e$_2$-muš$_3$-še$_3$		18	**nin munus*****
	Gan-ki		4½	
	E$_2$-mete		4	**ar$_3$-tu munus**
	Nin-u$_3$-ma		2	**ar$_3$-tu munus**
	Šeš-a-mu		2	**ar$_3$-tu munus**
	Nin-uru-da-kuš$_2$		2	**ar$_3$-tu munus**
VS 25, 70 (UL1)	Ki-tuš-lu$_2$	Unspecified	18	**dam Il$_2$ dub-sar; nin munus******
	E$_2$-mete	Unspecified	6	**ar$_3$-tu munus**
	Geme$_2$-šu-ga-lam-ma	Unspecified	6	**ar$_3$-tu munus**
HSS 3, 40 (UL1)	Ki-tuš-lu$_2$	**gan$_2$ apin-la$_2$**	17¾	**dam Il$_2$ dub-sar mah**
	Ku$_3$-ge-pa$_3$	**gan$_2$ apin-la$_2$**	18½	**dam Du-du dub-sar; nin ensi$_2$-ka*******
	E$_2$-mete	**gan$_2$ šuku**	6	**ar$_3$-tu munus**
	Geme$_2$-šu-ga-lam-ma	**gan$_2$ šuku**	6¼	**nu-gig**
DP 583 (UL2)	No name	Unspecified	36?	**ama munus**
VS 25, 93 (UL2)	Ki-tuš-lu$_2$	**gan$_2$ apin-la$_2$**	18	**dam Il$_2$**
DP 580 (UL3)	No name	**gan$_2$ šuku**	6	**nu-gig**
DP 587 (UL4)	Nin-nig$_2$-mu	**gan$_2$ 5-tuku**	1½	**kar-kid$_3$**
DP 592 (UL4)	Ki-tuš-lu$_2$	**gan$_2$ 10-tuku**	9	**dam Il$_2$ dub-sar**
TSA 7 (UL4)	No name	**gan$_2$ 5-tuku**	18	**ama munus**

* Bara$_2$-a-ra$_2$-nu$_2$ = **dam** Lugal-mu-da-kuš$_2$ (DP 127); ** Geme$_2$-ub$_5$-ku$_3$-ga = **ama munus** (VS 27, 81); *** Nin-e$_2$-muš$_3$-še$_3$= **nin munus** (DP 170); **** Ki-tuš-lu$_2$ = **nin munus** (DP 127); ***** Ku$_3$-ge-pa$_3$ = **nin ensi$_2$-ka** (DP 127).

2 Female members of ruling families with land

2.1 Queen's mother (ama munus)

Geme$_2$-ub$_5$-ku$_3$-ga in the above list is identified as the **ama munus** "queen's mother" (VS 27, 81: obv. i 3–4; dated to L3), namely the mother of Baranamtara, Lugalanda's wife. In a text dated to L4, she was allotted 36 **iku** of subsistence land (VS 14, 72: obv. ii 4–5).

Another **ama munus** "queen's mother," who should be identified with the mother of Sasa, Urukagina's wife, was also probably allotted 36 **iku** of land – not specified in the text but most likely **gan$_2$ šuku** (DP 583: obv. i 1–2; dated to UL2) and 18 **iku** of leased land qualified as **gan$_2$ 5-tuku** "field that yields 720 **sila$_3$** per **iku**"[9] (TSA 7: rev. i 6–7; dated to UL4).

2.2 Sister of the queen or ruler

In a text dated to L5, Nin-e$_2$-muš$_3$-še$_3$ is identified as the "queen's sister" (**nin munus**), namely the sister of Baranamtara (DP 170: obv. ii 1–2).[10] In the aforementioned text VS 14, 72, in which Baranamtara's mother Geme$_2$-ub$_5$-ku$_3$-ga was listed with 36 **iku**, Nin-e$_2$-muš$_3$-še$_3$ is allotted 18 **iku** of subsistence land (VS 14, 72: obv. iii 1).

Ki-tuš-lu$_2$ was another sister of Baranamtara, identified as **nin munus** in a text dated to Lugalanda's reign (DP 127: obv. iv 8–9).[11] Ki-tuš-lu$_2$ in a later text, HSS 3, 40 dated to UL1, is identified as the wife of the chief scribe Il$_2$ (**dam Il$_2$ dub-sar-mah**). She is mentioned in three documents from UL1 and UL2 with 17¾ or 18 **iku** of **gan$_2$ apin-la$_2$** (HSS 3, 40: obv. iii 12–15 and VS 25, 70: rev. iii 8–10; VS 25, 93: obv. i 1–3) and in UL4, with 9 **iku** of **gan$_2$ 10-tuku** "field that yields 1440 **sila$_3$** per **iku**" (DP 592: rev. iii 7–10).

Ku$_3$-ge-pa$_3$, who was identified as the "wife of the scribe Du-du" (**dam Du-du dub-sar**), rented 18½ **iku** of **gan$_2$ apin-la$_2$** (HSS 3, 40: rev. ii 13–16). She most likely should be identified with the Ku$_3$-ge-pa$_3$-da who is mentioned among Lugalanda's sisters (**nin ensi$_2$-ka-me**) in DP 127 (obv. ii 6 and 11). This

---

9 The term **gan$_2$** X-**tuku** means that the field concerned was on the level of productivity of X **gur-sag-gal$_2$** per **iku** (Nakahara apud Maekawa 1977: 4).

10 **Nin** (instead of **nin$_9$**) signifies "sister" in the Presargonic Lagaš texts (Beld 2002: 190, n. 88).

11 This text is dated to **Lugal-an-da-nu-hun-ga$_2$**: no year number is given but it should be dated to the early years of Lugalanda (Selz 1989: 265–266, 544; 1995: 24).

is one of the so-called **ereš-dingir** ration texts of which four have been preserved (Beld 2002: 184–187); the other three are Nik 1:53 (AWEL 53), RTC 61, and DP 134, in all three of which Lugalanda's sisters were, instead, designated as the **lukur** (MUNUS+ME) (Steinkeller 1981: 85).[12]

2.3 Other elite women

The wife of Lugal-mu-da-kuš$_2$ (**dam Lugal-mu-da-kuš$_2$**) rented 9 **iku** of **gan$_2$ apin-la$_2$** (RTC 75: obv. iv 6–rev. i 1). This person is identified by name in a **maš-da-ri-a** text (DP 59: rev. ii 18–19) and an **ereš-dingir** ration text (DP 127: obv. iii 5–6) as **Bara$_2$-a-ra$_2$-nu$_2$ / dam Lugal-mu-da-kuš$_2$**. In three **ereš-dingir** texts (Nik 1, 53; RTC 61; DP 134), she is mentioned only by name with no reference to her family relation. All the **ereš-dingir** texts ranked her fourth, the first being the **ereš-dingir** priestess of the Goddess Baba (**ereš-dingir ^{d}Ba-ba$_6$**),[13] and the second and third being the two "men of the **ereš-dingir**" (**lu$_2$ ereš-dingir-me** in DP 134: obv. i 11). This points to her remarkably high social status and the strong possibility that she was an important member of the ruling family. Besides 9 **iku** of leased land, she held 1 **iku** of **ki-šum$_2$-ma** "onion field" (DP 406: obv. i 1–2).[14] As for her husband, several persons by the name of Lugal-mu-da-kuš$_2$ are attested, but none of them can be identified with him with certainty.

Next we turn to a woman named Gan-ki, who was recorded as having 4½ **iku** of subsistence land in VS 14, 72: obv. iii 4 following the names of Geme$_2$-ub$_5$-ku$_3$-ga (see 2.1), A-en-ra-DU (Lagalanda's son), Nin-e$_2$-muš$_3$-še$_3$ (see 2.2), and Šubur-^{d}Ba-ba$_6$ (Urukagina's son and **gala**-cantor). With regard to her identity, I wonder whether she can be identified with one or more of the individuals of the same name listed chronologically below:

1. Gan-ki-ku$_3$, who sold her son Gu$_3$-bi-dug$_3$ as **gala**-singer to Dimtur, wife of Enentarzi, during her husband's reign (RTC 17). The name Gan-ki-ku$_3$ is supposedly a longer form of Gan-ki (Foxvog 2011: 64, 67, and 94).
2. Gan-ki-ku$_3$-ga, who is mentioned in the **ereš-dingir** texts Nik 1, 53 (obv. iv 13; dated to L1), RTC 61 (obv. vi 1; dated to L1), and DP 134 (obv. v 20; dated to L[...]). In these texts occur the four royal family members (Geme$_2$-ub$_5$-

12 See **munus-me** (Beld 2002: 214); for **lukur**, see Sharlach 2008.

13 She might have been the wife of the ruler (Maekawa 1996: 172); cf. Steinkeller 1999b: 120, n. 54.

14 Otherwise she is mentioned as a sender of a **maš-da-ri-a**-gift (DP 59) and receiver (?) of 144 **sila$_3$** of barley (BIN 8, 12: rev. i 2).

ku$_3$-ga, A-en-ra-DU, Nin-e$_2$-muš$_3$-še$_3$, and Šubur-^{d}Ba-ba$_6$) who are also listed with the landholding Gan-ki (VS 14, 72; see above).

3. Gan-ki, the "wife of the leatherworker Gišgal-si" (**Gan-ki / dam Gišgal-si / ašgab-ke$_4$**). She was one of the three creditors to whom Baranamtara reimbursed the money she had borrowed to buy a **gala**-singer (Nik 1, 17 = SRU 45; dated to L3). That Gan-ki's husband Gišgal-si might have been a person of some importance can be deduced from the sale contract DP 31 (SRU 31; Beld 2002: 70–73). This document mentions A-sa$_6$, the wife of Baranamtara's father,[15] as the seller of the house and Enentarzi as its buyer, and listed, among witnesses, **Gišgal-si / ašgab** (DP 31: iv 15–16) as well as Enentarzi's son Lugalanda (DP 31: v 18–19), the future husband of Baranamtara.[16]
4. Gan-ki, the "wife of Lugal-ra" (**Gan-ki / dam Lugal-ra**). She is listed in two texts, DP 128 (obv. ii 6–7; dated to UL2) and DP 129 (obv. ii 6–7; dated to UL3), which are classified as **ziz$_2$-ba ušur$_3$ nam-dumu** "emmer rations to the friends of prince-ship." These texts included a **nu-gig** "midwife" (Civil 2011: 281–83) named Gan-ezem and a **kar-kid$_3$** named Ama-ab-e$_2$-ta, who will be discussed below in 3.3 and 4.

While there were at least two different Gan-ki (3 and 4), we cannot say exactly how many more, if any, had the name Gan-ki-(ku$_3$-ga). Our landholding Gan-ki should likely be identified with the Gan-ki-ku$_3$-ga of (2), who clearly belonged to the elite, presumably, the ruling family (see Beld 2002: 189). It is also possible that she might have been the same person as Gan-ki (1).

The unnamed "wife of the chief administrator Šubur" (**dam Šubur / [nu]-b[anda$_3$]**) received 12 **iku** of land (VS 14, 156: obv. iii 9–iv 1). We do not know exactly who she was. Being the wife of one of the chief administrators of the E$_2$-mi$_2$, however, she must have been a high-ranking woman. She provided a workforce for cutting and carrying 90 bundles of reed in L3 (DP 352: obv. i 1–3) and was given 12 **sila$_3$** of semolina (**dabin**) in L5 (VS 25, 89: obv. v 8–9).[17]

15 This person was not Baranabtara's mother, who was Geme$_2$-ub$_5$-ku$_3$-ga (Beld 2002: 70, n. 66).

16 Since Enentarzi was still **sanga** when the document was produced, Lugalanda was designated as "son of the temple administrator" (**dumu sanga**).

17 Cf. Hal-hal, the wife of the chief administrator En-ig-gal, who is known from the texts recording **maš-da-ri-a**-gifts (DP 86; Nik 1, 172 = AWEL 172; VS 14, 159 = AWL 176; VS 14, 179 = AWL 175).

3 Female servants (ar_3-tu munus) with land

3.1 Female servants (ar_3-tu munus)

Another group of women who were allotted subsistence land comprised "female servants" (**ar_3-tu munus**).[18] Before going into details, let us briefly consider the **ar_3-tu munus**. This term refers to female (royal household) servants, and in contrast to the elite women mentioned above in section 2, who were mostly identified by family relationships such as "queen's mother," "queen's sister," or "wife of so-and-so,"[19] the **ar_3-tu munus** were identified only by their own name.[20]

Female servants usually occur in Type II lists, "barley rations given to blind persons, carriers, and those registered in various tablets" (**še-ba igi-nu-du_8 il_2 $ša_3$-dub-didli**). As Maekawa (1973–74: 104, n. 36; 1987: 61; 1999: 85) has pointed out, women do not appear in Type I lists, "barley rations given to those who were allocated subsistence land" (**še-ba lu_2-šuku-dab_5-ba**) even though they held a subsistence land (**gan_2 šuku**). Female servants are also found in the so-called "pure milk and pure malt" (**ga-ku_3 $munu_4$-ku_3**) texts.[21] These texts recorded a gift-giving ceremony of milk and malt, which Gelb (1975: 72–73) schematically described as "offerings by about 50 men to the wives of 50 other men." Recipients were mainly the wives of high-ranking priests and officials and the givers were mostly men of "lower" rank (Beld 2002: 129–130). However, neither the givers nor the recipients were exclusively of the same sex. Notably, female servants are also listed among givers.[22] As a group, they are listed second to the givers designated as "the great **igi-$nigin_2$**-people" (**lu_2-igi-$nigin_2$ gal-gal-me**), who "are the most important or highest ranking people among the donors" (Beld 2002: 131). This order may speak for the relative importance of this female group in the E_2-mi_2 organizational machinery (Beld 2002: 137–141). Women mentioned in the first and second places in the ar_3-tu munus section of the "pure milk and pure malt" texts (Table 2) are found in the land allotment documents.

18 For the reading **ar_3-tu** for HAR.TU, see Steinkeller 1989: 130, n. 389; **ur_5/ar_3-tu** in Michalowski 2011: 227–228.

19 Foxvog (2011: 60) has counted 267 unnamed wives referred to by their husbands' names or titles among the 3,371 discrete individuals identified by him in the Lagaš **E_2-mi_2** corpus.

20 They may be called "independent" women; cf. Asher-Greve 2006: 57.

21 Discussed by Deimel (1931: 40–49), Gelb (1975), Selz (1995: 73–78), Beld (2002: 129–142), and Prentice (2010: 181–185) among others.

22 Five men were listed among recipients (Beld 2002: 133, with n. 25).

Tab. 2: First two female mentioned in the “pure milk and pure malt” texts.

Text (Date)	DP 226 (L4); VS 14, 173 (L4)*; DP 132 (L5)	DP 133 (UL1); TSA 5 (UL2)
Name #1	E$_2$-mete	E$_2$-mete
Name #2	Nin-uru-da-kuš$_2$	Geme$_2$-šu **nu-gig**

* Bauer (1967: 244) believes that VS 14, 173 was a first draft of DP 226, whereas Beld (2002: 135) thinks that the two texts represented two different occasions. According to Beld’s interpretation, the gift-giving of “pure milk and pure malt” was celebrated twice a year, in **ezem-še-gu$_7$-^{d}Nanše** (first month) and **ezem-munu$_4$-gu$_7$-^{d}Nanše** (ninth month), and these two texts dated to the same year testify to this.

3.2 E$_2$-mete, Nin-u$_3$-ma, Šeš-a-mu, and Nin-uru-da-kuš$_2$

In L4, E$_2$-mete was allotted 4 **iku** of subsistence land and the other three, Nin-u$_3$-ma, Šeš-a-mu, and Nin-uru-da-kuš$_2$, were allotted 2 **iku** each (VS 14, 72: rev. i 5–9). We know that the latter women had already been working in L1 as **ar$_3$-tu munus** and that each received 18 **sila$_3$** of emmer rations (DCS 8: obv. v 3–6). As for E$_2$-mete, her earliest attestation is in RTC 52 dated to L3, in which she worked as an overseer of female weavers.[23] E$_2$-mete, who joined the work force of female servants later, became its head, receiving an area twice as large as those of the other female servants. In UL1, the size of E$_2$-mete’s subsistence land amounted to 6 **iku** (VS 25, 73: rev. iv 3 and HSS 3, 40: rev. iii 10–11).

3.3 Geme$_2$-šu-ga-lam-ma and an unnamed midwife (nu-gig)

In UL1, Geme$_2$-šu-ga-lam-ma was given (**šum$_2$**) 6 **iku** (VS 25, 70: rev. iv 4–5), and her field was measured (**gid$_2$**) at 6¼ **iku** (HSS 3, 40: rev. v 6–7). It is noteworthy that in the letter Geme$_2$-šu-ga-lam-ma is specifically designated as “midwife” (**nu-gig**). She can be identified with the **nu-gig** Geme$_2$-šu attested in the “pure milk and pure malt” texts that date to UL1 and UL2 (DP 133: obv. iv 4–5 and TSA 5: obv. iii 12–13).

In UL3, an unnamed **nu-gig** was given 6 **iku** of subsistence land (DP 580: obv. ii 6). With whom should this person be identified? Besides Geme$_2$-šu-(ga-lam-ma), another **nu-gig** named Gan-ezem is mentioned in DP 128: rev. i 5–6 and DP 129: rev. i 7–8, dated to UL2 and UL3 respectively.[24] If we assume that

23 For E$_2$-mete’s career, see Karahashi 2014.
24 For DP 128 and DP 129, see 2.3 (4).

Geme$_2$-šu-(ga-lam-ma) was replaced by Gan-ezem in the **nu-gig**-function sometime during UL2, the unnamed midwife in DP 580 can probably be identified as Gan-ezem.

4 A kar-kid$_3$ with land

An exceptional case was a **kar-kid$_3$** named Nin-nig$_2$-mu who was given 1½ **iku** of leased land characterized as **gan$_2$ 5-tuku** "field that yields 720 **sila$_3$** per **iku**" (DP 587: obv. ii 9–iii 2; dated to UL4). We have no more information about her; however, another **kar-kid$_3$** named Ama-ab-(e$_2$-ta) is attested in DP 128 (obv. iv 2–3), where the aforementioned midwife (**nu-gig**) Gan-ezem is also found. This association of **kar-kid$_3$** and **nu-gig** reminds us of a Fara text, WF 74 (EDATŠ 6), in which **nu-gig**, **ša$_3$-zu** "midwife," and **geme$_2$-kar-kid** are mentioned.[25]

5 Comparison of male and female landholding

It is difficult to estimate how much area one individual held because if he/she held more than one plot, the total area given to that person was not necessarily recorded in a single tablet. For example, Šeš-lu$_2$-dug$_3$ was given 52 **iku** (26 **iku** of **gan$_2$** FN$_1$ and 26 **iku** of **gan$_2$** FN$_2$) in a **šum$_2$**-tablet (VS 25, 70: obv. i 8–10), but only 26 **iku** of subsistence land is mentioned for him in a **gid$_2$**-tablet (HSS 3, 40: iv 2). A similar recording situation is found in the cases of Inim-ma-ni-zi (48 **iku** in VS 25, 70; cf. 24 **iku** of subsistence land in HSS 3, 40) and Dam-dingir-mu (46 **iku** in VS 25, 70; cf. 23 **iku** of subsistence land in HSS 3, 40).[26]

In spite of these difficulties, let us attempt to evaluate the subsistence land allotment recorded in VS 14, 72. As we have already seen, the land of the queen's mother Geme$_2$-ub$_5$-ku$_3$-ga was measured at 36 **iku**. On the one hand, that was twice as much as the area held by other royal members, male (A-en-

25 For discussion about **kar-kid$_3$**, see Civil 1976; Pomponio 1986; Assante 1998; Cooper 2006; Cooper 2010; Heimpel 2010.

26 In other words, "there are no summation registers of all who received **šuku** land, instead, each group of fields is entered on a separate document ... Consequently, drawing comparisons between the landholding of individuals is difficult ..." (Prentice 2010: 73).

ra-DU and Šubur-^{d}Ba-ba$_6$) and female (Nin-e$_2$-muš$_3$-še$_3$). On the other hand, Geme$_2$-ub$_5$-ku$_3$-ga's area was quite small compared with that held by En-ig-gal, a chief administrator of the E$_2$-mi$_2$ (138 ¾ **iku**) and Šul-me, an **agrig**-administrator (90 **iku**).

The mother of Sasa the queen was probably allotted 36 **iku** of subsistence land, as was Baranamtara's mother, and also had 18 **iku** of leased land. Baranamtara's sister Ki-tuš-lu$_2$, who married a chief scribe, is attested only with leased land (18 **iku**).

What was the landholding situation of other male members of the ruling families? Giri$_3$-ni-ba-dab$_5$, brother of Baranamtara, is mentioned with 17 ¾ **iku** of leased land in HSS 3, 40: obv. iii 6–8 (dated to UL1) and 10 **iku** of leased land in Nik 1, 32: rev. ii 5–7 (dated to UL3). Two brothers of Sasa, Ur-^{d}Ba-ba$_6$ and Igi-zi, held both subsistence and leased land: the size of each field was either 18 or 24 **iku** (DP 583: obv. i 3–5, rev. i 1–3; DP 580: obv. ii 2–4). They and another brother, Me-an-ne$_2$-si, are listed with 18 **iku** of leased land each (TSA 7: rev. i 8–15).[27] The latter was also recorded with18 **iku** of subsistence land in HSS 3, 38: rev. ii 1–2.

E$_2$-mete, Geme$_2$-šu-ga-lam-ma and an unnamed midwife were allotted 6 **iku** of subsistence land. E$_2$-mete is known to have played the role of "overseer" of textile workers (Maekawa 1980: 87), although she is never explicitly designated as such in extant texts. Among seven female overseers of textile workers, she was the only one who was given land in addition to monthly rations. E$_2$-mete's male counterparts, Gišgal-si and ^{d}Nanše-da-nu-me-a, who are clearly designated as "overseers of textile workers" (**ugula ki-siki-ka-me**), were allotted 6 **iku** each (HSS 3, 40: obv. ii 3–5, dated to UL1; DP 578: rev. iv 2–4, dated to UL2).[28] As for the other male textile overseer, Ma-al-ga, no land allotment document is preserved. It is certain, however, that he was also given subsistence land because he fulfilled the work obligations of subsistence-land holders (**lu$_2$-šuku-dab$_5$-ba**), as Gišgal-si and ^{d}Nanše-da-nu-me-a did.

At the time when E$_2$-mete's allotment was 4 **iku**, the other female servants (**ar$_3$-tu munus**) were each allotted 2 **iku** of subsistence land, which was the smallest allotment unit (Yamamoto 1973: 29–30, n. 36; Steinkeller 1999: 295). Men, mostly members of the artisan group (**giš-kin-ti**), which included metalworkers (**simug**), leatherworkers (**ašgab**), fullers (**azlag$_3$**), carpenters (**nagar**),

27 For Me-an-ne$_2$-si and TSA 7, see Selz 2004: 239 [5].

28 In the matter of 6 **iku**: "Typically in southern Babylonia during the third millennium BC, an individual family held a tract of arable land as their subsistence land, which most commonly measured 6 **iku** or 2.1 ha of land" (Steinkeller 1999a: 303).

reed-mat weavers (**ad-kup$_4$**), rope-makers and braiders (**tug$_2$-du$_8$**), and so forth, seem to have been allotted 2 to 4 **iku** of subsistence land (VS 25, 70 and HSS 3, 40).

***

Even though there must have been more women holding subsistence land and/or leased land than have been discussed in this paper, attestations of such women are few. The data available for UL1, in which more than 120 individuals and groups are mentioned, shows that their number amounts to only about three percent. Among them elite women held subsistence land and/or leased land. One may wonder whether women made a profit by managing their leased land. Female servants seem to have been the only group of working women who received subsistence land. E$_2$-mete, who was the chief of the female servants and also the textile overseer, was allotted a land as big as those of the male textile overseers. Wet-nurses belonged to the same category, while others belonged to a lower one.

Abbreviations

E	Enentarzi
FN	Field Name
L	Lugalanda
PN	Personal Name
UL	Urukagina Lugal

Bibliography

Asher-Greve, Julia M. 2006. "Golden Age" of Women? Status and Gender in Third Millennium Sumerian and Akkadian Art. Pp. 41–81 in *Images and Gender: Contributions to the Hermeneutics of Reading Ancient Art*, ed. Silvia Schroer. OBO 220. Fribourg: Academic Press; Göttingen: Vandenhoeck & Ruprecht.

Assante, Julia. The kar.kid / *ḫarimtu*, Prostitute or Single Woman?: A Reconsideration of the Evidence. *UF* 30: 5–96.

Bartash, Vitali. 2014. E$_2$-mi$_2$ – "Women's Quarters": The Earliest Written Evidence. Pp. 9–20 in *House and Household Economies in 3rd Millennium B. C. E. Syro-Mesopotamia*, ed. Federico Buccellati Oxford: Archaeopress.

Bauer, Josef. 1967. Altsumerische Wirtschaftstexte aus Lagasch. Inaugural-Dissertation zur Erlangung der Doktorwürde der Philosophischen Fakultät der Julius-Maximilians-Universität zu Würzburg.

Beld, Scott G. 2002. The Queen of Lagaš: Ritual Economy in a Sumerian State. Ph. D. dissertation. The University of Michigan.

Civil, Miguel. 1976. Kar-AK = kar-kìd. *RA* 70: 189–190.

Civil, Miguel. 2011. The Law Collection of Ur-Namma. Pp. 221–286 in *Cuneiform Royal Inscriptions and Related Texts in the Schøyen Collection*, ed. Andrew George. CUSAS 17. Bethesda: CDL Press.

Cooper, Jerrold S. 2006. Prostitution. *RlA* 11: 12–21.

Cooper, Jerrold S. 2010. Blind Workmen, Weaving Women and Prostitutes in Third Millennium Babylonia. *CDLN* 2010: 005.

Deimel, P. Anton. 1931. *Šumerische Tempelwirtschaft zur Zeit Urukaginas und seiner Vorgänger: Abschluss der Einzelstudien und Zusammenfassung der Hauptresultate.* Analecta Orientalia 2. Rome: Pontificio Instituto Biblico.

Foxvog, Daniel A. 2011. Aspects of Name-Giving in Presagonic Lagaš. Pp. 59–97 in *Strings and Threads: A Celebration of the Works of Anne Draffkorn Kilmer*, eds. Wolfgang Heimpel and Gabriella Frantz-Szabó. Winona Lake: Eisenbrauns.

Gelb, Ignace J. 1975. Homo Ludens in Early Mseopotamia. *StOr* 46: 43–75.

Heimpel, Wolfgang. 2010. Left to Themselves: Waifs in the Time of the Third Dynasty of Ur. Pp. 159–166 in *Why Should Someone Who Knows Something Conceal It?: Cuneiform Studies in Honor of David I. Owen on His 70th Birthday*, eds. Alexandra Kleinerman and Jack M. Sasson. Bethesda: CDL Press.

Karahashi, Fumi. 2014. Overseers of Weavers in Presargonic Lagaš: E_2-mete and Her Colleagues. Paper presented at the 60th Rencontre Assyriologique Internationale in Warsaw.

Maeda, Tohru. 1984. Work Concerning Irrigation Canals in Pre-Sargonic Lagaš. *ASJ* 6: 33–53.

Maekawa, Kazuya. 1973–74. The Development of the é-mí in Lagaš during Early Dynastic III. *Mesopotamia* 8–9: 77–144.

Maekawa, Kazuya. 1977. The Rent of the Tenant Field (gán-APIN.LAL) in Lagaš. *Zinbun* 14: 1–54.

Maekawa, Kazuya. 1987. Collective Labor Service in Girsu-Lagaš: The Pre-Sargonic and Ur III Periods. Pp. 49–71 in *Labor in the Ancient Near East*, ed. Marvin A. Powell. American Oriental Series 68. New Haven: American Oriental Society.

Maekawa, Kazuya. 1996. The Governor's Family and the "Temple Households" in Ur III Girsu. Pp. 171–179 in *House and Households in Ancient Mesopotamia: Papers read at the 40^{e} Rencontre Assyriologique Internationale, Leiden, July 5–8, 1993*, ed. Klaas R. Veenhof. Istanbul: Nederlands Historisch-Archaeologisch Instituut.

Maekawa, Kazuya. 1999. The "Temples" and the "Temple Personnel" of Ur III Girsu-Lagaš. Pp. 59–102 in *Priests and Officials in the Ancient Near East: Papers of the Second Colloquium on the Ancient Near East – The City and its Life, Held at the Middle Eastern Culture Center in Japan (Mitaka, Tokyo)*, ed. Kazuko Watanabe. Heidelberg: Universitätsverlag C. Winter.

Marchesi, Gianni. 2011. Goods from the Queen of Tilmun. Pp. 189–199 in *Akkad is King: A Collection of Papers by Friends and Colleagues Presented to Aage Westenholz on the Occasion of His 70th Birthday 15th of May 2009*, ed. Gojko Barjamovic PIHANS 118. Leiden: Nederlands Instituut voor het Nabije Oosten.

Michalowski, Piotr. 2011. *The Correspondence of the Kings of Ur: An Epistolary History of an Ancient Mesopotamian Kingdom*. Winona Lake: Eisenbrauns.

Nakahara, Yomokuro. 1961.「シュメール土地制度における託営地について—折半小作と開拓地—」『西洋史学』50号, pp. 1–12.

Pomponio, Francesco. 1986. géme-kar-kìd: The Sumerian Word for "Prostitute." *Oikumene* 5: 63–66.

Prentice, Rosemary. 2010. *The Exchange of Goods and Services in Pre-Sargonic Lagaš*. AOAT 368.

Rubio, Gonzalo. 2010. Reading Sumerian Names, I: Ensuhkešdanna and Baba. *JCS* 62: 29–43.

Selz, Gebhard J. 1989. *Altsumerische Verwaltungstexte aus Lagaš*, Teil 1: *Die altsumerischen Wirtschaftsurkunden der Ermitage zu Leningrad*. FAOS 15/1. Stuttgart: Franz Steiner Verlag Wiesbaden.

Selz, Gebhard J. 1993a. *Altsumerische Verwaltungstexte aus Lagaš*, Teil 2: *Altsumerische Wirtschaftsurkunden aus amerikanischen Sammlungen*, 1. Abschnitt. FAOS 15/2-1. Stuttgart: Franz Steiner Verlag Wiesbaden.

Selz, Gebhard J. 1993b. *Altsumerische Verwaltungstexte aus Lagaš*, Teil 2: *Altsumerische Wirtschaftsurkunden aus amerikanischen Sammlungen*, 2. Abschnitt. FAOS 15/2-2. Stuttgart: Franz Steiner Verlag Wiesbaden.

Selz, Gebhard J. 1995. *Untersuchungen zur Götterwelt des altsumerischen Stadtstaates*. Occasional Publications of the Samuel Noah Kramer Fund 13. Philadelphia: The University of Pennsylvania Museum.

Selz, Gebhard J. 2004. Familiäres: me-an-ne$_2$-si šeš munus. Pp. 237–241 in *Von Sumer Nach Ebla und Zurück*, ed. Hartmut Waetzoldt. Heidelberger Studien zum Alten Orient, Band 9. Heidelberg: Heidelberger Orientverlag.

Sharlach, Tonia M. 2008. Priestesses, Concubines, and the daughters of men: Disentangling the Meaning of the Word lukur in Ur III times. Pp. 177–183 in *On the Third Dynasty of Ur: Studies in Honor of Marcel Sigrist*, ed. Piotr Michalowski. Boston: American Schools of Oriental Research.

Steinkeller, Piotr. 1981. More on the Ur III Royal Wives. *ASJ* 3: 77–92.

Steinkeller, Piotr. 1989. *Sale Documents of the Ur-III-Period*. FAOS 17. Stuttgart: Franz Steiner Verlag.

Steinkeller, Piotr. 1999a. Land-Tenure Conditions in Third-Millennium Babylonia: The Problem of Regional Variation. Pp. 289–321 in *Urbanization and Land Ownership in the Ancient Near East*, eds. Michael Hudson and Baruch A. Levine. Peabody Museum Bulletin 7. Cambridge, MA: Harvard University.

Steinkeller, Piotr. 1999b. On Rulers, Priests and Sacred Marriage: Tracing the Evolution of Early Sumerian Kingship. Pp. 103–137 in *Priests and Officials in the Ancient Near East: Papers of the Second Colloquium on the Ancient Near East – The City and its Life, Held at the Middle Eastern Cultural Center in Japan (Mitaka, Tokyo, March 22–24, 1996)*, ed. Kazuko Watanabe. Heidelberg: Universitätsverlag C. Winter.

Yamamoto, Shigeru.
1973.「シュメール都市国家ラガシュに置ける土地制度研究への一序論— P. A. Deimelの業績の再検討を中心に—」『オリエント』14: 1–32 (English summary, pp. 181–182).

Yamamoto, Shigeru. 1979. The "Agricultural Year" in the Pre-Sargonic Girsu-Lagaš (I). *ASJ* 1: 85–97.

Yamamoto, Shigeru. 1981. The lú-KUR$_6$-dab$_5$-ba People in Pre-Sargonic in the é-mí-e$_2$-^{d}Ba-Ú in Pre-Sargonic Lagaš. *ASJ* 3: 93–110.

Maria Giovanna Biga

The Role of Women in Work and Society in the Ebla Kingdom (Syria, 24th century BC)

The archives of Ebla, kept in the royal palace or rather in the complex of palatial buildings that housed those in power, tell us mainly about life at the court of Ebla and at other courts of Syrian capitals at the time.

The Ebla archives cover a period of roughly 50 years of the history of the city and kingdom. 26 kings of Ebla are known but it is only possible to reconstruct a detailed history of Ebla for the last three kings, who ruled over a period of 50 years. The third from last king, Igriš-halab, and his viziers Tir and Darmia, are attested in a limited number of texts; it is already possible to have some information about the life at the court of Ebla and also about women at the court. The reign of the penultimate sovereign Irkab-damu is much better documented. His vizier was Arrukum. But it is the reign of the last king Išar-damu (with his two viziers Ibrium and his son Ibbi-zikir) that is known best of all. The last king reigned for a period of approximately 36 years. The purpose of this paper is to give an outline of the role of women in the society of Ebla and of some of the female workers there.

1 Women of the Eblaite royal family

The court represents a privileged observation point from which we can view the political, diplomatic, religious, economic and commercial life of a 24th century BC Syrian kingdom and study the role of women in Eblaite society and at work in the court.

From the very beginning of Eblaite studies G. Pettinato was able to understand that with the word "DAM" the Eblaite scribes indicated women of differ-

Acknowledgements: I greatly enjoyed this conference on women in work and society because of the interesting exchange of opinions in a friendly atmosphere. Several articles on women at Ebla have already been written, see for example Archi 1996a, 2002a, 2002b; Biga 1987, 1988, 1991, 1995, 1996, 1998b, 1999, 2000, 2010a, 2010b, 2010c, 2014b; Catagnoti 1989; Dolce 2014; Matthiae 2014; Tonietti 1989, 2010, etc.

Maria Giovanna Biga, Sapienza Università di Roma; vanna.biga@gmail.com

ent rank living at the Ebla court. He was also able to identify the word for "queen" "*maliktum*" (whereas the word for "king" is the Sumerian logogram "EN").[1]

Some women of the Ebla court had an important role in Eblaite society, taking part in every event of the court, religious ceremonies, rituals etc. They did not live apart from men but were involved in all the affairs of the kingdom with them, except for war. Women at war are not attested at Ebla in my opinion.[2]

They participated with men at the festivals at the court, including those for the triumph of victorious generals back from war, wherein they offered gifts to the victor.[3]

To reconstruct the history of Ebla it is fundamental to study the relative chronology of the texts. For this purpose the study of the prosopography, tracing the lives and families of important figures and especially of people of the royal family in various periods, was essential. Also, people serving at the Ebla court were important for reconstructing the chronology.[4]

The study of the court ladies (DAM EN), consisting of the kings' secondary wives, concubines, aunts, sisters, wet-nurses etc. proved to be fundamental. Indeed, their study was more important than that of male personages. Especially in the monthly accounts of textiles there are lists of women of the court receiving textiles and wool. These women were listed according to their importance. It is possible to follow the lives of several women. Many of the events important to write the history of Ebla include women: births of princes and princesses, inter-dynastic marriages, marriages of princesses with Eblaite high functionaries, princesses going into some temples as priestesses, deaths of queens in other kingdoms, religious ceremonies according to specific rituals with participation of women of the royal family etc.[5]

The women of the vizier Ibrium and his daughters were also important for reconstructing the relative chronology of the Ebla texts. Azimu, principal wife of Ibrium and the mother of his son and successor as vizier, Ibbi-zikir, and also lady Tiludu, mother of other sons of Ibrium, are well known and often quoted in the texts. Their names were fundamental for Pomponio to understand that

1 See Pettinato 1980, MEE II s.v. "DAM" and "*maliktum*".

2 For another opinion see Tonietti 2010; Archi 2014; but see Biga in press 2.

3 See Biga 2011 for several examples.

4 See Biga-Pomponio 1990, 1993; Biga 1996, 2003a.

5 Pettinato 1988 was first able to recognize the importance of these "rites of passage" in the Ebla texts. For articles regarding women of the Ebla court see Biga 1987, 1991, 1996, 1998b, 2008, 2010a, b, 2014c.

Ibrium and Ibbi-zikir could not have been kings of Ebla as previously supposed by Pettinato.[6]

Some queens travelled a lot, like queen Tiša-lim, queen of Emar, perhaps an Eblaite, who was often present at Ebla, or Zugalum, the Eblaite princess married to the king of Harran.

The queen mother and the queen went on pilgrimages to some sanctuaries of the goddess Išhara (see § 5.1).

Textiles of different types were given to the court ladies and to women workers at the Ebla court on different occasions for particular ceremonies such as the ritual of royalty or other festivals. But often textiles given to women are registered without an occasion. These are not rations of textiles because they are not given regularly.[7]

Women of the Ebla court received textiles when moving from one palace to another, for example lady Anialudu who moved to the palace of Arugadu with a staff of some servants (GEME_2):

TM.75.G.1760+10130 (king Išar-damu,vizier Ibrium, month MAxGANA$_2$*tenû*-GUDU_4) obv iii 8-iv 3: 5 AKTUM-TUG_2 TI-TUG_2 1 GADA- TUG_2 HUL *A*-NI-*la-a-lu-du* DAM EN DU-DU *si-in A-ru*$_{12}$-*ga-du*^{KI} 10 GU-MUG-TUG_2 GEME_2-GEME_2-*sù*, "5 AKTUM-textiles, 1 linen textile to Anilaludu woman of the king to go to the city of Arugadu, 10 GU-MUG-textiles to her servants."

On the occasion of birth at the Ebla court or in one of the other palaces the king of Ebla had in towns around Ebla, such as 'Azan, Arugadu, etc.,[8] gifts were given to the mother of the prince or princess.

TM.75.G.2511+ 10139 (king Išar-damu, vizier Ibbi-zikir 2 year, month MAx-GANA$_2$*tenû*-GUDU_4) obv. vi 18-vii 8: 1 ZARA_6-TUG_2 2 *bu-di* ŠU_2+ŠA BAR_6:KU_3 *Téš-ma-zi-kir* DAM EN *'À-za-an*^{KI} *in* UD DUMU-NITA TU-DA, "1 ZARA_6-textile, 2 pins weighing 20 shekels of silver to Tešma-zikir woman of the king of the city of Azan when she gave birth to a son."

Wool was often given to women, including the important women of the court, to make fabrics, blankets, pillows, cushions, carpets or ropes and also textiles for deities.

Women of the court also had servants (GEME_2) at their service, but it is difficult to know if they were prisoners of war or not.

---

6 See Pettinato 1979: XXXIII; Pomponio 1987.

7 TM.75.G.2511+ 10139 (king Išar-damu. vizier Ibbi-zikir 2 year, month MAxGANA$_2$*tenû*-GUDU_4) obv. viii 17-ix 3: 1 ZARA_6-TUG_2 1 GID_2-TUG_2 *BU*$_3$-BAR_6:KU_3 DAM EN, "1 ZARA_6-textile, 1 GID_2-textile to Bu-barku woman of the king." See also Biga 2010d.

8 For these palaces see Biga 2013: 261–262.

Ladies of the royal court probably had ladies-in-waiting. When a girl of the family of vizier Ibrium married the son of the king of DUlu, she left with a retinue of 17 ladies-in-waiting supplied by 17 different state officers (Biga 2014c).

2 The queen mother Dusigu and the last queen of Ebla Tabur-damu

It is thanks to the study of the court ladies that it is possible to identify Išar-damu as the last king of Ebla (Biga-Pomponio 1987). The study of the life of lady Dusigu was important for this task and also for the reconstruction of several years of the history. Lady Dusigu became "great mother of the king" (AMA-GAL EN) when her son came to the throne. The identification of the last king of Ebla as son of Dusigu and of the penultimate king Irkab-damu was essential to begin the reconstruction of his long reign (around 36 years; Biga-Pomponio 1990, 1993). Further proof that Išar-damu was really the last king of Ebla came later by the prosopographical study of wet-nurses. K/Gisadu is quoted as wet-nurse of the king (GA-DU$_8$ EN) and of Išar-damu so the equivalence of Išar-damu with the king became certain (Biga 2000: 72–73; Biga-Capomacchia 2012; see also § 6.2).

The court ladies of king Irkab-damu are well known (Archi 1996a); some powerful figures are Kešdut[9] and Enna-Utu, but the name of the queen remains unknown.

Irkab-damu married and performed the ritual described in ARET XI, 1 with his wife (the queen). He had several sons and daughters by different wives and probably also by the queen. Their names are well known and their lives can be reconstructed.[10] One of the sons of king Irkab-damu was Išar-damu. He was probably his last son, born of the lady Dusigu, and he became Irkab-damu's successor.

Irkab-damu became a widower soon after his marriage; several texts of the period of Irkab-damu quote women of the court but not the queen.[11] At this

9 Kešdut was also important at the time of king Igriš-Halab and was possibly his wife. In that period no mother of the king (AMA-GAL EN) is mentioned. Only lady Dusigu had this title and she was the mother of king Išar-damu.

10 For some examples of the lives of princesses see Biga 1996: 63–72.

11 For the reconstruction of this part of Ebla's history see Biga-Pomponio 1990, 1993; Biga 1996. Pomponio and I were able to recognize several texts in which a queen of Ebla is not

point lady Dusigu[12] suddenly appears in the lists of women at the court and begins to be mentioned often. Then she takes the first place in the list of women. She was active in diplomatic affairs and the first of the ladies of the court when making cult offerings. It is clear that, at the same time she assumed her important role at court, Ibrium began to have an important place in the administration while vizier Arrukum was still alive.[13] Four sisters of Dusigu are well known and it is possible to follow their lives until their deaths.[14] The texts that mention Dusigu, above all the monthly textile lists, show that she acted like a queen. Despite her rapid rise to the position of first lady at court, Dusigu was never referred to with a title, nor was she ever called queen. During this period of some years no woman was given the title of queen. Irkab-damu probably did not bestow this title on his last wife. In several texts lady Dusigu is not referred to by her personal name and is designated as "great mother of the king" until her death.[15] After long study it was possible to verify that lady Dusigu took her new title in the same year that king Irkab-damu died (Biga-Pomponio 1990: 188–194). It was possible to conclude that, at the death of king Irkab-damu, Dusigu succeeded in putting her son Išar-damu on the throne. From that moment on she was omnipresent for several years. She was named even before her son the king. When vizier Arrukum died he was replaced by Ibrium. Dusigu became Ibrium's chief collaborator. The most plausible explanation for this is that Išar-damu became king while he was still a child and his mother, with the help of vizier Ibrium, acted as a sort of regent. The queen mother had a very powerful role at the Ebla court for the entire period of vizier Ibrium (around 18 years) and also for the first three years of vizier Ibbi-zikir.

During the years 12–13 of Ibrium as vizier, a girl named Tabur-damu appears in the lists of court ladies.[16] Tabur-damu is the daughter of Irib-damu, a brother of king Irkab-damu, so she is therefore a cousin of king Išar-damu. She

mentioned; they are from the time of vizier Arrukum and also of vizier Ibrium when a powerful figure began to emerge at the court, a woman named Dusigu.

12 For Dusigu as the most important woman at the Ebla court, see Biga 1987: 41–42; Biga 1991; Biga 2003a: 354–356.

13 Possibly she was a member of Ibrium's family but it is not mentioned in the texts. When both Ibrium and Dusigu died, and when funerary goods (textiles) were given on the occasion of a funeral service of a member of the royal family, Dusigu and Ibrium were both quoted (Biga 2007–2008: 263–264; Biga 2010a: 46).

14 Their quotations in several texts were important for the reconstruction of the relative chronology, see Biga-Pomponio 1990: 189.

15 A study of all the texts of the long life of lady Dusigu should be undertaken.

16 For the identification of Tabur-damu as last queen of Ebla see Biga-Pomponio 1990: 188–189.

soon occupied a place second only to that of the queen mother. From a passage of the text TM.75.G.2417 (parallel and contemporary to the text of the ritual ARET XI 2 and to the annual account of metals TM.75.G.1730 (= MEE VII 34) (Biga 1998a), it is evident that lady Dusigu selected the young girl as a bride for her son. Dusigu then asked for an omen. The omen was favorable, so Tabur-damu became queen of Ebla (Biga 1999).

In that year, year 14 of Ibrium as vizier, Tabur-damu married the young king, who had already been on the throne for fourteen years. The marriage is quoted only in an annual account of deliveries of metals, MEE VII 34. No monthly accounts of deliveries of textiles with the dowry (that was surely very rich) to Tabur-damu, nor the anointing of the head of the girl have been recognized in the Ebla texts. No text with the dowry has been identified, probably because it was given by the family of the bride's father. Those deliveries were not from the palace storerooms but from the storerooms of the house of Irib-damu, and therefore were not registered in the Eblaite palace archives.

After the wedding, in that same year, the new queen and the king her husband celebrated the complex ritual narrated in ARET XI 2.

Even after the marriage, when king Išar-damu went to war for the first time with vizier Ibrium in a military campaign against the kingdom of Zahiran, in year 16 of vizier Ibrium, the news of the Eblaite victory was immediately brought only to the queen mother (and not also to the queen) who was probably anxious for news.[17]

The queen mother and the queen had their own chariots, received regularly textiles for animals of the chariots[18] and travelled especially to visit some sanctuaries of the goddess Išhara. It is also possible that they had sedan-chairs (see § 5.1).

The chariot mentioned among the funerary array for the queen mother is probably the funerary chariot used for the ceremony, which was then interred in the tomb with the extremely rich funerary gifts that Dusigu received when she died.

Dusigu died in the third year of vizier Ibbi-zikir. Her death was an important marking event for the ordering of texts. The death of the queen mother

---

17 Biga 2010a. For a different opinion see Archi 2014: 22 where Archi states that the king never went with Ibrium on a military campaign.

18 See for ex. TM.75.G.2436+10138 (after the join a big tablet of monthly accounts of textiles almost complete, 10 columns on the obverse and 8 on the reverse, dated to the first three years of Ibbi-zikir as vizier, under the reign of king Išar-damu, month *i-rí-sa*) obv. x 5–16: 6 AKTUM-TUG$_2$ TI-TUG$_2$ DAM-GEME$_2$ EN 4 GADA-TUG$_2$ 4 IGI-NITA EN 4 GADA-TUG$_2$ 4 IGI-NITA AMA-GAL EN *wa ma-lik-tum*, "6 AKTUM-textiles to women and servants of the king, 4 linen textiles to 4 equids of the king, 4 linen textiles to 4 equids of the queen mother and of the queen."

and her very rich funerary array is recorded in an annual account of metals (which ends with this event that gives the name to the year and specifies that the event took place in the month *gasum*, see Archi 2002a) and in a poorly preserved monthly account of deliveries of textiles (TM.75.G.1962) that was joined from several fragments in the last years of study in the Idlib museum (see Biga 1996: 48–50; Biga 2007–2008: 261, 266 and n. 69; Biga 2010a: 53–54.)

3 Women in rituals

Eblaite women had great importance in rituals. The queen had a very important role in the ritual of the renewal of royalty and initiation of the royal couple. The name of the queen of Irkab-damu, who performed the ritual narrated in ARET XI 1, is not known. Queen Tabur-damu performed the ritual narrated in ARET XI 2 with her husband. The dresses, the jewels for the queen, the different objects used during the days of the ritual, the sacrifices, everything was strictly prescribed and had to be perfectly performed (see ARET XI 1 and 2).

Other administrative texts related to the ritual narrated in ARET XI 2 allow interpretation of the ritual as a festival of initiation of royalty for the royal couple, as well as a renewal of royalty for the king who had already reigned for 13–14 years.[19]

In a complex ritual in the place called AN-EN-KI (possibly to be read as ^{d}EN^{KI})"the place where some dead and deified kings of Ebla were buried", some anonymous women (DAM) had the role of receiving textiles and wool for the rite.[20]

Women also had an important role in other rituals. See for example the ritual for the deities of the night, in which several women are involved (Biga 2003b; Fronzaroli 2012).

4 Interdynastic marriages of Eblaite princesses

Eblaite princesses had a very important role in Syrian society as protagonists of interdynastic marriages.

19 For the different interpretations of the ritual and previous bibliography see Biga-Capomacchia 2012.

20 See Archi 2010 for the translation of several passages, but Archi considered the ritual as performed in honor of the god EN-KI (Hayya in Eblaite). See also Pasquali 2002; Biga 2012: 12–15.

The texts prove that the kings of Ebla often used interdynastic marriage, sending Eblaite princesses to several small kingdoms, to reinforce alliances.[21]

Several of these marriages have already been studied.[22] Marriages of Eblaite princesses with the kings of Burman, Lumnan, 'Ašu, Nirar, small kingdoms probably near the kingdom of Ebla, are already well known. Recently the marriage of the Eblaite princess Zugalum with the king of Harran in the first year of vizier Ibbi-zikir and the subsequent relationships between the two kingdoms have been studied in detail thanks to the established relative chronology and the joins of several texts.[23]

In the last years of the kingdom of Ebla several interdynastic marriages took place: that of princess Tagriš-damu with Ultum-HU.HU, a son of Nagar's king (Biga 1987: 46 and n. 24; Biga 1998b; Biga 2011: 482–483) and that of princess Kešdut, daughter of the king and queen, who married the son of the king of Kiš (Biga 1987: 45; Archi 1987: 121–122; Archi-Biga 2003: 26–29).

And also in the last years of Ebla, the marriage of the Eblaite princess Tamurdasinu, a cousin of vizier Ibbi-zikir, with the son of the king of DUlu (probably Byblos) took place (Biga 1987: 46 and n. 23; Biga 2014a: 97; Biga 2014c).

It seems that princesses of other kingdoms never came to Ebla to marry the king, a son of the king or high functionaries.[24] No ceremony of the marriage of an Eblaite prince with a foreign princess is attested in the texts. We cannot exclude the possibility that some foreign princesses came to marry Eblaite princes, but the ceremony probably took place in other cities or countries and the dowry for the princesses was given by the foreign court, and for this reason was not registered by Eblaite scribes. The last king of Ebla married a cousin, Tabur-damu, daughter of Irib-damu, a brother of the penultimate king Irkab-damu. At the end of the history of Ebla the heir to the throne, prince Ir'aq-damu, married Za'aše, a daughter of the last vizier Ibbi-zikir.

Other marriages of Eblaite princesses and of girls of important Eblaite families with high functionaries of the court are documented in the still unpublished texts. The rich dowries given to these princesses have yet to be studied.

---

21 Biga 2008. In a period in which wars were very frequent it was necessary to have allies ready to supply soldiers and food during military campaigns, or simply to permit the Eblaite army to go through their territories. Ebla had a group of constant allies who came there to swear allegiance and were ready to march with the Eblaite vizier in his almost annual military campaigns.

22 For the first information about some interdynastic marriages see Biga 1987: 45–47.

23 Archi 2002a: 166–170; Biga 2010a: 48–49; Biga 2010b. See also Tonietti 2010.

24 This reflection was stimulated by a discussion during the conference.

5 Women as priestesses

5.1 Women as priestesses and making offerings to divinities

Several Eblaite princesses were appointed as priestesses (DAM-DINGIR) in temples of the region of Ebla. They must have had an important religious, social, and economic role, considering the importance of these much venerated and visited temples.[25] They received rich gifts as dowries for entering the temple as priestesses. Some of these lists of goods have already been published (Archi 2002a), but several are still unpublished.

Text TM.75.G.1679 lists a long series of precious textiles, jewels and objects intended for Tiabarzu, a girl from the family of vizier Ibrium.[26] These were probably given on the occasion of her entering a temple as priestess, even if she is not defined as such in the text. The ceremony in which she is involved must be studied in more detail. The dowry for Tiabarzu is quite similar to those for princesses in marriage or for their tomb already published by Archi 2002a.

It should be noted that princess Tinib-dulum was accompanied by five princes when she went as priestess to the sanctuary of the god 'Adabal of the city of Luban. They probably carried (IL_2) her on a sedan-chair. It is quite probable that some important women of the court used a sedan-chair; this is well attested in the Mari texts.[27] The wonderful, perfectly preserved sedan-chair of the mother of pharaoh Chefren is displayed in the Cairo museum.

The queen mother and the last queen went on several pilgrimages. They especially travelled to visit three sanctuaries dedicated to the goddess Išhara in the cities of Zuramu, Uguaš and MaNE, in the region controlled by Ebla (see Biga 2015: 108 and Biga in press 1).

Women of the court used to send gifts to the different temples and gods; it is impossible to know if this happened on specific occasions and what these occasions were.[28]

---

25 For the DAM-DINGIR see Archi 1998; Biga 2006: 29–31.

26 See Biga in press 4.

27 For sedan-chair in the Mari texts see Durand 1988: 123; Groneberg 1990: 162; Arkhipov, 2010; Kogan 2012. I would like to thank very much Jean-Marie Durand and Ilya Arkhipov for their precious suggestions during some profitable discussions on this topic. For sedan-chairs destined to women of the royal Eblaite family and to the king of Ebla see Biga, in press 3.

28 For the offerings to the deities of Eblaite pantheon see Pomponio-Xella 1997. For ex. TM.75.G.2511+10139 (king Išar-damu, vizier Ibbi-zikir year 2, month $MAxGANA_2$*tenû*-$GUDU_4$) obv. viii 3–9: 1 $ZARA_6$-TUG_2 NIG_2-BA *Ma-za-a-du* DAM EN *'À-za-an*^{KI} ^{d}*Ra-sa-ap 'À-da*-NI^{KI}, "1 $ZARA_6$-textile gift of Maza'adu woman of the king of Azan to the god Rasap of the city of Adani."

5.2 An unidentifiable object in the Ebla texts or girls (and boys) given to temples (oblates)?

Several years ago, in 1987, A. Archi published text TM.75.G.2022, which is related to gifts given to princess Tinib-dulum when she was going to Luban as a priestess (Archi 1987: 115–120). Archi transcribed at obv. i 4: 1 TUR:SAL (and passim in the text) and translated the word as "an unidentifiable object" (Archi 1987: 116 and n. 7: "Small SAL" where SAL may be the abbreviation for KU_3-SAL). At the time I was surprised by this, and informed Archi as much, but I could not challenge his translation, given the fact that only a few Ebla texts had been published. Now, after many years and many more published texts, it must be concluded that the common reading "DUMU-MUNUS" of the two logograms is also possible in the quoted text. It could refer to girls given to the princess to be in her service and in the service of the temple.[29] It should also be noted that the adjective "TUR" "small" always follows the object or the worker it qualifies and is never in first position.

Not all the functionaries quoted in the text TM.75.G.2022 supplied a girl, but all of them gave textiles and pins for textiles.

Girls and boys (always anonymous) were often offered (NIG_2-BA) to deities of temples by members of the royal family, especially the king, the queen mother and the queen. It is quite possible that at least several of them were prisoners of war. Sometimes the texts register the silver payed (to whom?) for these girls and boys. ARET VIII 534 § 28–29: 30 (GIN_2 DILMUN) BAR_6:KU_3 NIG_2-SA_{10} 2 DUMU-MUNUS 1 DUMU-NITA NIG_2-BA *ma-lik-tum* ^{d}*Išḫara Su-ra-mu*^{KI} *Má*-NE^{KI} *U*$_9$-*gú-a-šu*^{KI}: "30 shekels of silver, value of 2 girls and 1 boy offered by the queen to the goddess Išhara in her sanctuaries of Zuramu, Mane and Uguaš."

In the text of the treaty with Abarsal, a long passage (ARET XIII 5 rev. ix 7-x 7) regulates the ransom[30] of boys (DUMU-NITA) and girls (DUMU-MUNUS), the sons and daughters of citizens of Abarsal, who were working as manservants (IR_{11}) and servants ($GEME_2$) of an Eblaite. They could have been prisoners of war, but it is also possible (but less likely) that they were debtors.

---

29 At the time Archi still considered Ibrium to be a king of Ebla (Archi 1987: 117, 121). At a conference held in Naples 9–11 October 1985, Pomponio presented a paper in which he reached the conclusion that Ibrium and Ibbi-zikir could not have been kings of Ebla. He reached this conclusion by studying the names of the sons, daughters and women of different kings and of Ibrium and Ibbi-zikir (Pomponio 1987).

30 For prisoners of war in this period see Steinkeller 2013; for ransom of prisoners see Catagnoti 2012.

Several examples of boys and girls offered to temples have already been published, see Pomponio-Xella 1997: 256 (ARET III 118); 302 (TM.75.G.1743: 1 textile, 1 boy, 1 girl offered by the queen to the god Rasap of Adani on occasion of an illness of the son of the queen), etc.[31]

Sometimes in the texts it is difficult to determine if the gift consisted only of textiles intended for servants of the temple or if the servant was also part of the gift. In text TM.75.G.2022 there is no doubt that every functionary also gave a servant; when some of them did not give a servant it is specified (see for example obv. i 7–8: 1 DUMU-MUNUS NU I_3-NA-SUM "1 girl not given").

The offering of male and female servants to the temples (oblates) is a well know practice. It is attested from texts of the 3rd millennium to the texts of Babylonia of the 1st millennium BC, in which the practice of *širkûtu* is well documented.[32]

6 Women at work

We know of different types of women at work in the palace, outside the palace and outside the city of Ebla who received gifts or rations of textiles, wool or food. The Ebla texts are laconic administrative documents listing fabrics, wool or food leaving the coffers of the state. The letters from the royal archives of Mari are without a doubt astonishing. They deal with numerous private and public events of the time in a wealth of detail, but the types of female workers attested at Mari are almost the same as those working at the Ebla court.[33]

6.1 DAM/DUMU-MUNUS PA_4-ŠEŠ

In the royal palace lived the king, the queen and the other wives, and also the king's aunts and sisters. There were also a number of anonymous maids, DAM/DUMU-MUNUS PA_4-ŠEŠ, who took care of the women of the court. They prepared

31 Pomponio and Xella translated the word "DUMU-MUNUS" as "subordonné".

32 For the offering of boys and girls to deities in the Ebla texts see Biga-Capomacchia 2008: 143–144: "Già dagli archivi di Ebla risulta che i membri delle principali famiglie donavano alla divinità dei ragazzi e delle ragazze. I testi sono al solito laconici e annotano che un ragazzo o una ragazza sono offerti alla divinità. E' ovvio che sono offerti in servizio al tempio di quella divinità e probabilmente in servizio permanente; questa di Ebla è la prima e più antica attestazione della pratica di dedicare persone ad una divinità ..."

33 See N. Ziegler in this volume.

perfumed creams and unguents for their daily hygiene and looked after their wardrobes. In their private apartments the queen and the queen mother had dozens of these maids. Given their proximity to the queen or queen mother they probably had a certain importance at court and received precious pieces of clothing when certain ceremonies were performed. The king had male PA_4-ŠEŠ servants who probably did the same work for him (Archi 1996b). Among them there was the son of the king of Ursaum, a king allied with Ebla (Biga 2008).

6.2 Wet-nurses (GA-DU_8), midwives, female doctors at the Ebla court

A fairly important role was also played by the wet nurses in the service of the ladies of the court, who breastfed and brought up their children (Biga 1997). They are mentioned by their personal names and they remained at court after they had finished nursing the prince or princess with whom they were entrusted. They clearly enjoyed a certain degree of importance on the social scale, since in the lists of women they appear immediately after the king's wives, sisters and daughters and are not included in the lists of anonymous women working at the court. The importance of wet nurses also in other contemporary Syrian kingdoms is proven by the beautiful inscribed seals (found in the palace of Tell Mozan/Urkeš) of the wet nurse Zamena, who is depicted sitting with the royal baby on her knees (Buccellati and Kelly Buccellati 1998; and Otto in this volume).

The wet nurse of the last king of Ebla, lady G/Kisadu, is well known. We can see her active in numerous texts. It was also due to the texts mentioning Kisadu, who spent her long life entirely at court, that many texts have been arranged in chronological order. Moreover, it was due to her quotation in two parallel texts that it was possible to verify that Išar-damu really was the last king of Ebla (Biga 2000; Biga-Capomacchia 2012; see also § 2).

Gida-naim, the merchant of the palace of Ebla who travelled along the Euphrates (Milano 2003), was the son of the wet nurse Gisadu, and was probably the same age as the last king.

There were also some midwives ($ŠA_3$-ZU, *mu-wa-li-tum*) at court. Their job was to assist the ladies during childbirth, and they receive textiles for their work.[34]

34 See Biga 1988, 1991.

During the last years of the city's life a female doctor (AZU-MUNUS) is also documented. She looked after the daughter born to the royal couple, princess Kešdut, who later married the son of the king of Kiš.[35]

6.3 Female dancers (NE.DI-MUNUS) and singers (NAR-MUNUS)

There were also number of female dancers and singers at court, although they were far fewer than the male dancers and singers.[36] They lived at court permanently, and received textiles, wool and food for their work. They performed at banquets on the occasion of important events of the court, such as the arrival of foreign kings to swear allegiance to Ebla etc.[37]

Female acrobats (HUB_2-KI) are not attested at Ebla.

6.4 Female elders (ABxAŠ_2-MUNUS)

The kings of Ebla were flanked by a council of elders, the wise men of the kingdom. Some elder women are also quoted. TM.75.G.1794+ARET III 469 rev. v 13–17: 1 TUG_2-NI-NI *Da-gú-sa* ABxÁŠ-munus *si-in* ÉxPAP.

6.5 Female cooks (MUHALDIM-MUNUS)

The king's food and that for his court was prepared by a group of around 13–14 cooks.[38] Even today women are excluded from elite cooking positions! The cooks are quoted, all by their personal names, in lists, and they received textiles from the palace administration.

Some anonymous female cooks are attested as well.

The role of cupbearer (LU_2-ŠE+TIN) was male; always mentioned by name, he served the beer that normally accompanied meals. No female cupbearer is attested in the Ebla texts.[39] In Greek, Etruscan, Roman banquets cupbearers were female.

---

35 See Biga 1988.
36 They were far fewer than those of the royal palace at Mari where dozens of beautiful and accomplished young dancers were requested and sent to the king.
37 For the lists of female dancers see Catagnoti 1989; Biga 1998b, 2011.
38 For a complete account on cooks at the Ebla court in different periods see Biga in press 5.
39 Gods of the Greek pantheon had a female cupbearer, Ebe.

There is also a cupbearer responsible for wine (LU_2-GEŠTIN), who was always male.

6.6 Wailing (*munabbītum*, EME-BAL, *rāzimtum*) and weeping women (DAM IGI:A)

Especially for certain important funerals some types of wailing women (*munabbītum*, EME-BAL, *rāzimtum*) and weeping women (DAM IGI:A) are attested.[40]

Professional mourners are widely attested in Near Eastern and Classical antiquity throughout the Mediterranean and still existed in Italy only a few years ago.

At the funeral of the queen mother Dusigu 10 wailing women were present.

6.7 Women working in textile production

Several female workers were involved in the preparation of fabrics (DAM/DUMU-MUNUS TUG_2-NU-TAG). Female dyers and apprentice dyers (DAM/DUMU-MUNUS-GUN_3) are also attested.[41]

Some (few) monthly accounts of textiles have long lists of female court workers receiving wool as ration/payment for their work. Some of these women work under the direction of important women or functionaries of the court to produce textiles. These female workers worked in weaving houses (*ʻa_5-za-ru_{12}*) in which different types of textiles were woven.[42]

6.8 Other female workers

The court depended on the labor of numerous anonymous workmen and women. We learn about them from the texts of deliveries of textiles, from the sections registering wool given as a ration/payment to these workers but especially from the texts of the small archive L. 2712 (see ARET IX s.v. DAM).

Women who were probably responsible for attending the fire (DAM NE-RA) are also attested.

40 See Pasquali-Mangiarotti 1999; Biga 2007–2008: 262.

41 For a recent study see Biga 2010d.

42 See Biga 1988, 2014b.

Many other female workers, all anonymous, are attested at the court of Ebla: women milling flour, cooking bread, working in the kitchen of the palace, preparing vegetables etc.

***

Women of the court of Ebla had an important role in Eblaite society, taking part in every event of the court, religious ceremonies, rituals etc. They did not live apart from men but were involved in all the affairs of the kingdom with them, except for war.

The study of the court ladies, consisting of the kings' secondary wives, concubines, aunts, sisters, daughters, wet-nurses etc. proved to be fundamental for the reconstruction of the relative chronology of the texts and for writing the history of Ebla.

For a long period of almost 20 years the most important woman at the Ebla court was the queen mother, lady Dusigu.

Many anonymous female workers, who were involved in different types of work, are attested. A complete account of female workers at the Ebla court has yet to be written.

Abbreviations

TM	Tell Mardikh
ARES	*Archivi Reali di Ebla: Studi.* Roma. Missione Archeologica Italiana in Siria 1988.
ARET	*Archivi Reali di Ebla: Testi.* Roma. Missione Archeologica Italiana in Siria 1981.
MEE	*Materiali Epigrafici di Ebla.* Napoli. Istituto Universitario Orientale 1979-.

Bibliography

Archi, Alfonso. 1987. Gifts for a Princess. *Eblaitica* 1: 115–124.

Archi, Alfonso. 1996a. Les femmes du roi Irkabdamu. Pp 101–124 in Durand 1996.

Archi, Alfonso. 1996b. Eblaita: *pāšišu* "colui che è addetto all'unzione; sacerdote purificatore; cameriere al servizio di una persona". *VO* 10: 37–71.

Archi, Alfonso. 1998. The High Priestess, dam-dingir, at Ebla. Pp. 43–53 in *'Und Moses schrieb dieses Lied auf ...'. Festschrift O. Loretz*, eds. Manfred Dietrich and Ingo Kottsieper. AOAT 250. Münster: Ugarit Verlag.

Archi, Alfonso. 2002a. Jewels for the Ladies of Ebla. *ZA* 92: 161–199.

Archi, Alfonso. 2002b. The Role of Women in the Society of Ebla. Pp. 1–19 in *Sex and Gender in the Ancient Near East. Proceedings of the XLVIIe Rencontre Assyriologique*

Internationale, Helsinki, July 2–6, 2001, eds. Simo Parpola and Robert M.Whiting, Helsinki: Helsinki University Press.

Archi, Alfonso. 2010. The god Hay(y)a (Ea/Enki) at Ebla. Pp. 15–36 in *Opening the Tablet Box. Near Eastern Studies in Honor of Benjamin R. Foster*. eds. Sarah C. Melville and Alice L. Slotsky. Leiden–Boston: Brill.

Archi, Alfonso. 2014. Who Led the Army of Ebla? Administrative Documents vs. Commemorative Texts. Pp. 19–25 in *Krieg und Frieden im Alten Vorderasien. 52e Rencontre Assyriologique Internationale. International Congress of Assyriology and Ancient Near Eastern Archaeology, Münster, 17.–21. Juli 2006*, ed. Hans Neumann AOAT 401. Münster: Ugarit Verlag.

Archi, Alfonso and Maria Giovanna Biga. 2003. A Victory over Mari and the Fall of Ebla. *JCS* 55: 1–44.

Arkhipov, Ilya. 2010. Les véhicules terrestres dans les textes de Mari. I. Le *nubalum*. Pp. 405–420 in *Language in the Ancient Near East. Proceedings of the 53e Rencontre Assyriologique Internationale. Vol. 1*, ed. Leonid Kogan Babel und Bibel 4. Winona Lake: Einsenbrauns.

Biga, Maria Giovanna. 1987. Femmes de la Famille Royale d'Ebla. Pp. 41–47 in *La Femme dans le Proche-Orient Antique. XXXIIIe Rencontre Assyriologique Internationale (Paris, 7–10 juillet 1986)*, ed. Jean-Marie Durand. Paris: Éditions Recherche sur les Civilisations.

Biga, Maria Giovanna. 1988. Frauen in der Wirtschaft von Ebla. Pp. 159–171 in Waetzoldt and Hauptman 1988.

Biga, Maria Giovanna. 1991. Donne alla corte di Ebla. *La Parola del Passato* 46: 285–303.

Biga, Maria Giovanna. 1995. I rapporti diplomatici nel periodo Proto-Siriano. Pp. 140–147 in *Ebla, Alle origini della civiltà urbana. Trent'anni di scavi in siria dell'Università di Roma "La sapienza"*, eds. P. Matthiae et al. Milano: Electa.

Biga, Maria Giovanna. 1996. Prosopographie et datation relative des textes d'Ebla. Pp. 29–72 in Durand 1996.

Biga, Maria Giovanna. 1997. Enfants et nourrices à Ebla. *Ktèma* 22: 35–44.

Biga, Maria Giovanna. 1998a. Rituali reali eblaiti e loro riflessi nei testi amministrativi. *ISIMU* I: 213–224.

Biga, Maria Giovanna. 1998b. The Marriage of Eblaite Princess Tagrish-Damu with a Son of Nagar's King. *Subartu* 4/2: 17–22.

Biga, Maria Giovanna. 1999. Omens and Divination at Ebla. *NABU* 1999/109: 103–104.

Biga, Maria Giovanna. 2000. Wet-nurses at Ebla: a Prosopographic Study. *VO* 12: 59–88.

Biga, Maria Giovanna. 2003a. The Reconstruction of a Relative Chronology for the Ebla Texts. *Or* 72: 345–367.

Biga, Maria Giovanna. 2003b. A Ritual from Archive L. 2712 of Ebla. Pp 54–69 in Marrassini 2003.

Biga, Maria Giovanna. 2006. Operatori cultuali a Ebla. *SEL* 23: 17–37.

Biga, Maria Giovanna. 2007–2008. Buried among the Living at Ebla? Funerary Practices and Rites in a XXIV cent. B.C. Syrian Kingdom. *Scienze dell'Antichità* 14: 249–275.

Biga, Maria Giovanna. 2008. Au-delà des frontières: guerre et diplomatie à Ebla. *Or* 77: 289–334.

Biga, Maria Giovanna. 2010a. War and Peace in the Kingdom of Ebla (24th Century B.C.) in the First Years of Vizier Ibbi-zikir under the Reign of the Last King Ishar-damu. Pp. 39–57 in *Ana turri gimilli, Fs W.Mayer, Vicino Oriente Quaderni* V, eds. Maria Giovanna Biga and Mario Liverani. Roma: Sapienza Università di Roma.

Biga, Maria Giovanna. 2010b. More on Relations between Ebla and Harran at the Time of the Eblaite Royal Archives (24th Century B.C.). Pp. 159–165 in *Veysel Donbaz'a Sunulan Yazilar* DUB.SAR É.DUB.BA.A. *Studies presented in Honour of Veysel Donbaz*, ed. Sevket Dönmez. Istanbul: Ege Publications.
Biga, Maria Giovanna. 2010c. Scrivere la storia con i testi di Ebla. Pp. 23–28 in *Scritti siriani dell'antichità. Testi Preclassici e classici*, ed. Gaia Servadio. Biblioteca di «Pasiphae» IX. Roma–Pisa: Fabrizio Serra Editore.
Biga, Maria Giovanna. 2010d. Textiles in the Administrative Texts of the Royal Archives of Ebla (Syria, 24 Century B.C.) with Particular Emphasis on Coloured Textiles. Pp. 146–172 in *Textile Terminologies in the Ancient Near East and Mediterranean from the Third to the First Millennium BC*, eds. Cécile Michel and Marie-Louise Nosch. Oxford: Oxbow Books.
Biga, Maria Giovanna. 2011. La fête à Ebla (Syrie, XXIVe siècle av. J.C.). *Journal Asiatique* 299(2): 479–494.
Biga, Maria Giovanna. 2012. Les vivants et leurs morts en Syrie du III millénaire d'après les archives d'Ebla. Pp 1–18 in *Les vivants et leurs morts. Actes du Colloque organisé par le Collège de France, Paris les 14–15 avril 2010*, eds. Jean-Marie Durand, Thomas Römer, and Jürg Hützli. OBO 257. Fribourg: Academic Press Fribourg, and Göttingen: Vandenhoeck & Ruprecht.
Biga, Maria Giovanna. 2013. Defining the *Chora* of Ebla: a Textual Perspective. Pp 259–267 in *Ebla and its Landscape. Early State foramtion in the Ancient Near East*, eds. Paolo Matthiae and Nicolò Marchetti. Walnut Creek: Left Coast Press.
Biga, Maria Giovanna. 2014a. Inherited Space-Third Millennium Political and Cultural Landscape. Pp. 93–110 in *Constituent, Confederate, and Conquered Space. The Emergence of the Mittani State*, TOPOI Berlin Studies of the Ancient World 17, eds. Eva Cancik-Kirschbaum, Nicole Brisch, and Jesper Eidem. Berlin: De Gruyter.
Biga, Maria Giovanna. 2014b. Some aspects of the Wool Economy at Ebla (Syria XXIV Century BC. Pp. 139–150 in *Wool Economy in the Ancient Near East and the Aegean*, eds. Catherine Breniquet and Cécile Michel. Oxford: Oxbow Books.
Biga, Maria Giovanna. 2014c. The Marriage of an Eblaite Princess with the King of Dulu. Pp. 73–79 in *From Source to History. Studies on Ancient Near Eastern Worlds and Beyond Dedicated to Giovanni Battista Lanfranchi on the Occasion of his 65th Birthday on June 23.2014*, ed. Salvatore Gaspa AOAT 412. Münster: Ugarit Verlag.
Biga, Maria Giovanna. 2015. La città di 'Arugu e la geografia del culto del regno di Ebla (Siria, XXIV sec. a.C.). Pp. 105–116 in *Homenaje a Mario Liverani, fundador de una ciencia nueva (II) Omaggio a Mario Liverani fondatore di una nuova scienza (II), ISIMU* 13, ed. Maria Giovanna Biga et al. Madrid: Servicio de publicaciones Universidad Autonoma de Madrid.
Biga, Maria Giovanna. in press 1. Pellegrinaggi a santuari del regno di Ebla (Siria, XXIV sec. a.C.). Atti del convegno *L'archeologia del sacro e l'archeologia del culto. Sabratha, Ebla, Ardea, Lanuvio*, Roma Accademia dei Lincei 8–11 ottobre 2013, ed. P. Matthiae.
Biga, Maria Giovanna. in press 2. Not Tonight Josephine! *NABU* 2016.
Biga, Maria Giovanna. in press 3. Sedan-chairs at Ebla.
Biga, Maria Giovanna. in press 4. Jewels for princess Tiabarzu.
Biga, Maria Giovanna. in press 5. Cooks at the Ebla court.
Biga, Maria Giovanna, and Anna Maria Gloria Capomacchia. 2008. *Il politeismo vicino-orientale. Introduzione alla storia delle religioni del Vicino Oriente antico*. Roma: Poligrafico dello Stato.

Biga, Maria Giovanna, and Anna Maria Gloria Capomacchia. 2012. I testi di Ebla di ARET XI: una rilettura alla luce dei testi paralleli. *RA* 106 (*Recueil d'études historiques, philologiques et épigraphiques en l'honneur de Paolo Matthiae – Première partie*): 19–32.

Biga, Maria Giovanna, and Francesco Pomponio. 1987. Ishar-Damu, roi d'Ebla. *NABU* 1987/106: 60–61.

Biga, Maria Giovanna, and Francesco Pomponio. 1990. Elements for a Chronological Division of the Administrative Documentation of Ebla. *JCS* 42: 179–201.

Biga, Maria Giovanna, and Francesco Pomponio. 1993. Critères de rédaction comptable et chronologie relative des textes d'Ebla. *MARI* 7: 107–128.

Buccellati, Giorgio, and Marilyn Kelly Buccellati. 1998. The Courties of the Queen of Urkesh; Glyptic Evidence from the Western Wing of the Royal Storehouse AK. *Subartu* 4/2: 195–216.

Catagnoti, Amalia. 1989. I NE.DI nei testi amministrativi degli archivi di Ebla. *Miscellanea Eblaitica* 2 (*QuSem* 16): 149–201.

Catagnoti, Amalia. 2012. In the Aftermath of the War. The Truce between Ebla and Mari (ARET XVI 30) and the Ramsom of Prisoners. *RA* 106 (*Recueil d'études historiques, philologiques et épigraphiques en l'honneur de Paolo Matthiae – Première partie*): 45–63.

Dolce, Rita. 2014. The Ebla Families. Pp. 193–206 in Marti 2014.

Durand, Jean-Marie. 1988. *Archives Épistolaires de Mari I/1* (*ARM* XXVI). Paris: Éditions Recherche sur les Civilizations.

Durand, Jean-Marie. (ed.). 1996. *Mari, Ébla et les Hourrites. Dix ans de travaux, première partie*. Amurru 1. Paris: Éditions Recherche sur les Civilisations.

Fronzaroli, Pelio. 2012. The Eblaic King's Supplication to the Gods of the Night. *RA* 106 (*Recueil d'études historiques, philologiques et épigraphiques en l'honneur de Paolo Matthiae – Première partie*): 165–176.

Groneberg, Brigitte. 1990. La culture matérielle à Mari, *MARI* 6: 161–180.

Kogan, Leonid. *Na'r 'garçon' dans une lettre mariote. *RA* 106 (*Recueil d'études historiques, philologiques et épigraphiques en l'honneur de Paolo Matthiae – Première partie*): 177–180.

Marrassini, Paolo (ed.). 2003. *Semitic and Assyriological Studies presented to Pelio Fronzaroli by Pupils and Colleagues*. Wiesbaden: Harrassowitz Verlag.

Marti, Lionel (ed.). 2014. *La famille dans le Proche-Orient ancien: réalités. symbolismes et images. Proceedings of the 55th Rencontre Assyriologique Internationale, Paris, July 6–9, 2009*. Winona Lake: Eisenbrauns.

Matthiae, Paolo. 2014. *Muliebris imago*: reines, princesses et prêtresses à Ebla. Pp. 207–226 in Marti 2014.

Milano, Lucio. 2003. Les affaires de monsieur Gida-na'im. Pp. 411–429 in Marrassini 2003.

Pasquali, Jacopo. 2002. Sul falco (buru$_4$-mušen) di ^{d}*ra-sa-ab* ^{d}en^{ki} ad Ebla. *NABU* 2002/33: 34–36.

Pasquali, Jacopo, and Pietro Mangiarotti. 1999. Eblaite *rāzimtum*, "Wailing woman". *NABU* 1999/7: 9.

Pettinato, Giovanni. 1979. *Catalogo dei testi cuneiformi di Tell Mardikh-Ebla*, MEE I, Napoli: Istituto Universitario Orientale

Pettinato, Giovanni. 1980. *MEE* II. Napoli: Istituto Universitario Orientale.

Pettinato, Giovanni. 1988. Nascita, matrimonio, malattia e morte ad Ebla. Pp. 299–316 in Waetzoldt and Hauptman 1988.

Pomponio, Francesco. 1987. La datazione interna dei testi economico-amministrativi di Ebla. Pp. 249–262 in *Ebla 1975–1985*, ed. Luigi Cagni. Napoli: Istituto Universitario Orientale Series Minor XXVII.

Pomponio, Francesco, and Paolo Xella. 1997. *Les dieux d'Ebla*. AOAT 245. Münster: Ugarit-Verlag.

Steinkeller, Piotr. 2013. An Archaic "Prisoner Plaque" from Kiš. *RA* 107 (*Recueil d'études historiques, philologiques et épigraphiques en l'honneur de Paolo Matthiae – Deuxième partie*): 131–157.

Tonietti, Maria Vittoria. 1989. Le liste delle dam en: cronologia interna. *Miscellanea Eblaitica* 2 (*QuSem* 16): 79–113.

Tonietti, Maria Vittoria. 2010. The Expedition of Ebla against Ašdar(um) and the Queen of Ḫarran. *ZA* 100: 56–85.

Waetzoldt, Hartmut, and Harald Hauptman (eds.). 1988. *Wirtschaft und Gesellschaft von Ebla*. HSAO 2. Heidelberg: Heidelberger Orientverlag.

Massimo Maiocchi

Women and Production in Sargonic Adab

The topic of productivity in the Sargonic Period – and especially the role played by women in it – has seldom attracted the attention of Assyriologists and Historians of the Ancient Near East. This is no doubt due to two facts: first, the archives of Akkad, as well as the city itself, are still to be located, forcing scholars to adopt a peripheral point of view in their analysis of this period; second, the sources presently available for the preceding period, i.e. the Early Dynastic IIIb period in Southern Mesopotamia, roughly corresponding to the Early Jezirah in Syria, are not only more abundant, but also more extensively studied. The same holds true for the subsequent Ur III period. Because of these facts, The Sargonic period seems to be packed between historical phases and areas that are better understood.

Nevertheless, the corpus of Sargonic tablets has increased considerably in recent years, bridging to some extent the gap in the available documentation.[1] As we shall see, recently published and forthcoming texts add significantly to our knowledge, especially in regards of the topic of textile production, and the social status of women in the Sargonic period. Assessing the impact of the supra-regional organization labeled "the first world empire" on women's life and productivity is therefore in order.

At present, the archives of Adab are perhaps the most significant sources for this period, in terms of both quantity of tablets and the amount of information embedded in them. Thanks to the new available data, it is in fact possible to get a fairly good idea on the historical developments that affected the site during the entire time span of the Sargonic period, broadly understood as to include the transition from Early Dynastic IIIb to Early Sargonic periods up to the so-called "Late Akkad" period (i.e. from the period of confusion after the

1 This paper is deeply in debt to the generosity of several scholars working on Sargonic texts, who allowed me to quote unpublished material: F. Pomponio and G. Visicato (texts in the Jonathan and Jeannette Rosen Ancient Near Eastern Studies Seminar in the Department of Near Eastern Studies at Cornell University, just appeared as CUSAS 20, cf. Pomponio and Visicato 2015); V. Bartash (texts in the Schøyen collection, Oslo); M. Molina (texts in the Carl Lippmann collection at the Real Academia de la Historia, Madrid, now published in Molina 2014). Special thanks go to A. Westenholz, who provided me with his preliminary transliterations of most of the Sargonic evidence quoted in this paper, and to Lucio Milano, who read a preliminary draft of this paper, offering further insight on the matter.

Massimo Maiocchi, University of Chicago; massimo.maiocchi@gmail.com death of Šar-kali-šarrī up to the rise of the Gutian dynasty).[2] This is a unique situation, since other Sargonic archives date either to the Early or to the Classical Sargonic period. Because of the great continuity of the available sources, and the importance of the site at political level, Adab may presently be considered as the best case study for the analysis of women and production in the Sargonic period. For reasons of space, I shall limit the discussion to the new evidence concerned with the production of textiles in Sargonic Adab.

1 Archaeological context

The archaeological context of most of the Adab tablets is either very roughly known, or entirely unknown. Such is the case of the Middle Sargonic tablets belonging to the weaver's dossier, discussed below, whose find spot(s) can only be guessed at on the basis of internal data, cursory archaeological reports, and the (recent) history of the site. Thus, we miss important information concerning the connection between archives and institutions they belonged to. In turn, this partly blurs our understanding of the modes of imperial control over local productive units, with special regards to those more closely tied with the activities of women, such as weaving.

The site was partly excavated in 1903–1905 by Edgard J. Banks and Victor S. Persons, of the Oriental Institute of the University of Chicago. In more recent years, Adab has been targeted by looters, who destroyed large parts of the Tell in between and shortly after the first and second Gulf wars (1991 and 2003).[3] As a consequence of these tragic developments, thousands of cuneiform tablets and other valuable artifacts from Southern Mesopotamia flooded the black market, eventually reaching private and institutional collections scattered all over the world. Needless to say, no information on the findspot of these objects is available to us. The same holds roughly true for the tablets excavated by Banks and Persons, since at that time the stratigraphic method was unknown. The "excavations reports" were published by Banks (1912), in narrative anecdotal form.

2 For an overview on the political history of Adab see Pomponio 2006; Biga 2005. In this contribution I adopt the following terminology to refer to the internal sub-phases of the Sargonic period: Early Sargonic, Middle Sargonic, Classical Sargonic, "Late Akkad" (abbreviated respectively as ES/MS/CS/LA). The "Late Akkad" period in turn may overlap with the Gutian period, but this is irrelevant for the present discussion. For reasons of clarity and consistency within this volume, Old Akkadian names appear in their Old Babylonian form (thus one finds for instance Šar-kali-šarrī, not Śar-kali-śarrē). No attempt has been made to transcribe Sumerian names, which appear in transliteration.

3 See most recently Molina 2014, 22–24.

It is fortunate that the data for this site have been recently re-evaluated by Wilson (2012). The new interpretation of the structures on Mound III in terms of a light industrial unit devoted to the production of textiles is particularly interesting here. As we shall see, it is possible that at least part of the weavers' dossier discussed below may actually stem from this mound, more precisely from the portion of it affected by recent looting.

This area is also known as the "Semitic quarter", according to a label attached to it by Banks (1912: 299–315), on the basis of the fact that several tablets written in Akkadian were recovered there, as well as bullae and cylinder seals belonging to individuals bearing Akkadian names. It is worth noticing that the names of both Narām-Sîn and Šar-kali-šarrī are attested on both bullae and seals, proving the continuity in the use of this area at least by the end of the Middle Sargonic Period. As noted by Wilson (2012: 63), the "Semitic quarter" may be older than that, since a group of Early Dynastic objects (including cuneiform texts and a cup) may be traced as coming from level 3, just below the middle Akkadian occupation level. Other archaeological finds from Mound III include installations to handle water, such as drains, cisterns, and what Banks mistakenly considered to be a bath. Contrary to this idea, there is consistent evidence for an interpretation in terms of structures devoted to the production of textiles. We would therefore have another example of an industrial complex dated to the Sargonic period, besides the one possibly found in Tell Asmar.[4] Be this as it may, there are some clues linking the weavers' dossier to the "Semitic quarter": the few archaeological information we have allows for such a provenance; the dating of the area corresponds to the one of the dossier; the content of the texts (production of textiles) is obviously related to the archaeological evidence (industrial complex); four weavers' supervisors out of nine bear an Akkadian name, in possible accordance with the ethnic connotation of this area.

2 Terminology

The two crucial terms for our understanding of weavers activity in the Sargonic period are **ki-siki** (also appearing in the plural form **ki-siki-ke$_4$-ne**, apparently

4 Foster (2010: 119) points out that "The only Akkadian structure sometimes identified with industrial production, in fact, industrial weaving, is the Northern Palace at Tell Asmar, ancient Ešnunna. There is, however, little archaeological basis for this proposal, such as numerous loom weights or other evidence for weaving one would expect to find."

meaning "(workers of) the place of wool") and (**geme$_2$**) **uš-bar**. The latter is a well-known and rather unproblematic term, related to Akkadian *išpartu* "female weaver",[5] also used to denote a type of fabric, possibly of second quality.[6] As for the former, to the best of my knowledge **ki-siki** is never attested in lexical lists.[7] It first appears in the Early Dynastic texts from Lagaš, that also make use of the term **uš-bar**, but only as a designation of a type of fabric, not as an occupational term. As already noted by Maekawa (1980: 81), the term **ki-siki** disappears after the Sargonic period, being replaced by **uš-bar**, with the exception of a rare personal name **Geme$_2$-ki-siki-ka.**

Given that the two terms coexist within the Sargonic period, they might not have been exact synonyms, especially because both are used within the weaver's dossier of Sargonic Adab. Most notably, the text MS 4233 lists groups of **geme$_2$** assigned to supervisors, which are known from other texts to be **ugula ki-siki-ka.**[8] The colophon provides the total workforce, stating that "they are female workers in service as **uš-bar**-weavers" (**[šu+nigin$_2$] 172 geme$_2$-gub-ba / uš-bar-me**).[9] Note that the total does not include the supervisors, but only their dependents. As a possible explanation, one may consider that **uš-bar** in the Sargonic period is used as a generic term for weaver, possibly employed for a limited period of time, as opposed to **ki-siki** in the sense of personnel primarily (but not exclusively) belonging to a specific workshop. According to Verderame and Spada (2013: 439–441), this connotation of the term **uš-bar** is also found in Ur III Umma. The apparent use of **ki-siki** in the sense of a generic worker in the Lagaš texts may be due either to a later semantic drift, or to a bias in the available documentation belonging to the palace archive.

Besides **geme$_2$ ki-siki** and **geme$_2$-uš-bar**, the Sargonic texts from Adab also mention **geme$_2$-gu**, albeit rarely. The term has been understood either as

5 For the translation cf. standard dictionaries and Waetzoldt (1972: 42 n. 27, 94 n. 50). The term **uš-bar** (written **bar:uš**) already occurs in Early Dynastic lexical lists of metal objects, probably referring to a tool for weaving, see also Westenholz 1975: 76 with previous references.

6 See most recently Molina 2014: 61 note *ad* no. 4 obv. 1.

7 On this term see most recently Prentice 2010: 53–58.

8 Cf. SCTRAH 186; SCTRAH 307; CUSAS 20: 66 *et passim*.

9 For the Sargonic period, other attestations of the term **uš-bar** as referring to workers are found in the following texts: Adab: **uš-bar iti 3-kam** (SCTRAH 204: rev. 4′, MS), **uš-bar** (SCTRAH 221: rev. 5, MS); Nippur: **ugula uš-bar-ke4-[ne]** (TMH 5, 205 = ECTJ 205: obv. 1′, CS); **[...] SAL / [u]š-bar** (OSP 1, 26: rev. ii′ 1, CS, possibly referring here to a kind of fabric); Tutub: **[x gem]e$_2$ uš-«bar»** (Tutub 14: obv. 1, CS, list of various workers, the second entry after the weavers is **igi-nu-tuku "PAP"** = blind workers + checkmark); Ur: **geme$_2$ uš-bar** (UET 2 supp., 33: rev. 1, CS, list of female workers); Umma: PN **ugula [geme$_2$ uš]-bar** (USP 62: obv. 4, receipt of wool).

"linen weaver" or "spinner",[10] although according to the Sargonic evidence, the more basic translation "flax worker" is perhaps to be preferred. Several texts in the Madrid collection deal in fact with allotments of flax (SCTRAH 108–118), in close connection with a certain **En-ra**, titled **šabra**, and other individuals related to the palace.[11] Most notably, MS 4208 lists groups of **geme$_2$** in connections with the relative supervisors, which are referred to in the colophon as "21 female workers in service, (including) 8 flax workers, (which are) in the field cutting (flax out of the plants)" **(šu+nigin$_2$ 21 geme$_2$ / geme$_2$ gub-ba-me / 8 geme$_2$-gu / ašag-ga mu-**SIG$_7$**)**.[12] As linen textiles are never explicitly mentioned in the texts dealing with the production of the **ki-siki** institution,[13] it seems likely that **geme$_2$-gu** is used here as a term that refers to an activity or occupation, not to a profession. As Prentice (2010: 59) points out, in Early Dynastic Lagaš texts **geme$_2$-gu** workers receive the lowest amount of rations, a fact that suggests non-specialized workforce is concerned here, also in the light of the fact that linen textiles, on the contrary, are very expensive items.

3 Workforce organization

As I mentioned above, women in Sargonic Adab are concerned with typical activities, most notably weaving. In this regard, new information comes from a group of roughly 80 tablets, known to specialists as the Mama-ummī "archive", from the name of the supervisor of female workers usually mentioned first in the administrative records concerned with textile production, work management, and rations.[14] The weavers are in fact organized in teams of workers, under the supervision of the **ugula ki-siki**, as customary for the

---

10 For the former translation see Selz 1993: 232, with previous references. As for the latter, see Prentice 2010: 58–59, discussing the term **ki-gu** in Early Dynastic Lagaš, an apparent abbreviation for ***geme$_2$-ki-gu**, which is in turn spelled **geme$_2$-gu** in Sargonic and Ur III texts.

11 The basic translation offered here is partially supported by the fact that the term **gu** = Akk. *qû* refers primarily to flax, not linen, according to CAD, s.v. On flax/linen see also: Waetzoldt 1980–83b; Michel – Veenhof 2010: 216–218; Molina 2014: 118 note ad no. 108: obv. 1 with previous references.

12 On the term SIG$_7$ in connection with agricultural terms see Molina and Such-Gutiérrez 2004: 4; Molina 2014: 64 note ad no. 11: obv. 2. A reading **si$_{12}$** for SIG$_7$ as a reference to the practice of blinding or marking workers (Heimpel 2009a; Molina 2014: 209) seems unlikely here.

13 For a list of the items produced by the **ki-siki** workshop see Molina 2014: 35; for the terminology see also Foster 2010.

14 Westenholz 2010: 457 lists 71 tablets as belonging to this archive. The figure has increased since then due to the identification of new fragments after cleaning and collation.

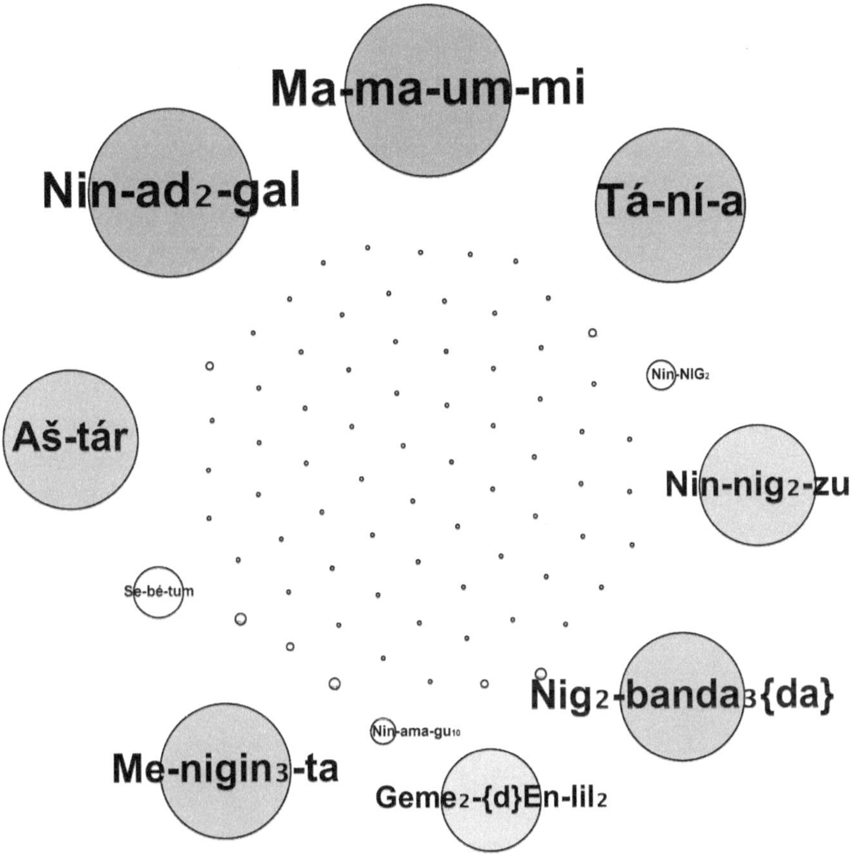

Fig 1: Frequency distribution of named individuals within the weaver's dossier. The large nodes in the periphery of the graph are associated with supervisors (**ugula ki-siki**). The small dots in the center represent low-ranking workers mentioned in rosters and ration texts. Many individuals are never mentioned by name in the dossier, the grand total, including named and unnamed individuals, reaching roughly 180 persons.

whole third millennium and beyond. The graph in Fig. 1 provides a view at a glance of all named individuals (supervisors and menial workers) within the **ki-siki** institution.

All supervisors, whose names occur with the greatest frequency in our texts, bear female names. The same seems true for their dependents, despite some difficulty in interpreting Sumerian personal names. Both groups relate to various institutions, such as the storehouse (**e$_2$-nig$_2$-gur$_{11}$**), the office of work management, as well as other productive units, such as the fuller workshop and various craft units (carpenters, smiths, reed workers, etc.), under palace control.

The total number of supervisors mentioned in the texts, as well as the composition of the teams, varies within the available documentation. Several texts mention 9 supervisors, usually quoted in fixed order,[15] a fact that suggests that 9 was in fact the normative number, with possible fluctuations. This may suggest the following ideal structure within the **ki-siki** institution: 180 weavers = 9 supervisors × 20 weavers. The figure of 20 individuals per team of workers is not surprising, the same happening in other contexts as well, as pointed out by Milano 1990. A partial exception to this rule is provided by MS 4233, where 172 workers are associated with only 8 supervisors, but there the team of Aštar seems roughly double in size when compared to the others, suggesting that two teams have been joined together, perhaps because of the absence of a supervisor.

Be this as it may, the number of actual workers within the **ki-siki** varies through time. For instance, smaller figures are provided by a couple of Cornell texts, having 13 or 14 workers per team, and 4 or 5 teams in total.[16] Rather than thinking about a drastic reshaping of the **ki-siki** institution, we may explain the lack of other teams in this text on the basis of the fact that the workers were in fact rather movable, performing for instance agricultural activities as well, if need be (see below).

The internal structure of the **ki-siki** institution seems very well organized, in terms of a top to bottom hierarchy, strictly controlled by the central bureaucratic office, belonging to the palace, which in turn was in contact with the imperial administration in Akkad.

PN	Frequency	PN	Frequency
Ma-ma-um-mi	47	**Nin-nig$_2$-zu**	33
Nin-ad$_2$-gal	46	**Geme$_2$-^{d}En-**	28
Tá-ní-a	42	**lil$_2$**	14
Aš-tár	38	*Se-bé-tum*	8
Me-nigin$_3$-ta	37	**Nin-NIG$_2$**	7
Nig$_2$-banda$_3$^{da}	35	**Nin-ama-gu$_{10}$**	...
		TOTAL:	83

15 For instance, SCTRAH 275 lists 9 supervisors, in this order: *Ma-ma-um-mi*, **Geme$_2$-^{d}En-lil$_2$**, *Aš-tár*, *Tá-ní-a*, **Nin-ad$_2$-gal**, **Nig$_2$-banda$_3$^{da}**, **Nin-nig$_2$-zu**, *Se-bé-tum*, **Me-nigin$_3$-ta**. The same order is found in SCTRAH 184, CUSAS 20 no. 227, *et passim*.

16 Cf. for instance CUSAS 20 no. 61 = CUNES 47-12-294, which reads: "14 **geme$_2$** / [*M*]*a-ma-um-mi* / [10]+4 **Geme$_2$-^{d}En-lil$_2$** / 10+⸢3?⸣ *Aš-tár* / (2 lines missing, possibly for one extra entry or a blank space and the total or indication of the month, reverse uninscribed).

4 Dating of the weavers' dossier

Most of the texts belonging to the weavers' dossier can be confidently dated to the Middle Sargonic Period, on the basis of both prosopography and paleography. Anchor points for framing the tablets in a chronological sequence are two texts of our dossier (SCTRAH 195, and MS 4233) mentioning a certain **Lugal-a-ĝu$_{10}$**, respectively as the **sanga** priest of Iškur, and **ensi$_2$** of Adab.[17] In this office, he succeeded a certain Šarru-ālī, who is known from other documents to have been the local governor in the early years of Narām-Sîn.[18] Therefore, the weavers archive must belong to the first half of the reign of this king (roughly 2250–2225 BCE), definitely before the great rebellion.[19] Assessing the time span covered by these texts in more precise terms is difficult, since no document is dated with a year name. This is however an important datum, which may allow us to understand continuity and change in the use of the **ki-siki** institution, as well as the possible impact of local political change on the daily life of women in Sargonic Adab. We should therefore rely on other criteria, including:

a) Morphographemic conventions show a certain degree of variability. Most notable is the alternation **e-na/ne-šum$_2$** ~ **an-na/ne-šum$_2$** "it was given to him/her/them", the former being the ES-MS spelling, the latter MS-CS spelling.[20]
b) Spellings of personal and month names may vary as well. One notes for instance the alternation *Aš-târ* / *Eš$_4$-târ* in the spelling of the personal name of one of the supervisors, as well as the alternation in the spelling of the intercalary month, for which see below under d).
c) Variation in the supervisor's hierarchy. A Madrid tablet (STCRAH 282) mentions new personnel (**geme$_2$-gibil**) introduced in the textile workshop. Sebettum, otherwise known to be a supervisor (**ugula ki-siki**), appears there under the supervision of **Geme$_2$-^{d}En-lil$_2$**. Given the rarity of this personal name, we must assume that this document was written earlier than the ones mentioning Sebettum as supervisor. Unfortunately the time span of her "ap-

17 Cf. discussion in Molina 2014: 29–32. The former is a small document concerned with a delivery (**e-na-šum$_2$**) of garments to one of the weaver's supervisors (**Me-nigin$_3$-ta**), under the supervision (?) of **Lugal-a-gu$_{10}$**, the **sanga** priest of Iškur. The same individual, titled **ensi$_2$**, is mentioned in the colophon of MS 4233, a roster of people assigned to the weavers' supervisors, possibly on the occasion of his installment as city governor.

18 Biga 2005: 34; cf. also the contribution by Pomponio 2006: 54–55, and the discussion in Pomponio and Visicato 2015, note *ad* no. 98: obv. 4, rev. 1–3.

19 As already concluded by Molina 2014: 29–32.

20 For the possible alternation **geme$_2$ gub-ba-am$_3$** ~ **geme$_2$ gub-ba-me** see below sub e).

prenticeship" is unknown. We may think about two to five years is a reasonable guess. Other variations in the normative sequence of supervisors are perhaps best explained on the basis of contingent reason, see below § 9.

d) The intercalary month (Maiocchi and Visicato 2012: 18) is mentioned 3 times within the weavers' dossier. In two instances, the tablets concern arrears (**la$_2$-NI**), either of wool (TCABI 137) or of textiles (TCABI 141). The third document (SCTRAH 201) concerns again textiles, with indication of their weight, but technical terms (such as **e-na-šum$_2$**, **la$_2$-NI**, etc.) are missing. The month name is spelled either **iti šuba$_x$**(MUŠ$_3$×ZA)-**nun iti ab-us$_2$-a**, **iti šuba$_x$**(MUŠ$_3$×ZA)-**nun ab-us$_2$-a**, or **iti šuba$_x$**(MUŠ$_3$×ZA)-**nun** // **ab-us$_2$-a** (i.e. on two different lines). Given the rather limited amount of tablets composing the dossier under present inquiry, the frequency of the intercalary month is rather surprising. Two explanations may apply: 1. we are dealing with an incomplete documentation, missing several texts, that originally covered a time span of some 16 to 24 years (depending on whether two documents discussed here were written in the same year or not, an intercalary month being expected every 8 years); 2. Contrary to this, on the basis of the fact that occurrences of intercalary months may be very irregular, as it happens in the Ur III and Old Babylonian periods, we may deal here with a much more limited time span. To an extreme, the documents of the Mama-ummī dossier might have been written over a period of 2 or 3 years, each including an intercalary month. This may be regarded as an exaggeration, but in fact one may think about similar practices from later periods, which may be motivated by the will of synchronizing calendars belonging to different cities. This would be in accordance with the three **e-na-šum$_2$** texts dated to the 6th month (**iti ab-e$_3$-zi-ga** see below),[21] and would imply that we have at our disposal most of the documentation actually produced by the scribes.

e) The term **ki-siki** is also mentioned in a Cornell text (CUSAS 23, 190), a very fragmentary document that reads: [... / x]+10 **ki-siki-me** / **geme$_2$ gub-ba-am$_3$** "[...] N weavers, ready to work". The tablet has been assigned to the CS/LA period on the basis of its paleography, and perhaps because of the spelling **geme$_2$ gub-ba-am$_3$** as opposed to **geme$_2$-gub-ba-me** found in MS 4208, even though the structure of the latter may be slightly different, therefore requiring a different use of the enclitic copula. On the basis of prosopographical connections, the document is perhaps to be re-assigned to the MS/CS period, but this speaks at least for a different scribal hand within the sub-group of the documents belonging to the office of personnel management.

---

21 Two out of three of these texts seem partly parallel, in the sense that they are small tablets recording wool given to **Me-nigin$_3$-ta** alone (CUSAS 20: 228), or to her and *Aš-tár* (SCTRAH

f) Mama-ummī is mentioned in MS/CS texts that are not part of the weavers' dossier proper, cf. for instance CUSAS 13, 43.
g) The script is consistent with MS standards, with minor deviations.[22] An in-depth treatment of the paleographical repertoire attested in the **ki-siki** tablets would take more space than it is here permitted. It suffices to say that most texts feature signs belonging to the MS script, albeit some diagnostic variants of the CS script also sporadically appear. For instance, the sign ŠU and similar signs (such as DA, A_2, ŠU+$NIGIN_2$, etc.) appears both in the variant having the "thumb" pointing downward – a MS feature, as found for instance in CUSAS 20, 68 (= CUNES 50-03-173) – as well as in the one having the "thumb" perfectly flat – a CS feature, as found for instance in CUSAS 20, 64 (= CUNES 98-06-144).

To summarize, whereas the Mama-ummī dossier proper, which forms the largest portion of the group of tablets concerned with textile production, seems to cover a short time span in the first years of **Lugal-a-gu_{10}**'s governorship, it seems that the **ki-siki** institution survived to later periods, possibly even after the collapse of the Sargonic empire under Šar-kali-šarrī. In this regard, one notices here that a couple of CS tablets deal in fact with industrial production of textiles. CUSAS 23, 137 records for instance 720 garments of various typologies (**tug_2-hi-a**), referred to as **tug_2-šabra-ne** "textiles (for) the administrators / of **šabra** quality (or both)".[23]

5 Typology of texts

The tablets can be classified as belonging to 4 macro-groups, on the basis of their content: personnel, textiles, wool, and ration texts. These can be further sub-divided into several sub-groups, according to the technical terms men-

175). In addition, two **e-na-$šum_2$** complementary accounts (allotments to different supervisors) were recorded in the month **iti še-sag-sag_8-ga** (SCTRAH 59 and TCABI 129).

22 For an overview of methodological issues and script evolution in the Sargonic period see Maiocchi 2015.

23 On this quality of garments see Molina 2014: 61 note *ad* no. 4: obv. 1. The productivity here seems significantly higher than the MS one, and may perhaps be connected with an increase in the total number of animals within the herds gravitating in the surroundings of the city. A small CS Adab text (CUSAS 19, 74) mentions in fact 3,000 plucked sheep, which may perhaps yield 6,000 minas of wool, according to the estimate by Foster 2014: 117 – four times the amount of wool processed by the **ki-siki** weavers in three months, see below. However, the round numbers and the brevity of the tablet, having only four lines of text in total, may also suggest an interpretation of this short note in terms of a school text.

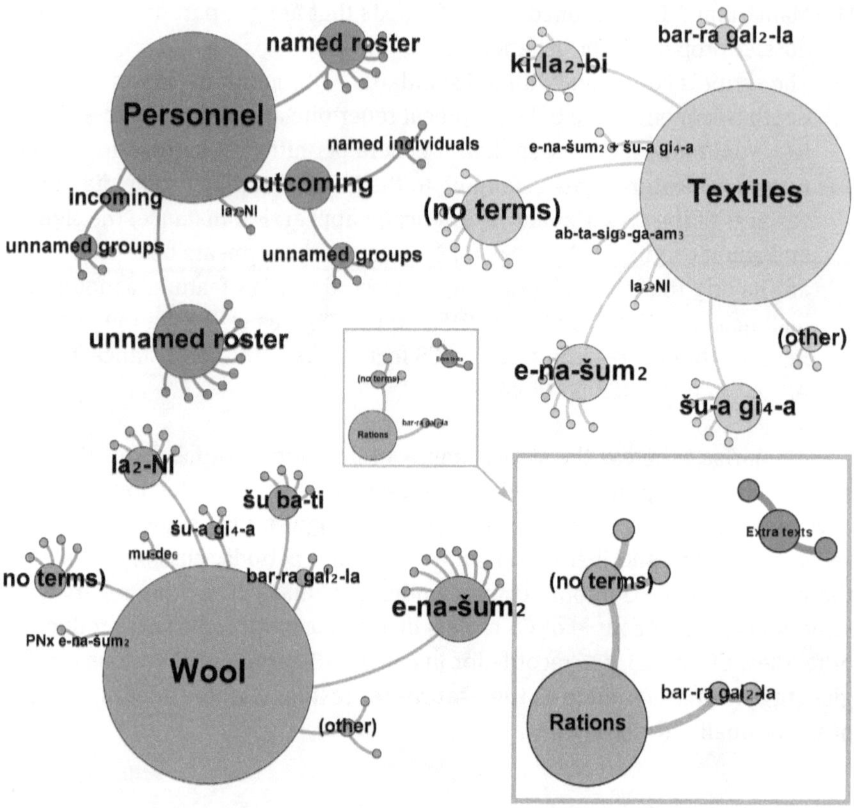

Fig. 2: Diagrammatic view of the textual typologies within the weaver's dossier. Size of dots and labels is proportional to the number of texts within each group or sub-group. Unlabeled nodes represent individual texts. The small cluster in the center represents ration and extra texts, i.e., miscellaneous administrative documents in which weavers' supervisors are mentioned, but not directly connected with the production of textiles.

tioned in the text, as well as the general format of the tablet. To the above-mentioned groups may be added an extra one, composed by miscellaneous texts that mention some of the weavers' supervisors, but are not related to the weavers' dossier proper, as well as the **dumu-nita dumu-munus** texts, that seem rather connected with the fullers' activities, which can't be discussed here for reasons of space. A view at a glance of the content of the dossier discussed in the present article is given in Fig. 2.

Some considerations are in order. As it appears from this classification, the weavers' dossier is very detailed. The movement of wool as well as of textiles produced by the people of this workshop was carefully recorded. During the proper season, a certain amount of wool was to be given to the weavers, in order to produce a certain amount of textiles. Such an amount was no doubt estimated in advance, hence the use of terms such as "arrears" (**la$_2$-NI**). The garments produced were not only counted, but also weighed, at least in some occasions, possibly to avoid theft of wool by the weavers, but this remains speculative, as there are no balanced accounts of wool within the available evidence. In any case, unused wool was to be returned to the central administration. Ration texts are rare, and definitely belong to a different administrative office. Weavers' supervisors (**ugula ki-siki**) were given rather substantial amounts, fluctuating between 30 and 180 liters of barley per month, the latter figure representing three times the average amount received by low-ranking male workers (60 liters per month).

6 Seasonality

Within the **ki-siki** dossier, 28 texts are dated to a given month. Only two month names are lacking in our dossier, namely the first one (**iti še-|ŠE.ŠE|.KIN-a**, probably to be read **še-saga$_x$-a**, cf. Maiocchi 2009: 12), and the last one (**iti še-KIN-kud**), see Fig. 3 below.

In all likelihood, the reason for this absence lies in the fact that during these two consecutive months intense agricultural activities were performed in the fields, the two month names probably meaning "month of reaped barley"

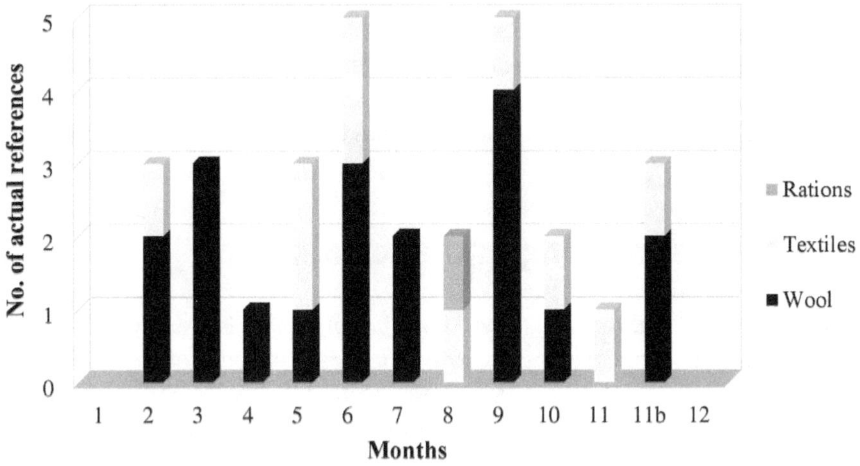

Fig. 3: Frequency distribution of texts dated to a month within the weavers' dossier. No texts record weaving activity for the first and last months of the calendar.

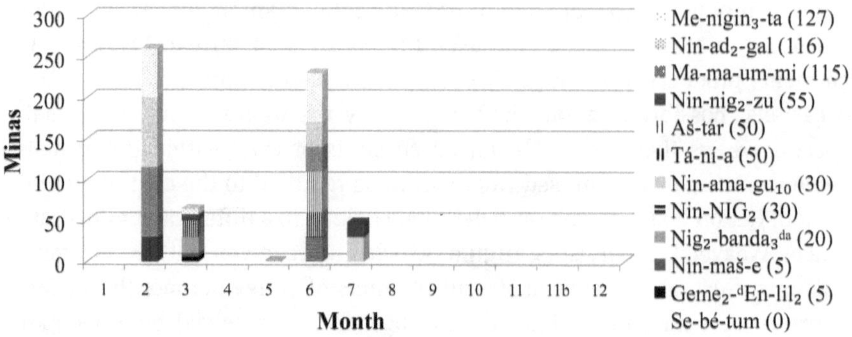

Fig. 4: Frequency distribution of wool allotted to supervisors in the **e-na-šum$_2$** texts dated to a given month. The numbers in parenthesis in the right side of the graph represent the total amounts received by the individual supervisors, measured in minas.

and "month of barley cutting(?)". During this period, the female workers usually employed as **ki-siki** weavers might have moved outside of the textile workshop to help in the processing of cereals, or to perform some other activities (see below § 8). If we now focus on the **e-na-šum$_2$** sub-corpus of texts, which seems to be the one in which the use of dating formulas appears with the greatest regularity, two distinct peaks emerge, in the second and six months respectively, see Fig. 4.

The first peak fits well in the agro-pastoral cycle of Southern Mesopotamia, at a time of seasonal contact between permanent farmers and movable shepherds, just after the harvest. The second one is perhaps to be explained in terms of administrative practices: the wool obtained in the second month is not immediately delivered in its totality to the weavers, nor it is allotted on a day-by-day basis, but it is instead parceled in two distinct occasions, at the beginning and at the middle of the textile productive cycle.

7 Weavers' ranking and specialization

A closer look at Fig. 4 reveals that Mama-ummī, which is usually mentioned first in the lists, is not the one receiving the largest amount of wool in the **e-na-šum$_2$** texts. A somehow similar pattern is found in other documents as well, such as SCTRAH 206 – a record of wool turned over (**šu-a gi$_4$-a**) dated to the ninth month – in which the order according to the amount of wool delivered is **Nig$_2$-banda$_3$^{da}** (15 1/3 mana), Aštar (15 mana), **Me-nigin$_3$-ta** (14 2/3 mana), Mama-ummī (11 3/4 mana), Tānia (12), **Nin-ad$_2$-gal** (12 1/3 mana), **Nin-nig$_2$-zu**

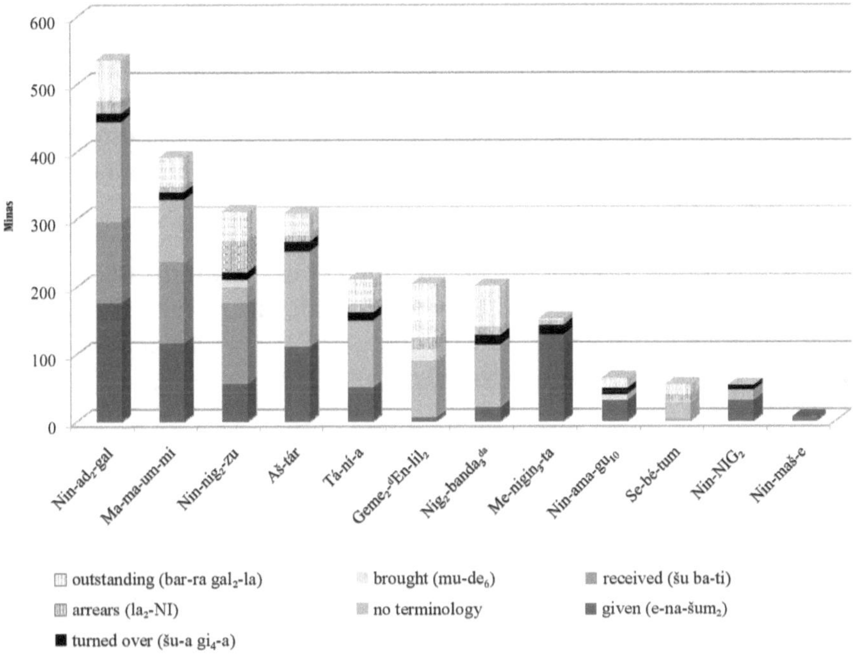

Fig. 5: Total amount of wool in connection with the weavers' supervisors – dated and undated texts.

(11 mana), and **Nin-**NIG$_2$ (7 mana). If however we consider the totality of the wool texts, yet another picture emerges, as illustrated in Fig. 5.

One may speculate that the fixed listing order of the documents, regardless of the amounts disbursed, is due to the physical arrangement of the weavers within the workshop, possibly in different rooms, as yet unidentified on Mound III.

It is also worth noticing that Me-nigin$_3$-ta, who is the supervisor receiving the largest amounts in the **e-na-šum$_2$** texts related to wool, is also the only one to whom considerable quantities of textiles (up to 157 **bar-dul$_5$ uš-bar** in a single text)[24] are delivered, again referred to as **e-na-šum$_2$**, probably to be

24 See for instance STCRAH 167, 192–195, and 209. The term **bar-dul$_5$** is equated with Akk. *kusītu*, possibly a full body garment, cf. Waetzoldt 1980–83a: 21; Michel and Veenhof 2010: 226, 234; Foster 2010: 130; Molina 2014 commentary ad no. 29: obv. 1. It appears that this garment or fabric could be manufactured in different qualities: it was rather expensive in Old Assyrian Aššur, whereas in Sargonic Adab it was allotted to low-ranking workers (cf. for instance SCTRAH 138).

altered or repaired using part of the wool received. This practice is unattested for the other supervisors, with the possible exception of the fragmentary CUSAS 20, 252, which is anyway concerned with small amounts of textiles. This fact may suggest that the workers belonging to **Me-nigin$_3$-ta**'s team were actually mostly involved in repairing, altering, or recycling textiles, as also suggested by CUSAS 20, 245, where Me-nigin$_3$-ta appears in connection with worn-out cloths (**tug$_2$ sumun**).

Other possible inconsistencies within our dossier are harder to explain. For instance, Sebettum is never mentioned in the **e-ne-šum$_2$** texts. However, in SCTRAH 177, which is dated to the second month, she receives (**šu ba-ti**) 2 talents of wool (= 120 mana), which is the same amount her colleagues get (Mama-ummī, **Nin-ad$_2$-gal**, and **Nin-nig$_2$-zu**).

8 Mobility

Workers can be transferred to other productive units, or sent to work in the fields. For instance, STCRAH 197 mentions 2 workers, belonging to the teams led by Mama-ummī and **Nin-ad$_2$-gal**, who are sent to the storehouse (**ganun**). STCRAH 217 and 309 are instead rosters of female workers connected with the usual weavers' supervisors who are given (**e-na-šum$_2$/an-na-šum$_2$**) to two scribes (**Adda** and **Ur-**UD.BU), apparently to perform an unknown activity. Administrative or contingent reasons may also explain why the normative sequence of supervisors is sometimes altered. For instance, in CUSAS 20, 64 the poorly attested **Nin-dalla** replaces **Nig$_2$-banda$_3$^{da}**. Similarly in SCTRAH 280 Me-me replaces **Nin-nig$_2$-zu**, and in SCTRAH 176 **Nin-**NIG$_2$ replaces **Geme$_2$-^{d}En-lil$_2$**.[25] As a further example of internal mobility, in MS 4049 Aštar is missing, the remaining list is shifted up, and **Nin-ama-gu$_{10}$** is mentioned at the end of the list, taking the now empty spot. Of particular interest here is MS 4208, seen above in § 3, which mentions workers sent to cut flax in the field (**ašag-ga mu-**SIG$_7$). We find here a clear indication that women working in the **ki-siki** workshop could also perform outdoor activities. This is obviously important in terms of social visibility of female workers. As it has been rather recently recognized, women in third millennium BC have access to a more varied array of job opportunities when compared to the situation from the second millennium onward.[26]

25 See also above note 14 for further examples of shifting within the normative sequence.
26 The data for the 3rd millennium BC primarily concern the Ur III sites of Garšana and Irisagrig, see Heimpel 2009b; Owen 2013; Lafont 2013.

9 Social visibility

This evaluation is in agreement with the fact that women in the Sargonic period could also act as witnesses. This fact was already established by Steinkeller (1982), who provided the edition of two very interesting documents from the Diyala region, recording the sale of a "house" (**e$_2$**, most probably to be interpreted as a room within a house, on the basis of the dimension of the sold property) and the purchase of an onager. In these texts, the witnesses are all female, and are referred to as SAL.AB×AŠ$_2$ (appearing also in the reduplicated form SAL.AB×AŠ$_2$.SAL.AB×AŠ$_2$). Steinkeller convincingly argues that this fact may be explained by assuming that these women belong to the same religious or professional group, also in the light of the high price of the room. Indeed, the presence of women within Sargonic legal corpus seems rather consistent. For instance, a Classical Sargonic text from Adab now in Cornell (CUSAS 19, 165), concerns the redemption of two people in debt slavery, featuring 8 witnesses, half of whom appear to be women (**E$_2$-sa$_6$** the singer, **Ama-šu** the wife of **Ur-eš$_3$**, **Me-bara$_2$** the wife of **E$_2$-sa$_6$**, and **Geme$_2$-e$_2$-dam**).[27] The relationship of these individuals with the two redeemed persons is not stated in the text. We might speculate that they are relatives of the people mentioned in the initial part of the tablet.

As far as Adab is concerned, it is interesting to note that one of the weavers' supervisors, namely **Geme$_2$-^{d}En-lil$_2$**, also appears as witness in a text recording a loan of barley (SCTRAH 307). This document is somehow different from the ones just mentioned, for two reasons: 1. **Geme$_2$-^{d}En-lil$_2$** is the only witness; 2. the presence of a woman is apparently not motivated by a relation of kinship with other participants in the transaction.

That women belonging to the **ki-siki** workshop enjoyed a relatively high social status is also evident from the fact that the documents occasionally mention quantities of silver in relation to wool and textiles (SCTRAH 188–190, 208). As the amount of silver doesn't follow any clear pattern in relation to the amount of wool and textiles mentioned in the texts, Molina (2014: 35) suggests that the precious metal could have been allotted to the weavers' supervisors so that they may buy extra raw materials or whatever was needed in the workshop.

27 There is room for a personnen keil in front of **Geme$_2$-e$_2$-dam**. Therefore, the interpretation "female workers of the **e$_2$-dam** institution", as a term denoting the individuals listed above, seems unlikely.

10 Evaluating the magnitude of production

As it is true for documents from different regions and periods, evaluating the amount of workforce employed in the productive process, as well as the amount of final products, is not an easy task. As we have just seen, MS 4233 provides the highest figure of people involved in the textile industry, namely 172 workers, presumably all women. To this figure, we must add 9 supervisors. In the light of the fluctuations mentioned above, one may wonder if the figure of 181 is to be considered final.

In this regard, we should now consider SCTRAH 204, perhaps the most informative document concerning the actual amount of garments produced by the **uš-bar** weavers over a period of three months. The colophon reads: **šu+nigin$_2$** 440 **la$_2$** 1 **tug$_2$ min-bi / uš-bar iti 3-kam** "total: 439 garments, as listed above: it is a three-month (delivery) of the *ušbar*-weavers". The text lists various kinds of textiles, mostly of second quality (**us$_2$**), including "ceremonial" garments (^{tug2}**nig$_2$-lam$_2$**),[28] loin-bands$^?$ (^{tug2}**ša$_3$-ga-du$_3$**),[29] toga-garments (^{tug2}**ša$_3$-gi-da$_5$**),[30] bags (^{tug2}*našparum*),[31] and "protective" garments with loin-bands$^?$ (^{tug2}**ša$_3$-ga-du$_3$** NIG$_2$.SU.A).[32] The total figure implies an average of 146 1/3 second-quality garments per month, which in turn implies 0.8 garments per woman per month. Keeping in mind that in this estimate the size of the textiles actually produced greatly varies from large (toga-like garments) to small (loin bands), the figure above may perhaps be reformulated as 0.4 large garments per women per month.

In order to be able to evaluate this figure, one has to rely on estimates made for other time periods. The most recent effort in this direction, based on both textual material from Ur III and Old Assyrian periods, as well as on experimental evidence, is provided by Michel 2014: she gives a figure of 2 to 2.5 large textiles (4 × 4.5 m) per year per woman, taking in consideration the time to process raw wool, spinning, and periods of inactivity throughout the year. This figure implies ~ 0.2 textiles per month (year of 12 months). Thus, it

---

28 Akk. *lam(a)huššû*, cf. Michel and Veenhof 2010: 229; Molina 2014 commentary *ad* no. 22: obv. 4.

29 Akk. *šakattû*. The term has been interpreted also as referring to an undershirt, cf. Foster 2010: 134–136.

30 For this interpretation see Steinkeller 1992: 48; Foster 2010: 133.

31 As suggested by Foster 2010: 139, the bags were probably used to store and/or transport the other garments listed here. Cf. also Molina 2014 commentary *ad* no. 20: obv. 3.

32 The terms NIG$_2$.SU.A refers to an item used as military equipment, cf. Schrakamp 2008: 700; *id.* 2010: 152.

seems that productivity in the **ki-siki** institution is higher than the one attested for the Old Assyrian traders, perhaps double in mere numerical terms. The figure of 439 garments in three months is to be compared with the three months delivery of wool to the **ki-siki** workers, attested in SCTRAH 184. The total reaches 554 minas, despite the difficulties in restoring the breaks in the text. This implies 184.67 minas per month, which in turn implies roughly 1 mina per person, which is 4 times the figure in Old Assyrian Aššur.[33]

Some considerations are in order. First, in a unique text (SCTRAH 206) the weavers actually return part of the wool that they had received (**šu-a-gi$_4$-a**),[34] in the amount of 10 to 15 minas per supervisor in a month, i.e. roughly half mina per subordinate worker. The latter figure is in accordance with an estimate of local productivity as double the Old Assyrian one. Second, we are concerned here with a period of continuous production, whereas the estimates for the Old Assyrian are yearly based, and take into consideration seasonal interruptions within the productive cycle. Third, it appears that a good deal of the production of the **ki-siki** workshop in Adab is connected to military equipment, at least according to the interpretation of relevant textile terminology by Molina 2014: 35. Therefore, we may deal here with relatively unsophisticated textiles that require less time to be produced, and presumably made with a yarn relatively lighter in weight.[35] Finally, we may deal with incomplete documentation, the total number of people involved in the textile production being higher than 180 individuals, but this is an argument *ex silentio* that it is impossible to substantiate on the basis of the present evidence.

Evaluating the profit generated by selling the textiles, if any, is difficult for this period, as there is very scarce evidence for textiles being sold. A Girsu text (RTC 202) provides the figure of 1 **gur** and 3 **ban$_2$** of barley, corresponding to either 270 liters ("standard" **gur**) or 330 liters (**gur** of Akkad) as purchase price

33 Calculating how much wool is implied in the above-mentioned 439 garments recorded in the colophon of SCTRAH 204 is difficult. According to the **ki-la$_2$-bi** texts in the weavers' dossier, a **bar-dul$_5$ uš-bar** garment weights 3 minas, whereas other kind of garments, such as loin bands, roughly 0.5 minas. Assuming an average of 1.5 minas per textile we obtain a figure of 831 minas, which is not too far from the 554 minas of wool mentioned in SCTRAH 184, which in turn would imply 1.26 minas per garment, without considering any loss in the production process.

34 The wool is referred to as **siki** $^{\text{[giš]}}$RI, a term of unclear meaning, cf. Molina 2014 commentary *ad* no. 206: obv. 1.

35 There is not enough space here for an in-depth analysis of the terminology of garments and wool in the Sargonic period. It suffices to say that the texts in our dossier refer to garment quality as **šabra**, **ensi$_2$**, **sag** and **us$_2$**. The last two terms are also used to denote wool, besides **mug** "of poor quality".

for 1 ^{tug2}**bar-dul$_5$**. Assuming that this item was manufactured by a weaver over a period of 6 months (i.e. assuming the same productivity as in Old Assyrian Aššur), we may perhaps calculate its cost in terms of grain rations allotted to the weaver to produce it as 180 liters (= 6 × 30 liters, the latter figure representing the standard monthly ration for a low-ranking weaver). The profit in this case is around 33 % to 50 % of the possible initial investment in grain, but this calculation does not take in consideration other rations (textiles and oil), which are in fact expected.[36] However, we should keep in mind that: 1. this is an isolated case, generalization being extremely dangerous; 2. this is the purchase price of a garment within the local economy. In order to build fortunes, entrepreneurs would no doubt export the goods to distant areas, as Old Assyrian traders certainly did.[37]

***

Because of the lack of archaeological information, it is not possible to state a final word on the modalities of centralized control during the Sargonic period. In this paper, I have tried to put forward the idea that the weavers' archive may stem from mound III. This is suggested by the early history of excavations and illicit digs there, as well as by the relatively small size of the buildings and their function, which is in accordance with the content of the text, and the presence of several women bearing Akkadian names as a senior supervisor of weavers, which is in accordance with Akkadian ethnic connotation (or rather nuance) of the quarter.

If this is the case, the presence of cylinder seals and seal impressions of high functionaries of the imperial court may suggest that at least part of the production was under direct control of the capital Akkad. In this regard, one notes that a handful of texts mentioning gifts sent to Akkad are now known, thanks to the edition of the Madrid texts by Molina 2014, including high quality textiles, sandals, oil, and silver objects. Nevertheless, the amount of textiles involved here is very limited, probably representing a standard set to dress a single person.

---

36 OIP 14, 160 provides perhaps the figure of 10 shekels of silver as value of 1 **tug$_2$** *gu-zi-tum*, which is never mentioned in the weavers' archive.

37 In another instance (STCRAH 1999–241), we are informed that the purchase price of 1 ^{tug2}NIG$_2$.S[U$^?$.A$^?$] is ½ shekel of silver. The identification of this textile is unclear, it may refer to some protective garment used by soldiers. The amount of work needed to produce it is unknown, but even if we are dealing with a small object, its price seems again rather low, especially when compared with the situation in Kaneš.

But even if we assume that the texts stem from another area of the site, and the link with the capital Akkad is a weak one, it is striking that the total number of people involved in the local production seems indeed rather modest, especially when compared to the big agencies known from Early Dynastic and Ur III periods, having much larger people employed in the local workshops. The maximum estimate of women working as weavers for the central administration of Adab at a given moment lies in fact around 180 persons. Higher numbers are attested in Sargonic Nippur, reaching 500 workers, who were certainly not all weavers, but the detail of the available documentation does not parallel the one we have for Adab.

In conclusion, by the end of Narām-Sîn's reign, the administrative structures for the management of textile production were in place, largely borrowing the modes of control already attested in the Early Dynastic period (**ki-la$_2$-bi** texts, roster texts, etc.). Despite the difficulties in achieving reliable estimates on local production, it may be true that the practice in Sargonic Adab focused on the intensity of production, rather than on large numbers as attested in other areas and periods, within a scenario of high mobility for female workers participating in the production process.

Abbreviations

ES	Early Sargonic
CS	Classical Sargonic
CUNES	Siglum of the texts in the Cornell University collection
CUSAS 13	See Maiocchi 2009
CUSAS 19	See Maiocchi and Visicato 2012
CUSAS 20	See Pomponio and Visicato 2015
CUSAS 23	See Bartash 2013
LA	Late Akkad
MS [number]	Siglum of cuneiform texts in the Schøyen Collection, Oslo
MS	Middle Sargonic
SCTRAH	See Molina 2014
TCABI	See Pomponio, Visicato, and Westenholz 2006
Tutub	Sommerfeld, Walter. 1999. *Die Texte der Akkade-Zeit: 1. Das Dijala-Gebeit: Tutub*. IMGULA 3/1. Münster: Rhema, 1999.

Bibliography

Banks, Edgard J. 1912. *Bismya or The Lost City of Adab*. New York: The Knickerbocker Press.

Bartash, Vitali. 2013. *Miscellaneous Early Dynastic and Sargonic Texts in the Cornell University Collections*. CUSAS 23. Bethesda: CDL Press.

Biga, Maria-Giovanna. 2005. A Sargonic Foundation Cone. Pp. 29–38 in *An Experienced Scribe Who Neglects Nothing: Ancient Near Eastern Studies in Honor of Jacob Klein*, ed. Yitschak Sefati *et alii*. Bethesda: CDL Press.

Foster, Benjamin R. 2010. Clothing in Sargonic Mesopotamia: Visual and written evidence. Pp. 110–145 in *Textile Terminologies in the Ancient Near East and Mediterranean from the Third to the First Millennnia BC*, eds. Cécile Michel and Marie-Louise Nosch. Oxford: Oxbow Books.

Foster, Benjamin R. 2014. Wool in the Economy of Sargonic Mesopotamia. Pp. 115–123 in *Wool Economy in the Ancient Near East and the Aegean, from the Beginning of Sheep Husbandry to Institutional Textile Industry*, eds. Catherine Breniquet, and Cécile Michel. Oxford and Philadelphia: Oxbow Books.

Heimpel, Wolfgang. 2009a. Blind Workers in Ur III Texts. *Kaskal* 6: 43–48.

Heimpel, Wolfgang. 2009b. *Workers and Construction Work at Garšana*. CUSAS 5. Bethesda: CDL Press.

Lafont, Bertrand. 2013. State employment of women during the Ur III period. Second and third REFEMA workshops, Tokyo (June 2013) and Carqueiranne (September 2013). http://refema.hypotheses.org/976.

Maiocchi, Massimo. 2009. *Classical Sargonic Tablets Chiefly from Adab in the Cornell University Collections*. CUSAS 13. Bethesda: CDL Press.

Maiocchi, Massimo. 2015. From Stylus to Sign: a Sketch of Old Akkadian Palaeography. Pp. 71–88 in *Current Research in Cuneiform Paleography. Proceedings of the Workshop held at the 60th Rencontre Assyriologique Internationale, Warsaw 2014*, ed. Elena Devecchi, Gerfrid G. W. Müller, and Jana Mynářová. Gladbeck: PeWe-Verlag.

Maiocchi, Massimo and Giuseppe Visicato. 2012. *Classical Sargonic Tablets Chiefly from Adab in the Cornell University Collections, Part II*. CUSAS 19. Bethesda: CDL Press.

Maekawa, Kazuya. 1980. Female Weavers and Their Children in Lagash – Pre-Sargonic and Ur –. *ASJ* 2: 81–125.

Michel, Cécile. 2014. The Economic Role of Women in the Old Assyrian Sources, Pp. 93–101 in *Le role économique des femmes en Mésopotamie ancienne (REFEMA) / Women's Role in the Economy of the Ancient Near East*, eds. Francis Joannès, and Fumi Karahashi. Tokyo: Japan Society for the Promotion of Science: International Collaborations.

Michel, Cécile and Klaas R. Veenhof. 2010. The Textiles Traded by the Assyrians in Anatolia (19th–18th centuries BC). Pp. 210–271 in *Textile Terminologies in the Ancient Near East and Mediterranean from the Third to the First Millenia BC*, eds. Cécile Michel, and Marie-Louise Nosch. Oxford: Oxbow Books.

Milano, Lucio. 1990. é-duru$_5$^{ki} = "one Score" (of People) in the Ebla Accounting", *ZA* 80: 9–14.

Molina, Manuel. 2014. *Sargonic Cuneiform Tablets in the Real Academia de la Historia: The Carl L. Lippmann Collection*. Madrid: Real Academia de la Historia.

Molina, Manuel and Marcos Such-Gutiérrez. 2004. On Terms For Cutting Plants And Noses In Ancient Sumer. *JNES* 63: 1–16.

Owen, David I. 2013. *Cuneiform Texts Primarily from Iri-Sagrig / Āl-Šarrākī and the History of the Ur III Period*. Nisaba 15. Bethesda: CDL Press.

Pomponio, Francesco. 2006. La storia politica di Adab. Pp. 52–57 in *Le tavolette cuneiformi di Adab delle collezioni della Banca d'Italia*, vol. 1, ed. Francesco Pomponio, Giuseppe Visicato, and Aage Westenholz. Roma: Banca d'Italia.

Pomponio Francesco and Giuseppe Visicato. 2015. *Middle Sargonic Tablets Chiefly from Adab in the Cornell University Collections*, CUSAS 20. Bethesda: CDL Press.

Pomponio, Francesco, Giuseppe Visicato, and Aage Westenholz (eds.). 2006. *Le tavolette cuneiformi di Adab delle collezioni della Banca d'Italia*, vol. I. Roma: Banca d'Italia.

Prentice, Rosemary. 2010. *The Exchange of Goods and Services in Pre-Sargonic Lagash*, AOAT 368. Münster: Ugarit-Verlag.

Selz, Gebhard. 1993. *Altsumerische Verwaltungstexte aus Lagash, Teil 2: Altsumerische Wirtschaftsurkunden aus amerikanischen Sammlungen*. FAOS 15/2. Stuttgart: Franz Steiner Verlag.

Schrakamp, Ingo. 2008. Review of Le tavolette cuneiformi delle collezioni della Banca d'Italia. I. Le tavolette cuneiformi di Adab delle collezioni della Banca d'Italia, ed. Francesco Pomponio, Giuseppe Visicato, and Aage Westenholz; Le tavolette cuneiformi delle collezioni della Banca d'Italia. II. Tavolette cuneiformi di varia provenienza delle collezioni della Banca d'Italia, ed. Francesco Pomponio, Marten Stol, and Aage Westenholz. *BiOr* 65: 661–712.

Schrakamp, Ingo. 2010. *Krieger und Waffen im frühen Mesopotamien. Organisation und Bewaffnung des Militärs in frühdynastischer und sargonischer Zeit*. Ph. D. Dissertation. Philipps-Universität Marburg.

Steinkeller, Piotr. 1982. Two Sargonic Sale Documents Concerning Women. *OrNS* 51: 355–368.

Steinkeller, Piotr. 1992. *Third-Millennium Legal and Administrative texts in the Iraq Museum, Baghdad. With Hand Copies by J. N. Postgate*. Mesopotamian Civilizations 4. Winona Lake: Eisenbrauns.

Verderame, Lorenzo and Gabriella Spada. 2013. Ikalla, Scribe of (Wool) Textiles and Linen. Pp. 425–444 in *From the 21st Century BC to the 21st Century AD. Proceedings of the International Conference on Sumerian Studies Held in Madrid 22–24 July 2010*, eds. Steven Garfinkle and Manuel Molina. Winona Lake: Eisenbrauns.

Waetzoldt, Hartmut. 1972. *Untersuchungen zur neusumerischen Textilindustrie*. Roma: Istituto per l'Oriente.

Waetzoldt, Hartmut. 1980–83a. Kleidung. Philologisch. *RlA* 6: 18–31.

Waetzoldt, Hartmut. 1980–83b. Leinen. *RlA* 6: 583–594.

Westenholz, Aage. 1975. *Early Cuneiform Texts in Jena: Pre-Sargonic and Sargonic Documents form Nippur and Fara in the Hilprecht-Sammlung vorderasiatischer Altertumer Institut fur Altertumswissenschaften der Friedrich-Schiller-Universitat, Jena*. Copenhagen: Munksgaard.

Westenholz, Aage. 2010. What's New in Town? Pp. 453–462 in *Opening the Tablet Box: Near Eastern Studies in Honor of Benjamin R. Foster*, eds. Sarah Melville and Alice Slotsky. Leiden: Brill.

Wilson, Karen. 2012. *Bismaya. Recovering the Lost City of Adab*. OIP 138. Chicago: Oriental Institute of the University of Chicago.

Adelheid Otto

Professional Women and Women at Work in Mesopotamia and Syria (3rd and early 2nd millennia BC): The (rare) information from visual images

Women have always, today as well as in antiquity, made up roughly 50 % of every society. Despite this banal fact, the search for pictorial representations of mortal women in the Ancient Near East is not easy. On the one hand, far less than half of the depicted humans are female; on the other hand, the existing representations are unevenly distributed over the periods and regions. While a considerable number of women were depicted as statues or on stelae and seals in 3rd millennium Mesopotamia, there is hardly a single one on such objects in 2nd millennium Mesopotamia, while in contemporary Syria, Elam and Anatolia there are many.[1] Conversely, numerous Old Babylonian terracotta plaques, cheap everyday items, show mortal woman. Why are there these differences?

There are some obvious reasons for this. First of all is the nature of the sources: the few images that have reached us so far from the Ancient Near East are but a tiny fragment of what formerly must have existed. Most of the sculptures and reliefs from the 3rd millennium discovered so far, are made of stone, which was not a common material in the lowlands of Mesopotamia, and most of them were found in temples. Terracotta was used mostly for simple figurines. Therefore we have to bear in mind that many of the representations made of perishable materials disappeared in the course of time; those made of metal were melted down, and those used in domestic contexts have not been discovered yet.

Furthermore, the sources reflect society in general in an unequal way and this is also true for pictorial representations of women, as H. Crawford has

1 The evidence investigated here dates from the Early Dynastic until the Old Babylonian / Old Syrian period. For the Uruk period see C. Breniquet in this volume.

Acknowledgements: I thank Ursula Seidl and Michael Roaf very much for their critical remarks and useful suggestions. The latter helped also to improve my English.

Adelheid Otto, Institut für Vorderasiatische Archäologie, Ludwig-Maximilians-Unversität München; aotto@lmu.de

described it recently for written sources: "The top echelon of society created most of the records that have survived and these deal largely with their own activities and concerns (...) The professional women in the middle ranks are not so well documented, and rural and nomadic women are barely mentioned at all" (Crawford 2013: 13).

Still more important are the intentions of Ancient Near Eastern art in general and, especially for this small study, the purpose of pictorial representations in 3rd and 2nd millennium Mesopotamia and Syria. Works of "major art", i.e. statues and reliefs, were not created with the intention of depicting real life, but were intended to enhance the roles or capacities of a limited number of persons through stereotypical renderings. They most often show people involved in cultic or ritual scenes that were deemed worthy enough to be depicted. They illustrate anything but "everyday life". Their purpose was to perpetuate the most spectacular and exceptional events of a small part of former societies.

The purpose of certain works of "minor art", especially of terracotta plaques, was clearly different. Some of them show at least a few depictions of daily life and work. But while many female figures seem to be represented, here again – as in the major arts of 2nd millennium Mesopotamia – only a small percentage of them depict mortal women.

Much has been written about the depiction of women in 3rd millennium Mesopotamia. The most comprehensive studies on Mesopotamian women during Uruk- to ED III-period are those of Julia Asher-Greve (1985; 2006; 2013) and during the Akkadian and Ur III periods those of Claudia Suter (2007; 2008; 2013); the most recent summary was written by Harriet Crawford (2014). All of them focus on the Mesopotamian area proper. The representations of women in Syria, especially in Ebla and Mari, have been investigated by Frauke Weiershäuser (2006; 2008), Rita Dolce (2008) and Stefania Mazzoni (2002).

Asher-Greve (2006) called the later Early Dynastic period (ca. 2700–2350 BC) the "Golden Age" of women. This is certainly correct, at least as far as the number of depictions in the Mesopotamian area is concerned. Still in the Akkadian period and continuing into Ur III times, there are numerous images of various female persons engraved on cylinder seals, represented as statues and carved on reliefs. The depiction of mortal women stops abruptly in works of major art and seals at the beginning of the 2nd millennium, and this may also be the reason why most scholarly works on women do not go beyond the end of the 3rd millennium.[2] By contrast, Syrian art continues to depict women

2 The extremely valuable collection of depictions of women by Claudia Suter (2008) ends more or less, despite the title of the article, around 2000 BC, because only a handful of cylinder seals can be attributed to the Isin-Larsa period.

into the 2nd millennium. The same is true for the arts of Anatolia and Elam, which however lie beyond the scope of this study.

In the following, I will try to categorize the depictions of female mortals during the 3rd and 2nd millennia according to the women's roles or professions. This is not an easy task, since only a few images bear inscriptions that clearly indicate the profession or title of the depicted person.

1 Queens and high-ranking women

1.1 Royal or high-ranking women engaged in cultic activities

It is supposed that the majority of the women depicted in 3rd millennium Mesopotamia belonged to the upper crust of society and have normally been identified as royal or high-ranking women. Claudia Suter summarized our knowledge about royal women in Mesopotamia of Akkadian and Ur III times in the following way: "royal women were represented in public in the form of statuettes set up in temples and they were depicted on public monuments, such as a stela. On seal images that circulated within state administration, they participate in state ceremonies or cult festivals alongside the king, are received in audience by a deified king, receive themselves subordinates in audience and direct women's cult festivals" (Suter 2008: 26).

Their superior status can be deduced either from the accompanying inscriptions or from the context, but only in very few instances is it explicitly stated which status, profession or rank the depicted woman had. A good example is the stela from al-Hiba (Lagaš), which commemorates the inauguration of the Ibgal Temple (Fig. 1).[3] The goddess for whom the temple was built, is depicted on the obverse. On the reverse the royal family of Ur-Nanše, **ensi$_2$** of the First Dynasty of Lagaš, is represented in a remarkable way: while Ur-Nanše himself is standing in the upper register clasping his hands and is followed by a small cup-bearer, Men-bara-abzu (on the right) and Nin-usu (on the left), Ur-Nanše's wife and daughter respectively, are sitting in the lower register. Each has long hair, which falls over her back and shoulders, and each is probably holding a cup in one hand and a branch in the other. It is certainly not by chance that their hairdos and the branches in their hands resemble those of the goddess. Their seated position also mirrors that of the goddess and designates their special status. Since the seated position indicates generally a role

3 Börker-Klähn 1982: no. 16; RIME 1.9.1.6a.

Fig. 1: Stela of Ur-Nanše, showing his wife and daughter seated (Asher-Greve 2006: 60, fig. 8).

superior to the standing one, the queen and princess seem to have played an important role, at least on this special occasion of the temple's inauguration. Unfortunately, we do not know whether in addition to being the wife and daughter of the ruler they were also priestesses in the service of the goddess: such a role was often fulfilled by members of royal families. [4]

The garments, the headdress or hairdo and the posture are usually the most explicit markers of the status of a depicted person. But it is often impossible to know whether certain clothes were typical of the profession, of the position held, of the momentary activity or situation the woman was represented in, or of the period or region. It is striking, for instance, that the main female person on a votive plaque from Ebla (Fig. 3) is wearing a smooth cloak over her head, while women on comparable votive plaques from central and southern

4 Several votive plaques are known from the same **ensi$_2$** Ur-Nanše. On one of them five of his children are shown approaching their father (Strommenger 1962: no. 73). ÁB-d[a?], Ur-Nanše's daughter, is standing ahead of the son Akurgal (his role as crown prince possibly expressed by his hairknot), and three other brothers. Because the daughter is heading the row, is depicted larger than her brothers, is the only one (except her father) wearing a tufted garment, shows one breast and because the Sumerian word **dumu** can mean either son or daughter, many scholars have argued that in fact another son or a male diviner was depicted: this was rejected convincingly by Strommenger 1962: 67; Asher-Greve 1985: 90–92 and Selz 2010: 189.

Fig. 2: Votive plaque from Khafaji (Strommenger 1962, pl. 45).

Fig. 3: Votive plaque from Ebla, Palace G (Pinnock 2013, fig. 28.13).

Mesopotamia (Fig. 2) wear pinned-up hair without a cloak.[5] Rita Dolce suggested that the cloak, worn over the head, "was chosen for banquets tied to funerary ceremonies" and was "perhaps connected to the cult of the dead" (Dolce 2008: 72). The different garments could be also regarded as regional peculiarities or as garments worn on special occasions. Since the cloak was worn by various women on Syro-Hittite reliefs in a ritual cultic context and on funerary monuments, Dolce supposes also "a deliberate use of the cloak in a sacred ritual sphere, at least in the Syro-Anatolian area" (Dolce 2008: 71). It cannot be excluded, though, that this special garment was meant to identify a woman as a priestess, as a widow, as a former queen, as an elderly woman or something else.

Many images of women without divine attributes – thus probably mortals – have been preserved from the later Early Dynastic period. Many of the votive statuettes, so-called "Beterstatuetten", are female. Several stelae clearly render the high status of the depicted women. The early ED stele of Ušumgal, **pa$_4$-šeš**-priest of Šara(?), for instance, commemorates the transactions of fields, houses and livestock, in which Ušumgal's daughter Šara(?)-igizi-Abzu was prominently involved.[6] She is depicted as tall as her father opposite her.

5 There is however a rather late votive plaque, presumably from Umma, which shows a woman with her head covered: Boese 1971, UM 1.

6 Gelb, Steinkeller, and Whiting p. 43–47; Evans 2003a: no. 20.

Four other high-ranking persons are involved in the transactions, but since they are depicted much smaller, their status or their role in the relevant deal was probably less important. Among these four persons are the chief of the assembly, the foreman of the assembly, the chief herald, and another woman named IGI.RU$^{?}$.NUN, daughter of Mesi, **pa$_4$-šeš**-priest of the temple Enun. Again the size and position of the woman do not differ from those of the men. Both women are called ÈS.A, the meaning of which is obscure.

Women (and men) as principal participants in banquets were a common motif on votive plaques (Figs. 2, 3). It seems as if no individual rendering of specific people was depicted on votive plaques, although they were given by individuals, since there are many plaques which are more or less identical.[7] They seem to be stereotype icons of feasts, and they served to commemorate the most important political and social events. The main protagonists were usually rendered as two sitting and drinking persons, a female and a male (Fig. 2). This was probably meant as *pars pro toto* for a larger number of banqueters, since occasionally more than two seated main persons were depicted.[8] The banqueters are served by several standing female and male attendants and are surrounded by female and male musicians (the other depictions such as the wrestling, wagon or boat scenes are not mentioned here, since there are no women involved). These plaques were common at least from Susa in the East to Ebla in the West, where a fragmentary limestone plaque was found below Palace G (Fig. 3) (Dolce 2008, Pinnock 2013).

Several queens, secondary wives and princesses of the Ur III royal house are depicted on their own cylinder seals (Weiershäuser 2006; Suter 2013). At least three "Royal Gift Seals" are known, which were given to women, each called lukur by Šulgi and Šu-Suen respectively (Mayr and Owen 2004, p. 149–151, nos. 1, 2, 8). The distinguished status of the women becomes obvious through their position directly in front of the king with their hands outstretched towards him – a gesture that has never been found with men – perhaps indicating the special relationship between them. The seal of Geme-Ninlila, beloved consort of Šulgi, shows her standing in front of the warlike king

7 Our Fig. 2 shows the fragmentary votive plaque from the Sîn-Tempel at Khafaji, the image of which can be restored with the help of the similar plaque from Ur: Boese 1971, CT 2 + U1 (this had been recognized already before by many scholars such as Frankfort, Hansen, Moortgat and others). This plaque is just one of many examples.

8 E.g. Boese 1971: AG 1 shows two women and a man in the upper register and two more men in the middle register; N 5 and N6 show at least two pairs of female and male drinkers. Also other media such as cylinder seals and standards, e.g. the standard of Ur, depict banquets with many participants.

Fig. 4: Seal impression of Geme-Ninlila, beloved consort of Šulgi (Suter 2013, fig. 10.13).

and holding the small vessel, which is usually held by the king, in her outstretched hand (Fig. 4).[9] There occurs a prominent tree, an element, which seems to have had a specific symbolic value in relation to women.[10]

1.2 The women with high polos and cape = a priestess, the queen or another high-ranking woman?

Seated women, wearing a high polos with a cloak above it, were interpreted as priestesses until recently. Examples are known from Mari as statuettes (e.g. Fig. 5). Sitting or standing women wearing a polos and no cloak above it are more frequent,[11] but it is not known, if these are depictions of the same person.

9 The scene is unique in many ways. Usually the lion headed club is a typical weapon of deities, but here it is the king's attribute.

10 It seems striking to the present writer that several seals belonging to women or their servants show this tree, e.g. the seal of Dada, the estate manager of Šarkališarri's consort (Suter 2013: fig. 10.14), and many more Akkadian seals, see here Fig. 31. It seems possible that this tree, which is never related to the main scene, might be a symbol especially apt for women, e.g. meaning fertility; but this has to be investigated further.

11 For multiple examples from the Ištar temple at Mari see Parrot 1956: pl. XXXVI–XXXVII; Evans 2003c: no. 92.

Fig. 5: Seated female figure with cloak over a polos from Mari, Ninni-zaza temple (Evans 2003c: 153, no. 92a).

Fig. 6: Seal impression of the queen of Mari (Beyer 2007: 239, fig. 4c).

Since the impression of the magnificent seal of the queen of Mari[12] (Fig. 6) has come to light, it seems probable that the sitting woman with cloak should be interpreted as the queen. The Mari seal shows her in the upper register, seated and holding a vessel in one hand and a branch in the other. She is sitting opposite another seated person who could be the king or another high-ranking woman.[13] Were the image intact, she would be surrounded by more than twenty court ladies and female musicians. If her identity as the queen of Mari is correct, the other examples of women with a cloak over their heads may be considered the queens of Ebla and Mari respectively (Figs. 3, 5, and 6).

The depiction of royal and high-ranking women seems to end in Mesopotamia with the end of the 3rd millennium, but it continues in Syria. Several representations are known from stelae, statues, and carved basins. The most elaborate depiction of a banquet of the queen and the king is found on the basalt basin in the cella of Temple D at Ebla (Fig. 7). The upper register of the front side shows a seated woman, dressed in a hatched garment, her head covered with a hat and a scarf, holding a beaker in her right hand. She is sitting opposite the king, marked as such by his peaked cap; between them is a table. Two

12 The names of the queen and the king have not yet been deciphered, but the inscription designates her as the wife (**dam**) of the king (**en**) of Mari.

13 These possibilities are evident in analogy to seals from the Ur cemetery and other sites.

Fig. 7: Basalt basin from Temple D at Ebla (Matthiae 1977: fig. 127)

women, dressed in calf-length garments, held by a belt, their hair tied up, are bringing buckets. Three men, holding a staff and spears or standards respectively, are their counterparts behind the king. The scene shows a striking continuity to the 3rd millennium depictions of banquet scenes, where the main couple is assisted by female and male attendants or courtiers.

Two basalt statues of women in elaborate cloaks, one with a fringed edge and the other with a swollen edge (early and late 18th century respectively), presumably representing the queen or a priestess, were found in Ebla in the sacred area near Temple P2.[14] The cloak with the swollen edge of the headless statue (Fig. 8) falls over her right shoulder and covers the right arm until the elbow, but covers her left arm completely. A quite similar cloak is worn by a woman depicted on a Classic Syrian cylinder seal in the mid-18th century Yamhad court style (Fig. 9)[15]. She is standing opposite the king of Yamhad in his typical cloak made from fur, and they each lift one hand in front of their faces.[16]

14 Matthiae 2010: 285–286, fig. 146, pl. XX–XXI; Matthiae 2013: 376–379, figs. 198, 202.

15 Tokyo Museum III-7-14; Ishida 1991: 52; Otto 2000: 96, pl. 28, no. 355.

16 For the king in the cloak from fur ("König im Fellmantel") as a typical representation of the king of Halab see Otto 2000: 232–233.

Fig. 8: Headless statue of a woman in an elaborate cloak; Ebla, sacred area P (Matthiae 2013: 377, fig. 198).

Fig. 9: Syrian cylinder seal showing the queen (?) opposite the king of Yamhad (Ishida 1991: 52).

2 Court ladies and female attendants

Many votive plaques and seals of 3rd millennium Mesopotamia show standing female persons in front of or behind the seated women. They hold various objects in their hands, among which are vessels and fans (Fig. 2). These women are often called female servants or attendants, and their male counterparts are also servants or attendants. Their lower rank in relation to the seated main persons is evident. But since they are often wearing the same garments and the same hairdo as the seated female, they must be considered not as simple servants, but as high-ranking court ladies.

The best illustrations of the numerous women who lived together at the court are found on the various seals which were worn by the court ladies in the Ur cemetery and by the seal from Mari, which shows the queen, court ladies, musicians and dancers in three registers (Fig. 6). In the Syrian orbit court ladies continue to be depicted in the 2nd millennium, see above (Fig. 7).

3 Priestesses

The secure identification of certain priestesses was made possible by Enheduana's disk (Fig. 10). The main figure on the badly damaged object is identified as the **en**-priestess of the moon god by the inscription on the back of the disk.

Fig. 10: The **en**-priestess Enheduana on her disk (before restauration) (Hatz 2003: 200, fig. 60).

Fig. 11: Statuette of an **en**-priestess (Weiershäuser 2006: 20, 2).

She is dressed in a flounced garment and wears long hair, which is held by a broad rounded headband. Also Enanatum, daughter of Išme-Dagan of Isin, **en**-priestess at Ur, is depicted wearing a flounced garment (Spycket 1981: 176). Several more statuettes, and a wall plaque from Ur show a woman with this same costume, which has been convincingly interpreted as the standard costume of the **en**-priestess (Pinnock 1998; Seidl 2005: 646; Weiershäuser 2006; Suter 2007). They all wear as their professional dress their long hair held by a broad headband[17] and a flounced garment (Figs. 10, 11). Otherwise the flounced garment is reserved for deities or deified persons. Only the **en**-priestess is allowed to wear it, presumably because she was considered the god's spouse.

Already a late Early Dynastic votive plaque from the Giparu in Ur (Fig. 12)[18] shows a priestess with broad headband, represented frontally, in the center of the lower register and three other priestesses approaching the seated god in the upper register. Winter (1987) took it as an argument for the existence of the ritual office of **en**-priestess of Nanna already in the late Early Dynastic period. She is certainly right to identify the three cloaked women in the upper register of Fig. 12 wearing broad headbands around their long hair, as priestesses, doing service at the sanctuary of the moon god. Also a late Early Dynastic cylinder seal shows a priestess with the characteristic headband, carrying a bucket and being assisted by a libating servant (Moortgat 1940: no. 144).

17 Enheduana herself mentions in her hymn to Inanna the **aga-zi/nam-en-na**, the true cap/the sign of **en**-ship; see Winter 1987: 192 with note 20.

18 Votive plaque; British Museum; limestone, H: 22 cm; Boese 1971, U4; Evans 2003b: no. 33.

Fig. 12: Votive plaque from the Giparu in Ur depicting various priestesses (Evans 2003b: 74, no. 33).

I would like to argue that also on Enheduana's disk two other women (not men, as usually argued) were depicted following her and bringing votive gifts; the first one probably wore her hair tied up like the woman on Fig. 12, bottom left; the second one held a bucket – an offering typical of women.[19]

An Akkadian or Ur III statuette of an **en**-priestess (Fig. 11) illustrates explicitly the intellectual abilities and the high educational level of these elite persons: there is a flat rectangular object, probably a cuneiform tablet, lying on the lap of the seated priestess.[20] If this is not an image of Enheduana herself, it reminds us at least of her fame as a gifted poet.

A Neo-Sumerian fragmentary votive plaque from Ur also shows a seated woman wearing the flounced garment (Boese 1971: K 12; Seidl 2005: 646, fig. 4; Weiershäuser 2006: pl. 20.4). Her long hair falls down over her shoulders and is held by the rounded headband. Usually, the person is interpreted as the

19 These two persons are usually considered to be male servants. But the last one, of which only the bucket in the hand has been preserved, was certainly a woman, since only women carry buckets (containing what?) in Early Dynastic and Akkadian ritual scenes, while men carry animals. Also the person immediately following Enheduana must be female, since the photo of the disk before restoration (Fig. 10) shows a protrusion on the backside of the person's head, which is impossible for a clean-shaven male, but matches well the tied-up hair of women.

20 Statuette, Museum Berlin, H: 11. 6 cm; see Weiershäuser 2006: 265, pl. 20.2.

Fig. 13: Stela from Mardikh, showing a priestess in front of the Storm God (Matthiae 2010: fig. 148).

priestess of the goddess Ninsun, whose name is the only remaining trace of the former inscription. Following the proposition of F. Weiershäuser (2006: 271), Šulgi-simti, the queen of Ur during the time of Šulgi, could be represented here in her cultic role, since one of her cultic duties consisted of regular offerings for the goddess Ninsun, the divine mother of the kings of Ur.

Several Ur III audience scenes of **lukur**-priestesses were depicted on seals, which had been donated by the king, e.g. the seal of Ea-niša, beloved consort of the king (the secondary wife of Šulgi) and of Simat-Ištaran, daughter of Amar-Sîn, called by Šu-Suen "his beloved sister" and "his **lukur**" (Mayr 2002; Mayr and Owen 2004, p. 150). Well attested on Ur III seals is also the important priestess Geme-Lamma, **ereš-dingir**-priestess of the goddess Baba at Lagaš (Fischer 1997: 174, no. 4). Her seal shows an audience scene. The priestess, her hair tied up and with one hand held in front of her face, is standing before the goddess, depicted *en face*, enthroned and holding a vessel from which water is flowing. To judge from the impressions, the seal must have been a very fine one, cut with greatest precision and held by granulated golden caps, which itself is a marker of status.[21]

For 2nd millennium depictions we must again switch to Syria. The fragmentary stele TM.88.S.500 (Fig. 13) was found in the village of Mardikh, but had

21 The quality of her seal is especially evident, since her seal may be compared to a seal which belonged to one of her male servants. The seal of "Atašuta, servant of Geme-Lamma, **ereš-dingir**-priestess of Baba" shows an introduction scene in front of a seated goddess, but the carving is not as fine and it had no cap setting (Fischer 1997: 174, no. 3). The same difference in quality can be observed on other seals of Geme-Lamma's servants (Fischer 1997: 175, nos. 10 and 11).

Fig. 14: Syrian seal with priestess in front of the standard with heads (Eisen 1940: no. 132).

certainly been erected in Ebla (Matthiae 1993). Only one register is partially preserved. It shows the Storm God as the largest figure, behind whom a standing and a sitting person are depicted. Because their heads are missing and their garments are quite similar, it is difficult to interpret them. Matthiae proposed that they are the king and queen of Ebla. In front of the Storm God and opposite a rectangular block, on top of which an incense burner is depicted, stands a woman dressed in a long garment. Her head is covered by a long veil, under which her long hair appears and falls down her back down to her hips. She holds a small bowl in her right hand. Because of this gesture, her garment and size (only 2/3 the size of the god), Matthiae convincingly interpreted her not as a goddess, but as a priestess.

If this interpretation is to be accepted, many other similar depictions of female persons should also be interpreted as priestesses. Some Old Assyrian seals from Karum Kaneš II and many Old Syrian Cylinder seals from the 19th/ 18th century show a woman wearing long hair or a veil (Fig. 14):[22] she is usually depicted standing, rarely sitting, is dressed in a flounced or plain garment, and lifts one hand in front of her face or carries a branch or a vessel.[23] On several seals she stands with one hand raised in front of a bull or the (double-) headed *semeion*-standard.[24] It is difficult to determine whether the "woman with long hair" depicts a goddess or a priestess, because her attitudes and positions often resemble closely those of goddesses and because divine fig-

22 Eisen 1940: no. 132; Otto 2000: no. 181.

23 For this woman see Otto 2000: 212–214.

24 For this enigmatic standard with one or two human heads see Matthiae 2015 and Otto 2015. For seals from Karum Kaneš II depicting the woman with long hair in front of this standard see Teissier 1994: nos. 536, 537. For the woman in front of the bull see e.g. Özgüç 2006: pl. 83, CS 820; pl. 84, CS 823.

ures in Syria and Anatolia do not necessarily wear horned crowns. But if we consider that priestesses in the 3rd millennium were sometimes depicted with divine attributes, an intended similarity of the images of priestesses and goddesses seems plausible.

4 Female musicians and dancers

Many Early Dynastic votive plaques show female or male musicians accompanying the banquets with their music, played on bull-headed lyres or harps.[25] On the Mari queen's seal (Fig. 6) at least two women are depicted playing harps, two are beating curved sticks, and at least two are clapping their hands. Also ED seals from Fara, Tutub and other sites show female musicians (e.g. Amiet 1981: nos. 1200, 1201). Many seals which were found in the Ur cemetery, especially those which were found among the larger groups of court people, depict banquets in the upper register and musicians and dancers in the lower register. 68 female and 5 male servants and musicians were buried in PG 1237, the "Great Death Pit". An exceptional seal, inscribed **dumu-kisal** ("son or daughter of the court"), was found under the skeleton of no. 7, which lay close to three large lyres (Fig. 15). In the lower register of the seal a group

Fig. 15: Female musicians and dancers on a cylinder seal from the Great Death Pit at Ur (Zettler and Horne 1998, fig. 19).

25 E.g. the votive plaque from Nippur, Inanna Temple (ED III), dedicated by the stonemason Lumma to Inanna; Boese 1971, N6.

Fig. 16: Old Babylonian terracotta plaque showing dressed female or more probably male harp-player (Barrelet 1968: pl. 75, no. 775).

Fig. 17: Old Babylonian terracotta plaque showing singing female harp-player (Rashid 1984: fig. 65).

of 9 musicians and dancers is depicted: a woman playing a bull-headed lyre is depicted in the center; the woman behind her is playing a flute, and behind her a woman is shaking a percussion instrument – one of the earliest representations of a sistrum. On the other side of the large lyre, three more women are depicted with their lower bodies in motion (depicted as a wavy long skirt) with one foot raised off the ground: they clap their hands in front of their faces – a very lively representation of dancing and singing women. In even wilder movement are two small figures dancing below the lyre.

Female musicians are a fairly common motif on Old Babylonian terracotta plaques, which have been found in most excavated Old Babylonian sites. The female musicians appear either naked or clothed. Many of the dressed women wear long garments, their hair is covered by a cap, and they are sitting on stools playing the harp (Fig. 16).[26] A fragmentary plaque from the Iraq Museum shows a dressed female harp-player, whose hair is worn in a bun: her mouth is open and she is apparently singing (Fig. 17).[27]

26 Barrelet 1968: no. 775. This complete and most detailed plaque unfortunately comes from the art market. Many more examples were assembled by Rashid 1984: 80–84.
27 Rashid 1984: fig. 65. Iraq Museum IM 11135, without provenience.

Hundreds of terracotta plaques and moulded figurines from Babylonia, Elam and Syria show naked female musicians or dancers. They are usually not playing a harp or a lyre,[28] but a tambourine (e.g. Barrelet 1968: pls. XXXIII–XXXVII). A plaque from Larsa shows a naked woman with a tambourine with a male lute-player in a terribly twisted sexual intercourse (Barrelet 1968: 320, pl. LVI.591, and fig. 7 of J. Cooper in this volume). Blocher (1987: 231) interprets them as jugglers, comedians and musicians, who performed during rituals. Several terracotta figurines of naked female musicians were found inside and outside the "Grand Palais" at Mari (Fig. 18).[29] They are rendered *en face*, adorned with elaborate hairdos and necklaces and holding tambourines. Since similar figurines with naked male lute-players were also found in the Mari palace (Parrot 1959: M. 1022), their earlier interpretation as a group of musicians, who may have been associated with fertility rites (Collon 1986: 132), seems convincing. These naked female musicians, however, are but a part of the large group of depicted "Naked Women" – a terribly complicated issue that has been treated recently by Candida Felli (2015). Since many female musicians are well attested for the Mari palace by the texts (Ziegler 2007), it would be interesting to know why some musicians were depicted with and some without garment.

5 Naked women and women as sexual partners

Much has been written about the "oldest profession in the world" (for recent summaries see Assante 2006; Cooper 2006; Felli 2015). As concerns depictions, the challenge is to distinguish between the various forms of nudity and nakedness (Uehlinger 1998; Asher-Greve and Sweeney 2006). The identity of the so-called "Naked Woman" / "Nackte Frau" has been discussed at length by many scholars (for the most recent summary see Felli 2015). As a result of these studies, the general trend today is to see her not as a prostitute or any other kind of mortal woman, but either as a supernatural creature or as a personification or symbol. Therefore I will not treat the well-defined type of the "Nackte Frau" here.

---

28 Exceptions are a few plaques showing a naked woman with a lyre with a dancing man holding a tambourine (Rashid 1984: 76–77).

29 M. 990 (Fig. 18) was found in salle 104; the findspot of M. 761 is given as "palais, extérieur" (Parrot 1959: 71).

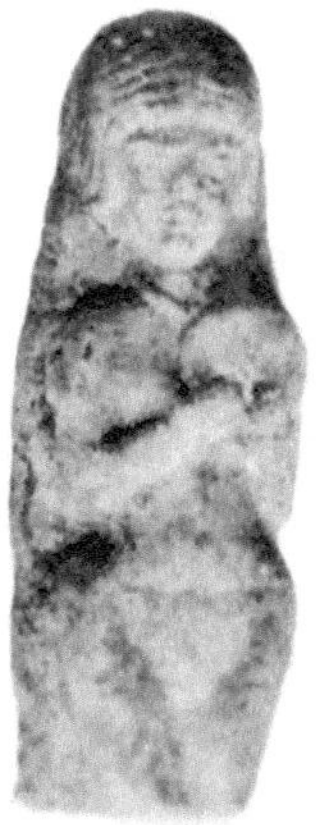

Fig. 18: Terracotta figurine of naked female musician, holding a tambourine (Parrot 1959: 71, fig. 18).

Fig. 19: Old Babylonian terracotta plaque from Susa showing sexual intercourse with a drinking woman (Trümpelmann 1984: pl. IIa).

To be distinguished from this type is another type of nude female. Quite certainly the standing woman, bent over a beer jar and drinking from it, while having sexual intercourse, can be interpreted as a prostitute (Fig. 19), especially since a context in Susa might suggest the association of such images with a pub (Trümpelmann 1984). But it is still debated whether the naked women, lying on Old Babylonian terracotta bed models together with a man, are indeed depictions of prostitutes, or illustrations of a (sacred) marriage, or symbols for the abstract concepts of procreation and fertility.

6 The woman as mother and the wet-nurse

The excavations at Tell Mozan have furnished excellent depictions of the queen's various roles, of her family life, and of female professions at the royal court of Urkeš during the Akkadian period (Buccellati and Kelly-Buccellati 1995–1996; Kelly-Buccellati 2015). Several seals of queen Uqnitum, the wife (**dam**) of the ruler of Tupkiš, depict her in an intimate "family scene" with a small child on her lap (Fig. 20), or being touched by a small child standing in front of her (Kelly-Buccellati 2015: 120, Fig. 7). Associated are either the king and another child, or musicians and court ladies or servants. As Kelly-Buccellati already remarked (2015: 120), only women occur on most of these seals in which these intimacies are rendered. Until recently it was not clear if the

Fig. 20: Seal impression of queen Uqnitum of Urkeš with her family (Kelly-Buccellati 2015: 113, fig. 1).

Fig. 21: Seal impression of Zamena, the nurse (Kelly-Buccellati 2015: 120, fig. 8).

mother or a wet-nurse was depicted on these seals. But in the light of a seal from Urkeš it seems probable that the woman with the child on her lap is indeed the queen and mother. The seal belongs to Zamena, the nurse (**eme$_2$-da**) (Fig. 21). It shows the same seated woman with long hair, holding a child on her lap, and a standing woman in front of her, who grasps both hands of the child.

More Akkadian seals show similar intimate scenes of a woman associated with a child sitting on her lap (Fig. 22).[30] Since all four women on the seal from Ur (Fig. 22) are wearing the same garments with fringed borders and the same bun, a similar social rank may be deduced.[31]

Very similar depictions of a seated woman with a child on her lap continue to be depicted on Old Babylonian terracotta plaques. The mother on a plaque found in Isin (Fig. 23)[32] although apparently breastfeeding the child is dressed

Fig. 22: Akkadian cylinder seal from Ur (Woolley 1934: no. 291).

30 Woolley 1934: 97–98, no. 291 (U. 10757); Boehmer 1965: no. 1301.
31 For the social status of a wet-nurse and nurse see Stol 2000, 181–190.
32 Hrouda 1977: 49, pl. 24, IB 314.

Fig. 23: Terracotta plaque from Isin showing mother or wet-nurse with a child on her lap (Hrouda 1977: pl. 24, IB 314).

Fig. 24: Terracotta plaque from Girsu showing mother or wet-nurse breastfeeding a child (Genouillac 1936: pl. 102,3).

in a long garment. The woman on a plaque from Girsu is depicted while breastfeeding her child (Fig. 24).[33] Since there is no inscription, this might be the depiction of a mother or of a wet-nurse.

A few seals certainly depict wet-nurses and nursemaids (e.g. Suter 2008: 19, S 39 and S 48). An Akkadian seal – the carving of which is extremely delicate and exquisite and which is made of lapis lazuli – was the property of Takunai, the wet-nurse of the daughter of Timmuzi, female estate administrator.[34] The goddess Lama introduces a woman dressed in a rather unusual, vertically pleated robe to the goddess Ninhursag and another woman dressed in the more usual fringed robe is following her carrying a pail in her left hand. Both mortal women wear their hair tied up, but their garments differ, and the introduced woman seems to wear multiple necklaces. Suter, following Collon and contradicting other interpretations, convincingly interprets the introduced woman as the seal-owner, since this "not only agrees with the general rule that the presentee represents the seal owner, but also makes more sense for the custom-made seal of a wet-nurse, since Ninhursag is the nurturing goddess" (Suter 2008: 19). This means that one of the finest Akkadian seals that has survived, made of *the* prestigious material *par excellence*,

33 Genouillac 1936:pl. 102.3.

34 3.29 by 1.86 cm (Jerusalem, Bible Lands Museum). Collon 1987: no. 642; Suter 2008: Seal 48.

belonged to a wet-nurse. It demonstrates again that the rank of this profession could vary. While normal wet-nurses seem to have had a fairly low rank, those who had wet-nursed the princesses or princes were among the ladies of the highest rank in court (Biga 1991: 297–298 and in this volume; Stol 2000: 186–189).

7 Female kitchen personnel, female brewers and women in a garden

Several seals from Tell Mozan show the personnel of queen Uqnitum at the court of Urkeš. The seal of Tuli, the chief cook, depicts the cook himself about to butcher a sheep or goat, the results of his butchering (two animal's legs hang from the ceiling) and a woman (Fig. 25). She is depicted with her upper body bent forwards and stirring with two sticks something in two narrow-necked jars, presumably making butter or cheese.[35] Several Akkadian seals show brewing women with larger jars including one in a stand, from which a liquid is flowing into a jar below it – the usual depiction of a beer jar (Fig. 26).[36] Woman active in a palm tree garden are rendered on a few Akkadian

Fig. 25: Seal of Tuli, the chief cook, showing male and female kitchen personnel (Kelly-Buccellati 2015: 121, fig. 9).

35 Buccellati and Kelly-Buccellati 1995–1996: Fig. 14; Kelly-Buccellati 2015: 121, Fig. 9.
36 Boehmer 1965: no. 1279, Fig. 549; Kunsthistorisches Museum Wien. See also a cylinder seal in the Louvre with a female brewer (Boehmer 1965: no. 1297, Fig. 555) and a seal in the de Clercq Collection with a male brewer (Boehmer 1965: no. 1299, Fig. 557).

Fig. 26: A female brewer and a woman and a man bringing a bucket and a kid to a seated woman (Boehmer 1965, fig. 549).

Fig. 27: Akkadian seal showing three women in garden with various plants and birds (Boehmer 1965, fig. 709).

seals (Fig. 27).[37] Since the palms are quite small in relation to the women, and since the women seem to touch the date clusters, one wonders if real agricultural work or perhaps a symbolic act of fertilization is depicted. A seal from an ED level at Tall Mozan show four standing women involved in some action with a large rectangular object above a flat object, presumably textiles or vessels (Dohmann-Pfälzner 2013: 231, Fig. 103.8).

8 Female textile workers

The depiction of textile work is extremely rare. Exceptions are the spinning women on the mosaic panel from Mari (see Fig. 33), a woman bringing a ball

37 Boehmer 1965: no. 1676, Fig. 709; see also the secondary scene of a seal in Moscow: Boehmer 1965: no. 952, Fig. 383.

Fig. 28: Cylinder seal from the Ištar Temple at Mari, showing a weaving woman in front of a vertical loom (http://cartelfr.louvre.fr/cartelfr/visite?srv=car_not_frame&idNotice=9617).

of thread on a seal from Tall Mozan (Kelly-Buccellati 2015: 122, fig. 11) and an ED III seal from the Ištar temple at Mari (Fig. 28).[38] It shows only women: in the upper register a symposium of two women accompanied by a female servant or court lady, and in the lower register a woman sitting in front of a large vertical loom.

9 An exceptional profession

A unique position was held by the deaf lady Aman-Aštar, who must have had despite (or because of) her handicap a high position with regard to her boss, the *ēntu*-priestess Tutanapšum, daughter of Naram-Sin (Fig. 29). The inscription reads: "Tutanapšum, *ēntu*-priestess of the god Enlil: Aman-Aštar, the deaf lady, the *prattler*, (is) her female servant" (Frayne 1993: 175, no. 2017).[39] The high-priestess is rendered like a goddess, enthroned on a block on top of a three-stepped dais, and wearing the flounced garment. Only the horned crown is missing. The deaf lady appears directly in front Aman-Aštar, which reveals her high status and a strong relationship to the *ēntu*-priestess. Aman-Aštar holds a strange instrument in her hands, which has been interpreted as a musical instrument or as "something used to perform amusing tricks" (Asher-Greve 2006: 68). A medical instrument seems a better interpretation. The object is unique, but somewhat similar to the medical tools on an equally exceptional

38 Parrot 1956: 194, pl. LXVI, M. 1071.

39 The translation is uncertain. According to Asher-Greve 2006: 68 she could be dumb not deaf. But I wonder if a dumb person would have owned a seal, which can be used in legal affairs.

Fig. 29: Cylinder seal of the deaf lady Aman-Aštar with her (medical?) instruments (Collon 1987: fig. 530).

seal (Collon 1987: no. 638), belonging to a male doctor who – according to the inscription – prays to Edin-mugi, vizier of the god Gir, who assists mothers in childbirth. Therefore it seems possible that the Aman-Aštar-seal is the only known depiction of a female physician so far.

10 Midwives and women giving birth

Professional midwives were depicted on cylinder seals. But the Neo-Sumerian seal of Ninkala, midwife of the goddess Baba, shows a standard introduction of the midwife to the enthroned goddess.[40] Only the lower register alludes explicitly to her profession, since it shows geese, the attributive animals of Baba, floating on water, and scorpions, the animals of Išhara, as symbols of fertility.[41]

It may be that midwives in action during childbirth were depicted.[42] Let us begin with a fascinating cylinder seal from the late ED III or Akkad period, the depiction of which has not previously been properly understood (Fig. 30).[43] In the lower register a woman in a long garment and with a bun lies on a bed that is decorated with bull's legs. Two people, one with long hair and the other

40 Neo-Sumerian seal, formerly Erlenmeyer collection, Basel; Asher-Greve and Goodnick Westenholz 2013: 402, Fig. 48.

41 For the frequent association of the scorpion with Išhara and with bed scenes see Zernecke 2008 (I am grateful to Alexander Tamm for this reference).

42 I owe this idea to a fascinating lecture by Ursula Seidl about birth in Urartu. She is presently preparing the publication.

43 Chicago: A 27 902; Asher-Greve 1985: no. 593. After I finished this article, B. Lion and C. Michel pointed out to me two articles by Laura Battini, where she already suggested that the two seals (here Figs. 30 and 31) show a woman giving birth: Battini 2002 and Battini 2006. I regret that I had not known these articles before, but I am happy that Battini and I arrived at the same conclusion.

Fig. 30: Cylinder seal showing a woman giving birth and a midwife in action (Asher-Greve 1985, pl. 30, no. 593).

with short or no hair, are standing near the curved headboard. A woman, her hair fashioned in a similar bun, is squatting at the lower end of the bed and is stretching her hands towards the feet of the lying woman. Below the bed is a scorpion, symbol of fertility, above it a star and a crescent.

The scene has been interpreted as a *hieros gamos* (Asher-Greve 1985: 113–114) or as an oneiromancy (Asher-Greve 1987). Both interpretations are implausible; the first one because a man is missing, and the second one, because the lying woman is holding her head actively up with her arm raised in front of her face, which would be an inappropriate position for dreaming, but is a typical posture during childbirth in many cultures. Since the woman squatting on the ground is by far the largest person and is placed in the center of the scene, i.e. below the central hero of the contest scene in the upper register, we suggest that this seal belonged to this person, i.e. to the midwife. This is one of the most explicit and detailed renderings of this female profession to date.

This seal is not unique in showing a woman giving birth, since at least one other Akkadian seal[44] shows a lady lying on a bed with bull's legs and a scorpion below the bed (Fig. 31).[45] Interestingly, many vessels and trees or plants are depicted there – apparently important elements of female equipment or symbols of the female world, since they frequently occur on women's seals (see below).

A late Early Dynastic votive plaque from the Abu Temple in Tall Asmar (Ešnunna) shows a similar scene in the upper register (Fig. 32)[46]: Two women

44 Boehmer 1965: no. 1656, Fig. 690 = Buchanan 1981: no. 458.

45 Buchanan 1981: 176–177, no. 458.

46 Limestone plaque from Tell Asmar, Abu Temple; Iraq Mus. IM 15547; Selz 1983: pl. IX, no. 110. Earlier interpretations speak of a *hieros gamos* or of the slaughtering of an animal (Asher-Greve 1985: 101–102).

Fig. 31: Cylinder seal with a woman lying on a bed with bull's legs, oil vessels and the birth plant (Buchanan 1981: no. 458).

Fig. 32: Votive plaque showing a midwife and a birth-giving woman (right) and two banqueting women (left) (Selz 1983: pl. 9, no. 110).

are sitting on the left side. On the right side, there is a table with bull's legs, covered with a flounced cloth. A horizontal figure is lying on top, and another smaller object on top of it. Seven lancet-shaped objects (plants?[47]) appear above the scene. Exactly in the middle of the upper register is depicted the

47 Selz (1983: 207–208) interprets them as the 7 heads of a serpent-dragon, which had been cut off and were to serve as apotropaic objects.

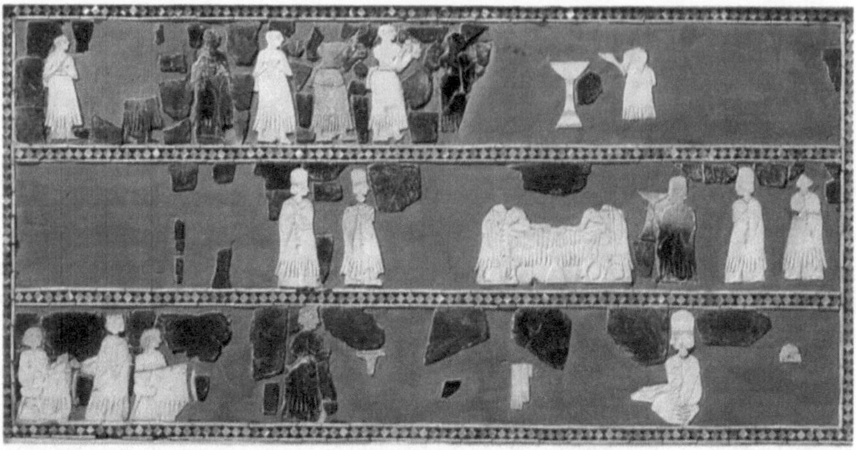

Fig. 33: Tentatively reconstructed mosaic panel from Mari showing female and male persons carrying goods, spinning women and a bed.

midwife: she is standing at the end of the bed, is inclined towards the bed and stretches her hands to the mother. Perhaps – if the object on top of the woman is the child who lies on the mother's belly – she has just given birth.

A mosaic panel from Mari (Fig. 33), the "Panneau des rites" M. 303 was excavated in room 10 of the so-called "secteur dit des dépendances du temple de Dagan." Unfortunately, the pieces when found were completely dispersed which is why Parrot's reconstruction is only a guess (Parrot 1962: 163–169; Couturaud 2014). Parrot assembled the figures of several female and male people, who are carrying goods. At least five of the women wearing a high polos, a long garment and a shawl covering their shoulders are bringing large vessels on a stand. Another five women in the lower left corner have their hair covered by a turban and are busy with spinning.

Very different is the largest piece of the panel (Fig. 34). It features two headless figures bending over a large bed with bull's legs, which is covered with a tufted cloth. The two persons are characterized as women by their coats, which are held together by a large pin from which beads or seals are hanging down. The ladies are stretching their hands towards a vertical stick, which emerges from a conical base, or are about to do something with the covered bed. Since the position of their bent upper body is unusual, their activity must have been an important one, worth being depicted, and the scene must have had a crucial meaning for the whole panel. This scene was interpreted before as a *hieros gamos* (Asher-Greve 1985), or as a female oneiromancer (Asher-Greve 1987). Crawford (2013: 18) recently suggested, without further argu-

Fig. 34: Detail of the panel: Two midwives busy with the childbed (Parrot 1962, fig. 13).

ments, to see in them "perhaps" the representation of midwives – an interpretation, that seems extremely probable in the light of the afore-mentioned plaque and seal.

This re-interpretation leads to a new understanding of the mosaic plaques in general, the iconography of which differs distinctly from that of other media. The intention of the Mari panel was probably to depict the childbirth of a high-ranking woman – perhaps the queen – and the related festivals, especially the offering of gifts to the woman in childbirth by an impressive number of high-ranking women and men. Contemporary texts from Ebla note ample festivities and presentation of gifts on the occasion of the childbirth of a queen; and not only royal women but also other high-ranking women received gifts on the occasion of their birth-giving.[48] If we compare this interpretation of the plaque to the interpretations of other mosaic panels, for example the so-called Standard of Ur, we may recognize that these mosaic panels commemorate and celebrate the most essential and perhaps also the most life-threatening events in the lives of women and men, the victorious return from a battle and the successful birth of a healthy child.

A fragmentary Akkadian seal from Ur shows the most explicit rendering of a woman giving birth (Fig. 35).[49] The woman, with her hair in a bun and wearing a fringed robe, sits on the front edge of a bed with bull's legs and holds a

48 Biga 1991: 294; Weiershäuser 2008: 189–193; Sallaberger 2003: 619.

49 BM 119219; Boehmer 1965: no. 1658; Collon 1982: 74–75, no. 143, pl. XX. I am grateful to Ursula Seidl who pointed this seal out to me, since the published illustrations are not very clear. I thank Rainer Michael Boehmer for kindly providing me with a better photo, which he made for his dissertation.

Fig. 35: Akkadian seal from Ur showing a woman giving birth (to the right), assisted by two midwives (Photo courtesy R. M. Boehmer).

cup in her right hand, while her left lies in her lap. Her feet rest between the knees of a smaller woman who sits on a stool. This smaller woman is grasping towards the woman's feet with both hands. A third woman stands behind her and holds a towel in her right hand and something (the seal is broken here) in her left hand.

In order to substantiate our interpretation of these scenes as renderings of childbirth, we may have a look at some Old Hittite relief vases (Figs. 36–37). These exceptionally large, colorful vases were splendidly decorated with narrative depictions of festivals, including sacrifices, banquets, ritual sex, and offerings, all of which were accompanied by music, dance and acrobats. Examples are known from Inandik, Bitik, Boğazköy and Hüseyindede Tepesi (Sipahi 2001; Yıldırım 2008). The partly damaged scene on the Inandik vase (Fig. 36), where two people are crouching on a bed opposite each other, has been interpreted as a sacred marriage[50] or as the representation of a couple of gods or goddesses or the king and the queen (for a summary see Yıldırım 2008: 844). But a similar, completely preserved depiction on the Hüseyndede vase (Fig. 37) clearly shows that the two people on top of the high bed are far from having sexual intercourse, they are not even touching each other. Two crouching persons are depicted. The one in a white garment with long hair has her legs tightly tucked up, is leaning backwards, and holds a bowl in one hand. Her head is higher than the head of the other person, who is wearing a black dress and has her head covered by white scarf. She seems to be busy with the person

50 The interpretation as sacred marriage is especially strange, since this is already depicted in the upper register exactly above the bed scene.

Fig. 36: Detail of the Old Hittite Inandik vase showing two people crouching on a bed opposite each other (Özgüc 2002: 253).

Fig. 37: Detail of the Hüseyndede vase showing a midwife and a woman giving birth (Alparslan – Dogan-Alparslan 2013: 227).

opposite her, since one hand is emerging from the amorphous mass of her body. Obviously – as has been described already by Yıldırım – two women are depicted. The most logical interpretation is that of a birth scene, in which a midwife and a woman giving birth are involved. There is a striking similarity between these birth scenes and those from 3rd millennium Mesopotamia including such details as the beds with bull's legs and the sophisticated blankets covering them.

When I presented this interpretation during the conference in Nanterre, various scholars rightly uttered their doubts, because "the brick of birth" is considered the crucial object during childbirth in ancient Babylonia and Egypt and was used until recently in remote areas of the Near East. The woman leaves her bed for the delivering of the baby and takes place in a crouching position on two sets of bricks on either side, which leave a space in the middle for the baby to come out (Stol 2000: 118–122). However, the earliest attestation for the birth bricks is – according to Stol – from the Old Babylonian period. The Mesopotamian depictions so far recognized and discussed here are earlier. Therefore, and because of pictorial representations, I am very much inclined to think that an uncomfortably hard brick was not the only possible accessory which was used for giving birth throughout Near Eastern history. Indeed, birth-stools are attested from the Hittite period onwards; the stool "consisted of a 'bowl' upon which the mother sat (and) two pegs which the woman grasped during her delivery ... It was purified before being used ..." (Stol 2000: 121–122). A Hittite birth ritual describes it in the following way: "[When] a woman is giving birth, then the midwife prepares the following: [two sto]ols (and) three cushions. On each stool is placed one cushion. And one spreads [on]e cushion between the stools on the ground. When the child begins to fall, [then] the woman seats herself on the stools. And the midwife holds the receiving blanket with (her) [ha]nd." (Stol 2000: 122).

This birth-stool is probably depicted on the mentioned images: it is covered with cushions (Figs 32, 34, 36, 37); it was purified (Fig. 34); there were pegs which the woman could grasp (Fig. 34); and a towel was prepared (Fig. 35). Also the frequently associated depictions of plants and vessels (Fig. 30, 31, 33, 36) are understandable, since certain plants were thought to promote pregnancy and birth (Stol 2000: 52–59), and "oil has always been a very important ingredient in easing deliveries" (Stol 2000: 124). The cup in the hand of the mother (Figs. 35, 37) illustrates perhaps the medicine which was consumed by the women in labour (Stol 2000: 52–59).

***

This short survey has shown that the following female professions and activities were depicted during the 3rd and early 2nd millennium BC in Mesopotamia and Syria:

- Royal and high-ranking women
- Court ladies and female attendants
- Priestesses
- Female musicians and dancers
- Prostitutes and perhaps other women having sexual intercourse or indulging in other sexual activities
- Women as mothers and as wet-nurses
- Female kitchen personnel and female brewers
- Female textile workers
- Midwives
- Women in childbirth or childbed.

Generally, mortal females are represented in Mesopotamia quite frequently in the 3rd millennium on works of major art and cylinder seals. The majority of depicted women belongs to the upper class. This stops abruptly at the beginning of the 2nd millennium in Mesopotamia, but it continues in Syria, Anatolia and Elam. In the first half of the 2nd millennium mortal women are mainly depicted on thousands of cheap terracotta images, which were present in domestic and the every-day contexts in every Mesopotamian settlement. Many of them, especially specific types of naked women and musicians, probably prostitutes and itinerant artists, do not seem to have been part of the upper social class. The lack of representations in Babylonia in the major arts might be explained by the fact that several female activities seem to have been transferred to the divine world, not only, but especially, in the 2nd millennium. If we look at the scenes on Old Babylonian cylinder seals, which are our richest source of pictorial representations, we register a multitude of goddesses and gods, who might have covered a wide range of everyday concerns of the mortal women. Thousands of representations of Ištar and other armed goddesses, of the rain goddess accompanying the weather god, of the goddess holding a water vessel, of Gula and of many others, may refer to war and love, fertility, surgery[51], and other fields in which women were active. But – as stated at the beginning – only professions and activities that were deemed important enough were depicted.

The biggest difference between the representations of the 3rd and the 2nd millennium is a fundamental one, which has nothing to do with a possibly changed status of women. All pictorial genres of the 3rd millennium generally feature individual women and men. This equally applies to stelae, reliefs, statues and seals of the Early Dynastic, Akkadian and Neo-Sumerian periods. In Old Babylonian major art and seals, by contrast, hardly any individuals were depicted any more. The few mortals being represented at all (especially the king in many variations) are little more than stereotypical formulas for abstract characteristics such as the strength of kingship, the justice of the ruler, piety or fertility.[52] The individual disappears. It is mainly on the cheap terracotta plaques that we find images of mortals in scenes, which are related to everyday life.

The most astonishing result of this study is the discovery of scenes depicting women in childbirth or giving birth assisted by midwives. Since depictions are known from Mari, the Diyala region, Ur and Anatolia during the 3rd and 2nd millennia, they may have existed at other times and in different regions, but have not yet been recognized as such. The associated scenes always show large festivals, where numerous female and male persons are bringing various gifts, accompanied by music and dance. Cuneiform sources from various periods tell us about the celebrations for the birth of a child, but these are the first known depictions of this celebratory as well as life-threatening event in the lives of Near Eastern women.

---

51 Female physicians are attested e.g. at Ebla (see Biga, this volume).

52 For the codification of the king's main characteristics on cylinder seals see Otto 2013.

Bibliography

Alparslan, Metin and Meltem Dogan-Alparslan (eds.). 2013. *Hittites – An Anatolian Empire / Hititler – Bir Anadolu Imparatorlugu*. Istanbul: Tüpraş.

Amiet, Pierre. 1981. *La glyptique mésopotamienne archaique*. 2nd ed. Paris.

Aruz, Joan (ed.). 2003. *Art of the First Cities: The Third Millennium B.C. from the Mediterranean to the Indus*. New York: Metropolitan Museum of Art.

Asher-Greve, Julia M. 1985. *Frauen in altsumerischer Zeit*. BiMes 18. Malibu: Undena Publ.

Asher-Greve, Julia M. 1987. The oldest female oneiromancer. Pp. 27–31 in Durand 1987.

Asher-Greve, Julia M. 2006. 'Golden Age' of Women? Status and Gender in Third Millennium Sumerian and Akkadian Art. Pp. 42–81 in Schroer 2006.

Asher-Greve, Julia M. 2013. Women and Agency: A Survey from Late Uruk to the end of Ur III. Pp 359–377 in Crawford 2013.

Asher-Greve, Julia M. and Deborah Sweeney. 2006. On Nakedness, Nudity, and Gender in Egyptian and Mesopotamian Art, Pp. 125–176 in Schroer 2006.

Asher-Greve, Julia M. and Joan Goodnick Westenholz. 2013. *Goddesses in Context. On Divine Powers, Roles, Relationships and Gender in Mesopotamian Textual and Visual Sources*. OBO 259. Fribourg: Academic Press and Göttingen: Vandenhoeck & Ruprecht.

Assante, Julia. 2006. Undressing the Nude: Problems in Analyzing Nudity in Ancient Art with an Old Babylonian Case Study. Pp. 177–207 in Schroer 2006.

Barrelet, Marie-Thérèse. 1968. *Figurines et reliefs en terre cuite de la Mésopotamie antique I, Potiers, termes de métier, procédés de fabrication et production*. Paris: Geuthner.

Battini, Laura. 2002. De l'étude des sceaux: quelques nouvelles pistes en partant de l'analyse du sceau A 27902 de l'*Oriental Institute Museum* de Chicago. *Akkadica* 123: 153–161.

Battini, Laura. 2006. Les images de la naissance en Mésopotamie. Pp. 1–37 in *Médecine et médecins au Proche-Orient ancien*, Laura Battini and Pierre Villard eds. BAR 1528. Oxford.

Beyer, Dominique. 2007. Les sceaux de Mari au IIIe millénaire. *Akh Purattim* I: 231–260.

Biga, Maria Giovanna. 1991. Donne alla corte di Ebla. *La parola del passato* 46.

Blocher, Felix. 1987. *Untersuchungen zum Motiv der nackten Frau in der altbabylonischen Zeit*. Münchener Universitäts-Schriften 4. München and Wien: Profil-Verlag.

Boehmer, Rainer M. 1965. *Die Entwicklung der Glyptik während der Akkad-Zeit*. UAVA 4. Berlin: de Gruyter.

Boese, Johannes. 1971. *Altmesopotamische Weihplatten, Eine sumerische Denkmalsgattung des 3. Jahrtausend v. Chr.* UAVA 6. Berlin: de Gruyter.

Börker-Klähn, Jutta. 1982. *Altvorderasiatische Bildstelen und vergleichbare Felsreliefs*. BaF 4. Mainz am Rhein: Zabern.

Buccellati, Giorgio and Marilyn Kelly-Buccellati. 1995–1996. The royal storehouse of Urkesh. The glyptic evidence from the southwestern wing. *AfO* 42/43: 1–32.

Buchanan, Briggs. 1981. *Early Near Eastern Seals in the Yale Babylonian Collection*. New Haven and London: Yale University Press.

Ciafardoni, Paola and Deborah Gianessi (eds.). 2015. *From the Treasures of Syria. Essays on Art and Archaeology in Honour of Stefania Mazzoni*. Leiden: Nederlands Instituut voor het Nabije Oosten.

Collon, Dominique. 1982. *Catalogue of the Western Asiatic Seals in the British Museum. Cylinder Seals III. Akkadian – Post Akkadian – Ur III Periods*. London: British Museum Publications.

Collon, Dominique. 1986. *Catalogue of the Western Asiatic Seals in the British Museum. Cylinder Seals II. Isin-Larsa and Old Babylonian Period.* London: British Museum Publications.

Collon, Dominique. 1987. *First Impressions.* London: The British Museum Press.

Collon, Dominique. 1999. Depictions of Priests and Priestesses in the Ancient Near East. Pp. 17–46 in *Priests and Officials in the Ancient Near East: Papers of the Second Colloquium on the Ancient Near East – the City and its Life, held at the Middle Eastern Culture Center in Japan (Mitaka, Tokyo), March 22–24, 1996*, ed. Kazuko Watanabe. Heidelberg: Winter.

Cooper, Jerrold. 2006. Prostitution. *RlA* 11: 13–21.

Couturaud, Barbara. 2014. L'image et le contexte: nouvelle étude des panneaux figuratifs incrustés de Mari. *Syria* 91: 77–97.

Crawford, Harriet. 2013. (ed.) *The Sumerian World.* London: Routledge.

Crawford, Harriet. 2014. An Exploration of the World of Women in Third-Millenium Mesopotamia. Pp. 10–27 in *Women in the ancient Near East: A Sourcebook*, ed. Mark W. Chavalas. London: Routledge.

Dohmann-Pfälzner, Heike. 2013. Siegel des dritten Jahrtausends v. Chr. in der syrischen Gazira. Pp. 215–234 in Orthmann, al-Maqdissi, and Matthiae 2013.

Dolce, Rita. 2008. Ebla before the Achievement of Palace G Culture: an Evaluation of the Early Syrian Archaic Period. Pp. 65–80 in *Proceedings of the 4th International Congress of the Archaeology of the Ancient Near East*, eds. Harmut Kühne, Rainer M. Czichon, and F. Janoscha Kreppner. Wiesbaden: Harrassowitz.

Durand, Jean-Marie (ed.). 1987. *La femme dans le Proche-Orient antique: Compte rendu de la XXXIIIe Rencontre assyriologique internationale, Paris, 7–10 juillet 1986.* Paris: Editions Recherche sur les Civilisations.

Eisen, Gustavus A. 1940. *Ancient Oriental Cylinder and other Seals with a description of the Collection of Mrs. William H. Moore.* OIP 47. Chicago: The University of Chicago Press.

Evans, Jean M. 2003a. Stele of Ušumgal. P. 53 in Aruz 2003.

Evans, Jean M. 2003b. Wall plaque with libation scenes. P. 74–75 in Aruz 2003.

Evans, Jean M. 2003c. Female figures wearing tall headdresses. P. 153–154 in Aruz 2003.

Felli, Candida. 2015. On Naked Woman: A Case Study. Pp. 217–239 in Ciafardoni and Gianessi 2015.

Fischer, Claudia. 1997. Siegelabrollungen im British Museum auf Ur-III-zeitlichen Texten aus der Provinz Lagaš. Untersuchungen zu den Verehrungsszenen. *BaM* 28: 97–183.

Frayne, Douglas. 1993. *Sargonic and Gutian Periods 2334–2113.* Royal Inscriptions of Mesopotamia, Early periods 2. Toronto: University of Toronto Press.

Gelb, Ignace J., Piotr Steinkeller, and Robert M. Whiting Jr. 1991. *Earliest Land Tenure Systems in the Near East: Ancient Kudurrus*, OIP 104. Chicago: The Oriental Institute of the University of Chicago.

Genouillac, Henri de. 1936. *Fouilles de Telloh II, Époque d'Ur IIIe Dynastie et de Larsa.* Paris: Paul Geuthner.

Hatz, Melanie J. 2003. Disk of Enheduanna, daughter of Sargon. Pp. 200–201 in Aruz 2003.

Hrouda, Barthel (ed.). 1977. *Isin – Išān Bahriyāt I. Die Ergebnisse der Ausgrabungen 1973–1974.* München: Bayerische Akademie der Wissenschaften.

Ishida, Keiko. 1991. Ed. *Ancient Near Eastern Seals in Japan.* Tokyo: Ancient Orient Museum.

Kelly-Buccellati, Marilyn. 2015. Power and Identity Construction in Ancient Urkesh. Pp. 111–130 in Ciafardoni and Gianessi 2015.

Matthiae, Paolo. 1977. *Ebla, Un Impero Ritrovato.* Torino: Einaudi.

Matthiae, Paolo. 1993. A Stele Fragment of Hadda from Ebla. Pp. 389–397 in *Aspects of Art and Iconography: Anatolia and its Neighbors. Studies in Honor of Nimet Özgüç*, eds. Machteld J. Melling, Edith Porada, and Tahsin Özgüç. Ankara: Türk Tarih Kurumu Basimevi.

Matthiae, Paolo. 2010. *Ebla. La città del trono: Archeologia e storia*. Torino: Einaudi.

Matthiae, Paolo. 2013. Stone Sculpture of the Second Millennium BC. Pp. 375–394 in Orthmann, al-Maqdissi, and Matthiae 2013.

Matthiae, Paolo. 2015. Notes et études éblaites, I: le semeion de Hiérapolis dans l'Ébla paléosyrienne. *RA* 108: 93–120.

Mayr, Rudi. 2002. The Depiction of Ordinary Men and Women on the Seals of the Ur III Kingdom. Pp. 359–366 in Parpola and Whiting 2002.

Mayr, Rudi and David Owen. 2004. The Royal Gift Seal in the Ur III Period. Pp. 146–174 in *Von Sumer nach Ebla und zurück. Festschrift Giovanni Pettinato zum 27. September 1999 gewidmet von Freunden, Kollegen und Schülern*, ed. Hartmut Waetzoldt. HSAO 9. Heidelberg: Heidelberger Orientverlag.

Mazzoni, Stefania. 2002. The Squatting Woman. Between Fertility and Eroticism. Pp. 367–377 in Parpola and Whiting 2002.

Moortgat, Anton. 1940. *Vorderasiatische Rollsiegel*. Berlin: Mann.

Orthmann Winfried, Michel al-Maqdissi and Paolo Matthiae (eds.). 2013. *Archéologie et Histoire de la Syrie, Vol. I: La Syrie de l'époque néolithique à l'âge du fer*. Wiesbaden: Harrassowitz.

Otto, Adelheid. 2000. Die Entstehung und Entwicklung der Klassisch-Syrischen Glyptik. *UAVA* 8. Berlin and New York: Walter de Gruyter.

Otto, Adelheid. 2013. Königssiegel als Programm – Überlegungen zum Selbstverständnis altorientalischer Herrscher und zur Deutung der Tierkampfszene. *ZA* 103: 45–68.

Otto, Adelheid. 2015. 9,000 Years of Cultic Traditions in Northern Mesopotamia and Syria? Thoughts about the crescent, the bull and the pole with human heads. Pp. 185–202 in Ciafardoni and Gianessi 2015.

Özgüç, Nimet. 2006. *Kültepe-Kaniš/Neša: Seal Impressions on the Clay Envelopes from the Archives of the Native Peruwa and Assyrian Trade Usur-ša-Ištar son of Aššur-imitti*, Ankara: Türk Tarih Kurumu.

Özgüç, Tahsin. 2002. Die Keramik der althethitischen Zeit. Kultgefäße. Pp. 248–255 in *Die Hethiter und ihr Reich*, ed. Kunst- und Ausstellungshalle der Bundesrepublik Deutschland GmbH. Stuttgart: Konrad Theiss Verlag.

Parpola, Simo and Robert Whiting (eds.). 2002. *Sex and Gender in the Ancient Near East. Proceedings of the XLVIIe Rencontre Assyriologique Internationale, Helsinki, July 2–7, 2001*. Helsinki: Helsinki University Press.

Parrot, André. 1956. *Le temple d'Ishtar. Mission Archéologique de Mari II/3*. Paris: Geuthner.

Parrot, André. 1959. *Les Palais III. Documents et monuments. Mission Archéologique de Mari I*. Paris: Geuthner.

Parrot, André. 1962. Les fouilles de Mari, 12e campagne (automne 1961). *Syria* 39: 151–179

Pinnock, Frances. 1998. The Iconography of the Entu-Priestesses in the Period of the Ur III Dynasty. Pp. 339–346 in *Intellectual Life of the Ancient Near East. Papers Presented at the 43rd Rencontre Assyriologique Internationale Prague, July 1–5, 1996*, ed. Jiří Prosecký. Prag: Oriental Institute.

Pinnock, Frances. 2013. Sculpture and Minor Arts of the Early Dynastic and Akkade Periods and Their Relation to Mesopotamian Art. Pp. 199–214 in Orthmann, al-Maqdissi, and Matthiae 2013.

Rashid, Subhi Anwar. 1984. *Mesopotamien. Musikgeschichte in Bildern*, Band II: Musik des Altertums, Lieferung 2, ed. Werner Bachmann. Leipzig: VEB Deutscher Verlag für Musik.

Sallaberger, Walther. 2003. Nachrichten aus dem Palast von Ebla. Eine Deutung von níĝ-mul-(an) Pp. 600–625 in P. Marrassini (ed.), *Semitic and Assyriological Studies Presented to Pelio Fronzaroli by Pupils and Colleagues*. Wiesbaden: Harrassowitz.

Schroer, Silvia (ed.). 2006. *Images and Gender. Contributions to the Hermeneutics of Reading Ancient Art*. OBO 220. Fribourg: Universitätsverlag Academic Press and Göttingen: Vandenhoeck & Ruprecht.

Seidl, Ursula. 2005. Priester. B. I. Nach archäologischen Quellen. Mesopotamien, *RlA* 10: 643–647.

Selz, Gebhard J. 2010. Immer nur Söhne und keine Töchter? Zu einem Familienrelief des Ur-Nanše (Urnanše 20 = RIME 1 E1.9). Pp. 187–196 in *Von Göttern und Menschen. Beiträge zu Literatur und Geschichte des Alten Orients. Festschrift für Brigitte Groneberg*, eds. Dahlia Shehata, Frauke Weiershäuser and Kamran V. Zand. CM 41, Leiden and Boston: Brill.

Selz, Gudrun. 1983. *Die Bankettszene*. FAOS 11. Wiesbaden: Franz Steiner.

Sipahi, Tunç. 2001. Eine althethitische Reliefvase vom Hüseyindede Tepesi. *Istanbuler Mitteilungen* 50: 63–85.

Spycket, Agnes. 1981. *La Statuaire du Proche-Orient Ancien*, Handbuch der Orientalistik 7, Leiden and Köln.

Stol, Marten. 2000. Birth in Babylonia and the Bible. CM 14. Groningen: Styx.

Strommenger, Eva. 1962. *Fünf Jahrtausende Mesopotamien*. München: Hirmer Verlag.

Suter, Claudia E. 1991–93. A Shulgi statuette from Tello, *JCS* 43–45: 63–70.

Suter, Claudia E. 2007. Between Human and Divine: High Priestesses in Images from the Akkadian to the Isin-Larsa Period. Pp. 315–359 in *Ancient Near Eastern Art in Context: Studies in Honor of Irene J. Winter*, eds. Marian H. Feldman and Jack Cheng. Leiden: Brill.

Suter, Claudia E. 2008. Who are the women in Mesopotamian art from ca. 2334–1763 BCE?, *KASKAL* 5: 1–55.

Suter, Claudia E. 2013 Kings and Queens: Representation and Reality. Pp. 201–226 in Crawford 2013.

Teissier, Beatrice. 1994. *Sealings and seals on texts from Kültepe Karum level 2*. Istanbul and Leiden: Nederlands Historisch-Archaeologisch Instituut.

Trümpelmann, Leo. 1984. Eine Kneipe in Susa. *Iranica Antiqua* 16: 35–48.

Uehlinger, Christoph. 1998. Nackte Göttin. B. In der Bildkunst, *RlA* 9: 53–64.

Weiershäuser, Frauke. 2006. Die bildliche Darstellung königlicher Frauen der III. Dynastie von Ur und ihre sozialpolitische Aussage. Pp. 263–279 in Schroer 2006.

Weiershäuser, Frauke. 2008. *Die königlichen Frauen der III. Dynastie von Ur*. Göttinger Beiträge zum Alten Orient 1. Göttingen: Universitätsverlag.

Winter, Irene. 1987. Women in Public. The Disc of Enheduanna, the Beginning of the Office of En-Priestess, and the Weight of Visual Evidence. Pp. 189–201 in Durand 1987.

Woolley, Leonard. 1934. *Ur Excavations Vol. II, The Royal Cemetery*, Philadelphia.

Yıldırım, Tayfun. 2008. New scenes on the second relief vase from Hüseyindede. *Studi micenei ed egeo anatolici* 5: 837–850.

Zernecke, Anna E. 2008. Warum sitzt der Skorpion unter dem Bett? Überlegungen zur Deutung eines altorientalischen Fruchtbarkeitssymbols. *Zeitschrift des Deutschen Palästina-Vereins* 124: 107–127.

Zettler, Richard L. and Lee Horne. 1998. *Treasures from the Royal Tombs of Ur*. Philadelphia: University of Pennsylvania Museum.
Ziegler, Nele. 2007. *Les Musiciens et la musique d'après les archives de Mari*. Florilegium marianum IX. Mémoires de NABU 10. Paris: SEPOA.

Bertrand Lafont

Women at Work and Women in Economy and Society during the Neo-Sumerian Period

Until recently, cultural and law-centered approaches have dominated most studies on the role of women in ancient Mesopotamia. The aim of the REFEMA program (*Rôle Économique des Femmes en Mésopotamie Ancienne*, 2012–2015) was to address the social and economic dimensions of this topic and to try to learn more about the "condition féminine" in the ancient Near Eastern context, in the flow of current gender studies.

This contribution will summarize some main data and results obtained and discussed during the three years of this program[1] and will propose some conclusions. Focused on the Neo-Sumerian period, at the end of the 3rd millennium BC, it addresses the following topics: women's economic activities both at home and outside the home; state employment of women; and the question of the constitution, conservation and inheritance of the assets of women belonging to the elite.[2]

1 Economic activities of women at home

During the whole Sumerian period, women as well as men were the holders and guardians of social and economic traditions inside the family sphere. Both women and men can be regarded as economic agents in terms of wealth production.

The social framework within which the experiences, roles, and realities of women's lives and contributions can be best evaluated was the *household* (**e$_2$**), whether a domestic unit or an institutional establishment, such as the royal palace or a temple. This notion of the household, well characterized and stud-

1 See the "Carnet de REFEMA", http://refema.hypotheses.org.

2 On all these issues, see also Agnès Garcia-Ventura's recent bibliography (and her contribution to this volume), as this author has published a lot during the last five years on similar themes.

Bertrand Lafont, CNRS, Archéologies et Sciences de l'Antiquité; bertrand.lafont@mae.cnrs.fr

ied by I. J. Gelb some 35 years ago[3] and more recently reassessed by J. D. Schloen,[4] is particularly meaningful and useful for the kind of historical investigation undertaken here.

Moreover, and without fear of being too much influenced by our own conceptions of what is a "family," it is well known that that Sumerian society of that time was based on nuclear families practicing monogamy, with a relatively small number of children (in contrast with what is known for *royal* families). Each of them was an "**e_2**" of an often limited size, as shown by the following examples: husband, wife, and five children in UET 3, 93 [P136410];[5] husband, wife, and three children in BM 105377 [P112634]; a widow, mother of five children in BAOM 2, 26 26 [P104889], etc.

Nevertheless, in Ur III, all women did not systematically belong to an official or family "**e_2**." Thus, we do find frequent attestations of women qualified as **$geme_2$-kar-KID**: these women were not necessarily "prostitutes" as often said, but rather independent women, not living under male authority, or not part of a patriarchal household. They had to support themselves in any number of ways (and some may in fact have been prostitutes).[6]

Be that as it may, the problem is that usual domestic life and work are very poorly documented and largely escapes us in the kind of archives that we have. However, large family households (**e_2**) or princely domains and estates of individuals belonging to the elite are better known in our archival texts, as documented for example with this household inventory of the assets of the son of the Girsu governor, drawn up in year Ibbi-Sîn 2. This tablet[7] records the following items:

- 5 hectares of orchard
- 200 slaves (half of them being women)
- 3700 heads of livestock, 250 heads of cattle
- objects in silver, non-precious metals, stone, wood, and reed
- clothes, drapery, and skins
- perishable goods

Apparently, the wealth of this princely and very large domain originated mainly in animal husbandry. But a more detailed look at the description of this household estate (inventoried on the occasion of seizure proceedings, as pro-

3 Gelb 1979.
4 Schloen 2001.
5 P-numbers given in this article are id numbers of the CDLI database cdli.ucla.edu.
6 See Assante 1998; Cooper 2010 and in this volume; Démare-Lafont, *in press*.
7 Maekawa 1996: 167–168 n° 9 [P102665].

posed by K. Maekawa)[8] shows that more than 200 garments, nearly 500 kilos of wool and large quantities of oil, honey, wine, cheese, dates and aromatics were also counted.

The list of these goods, together with common sense, prompts us to conclude that the women in this household, including maids and slaves, were mainly the ones who transformed all of these raw materials into the products needed for everyday life. They were probably busy first of all with providing members of the household with their basic needs in terms of food, clothing, and care. But the problem is that their work remains "invisible" as there is never any mention of it in our archives. This kind of work was neither recognized, nor measured, nor recorded, nor paid.

Therefore, during the Ur III period, the domestic arena was clearly the place of productive and economically significant activities for women, enabling them to provide members of the household – great or small – with their basic needs. But in this regard, it must be noted that we never see any surplus of goods produced at home by women that could have fed external economic channels. Furthermore, there is no information in any of our texts regarding the potential participation in market activities of women belonging to family households. But on that point, attention must be paid of course to the argument that silence and the lack of documentation does not necessarily mean that there was no surplus sold in local markets ...

Regarding again this notion of "household" and the role of women inside it, a lot of new information has been recently provided by the Garšana archive.[9] Revealing the organization of a huge "private" household or estate under the authority of princess Simat-Ištaran, sister of king Šu-Sîn, (after her husband's death), this archive provides unprecedented data on the role of women in the Neo-Sumerian economy and society, as we can observe in productive activities including orchard work, brewing, weaving, animal husbandry, leather-working, and extensive building works.[10]

If one considers the labor force at work in this household, it has been noticed that, in the Garšana archive, working women exceeded in number working men.[11] Moreover, these texts highlight especially the role of women, both as heads of the household and in the capacity of supervisors, administrators (some of them have seals), and laborers in many sectors of the estate.

8 Maekawa 1996 and 1997. See also Heimpel 1997.
9 Owen and Mayr 2007.
10 See Owen and Mayr 2007; Kleinerman and Owen 2009; Heimpel 2009; Owen 2011.
11 Heimpel 2009: 47.

Thus, for example, various women supervised construction gangs consisting of both men and women:[12] such positions in such a sector of society were, until now, unattested within the existing Ur III records.

In the upper part of society, we have several examples of estates belonging to important women. At Garšana, if we just have a look at the possessions owned by princess Simat-Ištaran, we see that she had at her disposal a complete estate (**e_2**), with villages (**e_2-$duru_5$**), orchards (**$kiri_6$**), boats (**ma_2**), many slaves and servants, and a large wardrobe consisting of many luxurious clothes.[13]

At Irisagrig, an emerging batch of tablets provides new data on the role of a prominent woman at the head of another large household: this woman, named Ninsaga, was the daughter of the governor (**$ensi_2$**) of Irisagrig, Ur-mes. She managed her own huge estate in that city and three texts about it deserve attention:

- The tablet Nisaba 15, 953 [P454138]) is a complete inventory, in twelve columns, of hundreds of named male and female slaves (**$arad_2$** and **$geme_2$**) belonging to the household of Ninsaga in year Ibbi-Sîn 3. Each of them received between 10 and 75 liters of barley rations monthly. At the end, we find recorded: 74 **guruš**, 48 **$geme_2$**, 47 **dumu-$nita_2$**, 56 **dumu-munus** (= 122 adults, 103 children, that is, 225 men and women). All these dependents of this private household are clearly characterized as "slaves" or servants (**$geme_2$ $arad_2$**) of Ninsaga.
- A second text (Nisaba 15, 797 [P387850]) shows that, one year before (in Ibbi-Sîn 2), a general (**šagina**) had taken away 50 slaves who had been removed from the household of Ninsaga, probably to bring them to the king (or maybe to a memorial of the late king), since these slaves are characterized as being assigned to the throne (**$arad_2$ $geme_2$ nam-^{geš}gu-za**).[14]
- It is interesting to find again exactly this same information quoted in another text (Nisaba 15, 1038 [P454190]), which summarized other withdrawals made from Ninsaga's household staff.

Finally, the role of women as managers of wealthy family households is well illustrated by a text that is truly unique among the Neo-Sumerian archival documents. This is a letter, probably written by a woman who could be called a

12 Heimpel 2009: 75.

13 Kleinerman-Owen 2009: 546–547.

14 For commemorations to the throne of the dead kings, see Sallaberger 1993: 28–29, 147–148, and Michalowski 2013: 319–320.

"desperate housewife."[15] She speaks of her children (l. 4) and of the way she manages daily life in the household (l. 8–13). As the situation of the household is critical, she tries to explain the causes of the situation and to deny any personal responsibility for the crisis: perhaps she had been accused by her husband Ki'ag (?) for mismanaging the household.

In the end, thanks to all this evidence, and especially new information which sheds light on a hitherto undocumented aspect of society of that period (Garšana), we can see that women in Ur III society and in family households may have had more authority and influence than previously recognized.

2 Outside the house: Women at work alongside men

Chapter VII of Xenophon's *Oeconomicus* asserts that, "naturally", women should devote themselves to indoor activities and men to outdoor ones:[16]

> Because both the indoor and the outdoor tasks require work and concern, I think the god, from the very beginning, designed the nature of woman for the indoor work and concerns and the nature of man for the outdoor work. For he prepared man's body and mind to be more capable of enduring cold and heat and travelling and military campaigns, and so he assigned the outdoor work to him. Because the woman was physically less capable of endurance, I think the god has evidently assigned the indoor work to her.

But we must admit that the available Sumerian documentation challenges this usual and traditional view, according to which men worked outdoors for the primary productive sector of the economy (mainly in the fields and in animal husbandry), while women were occupied in the secondary productive sector (indoors, to produce flour, oil, clothing, and so on). This gender dimension of labor division does not fit information provided by the texts, as we can find for example:

- male weavers (**guruš uš-bar**) next to female weavers (**geme$_2$ uš-bar**), as in the tablet UET 3, 1449 [P137774]
- male millers working alongside female millers (BCT 2, 49 [P105290])
- or on the contrary, many women involved in agricultural and several other outdoor activities (*passim*).

15 MVN 11, 168 [P116181]. Studied in Owen 1980a; and reassessed in Hallo 2003: 295; Neumann 2006: 17–19; and Michalowski 2011: 15–17.

16 Translation: Pomeroy 1995: 141–147. See also Sebillotte Cuchet in this volume. Thanks to Brigitte Lion who drew my attention to this text.

Regarding these mixed "indoor"/"outdoor" activities, it is noteworthy that the female population working in the *indoor* mills and workshops was split into several categories depending on their professional skill, but that all of them were in fact often performing *outdoor* tasks far from their primary specialty. This is shown by the texts formerly studied by R. K. Englund,[17] and by the following table, drawn up from the Garšana data. Here, it is clear that the titles and occupations qualifying the registered women are not the same as the actual activities they were involved in according to the administrative records:

All the professional occupationsqualifying women in Garšana texts (Kleinerman and Owen 2009: 721)	Real occupations recorded for these women in administrative Garšana texts (Kleinerman and Owen 2009: 735–740)
– $geme_2$ ar_3-ra, "grinder" – $geme_2$ $kikken_2$, "miller" – $geme_2$ $^{geš}i_3$-sur-sur, "oil presser" – $geme_2$ gu, "spinner/flax worker" – $geme_2$ uš-bar, "weaver" – $geme_2$ kisal-luh, "(temple) sweeper"	agricultural work; construction work; transportation and boat towing; flour and food processing; mourning in mortuary ceremonies

This clearly indicates that, during the Neo-Sumerian period, the "status" or the profession of these women did not confine them to a single, particular and basic activity: they were also employed in many occupations having nothing to do with their original specialty in order to suit the needs of the economic organization.

Moreover, some of them could have had professional skills equal to those of men, which they could, and often did, exercise outside the family home. To illustrate this point let us simply examine the list of women's professions and specializations recorded in the recently discovered archives of Garšana and Irisagrig.[18] Thanks to this new data, we can now assert that women held many positions hitherto documented only for men. These specialized occupations include:

– **$geme_2$ $azlag_2$** cf. usually male **lu_2-$azlag_2$**, "fuller, washerman"
– **$geme_2$/munus muhaldim** cf. usually male **muhaldim**, "cook"
– **$geme_2$ i_3-du_8** cf. usually male **i_3-du_8**, "doorkeeper"
– **$geme_2$ kisal-luh** cf. usually male **kisal-luh**, "(temple) sweeper"

17 Englund 1990 and 1991. As noted by this author, "the range of activities of the female millers in agriculture was very broad, covering nearly all the tasks performed by their male counterparts, the **guruš**." (Englund 1991: 274).

18 Kleinerman-Owen 2009: 735–740; Owen 2013: 425–463.

- **geme$_2$/munus nar** cf. usually male **nar**, "singer, musician"
- **munus a-zu** cf. usually male **a-zu**, "physician"
- **munus dub-sar** cf. usually male **dub-sar**, "scribe"
- **munus gudu$_4$** cf. usually male **gudu$_4$**, "purification priest"

The last three professions are particularly interesting, because they are highly specialized and they were not previously attested much for women.[19]

Outdoors, women were involved in agriculture and irrigation, hauling boats, removing grain, making and carrying bricks, and construction projects. In these activities they contributed in the same way as men for the same kinds of collective work. They were employed in a large number of jobs, sometimes in unexpected sectors, as for example the female workers (**geme$_2$**) who "built the house of Amar-Suen."[20] Most of these activities probably had something to do with the *corvée*-duty. According to P. Steinkeller,[21] only heads of families owed such a service to the state, but it is clear that women were also involved in the same collective projects. Therefore, could we assume that they fulfilled these labor obligations on behalf of the heads of households, who generally tried to avoid performing these services themselves?

Indoors, women were spinning, weaving, milling flour and extracting oil, occupations traditionally considered to be the domain of women. The real feature that was quite unique to that time was the transposition into mass production of these tasks which were considered to be female roles within the family unit, since these activities were clearly organized collectively on an "industrial" scale.

Thus, all around the country, some large workhouses/factories employing female workers were created especially for the production of garments (with the **geme$_2$ uš-bar**), flour (with the **geme$_2$ kikken$_2$**) and oil (with the **geme$_2$ i$_3$-sur**). Women were probably employed there to meet the huge needs of the state and institutions. Through their labor they supplied the current ration allotment system. In or around the main cities of the kingdom, some "industrial" centers combining these various activities operated, as in Garšana, where a unique triple complex was established in the form of a "brewery-mill-kitchen build-

19 New professional female occupations, previously unattested at Ur III, appeared in recently published texts as this ^{munus}*qa$_2$-di$_3$-iš-tum*, "midwife?" (Sumerian **nu-gig**) in Nisaba 15 1066 [P387874] who was only attested until now in the recently published new parts of the Codex Ur-Namma (§ E2 see Civil 2011: 281–284). See also some new attestations at Ur III of *sà-bí-tum*, "innkeeper".

20 **e$_2$ ^{d}amar-^{d}suen-ka du$_3$-a** (NYPL 138 [P122674]). See also all the construction work texts studied in Heimpel 2009, in which women are largely involved.

21 Steinkeller 2013: 360.

ing" (**e$_2$ lunga e$_2$ kikken$_2$ u$_3$ e$_2$ muhaldim**).[22] In the same place another double complex was built in the form of a "textile mill and craftsmen's building" (**e$_2$ uš-bar u$_3$ e$_2$ gašam-e-ne**).[23]

In that context, weavers, millers and oil pressers were often associated, as shown by the Ur tablet UET 3, 1504 [P137830]: viii 28–29 where they received their allotted rations together: **nig$_2$-ba geme$_2$ uš-bar geme$_2$ i$_3$-sur u$_3$ geme$_2$ kikken$_2$**, "allotments for female weavers, oil pressers and millers."[24]

These installations, aggregated in unique places, seem to have been managed under the direct supervision of the "great organizations" (temples, local and royal palaces), which appear to have been the first employers of women and children, as well as men. Tens of thousands of female workers have thus been identified in the institutional workshops of Ur, Girsu and Umma, thanks to the thorough studies of H. Waetzoldt, K. Maekawa, J.-P. Grégoire, and others.[25]

General conditions in these "factories" were harsh and restrictive, as shown by the need of porters/doorkeepers (**i$_3$-du$_8$**) to control inputs and outputs of workers, and the frequent mention of fugitives (**zah$_3$**) that were pursued and caught (**^{geš}tukul-e dab$_5$-ba**) on many occasions, or workers who died (**uš$_2$**). One text from Ur, for example, records up to 134 of these fugitive women (**geme$_2$ zah$_3$**) who were returned to the palace (**e$_2$-gal-la gi$_4$-a**) from which they had escaped (UET 3, 1018 [P137343]). Another example can be found in an interesting text from Girsu where sisters and wives are held responsible for the flight of their brothers or husbands and are obliged to replace them at work in the factory (HLC 374 [P110244]). This is another illustration of the fact that, from the administration's point of view, there was no difference between male and female work.

This pressure exerted by the state administration and its strong will for control shown by the texts should probably be analyzed in the context of a scarcity of labor during the Ur III period, as P. Steinkeller has suggested some years ago.[26]

It is well known that workers were usually compensated on the basis of a number of factors, such as the kind of task involved, the worker's age and the worker's gender. But W. Heimpel has shown that, at Garšana, males performing

22 Kleinerman and Owen 2009: 705–710.

23 Kleinerman and Owen 2009: 701–702.

24 Other examples where female weavers, millers and oil pressers are associated: UET 3, 1422: 7–8 [P137747], or TLB 3, 71: rev. 1 [P134212].

25 Waetzoldt 1972; Maekawa 1980, 1987, 1989, 1998; Grégoire 1999.

26 Steinkeller 2002. See also the discussion in Adams 2010, and Garfinkle 2012: 25 n. 37.

tasks that were usually carried out by females were compensated and included in totals as if they were female![27]

In total, the professional specialization was more or less the same for women as for men, and we can see both men and women doing their job inside or outside the domestic sphere, for various tasks of production or service, including within the framework of the *corvée*-duty which made no gender distinction, as summarized in the following chart:

Tab. 1: A chart of male and female outdoor/indoor activities.

Occupations			**Female activity**	**Male activity**	**Remarks**
1) Outdoor activities					
– agriculture and animal husbandry			x	x	
– maintaining irrigation systems			x	x	
– carrying, removing grain, bricks, etc.			x	x	
– boat loading, hauling and towing			x	x	
– construction works			x	x	
etc.					
2) Indoor activities					
potter	**bahar**$_2$			x	mentioned all together in the *Laws of Ur-Namma*, §D1 (see Civil 2011) for their payment. These craftsmen are also mentioned all together in the industrial workshops of Ur (see for ex. UET 3, 1498)
smith	**simug**			x	
carpenter	**nagar**			x	
reed craftsman	**ad-KID**	*Organized*		x	
leather worker	**ašgab**	*in industrial*		x	
fuller	**azlag**$_2$	*workshops*		x	
braider	**tug**$_2$**-du**$_8$			x	
goldsmith	**ku**$_3$**-dim**$_2$			x	
porter	**i**$_3$**-du**$_8$		(x)	x	**geme**$_2$ **i**$_3$**-du**$_8$ *are attested*
cook	**muhaldim**		x	x	
beer producer	**kaš-a gub-ba**		x	x	
spinner/ flax worker	**gu**		x		
weaver	**uš-bar**	*Organized*	x	(x)	**guruš uš-bar** *are attested*
miller	**kikken**$_2$	*in industrial*	x	(x)	**guruš kikken**$_2$ *are attested*
oil presser	**i**$_3$**-sur-sur**	*workshops*	x		
courtyard sweeper	**kisal-luh**		x		

27 Heimpel 2009: 47.

The same women could therefore move from one job to another and were sometimes obliged to do so, as shown by the following three examples:

- An Umma tablet (Nisaba 11, 33 [P201735]) records rations allocated to women. Two of them are said to have "left their function of musician to return as weavers" (**nam-nar-ta ib$_2$-ta-e$_3$ uš-bar i$_3$-in-gi$_4$**, rev. i 7–10)
- In a Girsu tablet (TCTI 2, 3658 [P132869]), a woman has no other choice than to enter the weaving mill after the death (execution?) of her husband; the tablet is a wool withdrawal, "because Ur-Iškur has been killed and his wife has entered the weaving mill" (**mu ur-^{d}iškur ba-gaz-še$_3$ dam-ni e$_2$ uš-bar ba-an-ku$_4$-ra-še$_3$**).
- The Umma tablet MCS 3, 54 [P112668], like many other texts, shows that female millers (**geme$_2$-kikken$_2$**) were employed in textile activities. On the contrary, the table on p. 160 below shows that weavers and oil pressers were at work in a mill producing flour.

The work of women in "factories" can be seen in two large tablets, among many others, the first of which concerns textile production and the second pertains to cereal processing.

Textile: Women's work in textile factories (**e$_2$ uš-bar**) was intensively analyzed by H. Waetzoldt more than forty years ago.[28] As an illustration, let us consider the tablet BM 28417,[29] which is a huge accounting text calculating the amount of barley distributed to personnel working in the various public weaving mills in the province of Lagaš in year Šulgi 48. This text makes a clear distinction between:

- those receiving monthly rations, as they were supposed to work only part-time in the workshop (note that some of them were receiving more than the usual average rations)
- those receiving yearly grain rations, probably because they didn't belong to families holding allotment plots for cultivation.

In total, the text counts more than 10,000 individuals working in the weaving mills of the province of Lagaš in year Šulgi 48. Almost two thirds of them were female weavers, but men, children and elders were also categorized, divided according to the quota of rations they received (from 100 liters to 10 liters per person, per month).

28 Waetzoldt 1972: 91–108.

29 Maekawa 1998: 108 n° 7 [P120650]. Text reassessed by Uchitel 2002: 625–628. The chart above is adapted from his own. This text is to be completed with UNT 18 [P141849].

Tab. 2: BM 28417 [P120650]. Account of barley distributed in the weaving mills of Lagaš in year Šulgi 48.

Numbers of workers / Monthly rates (liters of barley)				**Total workers**	**Total grain**
1) Those receiving monthly rations (**še-ba iti-da**)					
geme$_2$ uš-bar (female weavers)				6423 **geme$_2$**	295,130 liters
– at 100 liters:	17	women (**geme$_2$**)		109 **guruš**	= ca. 183 tons
– at 60 liters:	209	women (**geme$_2$**)		3141 **dumu**	barley, for
– at 50 liters:	19	women (**geme$_2$**)		198 **šu-gi$_4$**	year Š 48,
– at 40 liters:	1574	women (**geme$_2$**)			as monthly
– at 40 liters:	61	men (**guruš**)			grain rations
– at 30 liters:	4604	women (**geme$_2$**)			
– at 30 liters:	48	men (**guruš**)			
– at 20 liters:	473	children (**dumu**)			
– at 15 liters:	1035	children (**dumu**)			
– at 10 liters:	1633	children (**dumu**)			
– at 20 liters:	198	elderly women (**geme$_2$ šu-gi$_4$**)			
un-IL$_2$ e$_2$ uš-bar (menials of the weaving manufacture)				326+ **guruš**	
– at 60 liters:	260+	men (**guruš**)			
– at 50 liters:	22+	men (**guruš**)			
– at 40 liters:	44+	men (**guruš**)			
gir$_3$-se$_3$-ga e$_2$ uš-bar (personnel of the weaving manufacture)				59 **guruš**	
– at 60 liters:	29	men (**guruš**)		16 **dumu**	
– at 50 liters:	14	men (**guruš**)			
– at 40 liters:	7	men (**guruš**)			
– at 30 liters:	9	men (**guruš**)			
– at 20 liters:	2	children (**dumu**)			
– at 15 liters:	6	children (**dumu**)			
– at 10 liters:	8	children (**dumu**)			
2) Those receiving yearly rations (**še-ba zag-mu-ka**) They are **nu-dab$_5$** (= **gan$_2$ šuku nu-dab$_5$**, "not holding allotment plots")					
– at 1,200 liters:	11	men	porters (**i$_3$-du$_8$**), fullers (**azlag$_2$**)	21+ **guruš**	55,200 liters
– at 720 liters:	6	men			= ca. 34 tons
– at 600 liters:	1	men			barley as
– at 720 liters:	2+	spinners/flax workers (**lu$_2$-gu**)			yearly grain
– at 720 liters:	1+	braiders (**tug$_2$-du$_8$**)			rations

Flour production: For a mill producing flour and employing female workers, let us have a look at the tablet BM 18344.[30] This is a comprehensive list of various workers receiving grain rations (see next page). It can be completed

30 CT 3, pl. 9–10 [P108467].

Tab. 3: CT 3, pl. 9–10, BM 18344 [P108467], col. i–iv.
List of the various workers receiving grain rations and assigned to Lu-Ninšubur, head of the **e_2 $kikken_2$ gu-la** ("great mill"). Girsu, year Šulgi 48.

Numbers of workers receiving rations		Supervisors
1) 490 millers (**$kikken_2$-me**):	364 **$geme_2$** 69 **dumu** 56 **guruš** 1 **$geme_2$ šu-gi_4**	(8 teams. PN **i_3-dab_5**:) – An-ki-da – Lugal-ki-ag_2 – Lugal-$anzu_2^{mušen}$ – Da-a-da-ni – Ur-^{d}utu – Lu_2-^{d}utu – Hu-u_2-u_2 – Ur-e_2-an-na lu_2-lunga
2) 11 oil pressers (**$^{geš}i_3$-sur-sur-me**):	4 **$geme_2$** 7 **dumu**	– $Arad_2$-mu
3) 23 weavers (**uš-bar-me**):	21 **$geme_2$** 2 **dumu**	
4) 54 various personnel (**gir_3-se_3-ga-didli**):		
– scribes (**dub-sar**):	2	
– overseer of millers (**ugula $kikken_2$**):	1	
– scribe of the arsenal (**dub-sar mar-sa**):	1	
– porters (**i_3-du_8-me**):	3	
– maltsters (**$munu_4$-mu_2-me**):	4 **guruš** 1 **$geme_2$**	
– mat makers (**ad-KID-me**):	4	
– carpenter (**nagar**):	1	
– leather workers (**ašgab-me**):	2	
– potters (**$bahar_2$-me**):	3	
– cook (**muhaldim**):	1	
– swineherd (**sipa $šah_2$**):	1	
– boat towers (**ma_2-gid_2-me**):	27	
– masons (**šitim-me**):	2	
– menial (**un-IL_2**):	1	
5) 49 personnel of the gardens (**gir_3-se_3-ga $^{geš}kiri_6$-me**)		
6) 6 xxx (**KA-gaz**) ?		
7) 25 workers stationed at the arsenal (**mar-sa gub-ba-me**)		
TOTAL: 392 women (**$geme_2$**), 186 men (**guruš**), 79 children (**dumu**), 1 elder (**šu-gi_4**) = 658		

based on several other similar large accounts from Girsu. This text provides a good example of how a mill was organized.

This "great millhouse" (**e_2 $kikken_2$ gu-la**) at Girsu seems to have employed 658 people in total. Two thirds of them were female millers, counted with their children, but some others were employed as weavers and oil pressers. Those in 1), 2) and 3) represent the workers in charge of producing goods. But the text also records people belonging to the regular staff in charge of maintenance and supervision of the mill, especially craft workers, boat towers, gardeners and specialists in boat construction, most of whom were male, recorded in 4), 5), 6) and 7). We therefore see that, besides the female millers who constituted the core of the workshop, a variety of craftsmen supported their activities.

The question that can be asked here is: who were these state-dependent women working in outdoor activities or in these various mills? And what do we know about them or about their origin?

3 State dependent women

To explore this matter, let us start with an important royal inscription of king Šu-Sîn, after his victorious military campaign against Šimanum in the Zagros mountains.[31] An excerpt of this inscription states that:

> The king blinded the young men of those cities, whom he had overtaken. And the women of those cities, whom he had overtaken, he offered as a present to the weaving mills.

As we can see, after this military campaign, male and female prisoners were separated. And whereas the male captives were blinded (probably to avoid any revolt without losing such a labor force), the female ones were not mutilated, but sent off to textile mills of the inner kingdom. It is therefore clear that the labor force of Neo-Sumerian textile mills consisted in part of prisoners of war. This situation is not without parallel, as for example at Mari in the Old Babylonian period with its "ergasterions" (*nepārātum*), that were large prison-workshops where mass productions were organized.[32]

In brief, from all the documentation it appears that women working in these Ur III factories included:

- war-captives as booty (**nam-ra-ak**),[33]
- purchased or indebted slaves (**geme$_2$** // **arad$_2$**)
- donated personnel (**a-ru-a**),[34]
- women of the impoverished classes and outcasts of society.

31 RIME 3/2.1.4.3: 129′–145′ [P432280].

32 See Durand 2000: 250; Cooper 2010.

33 For the prisoners of war sent to Ur III workhouses (as to the *nepārātum* of Old Babylonian Mari, cf CAD *nupāru*), we do have some examples of "**geme$_2$ nam-ra-ak**" probably sent to such places (see CDLI and BDTNS databases). See also Maekawa 1980: 125 n. 63, with the text TuT 159: v 5 [P135732]. Three texts quoted in Gelb 1973 are crucial concerning female prisoners of war, and among them is the important tablet TCL 5, 6039 [P131753].

34 Gelb 1972.

Yet these categories of women certainly did not represent the entire workforce inside the state-run workshops. They would have been in insufficient number to meet the economic needs of the state. In all likelihood, many of the female workers employed in the mills were simply state-dependents, working part-time or full-time for rations and salaries, like their male counterparts.

M. Van de Mieroop calculated that more than 13,000 female weavers were active at a single time in the workshops of Ur.[35] Such a huge number is consistent with a text from Ur quoted above (UET 3, 1504 [P137830]), where wool is distributed to female workers involved in the factories of that city for a total of 8,542 kg of wool. H. Waetzoldt calculated that at the rate of 1 mina of wool per capita (which is likely, according to parallels), more than 17,000 female workers could have been involved and employed as weavers, millers and oil pressers.[36] In the same way, he also calculated that, at Lagaš/Girsu, 15,000 persons were employed in the weaving industries of the province.[37] Among them, 6,466 female weavers are explicitly recorded in two Girsu administrative texts dated to the year Amar-Suen 1 (SAT 1, 279 [P131388] // HSS 4, 3 [P110276]). These two tablets inform us that, among the three main urban centers of the province of Lagaš (Girsu, Kinunir and Gu-abba), the greatest weaving mills were situated in Gu-abba. Such huge numbers explain why we can eventually find in summary accounting tablets some amazing records of more than 120,000 (!) "female workdays" (**geme$_2$ u$_4$ 1-še$_3$**) at a time for one given activity.[38]

According to P. Steinkeller, two categories of workers are to be distinguished in Ur III society: those belonging to the **eren$_2$** class, who received royal land and rations in exchange for part-time service, and those who were semi-free workers (**un-IL$_2$**, **geme$_2$**), working year round as unskilled laborers in exchange for rations.[39] In all likelihood, men and women belonging to the second of these categories were often employed in the mills.

As for the unskilled workers, it is interesting to find in administrative texts some (less frequent) instances of female menials (**geme$_2$ un-IL$_2$**) parallel to well-known male **un-IL$_2$**. Sometimes their occupations or origin are given:

---

35 Van de Mieroop 1989: 64.

36 Waetzoldt 1972: 106.

37 Waetzoldt 1972: 99.

38 See for example TCNU 685: vi 2 [P218075], recording in total not less than 129,123 **geme$_2$ u$_4$ 1-še$_3$** in flour milling activities (Umma, year Amar-Suen 8). Note however that in Ur III administrative terminology, such a huge number does not mean that 129,123 women were individually recorded. The purpose of such texts was only to calculate the total of "workdays".

39 Steinkeller 2003: 44–45, and 2013: 351, 364–365. See also Pomponio 2013: 220–223.

- **geme$_2$ un-IL$_2$ mar-tu** "menial Amorite women"
- **geme$_2$ un-IL$_2$ amar-e gub-ba**, "menial women on duty for the calves"
- **geme$_2$ un-IL$_2$ e$_2$ gu$_4$ niga-ka** "menial women of the house of fattened cattle".

In total, thousands of women, in every province of the kingdom, were involved in state-run activities. This must reflect a significant part of the population. However, it remains impossible to assess what percentage of the total female population was thus employed, or to estimate the importance of their contribution to the global economy, even if it may have been substantial. It is also difficult to differentiate groups of women in terms of social hierarchy.

Another interesting point concerns the family situation of these women. I. J. Gelb noticed that, in many Ur III administrative texts, women are recorded along with their children, without any accompanying man. He called these lists of rations for women and their children the "**geme$_2$-dumu** texts", and he asked the question: "where are the husbands and fathers?"[40] We must confess that, forty years later, this important question remains unanswered. We know almost nothing about the family life of these thousands of **geme$_2$** employed in these large weaving and milling factories and working there with their children. Were there dormitories or barracks for them around the factories? Or did they return home every evening to their families in nearby villages? We have no information regarding these questions, but we can consider that, depending on the status of these women, individual situations might have varied: prisoners and slaves were probably confined to barracks, while "free" workers had their own home and independent family life, and came to work every day with their young children.

How were these women paid? As is well known, the "ration system," with its amounts of barley, oil and wool issued to dependents, was a hallmark of early Mesopotamian history and is especially well documented in the Ur III period. It is mainly because of such rations that we have such a huge amount of written documentation. In this system, women were paid distinctly less than men, a phenomenon already attested elsewhere (Ebla) and in earlier periods (Fara, Lagaš II): while the **guruš** received an average of 60 liters of grain per month, women usually received only 30 to 50 liters.

But as we just saw, only some people worked full time for the state. We can imagine that some of these women were married or related to members of the **eren$_2$** class. They would have belonged to families that held plots of sub-

40 Gelb 1973: 75.

sistence land and they could have stayed at home or worked only part-time for collective public works. As a matter of fact, we do find texts in which women could, like men, be "hired" (**hun-ga$_2$**) for some period of time,[41] and many texts record real "salaries for women" (**a$_2$ geme$_2$**) instead of rations.

A last observation will be made about positions of authority that these women could hold in such a context of "public" work. It is not infrequent to find forewomen at the head of teams of workers (consisting of both males and females), as for example in the text MVN 16, 727: 11–12 [P118775]. Sometimes women could hold high administrative positions at the same level as men and could seal tablets, as shown by several seal impressions and the attested title of **munus dub-sar** (as in Nebraska 45 [P121730]). This is also the case, as we saw, at Garšana: the best example is that of a woman named Aštaqqar, who ended up managing the entire textile industry as the supervisor of the weavers (**ugula uš-bar**, a function usually occupied by men) and who had her own seals, with which she sealed dozens of tablets.[42]

To conclude, **guruš** and **geme$_2$**, women and men, contributed side by side and in the same way to economic life. We can emphasize right away the phenomenon of a complete mixed management of human resources employed by the state. The economic role played by women was therefore multifaceted, both inside and outside their family home.

4 The managerial autonomy of women inside wealthy families

Inside the family, it is clear that women could experience some managerial autonomy, especially when they belonged to the upper classes of society. First, let us mention as a reminder the case of some well-known women managers of large state institutions in Sumer during the 3rd millennium, such as the queens at the head of the **e$_2$**-MI$_2$ in Presargonic Lagaš, or the estates managed by queen Šulgi-simti in Drehem,[43] or by princess Simat-Ištaran in Garšana during the Ur III period.[44] The households that they headed were run by them on the same basis as the king's household. Law codes as well as historical texts

41 Two examples of texts with **geme$_2$ hun-ga$_2$**, "hired women", are BPOA 1, 562 [P339218], and BPOA 7, 1669 [P290993], both from Umma.

42 Owen and Mayr 2007: 431.

43 See Weiershäuser 2008; Paoletti 2012.

44 See Owen and Mayr 2007; Kleinerman and Owen 2009; Owen 2011.

often take into account situations where women were managers of families or private estates at that time.

This issue is explicitly considered in, for example, some inscriptions of Gudea, the Codex of Ur-Namma, and the Codex of Lipit-Ištar:

- Gudea, Satue B, vii 44–45 [RIME 3/1.1.7, St B = P431884][45]
  e_2 dumu-$nita_2$ nu-tuku dumu-munus-bi i_3-bi_2-la-ba mi-ni-ku_x (KWU 634)
  "For a household not having a son, I let the daughter (of the house) become its heir."
- Codex Ur-Namma, § E4 [P432130 e025][46]
  tukum-bi lu_2 ba-$uš_2$ dam-PI-ni ibila 1-gin_7 e_2-a he_2-dim_2
  "If a man dies, his wife will act in the house like a single heir"
- Codex Lipit-Ištar, § 18 [P464355]
  tukum-bi lugal e_2-a u_3 nin e_2-a-ke_4 ...,
  "If the master or the mistress of an estate ..."

This is also reflected in some trial texts, such as the following one, which treats a dispute for reimbursing a loan. In the first three lines of the text we learn that two women were involved:[47]

> Geme-Suen said to the wife of Ur-lugal the gardener that she had a credit of 2 minas of silver with her.

In his synthesis on Ancient Near Eastern Law,[48] R. Westbrook has shown that a woman's private property could have had three main sources in the Ur III period:

- dowries (**sag-rig_7**) received from their father. According to M. Civil,[49] the **sag-rig_7** is always owned by women and it consists mainly of slaves, orchards, houses, and rarely sheep. The fact that the husband cannot dispose freely of the **sag-rig_7** of his wife is explicitly specified in § B8 of the Codex Ur-Namma[50]
- gifts given by their husband
- personal purchases made on their own property.

45 See also the parallel in Gudea's Cylinder B: xviii 8–9 [P431882].
46 § E4 in Civil 2011: 252.
47 Molina, Fs Owen: 201–202, no. 1 [P200743]. Umma, no date.
48 Westbrook 2003: 208.
49 Civil 2011: 270–271.
50 § B8 in Civil 2011: 249

Illustrations can be given through the following texts: the first one shows how a rather rich father distributed gifts to his wife, his two daughters and his son, giving them slaves, livestock and real estate:[51]

> Ur-nigar gave to his wife as a gift: 1 ox [...], 1 house [...], (slaves) PN_1, PN_2, PN_3 (and) PN_4, *n* pregnant sheep, *n* pregnant goat(s), 1 house in **KI-AN** with its furniture, (and) 1 mill-stone with its upper stone.
> 10 sheqels of ring silver and (the slave) PN_5 are the gifts for (his) daughter Baza; (the slave) PN_6 is the gift for (his) daughter Nin-batuku; (and the slave) PN_7 is the gift for (his son?) Hala-abbana: Ur-nigar gave (all this) to his children.

The reasons for such gifts given by the head of the family are unknown. It could have been an arrangement before his death, before a journey, or before going to war, to protect his family. The second example is a trial that shows again that this independent property of women could come from a marital gift. In this case, we see a son who turned against his mother after his father's death, demanding a cow and two slaves. The woman denied the request, saying she had received these goods as a personal gift during the lifetime of her husband:[52]

> Dugudaga brought a legal case against Gemegu his mother. (Concerning) 1 milk-producing cow named Gemeguedena, 1 male slave named Šuna (and) 1 female slave named Matu, Gemegu declared: "My husband gave them as a gift to me."

Another example can be given along the same lines: an action brought by a widow to defend her property and rights after the death of the head of the family against his heirs:[53]

> Final judgement (concerning) 2 **sar** and ⅚ of a house-[x]: Innasaga, wife of Dudu the son of Titi, bought it with silver from her own hand on her own initiative ...

Moreover, we see quite frequently women involved in lending, borrowing, buying or selling things, such as silver, livestock, slaves, orchards or houses, just as men did, as illustrated by the following two examples:

- Women lending or borrowing:[54]

> Amasaga and her son Mašgula received ½ mana and 2 shekels of silver at an interest rate of 1 shekel per each 5 shekels.

51 BM 105377 [P112634]. Umma, Amar-Suen 4. See Wilcke 1998: 49.
52 Molina, Fs Owen: 213 no. 9 [P375930]. Umma, no date
53 ITT 3, 5279 [P111162]. Girsu, Šu-Sîn 4. See Lafont 2000: 53 n° 12; and Wilcke 1998: 50–51.
54 NRVN 1, 96 [P122311]. Nippur, Šu-Sîn 6.

- Women buying or selling:[55]

> Geme-Nanna bought from Šat-Sîn 1 female slave – her name is Enne-Laz – for 1 ⅓ shekel of silver, her full price."

Several pieces of evidence can also be found that show women (often widows)[56] disposing of their property, without interference from the men of their family. For example, the following text concerns a widow in charge of the subsistence field (**šuku**) of her deceased husband. The land was linked to a duty to perform services (**dusu**), and this duty was given to a man in return for a payment in silver, but it seems that the land remained in the hands of the widow. The following text comes from Nippur and is dated to Šu-Sîn 1:[57]

> Concerning 3.22 ha of field, subsistence field of Lugal-kagina, Geme-Suen his wife and Pešturtur his daughter approached Lugal-hegal. She said to him: "Bear the obligation of my subsistence field". Lugal-hegal gave to Geme-Suen, wife of Lugal-kagina, and to Pešturtur his daughter 5 shekels of silver for the subsistence field.

Another important text on the same topic illustrates the rights of widows, but this time it also addresses the thorny issue of land ownership. Without entering the debate over the status of agricultural land during the Ur III period, it seems that "in itself this text is sufficient to prove the existence of arable land in private hands."[58] The following text is from Nippur and dated to Šu-Sîn 8:[59]

> Alala together with Ur-Dun were heirs (and) had divided the estate of their father. (Then) Ur-Dun died. Geme-Suen, the wife of Ur-Dun, entered into litigation with Alala under the jurisdiction of Dada, the governor of Nippur, concerning [the field], the house, the furnishing (representing) the inheritance portion of Ur-Dun. (...).

---

55 FAOS 17, n° 117* [P116217]. Nippur, Ibbi-Sîn 2.

56 Note, however, that among so many administrative Ur III texts, and according to CDLI and BDTNS, only a dozen texts mention widows (**nu-mu-su**, **nu-ma-su**, Akk. *almattu*).

57 NATN 258 [P120956]. See Démare-Lafont 1998: 535; and Wilcke 1998: 55–56.

58 So G. van Driel, quoted in Garfinkle 2012: 21 n. 17. But according to M. Civil, "women could not inherit agricultural land" (Civil 2011: 268, concerning Codex Ur-Namma § B3). It seems, however, that from Old Sumerian times until Ur III, we have some attestations of women holding agricultural land inherited from their husband or their father. And we can find some examples where women (widows?) can dispose of their land and property without interference from men in their family. On the same topic "fields and women", see also the difficult letter of the "Ur III angry wife" (Owen *MVN* 11, 168 [P116181]) quoted above (see n. 15). And add finally Michalowski 1993: 80 n° 131 [P145730].

59 Owen *NATN* 302 [P121000]. See Owen 1980b; Steinkeller 1989: 203; and Lafont 2000: 50–51 n° 10. The restitution **a-ša**$_3$, "field" in the break of line 8 is quite certain because of the following lines of the text, not given here but that mention **a-ša**$_3$.

In summary, there were some clear opportunities for women to control and transmit personal property, as is explicitly substantiated now thanks to the newly published paragraphs of the Codex Ur-Namma. But perhaps this was only true in some specific situations (for widows, for example), or for some specific kinds of personal estate and property, as it is not completely clear whether a woman could usually act without her husband's consent.

***

In traditional societies, it is usual to consider that the division of labor is established according to two essential criteria: age and gender. Children keep herds, elders stay at home while the male adults hunt, fish, work in the fields and ensure collective tasks. Only some occupations are reserved for women aside from their management of everything related to the domestic space. It is clear, however, that this scheme does not fit the situation here described for the Ur III period.

Yet let us notice that the domestic sphere was clearly the place of productive and economically significant activities, within which women would provide members of the household with their basic needs of food, clothing and care. Even if this kind of work remained "invisible", unrecognized, unmeasured, unrecorded, and unpaid, it contributed of course to wealth creation. In the trend of the reflections of B. Lion,[60] it corresponds to *indirect* contributions of women to the economy, as opposed to the *direct* contributions documented when rations, salaries or products were recorded. But on this point, it must be noticed that we never see any surplus of goods produced at home by women that could have fed external economic channels.

We must not imagine, however, any exclusive assignment of women to the domestic realm only. As noted by M. Van de Mieroop, "for several decades it was popular in scholarship to see an opposition of public/private along male/female gender lines. This approach asserted that women were reduced to the domestic, private sphere in their activities, while men acted in the public sphere and therefore were more visibly engaged in cultural, political, scientific and other developments that define cultures."[61] This view is now outdated, especially since progress in gender studies has shown that family, marriage or the household are not restricted to women and that women were not only defined by their roles within families: they were employed alongside men in all

60 Lion 2007.
61 Van de Mieroop 1999: 159.

kinds of indoor and outdoor work and activities. The same author, already fifteen years ago, was right to observe that the participation of women in the economic sphere was real, separate from their husbands and on the same terms, although on a smaller scale. Therefore, from an economic point of view, the possible inequality of women "was one of scale, not of area of activity."[62]

In this regard, it is symptomatic to observe that the concept of professional skill or specialization was real for women as well as for men (cf. above the list of some professions practiced by women). We can see both men and women doing their jobs inside or outside the domestic sphere, for various tasks of production or service, including within the framework of the *corvée* obligation which made no gender distinction. In this *corvée* service we can observe that women were employed to do the same hard work as men: working in the fields, towing boats, hauling bricks, constructing buildings, etc.

Milling, weaving and oil pressing were essentially institution-run activities. They were organized on an "industrial" scale and performed by state-dependent women working collectively in large production units in which weavers, millers and oil pressers were often associated.

The pressure exerted by the state administration on such collective works and its strong will for control documented by the texts should probably be analyzed in the context of a scarcity of labor during the Ur III period – according to P. Steinkeller's idea –, as it was necessary to meet the huge needs of the state institutions for the "ration allotment" system provided to state dependents.

However, it would be wrong to consider "women" as if they were a social group! We should be wary of adopting a depreciating vision according to which only poverty or enslavement could explain and justify the collective work of women in factories. Texts show the same intensive use of male and female workers belonging to various categories of society throughout the entire kingdom. Finally, we can assert that, especially during this time, economic activities and the visibility of individuals in the sources depends more on their social rank than on gender categories.

For the most privileged women (and this situation has been known for quite a long time), it was possible to own property and to manage it freely, at least in some situations. They had full legal and economic rights, with the same management autonomy as men: they could sell, buy, lend, borrow, and sue for economic redress, all with the same legal capacity. To illustrate such a situation, we can also mention that more than a hundred seals are known to have been owned by women in the Ur III period.

62 Van de Mieroop 1999: 155.

Ultimately, are these data sufficient to validate or invalidate the commonly asserted idea that the living conditions of women deteriorated over time in Mesopotamian history after the 3rd millennium BC? It is possible at least to assert that, during the Ur III period, these conditions were more or less the same as those for men, and that a change in this situation occurred at the beginning of the 2nd millennium. This should motivate us to avoid a mistaken conception of history according to which any historical period necessarily inherits from the former one.

Abbreviations

BAOM *Bulletin of the Ancient Orient Museum* (Tokyo 1979 ff.).
BCT P. J. Watson, *Catalogue of cuneiform tablets in Birmingham City Museum*, Birmingham: Aris & Philips Ltd.
HLC G. Barton, *Haverford Library Collection of Cuneiform Tablets* (Philadelphia 1905–1914).
NYPL H. Sauren, *Les Tablettes Cuneiformes de l'Époque d'Ur de la New York Public Library*, 1978. Leuven: Peeters.

Bibliography

Adams, Robert McC. 2010. Slavery and Freedom in the Third Dynasty of Ur: Implications of the Garšana Archive. *CDLJ* 2010: 2.

Assante, Julia. 1998. The kar.kid / *harimtu*, Prostitute or Single Woman? A Reconsideration of the Evidence. UF 30: 5–96.

Civil, Miguel. 2011. The Law Collection of Ur-Namma. Pp. 221–287 in *Cuneiform Royal Inscriptions and Related Texts in the Schøyen Collection*, ed. Andrew George. CUSAS 17. Bethesda: CDL Press.

Cooper, Jerrold. 2010. Blind Workmen, Weaving Women and Prostitutes in Third Millennium Babylonia. *CDLN* 2010: 5.

Démare-Lafont, Sophie. 1998. Le Proche-Orient. Pp. 517–630 in *Les féodalités*, ed. Eric Bournazel, and Jean-Pierre Poly. Paris: PUF.

Démare-Lafont, Sophie. In press. Women. In *A Handbook of Ancient Mesopotamia*, ed. Gonzalo Rubio. Berlin: de Gruyter.

Durand, Jean-Marie. 2000. *Documents épistolaires du palais de Mari. Tome 3*. LAPO 18. Paris: Les Éditions du cerf.

Englund, Robert K. 1990. *Organisation und Verwaltung der Ur III-Fischerei*. BBzVO 10. Berlin: Dietrich Reimer Verlag.

Englund, Robert K. 1991. Hard Work – Where will it get you? Labor Management in Ur III Mesopotamia. *JNES* 50: 255–280.

Garfinkle, Steven J. 2012. *Entrepreneurs and Enterprise in Early Mesopotamia. A Study of Three Archives from the Third Dynasty of Ur (2112–2004 BCE)*. CUSAS 22. Bethesda: CDL Press.

Garfinkle, Steven J. and Manuel Molina (eds.). 2013. *From the 21st Century B.C. to the 21st Century A.D.Proceedings of the International Conference on Sumerian Studies Held in Madrid 22–24 July 2010.* Winona Lake: Eisenbrauns.
Gelb, Ignace J. 1972. The a-ru-a institution. *RA* 66: 1–32.
Gelb, Ignace J. 1973. Prisoners of War in Early Mesopotamia. *JNES* 32: 70–98.
Gelb, Ignace J. 1979. Household and Family in Early Mesopotamia. Pp. 1–98 in *State and Temple Economy in the Ancient Near East. Proceedings of the International Conference organized by the Katholieke Universiteit Leuven from the 10th to the 14th of April 1978*, ed. Edward Lipinski. OLA 5. Leuven: Peeters.
Grégoire, Jean-Pierre. 1999. *The Grain-Grinding-Households* (e2-HAR.HAR) of Southern Mesopotamia at the End of the 3rd Millennium BCE. *Bulletin of the Anglo-Israel Archaeological Society* 19: 7–37.
Hallo, William W. 2003. *The Context of Scripture. Archival Documents from the Biblical World.* COS 3. Leiden: Brill.
Heimpel, Wolfgang. 1997. Disposition of Households of Officials in Ur III and Mari. *ASJ* 19: 63–82.
Heimpel, Wolfgang. 2009. *Workers and Construction Work at Garšana.* CUSAS 5. Bethesda: CDL Press.
Heimpel, Wolfgang. 2010. Left to themselves. Waifs in the Time of the Third Dynasty of Ur. Pp. 9–13 in *Why Should Someone Who knows Something Conceal it? Cuneiform Studies in Honor of David I. Owen on His 70th Birthday*, eds. Alexandra Kleirnermann and Jack M. Sasson. Bethesda: CDL Press.
Kleinerman, Alexandra and David I. Owen. 2009. *Analytical Concordance to the Garšana Archives.* CUSAS 4. Bethesda: CDL Press.
Lafont, Bertrand. 2000. Les textes judiciaires sumériens. Pp. 35–68 in *Rendre la justice en Mésopotamie. Archives judiciaires du Proche-Orient ancien (IIIe–Ier millénaires av. J.-C.)*, ed. Francis Joannès. Saint Denis: Presses Universitaires de Vincennes.
Lion, Brigitte. 2007. La notion de genre en assyriologie. Pp. 51–64 in *Problèmes du genre en Grèce ancienne*, ed. Violaine Sebillotte and Nathalie Ernoult. Paris: Publications de la Sorbonne.
Maekawa, Kazuya. 1980. Female Weavers and Their Children in Lagash – Pre-Sargonic and Ur III –. *ASJ* 2: 81–125.
Maekawa, Kazuya. 1987. Collective Labor Service in Girsu-Lagash: The Pre-Sargonic and Ur III Periods. Pp. 49–72 in *Labor in the Ancient Near East*, ed. Marvin A. Powell. AOS 68. New Haven: American Oriental Society.
Maekawa, Kazuya. 1989. Rations, Wages and Economic Trends in the Ur III Period. *AoF* 16: 42–50.
Maekawa, Kazuya. 1996. Confiscation of Private Properties in the Ur III Period: A Study of é-dul-la and níg-GA. *ASJ* 18: 103–168.
Maekawa, Kazuya. 1997. Confiscation of Private Properties in the Ur III Period: A Study of é-dul-la and níg-GA (2). Supplement 1. *ASJ* 19: 273–291.
Maekawa, Kazuya. 1998. Ur III Girsu Records of Labor Forces in the British Museum (1). *ASJ* 20: 63–110.
Michalowski, Piotr. 1993. *Letters from Early Mesopotamia.* SBL WAW Series 3. Atlanta: Scholars Press.
Michalowski, Piotr. 2011. *The Correspondence of the Kings of Ur.* MC 15. Winona Lake: Eisenbrauns.

Michalowski, Piotr. 2013. Of Bears and Men. Thoughts on the End of Šulgi's Reign and on the Ensuing Succession. Pp. 285–320 in *Literature as Politics, Politics as Literature. Essays on the Ancient Near East in Honor of Peter Machinist*, eds. David S. Vanderhooft and Abraham Winitzer. Winona Lake: Eisenbrauns.

Neumann, Hans. 2006. Sumerische und akkadische Briefe des 3. Jt. v. Chr. Pp. 1–20 in *Briefe*, ed. Michael Lichtensten. TUAT, Neue Folge 3. Gütersloh: Gütersloher Verlagshaus.

Owen, David I. 1980a. A Sumerian Letter from an Angry Housewife. Pp. 189–202 in *The Bible World. Essays in Honor of Cyrus H. Gordon*, eds. Gary Rendsburg, Ruth Adler, Milton Arfa, and Nathan H. Winter. New York: KTAV 1.

Owen, David I. 1980b. Widow's Rights in Ur III Sumer. *ZA* 70: 170–184.

Owen, David I. (ed.). 2011. *Garšana Studies*. CUSAS 6. Bethesda: CDL Press.

Owen, David I. 2013. *Cuneiform Texts Primarily from Iri-Sagrig/Al-Šarraki and the History of the Ur III Period*. Nisaba 15/1 and 15/2. Bethesda: CDL Press.

Owen, David I. and Rudolf H. Mayr. 2007. *The Garšana Archives*. CUSAS 3. Bethesda: CDL Press.

Paoletti, Paola. 2012. *Der König und sein Kreis. Das staatliche Schatzarchiv der III. Dynastie von Ur*. BPOA 10. Madrid: CSIC.

Pomeroy, Sarah B. 1995. *Xenophon, Oeconomicus. A Social and Historical Commentary, with a New English Translation*. Oxford: Clarendon Press.

Pomponio, Francesco. 2013. The Ur III Administration: Workers, Messengers, and Sons. Pp. 221–232 in Garfinkle and Molina 2013.

Sallaberger, Walther. 1993. *Der Kultische Kalender der Ur III-Zeit*. UAVA 7/1. Berlin: de Gruyter.

Schloen, J. David. 2001. *The House of the father as fact and symbol: patrimonalism in Ugarit and the ancient Near East*. Studies in the Archaeology and History of the Levant 2. Winona Lake: Eisenbrauns.

Steinkeller, Piotr. 1989. *Sale Documents of the Ur III Period*. FAOS 17. Stuttgart: Franz Steiner Verlag.

Steinkeller, Piotr. 2002. Money-Lending Practices in Ur III Babylonia: The Issue of Economic Motivation. Pp. 109–138, in *Debt and Economic Renewal in the Ancient Near East*, ed. Michael Hudson and Marc Van De Mieroop. Bethesda: CDL Press.

Steinkeller, Piotr. 2003. Archival Practices in Third-millennium Babylonia. Pp. 37–58 in *Ancient Archives and Archival Traditions. Concepts of Record Keeping in the Ancient World*, ed. Maria Brosius. Oxford Studies in Ancient Documents. Oxford: Oxford University Press.

Steinkeller, Piotr. 2013. Corvée Labor in Ur III Times. Pp. 347–424 in Garfinkle and Molina 2013.

Uchitel, Alexander. 2002. Women at Work: Weavers of Lagash and Spinners of san Luis Gonzaga. Pp. 621–632 in *Sex and Gender in the Ancient Near East. Proceedings of the 47ᵉ Rencontre Assyriologique Internationale, Helsinki*, eds. Simo Parpola and Robert M. Whiting. Helsinki: The Neo-Assyrian Text Corpus Project.

Van De Mieroop, Marc. 1989. Women in the Economy of Sumer. Pp. 53–66 in *Women's Earliest Records from Ancient Egypt and Western Asia*, ed. Barbara S. Lesko. Atlanta: Scholars Press.

Van De Mieroop, Marc. 1999. Gender and Mesopotamian History. Chapter 5, pp. 138–160 in *Cuneiform Texts and the Writing of History*. London, New York: Routledge.

Waetzoldt, Hartmut. 1972. *Untersuchungen zur neusumerischen Textilindustrie*. Studi Economici e tecnologici 1. Roma: Istituto per l'Oriente.

Weiershäuser, Frauke. 2008. *Die königlichen Frauen der III. Dynastie von Ur*. Göttinger Beiträge zum Alten Orient 1. Göttingen: Universitätsverlag Göttingen.

Westbrook, Raymond, ed. 2003. *A History of Ancient Near Eastern Law* (2 vol.). HdO 72. Leiden: Brill.

Wilcke, Claus. 1998. Care of the Elderly in Mesopotamia in the Third Millennium B.C. Pp. 23–57 in *The Care of the Elderly in the Ancient Near East*, eds. Maten Stol and Sven Vleeming. Leiden: Brill.

Agnès Garcia-Ventura

The Sex-Based Division of Work *versus* Intersectionality: Some strategies for engendering the Ur III textile work force

One of the approaches most commonly used to elucidate the role of women in work and society in Antiquity is to analyze what is known as the sex-based or gender-based division of work. The starting point is the assumption that we are likely to find men and/or women performing certain tasks. Then, we usually concentrate on the activities carried out by one of these groups: women. We look for women in our primary sources; when we find them, we feel that we are able to make them visible and to describe their roles in society. This is undoubtedly a useful strategy, but it is not the only one – nor the best one in many cases.

In order to develop my argument, in this paper I will discuss the relevance of the sex-based or gender-based division of work and of intersectionality when scrutinizing Ur III texts (2112–2004 BCE) describing the work force, especially in the textile sector. I aim to show some weaknesses of the first of these approaches and suggest how the second one can help us to overcome them. Furthermore, I aim to show how the application of two possible gender studies perspectives leads us to different interpretations of the sources, and thus provides us with different pictures of women at work.[1]

1 The main aim of this paper is not to present a comprehensive study and compilation of Ur III texts dealing with textile production, but to use a small number of these texts as a pretext to show how the choice of the theoretical frameworks applied to our research might either reinforce or deconstruct some preconceptions. In other words, the case studies developed here aim to provide the background of the theoretical frameworks here discussed as well as some reflections for future research. Confronting large numbers of texts is beyond the scope of the present paper. Nevertheless, for readers who are interested in charts confronting these data regarding Ur III textile production, see for example Verderame and Spada 2013.

Acknowledgements: This paper was prepared during a Postdoctoral scholarship awarded by the Beatriu de Pinós programme (modality A), with the support of the Secretariat for Universities and Research of the Ministry of Economy and Knowledge of the Government of Catalonia.

Agnès Garcia-Ventura, Sapienza, Università degli Studi di Roma, Italy; agnes.ventura@gmail.com

1 Sex-based / gender-based division of work

The so-called sex-based or gender-based division of work starts from the premise that certain activities were performed exclusively or mainly by men, exclusively or mainly by women, or by both equitably in a more or less fixed way. From this perspective, then, the aim is to identify which activities were performed by men, by women, or by both, in what proportions, and the reasons why they were organized in this way.

The choice of one of the two possible labels mentioned above, i.e. sex-based or gender-based division of work is not a matter of chance. It reflects different points of view with regard to what is known as the sex-gender system.[2] The label "division of labor by sex" has been used in anthropology since the 1960s and 1970s to analyze why men and women, in an assumed binary sex system, performed different tasks. In this framework, underlying all the explanations was the assumption of a biological difference between the sexes understood as essential and naturalized: women's reproductive work conditioned their productive work and, consequently, the sex-based division of labor. A key reference work in this trend is the paper by George P. Murdock and Caterina Provost, *Factors in the Division of Labor by Sex: a Cross-cultural Analysis*, published in 1973. In this paper, the authors held that factors like physical strength, the kind of raw materials available or the use of the final product dictated whether a task was performed mainly or exclusively by males or by females, in a variety of geographies and chronologies. To give an example from the textile sector, these scholars came to the conclusion that women worked mainly with soft materials and men with harder ones. This helped to explain why in the societies they analyzed women spun and wove wool for textiles almost exclusively while men, also almost exclusively, worked as rope makers. All these cultural choices, again, were considered to be conditioned by biological and essentialist factors. This claim, as we will see below,[3] was contested by third wave gender studies.

In close association with the emergence and consolidation of these third wave gender studies and the emergence of gender archaeology,[4] in the 1980s

2 See Díaz-Andreu (2014: 25) for a summary of the adoption of the terms "sex" and "gender" in anthropology and archaeology.

3 See Brumfiel and Robin 2008: 2–3, referring to this study and the criticisms made of it from a gender archaeology perspective.

4 For a survey of gender archaeology in several contexts, including literature written in languages other than English, see Díaz-Andreu (2014). For a detailed description of these waves, the main scholars, and their publications, see Bahrani (2001: 14–25).

and the 1990s some scholars began to use "gender" instead of "sex" to refer to the distribution of tasks between men and women. Sandra Harding (1986: 17), one of the main theoreticians of the so-called feminist epistemologies,[5] proposed the use of "division of labor by gender." With this option Harding defended the validity of the sex/gender pairing, arguing that biological sex is dual, while gender presents several gender categories that are built socially and culturally. The aim of her strategy was to denaturalize the distribution of tasks and to highlight how previous studies, especially the ones from anthropology mentioned above, assumed that biology conditioned a great part of this distribution.

In ancient Near Eastern studies the proposals by Susan Pollock in the 1990s point in the same direction. Pollock (1999: 24–25) uses labels such as "gendered tasks" and "gendered division of labor" to stress that "whereas biological sex is an attribute that is independent of the culture or society that a person is born into, gender is a thoroughly sociocultural creation" (Pollock 1999: 24).

Furthermore, some authors working precisely from a feminist standpoint, and taking particular account of certain premises of the third wave, defended the use of the term "sex-based" instead of "gender-based". Those who proposed the term "sex-based" tended to question the validity of the sex-gender system, arguing that both sex and gender are culturally constructed. We see, then, that both labels are currently used in gender studies to contest essentialist discourses like the one proposed by Murdock and Provost. However, while those who use the label "gender-based" tend to defend the sex-gender system, i.e. that sex is biological while gender is culturally constructed, those who use the label "sex-based" challenge the system's validity.

Those who refer to "sex-based division of work" in a critical way question the assumption of a "natural", dual, biological sex versus a constructed, multiple, cultural gender. In their view, sex is also multiple and cultural.[6] As early as 1975 Gayle Rubin summarized the issue as follows, discussing some proposals by Lévi-Strauss about the division of labor by sex which "can therefore be seen as a 'taboo': a taboo against the sameness of men and women, a taboo dividing the sexes into two mutually exclusive categories, a taboo which exacerbates the biological differences between the sexes and thereby creates gender" (Rubin 1975: 178). From this position, referring to the "sex-based division

---

5 On feminist epistemologies and their potential application to Assyriology, see Garcia-Ventura (forthcoming) with previous references.

6 Rubin 1975, especially pp. 178–179; see Fausto-Sterling 2000 (with previous references), for a discussion on sex categories broader than two.

of work" draws attention to the corporeality underlying this particular organization of work. Far from denying biological differences, it helps to highlight how the cultural construction of these biological differences, i.e., of sex, leads to the cultural construction of gender as well.

Nancy Hartsock (2004: 40–44), another leading theoretician of the feminist epistemologies, also argued that the basis of the sexual division of work lies in activities that cannot be chosen and are performed only by females: that is to say, gestation and childbirth (see Haraway 1991: 140). Starting from these preordained biological issues, a certain division of work is defended and naturalized even though it is not totally dependent on biology and is thus a matter of choice. An example is childrearing, a task customarily assigned to women although it can be performed by both men and women. I agree with Hartsock here: without taking this starting point into account, it is impossible to understand how the division of work by sex has been organized, naturalized and justified in a wide variety of contexts. Indeed, it was also the starting point of the anthropological literature of the 1960s and 1970s, despite the diversity of its aims.

This debate is in turn closely linked to the discussion on productive *versus* reproductive work, a debate that highlights the main difference between men's and women's work: namely, that women's work can be both productive and reproductive, while men's work can only be productive (Hartsock 2004: 41). At the same time, research on work organization tends to consider only productive work and to ignore reproductive work. This is because, as suggested above, reproductive work is naturalized, in a strategy which has its roots in the much debated dichotomy "men-culture *versus* women-nature."[7] To turn this situation around, some feminist Marxist proposals see reproduction as just another kind of production, thus presenting men's and women's working conditions in the same terms and using the same theoretical framework to explain the two.[8]

Following this line of thought, another suggestive (and provocative) theoretical proposal tries to explain a certain sex-based division of work. Studies like the one by Murdock and Provost quoted above suggest that some activities

7 See Longino 1995: 27, with previous references.

8 The definition proposed by Haraway 1991: 132 for "sexual division of labor" is interesting in this respect: "Marx and Engels' naturalization of the sexual division of labour, in their assumption of a pre-social division of labor in the sex act (heterosexual intercourse), its supposed natural corollaries in the reproductive activities of men and women in the family, and the consequent inability to place women in their relations to men unambiguously on the side of history and of the fully social."

performed exclusively by women are perceived as subordinate to, or dependent on, others that are associated with men. To explain this, it might be helpful to consider the interaction between productive tasks, reproductive tasks, and factors in the division of labor by sex. This has been summarized under the term the "sexual contract," a label that echoes Rousseau's well-known "social contract."[9] The "sexual contract" presents women as subordinate to men, as it suggests that women have accepted this position in certain productive tasks in exchange for protection in order to be able to accomplish their reproductive duties. Of course, I am not defending these ideas of subordination or the assignation of a higher or a lower value to different tasks, but I think this idea of the sexual contract might help to explain some of the most common interpretations we find when dealing with the sex-based division of work.

2 Questioning the sex-based division of work: towards intersectionality

Despite the nuances in the use of sex-based or gender-based division of work summarized above, the common denominator underlying the application of the theoretical proposals presented in the previous section is their consideration of the centrality (or even the uniqueness) of sex or gender to organize work. However, there are other theoretical proposals that view sex or gender not as the central factor, but rather as one among several that should be taken into account alongside status, race or age. As we will see below, some of these theoretical proposals have been characterized by their emphasis on "decentering."[10]

Applying this "decentering" methodology, some studies in the areas of archaeology and ancient history[11] show how considering the sex-based division of work as one category of analysis among several, rather than as the central (or the only) one, would help us to find more complex interpretations. These proposals argue against the central and univocal use of the sex-based

9 The use of "sexual contract," echoing the Rousseauian "social contract" was also a topic of discussion for Wittig 1989. See Nuño Gómez 2010: 37–56, especially p. 45 for this argument, with previous references.

10 Spencer-Wood 2006: 60–61 and 86. See also Mann and Huffman 2005: 57, which also mention "difference" and "deconstruction" as the other features shaping the new theoretical frameworks that emerge from this moment onwards.

11 For a classical reference, see Nelson 1997: 85–111.

division of work as a category and framework of analysis. Two especially illuminating examples are the studies by Karen O. Bruhns (1991: 427) and Elizabeth M. Brumfiel (2006), which both focus on Mesoamerican material culture and on activities traditionally considered as female.

Bruhns' study of textile production and grinding grain showed that some age groups working in these sectors were considered outside gender categories. In this situation, the use of the sex-based division of work as the starting point of the study would exclude these groups from the analysis. Bruhns also noted that if we link a tool or a space to a specific task or a specific worker – a common practice in research applying the sex-based division of work – we disregard the fact that both tools and spaces are multipurpose and multifunctional. For her part, Brumfiel studied textile production over a long period of time. She saw that, for some periods, gender was the most significant factor, the one articulating production; however, in other periods gender was less relevant than class. Only by considering all these factors, without prioritizing any of them before scrutinizing the sources, was it possible to arrive at findings of this kind.

The case studies and scholars mentioned so far can be framed in the context of what has been termed "gender archaeology." Born on the cusp between second and third wave feminism, gender archaeology[12] was embraced by certain scholars who put forward pertinent criticisms of how we consider sex-based or gender-based division of work when studying the past. Two of its pioneers, Margaret W. Conkey and Janet D. Spector, published a joint paper in 1984 which is now considered one of the foundational texts of gender archaeology. They stated that "a division of labor between males and females should not be assumed but rather be considered a problem or a feature of social structure to be explained" (Conkey and Spector 1984: 9).[13]

Along the same lines, Sarah Milledge Nelson (1997: 85–88) warned about the assumptions that usually underlie the sex-based division of work, and

---

12 For a survey on gender archaeology see Díaz-Andreu 2014, and Montón Subías and Meyer 2014, both with previous references.

13 See Conkey and Spector (1984: 7): "[...] issues to be considered in a review of archaeology and the study of gender. These major issues include: 1. the prevalence of gender-specific models that result in gender-exclusive rather than gender-inclusive reconstructions of past human behavior; 2. the common assumption of a relatively rigid sexual division of labor that results in the sex linking of activities with one sex or the other, which in archaeology is often compounded by assuming sex linkages artifactually (e.g., projectile points as male, ceramics as female); and 3. the differential values placed on the different (and usually sex-linked) activities, such that there is a prevailing overemphasis on those activities or roles presumed to be male associated."

highlighted two of them for special mention. First, she noted that when applying this theoretical framework the category of analysis "women" is often used as an equivalent of "mother," supposing that the mothering role conditions all labor choices made by women throughout their entire lives. Second, "the division of labor is absolute: if men do it, women can't, or don't, or are prohibited from doing it, and vice versa" (Nelson 1997: 86). However, if we try to confer complexity on our analyses of the past, it is clear that these assumptions operate in the opposite direction, since they defend univocal, unidirectional explanations.[14]

Appraising the main contributions of gender archaeology and feminist anthropology some years later, Elizabeth M. Brumfiel and Cynthia Robin (2008: 1) listed some of the assumptions underlying research and described how these disciplines had managed to overcome them: "1. binary and exclusive models of gender roles and identities, 2. an expectation of fixed routines of domestic labor even in the face of significant economic and political change in wider society, and 3. an expectation that gender identity will always constitute a key axis of social organization."

Specifically in the field of ancient Near Eastern studies, some of the papers in the volume *Gender through time in the Ancient Near East* (2008) set themselves the same task. In her introduction to the volume, the editor Diane Bolger (2008: 14–15) summarizes the common points of some of the contributions: gender as "dynamic, rather than static, and therefore subject to considerable variation through time and space;" and "the recognition that gender is an important aspect of social identity which interfaces with other factors such as age, rank, class, and ethnicity."

We see, then, that some of the proposals referred to here claim that gender, status, race or age cannot be isolated or analyzed independently, because they are shaped through the relationships that they bear to each other. This gives a new twist to what was already proposed at the time of the shift from second to third wave feminism: we need not only to "decenter" sex, gender, or the sex-based division of labor, but also to consider the relationships between all the factors. Indeed, it is their interplay that shapes them; they cannot be analyzed in isolation. Putting the focus on this interplay, on constantly changing features and factors, on fluidity, is the kernel of the theoretical framework currently known in gender studies as "intersectionality."

---

14 In this regard, see also the proposals from the "archaeologies of complexity," which share some common points with gender archaeology. For a presentation of this proposal and its application to some case studies, see Chapman 2003.

The differences between the several approaches mentioned so far have been summarized and labeled by Ange-Marie Hancock (2007: 64, table 1) as the unitary approach, the multiple approach, and the intersectional approach. According to Hancock, the unitary approach considers only one central category of analysis (in our case here it might be gender, sex, or the sex-based division of labor: see § 1). The multiple approach considers several categories of analysis: it assumes that gender, class or age, for example, might be meaningful, and it assumes as well that there is a predetermined relationship between them. The intersectional approach acknowledges that diverse categories are equally important, just as the multiple approach does, but considers the relationship between these diverse categories to be fluid and changing. Consequently, it is important not to take anything for granted; everything must be explored in its specific historical context.

Bonnie Thornton Dill and Marta H. Kohlman (2012: 154) defined intersectionality as a perspective which "emphasizes the interlocking effects of race, class, gender and sexuality, highlighting the ways in which categories of identity and structures of inequality are mutually constituted and defy separation into discrete categories of analysis. Intersectionality provides a unique lens of study that does not question difference; rather, it assumes that differential experiences of common events are to be expected."

The concept of intersectionality emerged in close connection with what were termed "black feminisms." Indeed, it was the African-American scholar Kimberlé W. Crenshaw who coined the term. At the same time as some other scholars in the arena of gender archaeology,[15] Crenshaw charged that "remedial feminism," summarized by the notorious "add women and stir" (Tringham 1991: 95), was insufficient to engender research. Crenshaw claimed that it was necessary, indeed, to propose new theoretical frameworks instead of adding "women" or even "black women" to a set of existing ones. One of these possible new research frameworks was intersectionality, presented as a new research paradigm rather than a content specialization (Hancock 2007: 64 and 74–75).[16] In her pioneer paper Crenshaw (1989: 140) defined intersectionality as follows:

> "I argue that Black women are sometimes excluded from feminist theory and antiracist policy discourse because both are predicated on a discrete set of experiences that often

15 On the current debates regarding the relationship between gender archaeology and intersectionality, see Montón Subías and Meyer 2014: 2372–2381.

16 The same has been (and still is) claimed by those who apply diverse trends of gender studies to research. For some arguments and reflections, see Garcia-Ventura forthcoming.

> does not accurately reflect the interaction of race and gender. These problems of exclusion cannot be solved simply by including Black women within an already established analytical structure. Because the intersectional experience is greater than the sum of racism and sexism, any analysis that does not take intersectionality into account cannot sufficiently address the particular manner in which Black women are subordinated."

Although Crenshaw coined the term "intersectionality," its main elements could be said to have been present several decades earlier. We find a precedent in the famous speech "Ain't I a woman?" given by Sojourner Truth[17] at a meeting for women's rights held in Ohio as early as 1851. As Mercedes Jabardo Velasco (2012: 28) noted, this speech is not only considered the foundational one for black feminisms, but also the pioneer in what would become, more than 100 years later, the theory of intersectionality. On that occasion, the African American Sojourner Truth denounced that discrimination might be manifold: it could happen because you are a woman, because you are a black woman, or even more if you are a black woman and you are poor.[18]

Following this line of thinking, about 100 years later, during the 1960s and the 1970s, the so-called black feminisms denounced that what we know as second wave feminism was not representing them, that this feminism, the main one developed in the academia, was ethnocentric and representing only white, middle-class women. It was noticed that even the centrality of gender or the concern for the sex-based division of work were characteristic of "white feminism" (Oyewumi 2010, with previous references).

In the 1980s and 1990s these complaints had repercussions on new theoretical frameworks like the ones proposed by *queer* studies or post-colonialism. If *queer* studies questioned the use of "woman" as a feasible category of analysis, postcolonial studies questioned the implicit ethnocentrism present overall in research. For all these, main scholars like Judith Butler or Gayatri Spivak,[19] to quote one representative of each trend respectively, are among the main references to consider when applying intersectionality to our research.

We see, then, that intersectionality as a theoretical proposal has some links with postmodernism as well. However, as we have seen, what emerged so re-

---

17 The speech we can read today was not written by Sojourner Truth herself, but by a member of the audience at a later date. For some excerpts of the discourse, its contextualization and commentary see Crenshaw (1989: 152–160) and Hill Collins (2000 [1990]: 14–15). Crenshaw, meanwhile, explains that Sojourner Truth's speech was not scheduled at the meeting and that, paradoxically, some white women were reluctant to let her speak as they were worried that concentrating on black women's concerns might divert attention from those of white women.

18 See Crenshaw 1989: 151.

19 Reference works by these authors which are particularly relevant to the arguments put forward here are Butler 1990 and Spivak 1988.

cently is the term and the build-up of the theory summarized in this term, but not the kernel of what we defined above as "intersectionality." In this direction, Susan Pollock (1999: 218) claims that what is here presented as "intersectionality" is just what summarizes the aims of feminist research, which is presented as research that addresses the social construction of difference in its diverse formats like sex, gender, age, status, etc., that leads to addressing complexity as well (see Crenshaw 1989: 166–167).

3 The sex-based division of work *versus* intersectionality as strategies for engendering the Ur III textile work force

The period known as the Third Dynasty of Ur, or Ur III, lasted for roughly 100 years (ca. 2112–2004 BC). From this period we have a large number of cuneiform texts (about 120,000) written in Sumerian, most of which have to do with administrative matters. A significant proportion of these texts are related to the textile sector.[20] Although these texts provide us with a wealth of data, the information is extremely schematic. Consequently, our reading and interpretation of the texts is strongly influenced by our theoretical framework (always present, even when it is not explicit), as I intend to show below.

To begin, let us consider the approach presented in the first section: the sex-based division of work. As already outlined, it starts from a consideration of sex or gender as being central to the management of the work force, and therefore to our interpretations. If we look at Ur III texts dealing with textile production and textile workers, we see that for some of them the sex-based division of labor indeed seems to be the criterion used to record the workers in segregated lists. An example is the following text from Umma (SAT 2, 509):

	obverse	*obverse*
1.	**12 geme$_2$ 30 sila$_3$ u$_4$ 1-še$_3$**	12 female workers (receive) 30 **sila$_3$** for one day of work
2.	**udu ur$_4$-ra-a**	to shear sheep

20 The main reference to the Ur III textile sector today is still the volume edited by Waetzoldt 1972. Subsequent studies have added more information or have tried to summarize and interpret some of the data that Waetzoldt discusses. With a specific focus on the work force, see, among others Garcia-Ventura 2014a; Lafont 2013; Verderame and Spada 2013, with previous references.

3.	**ša$_3$ e$_2$-maš**	at the sheepfold
4.	**ugula Da-da-ga**	foreman: Dadaga
	reverse	*reverse*
5.	**kišib ensi$_2$**	sealed by the governor
6.	**iti min-eš$_3$**	month: 7
7.	**mu ki-maš^{ki} ba-hul**	year: Š 46
	+ *seal*	+ *seal*

This text lists female workers using the Sumerian word **geme$_2$**. It is an example of the texts in which low rank female or male workers (in this case only female workers) are required to carry out seasonal duties such as digging channels or shearing sheep. These workers are usually divided by sex, without specifying their specialization or age. Many other lists of workers, besides the ones referring to seasonal duties, follow the same pattern.[21]

In supervisory positions the situation may vary, as shown in the following text from Ur (UET 9, 38):

	obverse	*obverse*
1.	**11 ugula uš-bar**	11 foremen/forewomen of the textile workshop
2.	**5 sila$_3$-ta**	(receive) 5 **sila$_3$** each one
3.	**5 sila$_3$ Ur-AB šar$_2$-ra-ab-du**	5 **sila$_3$** (for) Ur-abba, **šar$_2$-ra-ab-du**[22] official.
	reverse	*reverse*
4.	**iti a$_2$-ki-ti**	Month: 7
5.	**mu us$_2$-sa bad$_3$-gal ba-du$_3$ mu us$_2$-sa-bi**	Year: 8th of Ibbi-Suen's Reign

In this text, 11 **ugula** at the textile workshop receive a payment. It is not specified whether they are male or female; nor are their proper names listed. For this reason, I propose that the translation should include both possibilities: foremen or forewomen. Nor do we have any information about the sector of

21 See, for example, the text UTI 3, 2282, from Umma, listing payments delivered to low rank full-time and part-time female workers, broken down by month, in the 3rd year of Šu-Suen's reign.

22 I opt not to translate the term. However, following Waetzoldt (1987: 136) it might be described as "a functionary with a scribal education who appears in the documents in the capacity of an inspector."

the workers under their charge, or even about the specific tasks that these overseers performed. Indeed the only information explicitly given through the Sumerian term **ugula** is their position, which suggests a concern with hierarchy. At this point, then, what happens if we approach this text taking into account only the sex-based division of work? Probably we will look for males or for females without realizing that this information is absent, and without realizing that this information, in this context or regarding the use of this word, **ugula**, may not be relevant.[23]

The other trap lying in wait for us is that we might apply certain assumptions about the sex-based division of work, as mentioned above (§ 2). A number of proposals consider a sexual division of work based on hierarchy, tending to link higher positions with men and lower positions with women. Perhaps for this reason, even though there are not always data on the sex of these supervisors, in the secondary literature it is usually assumed that **ugula** were mainly or even exclusively males.[24] But given that **ugula** is neutral as regards grammatical gender,[25] why do we not have to prove that the supervisors were male, but do have to prove that they were female? In my view, this occurs because sometimes a preconception prevails that assumes that males are the expected overseers, while females are not.

I suggest that in order to avoid these situations and traps alluded to here, it might be useful to question the centrality of the sex-based division of work as a means to explain how the work force was named, registered and organized. My proposal, at this point, is not to dismiss the idea of the sex-based

---

23 My main aim with this example is to highlight the lack of information, in some texts, about the sex of those who hold supervisory positions, rather than to prove the actual presence of forewomen in the texts. Nevertheless, it is worth noting that there are some examples of actual forewomen in Ur III texts, clearly identifiable by their proper names. For a commentary on the case of Aštaqqar and Kun-Simat (attested in the Garšana texts) and of Ummi-tabat (attested in Nippur texts), see Garcia-Ventura 2013: 12–17, with previous references. The fact that this presence of forewomen is mostly attested in Garšana texts (dealing with textile production and with construction work) has been interpreted as something linked to the more "private" nature of the production attested in these texts. As stated by Waetzoldt referring to the presence of forewomen as exceptional, "Diese Besonderheit hängt möglicherweise mit dem halb privaten Charakter der Weberei in Garšana zusammen" (Waetzoldt 2011: 442). However, the validity of the dichotomy public/private as a category of analysis has been widely discussed in both gender studies (for a classical reference, see Helly and Reverby 1992) and in Ur III studies (see for example Verderame and Spada 2013, especially 441–442). Consequently, the reason for this has yet to be better discussed.

24 For a classical reference, see Waetzoldt 1972: 92–108. See also Sallaberger 2009: 245: "In einer Weberei konnten hunderte von Frauen unter den männlichen Aufseher beschäftigt sein."

25 As with many other Sumerian words, for instance **uš-bar** and **dumu**. See discussion below.

division of work, but just to consider that this category of analysis is not the only one applicable, nor in many cases the central one. With this aim in mind, I propose to examine what happens if we apply the idea of intersectionality, instead of starting from the centrality of the sex-based division of work. As I intend to show, this approach opens up the possibility of new interpretations. We have already noted one example, the question of foremen and forewomen.

The weavers and millers in Ur III texts provide another example. As I said before (§ 1), some traditional arguments explaining the sexual division of work are based on essentialist assumptions of gender roles and features. For instance, tasks requiring physical strength tend to be attributed to males and child rearing to females. Indeed, these two attributes have been used several times to justify that weaving and milling were exclusively female tasks, because it is argued that weaving and milling require little physical strength and are easily compatible with child rearing.[26] However, if we examine certain written sources in more detail, we see that these assumptions may just be preconceptions that we are able to question and to refute.

Referring to weaving, from the point of view of grammatical gender, **uš-bar** (the Sumerian term for "weaver") is neutral. Therefore, if it appears alone, we cannot be 100 % sure whether these weavers were males or females. Moreover, even if we accept that most weavers in Ur III were women, certain texts show that some were probably males. One example is a text from Ur, dated in Ibbi-Suen's reign (UET 3, 1449), which presents a list of four teams of low-rank male workers, all of them listed with personal names and the name of the overseers controlling each team. At the very end of the text, rev. ii 16, we read **guruš uš-bar-me**, that is, "the male workers are weavers," referring to all workers (weavers in this case) listed above.[27] As far as milling is concerned, as Bertrand Lafont also noted,[28] both male and female millers are attested in written sources, though women were more numerous. Indeed, at least three texts from Garšana (CUSAS 3, 291, 292 and 304) list low-rank male workers (**guruš** ^{lu_2}**kinkin**) and low-rank female workers (**geme**$_2$**-kinkin**) together as millers.

26 For a classical reference, discussed above (§ 1), see Murdock and Provost 1973.

27 I referred to this text as a case study in a meeting on textile trade and production held in Marburg in April 2013 (see Garcia-Ventura 2014a: 137). Lafont 2013 also uses this text as an example in the same direction. However, Waetzoldt (1972: 94) defended an alternative interpretation for male workers listed in this text: "Das Weben war in der Ur-III-Zeit Frauenarbeit. Die in einigen Texten bezeugten $^{(\text{guruš})}$**uš-bar** sind Aufsichtpersonen, wie es eindeutig aus UET III 1449 iv 14 hervorgeht."

28 Lafont 2013. See also Garcia-Ventura 2014a: 137–138.

Finally, let us look at the example of a text from Girsu (SAT 1, 276). In this text we see how gender and age intersect; identity, and more specifically gender identity is not fixed but constantly changing:

	obverse	*obverse*
1.	**18 geme$_2$ 0.0.5 še lugal**	18 female workers, 50 **sila$_3$** of barley each one
2.	**134 geme$_2$ 0.0.3-ta lugal**	134 female workers, 30 **sila$_3$** each one
3.	**5 geme$_2$ a$_2$ 1/2 0.0.3-ta**	5 female workers, part time workers, 30 *sila* each one
4.	**4 geme$_2$ šu-gi$_4$ 0.0.2-ta**	4 old/retired female workers, 20 **sila$_3$** each one
5.	**19 dumu 0.0.2-ta**	19 children, 20 **sila$_3$** each one
6.	**25 dumu 0.0.1 5 sila$_3$-ta**	25 children, 15 **sila$_3$** each one
7.	**43 dumu 0.0.1-ta**	43 children, 10 **sila$_3$** each one
	reverse	*reverse*
8.	**1 guruš šu-gi$_4$ i$_3$-du$_8$ 0.0.5**	1 old/retired male worker, doorkeeper, 50 **sila$_3$**
9.	**še-bi 21.1.2 5 sila$_3$ gur**	their barley is 6.385 **sila$_3$**
10.	**še-ba geme$_2$ uš-bar**	as barley allocation for the female weavers
11.	**ugula Ur-^{d}Da-mu**	foreman Ur-Damu
12.	**iti še-sag$_{11}$-ku$_5$**	Month: 11
13.	**mu Ša-aš-ru-um^{ki} ba-hul**	year: Š 42

In this text several Sumerian words give us information about rank, age, and at the end, the productive sector (rev. 10). However, neither do all the words provide us with all these details, nor does each word provide us with the same information. The Sumerian word **geme$_2$**, as noted above, provides information about sex and rank: it refers to low rank female workers. When it appears next to **šu-gi$_4$**, information about age has to be added to the previous features. In the case of **dumu**, however, no information about sex or rank is provided, only information about age. Finally, the word **ugula**, also discussed above, provides information about rank, but not about sex, age or specialization.

I argue that, if we analyze this text under the light of the sexual division of labor, it is difficult to grasp the nuances of all these terms. Only if we consider all the features that intersect, without assigning centrality *a priori* to one of them (i.e. sex or gender in the case of the sex-based division of work) will we be able to present a more complex picture. The case of **dumu**, here translated as "children," is especially interesting. I argue that it allows us to reflect on how age affects the construction of gender identity and also how, at certain moments (as is the case of children), gender is not considered relevant and maybe for this reason is not specified in some texts (see Henriksen 2012).

***

In this paper I aimed to show how the various proposals for applying gender perspectives to our analysis may lead to diverse results. More specifically, I discussed two of these proposals: the sex-based (or gender-based) division of work and intersectionality.

As far as the sex-based division of work is concerned, the examples and reflections presented here are intended to show that it is just one of many categories that we might take into account when analyzing the data at our disposal. It is a useful category of analysis, but exaggerating its significance may lead us to miss some important information; obviously, if we automatically take for granted that a particular task was carried out by either males or females we will never establish who was actually responsible for it or whether there was really a clear cut division of the tasks between the sexes. Some of the texts and contexts discussed here suggest that there was no obvious division of this kind.

The use of the sex-based division of work as a category of analysis over several decades has helped to draw attention to women and women's occupations. Ironically, however, in trying to combat the pigeonholing of women into traditional roles, the ascription of certain qualities as female in order to attribute value to them eventually did no more than strengthen their naturalization. As a result, some gender studies, or more specifically women's studies, not only fail to challenge Western preconceptions, but actually reinforce them. For this reason, I think that proposals like the idea of intersectionality discussed here can help us to avoid preconceptions and to place the emphasis on difference and complexity.

As Crenshaw (1989: 156) points out, the feature underlying the emphasis on the centrality of the sex-based division of work in most of our research is the need to highlight how ancient women worked "outside the home." At the same time, it corresponds to the need to denaturalize the link between women and the home, another assumption that does not necessarily work for our primary sources. Needless to say, I argue that the assumption "women at home as housewives" versus "men as breadwinners" is invalid for most of our ancient Near Eastern sources, at least for Ur III Mesopotamia (see Garcia-Ventura 2014b). In my view, intersectionality can help us to decenter not only sex and gender, but also the ethnocentrism and Western preconceptions underlying our research. As Kurtis S. Lesick (1997: 39) stated some years ago, I feel that we need to do research "beyond the 'Western battle of the sexes'," a battle which, I hold, is embedded in the assumption of the centrality of the sex-based division of work.

Nevertheless, there is a risk that intersectionality may be perceived just as another buzzword.[29] I accept this caveat, but I would also argue that we need new words to conceptualize new theoretical frameworks. We cannot avoid using new terms of this kind, especially in feminist research and in gender studies. Indeed, the aim of these perspectives is to find a place in our analyses and discourses for agents who have been traditionally excluded, or included but stereotyped by research. Women represent an obvious example. One of the multiple means to achieve this goal might be, as I suggest in this paper, to question the centrality of the sex-based division of work and to embrace the potentialities of intersectionality. We are not just adding a new element to the analysis, but proposing a new framework that can make our analysis sharper, more complex and more meaningful.

Abbreviations

CUSAS 3	Owen, David I., and Rudolf H. Mayr. 2007. *The Garšana Archives*. Bethesda, Maryland: CDL Press.
SAT 1	Sigrist, Marcel. 1993. *Sumerian Archival Texts I: Texts from the British Museum*. Bethesda, Maryland: CDL Press.
SAT 2	Sigrist, Marcel. 2000. *Sumerian Archival Texts II: Texts from the Yale Babylonian Collections, part 1*. Bethesda, Maryland: CDL Press.
UTI 3	Yildiz, Fatma, and Tohru Gomi. 1993. *Die Umma Texte aus den Archäologischen Museen zu Istanbul, Band III (Nr. 1601–2300)*. Bethesda, Maryland: CDL Press.

Bibliography

Bahrani, Zainab. 2001. *Women of Babylon. Gender and Representation in Mesopotamia*. London: Routledge.

Bolger, Diane. 2008. Introduction. Pp. 1–20 in *Gender through time in the Ancient Near East*, ed. Diane Bolger. Lanham–New York–Toronto–Plymouth: Altamira Press.

Bruhns, Karen O. 1991. Sexual Activities: Some Thoughts on the Sexual Division of Labor and Archaeological Interpretation. Pp. 420–429 in *The Archaeology of Gender*, eds. Dale

29 For a critique of the use of "intersectionality" and its characterization as a mere "buzzword," see Davis 2008.

Walde and Noreen D. Willows. Canada: Proceedings of the 22nd Annual Chacmool Conference. The Archaeological Association of the University of Calgary.
Brumfiel, Elisabeth M. 2006. Cloth, Gender, Continuity, and Change: Fabricating Unity in Anthropology. *American Anthropologist* 108, 4: 862–877.
Brumfiel, Elisabeth M. and Cynthia Robin. 2008. Gender, Households and Society: an Introduction. *Archaeological Papers of the American Anthropological Association* 18(1): 1–16.
Butler, Judith. 1990. *Gender Trouble. Feminism and the Subversion of Identity*. London–New York: Routledge.
Chapman, Robert. 2003. *Archaeologies of Complexity*. London–New York: Routledge.
Conkey, Margaret W. and Janet D. Spector. 1984. Archaeology and the study of gender. Pp. 1–38 in *Advances in Archaeological Method and Theory*, ed. Michael B. Schiffer. New York: Academic Press.
Crenshaw, Kimberle. 1989. Demarginalizing the Intersection of Race and Sex: A Black Feminist Critique of Antidiscrimination Doctrine, Feminist Theory and Antiracist Politics. *The University of Chicago Legal Forum*: 139–167.
Davis, Kathy. 2008. Intersectionality as buzzword. A sociology of science perspective on what makes a feminist theory successful. *Feminist Theory* 9(1): 67–85.
Díaz-Andreu, Margarita. 2014. Historia del estudio del género en Arqueología. Pp. 25–32 in *Desmuntant Lara Croft. Dones, arqueologia i universitat*, eds. Antonio Vizcaíno, Sonia Machause, Vanessa Albelda, and Cristina Real. València: Saguntum. Papeles del Laboratorio de Arqueología de Valencia, Extra 15, Departament de Prehistòria i Arqueologia, Universitat de València.
Fausto-Sterling, Anne. 2000. The Five Sexes Revisited. *The Sciences*: 18–23.
Garcia-Ventura, Agnès. 2013. Trabajar en tiempos de guerra en Mesopotamia. Pp. 1–25 in *Más allá de la batalla. La violencia contra la población en el Mundo Antiguo*, eds. Jordi Vidal and Borja Antela-Bernárdez. Zaragoza: Libros Pórtico.
Garcia-Ventura, Agnès. 2014a. Weaving in Ur III Mesopotamia: Women's Work? Pp. 135–140 in *Textile Trade and Distribution in Antiquity / Textilhandel und -distribution in der Antike*, ed. Kerstin Droß-Krüpe. Wiesbaden: Harrassowitz Verlag.
Garcia-Ventura, Agnès. 2014b. Mano de obra y relaciones de parentesco en Mesopotamia: madres trabajadoras versus hombres "ganadores de pan". *Arenal. Revista de historia de las mujeres* 21(2): 297–316.
Garcia-Ventura, Agnès. forthcoming. Postfeminism and Assyriology: an (im)possible relationship? In *Gender, Methodology and the Ancient Near East*, eds. Saana Svärd and Agnès Garcia-Ventura. Winona Lake, Indiana: Eisenbrauns.
Hancock, Ange-Marie. 2007. When Multiplication Doesn't Equal Quick Addition: Examining Intersectionality as a Research Paradigm. *Perspectives on Politics* 5(1): 63–78.
Haraway, Donna. 1991. "Gender" for a Marxist Dictionary: The Sexual Politics of a Word. Pp. 127–148 in *Simians, Cyborgs, and Women. The Reinvention of Nature*, ed. Donna Haraway. London–New York: Routledge.
Harding, Sandra. 1986. *The Science Question in Feminism*. Ithaca–London: Cornell University Press.
Hartsock, Nancy. 2004. The Feminist Standpoint: Developing the Ground for a Specifically Feminist Historical Materialism. Pp. 35–53 in *The Feminist Standpoint Theory Reader. Intellectual and Political Controversies*, ed. Sandra Harding. London–New York: Routledge. Original edition, 1983.

Helly, Dorothy O. and Susan M. Reverby. 1992. *Gendered Domains. Rethinking Public and Private in Women's History. Essays from the seventh Berkshire Conference on the History of Women*. Ithaca–London: Cornell University Press.
Henriksen Garroway, Kristine. 2012. Gendered or Ungendered? The Perception of Children in Ancient Israel. *Journal of Near Eastern Studies* 71(1): 95–114.
Hill Collins, Patricia. 2000. *Black Feminist Thought. Knowledge, Consciousness, and the Politics of Empowerment*. New York–London: (revised Tenth Anniversary Edition), Routledge. Original edition, 1990.
Jabardo Velasco, Mercedes. 2012. *Feminismos negros. Una antología, Mapas*. Madrid: Traficantes de sueños.
Lafont, Bertrand. 2013. State employment of women during the Ur III period. *Second and third REFEMA workshops, Tokyo (June 2013) and Carqueiranne (September 2013)* http://refema.hypotheses.org/976 (accessed April 2015).
Lesick, Kurtis S. 1997. Re-engendering gender: some theoretical and methodological concerns on a burgeoning archaeological pursuit. Pp. 31–41 in *Invisible People and Processes. Writing Gender and Childhood into European Archaeology*, eds. Jenny Moore and Eleanor Scott. London–New York: Leicester University Press.
Longino, Helen E. 1995. To see feelingly: Reason, Passion, and Dialogue in Feminist Philosophy. Pp. 19–45 in *Feminisms in the Academy*, eds. Donna C. Stanton and Abigail J. Stewart. Ann Arbor: The University of Michigan Press.
Mann, Susan Archer and Douglas J. Huffman. 2005. The Decentering of Second Wave Feminism and the Rise of the Third Wave. *Science & Society* 69(1): 56–91.
Montón Subías, Sandra and William Meyer. 2014. Engendered Archaeologies. Pp. 2372–2381 in *Encyclopedia of Global Archaeology*, ed. Claire Smith. New York: Springer.
Murdock, George P. and Caterina Provost. 1973. Factors in the Division of Labor by Sex: a Cross-cultural Analysis. *Ethnology* 12(2): 203–225.
Nelson, Sarah Milledge. 1997. *Gender in Archaeology*. California: AltaMira Press.
Nuño Gómez, Laura. 2010. *El mito del varón sustentador. Orígenes y consecuencias de la división sexual del trabajo, Género y sociedad*. Barcelona: Icaria.
Oyewumi, Oyeronke. 2010. Conceptualizando el género: Los fundamentos eurocéntricos de los conceptos feministas y el reto de la epistemología africana. *Africaneando* 4: 25–35.
Pollock, Susan. 1999. *Ancient Mesopotamia. The Eden that Never Was*. Cambridge: Cambridge University Press.
Rubin, Gayle S. 1975. The Traffic in Women: Notes on the "Political Economy". Pp. 157–210 in *Toward an Anthropology of Women*, ed. Rayna R. Reiter. New York–London: Monthly Review Press.
Sallaberger, Walther. 2009. Von der Wollration zum Ehrenkleid. Textilien als Prestigegüter am Hof von Ebla. Pp. 241–278 in *Der Wert der Dinde. Güter im Prestigediskurs*, eds. Berit Hildebrandt and Caroline Veit. München: Münchner Studien zur Alten Welt, Herbert Utz Verlag.
Spencer-Wood, Suzanne M. 2006. Feminist Theory and Gender Research in Historical Archaeology. Pp. 59–104 in *Handbook of Gender in Archaeology*, ed. Sarah Milledge Nelson. Lanham MD: AltaMira Press.
Spivak, Gayatri Chakravorty. 1988. Can the Subaltern Speak? Pp. 271–313 in *Marxism and the Interpretation of Culture*, eds. Cary Nelson and Lawrence Grossberg. Urbana: University of Illinois Press.
Thornton Dill, Bonnie and Marla H. Kohlman. 2012. Intersectionality. A Transformative Paradigm in Feminist Theory and Social Justice. Pp. 154–174 in *Handbook of Feminist*

Research. Theory and Praxis, 2nd ed., ed. Sharlene Nagy Hesse-Biber. Los Angeles–London: SAGE.

Tringham, Ruth. 1991. Households with Faces: the Challenge of Gender in Prehistoric Architectural Remains. Pp. 93–131 in *Engendering Archaeology*, eds. Joan M. Gero and Margaret W. Conkey. Oxford: Blackwell.

Verderame, Lorenzo and Gabriella Spada. 2013. Ikalla, Scribe of (Wool) Textiles and Linen. Pp. 425–444 in *From the 21st Century B.C. to the 21st Century A.D.* eds. Steven J. Garfinkle and Manuel Molina. Winona Lake, Indiana: Eisenbrauns.

Waetzoldt, Hartmut. 1972. *Untersuchungen zur neusumerischen Textilindustrie*. Roma: Centro per le Antichità e la storia dell'arte del Vicino Oriente.

Waetzoldt, Hartmut. 1987. Compensation of Craft Workers and Officials in the Ur III Period. Pp. 117–141 in *Labor in the Ancient Near East*, ed. Marvin A. Powell. New Haven: American Oriental Society.

Waetzoldt, Hartmut. 2011. Die Textilproduktion von Garšana. Pp. 405–454 in *Garšana Studies*, ed. David I. Owen. Bethesda, Maryland: CDL Press.

Wittig, Monique. 1989. On the Social Contract. *Feminist Issues* 9(1): 3–12.

Cécile Michel

Women Work, Men are Professionals in the Old Assyrian Archives

The Old Assyrian private archives are predominantly of a commercial nature; however, compared to other cuneiform corpuses, they include a large proportion of texts related to women and their activities. These texts show that wives and daughters of the Assyrian merchants, both at Aššur and Kaneš, enjoyed considerable independence both socially and economically. Various types of family records, such as marriage and divorce contracts, as well as testaments, bear witness to the status of Assyrian women, mainly in Kaneš. The letters Aššur women sent to their relatives in Kaneš reflect their preeminent role on the home front as well as their contribution to long distance trade. In addition, a few texts refer to the activities of the Anatolian women in Kaneš, especially those married to Assyrian merchants.

This essay focuses on the gender-specific division of work in Old Assyrian sources, and how female activities were perceived. After some definitions and a quick presentation of the sources and their authors, an inventory of male and female professions will be given and the rare female professions attested will be compared with women's activities in various spheres.

1 Definitions and sources

1.1 Occupation, profession, work and job

There are many English words referring to human activities, which need to be clarified before studying women's work in the Old Assyrian period from a gender perspective; among these are profession, job, occupation and work. A "profession" is understood as an activity performed by a person who went through a specific training or education.[1] The words "job" and "occupation" include

1 For these definitions, see http://dictionary.cambridge.org/dictionary/essential-british-english/.

Acknowledgements: I address my warmest thanks to Benjamin Foster who kindly corrected the English of this article.

Cécile Michel, CNRS, Archéologies et Sciences de l'Antiquité, Nanterre;
cecile.michel@mae.cnrs.fr

profession; they correspond to an activity performed for compensation. "Work" has an even wider meaning: it corresponds to a task assigned either by oneself or by someone else and which has to be accomplished. Work can be interpreted quite broadly; it includes, for example, house work. A job or an occupation is thus work that is paid, independent of any training or qualification. It is also important to distinguish between occupation and status, which is an accepted or recognized social, legal or economic position. For example, the word *hapirum* refers, in the beginning of the 2nd millennium BC, to displaced persons; these persons could occasionally be ascribed to specific occupations (Durand 2005). In this paper, which explores the work performed by women and men in the Old Assyrian sources, the word profession will be used when referring to specific designations as "weaver", "cook", "midwife", etc.

1.2 The Old Assyrian Sources: what they say, what they don't say

The 22,500 Old Assyrian tablets excavated in the lower town of Kültepe belonged mainly to three generations of Assyrian merchants who settled there during the first half of the 19th century BC. The great majority of the dated texts – which represent 5% of the available sources – are concentrated in a sixty-year period (ca. 1895–1835), and it has been suggested that this is the case for the bulk of our documentation.[2]

According to modern categories, they can be classified into several text genres: letters, contracts and juridical texts, personal memoranda, lists, and a few non-commercial texts.[3] The letters form the largest group, being the private correspondence exchanged among the Assyrian merchants in Kaneš and their families and colleagues in Aššur or in other Assyrian towns in Anatolia.[4] Numerous commercial and family contracts excavated at Kaneš involve both the Assyrians and the Anatolians established in the lower town. Like other legal texts – verdicts, proceedings, private summons –, they deal with commercial and financial matters (Hertel 2013). The remaining group of tablets written for commercial purposes consists of anonymous private accounts, memoranda,

2 Barjamovic et al. 2012. Note however that some groups of letters are the oldest texts kept in archives, Michel 2008b.

3 For studies on the Old Assyrian archives, see for example Michel 1998; Larsen 2002; Veenhof 2003; Larsen 2008; Michel 2008a; Veenhof 2013. More generally, see the catalogue of Old Assyrian tablets and the bibliography in Michel 2003; Michel 2006a and Michel 2011a.

4 Michel 2001, with an overview of letters written to or by women, 417–511.

lists of names, or distribution of goods to various people (Ulshöfer 1995). All these texts are predominantly connected with the long distance trade the Assyrians initiated between Aššur and Central Anatolia. However, because of the displacement of families between Aššur and Anatolia, they also document family matters and everyday life both in Aššur and in Kaneš.

Before analyzing the role of women in work and society through the Old Assyrian archives, one needs to understand who wrote the texts, what these texts tell and what they do not tell.

How many individuals were involved in writing so many tablets? School texts document a scribal education for some merchants who produced neatly written tablets with well-formed signs. It has been suggested that, because of the enormous number of letters found at Kaneš, a significant percentage of the Assyrian population was able to read and write (Michel 2008c). Indeed, the Old Assyrian syllabary is quite simple and limited, and could be learned without following specific courses and long training. The grammar and syntax of letters are sometimes substandard, and they use vernacular language. These letters seem to have been mostly written by the merchants themselves, who were traveling extensively and could not always have a scribe at hand. Many women sent letters from Aššur; their prose is often full of emotion (Larsen 2001). They were themselves involved in commercial and financial operations and owned personal archives. Several women were able to read, classify and write tablets; a legal document explicitly mentions a commercial tablet written down by a woman (Michel 2009a, 268–269).

The great majority of the texts were produced by men, documenting a male world and male occupations, mainly linked to trade. Women, participating less than men in international trade, are thus less visible. Also, the family trees reconstructed by Assyriologists regularly lack female members. Women are however still visible, especially those living alone in Aššur and sending letters to Anatolia. The archive unearthed in 1993, belonging to Ali-ahum and his son Aššur-taklāku, is a good case study; it shows that documented married women are those who entered the family by marriage. Unmarried young girls are rarely mentioned, usually only on the occasion of their marriage; they then leave the family to enter their husband's family (Michel 2015a). The activities of women attested in this archive are those more generally observed for Assyrian women in the Old Assyrian sources. Married women in Aššur managed their households and participated in textile production and export to Anatolia. Married women in Kaneš were in charge of the household – including the archives – when their husbands were away. Unmarried adult women, usually consecrated to a deity, acted independently in financial matters and were involved in the disposition of their fathers' estates.

1.3 Old Assyrian society and Old Anatolian society

The Aššur population was divided among Aššur, Kaneš and other trade settlements in Anatolia. Various studies have been published trying to estimate the Assyrian population in Aššur and Kaneš, as well as the total Kaneš population. Even if the Old Assyrian levels in Aššur have not been excavated, it seems to be accepted that, at the beginning of the 2nd millennium BC, the city did not exceed 55 hectares, and was composed of between 7,000 and 10,000 inhabitants (Larsen 2000, 79). Kaneš was much bigger, between 170 and 230 hectares, and its population amounted to 25,000 or 30,000 persons (Barjamovic 2014), including some 3,000 to 3,500 inhabitants living in the 9 hectares of the lower town commercial district. Among these, there was a majority of Assyrians, all of them involved in trade (Hertel 2014). Since the documentation was found in the houses of these merchants, our data give a picture restricted to the people in Aššur and in Kaneš mainly involved in long distance commerce. For Aššur, we find, in connection with international exchanges, the king and his sons, the eponyms and other high officials, priests and temples' staff, heads of wealthy families, etc. As a consequence, many attested occupations are directly linked to trade and caravan enterprises. The same observation can be made for the population of the Kaneš lower town since we have only the archives of the commercial district.

The data concerning Anatolian society are even more biased since it is documented only through its contacts with the Assyrian population. Indeed, very few Anatolians left archives. Written in a borrowed language and script, these archives are mainly made up of contracts, especially loan contracts, and a few family contracts (Michel 2011b). So our data concerning Anatolian occupations are to be found in the Assyrian archives. Besides the exercise of authority and trade activities, the Anatolians provided food to the Assyrians who were not involved in agriculture and herding.

All these observations concerning the authors and owners of archives must be taken into account when analyzing the role of women in work and society in a gender-oriented perspective.

2 Male and female professions in the Old Assyrian Sources

Professions attested in the Old Assyrian sources have already been inventoried (Michel 2015b); the results of this study are summarized below. Professions are usually mentioned in distribution lists or other laconic contexts which do not give details about the activities of professionals; these are usually anonymous.

I will leave aside all the officials, both Assyrians and Anatolians. Their titles could sometimes be linked to a professional occupation. However it is interesting to note that all the Assyrian officials mentioned in the texts are men (Dercksen 2004), and no queen is attested at the side of the kings of Aššur. Assyrian authorities and officials in Anatolia – *hamuštum*, *šiprum*, *ṭupšarrum*, etc. – are also only men. As for the Anatolians, the fifty known Anatolian officials are all men (Veenhof 2008, 220–233; Michel 2014b, 120–122). However, we must take into account that the local dialect did not make any gender distinction and we cannot completely exclude that some male official titles could have exceptionally concealed some women. This is suggested by the fact that some towns were ruled by a royal couple or by a queen alone (Michel 2001, 163–167).

As already observed, Old Assyrian texts focus on trade, thus trade professionals and jobs linked to international trade are the most frequent: bankers, traders, transporters, freighters, donkey drivers, porters, agents; all these are male professions.

When we look at professions concerned with food production and preparation, there is a little more diversity. When a professional is mentioned, his ethnicity is not necessarily given, be it Assyrian or Anatolian. It was possible to identify a male Anatolian cook (*nuhittimum*), two male Assyrian confectioners (*kakardinnum*), a male Anatolian oil peddler (*pāširum ša šamnim*) and an oil trader (*ša šamnim*), a male salt trader (*ša ṭābtim*), male Anatolian gardeners (*nukiribbum*), and male Anatolian shepherds (*rē'um*). The only female occupation in food preparation is the flour grinder (*tē'ittum*), but flour grinders are usually slaves.[5] Inn-keeper was the only job exercised by both men and women: an Assyrian male inn-keeper (*sābium*) is known at Kaneš and an Amorite female inn-keeper (*sābītum*) is attested at Hattuš.[6]

The world of craft professionals looks again like a purely male one. Bricklayer (*itinnum*), metallurgist (*nappāhum*), carpenter (*naggārum*), bow maker (*šasinnum*), seal engraver (*parkullum*), potter (*pahhārum*), and leatherworker

5 TC 3, 88:10–15, *a-pu-tum i-na* u_4*-mì-*[*im*], *ša ṭup-pá-am ta-ša-*[*me-ú*], é^{tí} 2 géme$^{hi\text{-}tí}$*-kà*, *ki-lá-al-tí-ma*, *ù ṭé-i-té-en*$_6$ *ki-la-a*[*l*]*-tí-m*[*a*], *a-na* [*ší-mì-im dí-ma*], "Please, the very day you hear (this) tablet, offer for sale the houses, both of your slave girls and both of the grinding girls." Text edited by Larsen 2002, no. 40.

6 For a recent study on Old Babylonian inn-keepers, see Lion 2013.

(*aškāpum*) are all jobs attested in the masculine, both in Aššur and Kaneš. Even professions linked to textile production are known only with the masculine gender: an Assyrian male weaver (*ušpārum*), as well as the cleaner specialized in the finishing and washing of textiles (*ašlākum*). There is also mention of a male barber (*gallābum*).

Few legal occupations are known; they are all held by men: judge (*dayyānum*), attorney (*rābiṣum*), scribe (*ṭupšarrum*).

Female jobs are linked with social life, more precisely, as one might expect, with the care of children. Thus we find the following professions: midwife (*šabsūtum*), nurse (*ēmiqtum*) and wet-nurse (*mušēniqtum*), which is the only gender-based profession.

In the religious sphere, we find women as well, but these are not clearly associated with the temples, contrary to men. The temple was administered by the *sangûm*. A *sangûm* gave his name to a year as eponym (Elālī). Priests (*kumrum*) of Adad, Aššur, Ištar, Suen, Šamaš, and Šarra-mātēn are mainly referred to for their role in trade (Hirsch 1972, 55–59). It is interesting to note that women involved in the public life of Aššur were concentrated in the religious sphere; several occupations linked to religious practices were traditionally held by women, such as dream diviner (*šā'iltum*) and omen diviner (*bārītum*). These professionals were consulted by women as well (Michel 2009b). The consecration of a girl as *gubabtum* or *qadištum* conferred her upon a special social and religious status which certainly entailed specific responsibilities or tasks, but these were not necessarily compensated, so we usually see the *gubabtum* women living independently in Aššur and acting as businesswomen, initiating commercial and financial operations.

This inventory of occupations is very incomplete because of the nature of the sources. Many other professions are implied by the texts but are not explicitly mentioned. For example, distribution lists of breads suggest the existence of professional bakers (Michel in press b).

3 Women's activities not referred to as professions

In contrast to men, women seem to be rarely attested as professionals in Old Assyrian sources. However, they appear very active in various domains. To understand this paradox, we need to explore female activities.

3.1 Housewives: unrecognized and unpaid work

From an Assyrian man's perspective, the basic duties of a wife were to give him children, to keep house, to serve her husband and to prepare his meals, as we read in the following letter sent by Puzur-Aššur to his fiancée Nūhšatum:[7]

> "Your father wrote to me about you that I marry you, and I sent my servants and my letter about you to your father so that he lets you go. Please, the day you hear my tablet there, appeal to your father (so that he agrees), set out and come here with my servants. I am alone. There is no one to serve me and set my table."

Women, who did not accompany their husbands to Anatolia remained at Aššur in charge of their households. Their loneliness was well known, as witness the remark of Aššur-malik reproaching Aššur-idī for having forgotten him:[8]

> "Why have you kept me confined inside the City (of Aššur) for 10 months, like a woman?"

These women were active in various capacities that reflect the daily life of women at home, as well as their roles as heads of families: education of children, care of the elderly, management of servants, supplying food to the household, maintenance of the house, weaving textiles for members of the household to wear, etc. Besides these typical housewife's tasks, they had to represent their husbands in various business transactions and to produce textiles for export to Anatolia (see section 3.2).

In Kaneš, wives had also to deal with their husbands' frequent absences. Beside the duties of a housewife, they had to keep track of everything in the home: furnishings and utensils, documents, and merchandise.

The manifold activities of women as housewives were never recognized as "work".

---

7 Michel in press a, no. 3 (BIN 6, 104): 3–18, *a-bu-ki : a-šu-mì-ki* [*a-na*], *ṣé-ri-a a-na a-ha-*[*zi-ki*], *iš-pu-ra-am ù a-na-ku, ṣú-ha-ri-a ù na-áš-pè-er-tí, a-ṣé-er : a-bi-ki : a-šu-mì-ki, a-na šé-ṣú-i-ki, áš-ta-áp-ra-am a-pu-tum, i-na* ^{d}utu^{ši} *ṭup-pí, ta-áš-me-i-ni : a-ma-k*[*am*], *a-na a-bi-ki : pu-nu-*[*i-ma*], *iš-tí ṣú-h*[*a*]*-ri-a, té-eb-e-ma a-tal-ki-im, we-da-ku : ma-ma-an : ša i-/na, re-šé-e-a : i-za-zu-ma, pá-šu-ra-am : i-ša-kà-na-/ni, lá-šu.*

8 CCT 4 45b:16–19, *mì-šu-um : ki-ma, sí-ni-iš-tim : iš-tù* iti-10-kam, *i-qé-ra-âb : A-lim*^{ki}, *ta-áp-ta-ah-a-ni-i.* Both names are very common and we do not know if these two merchants belonged to the same family.

3.2 Textile production: Women acting as professionals but not recognized as such

The inventory of professionals attested in Old Assyrian sources includes men specialized in weaving and finishing textiles, but no feminine profession linked to textile production in mentioned. We know very well, of course, that Aššur women spent much of their lifetime producing textiles for the international trade with Anatolia, and that they were paid in return for their production. They are, however, not referred to as weavers in the texts![9] Even if there is scarce documentation on the organization of the private textile production in Aššur, it is possible to estimate the income women could earn from it; this may be summarized as follows.[10]

In healthy households, a dozen women, including children, elderly women and slaves, spun and wove throughout the year both the clothes for the family and textiles to be sent to Anatolia.[11] Letters give recommended dimensions for a *kutānum*-textile to be sent to Anatolia: 4 × 4,5 meters, which corresponds presumably to two sewn pieces. According to transport contracts, such a *kutānum*-textile weighed about 5 minas (2.5 kg).

Washing the wool and preparing 5 minas for spinning would have taken some 20 days of work for one person.[12] Experiments carried out at the *Centre for Textile Research* in Copenhagen have shown that it is possible, using ancient tools, to spin some 50 meters of thread per hour.[13] To weave a square meter of fabric, one needs about 2 km of thread, plus 2 to 5 % for the setting of the loom. To obtain these 2 km of thread, a woman would have to spin for 5 days.[14] The Assyrian textiles measuring 18 m^2 required 36 km of thread for the weaving, and about 3 months of spinning for a single woman, while the

9 Michel 2006b; Michel 2013; Thomason 2013.

10 Michel 2013; Michel in press a, chapter 4: "Businesswomen"; sub-chapter: "Weaving as a lucrative profession."

11 We suppose that in the context of private production for the international trade, production ran throughout the year.

12 According to an Ur III text, a person would prepare about 125 g of wool a day, see Waetzoldt 2010, 207.

13 Andersson Strand 2012, 34. This research is in progress; it includes a study of Kültepe textiles imprints and textiles tools by E. Andersson Strand, C. Breniquet and C. Michel. It is carried out within the framework of the Groupe de Recherche International *Ancient Textiles from the Orient to the Mediterranean* (ATOM 2015–2018), http://www.mae.u-paris10.fr/gdri-atom-presentation-eng/.

14 Nowadays, women maintaining a traditional production of textiles in the Near East weave for sixth to eight hours a day besides their domestic tasks, according to interviews with women in Bani Hamida (Jordan) and Çavdar (Turkey).

setting of the two looms required 4 more days of work. According to hands-on experiments, one person can weave about 50 cm per day of work, depending, of course, on the width of the loom (Andersson Strand 2012, 35). So we obtain the following figures:

Tab. 1: Number of day's work for an Assyrian to produce a *kutānum*-textile.

Tasks to produce a woolen textile weighing 5 minas and measuring 4 × 4,5 meters	Number of day's work for one woman
Cleaning and combing	20
Spinning	94
Setting of the loom(s)	8
Weaving	20
Total of working days/woman	142 [4 ¾ months]

Thus a woman could finish some 2 ½ such textiles a year, and a wealthy household would produce about 25 textiles a year. Of these, 5 large pieces would be necessary to clothe the members of the household. Thus, 20 textiles could be sent to be sold in Anatolia.[15]

The sale of their textiles in Anatolia assured an income to Aššur women. They were paid by the piece, allowing computation of the income per garment. The current *kutānum*-textile produced by Aššur women was sold 15 shekels at Kaneš. After taxes were deducted, women could hope to get back 10 to 12 shekels per piece. The price of the wool in Aššur was about 15 minas per shekel, and the loss during cleaning was about 30 % of the original wool; thus with 1 shekel of silver it might have been possible to acquire about 10 minas of cleaned wool, which could be used to weave 2 textiles. Taking into account that a third of the sale price of a textile was invested in the purchase of wool to produce new textiles, we may estimate that a household producing yearly some 20 textiles sent for trade to Anatolia would receive between 3 ½ and 4 minas of silver per year as gross income, corresponding to the price of a small house in Aššur (Veenhof 2011). Regular shipping of textiles guaranteed Aššur women a substantial annual income.

15 Such an estimation was confirmed by Lamassī's letters showing that, within a year, she was able to send 25 textiles to her husband including those for his own garde-robe (see Michel in press a, chapter 4: "Businesswomen"), Michel 2013; Michel 2014a, 95–96.

3.3 Women as actors in trade and finance

No profession connected with trade and finance concerns women, although they were quite active in both.

Tab. 2: Old Assyrian loan contracts involving men and women.

	Only men	Couples or families	Women	Women as creditors	Women as debtors
Interest free loans (14.5 % of the loans)	69.5 %	21.5 %	9 %	5.5 %	3.5 %
Loans with interest (25 % of the loans)	92 %	5 %	3 %	3 %	0 %
Loans with default interest (60.5 % of the loans)	86.5 %	6.5 %	7 %	5 %	2 %
average	85 %	8.5 %	6.5 %	4.5 %	2 %

There are about 400 published loan tablets excavated at Kaneš;[16] 6.5 % of these loan contracts involve at least one woman; in two-thirds of these she is a creditor and in one-third a debtor.

Women could lend silver either to men or women, Assyrians or Anatolians, but their loans tended to be smaller than those of men.[17] They appear both in interest-free short term loans and in loans with default interest. They could also act as creditor in loans with interest, but were never debtors in such loans – being usually commercial and linked to the international trade – because they did not act as travelling agents. But this does not mean that they did not take part in the trade. A specific type of loan, the *tadmiqtum*-loan, was more typical for women. To send their textiles to Anatolia, they entrusted their textiles on favorable terms as a *tadmiqtum* or "good-faith consignment loan" to members of their families or agents travelling to Anatolia.

16 For OA loan contracts, http://www.d-o-c.fr/.
17 Michel 2014a, 97–98; Michel in press a, chapter 4 "Businesswomen," section "Women lend, buy and invest." Ahatum lent silver to Assyrian men at least four times. The four loans are dated within 9 years (TC 3, 228; BIN 4, 153; KTS 1, 45b; RA 59, 36). Šāt-Ana lent a total of 1 mina and 27 shekels of silver to different men according to three contracts (TC 3, 235; CCT 5, 20c; TC 3, 220).

Beside their textile production, some women were clearly involved in long-distance trade, buying merchandise in Aššur to be sent for sale in Kaneš.[18] They could invest in a caravan enterprise.[19] There are also some rare mentions of women owing shares in joint-stock companies. Such a partnership involved several persons investing silver, which was made available to an agent on long term to gain profit from overland trade. Ahaha, the consecrated daughter of Pūšu-kēn, writes several letters to her brothers concerning her share in at least two such joint-stock companies (Michel 2001, nos. 225–226). The wife of Salliya bought a share in a joint-stock company administered by Iddin-Ištar.[20] Contracts of this type regulated the relationships between the investors of Aššur and the agents in Anatolia; this was the main financing mode for the Assyrian trade in Anatolia.[21]

We also see women travelling on business (Michel 2008d), for example, the widow Ennam-Ištar who wrote to her son as follows:[22] "In your presence, in Burušhattum, I gave 10 shekels of silver to Aššur-ṭāb. (Then) in Kaneš, I gave him a single *kutānum*-textile."

Single women, either consecrated or widows, as well as married women, were involved in financial operations similar to those operated by men. Some appear to have been excellent accountants. But they are less attested in such a role, and when they invest capital in gold or silver, the amount is usually smaller than the capitals invested by men. In any case, they are not considered professionals in these activities.

3.4 Agricultural tasks of Anatolian women

When the Assyrian merchants settled in Kaneš, they arrived alone, and some took Anatolian women as second wives there. As they were traveling within Anatolia or to Aššur, they sent letters to their Anatolian wives referring to their activities. Contrary to the main preoccupations of the women of Aššur, mostly eager to learn what was happening with their textile production, the Anatolian

---

18 A small contract lists consigned merchandise among which silver, textiles, wool, copper and donkeys belonging to the woman Bazaya; Michel in press a, no. 196, previously published by Bayram and Çeçen 1996, no. 5 (Kt 76/k 2).

19 Kulšan lend silver to merchants going on for one or two round trip caravan: Michel in press a, no. 188, previously published by Uzunalimoðlu 1992, 53–54 (Kt n/k 860).

20 CTMMA 1 85.

21 Larsen 1977; Hecker 1999; Veenhof 1999.

22 AKT 6a, 223:3–8, *ma-ah-ri-kà-ma, i-na Bu-ru-uš-ha-tim*, 10 gín kù-babbar : *a-na A-šùr*-du$_{10}$, *a-dí-in i-na Kà-ne-eš*$_{15}$, *iš-té-en*$_{6}$ túg *ku-ta-nam, a-dí-šu-um.*

women of Kaneš never speak about textile production. However, some texts, as well as archaeological artifacts excavated in Kültepe's lower town, such as spindle whorls and loom weights, announce such a production. As with the women in Aššur, the occupations of the Anatolian wives are domestic or commercial. But unlike Assyrian women, Anatolian women also performed agricultural work (Michel 2008e). Šišahšušar, Aššur-nādā's wife, bought oxen and had to find enough fodder for them; then she got them ready for ploughing. She also bought straw, wood, reeds and many tools for the house and for field work.[23] Kunnanīya received instructions from her husband Aššur-mūtappil about the pigs she was breeding.[24] As was still the case in France half a century ago, the agricultural activities of women were not recognized as professional in nature.

***

The inventory of professions occurring in Old Assyrian texts shows predominantly men at work. They were brought up as professionals, often learning their future job from their fathers. They practiced their profession outside the home, in a workshop, in institutional buildings, or by travelling.

Women are rarely mentioned as professionals, except in specific spheres. In the context of food preparation and sale, we find flour grinders and tavernkeepers. Diviners and dream diviners belonged to the religious sphere. Midwives, nurses and wet-nurses undertook the care of children. However, Assyrian women appear as very active, both as housewives and heads of households, and in their contribution to the international trade. When producing textiles for Anatolia, they acted as true professionals. Indeed, their skills were recognized abroad, and they were paid for their work as weavers. With the money they earned, which built up their personal assets, independent of their husband's, they invested in trade and initiated financial operations. However, they are never mentioned as "professional" weavers. Perhaps we can see here the idea that work done at home is not considered a job, an idea later developed by Xenophon (*Oeconomicus*, chap. VII) in Greece.

---

23 See TC 2, 47; translated by Michel 2001, no. 358 and Larsen 2002, no. 52, and VS 26, 20; edited by Larsen 2002, no. 58.

24 BIN 6, 84 mentioned by Michel 2006c, 171, n. 7.

Abbreviation

AKT 6a Larsen, Mogens T. 2010. *The Archive of the Šalim-Aššur Family. Volume 1: The First Two Generations*. Kültepe Tabletleri VI – a. Ankara: Türk Tarih Kurumu Basımevi.

Bibliography

Andersson Strand, Eva. 2012. The Textile chaîne opératoire: Using a Multidisciplinary Approach to Textile Archaeology with a Focus on the Ancient Near East. Pp. 21–40 in *Prehistory of Textiles in the Ancient Near East*, eds. Catherine Breniquet, Margareta Tengberg & Eva Andersson Strand with the collaboration of Marie-Louise Nosch. *Paléorient* 38: 21–40.

Atıcı, Levent, Fikri Kulakoğlu, Gojko Barjamovic, and Andrew Fairbairn (eds.). 2014. *Current Research at Kultepe/Kanesh. An Interdisciplinary and Integrative Approach to Trade Networks, Internationalism, and Identity*. JCS Supplemental Series 4. Atlanta: Lockwood Press.

Barjamovic, Gojko. 2014. The Size of Kanesh and the Demography of Early Middle Bronze Age Anatolia. Pp. 55–68 in Atıcı *et al.* 2014.

Barjamovic, Gojko, Thomas K. Hertel, and Mogens T. Larsen. 2012. *Ups and Downs at Kanesh. Chronology, History and Society in the Old Assyrian Period*. Old Assyrian Archives Studies 5. PIHANS 120. Leiden: Nederlands Historisch-Archaeologisch Instituut Leiden.

Bayram, Sabahattin and Salih Çeçen. 1996. The Institution of Slavery in Ancient Anatolia in the Light of New Documents. *Belleten* 60: 606–645.

Dercksen, Jan Gerrit. 2004. *Old Assyrian Institutions*. PIHANS 98. Leiden: Nederlands Historisch-Archaeologisch Instituut Leiden.

Durand, Jean-Marie. 2005. Assyriologie. Le problème des haBirum et l'étymologie du terme "hébreu". *Cours et travaux du Collège de France*, 563–584 http://www.college-de-france.fr/media/jean-marie-durand/UPL19772_durandres0405.pdf.

Fares, Saba, Françoise Briquel-Chatonnet, Brigitte Lion, and Cécile Michel (eds). 2009. *Femmes, cultures et sociétés dans les civilisations méditerranéennes et proches-orientales de l'Antiquité*. Topoi Suppl. 10.

Hecker, Karl. 1999. In nova ... *ArOr* 67: 557–565.

Hertel, Thomas K. 2013. *Old Assyrian Legal Practices. Law and Dispute in the Ancient Near East*. Old Assyrian Archives Studies 6. PIHANS 123. Leiden: Nederlands Historisch-Archaeologisch Instituut Leiden.

Hertel, Thomas K. 2014. The Lower Town of Kültepe: Urban Layout and Population. Pp. 25–54 in Atıcı *et al.* 2014.

Hirsch, Hans. 1972. *Untersuchungen zur altassyrischen Religion*. AfO Beiheft 13/14. Graz: Im Selbstverlage des Herausgebers.

Larsen, Mogens T. 1977. Partnerships in the Old Assyrian Trade. *Iraq* 39: 119–149.

Larsen, Mogens T. 2000. The Old Assyrian City-State. Pp. 77–87 in *A Comparative Study of Thirty City-Sate Cultures*, ed. Mogens H. Hansen. Copenhagen: Kongelige Danske Videnskabernes Selskab.

Larsen, Mogens T. 2001. Affect and Emotion. Pp. 275–286 in *Veenhof Anniversary Volume. Studies Presented to Klaas R. Veenhof on the Occasion of his Sixty-Fifth Birthday*, ed. Wilfred H. van Soldt. PIHANS 89. Leiden: Nederlands Historisch-Archaeologisch Instituut Leiden.

Larsen, Mogens T. 2002. *The Aššur-nādā Archive*. Old Assyrian Archives 1. PIHANS 96. Leiden: Nederlands Historisch-Archaeologisch Instituut Leiden.

Larsen, Mogens T. 2008. Archives and Filing Systems at Kültepe. Pp. 77–88 in *Old Assyrian Studies in Memory of Paul Garelli*, ed. Cécile Michel. Old Assyrian Archives Studies 4. PIHANS 112. Leiden: Nederlands Historisch-Archaeologisch Instituut Leiden.

Lion, Brigitte. 2013. Les cabarets à l'époque paléo-babylonienne. Pp. 393–400 in *L'alimentation dans l'Orient ancien: Cuisines et dépendances*, ed. Cécile Michel. Cahiers des thèmes transversaux d'ArScAn. Vol. XI, 2011–2012. Nanterre: Archéologies et Sciences de l'Antiquité. http://www.mae.u-paris10.fr/arscan/IMG/pdf/Cahier_des_ThemesXI_Th_9_Lion.pdf.

Michel, Cécile. 1998. Quelques réflexions sur les archives récentes de Kültepe. Pp. 419–433 in *3. Uluslararası Hititoloji Kongresi Bildirileri*, eds. Sedat Alp and Aygül Süel. Ankara: Uyum Ajans. http://halshs.archives-ouvertes.fr/halshs-00708857.

Michel, Cécile. 2001. *Correspondance des marchands de Kaniš au début du IIe millénaire av. J.-C.* Littératures du Proche-Orient ancien 19. Paris: Editions du Cerf.

Michel, Cécile. 2003. *Old Assyrian Bibliography of Cuneiform Texts, Bullae, Seals and the Results of the Excavations at Aššur, Kültepe / Kaniš, Acemhöyük, Alişar and Boğazköy*. Old Assyrian Archives Studies 1. PIHANS 97. Leiden: Nederlands Historisch-Archaeologisch Instituut Leiden.

Michel, Cécile. 2006a. Old Assyrian Bibliography 1 (February 2003–July 2006). *AfO* 51: 436–449.

Michel, Cécile. 2006b. Femmes et production textile à Aššur au début du IIe millénaire avant J.-C. *Techniques & culture* 46: 281–297. http://halshs.archives-ouvertes.fr/halshs-00821277.

Michel, Cécile. 2006c. Les suidés dans la documentation de Kaniš au début du IIe millénaire avant J.-C. Pp. 169–180 in *De la domestication au tabou: le cas des suidés au Proche-Orient ancien*, eds. Brigitte Lion and Cécile Michel. Travaux de la Maison René-Ginouvès 1. Paris: De Boccard. http://halshs.archives-ouvertes.fr/halshs-00518271.

Michel, Cécile. 2008a. The Alāhum and Aššur-taklāku archives found in 1993 at Kültepe Kaniš. *AoF* 35: 53–67 [abstract p. 359]. http://halshs.archives-ouvertes.fr/halshs-01186428.

Michel, Cécile. 2008b. La correspondance des marchands assyriens du XIXe s. av. J.-C.: de l'archivage des lettres commerciales et privées. Pp. 117–140 in *La lettre d'archive. Communication administrative et personnelle dans l'Antiquité proche-orientale et égyptienne*, ed. Laure Pantalacci. Topoi Suppl. 9. Le Caire: IFAO. http://halshs.archives-ouvertes.fr/halshs-00644198/fr/.

Michel, Cécile. 2008c. Écrire et compter chez les marchands assyriens du début du IIe millénaire av. J.-C. Pp. 345–364 in *Muhibbe Darga Armağanı*, eds. Taner Tarhan, Aksel Tibet, and Erkan Konyar. Istanbul: Sadberk Hanım Müzesi. http://halshs.archives-ouvertes.fr/halshs-00443900/fr/.

Michel, Cécile. 2008d. Femmes au foyer et femmes en voyage: le cas des épouses des marchands assyriens au début du IIe millénaire av. J.-C. *Clio, Histoire, femmes et sociétés* 28: 17–38. http://clio.revues.org/index7603.html.

Michel, Cécile. 2008e. Les Assyriens et leurs femmes anatoliennes. Pp. 209–229 in *Anatolia and the Jazira during the Old Assyrian Period*, ed. Jan Gerrit Dercksen. Old Assyrian Archives Studies 3. PIHANS 111. Leiden: Nederlands Historisch-Archaeologisch Instituut Leiden. http://halshs.archives-ouvertes.fr/halshs-00667570.

Michel, Cécile. 2009a. Les femmes et l'écrit dans les archives paléo-assyriennes (XIXe s. av. J.-C.). Pp. 253–272 in Fares et al. 2009. http://halshs.archives-ouvertes.fr/halshs-00644211/fr/.

Michel, Cécile. 2009b. Les filles de marchands consacrées. Pp. 145–163 in Fares *et al*. 2009. http://halshs.archives-ouvertes.fr/halshs-00644209/fr/.

Michel, Cécile. 2011a. Old Assyrian Bibliography 1 (July 2006–April 2009). *AfO* 52: 396–417.

Michel, Cécile. 2011b. The Private Archives from Kaniš Belonging to Anatolians. Pp. 94–115 in *Archival, Scribal, and Administrative Spaces among the Hittites*, ed. Maria E. Balza. *AoF* 38. http://halshs.archives-ouvertes.fr/halshs-01186438.

Michel, Cécile. 2013. Assyrian Women's Contribution to International Trade with Anatolia. *Second International Workshop of the French-Japanese ANR programme Chorus REFEMA (Rôle économique des femmes en Mésopotamie ancienne), Tokyo, June 2013*. Online publication October 2013. http://refema.hypotheses.org/850.

Michel, Cécile. 2014a. The Economic Role of Women in the Old Assyrian Sources. Pp. 93–101 in *Le role économique des femmes en Mésopotamie ancienne (REFEMA) / Women's Role in the Economy of the Ancient Near East*, eds. Francis Joannès and Fumi Karahashi. Japan Society for the Promotion of Science: International Collaborations. Bilateral Joint Research Project with France (ANR). Report: December 31, 2011–December 30, 2014. Tokyo.

Michel, Cécile. 2014b. Central Anatolia in the Nineteenth and Eighteenth Centuries BC. Pp. 111–136 in *Constituent, Confederate, and Conquered Space. The Emergence of the Mittani State*, eds. Eva Cancik-Kirschbaum, Nicole Brisch, and Jesper Eidem. TOPOI. Berlin Studies of the Ancient World 17. Berlin: De Gruyter. http://www.degruyter.com/viewbooktoc/product/129816.

Michel, Cécile. 2015a. Women in the Family of Ali-ahum son of Iddin-Suen (1993 Kültepe archive). Pp. 85–93 in *Proceedings of the 1st Kültepe International Meeting, Kültepe, 19–23 September, 2013. Studies Dedicated to Kutlu Emre*, eds. Fikri Kulakoğlu and Cécile Michel. Kültepe International Meetings 1. Subartu XXXV. Turnhout: Brepols.

Michel, Cécile. 2015b. Were there only merchants at Aššur and Kaneš? Overview of professions attested in the Old Assyrian Sources. Pp. 171–184 in *Cahit Günbattı'ya Armağan. Studies in Honour of Cahit Günbattı*, eds. İrfan Albayrak, Hakan Erol and Murat Çayır. Ankara: Ankara Üniversitesi Basımevi.

Michel, Cécile. In press a. *Women from Aššur and Kaniš according to the private archives of the Assyrian merchants at beginning of the IInd millennium B.C.* Writings from the Ancient World. SBL. Baltimore.

Michel, Cécile. In press b. Le pain à Aššur et à Kaneš, *Festschrift NN*. AOAT, Stuttgart: Kevelaer and Neukirchen-Vluyn.

Thomason, Allison K. 2013. Her Share of the Profits: Women, Agency, and Textile Production at Kültepe/Kanesh in the Early Second Millennium BC. Pp. 93–112 in *Textile Production and Consumption in the Ancient Near East. Archaeology, Epigraphy, Iconography*, eds. Marie-Louise Nosch, Henriette Koefoed, and Eva Andersson Strand. Ancient Textiles Series 12. Oxford: Oxbow Books.

Ulshöfer, Andrea. 1995. *Die altassyrischen Privaturkunden*. FAOS Beiheft 4. Stuttgart: Franz Steiner Verlag.

Uzunalimoğlu, Ayşe. 1992. 1950 Yılında Kültepe Kazısında Bulunan 5 Adet Mahkeme Kararı. *Anadolu Medeniyetleri Müzesi Yıllığı* 1990: 44–53.
Veenhof, Klaas R.1999. Silver and Credit in Old Assyrian Trade. Pp. 55–83 in *Trade and Finance in Ancient Mesopotamia*, ed. Jan Gerrit Dercksen. PIHANS 87. Leiden: Nederlands Historisch-Archaeologisch Instituut Leiden.
Veenhof, Klaas R. 2003. Archives of Old Assyrian Traders. Pp. 78–123 in *Archives and Archival Tradition. Concepts of Record-Keeping in the Ancient World*, ed. Maria Brosius. Oxford: Oxford University Press.
Veenhof, Klaas R. 2008. The Old Assyrian Period. Pp. 13–268 in *Mesopotamia. The Old Assyrian Period*, ed. Markus Wäfler. OBO 160/5. Fribourg: Academic Press Fribourg and Göttingen: Vandenhoeck & Ruprecht.
Veenhof, Klaas R. 2011. Houses in the ancient city of Assur. Pp. 211–231 in *Correlates of Complexity. Essays in Archaeology and Assyriology Dedicated to Diederik J. W. Meijer in Honour of his 65th Birthday*, eds. Bleda S. Düring, Arne Wossink, and Peter M. M. G. Akkermans. PIHANS 116. Leiden: Nederlands Historisch-Archaeologisch Instituut Leiden.
Veenhof, Klaas R. 2013. The Archives of Old Assyrian Traders: their Nature, Functions and Use. Pp. 27–71 in Archives and archival documents in ancient societies: Trieste 30 September–1 October 2011, ed. Michele Faraguna. Legal documents in ancient societies IV. Trieste: Edizioni Università di Trieste.
Waetzoldt, Hartmut. 2010. The Colours and Variety of Fabrics from Mesopotamia during the Ur III Period (2050 BC). Pp. 201–209 in *Textile Terminologies in the Ancient Near East and Mediterranean from the Third to the First Millennia BC*, eds. Cécile Michel and Marie-Louise Nosch. Ancient Textiles 8. Oxford: Oxbow Books.

Jerrold S. Cooper

The Job of Sex: The social and economic role of prostitutes in ancient Mesopotamia

Prostitution certainly cannot be shown to be Mesopotamia's "oldest profession," but it is attested quite early, from at least the mid-third millennium.[1] It is an occupation that, in its practice, as Brigitte Lion has noted (2013: 398), "has left practically no written trace," and involved, again in her words, a "transaction (...) payable in cash, which made it unnecessary to document on a tablet." Of course, as Lion implies, this lack of documentation is not a peculiar feature of prostitution, but rather is just one example of the absence of documentation for all small-scale private transactions. People bought vegetables, had their shoes repaired, got haircuts, and satisfied their sexual needs, all without leaving a trace in the great mountain of cuneiform documentation.[2]

In their call for papers, the conference organizers reminded us that most women's work was in and around the home, and thus unmentioned and unremunerated. When women worked outside the home, in the great institutions, palace or temple, they were most likely to be found in the textile or grain mills, that is, working in sectors that specialized in just one of the tasks that were part of the traditional chores women did in the home. Might prostitution also be so considered? Was the prostitute earning her livelihood by merely commodifying a single task that other women performed only at home with their husbands? Can we speak of sex workers in ancient Mesopotamia? I ask this question knowing that the terms "sex work" and "sex worker" have become controversial among feminist theorists and activists (Howell 2008). Some seek to support and protect women who satisfy sexual desire for money, and understand the term "sex worker" to be more dignified than "prostitute." Others are outraged at any attempt to dignify activity that involves the objectification and commodification of women's bodies, and insist that such activity be called prostitution, with all of the opprobrium that the term connotes. A more academic version of this dispute exists in the field of classics, where some scholars

1 For a detailed discussion of Mesopotamian prostitution, see Cooper 2006, where can be found philological details and references that may have been omitted from this paper. See also Roth 2006.

2 E.g. Jursa 2010: 31. Note that Brunke 2011: 221–222, maintains that in Ur III, at least, fruits and vegetables were delicacies and not part of normal diets.

Jerrold S. Cooper, Johns Hopkins University; anzu@jhu.edu

Fig. 1: Grain grinding installation, Ebla, west palace, ca. 18th–16th centuries BC. After Matthiae et al. 1995: 173.

insist that we moderns need to shed our hang-ups and realize that prostitution was just an occupation like any other, whereas other scholars would say that it may have been legal, but for its ancient practitioners, it was degrading.[3]

In Mesopotamia, as in much of the world even today, most occupations involved, in some sense, selling one's body, since they were physically very taxing, whether involving working in the fields, clearing canals, hauling, construction, or grinding grain. One of the most depressing glimpses of the life of ancient women is afforded by Fig. 1, a room at Ebla in which, ca. 1700 BC, a group of women, probably captives, spent their days at hard, monotonous labor turning grain into flour. Yet, the kind of physical labor performed by prostitutes is different, more fraught, and was so perceived by the ancients. It may

3 Contrast McGinn 2014 with Cohen 2014.

not have been considered sinful (in the religious sense) for a single woman to express her sexuality outside of marriage (Cooper 2009), but prostitution was degrading and "prostitute" was used as an insult (Cooper 2006: 13–14). The unfavorable omen apodosis "the man's wife will become a prostitute" is preceded by "the man's wife will get her husband killed" and followed by "the man's wife will cast a spell on her husband" (Koch 2005: 108–109), all rather dire projections of male anxiety.[4]

At the end of the last century, there was an attempt to show that the word for prostitute in Akkadian, *ḫarimtu*, didn't mean prostitute at all, but rather signified a woman independent of male authority, who was free to enjoy her sexuality as she pleased (Assante 1998, also 2003). As important and interesting as this attempt was, I believe I have shown elsewhere that it was wrong (Cooper 2006: 20), and I was unexpectedly gratified to note that in his broadcast inaugural lecture, the current occupant of the chair in Mesopotamian civilization at the Collège de France enthusiastically supported the existence of prostitution in ancient Mesopotamia.[5]

Why prostitution?[6] It is nearly universal, especially in traditional urban societies. Demand for extra-marital sex existed in Mesopotamia and elsewhere due to, ironically, the centrality of marriage and the emphasis on women's premarital chastity and marital fidelity, in part to ensure the legitimacy of offspring (Cooper 2002).[7] Males in Mesopotamia married relatively later than females, resulting in a pool of young single men, and there were male travelers, military personnel, and workers away from home, yet most women – other men's wives and daughters, and religious celibates – were not sexually available. Demand was there. On the supply side, there were destitute vulnerable women – the widows and orphan girls whom rulers traditionally claimed to protect – as well, no doubt, as wives and daughters from impoverished families who saw no other alternative,[8] and dependent women whose parents or own-

---

4 It is this type of negative apodosis that is found in the oft cited "the *entu*-priestess will have anal intercourse to avoid pregnancy" (CAD E: 325), which should not be taken to mean that the priestess could have sexual relations as long as she didn't conceive, but, rather, that she will become so depraved that she will have illicit intercourse while cleverly concealing the fact. See similar apodoses which imagine the *entu*-priestess stealing sacred property, having intercourse with a temple administrator or fornicating in general (CAD E: 179).

5 But, in fairness to Assante, she denied only that the word *ḫarimtu* means "prostitute," but not the existence of prostitution in ancient Mesopotamia.

6 For a brief general survey of the question, see Howell 2008.

7 See also the discussion of Engels on the origin of monogamy and the importance of premarital chastity and female marital fidelity in Lerner 1986: 22–23.

8 In 18th century Europe, prostitution might be part of a poor family's economic survival strategy (Hufton 1995: 163). See below for the adoption of girls for the purpose of prostituting them in Mesopotamia.

ers might earn income from their sale of sexual favors.[9] A socially sanctioned outlet for male desire was necessary to protect proper wives and daughters from improper advances or attacks; hence, the Middle Assyrian Laws required that married women appear veiled in public, but forbade prostitutes from doing so, visually marking the sexually approachable and the unapproachable (Roth 1997: 167–169).[10] Sumptuary laws in medieval Europe accomplished a similar purpose.

The *locus classicus* for prostitutes and prostitution in Mesopotamia is the address of Enkidu to the prostitute in the Akkadian *Gilgamesh Epic*. Near the beginning of the epic, the wild man Enkidu was seduced by a prostitute who effected his transit from nature to culture, and to friendship with Gilgamesh. In tablet VII, when Enkidu realizes that he is about to die as punishment for offenses against the gods committed in the course of his adventures with Gilgamesh, he turns against the prostitute and curses her. She will never have a normal household or family life, and furthermore, he says,

> "The bed you delight in shall be a *bench*![11] The crossroads shall be where you sit! A field of ruins shall be where you sleep! The shadow of the city-wall shall be where you stand! Thorn and briar shall scratch your feet! Drunk and sober shall strike your cheek!"[12]

The very picture of the classic street whore, plying her trade on the city's outskirts, vulnerable to male violence. And it is precisely "to the shadow of the city-wall," that Ištar, the divine harlot, beckons young men to appease her insatiable desire according to an Old Babylonian song: "Seven for her midriff, seven for her loins (…), Sixty and sixty satisfy themselves in turn upon her vulva (…) The young men have tired, yet Ištar never tires." (Foster 2005: 678)

---

9 Lerner 1986: 133–134 sees the origin of prostitution in Mesopotamia 1. in exploitation of slaves by owners as prostitutes, and 2. in "the pauperization of farmers (…) which led to debt slavery. Children of both sexes were given up for debt pledges or sold for 'adoption.' Out of such practices, the prostitution of female family members for the benefit of the head of the family could readily develop. Women might end up as prostitutes because their parents had to sell them into slavery or their impoverished husbands might so use them. Or they might become self-employed as a last alternative to enslavement." See also her summary of the theories of Engels, who viewed "the institutionalization of prostitution (…) as an indispensable prop for monogamous marriage" (1986: 23).

10 See Cooper 2006: 14 for other distinguishing marks of a prostitute. Lerner 1986: 134–140 has a very insightful, if flawed, discussion of the MAL veiling regulations.

11 The translation of Akk. *dakkannu* remains a problem, despite George's note (2003: 303).

12 George 2003: 640, 115–119 and the more literary translation in George 1999: 58; cf. the MB version of the curse in George 2003: 298, where, in a fragmentary line, Enkidu mentions the prostitute's tavern (for which see below), and cf. Maul 2005: 104, utilizing unpublished Assur manuscripts.

But, returning to the Epic, when the sun-god reminds Enkidu that thanks to the prostitute, he has enjoyed the friendship of his beloved companion, Gilgamesh, Enkidu has a change of heart:

> "My mouth that cursed you shall bless you as well! Governors shall love you and noblemen too! At one league off men shall slap their thighs, at two leagues off they shall shake out their hair! No soldier shall be slow to drop his belt for you, obsidian he shall give you, lapis lazuli and gold! *Ornate* earrings shall be your gift! Ištar, the ablest of gods, shall gain you entrance to the man whose home is established and wealth heaped high! For you the wife shall be deserted, though mother of seven!"[13]

In contrast to the street whore of Enkidu's curse, we have the image of the high-class prostitute or courtesan, plied with precious metals and jewelry, patronized by nobles and high officials, and a threat to established marriages. Significantly, Enkidu's curse had been "a fate not to end for all eternity," (George 2003: 638, 103) so it must persist alongside the subsequent blessing. Enkidu's curse and blessing thus comprise an etiology for the two faces of prostitution, the street whore and the courtesan.

The only explicit Mesopotamian evidence for actual payment for sex is in a Sumerian literary text where Inana, the Sumerian equivalent of Ištar, advertises that her fee when standing against a wall is one shekel, but bending over it is one and a half shekels – a not inconsiderate sum if we realize that a hired man's salary in the Old Babylonian period was one shekel per month. However, Inana doesn't tell us if the wall she leans against is interior or exterior. The ordinary prostitute might well ply her trade at crossroads, the city's outskirts, on the street (Steinert 2014: 144–145), or, as the etymology of the Sumerian equivalent of *ḫarimtu*, **kar-kid**, reveals, dockside (Civil 1976: 190). Lexical texts imagine prostitutes working in fields, prowling the banks of watercourses and haunting ruin hills. The only indoor venue listed is the tavern (**eš$_2$-dam** = Akk. *aštammu*), and it is probably a tavern wall that Inana would lean against when selling her favors. Two Sumerian texts imagine Inana's appearance as the evening star to be like a prostitute entering a tavern in the evening, and in a third text, Inana identifies herself as a prostitute sitting at the tavern gate. The tavern gate is associated with an earthly prostitute in the Sumerian composition *Curse of Akkade*, where one result of the gods' curse is that "the prostitute will hang herself at her tavern's gate," and taverns and prostitutes are associated in Akkadian texts as well.[14]

---

13 George 2003: 642, 152–161, with the more literary translation in George 1999: 59.
14 For documentation for this paragraph, see Cooper 2006.

Fig. 2: Molded clay plaque, Old Babylonian, Girsu. Louvre AO 16681.
After Barrelet 1968: pl. 50, No. 527.

The reason for the association is, of course, the nexus of inebriation and sexuality that was recognized and exploited in ancient times as in our own. The images (Fig. 2) on early second millennium terra cotta plaques showing standing heterosexual coitus from behind while the female, bending forward, imbibes beer through a drinking tube,[15] are not to be taken literally, but, rather, are emblematic of the link between the consumption of alcohol and sexual activity. In the same way, a 17th century Dutch tavern or brothel scene (Fig. 3) places copulating canines next to a man being served alcohol by a woman, to make a similar point. On the interior of ancient Greek wine cups, couples are shown in poses similar to the Mesopotamian plaques (Fig. 4), and in other sexual postures as well, but since the medium is an actual wine cup, references to alcohol are unnecessary, hence absent, in the scenes themselves.

The Mesopotamian tavern, where beer was brewed and dispensed, and, probably, lodgers accomodated, was presided over by a *sābû* "innkeeper" or *sābītu* "alewife" as his female equivalent has been rendered since the early

15 A somewhat outdated catalog of such plaques can be found in Cooper 1975: 262–263.

Fig. 3: Tavern or Brothel Scene, Frans van Mieris the Elder, 1658. Courtesy of Mauritshuis, The Hague.

days of Gilgamesh translations – remember, it is Siduri (or Šiduri), the alewife at the end of the world, who wisely tries to discourage Gilgamesh from pursuing his quest for immortality (George 2003: 148–149).

Fig. 4: Attic Red-Figure wine cup, ca. 470 BC. Getty Museum, 86.AE.294.
Digital image courtesy of the Getty's Open Content Program.

Archeological evidence for taverns has been discussed recently by Xavier Faivre (2013), who called our attention to a wonderful illustration from Africa (Fig. 5) demonstrating that, yes, you *can* drink from such very long tubes, as did our Babylonian women (Fig. 2) and as did Early Dynastic banqueters (Fig. 6) as well.[16] Brigitte Lion (2013: 395) has drawn attention to something very peculiar in the distribution of references to male (*sābûm*) and female (*sābītum*) proprietors of taverns: whereas the male proprietors predominate by far in archival texts, nearly all references to women proprietors are to be found in the

16 Breniquet 2013 insists that most Early Dynastic representations of a vessel with what have been interpreted as drinking tubes projecting from it be reinterpreted as representations of wool processing, but she herself (363 n. 12) admits that our Fig. 5 is indeed a drinking scene, and I believe that, contrary to Breniquet, most of the ED representations are as well, while not excluding the possibility that some may be what she claims. See also the possible drinking tube in the mouth of a figure in the Gunduk banquet scene (Reade et al. 2013: 88–89).

Fig. 5: Tiriki men in Kenya drinking through tubes. Katz and Voigt 1986: 28.

Fig. 6: Early Dynastic stone plaque with drinking scene, Nippur, Inana Temple. 7N 408 (IM 66151). Excavation photo courtesy R. Zettler; cf. Hansen 1963: pl. 5; Boese 1971: 182, N3.

Old Babylonian law codes and decrees, where the male proprietor is absent. The women are responsible for any criminal conspiracies hatched at their establishments, and their activities as creditors are stringently regulated. Even though their male counterparts are known to have engaged in similar financial transactions, and taverns run by males could just as well be frequented by criminals, it is only the women that come under legal scrutiny.

It may be that these alewives had special dispensations from the authorities to operate their establishments, and hence were subject to special regulation.[17] Glassner (1991: 141) has discussed African women who, no longer benefitting from male support, open taverns, and in England and colonial America, licenses to operate inns were given to women without other means of support to prevent them from becoming burdens on the community. Or it may be simply a question of regulating women more strictly than men. But it may also be the case that establishments run by women could differ in some fundamental way from those run by men. One of the only references to a tavern as a *bīt sābītim* "house of an alewife" and not simply a *bīt sābîm* or *aštammu*, is in a famous Mari letter where Šamšī-Adad claims that deserters from his palace have gone to Mari "for partying, for the *bīt sābītim*, and for carousing."[18] Did the *bīt sābītim* promise special pleasures that a tavern run by a male might not? A Neo-Babylonian slave girl who opened a tavern, one Ishunnatu (Joannès 1992, Tolini 2013), acquired equipment and materials to make beer, as well as tables and beds – more beds than tables! We have no smoking gun here, but it is possible, given the association of prostitutes with taverns,[19] that taverns run by women, in some cases, at least, were brothels

17 A less likely possibility is that "female tavern keeper" implied male tavern keepers as well: "If (even) a *female* tavern keeper (...)" A support for special legal status of the *sābītum* could be the use of *bīt sābītim* in FM 5 3, where a list of witnesses in a legal document is followed by this statement: "These persons [were present] in the [*bīt*] *sābītim* [for the writing of this] tablet" (restorations by the editors based on another, unpublished, tablet).

18 ARM 1, 28, now LAPO 16, 2. The translation is very tentative, since it is not clear whether the verbs *bitallulum* and *mēlulum* refer to activities that the deserters want to observe or participate in. For the former possibility, note that *mēlulum* is the verb used to describe the performance of the *ḫuppû* acrobats or dancers (male only) at Mari (Ziegler 2007: 262).

19 Tolini 2013 follows Assante 2002: 32, who asserts that female figure in the scene on plaques like our Fig. 2 is Inana-Ištar, and thus the plaques have nothing to do with prostitution, nor do they link taverns and prostitution. But there is no evidence whatsoever that the figure is a goddess, nor is there evidence for the divinity of any of the figures on other types of sexual scenes on OB molded clay plaques. Deities on OB plaques are always portrayed with horned crowns, and one would not expect otherwise for a major deity like Inana-Ištar.

Fig. 7: Molded clay plaque, Old Babylonian, Larsa. Louvre AO 16924. Author's photo. Cf. Barrelet 1968: No. 591.

of sorts. This could make men especially liable to become indebted to the *sābītum* as opposed to the *sābû*, which might then explain the focus on the former – the *sābītum* – in the law codes and decrees. (This last paragraph is bristling with modals: should, could, may, might. Our documentation is tantalizing, but unspecific on precisely those details that we are interested in uncovering. We can't avoid speculation, but we should not build too much on it).

A major attraction of the Mari court was its music (Ziegler 2007), and the harem included large numbers of female musicians, many of whom were royal concubines. We know that Zimrī-Lîm paid close attention to the physical appearance of the captive girls chosen to be instructed in music: they must be without blemish from the tips of their toes to the tops of their heads; all others should be sent to work in the textile mills (Ziegler 2007: 169). The association of music and musicians with sexuality is ubiquitous; in many cultures, women musicians have turned tricks, and, more relevant to our topic, prostitutes of the better sort and courtesans have cultivated music (and other arts) for the entertainment of their patrons. In 18th century Paris, a parent whose ambition for her daughter was for her to become the mistress of a wealthy or noble patron, would enroll that daughter in the school of the Opéra (Kushner 2013: 80–82). In Mesopotamia, the association of music and sexuality was expressed in the portrayal of musicians, male and female alike, playing nude and even having sexual relations while playing their instruments (Fig. 7).

The women usually play drums and the men lutes; both shapes are suggestive. Note, too, the touches of exoticism, which may be linked to the cap-

Fig. 8: Molded clay plaque, Old Babylonian, uncertain provenance. Louvre AO 12457. Author's photo. Cf. Barrelet 1968: No. 772.

tive origins of some musicians: the nude male lutenist in Fig. 8 has a shaved head but for four long braids, and in a set of Middle Assyrian lead inlays from Assur (Assante 2007), which include copulating musicians, the male in at least two sexual scenes (though not the male musician) is wearing a so-called Phoenician cap (Assante 2007: 370, Cooper 1975: 264). In the improbably posed Fig. 7, the long, unusually patterned hair of the woman has led Ziegler (2007: 50 n. 202) to suggest – correctly I think – that this might be a *kezertu*, a class of women whom I believe to be prostitutes as well (Cooper 2006: 19), alongside the *ḫarimtu*.[20] If the representations we have of nude musicians on Old Babylonian plaques or Middle Assyrian inlays portray actual performance practice and are not simply emblematic of the sensuality of music, then it is difficult to imagine that the musicians were not also available for sexual services.

Was there entertainment in the tavern, provided by women musicians, singers accompanying themselves on the frame drum, who were also available to minister to the customers' physical desires? A mid-first millennium docu-

20 Shehata (2009: 101–103) wisely warns us against seeing both classes of women merely as prostitutes; they seem to have had musical roles as well (especially the *kezertu*).

ment from Uruk describing a raucous nighttime tavern scene that resulted in the arrest of several men and two female singers suggests a positive answer (Kessler 2005: 274–275). Was there lascivious entertainment in the palace at Mari, performances with sex and music so alluring that it tempted functionaries to desert their posts at a more austere court and join Yasmah-Adad's entourage? We don't have much textual evidence for secular musical performance at Mari or anyplace else,[21] no indication of where concerts or performances took place and how they were received, other than that they were supposed to bring pleasure to the monarch.[22] According to Assante (2007: 384), the scenes on the Assur lead inlays may depict a live sex show with music put on by captive foreign performers for the male Assyrian elite, in the palace of Tukultī-Ninurta I. If so, perhaps similar entertainment was provided a half-millennium earlier by Yasmah-Adad's captives at Mari as well.

Beautiful captive musician-concubines were objects of desire at Mari, and could be requested by and granted to other rulers (Ziegler 2007: 37–40). High officials also had harems, and they, too, desired and acquired beautiful women (Ziegler 2007: 40–42), as did, probably, other wealthy elite. The trafficking of captive women and girls was a not unimportant element in what Liverani (1990) might call the system of "prestige and interest" in the "époque Amorite," and certainly, though without the same richness of epistolary documentation, in other ancient Mesopotamian epochs as well.[23]

I would imagine that outside of the royal circle, a beautiful, talented concubine of a wealthy Mesopotamian man need not have been a captive, but may have been the *ḫarimtu* of Enkidu's blessing, the courtesan kept by high officials and wealthy men. But of such courtesans we hear little or nothing. There is an echo of Enkidu's blessing – "for you his wife shall be deserted" – in the worry or the fact that a king would be so captivated by his musician-concubines that he would send his legitimate wives to live outside the palace (Ziegler 2007: 36–37). We find more than just an echo in paragraph 30 of the Laws of Lipit-Ištar

21 Cf. Shehata 2007, to which add the just mentioned Kessler 2005 text.

22 E.g. Ziegler 2007 84 with n. 9: The king will hear (*šemû*) the music and rejoice (*ḫadû*). ARM 22 139 (= Durand 2009 p. 195) from the reign of Yahdun-Lîm records gifts of garments for two musicians (LÚ.NAR.MEŠ) when they performed for the king (*inūma zamāram šarram ušešmû*), while the king was entertaining an emissary from Ešnunna. This is to be kept apart from the *inūma za-mi-ri(-im)* notations from the reign of Zimrī-Lîm, which most likely refer to a midsummer festival (Jacquet 2011: 66–67).

23 Cf. Kuhrt 2001: 14–16. The Mari archives also document important limits to the trafficking of women, as shown by Ziegler 2014.

(Roth 1997: 32) which reads: "If a young married man takes up with a prostitute from the street, and the judges forbid him from going back to that prostitute, but afterwards he divorces his legitimate wife, even after he has paid her divorce settlement to her, he may not marry that prostitute." Archival documents attest to two other cases of married men whose love for another woman threatens their marriages, and in which the authorities enjoin the woman from having further contact with the man. These women are not prostitutes, but as with the law concerning the young married man and the prostitute, these cases testify to the danger that love can pose to marriage (Roth 2006: 29–32; cf. Westbrook 1984). Roth (2006: 35) is certainly correct to insist that the law as well as the actions of the authorities in the two other cases have nothing to do with sexual morality, and everything to do with the other woman's "threat to the economic integrity of marriage and inheritance and to the stability of the social fabric."[24]

But prostitution might also serve to bolster the integrity of marriage and inheritance (Roth 2006: 33–34). The Laws of Lipit-Ištar (Roth 1997: 31) describe a case in which a man's wife is barren but a prostitute "from the street" bears him a child, who becomes the man's lawful heir. The man is required to support the prostitute, but she may not live in his house as long as his legitimate wife is alive. At Nuzi, a woman married off her prostitute granddaughter in hopes of producing a legitimate heir for her property. Yet also at Nuzi, what Westbrook would have called a "wicked uncle" claimed that his deceased brother's son was not a legitimate heir because his mother was not a legitimate wife, but a prostitute. Illegitimacy, nonetheless, could cut both ways: At Old Babylonian Sippar, a man's maternal aunt and uncle insist that the man is not liable for his purported father's service obligations, because their sister had not been married to the man, and she slept with many other men in addition to the purported father, so their nephew's paternity is therefore unknown. Other documents show that prostitutes' children could be put up for adoption or raised by the prostitutes' family members.[25]

Prostitution was a survival strategy not only for impoverished women. A woman who was uncertain about her means of support in old age, or simply wanted to augment her income, might adopt a girl who would be bound to support her later on. In an Old Babylonian adoption contract it is specifically

---

24 Barberon (2012: 26–28) interprets one of the documents (BM 13912 = *RA* 69: 122) very differently: the woman is possibly a *nadītum* of Marduk who is trying to maintain her independence vis-à-vis a too eager suitor. See there for further bibliography.

25 For the cases in this paragraph, see the documentation in Cooper 2006: 15–16; Roth 2006: 33–34.

stated that the adopted girl will be made a prostitute and support her adoptive mother. In a Nuzi contract and a Middle Babylonian contract from Nippur, the adoptive mother may marry the girl off (and collect bride wealth in the process) or prostitute her. These transactions benefitted the birth parents as well, who received payment at the time of adoption, and perhaps were more needy than the adopting mothers. The latter, after all, could afford the initial investment. Again, at Nuzi, a palace decree forbids personnel from having their daughters practice "beggary and prostitution" (*ekûti u ḫarīmūti*) without the king's permission. The palace wants to insure that the royal purse, and not just the parents' pockets, benefit from the income of these activities. Sex work may have been a survival strategy for the very poor, but could also be an investment for the better off.[26]

Finally there is the question of prostitution and cult. I have recently argued (Cooper 2013) that the rites involving "prostitution" *ḫarīmūtum* and women whose activities I believe also involved sexual practices, the *kezertum*-women, at Old Babylonian Sippar and Kiš, show not that sex was performed in the cult, but, rather, that the temple might benefit from sexual activity overseen by temple personnel. Shehata (2009: 101–103) has, in the meantime, studied these rites in great detail, and stressed that the one specific activity that we know the *kezertum* performed was music, and that even the *ḫarimtum* may have been – also – a temple musician. Barberon (2012: 56–58) also emphasizes the role of the *kezertum* as entertainer, insisting that she is not necessarily a prostitute, and in her discussion of the Sippar and Kiš rituals seems to reject the idea that they involved sexual acts (Barberon 2012: 191–204).[27]

Nevertheless, I maintain my speculative conclusion that sexuality was not foreign to the temple. Note in the seal impressions in Fig. 9 from Early Dynastic Ur, the sexual activity above a temple entrance at the upper left. The scene at lower right is one of many that seem to play on the special hair-do of the *kezertum*, and at the upper right we find, again, the nexus of music and sexuality. The use of images from 2700 BC to interpret texts from 1700 BC is not entirely unproblematic (Cooper 2008), but the images are nonetheless very suggestive, if not wholly convincing.

---

26 See the documentation in Cooper 2006: 15–16. The historiola of the man who marries a prostitute and possibly profits from her tavern (MSL 1: 96–97) will be discussed in a forthcoming article. Cornelia Wunsch kindly informs me that the references given in Dandamaev 1984: 132–136 for NB slaves hired out as sex workers by their owners have been improperly interpreted by him.

27 Until the Ur-Utu archives from Sippar are published in their entirety, the rituals accounted for in these texts will remain more mysterious than they need be.

Fig. 9: Early Dynastic Sealings, Ur. Clockwise from top left, after Legrain 1936: Nos. 385, 369, 368, 370.

***

In conclusion, the social role of prostitution was to protect respectable wives and daughters by providing readily available outlets for male sexual desire. To the extent that prostitution was part of tavern life, it contributed, together with alcohol and music, to creating a convivial atmosphere for those men who socialized there. The economic role of prostitution was to provide a means of survival for women and even families with little other recourse, perhaps also providing the extra resources that made pursuing a career in music or dance feasible. If the alewife – *sābītu* – was really a brothel madam, then the institution of prostitution seems to have played some as yet difficult to define role in providing credit during the Old Babylonian period. And prostituting an adopted daughter or a slave was the source of an extra income stream for those with the resources to acquire the girl or slave in the first place.

Bibliography

Assante, Julia. 1998. The kar.kid/*ḫarimtu*, Prostitute or Single Woman? *UF* 30: 5–94.

Assante, Julia. 2002. Sex, Magic and the Liminal Body. Pp. 27–52 in Parpola and Whiting 2002.

Assante, Julia. 2003. From Whores to Hierodules: The Historiographic Invention of Mesopotamian Female Sex Professionals. Pp. 13–47 in *Ancient Art and Its Historiography*, eds. Alice A. Donohue and Mark D. Fullerton. Cambridge: Cambridge University Press.

Assante, Julia. 2007. The Lead Inlays of Tukulti-Ninurta I: Pornography as Imperial Strategy. Pp. 369–407 in *Ancient Near Eastern Art in Context: Studies in honor of Irene J. Winter by her students*, eds. Jack Cheng and Marian H. Feldman. Leiden: Brill Publishers.

Barberon, Lucile. 2012. *Les religieuses et le culte de Marduk dans le royaume de Babylone*. Mémoires de NABU 14. ARCHIBAB 1. Paris: SEPOA.

Barrelet, Marie-Thérèse. 1968. *Figurines et reliefs en terre cuite de la Mésopotamie antique*. Paris: Geuthner.

Breniquet, Catherine. 2009. Buvait-on de la bière au chalumeau en Mésopotamie à l'époque protodynastique? Pp. 359–365 in *L'alimentation dans l'Orient Ancien: De la production à la consommation*, ed. Cécile Michel. Cahiers des thèmes transversaux ArScAn 9. Thème 9. Habitudes alimentaires de l'acquisition à la consommation. Nanterre: ArScAn.

Boese, Johannes. 1971. *Altmesopotamische Weihplatten*. UAVA 6. Berlin: De Gruyter.

Brunke, Hagan. 2011. *Essen in Sumer. Metrologie, Herstellung und Terminologie nach Zeugnis der Ur III-zeitlichen Wirtschaftsurkunden*. Geschichtswissenschaften 26. Munich: H. Utz Verlag.

Civil, Miguel. 1976. *kar*-AK = *kar-kid*. *RA* 70: 189–190.

Cohen, Edward E. 2014. Sexual Abuse and Sexual Rights: Slaves' Erotic Experience at Athens and Rome. Pp. 184–198 in Hubbard 2014.

Cooper, Jerrold S. 1975. Heilige Hochzeit. B. Archäologisch. *RlA* 4: 259–269.

Cooper, Jerrold S. 2002. Virginity in Ancient Mesopotamia. Pp. 91–112 in Parpola and Whiting 2002.

Cooper, Jerrold S. 2006. Prostitution. *RlA* 11: 12–21.

Cooper, Jerrold S. 2008. Incongruent Corpora: Writing and Art in Ancient Iraq. Pp. 69–94 in *Iconography without Texts*, ed. Paul Taylor. Warburg Institute Colloquia 13. London–Turin: The Warburg Institute/Nino Aragno Editore.

Cooper, Jerrold S. 2009. Free Love in Babylonia? Pp. 257–260 in *Et il y eut un esprit dans l'Homme. Jean Bottéro et la Mésopotamie*, eds. Xavier Faivre, Brigitte Lion, and Cécile Michel. Paris: De Boccard.

Cooper, Jerrold S. 2013. Sex and the Temple, Pp. 49–57 in *Tempel im Alten Orient*, CDOG 7, eds. Kai Kaniuth, Anne Löhnert, Jared L. Miller, Adelheid Otto, Michael Roaf and Walther Sallaberger, Wiesbaden: Harrasowitz Verlag.

Dandamaev, Muhammad A. 1984. *Slavery in Babylonia*. Carbondale: Northern Illinois University Press.

Durand, Jean-Marie. 2009. *La nomenclature des habits et des textiles dans les textes de Mari*. ARM 30. Matériaux pour le Dictionnaire de Babylonien de Paris 1. Paris: CNRS Éditions.

Faivre, Xavier. 2013. La bière de la brasserie au cabaret: Approche archéologique. Pp. 375–392 in Michel 2013.

Foster, Benjamin R. 2005. *Before the Muses: An Anthology of Akkadian Literature*. Bethesda: CDL Press.

George, Andrew R. 1999. *The Epic of Gilgamesh. A New Translation*. London: Penguin.

George, Andrew R. 2003. *The Babylonian Gilgamesh Epic. Introduction, Critical Edition and Cuneiform Texts*. 2 vols. Oxford: Oxford University Press.

Glassner, Jean-Jacques. 1991. Les dieux et les hommes. Le vin et la bière en Mésopotamie ancienne. Pp. 127–146 in *Le ferment divin*, eds. Dominique Fournier and Salvatore D'Onofrio. Paris: Éditions de la Maison des sciences de l'homme.

Hansen, Donald P. 1963. New Votive Plaques from Nippur. *JNES* 22: 145–156.

Howell, Philip. 2008. Prostitution. Pp. 526–535 in *The Oxford Encyclopedia of Women in World History*, ed. Bonnie G. Smith. Oxford: Oxford University Press.

Hubbard, Thomas K. (ed.). 2014. *A Companion to Greek and Roman Sexualities*. Oxford: Wiley-Blackwell.

Hufton, Olwen. 1995. *The Prospect Before Her. A History of Women in Western Europe 1500–1800*. New York: Knopf.

Jacquet, Antoine. 2011. *Documents relatifs aux dépenses pour le culte*. Mémoires de NABU 13. FM 12. Paris: SEPOA.

Joannès, Francis. 1992. Inventaire d'un cabaret. *NABU* 1992/64 and 89.

Jursa, Michael. 2010. *Aspects of the Economic History of Babylonia in the First Millennium BC*. AOAT 377. Münster: Ugarit-Verlag.

Katz, Solomon H. and Mary M. Voigt. 1986. Bread and Beer: The Early Use of Cereals in Human Diet. *Expedition* 28/2: 23–34.

Koch, Ulla S. 2005. *Secrets of Extispicy*. AOAT 326. Münster: Ugarit-Verlag.

Kessler, Karlheinz. 2005. Zu den ökonomischen Verhältnissen von Uruk in neu- und spätbabylonischer Zeit. Pp. 269–287 in *Approaching the Babylonian Economy*, eds. Heather D. Baker and Michael Jursa. AOAT 330. Münster: Ugarit-Verlag.

Kuhrt, Amélie. 2001. Women and War. *NIN* 2: 1–25.

Kushner, Nina. 2013. *Erotic Exchanges: The World of Elite Prostitution in Eighteenth-Century Paris*. Ithaca: Cornell University Press.

Legrain, Leon. 1936. *Archaic Seal Impressions*. UE 3. London and Philadelphia: Trustees of the British Museum and The University Museum.

Lerner, Gerda. 1986. *The Creation of Patriarchy*. Oxford: Oxford University Press.

Lion, Brigitte. 2013. Les cabarets à l'époque paléo-babylonienne. Pp. 393–400 in Michel 2013.

Liverani, Mario. 1990. *Prestige and Interest. International Relations in the Near East ca. 1600–100 B.C.* HANES 1. Padova: Sargon srl.

Matthiae, Paulo et al. (eds.). 1995. *Ebla. Alle origini della civiltà urbana*. Milan: Electra.

Maul, Stefan. 2005. *Das Gilgamesch-Epos*. Munich: C. H. Beck.

McGinn, Thomas A. J. 2014. Prostitution: Controversies and New Approaches. Pp. 83–101 in Hubbard 2014.

Michel, Cécile (ed.). 2013. *L'alimentation dans l'Orient ancien: Cuisines et dépendences*. Pp. 303–415 in Cahier des thèmes transversaux ArScAn 11. Thème 9. Habitudes alimentaires de l'acquisition à la consommation. Nanterre: ArScAn.

Parpola, Simo and Robert M. Whiting (eds.). 2002. *Sex and Gender in the Ancient Near East*, 2 vols. CRRAI 47. Helsinki: The Neo-Assyrian Text Corpus Project.

Reade, Julian E. et al. 2013. Gunduk, Khanes, Gaugamela, Gali Zardak – Notes on Navkur and Nearby Rock-Cut Sculptures in Kurdistan. *ZA* 103: 69–123.

Roth, Martha T. 1997. *Law Collections from Mesopotamia and Asia Minor*. 2nd ed. SBL Writings from the Ancient World 6. Atlanta: Scholars Press.

Roth, Martha T. 2006. Marriage, Divorce, and the Prostitute in Ancient Mesopotamia. Pp. 21–39 in *Prostitutes and Courtesans in the Ancient World*, eds. Christopher A. Faraone and Laura K. McClure. Madison: University of Wisconsin Press.

Shehata, Dahlia. 2007. Privates Musizieren in Mesopotamien? *WZKM* 97: 521–529.

Shehata, Dahlia. 2009. *Musiker und ihr vokales Repertoire. Untersuchungen zu Inhalt und Organisation von Musikerberufen und Liedgattungen in altbabylonischer Zeit.* GBAO 3. Göttingen: Universitätsverlag.

Steinert, Ulrike. 2014. City Streets: Reflections on Urban Society in the Cuneiform Sources of the Second and First Millennium BCE. Pp. 123–169 in *The Fabric of Cities. Aspects of Urbanism, Urban Topography and Society in Mesopotamia, Greece and Rome*, eds. Natalie N. May and Ulrike Steinert. Culture and History of the Ancient Near East 68. Leiden: Brill.

Tolini, Gauthier. 2013. The Economic Activities of Isḫunnatu, a Slave Woman of the Egibi Family. *Carnet de REFEMA.* refema.hypotheses.org/766.

Westbrook, Raymond. 1984. The Enforcement of Morals in Mesopotamian Law. *JAOS* 104: 753–756.

Ziegler, Nele. 2006. La chronologie méso-élamite et la lettre de Berlin. *Akkadica* 127: 123–136.

Ziegler, Nele. 2007. *Les musiciens et la musique d'après les archives de Mari.* Mémoires de NABU 10. FM 9. Paris: SEPOA.

Ziegler, Nele. 2014. Kriege und ihre Folgen. Frauenschicksale anhand der Archive aus Mari. Pp. 887–907 in *Krieg und Frieden im Alten Vorderasien* (CRRAI 52), ed. Hans Neumann Münster: Ugarit-Verlag.

Van Dijk, Jan. 1986. Die dynastischen Heiraten zwischen Kassiten und Elamern: eine verhängnisvolle Politik. *Or* 55: 159–170.

Jana Matuszak

"She is not fit for womanhood": The Ideal Housewife According to Sumerian Literary Texts

When studying the role of women in work and society in pre-modern civilizations like Mesopotamia, scholars generally have to resort to an implicit presupposition, namely that, as a norm, their primary role in society was that of wives, and their work was mostly domestic.[1] Substantiating this – undoubtedly not altogether arbitrary – assumption with concrete data, however, tends to be rather difficult, since it is exactly the everyday domestic work that largely goes unnoticed by the textual record. Considering that it was absolutely unnecessary to draft administrative documents concerning basic daily activities, which were taken for granted, this hardly comes as a surprise. However, there is in fact a small group of Sumerian literary texts which specifically deal with typically female tasks, and present domestic work as a defining characteristic of the ideal woman.

1 Corpus

The corpus under investigation consists of a variety of Sumerian literary texts from the Old Babylonian period pertaining to different genres, exhibiting dif-

1 One relatively explicit indigenous description of the role of women is quoted in the opening statement of Harris (1989: 145), although it leaves the exact kind of work performed unmentioned: "In ancient Mesopotamia the center of women's activities was in the domestic sphere just as the locus of men's activities was community or society wide. Mesopotamian women's traditional roles are best summed up in a verse from the late Babylonian hymn to the goddess of healing, Gula, who declares: 'I am a daughter, I am a daughter-in-law, I am a spouse, I am a housekeeper.' And there is no reason to think that any would have wanted it otherwise."

Acknowledgements: I wish to express my sincere gratitude to Cécile Michel and Brigitte Lion for their generous hospitality, and for giving me the opportunity to contribute to this volume. I am also indebted to Konrad Volk for reading a draft of this article, to Pascal Attinger for discussing certain grammatical problems with me, and to Joshua Bowen for correcting my English. All remaining mistakes are, of course, my own.

Jana Matuszak, IANES – Abteilung für Altorientalische Philologie, Eberhard Karls Universität Tübingen, Germany; jana.matuszak@gmx.de

ferent stylistic features and registers, and each displaying different thematic priorities.[2] However, they all share as their ultimate goal the *ex negativo* definition of the ideal woman or, more specifically, the ideal wife. Since none of them are yet available in comprehensive editions, their content shall briefly be outlined.[3]

1.1 *Two Women B / Dialogue 5*

The most informative text regarding the role of women in work and society is indubitably the Emesal (ES) dialogue between two women known as *Two Women B* or *Dialogue 5*, henceforth *2WB*. Presumably a product of the teachers of the Old Babylonian Edubba'a, it has been preserved on more than 60 manuscripts and consists of 230 lines. In alternating speeches, often employing grossly insulting jargon, the two women accuse each other of not being a (good) woman by listing all shortcomings and crimes a woman could possibly be responsible for. The chief allegation is, however, libel, which will not be

2 There are – to my knowledge – no comparable Akkadian compositions. *A Field Full of Salt*, an Old Babylonian diatribe edited by George (2009: 60–66), shares many motives with Old Babylonian texts discussed here (*Ka hulu-a* and MS 2865 in particular), but focuses on character traits rather than work. Some aspects, however, are taken up in the omen literature, for which see the contribution by Virginie Muller in this volume.

3 The model of femininity, as depicted in the literature commonly attributed to the Old Babylonian Edubba'a, has already been discussed by Volk (2000: 16–20), who amply quotes from *2WB*, and includes some aspects not mentioned here. The two dialogues between women (*Two Women A* and *B*) now form the subject of the present author's dissertation, including a comprehensive edition of the latter. *Ka hulu-a* has been edited by the author as part of her MA thesis, which is currently being revised for publication, and an edition of MS 2865 is being prepared for a separate publication. Needless to say, much of what is presented here is still work in progress. Thus, the ultimate line count of *Two Women B* (= *2WB*) is still provisional, and lines are generally quoted from one (or, if necessary, more) representative, ideally published manuscript(s). However, since the majority of manuscripts are unpublished, this is not always possible, and quoting the unpublished sources is unavoidable. In this case, CDLI numbers will be provided for the reader's convenience. Thanks to the generosity of the curators of the University of Pennsylvania Museum of Archaeology and Anthropology, the Yale Babylonian Collection, the Oriental Institute of the University of Chicago, the Cuneiform Library at Cornell University, and the Library of Congress, all relevant tablets have been collated, and copies of the unpublished tablets have been prepared by the author. They will be published as part of her dissertation. The tablets pertaining to the Martin Schøyen Collection are quoted by kind permission of the owner; they will be published in Matuszak and Volk (forthcoming). Tablets published in BE 31 should always be consulted in combination with Kramer's (1940) collations, and the ones in TMH NF 3–4 together with the collations by Wilcke (1976). The great majority of the manuscripts have been identified by M. Civil, to whom I am much indebted.

dealt with here, but allows for the dialogue to end in what seems to be a model court case.[4]

Some of the speeches culminate in the rhetorical question **u$_3$ ze$_4$-e munus-me-en** "And you (think) you're a woman?!" and variations thereof, implying that the rival clearly fails at being a "proper woman," and a "functioning member of society."[5]

1.2 *Two Women A / Dialogue 4*

There are about a dozen mostly unconnected tablets and fragments grouped under the modern titles *Two Women A* or *Dialogue 4*, henceforth *2WA*. Their content is reminiscent of *2WB* (three tablets even contain rhetorical questions similar to the ones in *2WB* just quoted above), but cannot be reconstructed into a complete composition. The fragments therefore could have belonged to one or more Emesal dialogue(s) between women. Apparently, only the middle part of the composition(s), which contains the mutual accusations or insults, is preserved. Hence, it remains unclear whether there is an overarching theme deciding the outcome of the dispute similar to the import of libel in *2WB*.

1.3 *Ka hulu-a*

Named after its incipit, *Ka hulu-a* ("The Evil Mouth") is an unusual and highly complex moralizing composition, which possibly describes the misbehavior of an unnamed and thus paradigmatic woman as an insult or even sin against Inanna.[6] Although her wickedness and wrongdoings are explored in various areas of everyday life and often match the ones expounded in the Emesal dia-

---

4 One of the protagonists calls the other a **kar-ke$_4$**, which in this context can justifiably be translated as 'whore.' As a consequence, the maligned woman is left by her husband, and appeals to a judge in order to clear her reputation, hoping to attain a just verdict against her slandering rival. The court case is described in great detail and comprises roughly the last third of the text.

5 Compare, for instance, *RA* 24: 36 rev. 10, which also offers an Akkadian translation: ⸢*ù*⸣ *atti sí-in-ni-ša-a-at*. Two particularly telling variants comprise **lu$_2$ iri^{ki} tuš-u$_3$** // *ša a-li šu-šu-bi* "city dweller," that is, a civilized member of society, as opposed to non-sedentary "barbarians" (*RA* 24: 36 obv. 12), and indeed **lu$_2$-lu$_7$^{lu}** "human being" (Ni 2268 [BE 31: 28] rev. 10). The latter finds a parallel in debates between Edubba'a affiliates, where similar rhetorical questions occur; see Volk (2000: 25).

6 For the role of the gods in matters of common decency as described by the moralizing literature originating from the Old Babylonian Edubba'a see Matuszak (forthcoming).

logues, a certain focus seems to lie on the fact that she fails to satisfy in bed. While sharing certain structural similarities with hymns, the text is written in Emegir (EG), and thus apparently contains accusations uttered by a male speaker, who, however, also remains anonymous.

1.4 MS 2865

This unpublished tablet also contains insults against a woman. The text partly resembles *Ka hulu-a* in style, though it is much shorter and less complex. It is also composed in Emegir, and ends with a doxology praising Nissaba (and Inanna).[7] Although the composition shares a number of topoi and phrases with the texts introduced above, it does not seem to contribute much to the question of what constitutes a good housewife. Similar to the diatribes against men edited by Sjöberg (1972), the insults – though exceedingly gross – seem more general in nature and do not focus on the addressee's incompetence in household matters as does *2WB*. Solely rev. 8 evokes a topos of interest to the present discussion, which is also well known from *2WB*: **teš$_2$ nu-tuku-e nin e$_2$-a-gen$_7$ mi-ni-in-AK** "She has absolutely no shame, she's acting there as if she were the mistress of the house." The mention of **geme$_2$ urdu** "servants" two lines later likewise suggests a disdainful stance toward (indentured) laborers more elaborately voiced in the other texts (see below).

1.5 Proverbs

Lastly, whenever illustrative of a given point, entries from the so-called proverb collections will occasionally be adduced. This is not only warranted by the sententious nature of many of the assaults, but also by the fact that from the earliest examples of these compilations (dating to the mid-third millennium

7 The last line, rev. 19, reads **^{d}nissaba ⌜za$_3$⌝-mim ^{d}Inanna a-ra$_2$-zu ⌜mah-am$_3$⌝** "Nissaba be praise! Inanna, your ways are august." Since the **za$_3$-mim** doxology usually marks the end of a composition, the praise of Inanna may be a later addition, although the fact that it seems to be the uninterrupted continuation of the line beginning with **^{d}nissaba ⌜za$_3$⌝-mim** is suspicious. The "august ways" of Inanna would also form a nice contrast to the wicked ways of the woman addressed in the diatribe. Compare obv. 2: **ka sun$_7$-na a-ra$_2$-na ga-bi$_2$-ib-du$_{11}$-du$_{11}$** "Her arrogant mouth – I will make them (i.e., everyone?) speak of her ways," which forms the introduction to the verbal assaults which comprise most of the text.

and onwards), they also contained insults, and were demonstrably used as "rhetorical collections" for debates and diatribes.[8]

2 Work

Generally, all moralizing texts found in Sumerian literature emphasize the importance of diligence; the most commonly employed image for laziness is that of a person roaming about (usually expressed by the verbal base **nigen$_2$ / ni$_{10}$-ni$_{10}$**). However, it constitutes such a universal reproach in virtually every didactic text, be it a diatribe, debate, or "Edubba'a text," that it will not be discussed at length here.[9] Interestingly enough, though, prowling around seems to have been perceived as particularly typical of women, as is suggested by a variety of sources: for instance, the *Instructions of Šuruppak* ll. 228–9[10] describe nosily prowling around as a typically female activity: **e$_2$-e$_2$-a i-in-ku$_4$-ku$_4$-ku$_4$ / e-sir$_2$ e-sir$_2$-ra gu$_2$ mu-un-gi-gi-de$_3$** "She's constantly entering all houses, she's craning (her) neck in each and every street."[11] Unsurprisingly, it also figures as an insult in *2WB*. In l. 110 one woman blames the other: **sila-a gub-gub e-sir$_2$-ra ni$_{10}$-ni$_{10}$**[12] "(You are) perpetually standing about in the city

8 See Civil – Biggs (1966: 5–7), Alster (1991/92: 3), and Klein (2003) for *EDPC 1*, and Alster (1997: xxv–xxvi et passim) for the Old Babylonian collections. In my forthcoming edition of *Ka hulu-a* I provide a detailed discussion of its literary dependency on *EDPC 1* ll. 1–14.

9 Compare, for instance, *Father and Son* (Sjöberg 1973): **[sila-a nu-mu]-un-ni$_{10}$-ni$_{10}$-e-de$_3$-en** "You [shan't] prowl around [in the streets!]" (l. 13), **tilla$_2$ nam-ba-e-gub-bu-de$_3$-en / sila-a nam-ba-ni$_{10}$-ni$_{10}$-de$_3$-en / e-sir$_2$-ra dib-be$_2$-da-zu-ne igi nam-bar-bar-re-en** "You shan't stand about on the market place, you shan't prowl around in the streets. Don't look (everywhere) while walking through the alleys!" (ll. 29–31), and the references collected by Volk (2000: 21).

10 See Alster (2005: 98).

11 A proverb (SP 1.174 // SP 7.47) written in Emesal, thereby signaling it as a typical utterance of a woman, which even made its way into the collections of the first millennium, apparently attests to the same fact: **al-di-di-de$_3$-en nu-kuš$_2$-u$_3$-de$_3$-en / i$_3$-di-di-de$_3$-en u$_3$ nu-ku-ku-me-en** "I roam about, I never tire. / I roam about, I never sleep," see Alster (1997: 35) with reference to Lambert (1960: 237 iv 11–14). While the Akkadian translation from the first millennium clearly records the utterance of a first person speaker (*atallak* / [*ul*] *annaḫ* / [*adâ*]*l-ma* / [*ul aṣa*]*llal*), the original Sumerian is notoriously ambiguous. Therefore it is – at least in theory – equally possible to interpret the forms as 2nd singular, in which case the restless addressee need not necessarily be female – it could just as well be a typical saying of a wife to her philandering husband.

12 Quoted from BM 54241 (CT 58 58) rev. 5. *RA* 24 36 rev. 1 adds an Akkadian translation: *mutazzizat rebiātim sāḫirat sūqātim*.

squares, and constantly prowling around in the streets." Furthermore, the arrangement of entries in lexical lists implies a connection between roaming about and prostitution, which is also reflected in a number of literary texts such as *Enlil and Sud* (see Civil 1983), and probably explains why women in particular are so frequently accused of this offense. In the OB lexical list Proto-Lu ll. 713–719 (MSL 12: 59) the **kar-ke$_4$** "prostitute"-section leads to the entry **kar nigen$_2$** "roaming about (at) the harbor" in l. 720, which in turn is the first in a series of entries concerned with roaming about in different places, while in the aforementioned myth, Enlil mistakes Sud for a prostitute simply because she is standing in the streets.

As a matter of fact, admonitions to lead an industrious life expressly addressed to women can be traced back to roughly the mid-third millennium – and not only to the relevant passages in the *Instructions of Šuruppak*. The *Early Dynastic Proverb Collection 1* (henceforth *EDPC 1*, s. Alster 1991/92), for instance, contains the following saying (ll. 102–103): **munus tibir$_2$ nu-tuku / munus addir nu-tuku** "A woman without hands / (is) a woman without wages." This underlines the necessity of labor and implies the imminent threat of poverty if a woman is unwilling to put her hands to work.

The texts under study here are largely written in the same vein. Thus, for instance, one of the protagonists in *2WB* l. 68 criticizes her rival: **kig$_2$-e šu nu-mu-un-da-sa$_2$ / ku$_4$-ku$_4$ e$_3$-de$_3$ a-ab-l[a$_2$]**[13] "(Her) hand is not suited for work: the moment she's begun she already stops, and *lets things slide* (literally: entering, exiting – it [the unfinished work] is suspended)."

However, the professional activities mentioned in the compositions pertaining to the corpus outlined above fall into two groups: base work thought insulting to a (free) woman, and domestic work, which, if not mastered to perfection, would, on the contrary, serve to put any self-respecting woman to shame. In other words, the texts draw a clear distinction between honorable (or esteemed) and dishonorable (or despised) work.

2.1 Base work as an insult

Particularly hard physical labor such as grinding grain was evidently regarded as dishonorable work, since it serves as a recurring insult – the monotony of the task being aptly expressed by reduplicated, and sometimes even quadrupli-

13 Quoted from MS 3228 (unpublished; P342701) rev. 15–16.

cated verbal bases. It is, therefore, unsurprising that there is ample evidence that preferably slave girls were consigned to work in mills.[14]

Thus, in *2WB* l. 44 one of the protagonists sneers at the other: **⸢u$_5$-mu⸣ sur-sur / še ⸢sa-sa⸣-sa / ⸢inda$_3$⸣ gu-⸢la⸣ du$_8$ -du$_8$** [15] "(You are) perpetually pressing oil, roasting barley, baking big breads," while in l. 61 her opponent retorts: **a si a lu$_3$-lu$_3$ {{a}} zi$_3$ ar$_3$-ar$_3$-ar$_3$-ar$_3$-ra**[16] "(You are) drawing water, disturbing water, grinding flour non-stop."[17]

A few lines later, the matter is taken up once more. In l. 86 the first speaker mocks her rival: **⸢e$_2$⸣ inda$_3$ gal$_2$-la muhaldim gal-bi-im** // *bi-it a-⸢ka⸣-[lu i]-ba-aš-šu-ú na-ha-ti-ma-tum ra-bi-⸢tum⸣*[18] "Of the house where there is bread/food, you are its chief cook." Admittedly, it cannot be determined with certainty whether **inda$_3$**/*akalu* is to be understood as "bread" and the irony therefore lies in the discrepancy between the simple food and the title suggesting fancy cooking, or whether it signifies "food" and thus simply ridicules the woman as a service provider (see below). Still, the snarky remark prompts the other woman to return the insult and state gleefully in ll. 96 and 98 respectively: **ir-⸢da⸣ e$_2$-a-ni-im udun pa-⸢pah⸣-a-ni-[im]**[19] "The *pig-sty*[20] is her house, the oven is

14 See Stol (2009–11: 566) § 5: Arbeit, and, for further references, the literature compiled by Molina (2009–11: 563–564); particularly Gelb's (1973) classic study on prisoners of war and Englund's (1991) extensive treatment of female millers in the Ur III period. There is, however, also evidence for slave girls being employed as weavers, although textile work clearly was perceived as 'honorable' work, see below.

15 Quoted from VAT 12579 (FAOS 2: 180) iii 1–3.

16 Quoted from MS 3228 (unpublished; P342701) rev. 6.

17 The signs in the first half of the line are ambiguous in their syntactical relation. According to PSD A/I 163–64. s.v. **a-si-ga**, "clear water" (as opposed to "muddy water," **a lu$_3$-a**) is always written **a si-ga**. Both terms are clearly *ḫamṭu* participles (B+a, which, in the case of **si-g**, renders the *Auslaut* visible). However, none of the manuscripts for this line write **a si-ga**, and *marû* participles in parallelism to **zi$_3$ ar$_3$-ar$_3$-ar$_3$-ar$_3$-ra** are expected (here the final /a/ instead of the expected /e(d)/) is probably to be explained as influenced by the /a/ in the quadruplicated verbal base). As a matter of fact, two manuscripts (UET 6/2 158 obv. 6 and MS 3176/1 [unpublished; P274469] vi 15) correctly write **lu$_3$-lu$_3$** (as opposed to **lu$_3$-lu$_3$-a** in Ni 2268 [BE 31 28] rev. 11 and MS 3228 rev. 6). Therefore, it seems advisable to interpret both **si** (= *sabûm*) and **lu$_3$-lu$_3$** as *marû* participles, with **a** "water" as the respective direct object. The first half of the line thus seems to blame the addressee for disturbing, that is, muddying, the water she is supposed to draw, and hence is at least semantically close to 'muddying clear water,' which would have been the translation of ***a si-ga lu$_3$-lu$_3$**.

18 Quoted from *RA* 24: 36 obv. 3.

19 Quoted from Ni 445 (BE 31: 42) obv. 13.

20 Sumerian attestations for pig-sty (Akk. *irritum*) are rare. Although Erimhuš II 61 (MSL 17: 29) has **ir-dam** (the Sumerian entry in SIG$_7$ALAN VI i 16′ [MSL 16: 100] is not preserved), the fact that the parallelism in *2WB* l. 96 requires a building of some sort, combined with ample attestations of female swineherds and several references to pigs in *2WA* and *2WB* as well as in

her shrine," and: **^{na4}kinkin dam-a-ni(-im) ^{na4}šu-ŠU$_2$ du$_5$-mu-ni(-im)**[21] "The lower grindstone is her husband, the upper grindstone is her child." Although the (reading of) **^{na4}šu-ŠU$_2$** deserves further comment, its identification as the upper grindstone is beyond doubt – not least because of the evident parallelism, which highlights the respective proportions of the big lower and the smaller upper grindstone, matching those of husband and child.[22] The family metaphor maliciously underlines the fact that this base and repetitive task represents the woman's one and only activity, and probably leaves no time for a real family.[23] It is therefore of little wonder that there existed a proverb written in Emesal, which voices the agony of female grain grinders, and their wish to acquit themselves of their duty: MS 2065 (published by Alster 2007: 30, see also Civil 2006b: 122) reads:

i-lu-lu nu-zu u$_2$-gu da-an-de$_2$-e ša$_3$-mu nu-ge$_{17}$-ga-e-še
i-lu-lu nu-zu u$_2$-gu da-an-de-e ša$_3$-mu nu-ge-ga-e-še
e-ri-i qe$_2$-mi u$_2$-ul i-de-e u$_2$-ḫa-al-la-⸢aq⸣-[(ma)] u$_2$-ul i-ma-ar-ra-[aṣ] li-ib-[bi]

Ka hulu-a render the identification of **ir-da** with *irritum* "pig-sty" quite likely. The etymology seems to be unclear, though, as AHw 244 s.v. *erru(m)* II lists *erretu* as a Sumerian loanword, although the opposite seems more likely.

21 Quoted from CBS 6999 (unpublished; P230180) obv. 3; the copula (**-im**) is supplied by Ni 445 (BE 31: 42) obv. 15 and AO 4603 (TCL 15: 6) rev. 2–3.

22 On the **^{na4}šu-ŠU$_2$** see Civil (2006b: 132 f.), who identifies it with the muller (upper grindstone, normally **^{na4}šu**), and tentatively connects it with the much better attested **^{na4}(šu-)U**, since the line from *2WB* just quoted, as well as a few other sources enlisted by Civil, "point to a pronunciation /šuš/." In fact, both U and ŠU$_2$ have a reading /šuš/. Besides, according to Schuster-Brandis (2008: 448), the **^{na4}šu-U** (= *šû*)-stone was probably of diorite or basalt, and was used as a millstone, although the Akkadian word might argue against a final /š/. As it stands, both the **^{na4}šu-min$_3$** and the **^{na4}šu-U** are reasonably well attested, and were undoubtedly used as pounding stones, but all manuscripts of *2WB* known to me (CBS 10211 + N 3545 [unpublished; P265454] iii 4 and CBS 6999 [unpublished; P230180] obv. 3; Langdon's copy of Ni 445 in BE 31: 42 obv. 15 also has **šu$_2$**, while Kramer 1940: 250 reads **u**; the tablet needs to be collated again – if Kramer is right it would of course confirm Civil's suggested identification) clearly write **^{na4}šu-ŠU$_2$**, for which I know of no other OB attestations. Therefore one might tentatively propose that **^{na4}šu-ŠU$_2$** was a literary term (or writing/pun?) for **^{na4}šu-U**, perhaps based on the verb **šu$_2$** = *katāmum* 'to cover,' which would again point to an identification as the upper millstone. In any case, considering the monotony of grinding flour, a reduplicated form analogous to **kinkin** is not altogether unlikely (cf. **kinkin-šu-šu** = HAR *mar-ga-bi$_2$-su$_3$* AN.ŠE$_3$ "millstone (and) its muller above it," listed in ED HAR-ra 91, s. Civil 2008: 77).

23 For a slightly different family metaphor involving the millstone (**^{na4}kinkin**) as the brother of the sharpening stone (**^{na4}gul-gul**) see the *Song of the Millstone* ll. 14′–18′ (Civil 2006b: 125; 127). Interestingly, Bauer (1989/90 [1991]: 85 ad 77 I 3K), draws attention to the fact that the Aztec language knew the millstone as *metlatl* and the muller as *metlapilli* "child of the millstone."

> Sumerian: "As they say: I don't know the work song (sung while grinding flour). I want to get rid of it (the millstone), (for then) I will not grieve (any longer)."
> Akkadian: "I don't know the flour millstone. If I get rid of it, I will not grieve (any longer)."[24]

Incidentally, the motif of grain grinders lamenting their dire fate is already found in *Enki and Ninmaḫ* a 11, where, before the creation of mankind, the younger gods were forced to do the job:[25] **dingir im-⌜ar$_3$-ar$_3$⌝-re-[n]e ⌜zi⌝-bi enim [a]m$_3$-⌜ma-gar⌝-re-ne** "The gods were incessantly grinding (grain), they were complaining about their lives."

Returning to the dialogues, *Dialogue 2* is a witness to the fact that both flour grinding and "commercial" baking or cooking were considered an insult to the whole family. Thus, in l. 170, one of the protagonists taunts the other: **ama-zu inda$_3$ du$_8$-du$_8$ muhaldim iri^{ki}-ka**[26] "Your mother is one who incessantly bakes bread, she's the cook of the whole city!" and adds in l. 173: **nin$_9$-zu-ne lu$_2$ še sa-sa-me-eš**[27] "Your sisters are barley roasters!"

Perhaps it is due to the overt contempt vis-à-vis grain grinders that **zi$_3$-milla** (Akkadian *kukkušum*) "low-quality flour" is twice used as an insult.[28]

---

24 For the substitution of the work song (Sum.) by the flour millstone (Akk.) see Civil (2006b: 122). Contrary to his analysis and translation, I understand *uḫallaq* as a 1st sg. form corresponding to the voluntative/cohortative in the Sumerian line (**da-** as Emesal form of **ga-**, not **ha-**) – mainly because the factitive D stem of *ḫalāqu* means "to make disappear, cause a loss" (see CAD Ḫ: 36 s.v.), and because intentional discarding of the muller (even if it were just wishful thinking) fits the context better. It also allows for a smoother translation, since the direct object (**i-lu-lu**//*erî qēmi*), and the 1st sg. subject respectively, remain the same.

25 The line count follows the forthcoming edition by Manuel Ceccarelli, who generously shared his manuscript with me.

26 Quoted from HS 1606 (TMH NF 3: 42) iii 14′. The manuscript actually contains the non-orthographic spelling **du$_{12}$-du$_{12}$** for **du$_8$-du$_8$**, which is preserved in Ni 4140 (ISET 2: 107) rev.! 3′, N 3246 (unpublished; P278294) obv. 5′, and UET 6/2 153 rev. 10. For semantic reasons, I take the final **-ka** as an abbreviated form of the genitive + copula 3rd sg. rather than a double genitive (*"she of the cook of the city"), although the fact that no duplicate contains the full form (**-am$_3$**) is suspicious (compare, however, the copula 3rd sg. **gub-ba-am$_3$** in l. 171 and the copula 3rd pl. **sa-sa-me-eš** in l. 173). A comprehensive study might show whether the loss of the final /m/ could be caused by the preceding genitive. A good case in point is *Enlil A* l. 16 (7 × garaš$_2$-a-ka vs. 1 × garaš$_2$-a-kam), courtesy P. Attinger. Also see Delnero (2012: 171 with fn. 72), who compiled lines from compositions belonging to the *Decad*, in which all, or all but one or two of the preserved manuscripts, contain an abbreviated form of the copula.

27 Quoted from HS 1606 (TMH NF 3: 42) iii 17′.

28 Quoted from UET 6 157 + 640 rev. 4 (*2WB* l. 145) and CBS 7167 (unpublished; P262200) obv. 3 ("*2WA*"). The lines are indeed exactly the same in both compositions. Also compare SP 12 Sec. D 5: **lu$_2$ nig$_2$ tuku u$_2$-[...]-⌜bi he-gu$_7$⌝-e / uku$_2$ zi$_3$-milla he-g[u$_7$-e]** "The rich man shall eat ..., the poor man shall eat **zi$_3$-milla**-flour."

Interestingly, it is each time combined with **gegge-ga me-luh-ha$^{(ki)}$ dim$_3$**. At first sight, and from a modern perspective, this seems to constitute a downright racist slur, which might be best rendered into English as "black one from Meluhha, *weakling*[29]!" Note, however, that in *Enki and the World Order* l. 221 (see Benito 1969: 97), Enki addresses Meluhha as the **kur gegge** "black country" in his favorable determination of fate, and that in *Curse of Agade* l. 48 (see Cooper 1983: 52) Meluhhans are called the **lu$_2$ kur gegge-ga** "people of the black country," who are bringing luxury goods to Inanna. Therefore, the designation as 'black' – at least in these two compositions – cannot have been discriminatory.

Since by the Old Babylonian period Meluhha had become a largely mythic country synonymous with luxury, it is rather unlikely that it was associated with low-quality flour.[30] Direct commercial relations had ceased, and Meluhhan prisoners of war serving as grain grinders in Babylonia are just as unlikely as **zi$_3$-milla** being an article of long-distance trade. Perhaps "Meluhha(n)" had simply become metonymic with "foreigner," and "foreigners" were usually perceived by the Babylonians as "uncultured barbarians," who, in this case, as it seems, were thought incapable of producing anything but poor-quality flour. Incidentally, this would be in line with the snobbish slur concerning the baking of "big breads" quoted above, since these were also made using plain flour.[31] More likely, however, the joke lies in a manifold contrast of opposites: Meluhhan luxury vs. low-quality flour, black vs. white. Therefore, the line seems to condemn the fact that the poor produce of the addressee fails to match with her showy outward appearance: *Schein* prevails over *Sein*.[32]

Interestingly, also *EDPC 1* ll. 43–48 suggest that grinding grain was normally performed by women, while only the unmarried – scorned – man was forced to see to it himself: **dam nu-il$_2$ / dumu nu-il$_2$ / hulu he$_2$-da-tab-ba / zi$_3$ im-ar$_3$**[33] **/ numun$_2$ nu-tuku /** (only A:) **ug$_3$-da nu-šid** "He who does not support a wife, he who does not support a child – it is doubly bad for him: he grinds

---

29 The meaning of **dim$_3$** here seems to be somewhere in the range of the meanings 2–4 established by Civil (1984: 294 ad 123): 2. "weak, fragile, delicate" (*dunnamu, šerru, ulālu*); 3. "corpse," and, possibly, 4. "figurine."

30 See Heimpel (1993–97: 53–55).

31 Milano (1993–97: 29 § 6a).

32 The similar reproach quoted by Volk (2000: 18–19), however, does not pertain to a dialogue between women, since NBC 7805 does not contain ES forms.

33 Judging from photographs, there are more variants than Alster's (1991/92: 12) score transliteration suggests: manuscript A (Abs-T 218, OIP 99, 255) iii 12a writes **ŠE$_3$ IM HAR**, manuscript B$_1$ (VAT 12655 [SF 26; P010604]) **ŠE$_3$ IM ŠE$_3$ HAR**, and manuscript C$_1$ (VAT 12764 [SF 27; P010606]) ⸢**ŠE$_3$ IM HAR A**⸣. The second **ŠE$_3$** in B$_1$ could either be read **zi$_3$** (**zi$_3$-zi$_3$ im-ar$_3$**) or **še$_3$-** and taken as a verbal prefix (**zi$_2$ še$_3$-im-ar$_3$**).

flour, he doesn't even have grass (to eat?).[34] (A adds:) He is not reckoned among the people." According to this, flour grinding in itself – or rather, flour grinding which served just the immediate family – was not considered shameful, but one of the daily tasks of the ordinary wife quite simply taken for granted (unless she had servants to do the job for her). It only became a matter of scorn if a woman in a subordinate position did nothing but grinding grain all day long – perhaps in a workshop like the one found in L.3135 in the Western Palace Q of Ebla[35] – and supplied a set of clients.

There seems to be a similar background to the several lines in *2WB* which attest to the fact that being the "cook of the city" was considered shameful. Remarkably, there are also a number of indications that it was deemed equally despicable to purchase readymade food. Thus, in *2WB* l. 49 one woman accuses the other of **kaš sa$_{10}$-sa$_{10}$ ag$_2$-šeg$_6$-ga$_2$ gu$_7$-gu$_7$**[36] "buying beer, eating readymade food (literally: cooked things)" and, for further emphasis, repeats her reproach at the end of her speech (l. 54): **kaš sa$_{10}$-sa$_{10}$ ag$_2$-⌜šeg$_6$-ga$_2$ tum$_3$⌝-de$_3$**[37] "She's always buying beer, bringing readymade food." Presumably, only laborers who did not have the time or energy to cook for their own families would use the services of cook-shops – or is it another accusation of laziness? In any case, buying readymade food seems to be synonymous with bad care for the family (see below), since it does not occur as an insult in dialogues between men. Hence, being the 'cook of the whole city' was bad, but not cooking for one's own family was not any better.

Reviewing the references to "base" work collected above, one has to acknowledge that many of these expressions probably would not have been immediately recognized as insults, had they appeared out of context. In other

34 Alster (1991/92: 20) translated "he has no rushes (scl. to sleep on?)," suggesting that the rushes here denote an inadequate form of bedding. Considering that *EDPC 1* ll. 56–57 (quoted from B$_1$ iii 18–19) read **numun$_2$ lul-a / ša$_3$-gar nu si**, in the translation of Alster, "rushes are deceptive, (they) do not satisfy hunger," and that the context is that of a man being forced to look after his own alimentation, it seems more likely that they denote an inferior, insubstantial kind of food. Indeed, *Dumuzi-Inanna W* (s. Sefati 1998: 261/263) l. 32, however metaphoric it may be, suggests that **numun$_2$**-grass was fed to sheep: **u$_2$-gu$_{10}$ ^{u2}numun-gu$_{10}$ udu-gu$_{10}$ ha-ma-gu$_7$-e** "May my sheep eat my herbs, my alfalfa$^?$ grass." Also the fact that **u$_2$**, literally "plant," "grass," also has the wider meaning "food" (cf. CAD A/1: 239 s.v. *akalu* lex. sect.) speaks in favor of this interpretation.

35 Matthiae (1989^2) fig. 88. See the contribution by Jerrold Cooper, in this volume, p. 210.

36 Quoted from Ni 2268 (BE 31: 28) obv. 19. In CUNES 52-08-069 (unpublished): obv. i′ 9, part of the Akkadian translation is preserved: [*ākilat*$^?$] *bu-ša-li*. I am greatly indebted to A. Kleinerman for providing me with excellent photographs.

37 Quoted from Ni 2268 (BE 31: 28) rev. 4; **tum$_3$-de$_3$** is clearly visible in CBS 13917 (SEM 114) rev. 7, Ni 4599 (ISET 2: 89) obv. 10′, and MS 3228 (unpublished; P342701) obv. 15′.

words, identifying certain phrases as insults because we *know* the debates are insulting and sarcastic in nature, runs the danger of being a circular argument. However, some of the lines quoted above are directly associated with poverty or low social status, and it was made clear that paupers were considered as **lu$_2$ nu-kal-la** "scorned people."[38]

Thus, l. 44 (⸢**u$_5$-mu**⸣ **sur-sur / še** ⸢**sa-sa**⸣**-sa /** ⸢**inda$_3$**⸣ **gu-**⸢**la**⸣ **du$_8$ -du$_8$** "(You are) perpetually pressing oil, grinding barley, baking big breads") is directly followed by **lu$_2$ kig$_2$-DU AK du$_5$-mu du-ul-lum-ma mu uku$_2$-e-ne**[39] "Laborer, child of misery,[40] offspring of paupers." Similarly, the speech in ll. 96–102 contains both references to what has been identified as "base work" (l. 98), and to low origin (l. 99–101): **dam e-re-da ag$_2$-ur$_2^?$(//NE)-ra**[41] **gu$_7$-gu$_7$ /**

38 Compare *2WB* l. 30: **du$_5$-mu lu$_2$ nu-kal-la** "child of scorned people," quoted from CBS 14174 + UM 29-13-11-12 (unpublished; P269151) ii 4.

39 Quoted from LoC 36 (unpublished; P272558) rev. 15. The nine manuscripts, in which l. 45 is attested, contain numerous variants, among which the most important ones are: **mu-lu** for **lu$_2$** and **dumu-mumus** for **du$_5$-mu** in Ni 2268 (BE 31: 28) obv. 15. LoC 36 is exceptional in its plene-writing of **du-lum-ma**; Ni 2268 (BE 31: 28) obv. 15, CBS 13917 (SEM 114) obv. 3′, MS 3176/1 (unpublished; P274469) vi 3, and MS 3228 (unpublished; P342701) obv. 5′ write (as expected, considering the r-*Auslaut*) **uku$_2$-re(-e)-ne**.

40 The original meaning of **du-lum** is "toil," see the discussion by Alster (1997: 361 ad SP 2.14) and Römer (2004: 115 sub 105) for further references.

41 The reading and interpretation of this term poses some problems. While CBS 10211 + N 3545 (unpublished; P265454) iii 5 and CBS 6999 (unpublished; P230180) obv. 4 seem to write **UR$_2$(×X?)$^?$**, BM 54241 (CT 58 58) lower edge 3 clearly has **NE**. Ni 445 (BE 31: 42) is unclear and, despite Kramer's (1940: 250) collations, needs to be checked once again. Except for *Dialogue 1*, where the Emegir form **nig$_2$-ur$_2$-ra** occurs in exactly the same phrase, again without orthographic variants (compare, for instance, Ni 4207 [ISET 2: 86] iv 15′ as one representative manuscript), the term does not seem to be attested elsewhere (only the notorious **nig$_2$-ur$_2$-limmu$_2$** "quadruped", which seems unlikely to appear in this context). **nig$_2$-NE** could of course be read **nig$_2$-šeg$_6$** (Akk. *emmum* "hot"), which is in fact attested in three different recensions of Nigga (Nigga 37, Nigga Bil. A i 2′, and Nigga Bil. B 33, see MSL 13: 97, 113, and 115 respectively). Since eating hot or cooked, that is, readymade food, has negative connotations throughout this composition, this interpretation, based on BM 54241 (CT 58 58), seems to fit the context. However, the idea of the term denoting hot food is hardly supported by the other two manuscripts. Although **UR$_2$** and **NE** look rather similar, the texts normally distinguish them very clearly, and the signs are legible enough. Volk (2000: 16–17 with fn. 73) translates the phrase as "Spelzen essend," apparently based on **ur$_2$** = *išdum* "roots," although **ur$_2$** could of course also mean "loin" or "lap." So either the term denotes some poor-quality food (cf. the slur involving low-quality flour above), or the whole phrase conveys an idea similar to SP 2.77 (**anše ki-nu$_2$ ni$_2$-ba gu$_7$-gu$_7$** "Donkey eating its own bed," quoted both in *Father and Son* l. 162 and in *Dialogue 2* l. 127 [cf. HS 1606, TMH NF 3: 42, ii 43′]), in which case the woman would be accused of foolishly consuming something precious which would be needed in a different situation.

ga gu$_7$-a ⸢gi$_4$⸣-in-e-ne u$_3$-du$_2$-da e-re-de$_3$-ne / e$_2$ gi$_4$-in-e du$_3$-a e-re-da šu AK[42] "Spouse of a slave, eating ...! / Breastfed by slave girls, born among slaves. / House 'built' by slave girls, (and) *put up*[43] by slaves."

While alleging a family background of servants seems straightforward enough, the expression **e$_2$ du$_3$-a** "built house" refers to the stability of a house, possibly both in its literal as well as in its wider sense, including the conduct of its inhabitants, and the managing of the household, as a passage in *Dialogue 2* suggests: In l. 178 the expression is used in praise of a mother: **ama-gu$_{10}$ bur-šu-ma lu$_2$ e$_2$ du$_3$-a-kam**[44] "My mother, a wise woman, is a person of a 'built' (i.e. solid) house," which implies that a house built by wise (and wealthy) people is a good thing, but quite the opposite if achieved by a poor slave girl. The same speaker continues boastfully in l. 179: **geme$_2$-ta 10-am$_3$ igi-ni-še$_3$ al-su$_8$-ge-eš**[45] "Ten of the slave girls are standing before her (that is, working for her)," and adds in l. 182: **nin$_9$-gu$_{10}$-ne ame$_2$ ge-na ^{geš}ig-gen$_7$ ab-gub-gub-bu-ne**[46] "My sisters are standing in the solid women's quarters like a door." In this section of the debate, good family members are contrasted with bad ones: ll. 170–173 contain insults against the mother, father, brothers, and sisters of the opponent, while in ll. 178–182 the speaker exhorts the qualities of his own family members.

In fact, dismissive remarks concerning a poor family background are ubiquitous in the Sumerian literary debates and diatribes. Thus, in *2WB* ll. 13–14,[47] the opening section of the debate, one woman assaults the other as **gi$_4$-in dag-ge$_4$-a** "slave girl of the (whole) city quarter" and **du$_5$-mu mu-lu-ke$_4$-ne** "everybody's child", and jeers: **ša$_3$-gal-bi-eš$_2$(//-eš) u$_3$ nu-ku** "(she) cannot sleep for (worry about) sustenance" – in l. 123, toward the end of the dispute, it even says: **ša$_3$-gar-ta uš$_2$**[48] "(she's) dying from starvation." A line from

42 Quoted from CBS 6999 (unpublished; P230180) obv. 4–6.

43 See Attinger (2005: 250–251) for the various meanings of **šu AK** (no. 5.455).

44 Quoted from HS 1606 (TMH NF 3: 42) iii 21, see the collations by Wilcke (1976: 38).

45 Reconstructed from HS 1606 (TMH NF 3: 42) iii 22 and STVC 133 obv. ii 2′; **geme$_2$** instead of **nugun** according to Wilcke's (1976: 38) collations.

46 Reconstructed from HS 1606 (TMH NF 3: 42) iii 25 and STVC 133 obv. ii 5′.

47 Quoted from LoC 36 (unpublished; P272558) obv. 5′–6′. In l. 13, VAT 12579 (FAOS 2: 180) i 24, MS 3425 (unpublished; P252366) obv. 13, and UET 6/3 636 "obv." 6′ have the EG form **lu$_2$**, while N 3066 (+) N 3141 + N 4656 (cf. *UF* 42: 557) obv. 7′ and N 5478 (unpublished; P279697) obv. 1′ have the ES form **mu-lu**. The variant **-eš** in l. 14 is supplied by VAT 12579 (FAOS 2: 180) i 26.

48 Quoted from CBS 6999 (unpublished; P230180) rev. 9. The complete line reads **ehi-ta zi$_2$-[(...)] ša$_3$-gar-ta uš$_2$** "tearing (her hair) out because of lice, dying from starvation," which, except for the addition of **lu$_2$-IM** "liar," finds a verbatim parallel in *Dialogue 1* (see, among other duplicates, Ni 9865 [ISET 2: 92] obv. 1 and Ni 2771 [SLTNi 116] obv. 11). For **ehi zi$_2$** compare

"*2WA*" shows that even having friendly relations with servants was considered shameful enough, since **ma-la(-ga) gi$_4$-in-e-ne**[49] "friend of slave girls" clearly was meant as an insult. Lastly, in *Ka hulu-a* l. 8 the addressed woman is slandered as a **dumu-munus lu$_2$ nig$_2$ nu-tuku**[50] "daughter of a pauper (literally: a man who does not own a thing)."

Thus, reviewing the references presented so far, the texts propagate the general necessity of diligence, but at the same time show no appreciation for hard physical labor, since it was equated with low social status. Accordingly, (indentured) laborers are haughtily treated with contempt, regardless of which circumstances might have forced the poor into their current situation in the first place. However, the texts also seem – at least in part – to reflect a certain reality, since they confirm the connection between base work and low social status, which can be deduced, for instance, from records documenting the employment of slave girls in mills. In this respect, it might be noted in passing that overt contempt for (female) grain grinders is not limited to the texts discussed here. Compare *Lugale* ll. 457–462, where Ninurta decrees the fate of the Sharpening Stone (**^{na4}gul-gul**) and the Millstone (**sag-gar**):[51]

sag nu-kal-la si-ig ha-b[a]-ra-an-zi$_2$-ig$_3$
ša$_3$-gar kalam-ma-še$_3$ gar-ba-ni-ib šu iri^{ki}-za he$_2$-eb-si
sag he$_2$-šal ur-sag geme$_2$-e-ne he$_2$-me-en
ul$_4$-ab sar-ra-ab hu-mu-ra-ab-be$_2$ mu-bi he$_2$-e[b$_2$]-še$_{21}$
i$_3$-ne-eš$_2$ nam-tar-ra ^{d}nin-urta-ka
u$_4$-da ug$_3$-e kig$_2$ ge$_{17}$ di-še$_3$ ur$_5$ he$_2$-na-nam-me

A weak lowly worker will verily be assigned to you.
Be ready for the hunger of the country! They will place (you) into the hands of your city.
You shall be *slighted*, you shall be the hero of the slave girls!
"Hurry! Run!" they will say to you, thus they will call you.
And now the fate decreed by Ninurta:
"(As of) today, with regard to the people performing painful work, it shall be thus!"

OB Lu A 395 (MSL 12: 169): **lu$_2$ ehi zi$_2$-zi$_2$** = *bu-qu$_2$-mu* "deloused man" (cf. CAD B: 97 ff. s.v. *baqāmu* "to pluck") and Izi J ii 12 (MSL 13: 213): **ehi zi$_2$-zi$_2$** = *up-pu-lu* "deloused" (cf. CAD U and W: 187 s.v. *uppulu* B "to delouse"). The reading **ehi** is suggested by the variant **e-eh$^?$** // **e-hi** in Cavigneaux – al-Rawi (2002: 26 l. 21). According to P. Attinger (personal communication), the vocalic *Auslaut* is further evidenced by the fact that the ergative (-**e**) is never realized graphically. Also compare Peterson (2007: 257 ff., and 260 f. in particular).

49 Line reconstructed from CBS 15008 + N 3635 + CBS 15129 obv. 10′ (unpublished; P269587) obv. 19′, HS 1519 (TMH NF 4 38) obv. 1, and Ni 2377 (BE 31 36) obv. 13.

50 Quoted from WB 169 (OECT 1: 13) i 8.

51 The Sumerian is quoted using Civil's (2006: 133) eclectic text; for a score transliteration and a complete edition see van Dijk (1983).

The speech abounds in sarcasm. While **lu$_2$ nu-kal-la,** "lowly, scorned person" is a ubiquitous slur in the Sumerian dialogues and diatribes, a weak worker (**sag**) is naturally absolutely unfit for the laborious task of flour grinding. Considering that Ninurta decrees an evil fate, it cannot even be excluded that the passage suggests that it was deemed particularly insulting for a stone to be placed in the hands of women. While the suspicious Emesal form **zi$_2$-ig$_3$** instead of **šum$_2$** in l. 457, attested in all preserved manuscripts, already hints at the fact the weak lowly workers are likely to be female, l. 459 leaves no doubt about that: in **ur-sag geme$_2$-e-ne** "hero of the slave girls" the sarcasm could not be plainer. In this context, it is not altogether unlikely – though impossible to prove – that the use of Emesal in Ninurta's speech was a means of mockery in itself.

2.2 Domestic work regarded as defining of womanhood

While frowning upon base, repetitive, and physically exhausting work, for which no further qualifications were needed, the texts under study at the same time highlight the importance of tasks which did require certain skills, or involved more responsibility. Every self-respecting woman who at one point would be the female head of a family household was supposed to master them to perfection – to the extent that these tasks were regarded as the essence of womanhood. According to the texts, they comprised the management of the household, care for husband and children, textile work, as well as the sexual satisfaction of the husband and childbirth.

2.2.1 Management of the household

Considering the frequency of taunts targeted at an imprudent or even harmful management of the household, one can surmise that administering the family estate and fortune constituted one of the main tasks of the matron. Thus, one of the protagonists of *2WB* repeatedly accuses her rival of failing at properly managing the household, and the women's quarters in particular. In l. 41 she rants: **ame$_2$ nu-mu-un-ge-en e$_2$ a-ra$_2^!$-še$_3^!$ nu-mu-mar (//gar)**[52] "She didn't establish the women's quarters. As regards the management of the house, she doesn't set it to rights (literally: the house, as regards (its) ways, she did not set them)" – the importance of firmly establishing the women's quarters had

52 Quoted from Ni 2268 (BE 31: 28) obv. 11; 3 × **gar** vs. 2 × **mar**.

already been highlighted in *Dialogue 2* ll. 178 and 182 quoted above. In a subsequent speech (l. 50), she mockingly asks: **i-bi$_2$-za nu-um-ga$_2$-ga$_2$-an al$^!$-⸢gal$_2$⸣ nu-⸢ub-be$_2$⸣<-en>**[53] "Don't you pretend that everything is fine, although in fact you're incurring losses (literally: Don't you incur losses (and) say 'it is there')?" Finally, she returns to the topic toward the end of the dispute in l. 134: **e$_2$-a-na hulu ⸢ame$_2$-še$_3$⸣ la-ba-ab-du$_7$**[54] "In her house she is evil, she is not suited to (look after) the women's quarters."

It emerges from this that it was the responsibility of a wife to manage the household in such a way as to avoid financial loss, and, if possible, even to augment the family's wealth. The protagonists of *2WB*, however, frequently accuse each other of theft – also within their own household: Thus, in l. 23 one woman calls her rival **mu-zuh e$_2$-a-na**[55] "*robber* of her own house," and three lines later accuses her of **e$_2$-DUB-ba du$_8$-du$_8$**[56] "opening the storehouse." In l. 27, she seems to round off her argument in a more metaphorical way – if I am correct in understanding **^{geš}kun$_4$ ^{geš}bala-gen$_7$ e$_2$-a ga-ga-ga**[57] "(she's) bringing the ladder like a spindle into the house" as an allegation of trying to get access to things stored out of her reach instead of doing what she is supposed to do: spinning. The accused, however, seems unimpressed, and returns the reproach (l. 34): **šaha zuh-a gu$_7$-gu$_7$ ze$_2$-eh tur zuh-a šu-ni-še$_3$ ⸢la$_2$-a⸣**[58] "(She's) eating stolen pigs, (she's) *holding* a stolen piglet *in* her hand (literally: a stolen piglet is bound to her hand)," and adds in l. 36: **ge$_6$-gen$_7$ di-di ^{im}šu-rin-na-ta utul$_2$ titab$_2$ ir-ir**[59] "(She's) creeping about like the night, taking away

---

53 Quoted from MS 3228 (unpublished; P342701) obv. 10′. The (grammatically obligatory) **-en** at the end of the line is supplied by VAT 12579 (FAOS 2: 180) iii 13, Ni 4599 (ISET 2: 89) obv. 5′, and N 1736 (unpublished; P276857) i 4′.

54 Line reconstructed from UET 6 157 + 640 obv. 11′ and CBS 14174 + UM 29-13-001 (unpublished; P269151) iv 3′.

55 Quoted from UM 55-21-434 + UM 55-21-283 (unpublished; P257217) obv. 1. The term **mu-zuh(KA)** is not entirely clear, but will be discussed extensively in the forthcoming edition of *2WB*. Suffice it to say that within this context **mu-zuh** as Emesal word for **lu$_2$-zuh** or **ni$_2$-zuh** "thief" is likely, but cannot be proved with absolute certainty, since there is no pertinent entry in the Emesal Vocabulary.

56 Quoted from Ni 4509 (ISET 2: 22) obv. 3′. Also compare CBS 15008 + N 3635 + CBS 15129 (unpublished; P269587) obv. 10′//Ni 2324 (SLTNi 130) ii 7′//Ni 2377 (BE 31 36) obv. 4 ("*2WA*"): **e$_2$ ma-al taka$_4$^{a}** "*forcing open* the house." Since the previous line mentions a debt (**ku$_3$ ur$_5$-ra**), this might constitute a further reference to theft. A little later, the accusation seems to be more explicitly phrased in CBS 15008 + N 3635 + CBS 15129 rev. 2′//HS 1519 (TMH NF 4 38) obv. 15: **tur$_3$ bur$_3$-bur$_3$ ⸢amaš-e$^?$⸣ [(x)] zi$_2$-⸢ih$^?$⸣ zuh$^?$-zuh$^?$⸣** "Constantly burgling the animal stall."

57 Quoted from UM 55-21-434 + UM 55-21-283 (unpublished; P257217) obv. 4.

58 Quoted from Ni 2268 (BE 31: 28) obv. 5.

59 Quoted from Ni 2268 (BE 31: 28) obv. 7.

the bowl with the grains cake from the oven."[60] While a stealing wife, likely to ruin the whole family, certainly marks a peak in the spiteful rhetoric, it goes without saying – so the texts imply – that such a woman would probably also fail at the other tasks performed by a woman who actually deserves the title.[61]

2.2.2 Care for the family

Already in the ED version of the *Instructions of Šuruppak* AbSt 123′–124′ we find the saying **dam tuku še$_3$-du$_7$ / dam nu-tuku šer$_2$-dib$_2$ DU**, which in the "Standard Version" ll. 185–186 is expanded to **lu$_2$ dam tuku a$_2$ šu im-du$_7$-du$_7$ / dam nu-un-tuku še-er-tab-ba mu-un-nu$_2$**, on which relies Alster's (2005: 88) translation "A married man is well equipped; (but) an unmarried man sleeps in a haystack."[62] Although the change from DU to **nu$_2$** remains difficult to explain, the couplet evidently contains a comparison between the married and the unmarried man, equating the existence of a wife with care and comfort.

Care for the family, broadly speaking, encompassed three different things: first, it seems to have been the responsibility of a matron to feed her family. A distant reflection of this – abounding with sarcasm – can be found in *2WB* l. 53: **še deš sila$_3$-am$_3$ ⸢ab-pa$_3$-de$_3$⸣-en-⸢na-zu⸣**[63] "It's one liter of barley that you've found." To my mind, the allegation that the addressee depends on the off-chance of finding food somewhere in the street might suggest that she is too lazy to work and therefore does not receive her wage, viz. her allotment of

---

60 For **titab$_2$** see Sallaberger (2012: 318–320). The **utul$_2$**-bowl is also mentioned in *Dialogue 1*, where, however, the allegation seems to be clumsiness rather than theft: **^{dug}utul$_2$ ar-za-na ^{im}šu-rin-na-ta e$_{11}$-da-zu-ne / ba-e-de$_3$-gaz tu$_7$ / utul$_2$ al-bil$_2$-la-ta** "When you lift the **arzana**-bowl out of the oven, it breaks because of you (literally: with you), since the soup/bowl is boiling hot," quoted from HS 1536 (TMH NF 3: 43) obv. ii 10′–11′ and CBS 13387 (SEM 65) rev. 8–9. The unusual syntax with the predicate of the main clause at the beginning of the line probably highlights that everyone else knows that a bowl, which had been sitting in the oven, tends to be hot.

61 Incidentally, a wife stealing from her husband is recorded in the famous model court case first edited by van Dijk (1963: 70–77), reference courtesy of an anonymous referee. There, theft and adultery are named as the two chief allegations, which result in divorce and public humiliation.

62 Although **šu du$_7$** would have been expected on the basis of the OB parallel, the sign in Abs-T 323+393 (for a copy of the joined tablets see Civil 1984: 282–3, and for photographs see Alster 2005, pls. 26–27) is clearly **ŠE$_3$**, and therefore (if not a mistake for **ŠU**) seems to be a verbal prefix. The *Instructions of Šuruppak* provide ample attestations for ED **še$_3$-** vis-à-vis OB **ši-** or **ša-**.

63 Quoted from CBS 13917 (SEM 114) rev. 6.

barley, which results in her being unable to feed her family. Indeed, as Wilcke (1998: 27) has demonstrated, even old women received 20 liters of barley a month (0.66 liters per day), so one liter would scarcely have sufficed to feed a family.[64] However, instead of laziness, the taunt could also quite simply insinuate poverty. SP 1.5 might point in that direction, as it illustrates quite drastically the fate of the pauper, who will never find all he needs, and therefore arrives at the cruel conclusion that he had better be dead: **uku$_2$ ha-ba-ug$_7$ nam-ba-da-til$_3$-i / inda$_3$ i$_3$-pa$_3$ mun nu-pa$_3$ mun i$_3$-pa$_3$ inda$_3$ i$_3$-pa$_3$ / gazi i$_3$-pa$_3$ uzu nu-pa$_3$ uzu i$_3$-pa$_3$ gazi nu-pa$_3$ / i$_3$ i$_3$-pa$_3$ šagan nu-pa$_3$ šagan i$_3$-pa$_3$ i$_3$ nu-pa$_3$** "The pauper should die, he should not live. Whenever he finds bread, he finds no salt. Whenever he finds salt, he finds no bread. Whenever he finds condiments, he finds no meat. Whenever he finds meat, he finds no condiments. Whenever he finds oil, he finds no jar. Whenever he finds a jar, he finds no oil."

Secondly, care for the family surely must have included the raising of children, although for some reason this does not play a prominent role in the texts discussed here. *Ka hulu-a* l. 19 seems to be an exception here, but the break at the end of the line prevents a thorough understanding: **^{šaha}ze$_2$-eh tur nu-mu-un-zu-a ša$_3$-du$_{10}$-bi ga-ta TAR nu-mu-un-x-[x]**[65] "The ignorant little sow does not [...] its *weaned* piglets." Possibly, the irony lies in the fact that the sow itself is too inexperienced to provide proper care for its piglets. The line might also condemn avarice, which in these texts is sometimes hard to distinguish from simple carelessness. Incidentally, the same holds true for the following quote from *2WB* ll. 51–52: **dam-zu tu$_9$ nu-um-mu$_4$ ze$_4$-e $^{\text{tu}_9}$nig$_2$-dara$_2$-e ⌜mu$_4$⌝ / gu-du-zu am$_3$-ta-la$_2$**[66] "Your husband has no clothes to wear (literally: does not wear clothes); you yourself are wearing rags. / Your butt sticks out from them!" Is the woman, who – thirdly – is evidently responsible for her family's clothing, thoughtless, lazy, cold-hearted, and stingy, or simply too poor to afford new clothes?

---

64 I am grateful to both anonymous referees for their comments on this point, as well as for the reference to Wilcke (1998).

65 Line reconstructed from WB 169 (OECT 1: 13) i 19, MS 2354 (unpublished; P251573) obv. 19, and MS 2714 (unpublished; P251727) obv. 1–2.

66 Lines reconstructed from MS 3228 (unpublished; P342701) obv. 11′–12′ and CBS 13917 (SEM 114) rev. 5. Ni 4599 (ISET 2: 89) obv. 8′ writes **$^{\text{tu}_9}$ag$_2$-dara$_2$ mu$_4$-mu$_4$**.

2.2.3 Textile work

In fact, there are far more indications among the texts under study that the fabrication of textiles was considered a very important task of a wife. Already in *EDPC 1* l. 205 (see Alster 1991/92: 19) we find the exclamation: **e$_2$-gu$_{10}$ tu$_9$ (-gu$_{10}$) ga-tuku$_5$** "Let me weave (my) garments for my house!"[67]

According to SLHF vii (34–36), the "assigned work quota of 'womanhood' (**nam-munus**)" was 20 shekels of wool.[68] Considering that "womanhood" is at stake in both dialogues between women, as shown by the rhetorical questions quoted at the beginning, this entry further testifies to the fact that textile work was regarded as a specifically female task. Needless to say, the two protagonists in *2WB* frequently accuse each other of failure in this matter. Thus, in *2WB* l. 42 one slanders the other: **dam-a-ni in-TAR gu-⸢ni⸣ gu tab-ba$^!$ li-bi$_2$-in-tuku**[69] "She keeps her husband short: she only gives him (clothes made of) poor quality yarn (literally: she cuts her husband, she does not let his thread have a double thread)," which her opponent shrugs off a few speeches later, replying in l. 67: **siki nu-mu-un-da-peš$_6$-e / ^{geš}bala nu-mu-un-da-nu-nu**[70] "She cannot comb wool, she cannot operate a spindle." Textile work – as opposed to, for instance, grinding grain – does require a certain set of skills, and, while considered a typically female task, constituted an important contribution toward the welfare of the family. It is, therefore, easy to perceive why the aforementioned reproach could serve as such a devastating insult.

Taunts directed at a woman's inability to perform textile work, however, are not restricted to *2WB* alone. Although the following line of "*2WA*"[71] is too fragmentary to determine what might have been insulting about **siki i-ni-in-zi$_2$-zi$_2$** "she is always plucking wool there," it still presents textile work as a typically female task. Another line culled from manuscripts attributed to "*2WA*" is again targeted at, not so much lack of technical skill, but avarice: **$^{\text{tu}_9}$nu-la-**

67 Alster's ad loc. transliteration **e$_2$-mu túg-mu tug$_5$(TAG)-ga** and his (more or less) consequent translation "My house weaves my cloth" (p. 21) do not take into account that the verbal base, which should be read **tuku$_5$**, has a vocalic *Auslaut*, and thus renders ***tuku$_5$-ga** impossible. Rather, **GA** is to be understood as a cohortative prefix.

68 See Roth (1995: 53): **1/3 ma-na siki eš$_2$-gar$_3$ nam-munus al$^?$-x he$_2$-e** "20 shekels of wool, the assigned work quota of 'womanhood' ..."

69 Quoted from Ni 2268 (BE: 28) obv. 12.

70 Quoted from MS 3228 (unpublished; P342701) rev. 13–14.

71 Reconstructed from CBS 15008+N 3635 + CBS 15129 (unpublished; P269587) obv. 13′, Ni 2324 (SLTNi 130) ii 10′, and Ni 2377 (BE 31 36) obv. 7

zu dam-zu na-ab-ag$_2$-gen ša$_3$-zu-a he$_2$-en-kur$_2$[72] "You don't even grant your husband your ...-garment.[73] You really are wicked at heart!"

Also *Ka hulu-a* l. 46 contains a reference to textiles which was indisputably meant as an insult, although the exact interpretation of the imagery might escape the modern reader: **[x x I]B$^?$ ⌜tu$_9$$^?$⌝-ba-na gu-keše$_2$ nig$_2$-la$_2$-⌜na⌝**[74] "[*Ra*]*g*$^?$ *of her cloth ration, thread of her ribbon.*" The assault seems to operate in the same way as **zi$_3$-milla** "low-quality flour" discussed above, namely by equating the woman with her low-quality produce. But even without the purport of this line the evidence is sufficiently clear in presenting textile work such as combing wool, spinning, and weaving as crucial tasks typically performed by women – and every failure in this field as threatening a woman's claim to womanhood.

2.2.4 Sex and childbirth

The texts under investigation leave no doubt that both the sexual satisfaction of the husband, as well as childbirth, were considered as tasks of a 'professional' wife. Consider *Ka hulu-a* l. 7: **ša$_3$-dur$_2$-re**[75] **pa$_3$-da anše nu-mu-un-kuš-am$_3$**[76] "Destined to (make use of her) womb, but she's a donkey widow (that is, does not give birth as she is supposed to)." As mentioned above, *Ka hulu-a* lays a certain emphasis on satisfying a man in bed as being an important skill for a woman or (prospective) wife. Although unquestionably a prerequisite for having children, sex is by no means reduced to its reproductive function, but rather the good looks of a woman, and her willingness to give the man pleasure, also play an important role. Thus, in ll. 8–9 we read: **dumu-munus lu$_2$ nig$_2$ ⌜nu⌝-tuku galla$_4$^{la}-a-ni nu-mu-un-na-kal-la / munus lu$_2$ nu$_2$-da-a-ni nu-dul-dul dam-a-ni nu-keše$_2$-da**[77] "Daughter of a pauper, whose vagina is

72 The complete line of "*2WA*" is preserved in CBS 9863 (unpublished; P265166) rev. 3; more fragmentary duplicates are N 3505 (unpublished; P278534) obv. ii 4′, CBS 7910 (unpublished; P262873) rev. 2′, and perhaps UM 29-13-561 (unpublished; P255497) obv. 10′.

73 Apart from the entry **nu-la** = MIN (*al-ma-tu*) "widow", following **nu-siki** = *e-ku-t[u]* and **nu-siki** = *al-ma-tu* in the "unplaced Lu-fragment" ND 4373 vi 6′, I know of no other attestation of the term. Given the context, it probably denotes a poor-quality garment unfit for a (married) man.

74 Quoted from WB 169 (OECT 1: 14) ii 24; the beginning of the line might have once contained the **^{tu9}nig$_2$-dara$_2$(IB)** = *ulāpum* "rag."

75 **ša$_3$-dur$_2$** is here interpreted as an unorthographic spelling for **ša$_3$-tur$_3$** = *šassūrum* "womb."

76 Line reconstructed from WB 169 (OECT 1: 13) i 7, and MS 2354 (unpublished; P251573) obv. 7; the line is in fact inspired by *EDPC 1* ll. 18–19.

77 Line reconstructed from WB 169 (OECT 1: 13) i 8–9, and MS 2354 (unpublished; P251573) obv. 8–9.

worthless to him. / Woman who does not 'cover' the man who sleeps with her, who does not succeed in making her husband stay with her (literally: who does not bind her husband)." *Ka hulu-a* l. 15 metaphorically describes her genitals as a locked door, preventing men from tasting her pleasures: **ka$_2$-zu ka$_2$ ⌜kuru$_{13}$⌝-gen$_7$ al-keše$_2$-da lu$_2$ gu$_3$ de$_2$-a nu-gal$_2$**[78] "Your 'gate' is locked like a gate of a granary. (That's why) there is no prospective husband (literally: a chosen man)", while l. 17 states quite bluntly: **galla$_4$^{la} tur-tur-ra lu$_2$ nu$_2$-da-a-ni la-ba-an-hul$_2$-l[e]**[79] "No man who sleeps with her takes pleasure in her too small vagina."

Conspicuously, such insults are comparatively seldom found in the Emesal dialogues – maybe because it is not a male speaker who is raging against a woman he evidently despises, but (allegedly) two women harassing one another? In any case, *2WB* ll. 148–9 are written in virtually the same vein as the insults in *Ka hulu-a*, ridiculing both the looks and the sexual skills of the respective rival: **gu-du zara$_5$(BAD; //zar) galla$_4$^{la} tur siki galla$_4$$^{l[a]}$ gid$_2$-g[id$_2$] / pe-ze$_2$-er HAR lu$_2$ ša$_3$-la$_2$ pap-h[al]-la**[80] "... butt, (too) small vagina, (too) long

---

78 Quoted from WB 169 (OECT 1: 13) i 15. Admittedly, this slur could also be directed at her incapability of conceiving and bearing children.

79 Line reconstructed from WB 169 (OECT 1: 13) i 17, and MS 2354 (unpublished; P251573) obv. 17.

80 Quoted from CBS 10211 + N 3545 (unpublished; P265454) iv 6′–7′. The rare reading of BAD (cf. Ea II 82 [MSL 14: 250] **za-ra** = BAD = *ṭa-mu-u$_2$* "to spin, twist, braid, entwine", s. CAD Ṭ: 45 s.v.) is confirmed by ZAR in CBS 14174 + UM 29-13-001 (unpublished; P269151) iv 16′. *ṭamû* is usually used with cords and the like; its meaning in this context remains opaque. UET 6 157 + 640 rev. 7 writes **galla$_4$^{la}** instead of **ša$_3$-la$_2$**. The context and the similar line in UM 29-15-559 A (unpublished; P256317) suggest that **pe/be$_5$-zi$_2$-ir** in CBS 10211 + N 3545 iv 7′ and BM 16902 (CT 42 44) obv. 12 is a variant of **pe/be$_5$-en-zi$_2$-ir**, for which see Civil (2006a). As a Semitic loanword, **pe/be$_5$-zi$_2$-ir** seems to represent its Akkadian equivalent *biṣṣūrum* more faithfully than the dissimilated /pi/enzir/ or /bi/enzir/. Note that Civil (2006a: 58) proposes that, given its occurrence in dialogues and proverbs, "**be$_5$-en-zé-er** could very well be a 'vulgar' synonym of **gal$_4$-la**." The correct reading and interpretation of HAR, which qualifies **pe-ze$_2$-er**, is unclear in this context. **lu$_2$ ša$_3$-la$_2$** is probably identical with **lu$_2$ ša$_3$-la$_2$-la$_2$** = *ša ka-⌜ar-ša pe-ḫu-ú⌝* "one whose body/womb/innards is/are blocked" in OB Lu B vi 6 (MSL 12: 185); perhaps it is semantically similar to insults like **gu-du keše$_2$** "blocked butt" in *Dialogue 1* l. 11 (quoted from UM 55-21-315 [unpublished; P257384] obv. 11) and *Diatribe C* obv. 10′. Because of the highly elliptical syntax it is not quite clear how **lu$_2$ ša$_3$-la$_2$** and **pap-hal-la** relate to each other. Until now, a noun had been followed by a qualifying adjective. Therefore, **pap-hal** in this case probably does not denote "legs" (see CAD P: 517 ff. s.v. *purīdu* A), but rather something in the semantic range of *pušqu* (see CAD P: 543 s.v.) which has to do with narrowness. Since the two lines in question are mainly concerned with (too small or, apparently, blocked) body orifices, **ša$_3$** = *karšu* (cf. CAD K: 225 s.v.: "stomach, belly, womb, body") has been interpreted accordingly. Still, the translation offered above is tentative at best.

pubic hair / ... vagina, whose *very narrow genitals are blocked*!" While derogatory comments on the female rival's private parts can also be found in UM 29–15–559 A ("*2WA*") rev. 12: **[siki gal]la$_4$^{la} si$_4$-si$_4$ pe-en-⸢zi$_2$⸣-ir bu-ud-bar-r[a]**[81] "reddish pubic hair, *lame* vagina," there might be something else at stake in *2WB* ll. 148–9, which goes beyond mocking the bad looks and/or bodily deficits of the respective opponent. As a matter of fact, **galla$_4$^{la} tur** (literally, "small vagina") can be a term for virginity, as is evident from Ninlil's defensive reply to Enlil's advances in *Enlil and Ninlil* (see Behrens 1978) l. 30: **galla$_4$^{la}-gu$_{10}$ tur-ra-am$_3$ peš nu-um-zu** "My vagina is (too) young, it does not know how to stretch." While in *Ka hulu-a* l. 17 (see above), given the presence of the dissatisfied cohabitant (**lu$_2$ nu$_2$-da-a-ni**), this meaning seems unlikely (unless the cohabitant is but a potential or non-existent one, and the woman's virginity is the butt of the joke), it is certainly one possible way of understanding *2WB* ll. 148–9. In this case, the expression **galla$_4$^{la} tur siki galla$_4$^{la} gid$_2$-gid$_2$** would also jeer at the fact that the rival is still a virgin, although her long pubic hair suggests that she has long been fit for sexual intercourse and marriage – and marriage had been identified as the single most important aim in life of every (non-consecrated) woman!

Finally, the importance of marital procreation is emphasized in *2WB* l. 48, as it seems to equate fertility quite explicitly with prosperity: **ša$_3$ ku$_3$ til i-bi$_2$-za e$_2$-a-na**[82] "her pure womb is 'finished' – (it means) financial loss for her house."[83]

As financial loss takes us back to the first duty of the ideal matron, the prudent management of the household, seeking to maintain or augment the family's wealth and avoid incurring loss, it is time to review all the "crimes" and flaws listed in the speeches of the debating women. Indeed, considering the abundance of mutual accusations, it comes as no surprise that their verdicts concerning their respective adversary are shattering: Neither does she show any trace of decency, nor is she capable of performing the domestic work befitting her status. And isn't she a penniless slave anyway? Clearly, she is the **nu-ga nunus-e-ne** "unworthiest of women,"[84] and as such a disgrace to

81 The filling of the gap at the beginning of the line as well as the translation follows Civil (2006a: 56).

82 Quoted from Ni 2268 (BE 31 28). The **e$_2$** is clear in the other manuscripts; Ni 2268 is in need of collation.

83 In this respect it is interesting to observe that the late *Izbu Commentary* 526 f. also links I.BI$_2$.ZA to its possible outcomes: *ṣaltu* "quarrel" and, ultimately, *mūtu* "death," s. CAD I and J: 3 s.v. *ibissû*.

84 This expression in fact occurs twice, once in *2WB* l. 143 (quoted from BM 16902 [CT 42 44] obv. 6) and once in CBS 7167 (unpublished; P262200) obv. 5, one of the unconnected fragments

womankind: **ki-še-er nu-tuku na-ag$_2$-munus-e la-ba-DI(//du$_7$)**[85] "She knows no limit, she is not fit for womanhood." This, incidentally, is also the résumé of the two diatribes (*Ka hulu-a* and MS 2865).

3 Discussion and summary

Indeed, all texts discussed here propagate similar moral values. A woman is supposed to be a humble, caring, neat, and able wife, who looks after husband and children, while at the same time prudently managing the household. It is in her capacity as domestic administrator, cook, and textile worker that she can – and should – contribute to the family's welfare – an economic role which had already been emphasized by certain sayings collected in *EDPC 1* in the mid-third millennium. If she fails to behave as expected, all of the essentially didactic texts discussed here agree that such outrageous misconduct must be punished in one way or other.

However, as outlined in section 1, each composition also has its own thematic priority, which examines one specific area of womanhood, and also determines the course of the story. In this respect, *2WB*, being the best preserved of the literary debates, has proved to be the most informative with regard to the everyday work of a typical woman. This is not altogether surprising, since dialogues between members of the Edubba'a (when compared to diatribes against men) also focus more on professional skills (or superficially, the lack thereof), while the diatribes, at first sight, simply appear to be exercises in the most offensive insults imaginable; ultimately, however, they were also supposed to serve the moral education of the students.

Hence it can be said that the dialogues in particular, apart from setting a moral code advocating a humble and diligent life (which applies to men and women alike), also define different occupational profiles. Although the debates between Edubba'a affiliates and between women undeniably form two distinct subgroups, I regard them as complementary, in the sense that they all, by way of insults, outline the requirements of certain professions.[86] Considering the

attributed to "*2WA*." The only criterion for assuming CBS 7167 to contain a dialogue is the occurrence of Emesal forms; it contains phraseological parallels to both *2WB* and MS 2865.

85 *2WB* l. 66, quoted from CBS 14174 + UM 29-13-001 (unpublished; P269151) iii 3; 3 × **du$_7$** vs. 3 × **DI**.

86 As the so-called 'corpus of Edubba'a literature' is still in need of an exact definition, I am mainly referring to *Dialogues 1–3* when writing about debates between Edubba'a affiliates, because they bear the closest parallels to the debates between women. For *Dialogue 1* an edition by J. Cale Johnson and Mark E. Geller has been announced, for *Dialogue 2* an edition is

numerous references to domestic activities of women, which are presented as the essence of womanhood, there is no doubt that being a housewife was considered a proper job – and in fact the only job befitting a woman. Thus, just as scribes accuse each other of having problems writing cuneiform, or of being unable to speak Sumerian properly,[87] women sneer at their rival's incompetence in household matters. In other words, in the same way that only proficiency in every subject taught at the Edubba'a allows a scribe to carry the title,[88] accomplishment in domestic activities makes a woman a woman.

The choice of professions is, however, far from exhaustive, and betrays the scholastic origin of these texts: men are portrayed as scribes or musicians – that is, (aspiring) Edubba'a graduates – and women as housewives. This elitist perspective also becomes apparent in the barely concealed contempt for menial workers and other members of the lower classes.[89]

Hence, all the stylized characters, who populate the diatribes and dialogues, stem from a scribal milieu (with women at the domestic periphery), and all of them were indiscriminately derived from an *ex negativo* definition of paradigmatic types – the extensive use of this rhetorical device proving it to be an effective didactic ploy.

Still, considering the sheer abundance of insults, one needs to address the question – however anachronistic it may in part be – as to whether the taunts in the texts dealing with women should be classified as misogynistic.

Indeed, there is little reason to doubt that all these texts, including the Emesal dialogues, were written by men. This is strongly suggested by the structural, stylistic, and phraseological similarity of the texts, regardless of whether the protagonists or the addressee be male or female. Therefore, the conclusion is unavoidable that all of the texts studied here exhibit an essentially male perspective on what constitutes an ideal woman. Moreover, if accepting that it was in all likelihood the **ummia** who authored the literary debates between, and the diatribes against, men and women alike,[90] and most definitely schoolboys who copied them, it cannot be excluded that in a male-dominated place

being prepared by Manuel Ceccarelli. *Dialogue 3* has been partly edited by Römer (1988), a new comprehensive edition remains a desideratum.

87 See the references collected by Sjöberg (1975: 161–172), which need not be repeated here.

88 Compare the well-known proverb SP 2.47: **dub-sar eme-gi$_7$ nu-mu-un-zu-a / a-na-am$_3$ dub-sar e-ne** "A scribe who does not know Sumerian – what kind of scribe is he?"

89 Compare Alster (1997: xxiii–xxv) for a similar pitiless stance toward the underprivileged in the OB Sumerian proverb collections. Although the proverbs reflect many more occupations than the dialogues, they still express the view of the independent, wealthy classes, and look down on the poor.

90 Thus Volk (2000: 28 et passim).

like the Edubba'a teachers and students were having a laugh at the expense of the bickering women in the dialogues, and utterly despised the malicious ones which *Ka hulu-a* and MS 2865 brought to mind. But this is also difficult to prove.

In fact, the similarity of diatribes against, and dialogues between, women and Edubba'a affiliates, as well as the conformity of the gender-neutral insults they contain, might argue against it. The compositions centering on men are equally offensive, and abound in slurs ridiculing not only the rival's incompetence, but also his ugliness and poverty – very much like the texts discussed in this paper. However (and this is by no means insignificant), there is, to date, no diatribe against a man written in Emesal, and it is rather unlikely such a text ever existed. Apart from this, the only aspects in which the dialogues in particular differ are the taunts exposing the inability of the respective addressee to meet the requirements of his or her profession, as well as the setting – the Edubba'a in the case of scribes, and the domestic sphere in the case of women.

Moreover, both dialogues and diatribes, though superficially parading the flaws of stereotypical fools, were really addressed to an assumed audience in need of moral guidance (or so the teachers thought). Indeed, the students who copied these texts, which were quite amusing in many respects, were probably even encouraged to laugh at these impossible fools, hoping that, as a result, they would refrain from repeating their mistakes. Hence, the texts are not abusive as such, but fundamentally didactic compositions. If men did sneer at the female characters in these texts, it was merely a side effect, but certainly not the main motif for composing them.

But what was it then? Why where students assigned to study these texts, which were (superficially, at least) addressed to women? Knowing that **dam nu-gar-ra e$_2$-a til$_3$-la-am$_3$ / a$_2$-sag$_3$-e diri-ga-am** "an unreliable wife living in the house is worse than all diseases" (SP 1.154),[91] Volk (2000: 16) may well be right in assuming that the teachers presented their students with an outlook on which kind of woman would make a good future wife. This would also explain why only one profession was allowed for women in these texts: that of a housewife. Judging from the texts, celibate priestesses, for instance, quite simply did not exist. In fact, this appreciation of the wife and mother confirms Harris' (1989: 145, see above footnote 1) assumption that the profession of

91 OB Lu A 120–121 (// Lu B 11–12 and D 81–82, s. MSL 12: 161) render **lu$_2$ nig$_2$ nu-gar-ra** as *ša la kīnātim* "not established/right(eous)/trustworthy" and *ša nulliātim* "malicious/treacherous/foolish one," **dam nu-gar-ra** is probably an abbreviated variation of this term. How Alster (1997: 31) arrived at the translation "thriftless" is incomprehensible to me.

housewife was not only the natural vocation of a woman, but also the aspiration of virtually every woman, since it provided, apart from security, also a certain amount of responsibility and esteem.

Bibliography

Alster, Bendt. 1991/92. Early Dynastic Proverbs and other Contributions to the Study of Literary Texts from Abū Ṣalābīkh. *AfO* 38/39: 1–51.
Alster, Bendt. 1997. *Proverbs of Ancient Sumer. The World's Earliest Proverb Collections* I–II. Bethesda, Maryland: CDL-Press.
Alster, Bendt. 2005. *Wisdom of Ancient Sumer*. Bethesda, Maryland: CDL-Press.
Alster, Bendt. 2007. *Sumerian Proverbs in the Schøyen Collection*. CUSAS 2. Bethesda, Maryland: CDL Press.
Attinger, Pascal. 2005. A propos de AK « faire » I–II. *ZA* 95: 46–64 and 208–275.
Bauer, Josef. 1989/90 [1991]. Altsumerische Wirtschaftsurkunden in Leningrad. *AfO* 36–37: 76–91.
Behrens, Hermann. 1978. *Enlil und Ninlil: ein sumerischer Mythos aus Nippur*. StPohl SM 8. Rome: Biblical Inst. Pr.
Cavigneaux, Antoine and Farouk al-Rawi. Liturgies exorcistiques agraires (Textes de Tell Haddad IX). *ZA* 92: 1–59.
Civil, Miguel. 1983. Enlil and Ninlil: The Marriage of Sud. *JAOS* 103: 43–66.
Civil, Miguel. 1984. Notes on the „Instructions of Šuruppak". *JNES* 43: 281–298.
Civil, Miguel. 2006a. be_5/pe-en-zé-er = *biṣṣūru*. Pp. 55–61 in *If a Man Builds a Joyful House: Assyriological Studies in Honor of Erle Verdun Leichty*, ed. Ann K. Guinan *et al.* CunMon. 31. Leiden–Boston: Brill.
Civil, Miguel. 2006b. The Song of the Millstone. Pp. 121–138 in *Šapal tibnim mû illakū. Studies Presented to Joaquín Sanmartín on the Occasion of His 65th Birthday*, eds. Gregorio del Olmo Lete, Lluís Feliu, and Adelina Millet-Albà. AulaOr. Suppl. 22. Barcelona: AUSA.
Civil, Miguel. 2008. *The Early Dynastic Practical Vocabulary A (Archaic HAR-ra A)*. ARES IV. Rome: Missione Archeologica Italiana in Siria.
Civil, Miguel and Robert D. Biggs. 1966. Notes sur des textes sumériens archaïques. *RA* 60: 1–16.
Cooper, Jerrold S. 1983. *The Curse of Agade*. Baltimore: Johns Hopkins University Press.
Delnero, Paul. 2012. *The Textual Criticism of Sumerian Literature*. JCS Suppl. 3. Boston: American Schools of Oriental Research.
Englund, Robert K. 1991. Hard Work – Where Will It Get You? Labor Management in Ur III Mesopotamia. *JNES* 50: 255–280.
Gelb, Ignaz J. 1973. Prisoners of War in Early Mesopotamia. *JNES* 32: 70–98.
George, Andrew R. 2009. *Babylonian Literary Texts in the Schøyen Collection*. CUSAS 10. Bethesda, Maryland: CDL Press.
Harris, Rivkah. 1989. Independent Women in Ancient Mesopotamia? Pp. 145–156 in *Women's Earliest Records: From Ancient Egypt and Western Asia. Proceedings of the Conference on Women in the Ancient Near East*, ed. Barbara S. Lesko. Atlanta, Georgia: Scholars Press.

Klein, Jacob. 2003. An Old Babylonian Edition of an Early Dynastic Collection of Insults (BT 9). Pp. 135–149 in: *Literatur, Politik und Recht in Mesopotamien. Festschrift für Claus Wilcke*, ed. Walther Sallaberger *et al.* Wiesbaden: Harrassowitz.

Kramer, Samuel N. 1940. Langdon's Historical and Religious Texts from the Temple Library of Nippur – Additions and Corrections. *JAOS* 60: 234–257.

Lambert, Wilfred G. 1960. *Babylonian Wisdom Literature*. Oxford: Clarendon Press.

Matthiae, Paolo. 1989^2. *Ebla. Un impero ritrovato. Dai primi scavi alle ultime scoperte.* Torino: Guilio Einaudi.

Matuszak, Jana. Forthcoming. Don't Insult Inana! Divine Retribution for Offense Against Common Decency in the Light of New Textual Sources. *CRRAI* 60, Warsaw.

Matuszak, Jana and Konrad Volk. Forthcoming. *Sumerian Literary Texts in the Schøyen Collection* I. With the collaboration of A. R. George, C. Mittermayer, L. Vacín and A. Westenholz. Bethesda, Maryland: CDL Press.

Milano, Lucio. 1993–97. Mehl. *RlA* 8: 22–31.

Molina, Manuel. 2009–11. Sklave, Sklaverei A. Im 3. Jahrtausend. *RlA* 12: 562–564.

Peterson, Jeremiah. 2007. *A Study of Faunal Conception with a Focus on the Terms Pertaining to the Order Testudines*. Univ. dissertation University of Pennsylvania.

Römer, Willem H. Ph. 1988. Aus einem Schulstreitgespräch in sumerischer Sprache. *UF* 20: 233–245.

Römer, Willem H. Ph. 2004. *Die Klage über die Zerstörung von Ur*. AOAT 309. Münster: Ugarit-Verlag.

Roth, Martha T. 1995. *Law Collections from Mesopotamia and Asia Minor*. Writings from the Ancient World 6. Atlanta, Georgia: Scholars Press.

Sallaberger, Walther. 2012. Bierbrauen in Versen: eine neue Edition und Interpretation der Ninkasi-Hymne. Pp. 291–328 in *Altorientalische Studien zu Ehren von Pascal Attinger: mu-ni u_4 ul-li_2-a-aš ĝa_2-ĝa_2-de_3*, eds. Catherine Mittermayer and Sabine Ecklin. OBO 256. Fribourg: Academic Press – Göttingen: Vandenhoeck & Ruprecht.

Schuster-Brandis, Anais. *Steine als Schutz- und Heilmittel. Untersuchung zu ihrer Verwendung in der Beschwörungskunst Mesopotamiens im 1. Jt. v. Chr.* AOAT 46. Münster: Ugarit-Verlag.

Sefati, Yitschak. 1998. *Love Songs in Sumerian Literature. Critical Edition of the Dumuzi-Inanna Songs*. Ramat Gan: Bar-Ilan University Press.

Sjöberg, Åke W. 1972. "He Is a Good Seed of a Dog" and "Engardu, the Fool". *JCS* 24: 107–119.

Sjöberg, Åke W. 1973. Der Vater und sein missratener Sohn. *JCS* 25: 105–169.

Sjöberg, Åke W. 1975. The Old Babylonian Eduba. *AS* 20: 159–179.

Stol, Marten. 2009–11. Sklave, Sklaverei B. I. Altbabylonisch. *RlA* 12: 564–571.

van Dijk, Jan. 1963. Neusumerische Gerichtsurkunden in Bagdad. *ZA* 55: 70–90.

van Dijk, Jan. 1983. *LUGAL UD ME-LÁM-bi NIR-ĜÁL: Le récit épique et didactique des Travaux de Ninurta, du Déleuge et de la nouvelle Création*. Leiden: Brill.

Volk, Konrad. 2000. Edubba'a und Edubba'a-Literatur: Rätsel und Lösungen. *ZA* 90: 1–30.

Wilcke, Claus. 1976. *Kollationen zu den sumerischen literarischen Texten aus Nippur in der Hilprecht-Sammlung Jena*. Berlin: Akademie-Verlag.

Wilcke, Claus. 1998. Care for the Elderly in Mesopotamia in the Third Millennium B.C. Pp. 23–57 in *The Care of the Elderly in the Ancient Near East*, eds. Marten Stol and Sven P. Vleeming. SHCANE 14. Leiden–Boston–Köln: Brill.

The recent edition of Dialogue 1 by J. Cale Johnson and Markham J. Geller, entitled *The Class Reunion: An Annotated Translation and Commentary on the Sumerian Diaologue* Two Scribes (Brill 2015), unfortunately came out too late to be included in this study.

Ichiro Nakata

Economic Activities of *nadītum*-Women of Šamaš Reflected in the Field Sale Contracts (MHET II/1–6)

The *nadītum*-women of Šamaš in Sippar cannot be ignored in any discussion about the roles of women in work and society in the ancient Near East. They were particularly active in the real estate transactions as lessors as well as purchasers of fields during the Old Babylonian period. They were the object of exhaustive studies by R. Harris (1962, 1964 and 1975) and J. Renger (1967: 149–168). More recently, C. Janssen (1991),[1] M. Stol (1998),[2] G. Kalla (1999; 2000),[3] A. Goddeeris (2002)[4] and S. Richardson (2002 and 2010)[5] dealt extensively with the documents related to the *nadītum*-women in Sippar. Most recently L. Barberon published a thorough study of *nadītum*-women of Marduk in Babylon in which she frequently touched upon those of Šamaš in Sippar (2012).

The *nadītum* was a woman dedicated to a particular god and found in cities such as Sippar, Babylon, and Nippur, to mention a few in Babylonia in the Old Babylonian period. Except for the *nadītum*-woman of Marduk, they would normally reside in a cloister (Barberon 2012: 30). The most well-known *nadītum*-women were those of Šamaš in Sippar, but *nadītum*-women of Marduk in Babylon are also known through the paragraphs dealing with them in the Code

1 Janssen drew our attention to a letter of Samsu-iluna who had warned the officials of the cloister in Sippar about *nadītum*-women who had been sent to the cloister but not provided with sufficient food (1991: 3–11).
2 Stol dealt in depth with the care of the *nadītum*-women in their old age (1998: 84–116).
3 Kalla (1999) not only made a very detailed study of the history of acquisition and the possible provenances of the tablets in the various Sippar collections of the British Museum that were published by L Dekiere in his *Old Babylonian Real Estate Documents from Sippar in the British Museum*, Mesopotamian History and Environment, Series III, Texts. Volume II (Hereafter MHET II), Parts 1–6, but also reviewed them thoroughly, except for Part 6 (2000).
4 Goddeeris touched upon many texts related to *nadītum*-women in Sippar in her study of the rather neglected history of Northern Babylonia in the early Old Babylonian Period (ca. 2000–1800 BC).
5 Richardson, based on newly published documents, thinks that the cloister remained operative as an institution into the reign of Samsu-ditana (2002: 181–183; 2012: 332–333).

Ichiro Nakata, Chuo University and Ancient Orient Museum, Tokyo;
ichiro.nakata71@gmail.com

of Hammurabi (§§ 144–146, 182 for example). *Nadītum*-women of Marduk were able to get married but not allowed to bear children. Those of Šamaš in Sippar, on the other hand, kept their celibacy and resided in the cloister throughout their life.

It is believed that many of the *nadītum*-women in Sippar were from relatively wealthy families, some even from royal families. One of the reasons behind the establishment of this institution was to have a *nadītum*-woman pray for the welfare of her family. She was sometimes called *kāribtum*, "she-who-prays."[6] However, there may have been a more mundane reason, which was to keep the patrimonial estate intact as much as possible by not giving away a part of it as a dowry when a daughter was married. For example, a *nadītum*-woman of Šamaš, when she entered the cloister, brought with her a dowry often including a field or fields, but this land was usually inherited by her brother(s) when she passed away, thus avoiding alienating a part of the estate.

Harris estimated that "about 200 *nadītum*-women lived in the cloister at any one time." (1975: 304) Barberon estimated that almost 230 *nadītum*-women of Šamaš lived in the period from Immerum to Sîn-muballiṭ (c. 1880–1793 BC), about 300 *nadītum*-women lived during the period from the first regnal year of Hammurabi to the ninth regnal year of Samsu-iluna (1792–1740 BC) and more than 140 from Samsu-iluna's tenth regnal year to the end of Samsu-ditana's reign (1739–1595 BC) (2012: 66).

In the present paper I would like first to make a quick survey of these women in the field leasing business and then investigate how *nadītum*-women accumulated fields for leasing during their residency in the cloister (*gagûm*). A bequest in which a part of the patrimonial possessions was given in advance was one way of acquiring fields for leasing, but the most important way of doing so was by purchase. I would like to concentrate on the latter after a brief sketch of the bequest documents. My survey here will be limited to the documents published by Luc Dekiere (1994–1997) (see Woestenburg 1997/1998; Kalla 2000 for reviews).

1 Field Lease Documents

Luc Dekiere (1994–1997) published 364 field lease contracts.[7] In about 120 of them (about 33.0 %) the lessor is qualified or can be safely regarded as *nadītum*

6 See Batto (1974: 93–107) on this aspect in connection with Erišti-Aya, daughter of King Zimri-Lim of Mari, who probably lived as a *nadītum* of Šamas in Sippar.

7 The cases (envelopes) of MHET II/3, 404 and II/5, 579 were published as CT 4, 44c and CT 2, 32, respectively.

(LUKUR).[8] However, it is likely that most of the remaining women-lessors are also *nadītum*-women, judging from their name-types.[9]

The acreage of a field for leasing by a female field owner varies, when it is mentioned,[10] from 1 IKU, about 0.36 ha (5 contracts: MHET II/3, 366; 373; 463; II/4, 558 and II/5, 655) to 25 IKU[11] (1 contract: MHET II/5, 596). The most popular acreage of fields for leasing is 3 IKU (at least 40 contracts). The second most popular acreage of fields for leasing is 6 IKU (34 contracts). However, 9 IKU appears quite frequently (19 contracts) as well in the field lease contracts with a woman as lessor.

Twenty-two *nadītum*-women appear as lessors in three or more field lease contracts published in MHET II/1–6.[12] Only 16 of them are qualified as *nadītum*, but, again, it is probable that the other six are also *nadītum*-women, judging from their name-types. Most of them had two or more fields for leasing in multiple irrigation districts (A-GAR$_3$/*ugārum*) or locations over a period of time.

For example, Huzālatum, daughter of Sumu-Erah, leased a field of 6 IKU in a location called Šamkanim to one tenant (MHET II/2, 260) and leased another field of 4 IKU in the irrigation district of Nagûm to a different tenant (MHET II/2, 261) in Hammurabi's 35th year. Again, Ruttum, daughter of a certain Hammurabi, leased out a field of 14 IKU in the irrigation district of Gizanu to one tenant in Hammurabi's 24th year (MHET II/2, 209), while she leased out another field of an unspecified acreage (A-ŠA$_3$ *mala maṣû*) on the bordering area of Sippar (*i-na* GU$_2$ UD-KIB-NUN^{ki}) to a different tenant in the same year (MHET II/2, 212 [Case]).[13]

---

8 The term is used for a cloistered woman in ancient Babylonia, but in this paper "*nadītum*-woman" or "*nadītum*-women" is used for convenience.

9 See Stamm (1939: 122–126), Harris (1964: 126–128) and Barberon (2012: 8–12). Stone (1982: 57) even suggests that "the establishment of a *nadītu* at Sippar apparently involved a ritual in which a change of name occurred."

10 In some lease contracts phrases such as A-ŠA$_3$ *mala maṣû* (field as much as there is; e.g., MHET II/1, 125) or A-ŠA$_3$ *mala qāssu ikaššadu* (field as much as his hand reaches; e.g., MHET II/4, 483) are found instead of a specific acreage.

11 This is the acreage of one piece of field in the irrigation district of Ṭābum. However, according to MHET II/297 three fields of a total of 15 + X IKU located in three different irrigation districts were leased out by Ruttum, whose father is not identified, to Inib-erṣetim and Šamaš-tappê.

12 Strangely, only five of them are found in the list of the *nadītum*-women compiled by R. Harris (1962: 1–12). Harris lists 38 *nadītum*-women who are mentioned in at least three texts that were available at the time of the publication of her article.

13 A more detailed study on the field leasing by *nadītum*-women reflected in MHET II/1–6 has just been published in Nakata 2016. It may be noted here that H and h in Akkadian names and terms stand for Ḫ and ḫ in this paper.

2 Bequest Documents

One of the ways through which *nadītum*-women acquired fields for leasing was "bequest" according to L. Dekiere's terminology. They received a sort of dowry ("bequest") for their subsistence at the time of their entry into the cloister (*gagûm*) from their father, or their brother(s) if their father was deceased.

L. Dekiere published 48 bequest documents in MHET II/1–6, including four uncertain ones.[14] Of these 48 bequest documents, 37 contain a field or fields in the list of items for bequest. In 30 of them, the beneficiary of the bequest is a woman.[15] Many of the female beneficiaries of bequests are believed to have been *nadītum*-women, although only 13 of them (MHET II/1, 18, 19, 80; II/2, 171; II/3, 414; II/5, 568, 618, 663, 696, 851, 819; II/6, 881, 924) are noted as such.

The acreage of the fields contained in these bequest documents varies from 1 IKU (MHET II/5, 589) to 22 IKU (two fields of 10 IKU and 12 IKU in a location called Halhala, MHET II/1, 333), but many of them (18 documents [60 %]) fall in the range between 2 IKU and 6 IKU. However, 1 BUR_3 (= 18 IKU) is not unusual on the upper end of the scale (five bequest documents [16.6 %]: MHET II/1, 19, 20; II/5, 570, 720; II/6, 819).

Among the thirty documents in which the beneficiary of the bequest is clearly a woman, the number of fields for bequest is normally one, and is naturally located in one irrigation district or location. Only two documents show that two separate fields in two different locations were bequeathed to a woman (MHET II/1, 85: 4 IKU in Tawirtum ša Ilī-sukkal and 1.3 IKU in Tuhamum, and MHET II/2, 258: 7.5 IKU in Nagûm and 3 IKU by Irnina Canal).

In view of the fact that quite a few *nadītum*-women owned fields for leasing in two or more locations, probably because of the alternate fallow system in practice in Babylonia during the Old Babylonian period, as in earlier periods,[16] *nadītum*-women must have purchased additional fields in one or more irrigation districts or locations for leasing.

---

14 MHET II/1, 99; II/2, 197; 210; 333.

15 In MHET II/1, 99; II/2, 248, 333; II/5, 570, 616, 720 and II/6, 925, the beneficiary is either male or uncertain.

16 For the alternate fallow system during the Sumerian period, see Yamamoto (1979–80); Charles (1990: 47–49 and 60–61); LaPlaca and Powell (1990: 78–80) and Liverani (1990: 169; please note that the term "field" in this article corresponds to our irrigation district [cf. p. 157]) among others. For that of mid-20th century Iraq, see Buringh 1960: 71 and 249 and Poyck 1962: 19 and 38.

3 Field Sale Documents

L. Dekiere published 100 field sale documents,[17] of which 53 (53 %) have a woman as purchaser (see Table 1). In 35 of them, the female purchaser is either stated as a *nadītum*-woman or can be safely regarded as one. It is likely that most, if not all, of the remaining female purchasers were also *nadītum*-women.

Tab. 1: Number of field sale documents.

MHET	Number of Field Sale Documents	Number of Field Sale Documents with a Woman as Purchaser
II/1	38	19
II/2	15	13
II/3	12	7
II/4	4	3
II/5	26	8
II/6	5	3
Total	100	53

3.1 Dates of Field Sale Documents

Most of the field sale documents whose dates are preserved were written during the period between the reign of Sabium (1844–1831 BC)[18] and that of Samsu-iluna (1749–1712 BC), as Table 2 shows (see below).[19]

Seven field sale documents, in two of which a woman appears as purchaser, had been written before Sippar was completely incorporated into the administrative system of Babylon, namely during the reigns of Iluma-El and Immerum (for this period of Sippar, see Goddeeris 2002: 40–42). One of the female purchasers of these two documents is Innabatum, a *nadītum*-woman, the daughter of Ištar-rēmîm. She bought a field of 4 IKU in the irrigation district of Mahana (MHET II/1, 8) during the reign of Immerum. This may be one of the earliest field sale documents that testify the purchase of a field by a *nadītum*-woman. The other female purchaser is Narubtum, a NIN of Šamaš[20] (MHET

17 This number is based on my counting.

18 The regnal years in this paper are those of Oppenheim (1970: 337).

19 I follow the dating given by Dekiere 1994–1997.

20 L. Dekiere equates NIN ^{d}UTU with NIN.DINGIR ^{d}UTU (MHET II/1, p. 262). M. Stol suggests that NIN.DINGIR in Old Babylonian Sippar should be read as *nadītum* (2000: 458, n. 14).

Tab. 2: Number of field sales documents per reigns.

Date	Number of Field Sale Documents	Date	Number of Field Sale Documents
Ilum-Ila	2 (0)	Hammurabi	18 (16)
Immerum	5 (2)	Samsu-iluna	14 (7)
[Sumu-Abum][21]	0 (0)	Abi-ešuh	1 (1)
Sumu-la-El	3 (1)	Ammi-ditana	1 (1)
Sabium	10 (3)	Ammi-ṣaduqa	2 (1)
Apil-Sîn	9 (6)	Samsu-ditana	0 (0)
Sîn-muballiṭ	11 (8)	No Date/Date Lost	26 (9)

The figures in parentheses indicate the number of documents in which a woman appears as purchaser.

II/1, 6). She also purchased two fields of 12 IKU and 6 IKU during the reign of Immerum, but the location of these fields are unknown.

The sudden drop in the number of field sale documents after the reign of Samsu-iluna may reflect a possible decline in the field sales in general in Sippar area. However, the lease of a field or fields does not seem to have declined even after the reign of Samsu-iluna. Although we find only 4 (1)[22] field leasing contracts datable to the reign of Abi-ešuh (1711–1684 BC) in MHET II/1–6, there are 11 (4) field leasing contracts datable to the reign of Ammi-ditana (1683–1647 BC) and as many field leasing contracts as 62 (16) in MHET II/4 without counting damaged texts datable to the reign of Ammi-ṣaduqa (1646–1626 BC). The latest field leasing contract with a woman as lessor among those published in MHET II/1–6 is that of Princess Iltani (MHET II/4, 562), and is dated to the 19th year of Samsu-ditana (1625–1595 BC), the last king of the First Dynasty of Babylon.[23]

21 It is doubtful whether Sumu-abum was the first king of the First Dynasty of Babylon, although he appears as such in the Babylonian King List (hereafter BKL) B that preserves the names of the kings of the dynasty. One reason for doubt is that the BKL B does not state that Sumu-la-El, the second king of the Dynasty, is the son of Sumu-abum, unlike the rest of the kings of the dynasty each of whom is stated as the son of his predecessor. See Goddeeris (2002: 41; 2012: 300–301) for further information.

22 The figures in parentheses are the numbers of field lease contracts in which a woman appears as lessor.

23 Regarding the last phase of existence of the cloister (*gagûm*) in Sippar, C. Janssen suggests that the *nadītum*-women ceased to reside in the cloister and that its function as a habitation for the *nadītum*s may no longer have existed after the reign of Samsu-iluna (1991: 12). However, S. Richardson, based on newly published or identified documents that were not available to Janssen, is more positive about the continued existence of the cloister, and thinks that it re-

3.2 Acreage of Fields

The acreage of the fields purchased by a *nadītum*-woman varies greatly from 1/2 IKU (MHET II/6, 847) to 27 IKU (MHET II/5, 607), but the most popular acreage of the fields purchased by *nadītum*-women is 3 IKU (about 1.08 ha) and is attested in 12 field sale documents. The popularity of 3 IKU for the field sale documents coincides with the most popular acreage (3 IKU) for the field leasing contracts with a woman as lessor published in MHET II/1–6. The next most popular acreage is 4 IKU, and it is attested in six field sale documents. We find acreages in multiples of 3 IKU fairly often, as Table 3 shows (see also Stol 1998: 68).

Tab. 3: Acreage of the field purchased.

Acreage of field	Number of documents	Texts
1/2 IKU	1	MHET II/6, 847
1 IKU	2	MHET II/2, 170; II/5, 584[24]
2 IKU	2	MHET II/5, 584[25]; 829
2 IKU 16 2/3 SAR	1	MHET II/ 3, 446
3 IKU	12	MHET II/1, 48; 50; 108; II/2, 134; 161; 176; 184; 206; II/3, 417; II/5, 584[26]; 623; 822
4 IKU	6	MHET II/1, 8; 37; 107; 118; II/4, 519; II/5, 606
6 IKU	4	MHET II/27; II/2, 136; II/3, 427; II/5, 626
9 IKU	4	MHET II/1, 58; 103; II/3, 452; II/4, 475
12 IKU	3	MHET II/1, 6 (one of the three fields purchased); 14; MHET II/5, 729
18 IKU	2	MHET II/1, 70; II/6, 844
27 IKU	1	MHET II/5, 607

3.3 Location of Fields

Nadītum-women may have had a certain preference regarding the location of fields that they purchased. However, possible reasons for this preference are not known at the moment.

mained operative as an institution into the reign of Samsu-ditana, the last king of the First Dynasty of Babylon (2002: 181–183; 2010: 332–333).

24 MHET II/5, 584 is a summary of several purchases of fields of 1–3 IKU and some other types of land of small sizes by two *nadītum*-women and a man.

25 See footnote 24.

26 See footnote 24.

Five fields that *nadītum*-women purchased were located in the irrigation district (A-GAR$_3$) of "Nine IKU" (MHET II/2, 136; 176; 206; II/3, 446; 492). Interestingly, four fields leased out by four different *nadītum*-women (MHET II/4, 506; 528; 558 and II/5, 702) and one field that a *nadītum*-woman acquired through bequest (MHET II/1, 122) were also located in the irrigation district of "Nine IKU".[27]

Three fields that three different *nadītum*-women purchased were found in the irrigation district of Eble (MHET II/1, 27; II/2, 238 and II/5, 606 [written 0.1.0 IKU-TA-A]).[28] To be noted in this connection is that a *nadītum*-woman also received a field in the same irrigation district of Eble through bequest (MHET II/2, 171).

Three fields that three different *nadītum*-women purchased were found in the irrigation district of Buša (MHET II/1, 71; II/4, 482 and II/5, 626). Again, it is noted that the fields in ten field lease contracts of *nadītum*-women were located in the same irrigation district of Buša (MHET II/2, 227; 265; 271; 278; 280; 289; 291; II/3, 361; II/5, 644 and 648). Of these ten field lease contracts listed above, eight of them were probably concluded by Šāt-Aya, a *nadītum*-woman and daughter of Ikūn-pî, (and Amat/Geme-Aya[29]) as field owner(s). To be noted is that Šāt-Aya (and Amat/Geme-Aya) leased out fields of the same acreage (7 IKU) in the same irrigation district of Buša in Hammurabi's 40th year (MHET II/2, 278; 280; 289 and 291). However, these are entirely separate documents either with a different tenant, a different rate of rent, or different witnesses. Therefore, Šāt-Aya (and Amat/Geme-Aya) must have had four different fields of 7 IKU each in the same irrigation district of Buša in Hammurabi's 40th year.

Two fields purchased by *nadītum*-women are located in the irrigation district of Mahana (MHET II/1, 8; II/3, 377). Seven fields leased out by *nadītum*-women were also found in the irrigation district of Mahana (MHET II/2,148 [acreage unspecified]; 177 [acreage unspecified]; II/5, 712 [7 IKU]; 741 [6 IKU]; 745 [4 IKU]; 784 [... IKU] and 789 [9 IKU]). Four of these leasing contracts were concluded with Masmaratum, *nadītum*-woman and daughter of Ahušina as owner.

---

27 The Irrigation district of "Nine IKU" originally might have consisted of fields of nine IKU each. See Stol's discussion for the meaning of "Nine IKU" (1998: 68–69).

28 For the equation of A-GAR$_3$ 0.1.0 IKU-TA-A and A-GAR$_3$ Eble, see L. Dekiere, MHET II/5, p. 317.

29 The name of this woman is usually spelled GEME$_2$-^{d}*a-a* (MHET II/2, 227; 265; 271; 280 and 281), but variants such as GEME$_2^{me}$-*ia* (MHET II/2, 259; 310), *ge-me-*^{d}*a-a* (MHET II/213 and 269) and *ge-me-ia* (MHET II/2, 293) are also found. These variants may have reflected the pronunciation of her name in her time.

3.4 Prices of Fields

The price of a field for sale is rarely indicated in the field sale documents datable to the pre-Hammurabi periods. The following two earliest field sale documents are exceptional in this regard. The earliest field sale document in MHET II/1–6 is probably MHET II/1, 10 dated to the period of Immerum. According to this document, a man named Nūr-Šamaš bought a rather large field of 11 IKU for the price of 3 MA.NA and 2 1/3 GIN_2 (= 182 1/3 GIN_2 = 1518.5 g) of silver. If this is correct, the price of this field amounts to as much as 16.6 GIN_2 per IKU. The second earliest field sale document in our corpus is MHET II/1, 14. According to this document a *nadītum*-woman named Huššutum bought a field of 12 IKU for 1 1/3 MA.NA (= 80 GIN_2) of silver. This would be approximately 6.7 GIN_2 per IKU.

In the periods of Hammurabi (1792–1750 BC) and his successors, field sale documents usually recorded the price paid for the field. The price per IKU of a field, however, varies greatly from 1/3 GIN_2 (MHET II/2, 170) to about 8.3 GIN_2 (MHET II/2, 191). The average price per IKU among the prices that appear in 9 field sale documents datable to Hammurabi's reign is 3.7 GIN_2. (All these sales documents except one indicate that a *nadītum*-woman was the purchaser.) This average price per IKU, however, may not mean much because the price of a field is likely to have depended on the location, yield, and other factors of a particular field.

It may be added here that some *nadītum*-women purchased an additional field next to their own (MHET II/3, 446) or adjacent to their father's field (MHET II/1, 114; 118; 206; 338 [*nadītum*-woman?], 606, and 623).

3.5 Prominent *nadītum*-women in the field sale documents

Only three *nadītum*-women appear as purchasers in more than three field sale documents published in MHET II/1–6.

3.5.1 Huzālatum, daughter of Akšaya

Huzālatum, daughter of Akšaya, is attested as purchaser in four field sale documents.

Thus, Huzālatum accumulated fields of more than 39 IKU (approximately 14 ha), during her residency in the cloister.[30]

30 Goddeeris has collected six more documents of purchases of real estate by Huzālatum, but only one of them testifies her purchase of a field of 8 SAR (during the reign of Apil-Sîn) (CT 8, 31a) (2002: 66). See also Harris 1969: 134–135.

Tab. 4: Fields Purchased by Huzālatum.

Texts	Date	Field	Seller
MHET II/2, 172	Ha 14	a furrowed field ready for sowing (AB.SIN$_2$) of more than 4 IKU (4 +x IKU) in an unidentified irrigation district	Mār-Baya
MHET II/3, 240	Ha 31	16 IKU in Tawirtum of LUGAL.SAG.ILA$_2$	unidentified
MHET II/5, 584 (= CT 45, 111 and 113)	no date, but after Ha 17 according to Dekiere	two fields of 3 IKU each in Tawirtum and another location	Nūr-ahhī, son of Ibbi-Sîn
		a field of 1 IKU in Tawirtum	Aya-tallik (*nadītum*) and her brother Ilšu-ibbi
MHET II/5, 729	no date	a field of 12 IKU in [...]	Erșetiya, son of Rababānum

It may be added that she also purchased three houses on three different occasions:

- MHET II/1, 91 (Sm[31]): a house of 1 SAR.
- MHET II/5, 707 (Sm[32]): a house of an unknown size purchased from Nidnuša, a *nadītum*-woman, which she paid for with a silver ring of 1/2 MA.NA and 5 GIN$_2$ (= 35 GIN$_2$).
- MHET II/2, 165 (Ha 12): a house of 2 1/3 SAR for which she paid 1 MA.NA and 23 GIN$_2$ (= 83 GIN$_2$ = 691 g), which is a lot of money.

There is no document in MHET II/1–6 that testifies to our Huzālatum's activities in the field leasing business in Sippar.

3.5.2 Erišti-Šamaš, daughter of Sîn-tayyār

Erišti-Šamaš, daughter of Sîn-tayyār, is another such woman. She appears in five field sale documents as purchaser.

31 The specific regnal year is lost, but an oath was taken by the names of Šamaš, Marduk and Sin-muballiṭ (1812–1793 BC), the predecessor of Hammurabi.

32 The date is lost, but the name of Sin-muballiṭ may be restored in the oath.

Tab. 5: Fields Purchased by Erišti-Šamaš.

Texts	Date	Field	Seller
MHET II/ 2, 170	Ha 14[33]	1 IKU in the irrigation district of Tuhamum	Erīb-Sîn and his brother
MHET II/2, 184	Ha 15	2+1 IKU in the irrigation district of Tuhamum	Erīb-Sîn and his brother
MHET II/2, 238	Ha 30	8 IKU in the irrigation district of Eble	Iltani, *nadītum*, daughter of Erībam
MHET II/2, 334	Ha ...[34]	x IKU in an unidentified irrigation district	Būr-Sîn
MHET II/5, 584 (= CT 45, 111 and 113	no date, but after Ha 17 according to L. Dekiere	2 IKU of meadow (A-ŠA$_2$ U$_2$-SAL) near Irnina Canal	Abum-waqar, son of Ibbi-Sîn
		4 small meadows and other small plots of land again near Irnina Canal	Nūr-Ahhī and Abum-waqar, sons of Ibbi-Sîn

Thus, Erišti-Šamaš also acquired fields, totaling more than 12 IKU, in addition to other types of land in more than two irrigation districts during her residency in the cloister.[35] Incidentally, she also purchased a house of 5 1/2 SAR (approximately 199 m^2) and an empty plot (E$_2$.KI.GAL$_2$) of 20 1/2 SAR for a price of 24 GIN$_2$ of silver (MHET II/2, 181). This house was rather large and expensive. There is no document in MHET II/1–6 that testifies to Erišti-Šamaš' activities in the field leasing business in Sippar.

3.5.3 Bēlessunu, daughter of Ikūn-pî-Sîn

Bēlessunu, daughter of Ikūn-pî-Sîn, appears as purchaser of a field in four field sale documents. In all four, the seller of the field was a *nadītum*-woman.[36]

Although the four documents listed in Table 6 are dated to the reign of Samsu-iluna, our Belessunu appears in an adoption document dated to Hammurabi's 40th year (MHET II/2, 277). According to this adoption text, she was adopted by another *nadītum*-woman, named Hunābatum, whose father's name

33 Abbreviation for the 14th year of Hammurabi

34 The date is lost, but Dekiere assigns this text to the reign of Hammurabi (MHET II/2, p. 225).

35 See also R. Harris (1969: 135).

36 See also R. Harris (1969: 137–38).

is not preserved, and was given two fields of 12 IKU and 2 IKU in two different locations. Thus, it is highly likely that she owned a total of more than 27 IKU (approximately 9.72 ha) in more than four irrigation districts or locations during her residency in the cloister. Strangely, however, I cannot find any document in MHET II/1–6 that unequivocally testifies to her activities in the field leasing business.

Tab. 6: Fields Purchased by Bēlessunu.

Texts	Date	Field	Seller
MHET II/3, 417	Si 10[37]	3 IKU in the irrigation district of Gaminanum	Amat-Mamu, *nadītum*-woman
MHET II/3, 425	Si 13	x IKU in the irrigation district of Eble	Šerikti-Aya, *nadītum*-woman
MHET II/3, 427	Si 14	6 IKU in the irrigation district of Tawirtum	Elmeštum, *nadītum*-woman
MHET II/4, 606	Si xx[38]	4 IKU, next to her father's field in the irrigation district of Eble	Mannaši, *nadītum*-woman (?)

3.5.4 The Family of Akšaya, son of Sîn-rēmēni

Before concluding this study, I would like to comment on MHET II/5, 584 (= CT 45, 111 and 113) referred to above. As noted in footnote 24, this document is a summary of several purchases of pieces of land by two *nadītum*-women (Huzālatum, *nadītum*, daughter of Akšaya, and Erišti-Šamaš, daughter of Sîn-tayyār) and a man (Sîn-tayyār, son of Akšaya). MHET II/5, 584 is a "private" memorandum of some of the past real estate transactions and not an administrative record of a public institution. Thus, these three persons must have been members of a family or a group of some kind.

A prosopographical study of Sipparians in the early Old Babylonian period by A. Goddeeris confirms that this is indeed so (2002: 68). Huzālatum was the daughter of Akšaya, son of Sîn-rēmēni, while Erišti-Šamaš was the daughter of Sîn-tayyār, who himself was the son of the same Akšaya according to MHET II/5, 584 and other documents, and thus a niece of Huzālatum.

37 Abbreviation for the 10th year of Samsu-iluna.

38 The date is lost, but L. Dekiere assigns this text to the reign of Samsu-iluna (MHET II/5, p. 54)

Since Goddeeris limited herself in her book (2002) to the early Old Babylonian period, or more specifically only down to the generation of Ikūn-pî-Sîn and not beyond, it is not known from the "family tree" she reconstructed (2002: 68) whether our Bēlessunu was another member of Akšaya's family. However, in 1968 R. Harris established that Ikūn-pî-Sîn had a daughter named Bēlessunu who was a *nadītum*-woman of Šamaš on the basis of CT 45, 111 and 113 (=MHET II/5, 584) as well as other documents (1969: 136–138; 1975: 326).[39] Since our Bēlessunu was active during the reign of Samsu-iluna, there is no doubt that she was the daughter of Ikūn-pî -Sîn, the grandson of Akšaya, son of Sîn-rēmēni.

Thus, the three most prominent *nadītum*-women appearing in the field sale documents of MHET II/1–6 as purchasers happen to have belonged to the wealthy family of Akšaya, son of Sîn-rēmēni. These three *nadītum*-women testify to the activities of a family in Sippar over three generations during the Old Babylonian period.

At the same time, however, we must keep in mind that there were *nadītum*-women such as those who had to sell a part of their fields to Bēlessunu, their fellow *nadītum*-woman, as we noted above, though we do not know the reasons for such actions. These transactions took place during the reign of Samsu-iluna, and it is difficult not to associate them with the possible deteriorating situation surrounding *nadītum*-women the letter of King Samsu-iluna seems to imply (Janssen. 1991: 3–11).

***

To summarize, most of the field sale documents with a *nadītum*-woman as purchaser were written during the period between the reign of Sabium and that of Samsu-iluna, though *nadītum*-women continued their field leasing business actively through the reign of Ammi-ṣaduqa. The most popular acreage of fields purchased by them in one transaction was 3 IKU, but acreages in multiples of 3 IKU are found fairly often. Fields purchased by them tend to be found in irrigation districts of "Nine IKU", Eble, Buša and Mahana. The price per IKU of a field they purchased varied greatly, but the average price per IKU at the time of Hammurabi was 3.7 GIN_2 (approximately 30.8 g) of silver. The three most prominent *nadītum*-women that are attested as purchaser in more than three field sale documents published in MHET II/1–6 happen to have belonged to the Akšaya family that was very active in the real estate business in Old Babylonian Sippar over more than three generations.

---

39 See also Woestenburg (n.d.: 33).

Bibliography

Barberon, Lucile. 2012. *Les religieuses et le culte de Marduk dans le royaume de Babylone.* Archibab 1. Mémoires de NABU 14. Paris: SEPOA.

Batto, Bernard Frank. 1974. *Studies on Women at Mari*, The Johns Hopkins Near Eastern Studies: Baltimore–London: The Johns Hopkins University Press.

Buringh, Pieter. (1960). *Soils and Soil Conditions in Iraq, Baghdad*, The Ministry of Agriculture, Baghdad, Iraq.

Charles, Michael P. 1990. Traditional Crop Husbandry in Southern Iraq 1900–1960. *Bulletin on Sumerian Agriculture* 5: 47–64.

Dekiere, Luc. 1994–1997. *Old Babylonian Real Estate Documents from Sippar in the British Museum*, Part 1–6. Mesopotamian History and Environment, Series III, Texts. Volume II. Part 1: Pre-Hammurabi Documents, 1994. Part 2: Documents from the Reign of Hammurabi, 1994. Part 3: Documents from the Reign of Samsu-iluna, 1995. Part 4: Post-Samsu-iluna Documents, 1995. Part 5: Documents without Date or with Date Lost, 1996. Part 6: Documents from the Series 1902–10–11 (from Zabium to Ammi-ṣaduqa, 1997). Ghent: The University of Ghent.

Goddeeris, Anne. 2002. *Economy and Society in Northern Babylonia in the Early Old Babylonian Period (ca. 2000–1800 BC)*. OLA 109. Leuven–Paris-Sterling Virginia: Peeters.

Goddeeris, Anne. 2012. Sumu-abum. *RlA* 13/3–4: 300–301.

Harris, Rivkah. 1962. Biographical Notes on the *nadītum*-women of Sippar. *JCS* 16: 1–12.

Harris, Rivkah. 1964. The *nadītu*-woman. Pp. 106–135 in *Studies Presented to A. Leo Oppenheim*. Chicago: Oriental Institute.

Harris, Rivkah. 1969. Notes on the Babylonian Cloister and Hearth: A Review Article. *Or* 38: 133–145.

Harris, Rivkah. 1975. *Ancient Sippar. A Demographic Study of an Old-Babylonian City (1894–1595 B.C.)*. Leiden: Institut historique et archéologique néerlandais de Stamboul.

Janssen, Caroline. 1991. Samsu-iluna and the Hungry Nadītums. *NAPR* 5: 3–23.

Kalla, Gabor. 1999. Die Geschichte der Entdeckung der altbabylonischen Sippar Archiv. *ZA* 89: 201–226.

Kalla, Gabor. 2000. Review of L. Dekiere, MHET II/1–5, 139–152. *ZA* 90: 139–152.

LaPlaca, Pieter J. and Marvin A. Powell. 1990. The Agricultural Cycle and the Calendar at Pre-Sargonic Girsu. *Bulletin on Sumerian Agriculture* 5: 75–82.

Liverani, Mario. 1990. The Shape of Neo-Sumerian Fields. *Bulletin on Sumerian Agriculture* 5: 147–186.

Nakata, Ichiro. 2016. Nadītum-Women in the Field Lease Contracts from Sippar. *Orient* 56: 95–109.

Oppenheim, A. Leo. 1977. *Ancient Mesopotamia. Portrait of a Dead Civilization* (rev. ed.). Chicago–London: The University of Chicago Press.

Oppenheim, A. Leo. 1977. *Ancient Mesopotamia. Portrait of a Dead Civilization* (rev. ed.). Chicago–London: The University of Chicago Press.

Poyck, Augustus P. G. 1962. *Farm Studies in Iraq*, Mededelingen van de landbouwhogeschool te Wageningen, 62(1). Wageningen: H. Veenman & Zonen N.V.

Renger, Johannes. 1967. Untersuchungen zum Priestertum in der altbabylonischen Zeit. 1. Teil. *ZA* 58: 109–188.

Richardson, Seth F. C. 2002. *The Collapse of a Complex State: A Reappraisal of the End of the First Dynasty of Babylon, 1683–1597 B.C.*, 2 vols. PhD diss. Columbia University (UMI Number: 3053344).

Richardson, Seth F. C. 2010. A Light in the *gagûm* Window: the Sippar Cloister in the Late Old Babylonian Period. Pp. 329–346 in *Opening the Tablet Box. Near Eastern Studies in Honor of Benjamin R. Foster*, eds. Sarah Melville and Alice Slotsky. CHANE 42. Leiden–Boston: Brill.

Stamm, Johann Jakob. 1939. *Die akkadische Namengebung*, MVAG 44, Leipzig: J. C. Heinrichs Verlag.

Stol, Marten. 1998. The Care of the Elderly in Mesopotamia in the Old Babylonian Period. Pp. 59–117 in *The Care of the Elderly in the Ancient Near East*, eds. Marten Stol and Sven P. Vleeming. SHCANE 14. Leiden–Boston–Köln: Brill.

Stol, Marten. 2000. Titel altbabylonischer Klosterfrauen. Pp. 457–466 in *Assyriologica et Semitica. Festschrift J. Oelsner*, eds. Joachim Marzahn and Hans Neumann. AOAT 253. Münster: Ugarit-Verlag.

Stone, Elizabeth. 1982. The Social Role of the *nadītu*-women in Old Babylonian Nippur. *JESHO* 25: 50–70.

Woestenburg, Els. n. d. *Index: Personal Names of Old Babylonian Sippar*. Unpublished MS, rev. ed. of previous work by G. Th. Ferwerda, Leiden.

Woestenburg, Els. 1997/1998. Review of L. Dekiere, MHET II/1–4. *AfO* 44–45: 349–356; Review of L. Dekiere, MHET II/5. *AfO* 44–45: 356–360.

Yamamoto, Shigeru. 1979–80. The 'Agricultural Year' in Pre-Sargonic Girsu-Lagash. *ASJ* 1: 85–97 and *ASJ* 2: 169–187.

Katrien De Graef

Cherchez la femme!

The Economic Role of Women in Old Babylonian Sippar

Il y a une femme dans toutes les affaires; aussitôt qu'on me fait un rapport, je dis: « Cherchez la femme ! »
(Alexandre Dumas, 1889, *Les Mohicans de Paris*, p. 103)

Since Rivkah Harris's pioneering studies on Old Babylonian Sippar (1961, 1962, 1963, 1964, 1969, 1975 and 1989), it is well known that, although Old Babylonian women in general seem not to have been very economically active, one specific class of women, the *nadītu* priestesses of Šamaš, were particularly present in this domain. The extremely rich textual material from Sippar attesting the economic activities of the *nadītu*s even seems to imply that these women were predominant in economic affairs. Studies on the economic activities of (particular) *nadītu* priestesses of Šamaš, since then published by Van Lerberghe (1994), Stol (1998), Földi (2009) and Lahtinen (2011), amongst others, have only added to this image. Their economic predominance – generally considered as an anomaly in a patriarchal society – is explained away by the invocation of the unevenness of our documentation. According to Stone (1982), the overabundance of *nadītu*s attested in economic activities is caused by the fact that the illicit excavators of Sippar chanced upon a number of *nadītu* archives, preserved in houses in the *gagûm* where they are generally considered to have resided.

Time has come to put some things right and to tackle the following key issues:

a) Were these women really predominant in the economy of Old Babylonian Sippar? Their active presence in economy has certainly been stressed in the abovementioned studies. However, a general overview of their activities is still lacking. Recent studies focused on the activities of individual *nadītu*s (e.g. Van Lerberghe 1994 and Földi 2009) or on specific aspects of their economic activities (e.g. within the framework of the care of the elderly in Stol 1998: 84–116). Lahtinen (2011) made a praiseworthy overview of the business activities of *nadītu*s of Šamaš, but incorporated in her study only

Katrien De Graef, Ghent University, Department of Archaeology, Ghent;
katrien.degraef@UGent.be

the texts already treated by Harris. It goes without saying that nowadays we have many more texts at our disposal than Rivkah Harris had at her time, which might (or not) alter our image.

My first aim is therefore to form the first overall picture of the female contribution to the economy of Sippar throughout the Old Babylonian period. How large is the contribution of these women in comparison to men in the economic transactions recorded in our texts? Today, it is possible to obtain such a general overview on the basis of the Old Babylonian Sippar Database, elaborated at the research unit Assyriology and History of the Ancient Near East of Ghent University.[1] Currently, this database contains more than 9000 texts: all published administrative, economic and legal texts and letters from the so-called twin cities of Sippar, namely Sippar-Jahrūrum (Abu Ḥabbah) and Sippar-Amnānum (Tell ed-Dēr),[2] as well as unpublished texts from the British Museum and the late Old Babylonian archive of Ur-Utu, chief dirge singer of Annunītum, excavated by Léon De Meyer and Hermann Gasche at Tell ed-Dēr in the 1970s.[3]

b) Can the supposed predominance or at least presence of these women in one or more specific economic roles be explained away by the unevenness of the documentation, or are our (always incomplete) data a true reflection of the economic activity in Old Babylonian Sippar? Do nearly all documents involving *nadītus* originate from the archives which the illicit excavators chanced upon in their houses in the *gagûm* in Sippar-Jahrūrum, leading to a *nadītu*-centric and therefore biased view of Old Babylonian economy, as Stone (1982) asserts? In my paper 'Bewitched, Bothered and Bewildered. Girl Power in Old Babylonian Sippar', read at the 54th *RAI* in Würzburg in 2008, I put forward arguments to contradict Stone's theory. These were in part corroborated by Barberon (2009), who correctly concluded that Stone's theory had to be revised as many of the documents involving *nadītus* originate from Sippar-Amnānum – and not from Sippar-Jahrūrum where the *gagûm* was located – as the Belgian excavations at Tell ed-Dēr and Kalla's (1999) study on the Sippar tablets at the British

1 This database was initiated in the 1990s by M. Tanret and elaborated throughout the years by him and other members of the department. I wish to thank M. Tanret for giving me the opportunity to use this database, an indispensable tool without which the present study would not have been possible. It goes without saying that this database is a work in progress as more texts are being published, and even more are still waiting to be published, a work that will be continued in our department in the future.

2 Cf. Charpin 1988 and 1992.

3 Cf. Gasche 1989; Janssen, Gasche and Tanret 1994; Tanret 2004 and 2008.

Museum had shown. Barberon (2009) put forward the hypothesis that the archive of a *nadītu* of Šamaš consisted of two parts, one part – dowries, gifts and inheritances – kept in the family's archive in order to guarantee the integrity of the family estate, and another part – title deeds – in her own archive, as the property mentioned in these documents belonged to her personal estate. I do agree with the dichotomy between the family estate on the one hand and the personal estate on the other[4]. However, I believe this dichotomy to be more complex and not based on text genres, as I will show further on.

1 Female Contribution in the Economy of Old Babylonian Sippar

In order to form an overall picture of the active female contribution to the economy, three main economic transactions and their related roles were determined:
1. Sale transactions in which they can be seller and/or buyer;
2. Lease transactions in which they can be lessor and/or lessee;
3. Loan transactions in which they can be creditor and/or debtor.

The number of economic transactions in which women played one of these roles was counted and compared to the number in which men played the same role. As such, we will not only have an overall picture of the female economic activity in Old Babylonian Sippar and its evolution over time, but will also be able to look into the very specific nature of their economic activity.

1.1 Sale Transactions[5]

A search through our database revealed a total of 662 sale contracts. Within these 662 sale contracts, 1725 parties – both sellers and buyers – are attested.

4 See my contribution on this topic to the proceedings of the international colloquium on Gender, Methodology and the Ancient Near East held in Helsinki in October 2014 organized by S. Svärd and A. Garcia-Ventura.

5 Only sale transactions referred to in actual sale contracts (including formulae and witnesses), and not in other genres of texts such as litigations or inventories are considered in this overview.

As some of the parties involve multiple actors – relatives or partners selling or buying together – it is normal that the total amount of parties is larger than the double of the sale contracts.

553 of these parties are female, 1138 are male, 30 are as yet unidentified (name broken or not mentioned) and 4 are not persons but institutions (city, palace, temple) and therefore to be considered gender neutral. We can thus conclude that almost one third of the active parties in sale transactions is female: 32.05 % of the buyers and/or sellers are women vs. 65.97 % men – 1.98 % being as yet unidentifiable or gender neutral.

Women are far more represented in the buying role than in the selling role: in 63.84 % the female party is the buying party, whereas only in 36.16 % is she the selling party. As for the men, we see the exact opposite: in 69.33 % the male party is the selling party, whereas only in 30.67 % is he the buying party. This, however, does not mean that there was a general shift of property from men to women. Taking all sale contracts into account, we see that in almost 37 % of them both the selling as the buying party are men and in 13 % both the selling as the buying party are women. It is nevertheless remarkable that in 32 % of them men sell to women, whereas in only 5 % do women sell to men. In the other sale contracts (13 %) selling and/or buying parties consist of both men and women or are unidentifiable.

Some of these 553 female parties occur more than once, or in other words, some of these women were involved in different sale transactions during their lifetime. At least 50 women, identified each as one and the same person by means of their patronymic, were active as sellers and/or buyers on several occasions, ranging from twice to eighteen times.

About 85 % of all sale contracts are dated or can be attributed to a particular reign by means of the oath formula and/or prosopography. Three quarters of the dated sale transactions involving women can be dated during the reigns of Sîn-muballiṭ, Hammu-rabi and Samsu-iluna (75.49 %). 16.73 % of the dated sale transactions involving women are dated during the early Old Babylonian period, i.e. the reigns of the local Sippar kings such as Ilumma-ila and Immerum and the reigns of Sumu-la-el, Zabium and Apil-Sîn. This can easily be explained by the fact that we have fewer documents for this early period. It is however remarkable that only 7.78 % of the dated sale transactions involving women can be dated to the reigns of the late Old Babylonian kings Abi-ešuh, Ammi-ditana, Ammi-ṣaduqa and Samsu-ditana. It is true that we have more tablets from the middle Old Babylonian period compared to the late Old Babylonian period, but the difference is not such that this explains the striking decline of sale transactions involving women post Samsu-iluna, especially if we compare this to the amount of sale transactions involving men in the late

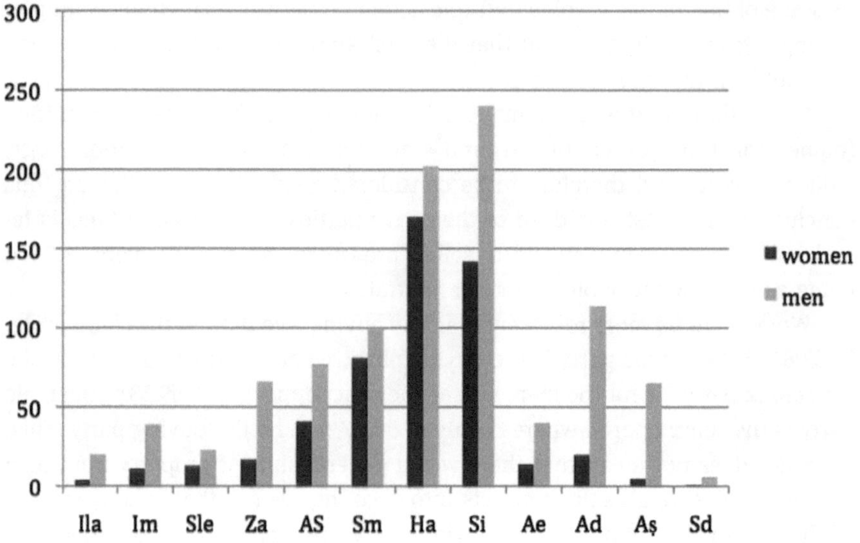

Fig. 1: Female vs. male transactors in dated sale contracts.[6]

Old Babylonian period, which obviously decreases but not dramatically: 22.87 % late Old Babylonian vs. 54.27 % middle Old Babylonian vs. 22.86 % early Old Babylonian.

We can thus conclude that female involvement in sale transactions peaked during the reigns of Sîn-muballiṭ, Hammu-rabi and Samsu-iluna, after which it came almost abruptly to an end.

1.2 Lease Transactions

A search through our database revealed a total of 839 lease contracts. Within these 839 lease contracts, 1877 parties – both lessors and lessees – are attested. As some of the parties involve multiple actors – relatives or partners – it is normal that the total amount of parties is larger than the double of the lease contracts.

567 of these parties are female, 1272 are male, 38 are as yet unidentified (name broken or not mentioned). We can thus conclude that in the lease trans-

6 The names of the Old Babylonian kings are abbreviated as follows: Ila = Ilumma-ila, Ams = Ammi-sura, Im = Immerum, Sle = Suma-la-el, Za = Zabium, AS = Apil-Sîn, Sm = Sîn-muballiṭ, Ha = Hammu-rabi, Si = Samsu-iluna, Ae = Abi-ešuh, Ad = Ammi-ditana, Aṣ = Ammi-ṣaduqa and Sd = Samsu-ditana.

actions 30.22 % of the lessors and/or lessees are women vs. 67.78 % men – 2 % being as yet unidentifiable. The lease figures correspond largely to the sale figures.

Women are far more represented in the leasing out role than in the leasing role: in 90.30 % the female party is the lessor, whereas only in 9.70 % she is the lessee. As for the men, we see the exact opposite: in 70.36 % the male party is the lessee, whereas in only 29.64 % is he the lessor. Taking all lease contracts into account, we see that in more than half of the cases (51.08 %) men lease from women. In 38.13 % men lease from men and in 3.84 % women lease from women. Women hardly ever lease from men (only in 1.44 %). In the other lease contracts (5.51 %) lessors and lessees are both men and women or are unidentifiable.

Several of these 567 female parties occur more than once, or in other words, some of these women were involved in different lease transactions during their lifetime. At least 53 women, identified each as one and the same person by means of their patronymic, were active as lessors and/or lessees on several occasions, ranging from twice to sixteen times.

About 84 % of the lease transactions are dated or can be attributed to a particular reign by means of the oath formula and prosopography. Three quarters of the dated lease transactions involving women can be dated during the reigns of Hammu-rabi and Samsu-iluna (74.42 %). Hardly any of the dated lease transactions involving women are dated pre Hammu-rabi (3.15 %). Post Samsu-iluna, in the so-called late Old Babylonian period, the amount of dated lease transactions involving women drops, but not as dramatically as the sale transactions (22.43 %). We even see a modest revival during Ammi-ditana and Ammi-ṣaduqa. As for the dated lease transactions involving men, we see a similar evolution for the pre Hammu-rabi period (2.32 %) vs. the reigns of Hammu-rabi and Samsu-iluna (44.76 %), but a tremendous increase post Samsu-iluna (52.92 %) with a peak during Ammi-ṣaduqa, partly due to the presence of the Ur-Utu archive and the fact that in the late Old Babylonian period the number of lessors and/or lessees per lease transaction seems to increase (see Fig. 2 below).

So, whereas female involvement in sale transactions peaked during the reigns of Sîn-muballiṭ, Hammu-rabi and Samsu-iluna after which it came almost abruptly to an end, female involvement in lease transactions peaked during the reigns of Hammu-rabi and Samsu-iluna, after which it dropped significantly but revived modestly during the reigns of Ammi-ditana and Ammi-ṣaduqa.

This could be explained as follows: since women start buying on a large scale from Sîn-muballiṭ onwards, they start leasing out their fields, houses and orchards soon afterwards, during Hammu-rabi. Whereas their buying activity

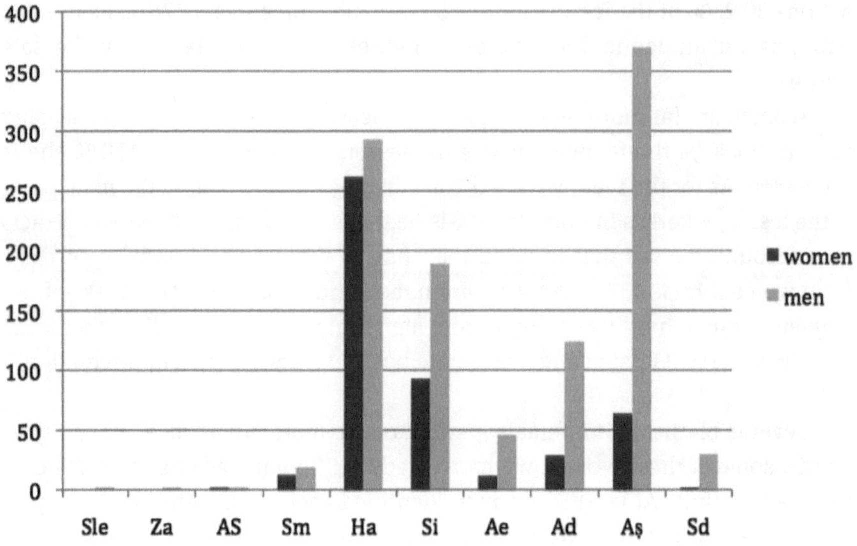

Fig. 2: Female vs. male transactors in dated lease contracts.

almost stops after Samsu-iluna, they keep on leasing out what they bought earlier, which is still in their or their (often female) heirs' possession. However, it is very hard to interpret these figures, as lease documents – contrary to sale documents – were only temporarily valid and those that we have are those that were either thrown away or were left in archives waiting to be sorted out.

1.3 Loan Transactions

A search through our database revealed a total of 787 loan contracts. Within these 787 contracts, 1719 parties – both creditors and debtors – are attested. As some of the parties involve multiple actors – relatives or partners – it is normal that the total amount of parties is larger than the double of the contracts.

221 of these parties are female, 1408 are male, 60 are as yet unidentified (name broken or not mentioned) and 30 are no persons but institutions (temple) and therefore to be considered gender neutral. We can thus conclude that female contribution to loan transactions was rather small: only 12.86 % of the creditors and/or debtors are women vs. 81.91 % men – 5.23 % being as yet unidentifiable or gender neutral.

Notwithstanding their small contribution, it is remarkable that, when involved, women are mostly creditors: in 69.68 % the female party is the creditor,

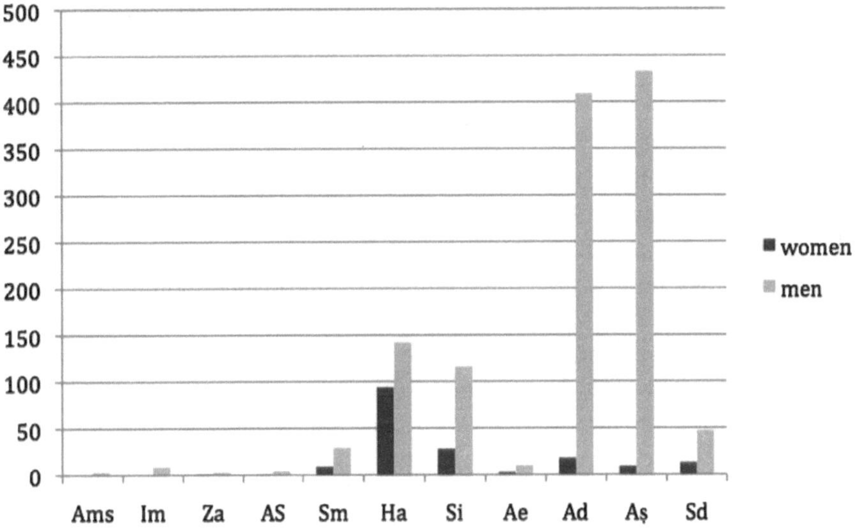

Fig. 3: Female vs. male transactors in dated loan contracts.

whereas in only 30.32 % is she the debtor. As for the men, the creditor/debtor division is more balanced: in 42.19 % the male party is the creditor and in 57.81 % is he the debtor.

At least 13 women, each identified as one and the same person by means of their patronymic, were active as creditor and/or debtor on several occasions, ranging from twice to thirty-three times.

About 84 % of the loan transactions are dated or can be attributed to a particular reign by means of the oath formula and prosopography. Almost 70 % of the dated loan transactions involving women can be dated during the reigns of Hammu-rabi and Samsu-iluna (69.32 %). 6.25 % of the dated loan transactions involving women are dated pre-Hammu-rabi and 24.43 % post-Samsu-iluna. As for the dated loan transactions involving men, we see a similar evolution for the pre-Hammu-rabi period (3.98 %) vs. the reigns of Hammu-rabi and Samsu-iluna (21.42 %), but again an even more tremendous increase post-Samsu-iluna (74.60 %) with a peak during the reigns of Ammi-ditana and Ammi-ṣaduqa. This is due to the large number of loan documents dating from the reigns of Ammi-ditana and Ammi-ṣaduqa kept in the Ur-Utu archive (see Fig. 3 above).

Apart from the peak of female contribution during the reigns of Hammu-rabi and Samsu-iluna, which is not only apparent in the loan transactions, but in all three categories of economic transactions, and which is partly due to the large amount of sources we have for that period, these figures are again hard to interpret. Like the lease documents, loans were only temporarily valid and our finds are those that were thrown away or were left in the archive waiting to be sorted out, especially so since we know that, as Charpin (2000) was able to show, greater numbers of unredeemed loans were kept from the time just before a royal edict.

The overall picture of the female active contribution to the Old Babylonian economy, as revealed in 662 sale contracts, 839 lease contracts and 787 loan contracts from Sippar, shows that almost one third of the active parties in sale and lease transactions were women, but that female involvement in loan transactions was rather small. As such, we cannot but conclude that there was no such thing as a predominance of female contribution in the Old Babylonian economy. This, however, does not mean that their presence was insignificant. On the contrary, women were a very significant minority in sale and lease transactions, especially during the reigns of Hammu-rabi and Samsu-iluna, when the active participation of women in sale and lease transactions nearly equals that of men.

1.4 Who were these women?

The major part of these female parties is specified or can be identified (through prosopography or the fact that they bear typical priestess names)[7] as belonging to a specific class of women. The overall majority are *nadītu* priestesses of Šamaš (LUKUR ᵈUTU, LUKUR *šá* ᵈUTU, NIN.DINGIR ᵈUTU, NIN ᵈUTU)[8], which does not come as a surprise as our corpus consists of texts from both Sippars and *nadītu*s of Šamaš are typical for Sippar-Jahrūrum, the city of the sun god's cult. A small minority belong to another similar class of priestesses: 8 *nadītu*s of Marduk (LUKUR ᵈAMAR.UTU), typical for the city of Babylon,[9] 5 *ugbabtu*s of Annunītum or *kulmašītu*s (NIN ᵈAnnunītum and NU.BAR)[10] – one of which (Tarbi-Annunītum, CT 47, 23 [Ha 14]) is specified as *kulmašītu* on the tablet but as ᶠ*nadītum* on the case[11] – typical for Sippar-Amnānum, and 4 *qad-*

7 See Barberon 2012: 9–10 for an overview of typical priestess names.

8 For the equation of LUKUR with NIN(.DINGIR), see Stol 2000: 457–458.

9 See Barberon's outstanding work on the *nadītu*s of Marduk (2012), especially pp. 74–77 for a list of *nadītu*s of Marduk attested in texts from Sippar. Barberon could identify 47 *nadītu*s of Marduk who are attested in texts from Sippar. Eight of them are involved in sale transactions.

10 See Barberon (2012: 70–73) for a list of *ugbabtu*s of Annunītum/*kulmašītu*s who are attested in texts from Sippar. Five of them are involved in sale transactions.

11 See Barberon (2012: 140–141) for the fusion of the titles *kulmašītu* and *nadītu* of Marduk from Ammi-ditana onwards. As in this case Tarbi-Annunītum is clearly dedicated to Annunī-

ištus (NU.GIG).[12] The overall majority of these women are – apart from their possible title – identified by a patronymic, which makes sense as it is generally assumed that *nadītus* of Šamaš were not allowed to marry and bear children. A minority of women are identified as being the mother, sister or wife of someone, especially when they act together with their child, brother or husband. As these women bear in most cases the same typical priestess names, we must assume that they also belonged to a particular priestly class, implying that in most cases they were not the biological mothers of their children.

It therefore seems safe to assume that the overall majority, if not all, of the women who were actively involved in economic transactions belong to specific classes, most of them being *nadītus* of Šamaš.

2 Do our Data Reflect a Real Situation?

In her article on the social role of *nadītu* women, Elisabeth Stone (1982) writes that the preponderance of *nadītu* texts from Sippar must be more the result of selective sampling than a true reflection of Old Babylonian activity in Sippar. She argues that in 97 % of the cases where a record exists of a transaction between a man and a *nadītu* the role of the *nadītu* is such that she would have been the one to keep the text, which proves, according to Stone, that the majority of *nadītu* tablets must have been found in the houses of *nadītu* women.

Apart from the fact that female economic activity in Old Babylonian Sippar was not preponderant but nevertheless significantly present, as is shown by the preceding overall picture, the question arises whether these data skew our view. Is the significant presence of women in sale and lease transactions, especially during the reigns of Hammu-rabi and Samsu-iluna, due to the fact that the illicit excavators chanced upon the houses – and thus archives – of women, or does this reflect a real situation?

Before asking ourselves whether these sale, lease and loan documents originate for the most part from the archives of the women involved – *in casu* largely of *nadītus* of Šamaš as our corpus consists of Sippar texts – as Stone believes, we have to dwell upon these women's archives: as *nadītus* of Šamaš

tum, as can also be determined from her name, and she probably was a *nadītu* of Marduk, as were Liwwir-Esagil and Lamassatum, combining this title with that of *kulmašītu* of Annunītum.

12 See Barberon (2012: 79–81) for a list of *qadištus* who are attested in texts from Sippar. Four of them are involved in sale transactions. One of them, Taram-Adad (MHET II, 320 [Ha]), is not attested with a title, but is identified as *qadištu* by Barberon based on her name having Adad as theophoric element.

were not married and can thus be considered to be independent – albeit small (one woman) – households or economic units, it seems logical that they kept their own archives in order to manage their estate.

2.1 Archives of *Nadītus* of Šamaš

According to Barberon (2009), tablets relating to dowries, gifts and inheritances (from a father to his daughter, a *nadītu* of Šamaš) were kept in the father's, brother's or other relative's house, in order to guarantee the integrity of the family estate, whereas the title deeds recording the fields, houses and orchards which the *nadītu* of Šamaš bought during her life were kept in her own house, *in casu* in the *gagûm*. CT 6, 6 (Aṣ 11) records the loss of the *ṭuppāt ummātim u šurdê* relating to a 2 EŠE$_3$ 3 IKU field in the Ašukum district which were placed in the *gagûm* in the presence of Aja-rīšat, *nadītu* of Šamaš, daughter of Ilšu-ibni, overseer of the merchants, after she bought the field (in Ad 3), and which her brothers and heirs needed to give to Ina-esagil-zērum, major-domo, son of Etel-pī-Ea, to whom they sold the field after her death.[13]

This division between dowries, gifts and inheritances to be kept in her father's house in order to guarantee the integrity of the family estate, on the one hand, and title deeds, to be kept in her own house, on the other, implies that the property mentioned in dowries, gifts and inheritances remained part of the family estate, whereas the property mentioned in sale contracts was part of the *nadītu*'s own estate. It moreover implies that in all *rēdit warkatīša* agreements or *nadītu* to *nadītu* inheritances, the *nadītu* testatrix and *nadītu* heiress were relatives. This might have been true in some cases, but was certainly not universal.

More than half of the dowries or gifts to *nadītu* daughters mention a fideicommissum,[14] in most cases one or more of her brothers. However, in some

13 CT 6, 6: 23–33: *ṭuppāt ummātim u šurdê īrissunūti-ma kīam iqbû umma šūnu-ma ina gagîm mahar Aja-rīšat nādit Šamaš aḫatīni šaknā-ma kīma aḫatni ana šīmtīša illiku ṭuppī šunūti nuba''i-ma ul nīmur ēma ṭuppū šūnu šaknū ul nīde ništenî-ma ninaddinâkkum annītam iqbû* "As he [= Ina-esagil-zērum, buyer] requested the *ummātim* and *šurdê* tablets from them, they [brothers/heirs of Aja-rīšat, sellers] spoke as follows: 'They were placed in the *gagûm* in the presence of Aja-rīšat, *nadītu* of Šamaš, our sister, and when our sister died, we looked for the tablets, but did not see (them). We do not know where these tablets are placed, but we will look (for them) and give (them) to you.' Thus they spoke."

14 "A gift under Roman law of property stipulated by the donor to be transferred by the donee at a given time or upon a stated condition to a third person for his benefit and made between living persons in contemplation of death or by will" according to the Merriam-Webster online dictionary.

dowries or gifts it is explicitly stated that the *nadītu* beneficiary may give her property to the heir of her choice (*ašar elīša ṭābu aplussa inaddin*).[15] The fact that they sometimes did, is shown by CT 47 63/a (Si 14),[16] a text replacing a set of lost documents, in which it is stated that Bēlessunu, *nadītu* of Šamaš, daughter of Mannium, appointed Amat-Mamu, *nadītu* of Šamaš, daughter of Sîn-ilum as her heiress. Two years after the *rēdit warkatīša* agreement between Bēlessunu and Amat-Mamu was drawn up, Bēlessunu's cousins, Amat-Šamaš, daughter of Ili-iqīšam and Nīši-īnīšu, daughter of Annûm-pī-Šamaš, both *nadītu* of Šamaš, pressed charges against their aunt Bēlessunu, stating that they should be the rightful heiresses of the fields included in Amat-Mamu's inheritance. After having examined the dowry document of Bēlessunu, which her father had given to her, the *rēdit warkatīša* agreement between Bēlessunu and her aunt Narāmtum, and the complaint by Amat-Šamaš and Nīši-īnīšu, Bēlessunu's cousins, the authorities of Sippar put Bēlessunu in the right, as both the dowry and the *rēdit warkatīša* agreement stated that Bēlessunu was free to dispose of the property as she pleased.[17]

Further on in the text is stated that after Bēlessunu's cousins, Amat-Šamaš and Nīši-īnīšu, were put in the wrong and a *ṭuppi lā ragāmim* (quitclaim tablet [literally: "tablet of not claiming again"]) was drawn up, and after Bēlessunu passed away, Amat-Mamu's father Sîn-ilum left the *ṭuppi aplūtim* (inheritance tablet) and the *ṭuppāt ummātim* (mother tablets[18]) of the fields and the houses

---

15 BAP 7 (Ha 39): 24–28: *mimma annîm ša Ašqudum abuša u Taram-sagila ummaša ana Dulluqtum mārtīšunu iddinu ašar elīša ṭābu aplussa inaddin* "All that Ašqudum, her father, and Taram-sagila, her mother, gave to Dulluqtum, their daughter, she may give her inheritance to whom she likes" and CT 48, 29 (AS): 19: *ūmi ša pī ṭuppim annîm lā iddinušim ašar elīša ṭābu aplussa inaddin* "The day he [= her brother] shall not give her as stated in this tablet, she may give her inheritance to whom she likes."

16 For comments on this text, see Harris 1969: 138–139 and 143; Yoffee 2000: 48–55; Charpin 2010: 63–65 and my contribution to the proceedings of the international colloquium on *Gender, Methodology and the Ancient Near East* held in Helsinki in October 2014 organized by S. Svärd and A. Garcia-Ventura.

17 CT 47, 63a: 41′–46′: *ṭuppāt nudunnê Bēlessunu nadīt Šamaš ša abuša mala libbīša ušamṣûši ṭuppāt aplūt Narāmtum ahat abīša ša aplussa iddinušim-ma ēma elīša ṭābu aplussa nadānam išṭuruši* "The tablets of the dowry of Bēlessunu, *nadītum* of Šamaš, in which her father has granted her authority to give her estate to whom she pleases, the tablets of inheritance of Narāmtum, sister of her father, who gave her inheritance to her and wrote her that she could give her inheritance to the heir of her choice."

18 The *ṭuppāt ummātim* or "mother tablets" are the tablets documenting the mother fields or houses which will become (give birth to) a new field or house. After the "birth" of the property (i.e. the moment it reaches the size in which it will be transmitted), all tablets recording transmission of the property are called *ṭuppāt šurdê*, viz. the documents that "follow" the present

Bēlessunu gave to Amat-Mamu, and the *ṭuppi lā ragāmim* of Bēlessunu's cousins in the house of his brother Ikun-pī-Sîn, where they disappeared.[19]

At the end of the text, it is stated that all these tablets, wherever they should appear, belong to Amat-Mamu alone, and the in the future, neither Ikun-pī-Sîn – Amat-Mamu's uncle in whose house the tablets where kept and got lost – and his children, nor the family of Bēlessunu, male or female, as many as there may be, may raise a complaint against Amat-Mamu.[20]

Three important conclusions can be drawn from this text:

1. As her dowry and the *rēdit warkatīsa* agreement between her and her aunt Narāmtum state that Bēlessunu is free to give her inheritance to whom she pleases, she bequeathed her estate by means of a *rēdit warkatīsa* agreement to a non-family member, viz. Amat-Mamu – even if there were family members to whom she could have transferred the estate, *in casu* Bēlessunu's cousins who raised a complaint but were put in the wrong by the authorities of Sippar.
2. This *rēdit warkatīsa* agreement between Bēlessunu and Amat-Mamu as well as the complete dossier relating to the estate transferred from Bēlessunu to Amat-Mamu, i.e. Bēlessunu's dowry, the *rēdit warkatīša* agreement between Narāmtum and Bēlessunu and the *ṭuppāt ummātim*, as well as the *ṭuppi lā ragāmim* stating that Bēlessunu's nieces were not entitled to inherit her estate, was stored by Amat-Mamu's father at his brother's house. At

transmission up to the mother tablets. See Charpin 1986, Janssen 1996 and Tanret and Janssen, forthcoming.

19 CT 47, 63a: 53′–60′: *ištu ṭuppi lā ragāmim ušēzibūšināti u Bēlessunu ana šīmātīša illiku ṭuppi applūtim ṭuppāt ummātim ša eqlim u bītim ša Bēlessunu ana Amat-Mamu mārat Sîn-ilum iddinu u ṭuppi lā ragāmim ša mārāt aḫḫi abīša šūzubā Sîn-ilum ana bīt Ikun-pī-Sîn aḫīšu ana maṣṣartim īziba ṭuppātum šīna ina bīt Ikun-pī-Sîn iḫliqā-ma* "After they had drawn up for them a *ṭuppi lā ragāmim* and Bēlessunu died, the *ṭuppi aplūtim* and *ṭuppāt ummātim* of the fields and houses which Bēlessunu gave to Amat-Mamu, daughter of Sîn-ilum, and the *ṭuppi lā ragāmim* which the daughters of the brothers of her father had drawn up, Sîn-ilum left these tablets in the house of his brother Ikun-pī-Sîn for safekeeping. In the house of Ikun-pī-Sîn these tablets disappeared."

20 CT 47, 63: 63–69: *ṭuppi aplūtim ṭuppi* (63a [case]: *ṭuppāt*) *ummātim u ṭuppi lā ragāmim ša Amat-Mamu mārat Sîn-ilum itti Bēlessunu laqiat ina bīt Ikun-pī-Sîn u ēma innammarā ša Amat-Mamu-ma mārat Sîn-ilum* UD.KUR$_2$.ŠE$_3$ *ša pī ṭuppi annîm Ikun-pī-Sîn mārūšu u nišūt Bēlessunu* nita *u* munus *mali ibaššû ana Amat-Mamu mārat Sîn-ilum ul iraggum* "The *ṭuppi aplūtim*, the *ṭuppāt ummātim* and the *ṭuppi lā ragāmim* which Amat-Mamu, daughter of Sîn-ilum, received from Bēlessunu, in the house of Ikun-pī-Sîn or wherever they will be seen, belong to Amat-Mamu, daughter of Sîn-ilum, alone. In the future, according to this tablet, Ikun-pī-Sîn, his children and the family of Bēlessunu, male or female, as many as there may be, shall not bring a complaint against Amat-Mamu, daughter of Sîn-ilum."

the latter's house they got lost. Although Amat-Mamu's father decided to store these tablets at his brother's house, they were not kept in the uncle's archive in order to guarantee the integrity of the family estate, as the properties described in these tablets did not belong to Sîn-ilum's family estate, but were transferred from another family estate, viz. Bēlessunu's family, to his daughter Amat-Mamu.

3. The authorities state that, should these tablets reappear, they belong to Amat-Mamu alone. This means that this whole dossier, including a dowry, two *rēdit warkatīsa* agreements, the *ṭuppāt ummātim* and the *ṭuppi lā ragāmim* was supposed to be kept in Amat-Mamu's archive, or in other words, that dowries and inheritances were kept in the archive of a *nadītu* of Šamaš, and not in her father's archive.

If not for the sake of the family estate's integrity, why did Amat-Mamu's father store these tablets in the house of his brother? The reason why the tablets were originally kept by Amat-Mamu's father might be Amat-Mamu's age at the time of the *rēdit warkatīša* agreement with Bēlessunu. If we assume that a *rēdit warkatīša* agreement implied an educational relation between the testatrix and the heiress – the elder *nadītu* introducing the younger one to the *nadītu*-ship – creating as such an artificial mother-daughter relation,[21] Amat-Mamu must have been a young girl at the time, taking her first steps into the *nadītu*-ship. Being a young girl, still living in her father's house,[22] she did not yet have her own archive. The fact that in CT 47, 63/a the authorities of Sippar assign the whole dossier of tablets – should they reappear – to her alone implies that in Si 14 she did have her own archive. Unfortunately we do not know the timespan between the date of the *rēdit warkatīša* agreement between Bēlessunu and Amat-Mamu and the date of the redaction of CT 47, 63/a. By then she certainly must have been an adult woman and experienced *nadītu*, as seven years earlier, she bought a 1 EŠE$_3$ 5 ½ IKU field in the Tēnunam district from another *nadītu*, Amat-Aja, daughter of Ipiq-Annunītum.[23] Moreover, CT 47, 63/a – replacing the set of lost tablets – would only have been written when Amat-Mamu decided to sell or bequeath (part of) her estate and therefore needed the lost tablets.

21 See my contribution to the proceedings of the international colloquium on Gender, Methodology and the Ancient Near East held in Helsinki in October 2014 organized by S. Svärd and A. Garcia-Ventura.

22 Girls seem to have been ordained as *nadītu* of Šamaš at a very early age, but did not actually enter the *gagûm* until ten years later when they were of a suitable age, see Harris 1964: 144.

23 Di 680 (Si 07).

The reason why Amat-Mamu's father decided to store the tablets in his brother's house is not clear to us. However, to store (a part of) one's archive in the house of another person was not uncommon as is shown by the Ur-Utu archive, in which parts of the archives of Pala-Adad, GALA, and of Marduk-mušallim, *abi* ERIN_2 – both unrelated to Ur-Utu's family – were kept (Tanret 2004: 256–257 and 260).

A similar situation is found in AbB 11, 55, a letter from Naramtāni, daughter of Ipqātum to Šamšīja in which she says that the inheritance of her cousin which she was entitled to – her cousin gave her her tablets, no doubt the *rēdit warkatīša* agreement between them and the whole dossier (*ṭuppāt ummātim* and *šurdê*) relating to the property to be transferred – was first claimed by her cousin's brother Nūrātum, who was put in the wrong as a *ṭuppi lā ragāmim* was drawn up, but was now being appropriated by her cousin's sister Alijātum. She wanted to sue Alijātum, but in order to do so she needed the tablets in question that are stored at her father's. Barberon (2009: 278) adduces this as proof that inheritance documents were not kept by the *nadītu* but by her father. However, Naramtāni says "*My* tablets are in the hand of my father, I will not litigate as long as my father does not come here",[24] which might imply that *all* her tablets, or in other words her complete archive, were stored at her father's, and not only the tablets relating to the inheritance. This would again imply that there was no division but that all tablets relating to a *nadītu*s estate – dowries, gifts, inheritances alongside sale, lease and loan documents – were kept together in one archive. The reason why Naramtāni's archive was stored at her father's is not clear, but as mentioned before, it was not uncommon to store one's archive at another person's house.

The idea of a division between "family estate" and "personal estate" is certainly interesting, especially since we know that *nadītu*s of Šamaš were keepers of the family estate on the one hand, but also developed a personal estate on the other.[25] However, this division cannot be made on the basis of the text genres, viz. dowries, gifts and inheritances (= family estate) vs. sale contracts (= personal estate). Indeed, property described in the dowries, gifts and inheritances was not necessarily part of the family estate (see CT 47, 63/a) or did not necessarily stay in the family (if the beneficiary was free to dispose of her property as she pleased). Moreover, property bought by *nadītu*s and thus described in their sale documents was not always but in most cases bought

24 AbB 11, 55: 23–25: *ṭuppātū'a ina qāti abīja-ma adi abi la illikam ul adân.*

25 See my contribution to the proceedings of the international colloquium on Gender, Methodology and the Ancient Near East held in Helsinki in October 2014 organized by S. Svärd and A. Garcia-Ventura.

with their "ring silver" (HAR KU$_3$.BABBAR or *šewerīša*), implying they (could have) had two kinds of means at their disposal: "ring silver" and "(ordinary) silver". As some of the dowries include an amount of silver explicitly indicated as "ring silver",[26] we can assume that the "ring silver" was given by their father and thus part of the family estate, whereas the "(ordinary) silver" was earned by themselves (by leasing out fields and lending out barley and silver) and thus part of their personal estate. In three of these dowries including "ring silver" a fideicommissary (mostly a brother of the *nadītu*) is appointed, implying that this "ring silver" or whatever is bought with it, will go to this fideicommissary after her death – which explains why *nadītus* distinguished between estate bought with "ring silver" and "(ordinary) silver" in their sale contracts.

Since the division between family estate and personal estate was not by definition based on the text genres – dowries, gifts and inheritances vs. sale contracts – but rather dependent on stipulations in these texts – inheritances could be part of the personal estate and sale contracts could be part of the family estate if bought with "ring silver" given in a dowry subject to fideicommissum – it seems more logical that all tablets relating to the estate – family and personal – of a *nadītu* were kept together in her archive, whether stored in her own house or in her father's or another person's.

2.2 A *nadītu*-centric View?

The question now is whether the sale, lease and loan documents involving these women originate for the most part from their archives, and thus lead us to an (unwarranted) *nadītu*-centric view of Old Babylonian economy, as Stone (1982) believes, or not. The answer to this question is threefold, as it concerns three different text genres – sale, lease and loan documents – each with their own specificities.

2.2.1 Sale Documents

As for the sale contracts, it is obvious that when a *nadītu* bought a field, orchard or house, she would have been the one to keep the sale document. Not

26 MHET II, 19 (Sle 13), CT 47, 30/a (Ha 10), CT 8, 5b (Ha 33) and CT 45, 79 (sd) – other dowries or gifts include an amount of silver not specified as 'ring silver'. For a discussion on these texts, see my contribution to the proceedings of the international colloquium on Gender, Methodology and the Ancient Near East held in Helsinki in October 2014 organized by S. Svärd and A. Garcia-Ventura.

only the document recording the purchase, for that matter, but the whole dossier of tablets relating to the plot she bought – all previous sale documents, exchange documents, gifts or inheritances, documenting the origin and evolution of the plot, its "chain of transmission"[27] – would have been given to her to keep in her archive. This means that if one or more women were involved in earlier transactions regarding to this plot, these tablets would not have been kept in *their* archives, but would have been given as part of the chain of transmission to the last buyer. Likewise, if the *nadītu* sold or bequeathed this field, orchard or house, she would have given the whole dossier, including her sale document, to the new owner. In other words, sale contracts are not necessarily found in the archive of the buyer.

The best way to illustrate this is the Ur-Utu archive. Within his archive 125 sale contracts have been found, 62 of which involve women. In the majority of sale contracts involving women the female party is the buyer (48) – in most cases (32) buying from one or more men, sometimes buying from another woman (11) or a mixed party (5) – in thirteen, she is the seller – alone (5) or together with male family members (8) – in one sale contract the name of the buyer is broken. The earliest sale contract involving a woman dates from the reign of Ilumma-ila, one of the early local Sippar kings,[28] the most recent one from the seventh year of reign of Ammi-ṣaduqa. The majority of sale documents involving women date from the reigns of Hammu-rabi and Samsu-iluna. So far, the data from the Ur-Utu archive correspond completely to the data from our general overview. As in none of the sale contracts involving women, Ur-Utu is the buying party – in five of them his father Inana-mansum is the buyer – all of these contracts belong to various chains of transmission.

Unfortunately is not possible to reconstruct all these chains, due to missing links – tablets that got lost in antiquity, that are too damaged to read, and of course also tablets that Ur-Utu managed to save during the fire in his house and took with him. It is, however, possible to reconstruct some (or parts) of the chains of transmission, such as the dossier relating to the house in Sippar-Amnānum that Ur-Utu inherited from his father, where he lived and where his archive was found, excellently described by Janssen, Gasche and Tanret (1994). Ur-Utu's father Inana-mansum bought this 6 SAR 15 GIN_2 house in Ad 28 from Lamassāni, *nadītu* of Šamaš, daughter of Rīš-Šamaš, SANGA of Annunītum (Di 1801), who bought it in Ad 7 from Mannium, RA.GAB, son of Šamaš-liwwir (Di 1800). This last one inherited the largest part of the plot from his sister, Šerikti-

27 See Charpin 1986; Janssen, Gasche and Tanret 1994; Janssen 1996; and Tanret and Janssen, forthcoming.
28 See Charpin 2004: 91–92.

Aja, *nadītu* of Šamaš who exchanged it with Erišti-Aja, daughter of Šamaš-rabi in Ha 39 (Di 1438),[29] thus enlarging her property as she already owned a neighboring house.[30] The remaining, smaller, part of the plot originates from the children of Ana-Sîn-taklāku, Bēltani, *nadītu* of Šamaš and her brother Halil-um, from whom the Šamaš-liwwir family must have bought it.[31]

Other (parts of) chains that can be reconstructed are those of a 2 EŠE_3 IKU field in the Tawirātum district in Kār-Šamaš, 1 EŠE_3 IKU of which was bought by Ina-libbi-eršet, *nadītu* of Šamaš from the children of Mār-Sippir during the reign of Abi-ešuh (Di 1802), who received it from Lamassāni, *nadītu* of Šamaš, daughter of Ibni-Amurru, who bought half of it from Amat-Šamaš, *nadītu* of Šamaš, daughter of Sîn-iqīsam in Si 30 (MHET I, 2) and the other half from Waqartum, *nadītu* of Šamaš, daughter of Sîn-napšeram 5 days earlier (MHET I, 1) – how this field came into the possession of Inana-mansum is not clear – and those of several fields in the Pahuṣum, Tēnunam and Buša districts – in part thanks to the certificates that were drawn up to replace tablets that got lost.[32]

The fact that all these sale contracts involving women were found in Ur-Utu's archive proves that the significant presence of women in sale transactions is not at all due to the fact that the illicit excavators chanced upon the archives of women. On the contrary: although these documents certainly started their life in a *nadītu* archive, most likely in Sippar-Jaḫrūrum, they moved from there, sometimes with a number of stops in between, to the Ur-Utu archive in Sippar-Amnānum. Unless a field bought by a *nadītu* never left her family – which would be exceptional – the real estate sales mentioning her has always moved to other archives and it is from these that they were excavated.[33]

We can therefore conclude that there was a significant presence of women in sale transactions in Old Babylonian Sippar, especially during the reigns of Hammu-rabi and Samsu-iluna, when the active participation of women nearly equaled that of men.

---

29 Not with the brother of Bēltani, as stated in Barberon 2009: 283.

30 This might have been the 4 SAR vacant plot adjacent to the Great (Annunītum?) Street she bought from Erišti-Aja, daughter of Sîn-māgir in Ha 32 (Di 1430), see also Janssen, Gasche and Tanret 1994: 106 n. 51.

31 On this point my reconstruction of the chain slightly differs from the one described in Janssen, Gasche and Tanret 1994. I will come back on this in a forthcoming article.

32 These are discussed in detail in Tanret and Janssen, forthcoming.

33 Older, obsolete, parts of chains, must have been discarded when an archive was sorted. This does not mean that they could not have been recovered by the illicit diggers, who dug indiscriminately through the floors under which the discarded tablets were buried.

2.2.2 Lease Documents

The situation of the lease contracts is somewhat different. A field, house or person was leased for a limited period of time, which means that the lease tablet lost its value when that period was over. In this respect they were different from the sale documents, which always kept their value since they were part of a chain of transmission. Moreover, we must take into account that for a lease, each party kept her/his own copy: one in the archive of the lessor, sealed by the lessee, and one in the archive of the lessee, sealed by the lessor. This excludes *a priori* that all documents mentioning the same *nadītu* woman as lessor were necessarily found in this *nadītus* archive: one would have been kept in her archive and one would have been kept in the archive of the lessee.

The leases found in the Ur-Utu archive illustrate this. Within his archive 74 lease contracts have been found, 13 of which involve women. The small number of lease documents in general and those involving women in particular – especially in comparison with the sale documents involving women in this archive – is due to the fact that all but two of the leases date from the reigns of Ammi-ditana and Ammi-ṣaduqa, a period in which female participation in lease transactions was lower. Most lease documents date between Aṣ 5 and 17 – thus belonging to Ur-Utu's living archive – in which he leases a field or a person from a woman (7) or leases out fields to women (2) and two date from Ammi-ditana's reign and involve his mother Ilša-hegalli as lessor and his father Inana-mansum as lessee. Two date from the reigns of Samsu-iluna and Abi-ešuh, one of which involves the son of his great-grandfather's brother as lessor. It goes without saying that all of these tablets would certainly have been sorted out if the house had not burned down and Ur-Utu had completed the reorganization of his archive.

We can thus conclude that if we have many documents on which *nadītu* women were lessors, this is not necessarily due to the chance finds of their archives. They could just as easily have come from the archives of their overwhelmingly male lessees. The truth of the matter may even be that these documents were not even retrieved from archives at all: they may have been found in rest archives or dumps, thrown away as useless by their owners.

Moreover, since women were actively involved in sale transactions, mostly as buyers, and therefore owned land, it is only logical that they leased out their land, and were thus actively involved in lease transactions, mostly as lessors.

2.2.3 Loan Documents

The loans, however, present another situation. It goes without saying that loan documents, sealed by the debtors, were kept in the archive of the creditors. This means that a loan document where the creditor is a *nadītu* was kept in her archive. But, as a loan document would have been broken after repayment, the loans kept in their archives were those that were not paid back by the debtors or unredeemed as a result of debt cancellation proclaimed in a royal edict (see Charpin 2000). This means that the majority of their loans, those that were paid back, have never been retrieved, as they would have been broken, implying that the female contribution to loan transactions might have been much larger in reality.

This is illustrated by the archive of Tarīb-ilīšu and Humṭi-Adad, *qadištu*, children of Ili-kīma-abīja, that was found in a jar in room 2 of house 11 of area U 106 in Sippar-Jahrūrum. It was excavated by an Iraqi team between 1978 and 1982 and published in Al-Rawi and Dalley 2000.[34] This archive contains eighteen loan documents in which Humṭi-Adad is creditor, all to be dated between the first and seventh year of Samsu-iluna,[35] which were cancelled by the royal edict Samsu-iluna issued in the third month of his eighth year of reign, as Charpin (2005: 156) was able to show. The most recent document in the archive dates from Si 8 and the house shows traces of a fire, implying the family had to leave it in (or shortly after) Si 8, taking with them their most important tablets, such as title deeds, but leaving those tablets that had lost their value for them, such as the cancelled loan documents.

The same goes for the 33 loan documents in which Erišti-Aja, *nadītu* of Šamaš, daughter of Ilšu-ibbīšu, is creditor. Although not excavated in a scientific way, it is clear that they must have been found together, as all of them belong to the same Budge collection (1902–10–11), acquired by the British Museum in 1902 and probably found shortly before. According to Kalla (1999: 216–217), four groups can be distinguished based on the location of real estate described in the tablets, two of which originate from Sippar-Jahrūrum and two of which from Sippar-Amnānum. Whether these tablets were found in both tells or in one tell, implying that parts of archives moved from one tell

---

34 For a detailed discussion of this archive see Charpin 2005: 154–157; and Barberon 2009: 279–281.

35 Al-Rawi and Dalley 2000, nos. 7 (Si 6), 8 (Si 7), 9 (Si 7), 10 (Si 6), 11 (Si 6), 21 (Si 7), 22 (Si 7), 23 (Si 6), 24 (sd), 30 (Si 7), 31 (Si 7), 32 (Si 7), 34 (Si 4), 35 (Si 7), 36 (Si 7), 37 (sd), 42 (Si 6) and 58 (Si 1).

Tab. 1: Loan documents in which Erišti-Aja is creditor.

Date	Text	Budge collection	Loan
Sm 11	BM 97819/A	Bu. 1902-10-11, 873/A	silver with interest
Sm 16 (or Ha 39?)	BM 97580/A	Bu. 1902-10-11, 634	silver and barley to be paid back in sesame with interest
Ḫa 09/11/15+x	BM 97628	Bu. 1902-10-11, 682	silver with interest
Ha 09/11/[...] (or Ha 33?)	BM 97371	Bu. 1902-10-11, 425	silver with interest
Ḫa 09 (or Ha 33?)	BM 97576	Bu. 1902-10-11, 630	silver with interest
Ḫa 10/10/17	BM 97589/A	Bu. 1902-10-11, 643/A	barley with interest
Ḫa 10	BM 97870/A	Bu. 1902-10-11, 924/A	silver with interest
Ḫa 11/9/-	BM 97837/A	Bu. 1902-10-11, 891/A	barley with interest
Ḫa 11/10/31	CT 33, 26b	Bu. 1902-10-11, 725	silver with interest
Ha 11/12d/-	BM 97395/A	Bu. 1902-10-11, 449/A	silver with interest
Ha 11/[...]/09	BM 97372/A	Bu. 1902-10-11, 426	silver with interest
Ḫa 11	BM 97524	Bu. 1902-10-11, 578	silver with interest
Ḫa 11	BM 97772	Bu. 1902-10-11, 826	silver with interest
Ḫa 11	BM 97805	Bu. 1902-10-11, 859	silver and barley with interest
Ḫa 11	BM 97860/A	Bu. 1902-10-11, 914/A	silver with interest
Ḫa 12/09/[...]	BM 97086/A	Bu. 1902-10-11, 10/A	barley with interest
Ḫa 12/10/-	BM 97674/A	Bu. 1902-10-11, 728/A	barley with interest
Ha 12/11/01	BM 97510	Bu. 1902-10-11, 564	barley with interest
Ḫa 12/11/-	BM 97744	Bu. 1902-10-11, 798	barley with interest
Ḫa 12/11/-	BM 97404	Bu. 1902-10-11, 458	barley with interest
Ḫa 12/ud.du/[...]	BM 97567	Bu. 1902-10-11, 621	barley with interest
Ḫa 12/ud.du/[...]	BM 97083/A	Bu. 1902-10-11, 137	barley with interest
Ha 12	BM 97452	Bu. 1902-10-11, 506	barley with interest
Ḫa 13?/[...]/-	BM 97703	Bu. 1902-10-11, 757	silver with interest
Ḫa 16?/ud.du/-	BM 97573	Bu. 1902-10-11, 627	barley with interest
Ḫa 16/11/-	BM 98049	Bu. 1902-10-11, 1103	barley with interest
Ḫa 32 or 42/07/06	BM 97587	Bu. 1902-10-11, 641	barley with interest
Ḫa 36?	BM 97600	Bu. 1902-10-11, 654	silver with interest
Ha (?)	BM 97703	Bu. 1902-10-11, 757	silver with interest
sd	BM 97532/A	Bu. 1902-10-11, 586	silver with interest
sd	BM 97842/A	Bu. 1902-10-11, 896/A	silver with interest
sd	BM 97793/A	Bu. 1902-10-11, 847/A	silver with interest
sd	BM 97570	Bu. 1902-10-11, 624	silver with interest
sd	BM 97689	Bu. 1902-10-11, 743	barley with interest

to the other in antiquity – as is the case with Ur-Utu's archive, part of which was moved from Sippar-Jahrūrum (see Tanret 2004) – is not clear. The fact that Erišti-Aja bought a 1 SAR 10 GIN_2 vacant plot in Sippar-ṣērim (= Sippar-

Jahrūrum[36]) from Eli-eressa, *nadītu* of Šamaš, daughter of Ilšu-bani during the reign of Samsu-iluna (MHET II, 434), might indicate she lived in Sippar-Jahrūrum.[37]

The majority of these loans must have been cancelled by the royal edict Hammu-rabi issued in his 13th year of reign and were therefore kept in Erišti-Aja's archive, where they were found in (or shortly before) 1902.

We can thus conclude that the loan documents in which a woman is creditor are the only documents that were retrieved from their archives. It is therefore not at all surprising that this is by far the smallest group of texts, as compared to the sale and lease documents involving women, especially since the loan documents that were kept were those not paid back or cancelled by a royal edict. It goes without saying that as women owned land that they leased out or could sell, it is only logical that they would have lent out the barley and silver they had at their disposal in order to make a profit. If we furthermore take into account that on average a *nadītu* who engaged in lending activities did this relatively frequently, the number of different *nadītu*s doing this is much smaller than the number of loans. It is these archives or their leftovers that were chanced upon by the mostly illicit diggers.

***

The preceding shows that our view on the active female contribution to the economy of Old Babylonian Sippar is not distorted by chance finds of the archives of women, but that our data – although always incomplete – give a fairly true reflection of the economic situation at the time. The economic role of women was not preponderant but their presence was nevertheless significant, especially in the sale and lease transactions. Their participation was particularly vital during the reigns of Hammu-rabi and Samsu-iluna, where we see a peak in all three economic activities.

Women start buying gradually from Zabium onwards and on a large scale from Sîn-muballiṭ onwards, and start leasing out their fields, orchards and

---

36 See Charpin 1988.

37 The same Erišti-Aja is attested in three more texts: an inheritance document, VS 9, 216/204 (sd), and two sale documents in which she is the buying party: TLB 1, 218 (AS) and TJDB pl. 59 (sd). The fact that all three sale documents belong to different museum collections (MHET II, 434 = Bu. 88-5-12 [British Museum], TLB 1, 218 = LB 1836 [Louvre] and TJDB pl. 59 = MAH 16516 [Geneva]) proves they were not found together but in different archives as part of a chain of transmission. The same goes probably for the inheritance document (VS 9, 216/204 = VAT 1449/1293 [Berlin]).

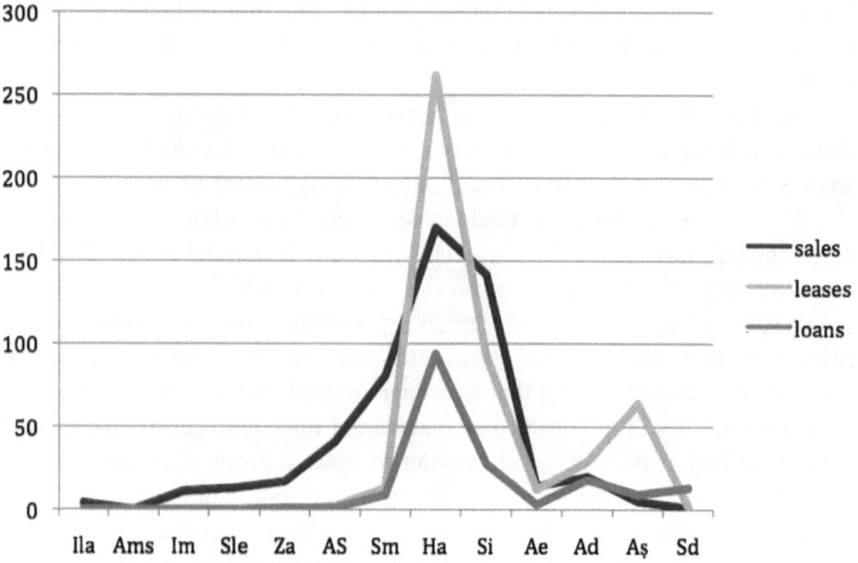

Fig. 4: Chronology of female participation in dated sale, lease and loan contracts.

houses, and lending out the yield of their estate soon afterwards, during Hammu-rabi and Samsu-iluna. At the end of Samsu-iluna's reign, female participation in economic transactions comes almost abruptly to an end, which is especially apparent in sale transactions. A possible answer lies in the letter published by Janssen (1991) in which Samsu-iluna raises the problem concerning *nadītus* whose families were not able to support them anymore as a result of which royal intervention was required. This is no doubt the precursor of the general regress in the economic activity that followed under Abi-ešuh. It seems that this crisis had repercussions on the economic situation of the upper class that caused at least part of them to largely abandon the system of property transfer in which women played a key role. This is not surprising, as throughout history, economic recessions have placed a disproportionate burden on women, who were not infrequently affected by increased responsibilities in all spheres of their life. However, the fact that a modest revival of female contribution to lease transactions is to be seen during the reigns of Ammi-ditana and Ammi-ṣaduqa, shows that women were still to a certain extent landowners and thus were still economically active, albeit on a smaller scale.[38]

38 See also Richardson 2010 for the survival of the thriving *nadītu* community in the late Old Babylonian period.

As mentioned before, part of these female economic players were involved in more than one economic transaction during their lifetime: at least 50 women were active in sale transactions on several occasions, at least 53 women were active in lease transactions on several occasions and at least 11 women were active in loan transactions on several occasions. It is, however, remarkable that most of these women were active in only one kind of economic transaction, whereas we would expect them to be active in all three kinds of transactions, assuming that they leased out the fields they acquired and lent out the yield of their fields in order to make a profit. The fact that only a small number of women were involved in loan transactions can be explained by the fact that only unredeemed loans were found, which obviously distorts our image of their actual lending activity.

Only 13 women were involved in both sale and lease transactions. The majority of women who were active as buyers, and were thus landowners, are not attested as lessors, which is odd, as they would certainly have leased out the fields they owned. The same goes for the majority of women who were active as lessors, but who are never attested as buyers. It goes without saying that women acquired a part of their estate through dowries, gifts and inheritances, but there seems nevertheless to be a mismatch, which can only be explained by the disparity of our texts, implying at the same time that female contribution to the Old Babylonian economy must have been larger.

Two women are involved in all three kinds of economic transactions: Bē-lessunu, daughter of Kassatum and Amat-Šamaš, daughter of Sîn-iddinam, both *nadītus* of Šamaš and both active during the reigns of Hammu-rabi and Samsu-iluna.

However incomplete and disparate our texts may be, I have looked for women in the economy of Old Babylonian Sippar and have found them, and as such have to say that *Monsieur Jackal* is right: *il y a une femme dans toutes les affaires*!

Bibliography

Al-Rawi, Farouk N. H. and Stephanie Dalley. 2000. *Old Babylonian Texts from Private Houses at Abu Ḥabbah, Ancient Sippir – Baghdad University Excavations.* É-DUB-BA-A 7. London: NABU Publications.

Barberon, Lucile. 2009. Les documents d'archives des religieuses en Babylonie ancienne: usage, transmission et conservation. Pp. 273–288 in *Femmes, cultures et sociétés dans les civilisations méditerranéennes et proche-orientales d'hier à aujourd'hui*, eds. Françoise Briquel-Chatonnet, Saba Farès, Brigitte Lion, and Cécile Michel. Paris: De Boccard.

Barberon, Lucile. 2012: *Les religieuses et le culte de Marduk dans le royaume de Babylone.* Mémoires de NABU 14. Paris: SEPOA.
Charpin, Dominique. 1986: Transmission des titres de propriété et constitution des archives privées en Babylonie ancienne. Pp. 121–140 in *Cuneiform Archives and Libraries: Papers Read at the 30ᵉ Rencontre Assyriologisue Intenrationale, Leiden, 4–8 July 1983*, ed. Klaas R. Veenhof. PIHANS 57. Istanbul – Leiden: Nederlands Historisch-Archeologisch Instituut.
Charpin, Dominique. 1988: Sippar: deux villes jumelles, *RA* 82: 13–32.
Charpin, Dominique. 1992: Le point sur les deux Sippar, *NABU* 1992/114.
Charpin, Dominique. 2000: Les prêteurs et le palais: les edits de *mīšarum* der rois de Babylone et leurs traces dans les archives privées. Pp. 185–211 in *Interdependency of Institutions and Private Entrepreneurs: Proceedings of the Second MOS Symposium (Leiden 1998)*, eds. A.C.V.M. Bongenaar and Govert van Driel. PIHANS 87. Istanbul–Leiden: Nederlands Historisch-Archeologisch Instituut.
Charpin Dominique. 2004: Histoire politique du Proche-Orient Amorrite (2002–1595). Pp. 25–480 in Dominique Charpin, Dietrich Edzard, and Marten Stol, *Mesopotamien. Die altbabylonische Zeit.* OBO 160/4. Fribourg – Göttingen. Academic Press – Vandenhoeck & Ruprecht.
Charpin, Dominique. 2005: Chroniques bibliographiques 5. Économie et société à Sippar et en Babylonie du nord à l'époque paléo-babylonienne, *RA* 99: 133–176.
Charpin, Dominique. 2010: *Writing, Law, and Kingship in Old Babylonian Mesopotamia.* Chicago: University of Chicago Press.
De Graef, Katrien. Forthcoming. Puppets on a String? On Female Agency in Old Babylonian Economy. in *Proceedings of the International Colloquium on Gender, Methodology and the Ancient Near East Held at Helsinki University, 27–28 October 2014*, eds. Saana Svärd and Agnès Garcia-Ventura.
Dumas, Alexandre. 1889. *Théâtre complet*, Paris: Michel Lévy frères.
Földi, Zsombor József. 2009. *Rībatum. The Archive of a Priestess from Old Babylonian Sippar* (unpublished thesis, accessed through www.academia.edu).
Gasche, Hermann. 1989. *La Babylonie au 17ᵉ siècle avant notre ère: approche archéologique, problèmes et perspectives.* MHEM 1. Wetteren: Cultura.
Harris, Rivkah. 1961: The Nadītu Laws of the Code of Hammu-rabi in Praxis. *Or* 30: 163–169.
Harris, Rivkah. 1962: Bibliographical Notes on the Nadītu Women of Sippar. *JCS* 16: 1–12.
Harris, Rivkah. 1963: The Organization and Administration of the Cloister in Ancient Babylonia. *JESHO* 6: 121–157.
Harris, Rivkah. 1964: The Nadītu Women. Pp 106–135 in *Studies Presented to A. Leo Oppenheim, June 7, 1964*, eds. Robert D. Biggs and John A. Brinkman. Chicago: University of Chicago Press.
Harris, Rivkah. 1969: Notes on the Babylonian Cloister and Hearth. A Review Article, *Or* 38: 133–145.
Harris, Rivkah. 1975. *Ancient Sippar. A Demographic Study of an Old Babylonian City (1894–1595 B.C.).* PIHANS 36. Istanbul – Leiden: Nederlands Historisch-Archeologisch Instituut.
Harris, Rivkah. 1989. Independent Women in Ancient Mesopotamia? Pp. 145–165 in *Women's Earliest Records from Ancient Egypt and Western Asia*, ed. Barbara S. Lesko. Atlanta: Scholars Press.
Janssen, Caroline. 1991. Samsu-iluna and the Hungry Nadītums, *NAPR* 5: 3–23.

Janssen, Caroline, Hermann Gasche, and Michel Tanret. 1994. Du chantier à la tablette. Ur-Utu et l'histoire de sa maison à Sippar-Amnānum. Pp. 91–123 in *Cinquante-deux reflexions sur le Proche-Orient ancien offertes en homage à Léon De Meyer* eds. Hermann Gasche, Michel Tanret, Caroline Janssen, and Ann Degraeve. MHEOP 2. Leuven: Peeters.

Janssen, Caroline. 1996. When the House is on Fire and the Children Are Gone. Pp. 237–246 in *Houses and Households in Ancient Mesopotamia: Papers Read at the 40e Rencontre Assyriologisue Intenrationale, Leiden, 5–8 July 1993*, ed. Klaas R. Veenhof. PIHANS 78. Istanbul–Leiden: Nederlands Historisch-Archeologisch Instituut.

Kalla, Gábor. 1999. Die Geschichte der Entdeckung der altbabylonischen Sippar-Archive, *ZA* 89: 201–226.

Lahtinen, Sara. 2011. *The nadītum as Businesswoman*, Saarbrücken: Lambert Academic Publishing.

Merriam-Webster online dictionary (Merriam-webster.com)

Richardson, Seth. 2010. A Light in the *Gagûm* Window: the Sippar Cloister in the Late Old Babylonian Period. Pp. 329–349 in *Opening the Tablet Box: Near Eastern Studies in Honor of Benjamin R. Foster*, eds. Sarah Melville and Alice Slotsky. CHANE 42. Leiden: Brill.

Stol, Marten. 1998. The Care of the Elderly in Mesopotamia in the Old Babylonian Period. Pp. 59–117 in *The Care of the Elderly in the Ancient Near East*, eds Marten Stol and Sven P. Vleeming. Leiden: Brill.

Stol, Marten. 2000. Titel altbabylonischer Klosterfrauen. Pp. 457–466 in *Assyriologica et Semitica. Festschrift für Joachim Oelsner anläßlich seines 65. Geburtstages am 18. Februar 1997*, eds. Joachim Marzahn and Hans Neumann. AOAT 252. Münster: Ugarit Verlag.

Stone, Elizabeth C. 1982. The Social Role of the Nadītu Women in Old Babylonian Nippur, *JESHO* 25: 50–70.

Tanret, Michel. 2004. Verba Volant, scripta non manent. Tablettes nomades dans les archives des gala.maḫ à Sippar-Amnānum. Pp. 249–270 in *Nomades et sédentaires dans le Proche-Orient ancien. Compte rendu de la XLVI*[e] *Rencontre Assyriologique Internationale (Paris, 10–13 juillet 2000)*, ed. Christophe Nicolle. Amurru 3. Paris: ERC.

Tanret, Michel. 2008: Open the Tablet Box ... New Aspects of Archive Keeping in Old Babylonian Sippar-Amnānum. Pp. 131–147 in *Studies in Ancient Near Eastern World View and Society Presented to Martel Stol on the Occasion of his 65*[th] *Birthday*, ed. Robartus J. Van der Spek. Bethesda: CDL Press.

Tanret, Michel and Caroline Janssen. Forthcoming. *Chains of Transmission*.

Van Lerberghe, Karel. 1994. The Ladies Amat-Aja and Šāt-Aja, Business Associates Under Hammu-rabi. *OLP* 25: 5–25.

Yoffee, Norman. 2000: Law Courts and the Mediation of Social Conflict in Ancient Mesopotamia. Pp. 46–63 in *Order, Legitimacy, and Wealth in Ancient States*, eds. Janet Richards and Mary Van Buren. Cambridge: Cambridge University Press.

Nele Ziegler

Economic Activities of Women According to Mari Texts (18th century BC)

In her unpublished doctoral dissertation, A. Millet Albà tried to estimate the population of the kingdom of Mari (Millet Albà 2001). She counted the people mentioned in the texts for the different towns, applied to the heads of families a ratio counting their wives and children and came to the number of 40,000 inhabitants for the best attested central districts of Mari during the reign of the last king, Zimrī-Lîm. Whatever the accuracy of this number may be, we can suppose that 50 % of the population of the kingdom of Mari were women or young girls, and that from the earliest age, these young girls were generally used to accomplish such tasks as looking after their smaller brothers and sisters, feeding or herding animals etc. As many other female tasks, these activities, actually, were not mentioned in texts and the only written information about these women concerned the food they consumed, the expenses for their amenities or well-being, or gifts they received. In fact, the palace archives from Mari mention the women that were related in some way to the royal administration or to the king because they were given wool and oil rations. This concerned first of all the 350 to 600 women who lived inside the royal palace and whom I studied 15 years ago in my book on the population of the "royal harem" (Ziegler 1999a). The administrative texts published in this study mention not only the amounts given to each woman, but enumerate them by profession or function inside the palace hierarchy, and provide good insight into the functioning of a royal palace in the 18th century BC. Besides this book, a good number of publications focused on the women of Mari. Some of these studies are devoted to women of the royal family (Dossin and Finet 1978; Batto 1980; Durand 1985b; Lafont 1987, Durand 2000: 259–504); an article deals with the women from the kingdom of Mari who had to take an oath (Bonechi 1997); others concern women as victims of war (Marello 1994; Ziegler 1999b; Ziegler 2014).

Given the limits of this paper, it is impossible to make a complete portrait of the economic role of women, so I chose to give glimpses of some women attested in the Mari archives. This data can be taken as paradigmatic for

Nele Ziegler, CNRS, UMR 7192, Proche-Orient – Caucase: langues, archéologie, cultures, Paris; nziegler@msh-paris.fr

others.[1] This presentation will start with the top of the palace society because those sources are the most varied: the first two women to be examined are Addu-dūrī, the queen mother, and Šībtu, one of the wives of Zimrī-Lîm. We will then look at two portraits of lower-ranking women: first Bazatum, a female musician from the palace who was married to one of Zimrī-Lîm's highest officials, and then the paper will be closed with Nanna, one of the lowest ranking women, who was a water carrier.

1 The queen-mother and the queen

The queen-mother and the queen were in charge of the palace and had under their command the female population and the manufactories of the palace. A sister of Zimrī-Lîm told him in a letter:[2]

> "I am fine! Adal-šenni, my lord (*scil.* husband) is fine! He has entrusted his big palace to my authority. He treated me (with respect), as I deserve it.
>
> 200 women, be they musicians, textile-workers or (palace) administrators do their job under my responsibility. They do what I order them (...)"

The wife of Adal-šenni, king of Burundum, tells in this letter that she had under her authority the concubines or musicians, the palace-servants and the women in the weaving mills of the palace, totaling 200 persons. In Mari, the population of the royal palace[3] exceeded this number: the female textile-workers did not live inside the palace and the royal household alone numbered more than 350 and, some years later, up to 600 inhabitants, nearly all women.

1.1 The queen-mother, Addu-dūrī[4]

Addu-dūrī was a princess from one of the Yaminite tribes. She was married to Hadnī-Addu, probably a son or brother of Yahdun-Lîm, and lived in exile dur-

1 An electronic edition of all the published texts from the royal archives of Mari here quoted in translation only can be found on http://www.archibab.fr (with bibliography). Excerpts of many unpublished texts mentioned in this contribution can be found in Ziegler 1999a (see index p. 294–295).

2 M.8161: 4–12 published by P. Marello 1994.

3 For the royal palace of Mari as architectural unit see Margueron 1982 and 2004, for the organization of the palace from textual evidence see Durand 1985a.

4 See Durand 2000: 273–295; Charpin and Ziegler 2003: 175 n. 36.

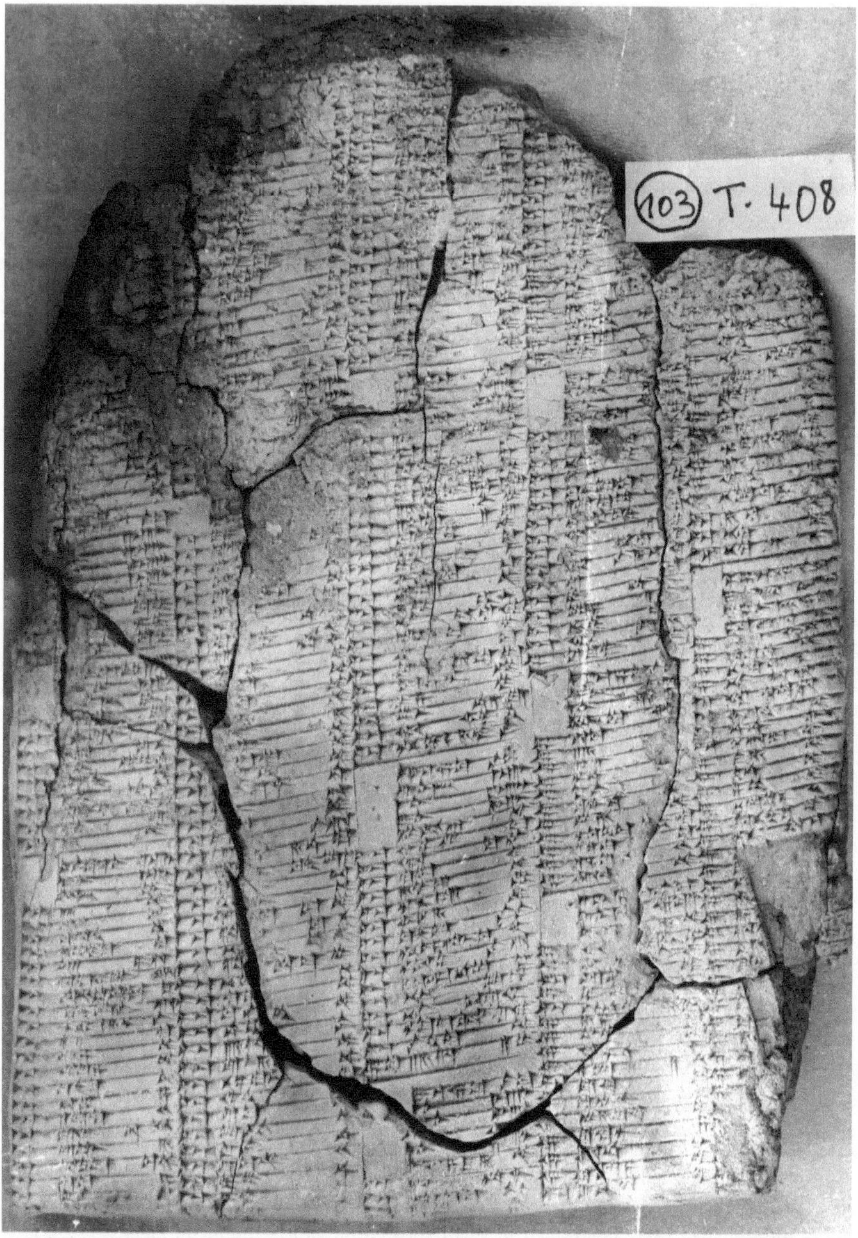

Fig. 1: The biggest account of oil rations, for more than 600 women living in the palace of Mari (FM 4, 13).

ing the years of Šamšī-Adad's reign. When Zimrī-Lîm reconquered the kingdom of his forebears, she regained Mari through his efforts. Except for a brief period at the very beginning of Zimrī-Lîm's reign, she didn't live with him in the royal palace of Mari,[5] but had a "house" of her own. This is clear from administrative texts, like the one that mentions a bronze knife from her house[6] or others that mention *burrum*-cereals delivered from her house to the kitchens of the royal palace.[7] Other texts enumerate textiles for her house.[8] We do not know where this building was situated. It is possible that it was in Mari itself or rather close to the capital. She wrote to the king (ARM 10 54):

> "The city of Mari, the temples and the palace are well. May the heart of my lord fear nothing."

This shows that she was aware of the situation in the capital and that she felt responsibility for the temples and the royal palace.

Outside Mari, the geographic horizon of her activities seems rather limited. Events in Ṣuprum[9] are mentioned, and her personal presence at the yearly Dērītum festival in Dēr is attested (ARM 10 142), but it is clear that she did not live there. Zimrī-Lîm told her about an official who was not allowed to stay in Terqa,[10] and she did mention a prophecy uttered in Hišamta (ARM 10 53 = ARM 26/1 195), but all this seems to be far away from her place of residence. Instead, cultic activity in Mari is attested by letters and administrative documents. The chapel of Bēlet-ekallim in the palace of Mari,[11] the sanctuary of Annunītum,[12] the cultic personnel of Itūr-Mêr (ARM 10 51) and Eštar-Bišri are mentioned in her correspondence, and sacrifices are recorded in administrative documents.[13]

---

5 This can be stated because of the "harem deliveries" edited by Ziegler 1999a; see p. 50–51 for Addu-dūrī not living inside the palace except for the time of redaction of the oldest document, FM 4 1.

6 M.8868 (ARM 32, p. 237–238) a bronze-knife from the "house of Addu-dūrī" (year ZL 3).

7 ARM 12, 141 and 146, FM 4, 49: *burrum*-cereals from the "house of Addu-dūrī" delivered to the royal kitchen, i.e. to Ilu-kān (year ZL 4).

8 M.6699 (ARM 30, p. 435): textiles for the "house of Addu-dūrī".

9 ARM 10, 150.

10 ARM 10, 148, see Durand 2000: 292.

11 She tells her dream about the palace chapel of Bēlet-ekallim and the priest of Eštar-Bišri (ARM 10, 50).

12 She reports about the temple of Annunītum (ARM 10, 55 and 50).

13 She must organize offerings for Eštar Dērītum (ARM 10, 142); for administrative texts, see ARM 21, passim.

She also exercised her authority by overseeing the maintenance of the royal palace.[14] Zimrī-Lîm asked her to organize and supervise construction works in the courtyard of the royal palace because he wanted to watch the white horses from Qaṭna from his apartment (ARM 10 147):

> "I heard about the white horses from Qaṭna and that these horses are splendid! Now, (...) in the courtyard of the painted house, at the door of [the guards, for protection] from the daylight there should be shadow. They shall make this! They shall cut [reed] and make a shelter for the horses. They shall [deliver to them] grain (...)"

On other occasions she acted as the representative of her son, the king Zimrī-Lîm, when he was absent from his capital. She had access to his personal belongings, and was able to give information about them[15] as shown by this letter to the official in charge of the goods and the workshops of the palace:[16]

> "I opened the box at the disposal of the king, but there is no silver-ring of 4 shekels (...)"

Addu-dūrī acted here as representative of her son and could manage the coffers containing his possessions. We know from another text that a box which held the king's belongings was stored in her house.[17]

Other texts show that she was in charge of her own household, which was clearly distinct from the royal palace or the king. Numerous people are enumerated as her servants and among them are not only women attached to textile-production,[18] but also people in charge of agriculture,[19] scribes,[20] and even a female physician.[21]

Addu-dūrī was involved in lending activities concerning large amounts of grain. A recapitulation written two years after her death, in the 8th year of reign of Zimrī-Lîm, states that she and her heir, the high-priestess Inibšina, had not recovered 6 *ugār* of grain, some 7,200 liters, which she had lent to different persons some four years earlier (Charpin 2008b). Since this text only mentions the debts that had not been recovered, we may assume that her lending activities took place on a much larger scale.

---

14 Other activities concern the instruction of female musicians (ARM 10, 148).
15 Data about metals and precious objects are given in ARM 10, 145. No. 146 mentions libation-vases for cultic purposes.
16 ARM 10, 61, see Durand 2000: 290, no. 1109. See also ARM 18, 1 and 4.
17 See for the *pisan šarrim ina bīt Addu-dūrī* M.8868 (ARM 32, p. 237–238).
18 *FM* 4, 35.
19 M.7454, M.7829+, cf. Ziegler 1999a: 51, n. 319.
20 M.7829+.
21 *FM* 4, 34: 16.

1.2 Queen Šībtu[22]

The queen-mother Addu-dūrī died at the beginning of the 6th year of Zimrī-Lîm's reign. She was replaced in the cultic activities by the second wife of Zimrī-Lîm, queen Šībtu, a princess from Aleppo.

Šībtu had been married to Zimrī-Lîm in his second year of reign. We have much data about this woman, including the preparations for the marriage, the negotiations of the bride-price, etc. Unfortunately, the only information that we do not have is the one thing that would help to evaluate more precisely her economic situation – that is, the contents of her dowry, which was given to her by her father in Aleppo and which she brought as her personal belongings to her new home. A comparison can be made with the dowries of other princesses, and for this one can consult the contributions of B. Lafont (1987) or D. Charpin (2008a). Princesses received as their dowry objects in precious metals, be it jewelry, small dishes, or table-ware in bronze, textiles, house furniture such as beds, stools or tables, and female servants. We can imagine that Šībtu came with such a dowry to Mari.

Her father, Yarīm-Lîm, was concerned about the installation of his daughter in her new home and discussed this matter with the envoy of Zimrī-Lîm, the high official and diviner, Asqūdum (ARM 26/1, 13):

> "Yarīm-Lîm addressed me as follows: '(...) Where will the household goods of my daughter go?'
>
> I (said): 'The house of your daughter is good.'
>
> He (said): 'The effects of my daughter may be placed in her house. (But) my daughter should live with her husband and for 5 or 6 days she may leave (the palace) and concern herself with her house. (...)'"

We know that the housing of the queen of Mari inside the palace was a matter of concern since Yahdun-Lîm had decided to make the queen live outside the royal palace. The reason for this installation of the main queen outside the palace was perhaps for the period of her menstrual impurity, but this is not the topic here. In any case, Asqūdum confirmed for the king of Aleppo that his daughter was endowed with a convenient house in Mari and that she could put her personal belongings there. In the same letter, Asqūdum gives more information about the house for Šībtu, as a collation of this text by J.-M. Durand revealed:[23]

---

22 Cf. Durand 1988: 95–117; Ziegler 1999a: 54–56, 96–98; Durand 2000: 304–355; Ziegler 2009–2011.

23 Durand 2004. See for the "house" of Šībtu also A.4670 (ARM 32, p. 371–372).

"Now, my lord must give instructions that they select the house of (general) Mut-Bisir* for his daughter, so that his servants, who will come with me (to Mari) will see it, and tell their lord about it. (...)

May my lord think about the house, and that they take care of the house that he gives to this young woman. (...)

And during my sojourn here (in Aleppo) may they prepare this house!"

Mut-Bisir was one of the highest ranking generals of Šamšī-Adad in Mari and he had had a palace in that town. This residence maintained the name of its famous former owner. We don't know if this was really this house that was finally selected for Šībtu, but it may have been.[24] In the following years, huge amounts of grain or other foodstuffs from this estate were delivered to the palace kitchens.[25]

So, Šībtu had two places to live in Mari:[26] an apartment in the royal palace, and a house outside the palace, perhaps the former residence of Mut-Bisir. Female servants worked in these two places.[27] Some of them are nominally known from the lists of the harem population. A part of these servants were devoted to house-keeping and cooking.

Šībtu gave birth to at least two children, perhaps twins,[28] and took the first place among the wives of Zimrī-Lîm. Even if another woman, Dām-hurāṣi, mother of Zimrī-Lîm's first-born son Yaggid-Lîm, seems to have held a more honorable position, it was Šībtu who was in charge of the royal palace. She wrote her husband letters like this one (ARM 10, 22): "Mari, the temples and the palace are well," and Zimrī-Lîm could call the royal palace "Šībtu's palace". After a victory he wrote to his wife the good news and closed his letter by the words:[29] "Rejoice! And give (this) good news to your palace!"

Indeed, Šībtu was at the head of the royal palace population. She was the one who had to decide the fate of deportees – to be admitted among the palace-musicians or among the textile-workers. She had access to all the rooms of the palace, and the administrators had to contact her for access to boxes or documents stored in these rooms.[30] For all these activities, her seal was important. We know that this seal was made from lapis lazuli and had a golden cap or

24 Note that Šībtu's presence in the "Smaller Eastern Palace" of Mari is attested in year ZL 10 (ref. in Ziegler 1999a: 56, n. 354)

25 E.g. ARM 12, 57 (date 1/xii/ZL 3); ARM 12, 15 (date 28/ix/ZL 4); ARM 12, 161 (date 14/xi/ZL 5); ARM 12, 433 (date 6/iv/ZL 6).

26 Ziegler 1999a: 56.

27 Ziegler 1999a: 96–98.

28 Ziegler 1997: 55.

29 ARM 10, 122+M.15083 (Durand 1987).

30 ARM 10, 12 and A.3413 (ARM 32, p. 358–359).

Fig. 2: Impression of one of the seals of queen Šībtu (after Parrot 1959: 167–168 and pl. XLVI, no. 69).

setting.[31] It is possible that she had more than one seal, since Zimrī-Lîm asked her (ARM 10, 119):

> "(...) seal it with your seal that is inscribed 'Šībtu, daughter of Yarîm-Lîm, wife of Zimrī-Lîm' and give it to Imgurrum (...)"

This detail indicates that Šībtu had another seal, which is a situation also known for other administrators (Charpin 1999).

Some other letters show that Šībtu was engaged in administrative affairs, but more generally she was concerned with the royal palace of Mari. Her letters informed the king about everyday events that had happened or about the women who lived in the palace. Sometimes she would discuss special foodstuffs with her husband, such as *hazannu*-garlic or wine. We don't see her involved in the organization of the weaving-mills, but this is, perhaps, because these workshops were outside of the palace and sources are lacking.

In any case, Šībtu had people in her service who made garments. She may have even produced textiles for her husband with her own hands, as this letter shows (ARM 10 17):

> "May my lord put on his shoulder the cloth and the shirt (**gu$_2$-e$_3$-a**) that I have made."

31 ARM 25, 349 (ARM 32, p. 268): "(...) 1 golden setting for the lapis lazuli seal of Šībtu" (date ZL 5).

Or in another letter she wrote to the king (ARM 10 18):

> "The palace is well. When I returned to Mari, the 5th day, I have sent the female physician Mammītum-ummī to my lord with 1 fine garment, 1 shirt and 1 *duḫšū*-coloured belt, the garments of my lord. (...)"

The queen was involved in many transactions, received or delivered goods, paid taxes, etc. She was active, and had, as many other women, the freedom to move from the royal palace to her own household or elsewhere. In the letter just quoted, she alluded to her return to Mari, showing by this that she had been absent. But Šībtu, unlike another wife of Zimri-Lîm, did not accompany Zimrī-Lîm on his longer trips. Even when he went to Aleppo, her former country, Šībtu stayed at home, looking after the palace. Clearly she felt her presence there more important than seeing her mother or brother again (Ziegler 1999a: 56).

From her private economic activities we almost know nothing. It is probable that these documents were stored in her personal house. One single exception is a loan document – it shows that Šībtu, like her mother-in-law, Addu-dūrī, could give credit and make benefice by this kind of activity (ARM 8, 76):

> "x shekel silver, its worth without interest, from Šībtu PN_1 has received. PN_2 is the guarantor of PN_1. Should PN_1 flee [...]"

2 Two women of middle and lower ranks

In the list FM 4, 13 (see above Fig. 1) more than 600 women from the royal palace are enumerated with their oil-rations. The amounts give insight about the social status of these women inside the palace hierarchy. We have just seen two of the highest situated women, the queen-mother and the queen. We will now turn to two other women who belonged to the "middle" and the "lower" classes, Bazatum and Nanna.

2.1 The musician Bazatum[32]

Bazatum belonged to the category of the "younger musicians" who, in the palace, were just below the highest-ranking ladies. Her rations of oil or wool in-

32 Durand 1990: 298–301; Ziegler 1999a: 74–76; Koppen 2002: 295.

creased during the first years of Zimrī-Lîm's reign, while she lived in the royal palace.[33]

Zimrī-Lîm apparently did not decide to make her one of his concubines, but gave her as a spouse to one of his highest officials, Sammêtar. She became his secondary wife and lived in his house in Zurubbān in the countryside.[34] Unfortunately, some months later her husband died; the royal palace then proceeded to make an inspection of all his belongings.[35] The administrative texts composed on that occasion distinguish the personal belongings of Bazatum from those of the palace and from those of her deceased husband. One of these inspection texts (FM 6, 33) established that the household of Bazatum consisted of 4 servants, 2 oxen and 25 *ugār* of barley (30,000 l) and ARM 9, 97 mentions 4 textile workers of Bazatum. Her cattle were grazing close to Terqa (ARM 24, 48). Other texts mention jewelry or precious dishes.[36]

We can thus see that a younger musician from the royal palace could be married outside the palace and acquire some wealth. Contacts with the women from the royal harem were not necessarily broken: Bazatum was entrusted with jewelry by one of her former colleagues, another musician from the palace, who meanwhile had gotten married as a lower ranking spouse to Zimrī-Lîm.[37] Bazatum took care of the jewels of her former colleague and friend, probably because the latter did not have a house of her own.

2.2 One of the poorest women

Let us close this overview with one of the less considered women who lived in the royal palace, a water carrier named Nanna. These women got the smallest rations of oil adult women could get, and were less highly esteemed since they performed hard work. In the harem lists, the water carriers (*hābêt mē*) are enumerated generally after the female door keepers, and before their male colleagues. I conclude from this that these women could cross the outer and inner gates of the harem (Ziegler 1999a: 113).

We don't know anything about the belongings of these women; they probably did not have much. But one letter of the queen Šībtu speaks about their activity (ARM 10, 129). She quotes a letter of Zimrī-Lîm:

---

33 Oil rations: FM 4, 3 (date 1-xi-ZL1): ½ **sila**$_3$, later FM 4, 13 (date ZL 5?): 1 **sila**$_3$. Wool rations: FM 4, 6 (date 2-vi-ZL 2): 7 **mana**, FM 4, 8 (date xi-ZL 2): 8 **mana**.

34 See ARM 9, 97: textile-production entrusted to Bazatum at Zurubbān (20-xi-ZL 7).

35 Koppen 2002: 292–293, 296–300.

36 ARM 25, 490; 748 (jewellery), M.15167+ (dishes), see Koppen 2002: 312, n. 117.

37 ARM 25, 353 (ARM 32, p. 334–335): jewels of Bēltāni with Bazatum in Zurubbān (8/xii/ZL 7).

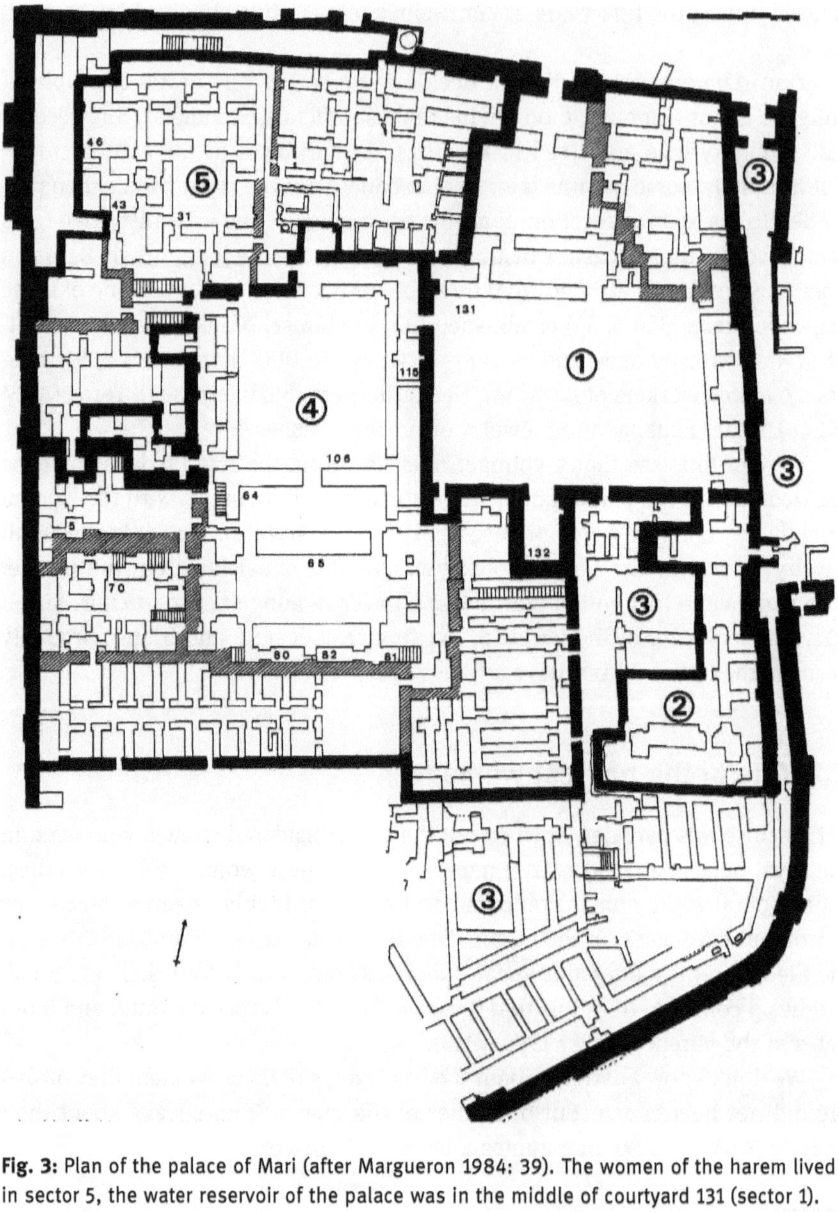

Fig. 3: Plan of the palace of Mari (after Margueron 1984: 39). The women of the harem lived in sector 5, the water reservoir of the palace was in the middle of courtyard 131 (sector 1).

> "I have heard: '(The water carrier) Nanna has a *simmum*-disease.' She is present in many places of the palace and many women can contract her illness. Give an order so that nobody shall drink from the vessel from which she is drinking; that nobody shall sit on the chair where she is sitting and that nobody shall sleep in the bed where she is sleeping. Many women live with her. She shall not infect them with her illness."

This letter of the queen shows that the water carrier's disease was particularly inconvenient, because that woman would bring water to the other rooms of the harem, had contact with many people and because she shared her living-space with many others: chairs, beds, dishes were used in common.

***

In this paper I have tried to give a glance of four women of different status, basing their presentation on the varied documentation available. Beyond these cases, the archives of Mari provide interesting insights into the economic situation of women. However, the documentation is unequal; we get more data about princesses or musicians than about weavers or slaves, but the same observation can be made about men.

Abbreviations

ARM 9	Birot 1960.
ARM 10	Dossin and Finet 1978.
ARM 12	Birot 1964.
ARM 18	Rouault 1977.
ARM 21	Durand 1983.
ARM 26/1	Durand 1988.
ARM 30	Durand 2009.
ARM 32	Arkhipov 2012.
FM 4	Ziegler 1999a.

Bibliography

Arkhipov, Ilya. 2012. *Le Vocabulaire de la métallurgie et la nomenclature des objets en métal dans les textes de Mari. Matériaux pour le Dictionnaire de Babylonien de Paris III*. ARM 32. Louvain/Paris/Walpole: Peeters.
Batto, Bernard F. 1980. Land Tenure and Women at Mari, *JESHO* 23: 209–239.
Birot, Maurice. 1960. *Textes administratifs de la salle 5 du palais*. ARM 9. Paris: Imprimerie Nationale.
Birot, Maurice. 1964. *Textes administratifs de la salle 5 du palais (2° partie)*. ARM 12. Paris: Geuthner.
Bonechi, Marco. 1997. Les serments de femmes à Mari. *Méditerranées* 10/11: 97–104.
Charpin, Dominique. 1999. Les propriétaires de deux sceaux à Mari, *NABU* 1999/78.
Charpin, Dominique. 2008a. La dot de la princesse mariote Inbatum. Pp. 159–172 in *Muhibbe Darga Armagani*, eds. Taner Tarhan, Aksel Tibet, and Erkan Konyar. Istanbul: Sadberk Hanım Müzesi.

Charpin, Dominique. 2008b. Archivage et classification: un récapitulatif de créances à Mari sous Zimrî-Lîm. Pp. 3–15 in *Proceedings of the 51st Rencontre Assyriologique Internationale, Held at the Oriental Institute of the University of Chicago, July 18–22, 2005*, eds. Robert D. Biggs, Jennie Myers, and Martha T. Roth. SAOC 62. Chicago: Oriental Institute.

Charpin, Dominique and Nele Ziegler. 2003. *Florilegium marianum V. Mari et le Proche-Orient à l'époque amorrite. Essai d'histoire politique*. Mémoires de NABU 6. Paris: SEPOA.

Dossin, Georges and André Finet. 1978. *Correspondance féminine*. ARM 10. Paris: Geuthner.

Durand, Jean-Marie. 1983. *Textes administratifs des salles 134 et 160 du palais de Mari*. ARM 21, Paris: Geuthner.

Durand, Jean-Marie. 1985a. L'organisation de l'espace dans le palais de Mari. Pp. 39–110 in *Le système palatial en Orient, en Grèce et à Rome*, ed. E. Lévy. Strasbourg: Centre de Recherches sur le Proche-Orient et la Grèce antiques.

Durand, Jean-Marie. 1985b. Les dames du palais de Mari à l'époque du royaume de Haute-Mésopotamie. *MARI* 4: 385–436.

Durand, Jean-Marie. 1987. La défaite de Zûzû, roi d'Apum. *MARI* 5: 621–622.

Durand, Jean-Marie. 1988. *Archives épistolaires de Mari I/1*, ARM 26/1, Paris: Editions Recherche sur les Civilisations.

Durand, Jean-Marie. 1990. Documents pour l'histoire du Royaume de Haute-Mésopotamie II. *MARI* 6: 271–301.

Durand, Jean-Marie. 2000. *Documents épistolaires du palais de Mari, tome III*. LAPO 18. Paris: Éditions du Cerf.

Durand, Jean-Marie. 2004. Une maison pour Šiptu à Mari, *NABU* 2004/52.

Durand, Jean-Marie. 2009. *La Nomenclature des habits et des textiles dans les textes de Mari. Matériaux pour le Dictionnaire de Babylonien de Paris Tome I*. ARM 30. Paris: Editions du CNRS.

Koppen, Frans van. 2002. Seized by royal order: The households of Sammêtar and other magnates at Mari. Pp. 289–372 in *Florilegium marianum VI. Recueil d'études à la mémoire d'André Parrot*, eds. Dominique Charpin and Jean-Marie Durand. Mémoires de NABU 7. Paris: SEPOA.

Lafont, Bertrand. 1987. Les filles du roi de Mari. Pp. 113–124 in *La femme dans le Proche-Orient antique. Compte rendu de la XXXIIIe Rencontre Assyriologique Internationale (Paris, 7–10 juillet 1986)*, ed. Jean-Marie Durand. Paris: Editions Recherche sur les Civilisations.

Margueron, Jean-Claude. 1982. *Recherches sur les palais mésopotamiens à l'âge du Bronze*. Paris: Picard / Edition Recherche sur les Civilisations.

Margueron, Jean-Claude. 1984. Le célèbre palais de Zimri-Lim, *Les dossiers histoire et archéologie* 80, february 1984: 38–45.

Margueron, Jean-Claude. 2004. *Mari. Métropole de l'Euphrate au IIIe et au début du IIe millénaire av. J.-C.*, 2 volumes. Paris: Geuthner.

Marello, Pierre. 1994. Esclaves et reines. Pp. 115–129 in *Florilegium marianum II. Recueil d'études à la mémoire de Maurice Birot*, eds. Dominique Charpin and Jean-Marie Durand. Mémoires de NABU 3. Paris: SEPOA.

Marello, Pierre. 1997. Liqtum, reine du Burundum. *MARI* 8: 455–459.

Millet Albà, Adelina. 2001. *La population du royaume de Mari à l'époque du roi Zimrî-Lîm d'après les archives du palais de Mari*. Unpublished PhD. Paris: EPHE.

Parrot, André. 1959. *Le palais. Documents et monuments. Mission archéologique de Mari II/3*. BAH 70. Paris: Geuthner.

Rouault, Olivier. 1977. *Mukannišum. L'administration et l'économie palatiales à Mari. Transcription, traduction et étude historique*. ARM 18. Paris: Geuthner.

Ziegler, Nele. 1997. Les enfants du palais. *Ktèma* 22: 45–57

Ziegler, Nele. 1999a. *Florilegium marianum IV. Le Harem de Zimrî-Lîm. La population féminine des palais d'après les archives royales de Mari*. Mémoires de NABU 5. Paris: SEPOA.

Ziegler, Nele. 1999b. Le harem du vaincu. *RA* 93: 1–26.

Ziegler, Nele. 2009–2011. Šībtum. *RlA* 12: 441–443.

Ziegler, Nele. 2014. Kriege und ihre Folgen: Frauenschicksale anhand der Archive aus Mari. Pp. 885–907 in *Krieg und Frieden im Alten Vorderasien. 52e Rencontre Assyriologique Internationale, Münster, 17.–21. Juli 2006*, ed. H. Neumann *et al.* AOAT 401. Münster: Ugarit Verlag.

Sophie Démare-Lafont

Women at Work in Mesopotamia: An attempt at a legal perspective

The starting point for this article is the observation that, when it comes to women's work in Mesopotamia, there is no specific legal point of view. While the sources related to the economic and administrative aspects of the subject are numerous, as shown by the workshops organized within the French-Japanese REFEMA project, those regarding the legal aspects are scarce.

An optimistic scholar would conclude that, in the realm of labor law, the Mesopotamian woman was a man like any other, which of course is wrong. Women were not always involved in the same types of work as men, at least in the "public" institutions (temple, palace), although they were compelled to do for instance the *corvée*-work;[1] they didn't have the same wages as men[2] and on many occasions, they performed ancillary tasks just like slaves. But these are sociological or economical features rather than legal ones.

Actually, the major difference between men and women in terms of labor law lies in the fact that economic activities of men are framed in a set of rather elaborated rules while no comparable regulations are attested for women. One could surmise that they were implicitly covered by the masculine standards of law, and this is true when they are in a position of employers: as far as we can see from the tablets involving queens, nuns or wealthy housewives, they resorted to the same methods as their male counterparts to run their estates and to hire their staff.[3]

But the picture is quite different when it comes to female workforce or employees. Their existence is well attested in the administrative documents, especially the lists of workers or of rations, but legally speaking, they are almost invisible.

1 See for Ur III Period Lafont 2014: 57–64 and his contribution in this volume, where he suggests, after Steinkeller, that only the heads of the households were liable to *corvée*-work, so that women would perform it on their behalf and not for themselves.

2 Judging from the administrative documents of the Ur III period, they received usually half the rations of men; see Waetzoldt 1988.

3 See for example the archives of princess Simat-Ištaran in Ur III Garšana (Owen and Mayr 2007; Lafont 2014: 71–74), of the Old Babylonian *nadītu*-nuns (Nakata 2014) or of princess Iltani in Qaṭṭara during the same period (Langlois 2014).

Sophie Démare-Lafont, Université Panthéon-Assas – École Pratique des Hautes Études; sodela@free.fr

The law collections mention some specific professions like innkeeper (*sābītu*), wet-nurse (*mušēniqtu*)[4] or prostitute (*ḫarimtu*), typically in criminal matters and without describing the legal basis of their trade. The *mīšarum*-edicts mention the female innkeeper but again in a very elliptical way. Legal deeds and documents testifying to their employment are notably few and shed a bit of light on the provisions of the codes, but many grey areas remain. For instance, it is striking that free women hardly appear in the Old Babylonian service contracts. This matches the idea that this kind of work was performed either by female slaves or within the family, thus without a contract.

On the other hand, the vocabulary can sometimes be ambiguous. For instance, female workers were sometimes called *ṣuhārtu*, regardless of their specific skills,[5] so that it is difficult to decide whether this word means "servant" or "employee"; from the point of view of their master or mistress, the difference is irrelevant because both of these statuses come down to a form of dependency. But we cannot exclude the possibility that among these women, some were hired without a written contract and received wages for their work in form of rations. Of course, it is not always a matter of postulating a contractual relationship between the female staff as a whole and the male or female head of the household. But we have to take into account the fact that most of the agreements were concluded orally, which means that a significant part of the legal reality escapes us.

Even the very conception of a labor contract seems debatable: like in other legal systems in Antiquity (especially the Roman law), Mesopotamia shaped the labor relations in the framework of a contract for services, using the same formulae for estates, animals and persons.[6] Indeed, the peculiarity of the labor contract as a category on its own is a very recent development in legal history, connected to the industrial revolution in the 19th century. The situation is complicated in Mesopotamia by the fact that many service deliveries are performed in connection with the repayment of a debt, through the mechanism of personal antichresis by which a creditor takes advantage of the work of his debtor or of a member of his family.[7]

---

4 Inkeepers and wet-nurses are among the rare female professions mentioned in the Old Assyrian private documents; see Michel in this volume.

5 For instance in Qaṭṭara, a female textile worker could be designated as *ṣuhārtum* rather than *išpartum* (OBTR 142; see Langlois 2014: 245). See also YOS 5 177 (from Larsa) recording the delivery of wool rations to the *ṣuhārātu ša bīt išpari* "working girls of the weaving workshop", and the more numerous occurrences in the Nuzi documents, where the *ṣuhārātu* are the young girls dependent on the palace, with or without specification of their task (see Lion 2016).

6 See the references in the CAD *agāru* "to hire, rent".

7 About this type of security for debts, see Westbrook and Jasnow 2001.

Thus, the legal basis for a labor relationship could vary, and in this picture, the situation of women appears as but one small aspect of a multifaceted reality. These caveats raise a methodological question as to the typicality of the legal deeds and provisions dealing with women at work. In this field more than in any other, the use of a written contract seems to meet the specific needs of the parties rather than the current practices.

With all of this in mind, we can review the legal data by trying to combine the information provided by law collections and legal documents.

As far as law is concerned, three main categories of feminine professions are attested, namely the weavers, the innkeepers and the wet-nurses.[8] Only the third one is a typically female occupation, while the two others are also attested for men.

1 Weavers

Female weavers are attested only in a Sumerian law collection published by P. Michalowski and C. Walker,[9] referred to as "Laws of X" in the edition of M. Roth[10] and henceforth incorporated in the *Code of Ur-Namma*.[11]

§ D8 states the wages for various works performed by female weavers:[12]

> The monthly (?) wages of a female weaver when washing will be [x sila]. The daily (?) wages of a female weaver of skilled (?) weaving will be twenty sila. The daily wages of a female weaver of *šutur*(?)-garments will be twenty sila.

Although the provision mentions women called **geme$_2$**, "female slave", free persons were also meant under this wide denomination that refers to a labor force rather than to a status in the Ur III administrative sources[13].

It is difficult to figure out the purpose of this provision, but one explanation would be that the public authorities wanted to regulate the salaries in the

8 Prostitutes are a fourth category, dealt with by J. Cooper in this volume. The legal side – if any – of their activities largely escapes us.

9 Michalowski and Walker 1989.

10 Roth 1997: 37–39.

11 Wilcke 2002: 291 and note 3.

12 Civil 2011: 251; **geme$_2$ uš-bar tan$_4$-tan$_4$-na a$_2$ iti$^?$ 1-a-ka-n[i...] geme$_2$ u[š-bar] ama-tuk$_5$-ka ⸢a$_2$ u$_4$$^?$⸣ 1-ni 0.0.2 geme$_2$ uš-[bar] ⸢šu$^?$⸣-dur$^?$-ka a$_2$ u$_4$ 1-[ni] 0.0.2.**

13 See for instance Englund 1991: 274, who notices that **geme$_2$** appears to be the female counterpart of **guruš** in the lists of workers. Elsewhere, **geme$_2$** has the meaning "female slave", as opposed to **arad$_2$**, "male slave".

"private" sector. These rates were probably to be enforced by employers entering into a contract with suppliers of female workers, who were therefore the objects of the contract and not the partners in it, which brings us back to the ordinary condition of women in the world of work.

The same ancillary condition can be perceived in the Mari documents: young girls taken as booty were sent to the weaving workshops of the palace,[14] where they probably learned their craft and increased the number of employees.

An Old Babylonian contract from Nippur (ARN 7) points to another situation: a slave woman is manumitted by her owners but has to continue serving them,[15] which probably means that she had to support them in their old age. Considering the attendance of three witnesses bearing the title of "overseer of the female weavers" (UGULA GEME$_2$.UŠ.BAR ll. 22–24), M. Stol has convincingly suggested that the freed woman would henceforth work in a weaving workshop and give her wages to her former masters, while dwelling in their house.[16]

2 Innkeepers

Women innkeepers have drawn the attention of the Sumerian and Babylonian lawgivers.[17]

The *Code of Ur-Namma* contains a provision setting an interest rate for the credit sale of beer (**§ D9**) by the woman innkeeper:[18]

> If a female tavern-keeper gives to someone a beer-jar of hers, at harvest time [she will receive] 50 sila of barley.

The *Code of Hammurabi* (**§ 111**) has exactly the same rule, in Akkadian:[19]

> If a woman innkeeper gives one vat of beer as a *qīptum*-loan, she shall take 50 sila of grain at the harvest.

---

14 See for instance ARM 13 21 (Durand 1997: 238 no. 99) or ARM 10 125 (Durand 2000: 351 no. 1167). I am grateful to Antoine Jacquet for these references.

15 ARN 7: 10–11 NA.AN.GA.TI.LA.AŠ IGI.NI.NE.ŠE$_3$ I$_3$.GUB.BU, "As long as they live, she shall stand before them (= serve them)".

16 Stol 1998: 83.

17 About brewers and innkeepers in general, see Cassin 1961; Röllig 1970; and Lion 2013.

18 Civil 2011: 244, 251; **tuk[um-b]i munus-lu$_2$-geštin-na-am$_3$ 1 ⸢pihu⸣-ka-ni lu$_2$-ra in-na-an-šum$_2$ [u$_4$] ⸢buru$_{14}$⸣-ke$_4$ 0.0.5 še [...] x.**

19 Roth 1997: 102, with an interrogation as to the legal nature of the contract: "one vat of beer as a loan (?)"; *šumma sabītum ištēn pīḫam ana qīptim iddin ina ebūrim* 5 *šūt še'am ileqqe.*

The comparison of the two texts reveals some slight differences but another source for **§ D9**, coming from Sippar, refers explicitly to the **šu-la$_2$**-loan, similar to the *qīptum*-loan mentioned in the *Code of Hammurabi*.[20] The legal nature of this type of contract is still a matter of discussion, especially because no interest is recorded in the documents despite their clear commercial background.[21] What is interesting for our topic is that these transactions usually involved a middleman who received the goods, mainly fungibles, probably as a capital from which further loans were to be made.[22] In both law collections, the innkeeper acts as a creditor and is part of a circulation process of goods initiated by the palace: she receives the grain, probably as a *qīptum*-loan, in order to produce the beer that she will sell, and then she pays a portion of the expected – and substantial – profits[23] to the palace in form of a tax.[24] In this network of production and distribution, she enjoys an important role as shown by the very fact that legal provisions deal with her business.

The *Laws of Ešnunna* also mention the alewife (*sabītum*) twice:

> § 15 A merchant or a woman innkeeper will not accept silver, grain, wool, oil, or anything else from a male or female slave.[25]
>
> § 41 If a foreigner, a visitor or an "acquaintance" wishes to sell his beer, the woman innkeeper shall sell the beer for him at the current rate.[26]

§ 15 includes the alewife and the *tamkārum*, "merchant" in the same prohibition: they should not receive silver, barley, wool or oil from a male or female

---

20 Civil 2011: 251 **1 pihu$_4$ lu$_2$-[ra] šu-la$_2$-a-še$_3$ in-[na-šum$_2$]** "she gives one beer-jar to someone on credit".

21 See Skaist 1994: 51 who concludes that the *qīptum* is a "commercial interest bearing loan" without any explicit amount noted in the contract "for some as yet unknown reason". Many scholars consider the *qīptum*-loan as a form of credit sale (see for instance Yaron 1988: 158) or as a deposit (Westbrook 2003: 403).

22 Such is the case for instance in the trial document from Sippar BE 6/1 103: a man received an amount of grain *ana qīptim* and was summoned by the creditor to give it back. He refused and claimed that he did not use the grain but gave it away *ana qīptim*, which seems to be the natural purpose of the operation.

23 Driver and Miles 1956: 207; Lion 2013: 394.

24 Stol 2004: 769; Lion 2013: 396. The situation is best illustrated by BE 6/1 103 quoted above (n. 22): the creditors were probably state agents trying to recover the grain lent as *qīptum* to the middleman-debtor. This would explain why the judges of Babylon had to intervene in a case brought in Sippar (Dombradi 1996: II 176 fn. 1257).

25 Roth 1997: 61; *ina qāti wardim u amtim tamkārum u sabītum kaspam še'am šipātim šamnam adi mādim ul imaḫḫar*. About the readings *adi mādim* (from *mādum* "much, numerous") or *adi māṭim* ("even in small quantity") see Yaron 1988: 52–53.

26 Roth 1997: 65; *šumma ubarum napṭarum u mudû šikaršu inaddin sabītum maḫīrat illaku šīkaram inaddinšum*.

slave, who are assumed to act in fraud of their owner's interests. The meaning of this provision is best understood against the background of the pattern described above: the innkeeper and the merchant involved in commercial transactions are but one link within a larger chain of persons or institutions. Therefore, accepting a suspicious partner in the network could produce a domino effect and cause financial losses to all participants. The fungible goods given by the slave are not a purchase price[27] but rather a capital entrusted in view of further commercial operations. In such a type of loan, there was no restitution in kind but a repayment in any accepted value, which makes this contract similar to a credit sale or a deposit. The whole system relied on trust and confidence, as is usual in partnership and trade relationship. The issue here is to prevent a slave from acting on his/her own,[28] not only because of their lack of legal capacity – such a general rule needs not to be repeated for the innkeeper or the merchant – but for fear of putting stolen goods on the market place, which might result in economic damages to downstream participants. The next provision (§ 16) completes the picture and implicitly addresses the alewife and the merchant: they are not allowed to give (instead of receiving in § 15) fungible goods as a *qīptum*-loan to an undivided son or to a slave.[29] Both are incapables, either by reason of age or of status.

Even if the real impact of the innkeeper's activities is difficult to clarify, the law collections at least acknowledge her economic role along with that of the merchant during the Old Babylonian period.

In § 41, she appears in her role of beer seller in connection with three groups of persons, all outsiders, who probably received beer as a salary and did not wish to consume the whole quantity; they would thus turn to the innkeeper to dispose of it for them; the law states that she had to obtain a fair price on her client's behalf because these alien residents or visitors, having no knowledge of the local market conditions, were open to exploitation by greedy traders.[30]

It is against this background that one should read § 108 of the *Code of Hammurabi* dealing with the *sabītum*:[31]

> If a woman innkeeper should refuse to accept grain for the price of beer but accepts (only) silver measured by the large weight, thereby reducing the value of beer in relation to the

27 Wool and oil were not current means of payment in Mesopotamia.

28 On the contrary, the contract is valid if the slave acts on behalf of his/her master.

29 **§ 16** Laws of Ešnunna: *mār awīlim la zīzu u wardum ul iqqīap* "The undivided son of a man or the slave shall not be given a *qīptum*-loan" (Roth 1997: 61).

30 For this interpretation, see Westbrook 1994: 45–46.

31 Roth 1997: 101; *šumma sabītum ana šīm šikarim še'am la imtaḫar ina abnim rabītim kaspam imtaḫar u maḫīr šikarim ana maḫīr še'im umtaṭṭi sābītam šuāti ukannušima ana mê inaddûši.*

> value of grain, they shall charge and convict that woman innkeeper and they shall cast her into the water.

Likewise, the *Edict of Ammi-ṣaduqa* § 18 incriminates the embezzlement perpetrated by the tavern keeper or the merchant, probably in similar circumstances:[32]

> The woman innkeeper or the merchant who ... dishonest [weight?] shall die.

The female innkeeper has thus to behave honestly in all the economic transactions she concludes. The fraud described in the text was all the more plausible if her partner was an outsider, who is not aware of the local rates of conversion.

These three provisions show that the commercial activities of the innkeeper were controlled by the state authority. This corroborates the information gained from other sources, pointing to registration formalities in order to obtain an operating license against the payment of a tax to the palace.[33]

Such a fee is mentioned in the *Edict of Ammi-ṣaduqa* § 16, stating that the arrears will not be reclaimed because of the debt cancellation proclaimed by the king:[34]

> The woman innkeeper of the rural areas (or suburbs) who (normally) pays the silver and/or barley of the innkeeper to the palace, because the king has established justice in the land, the collector shall not call for payment their arrears.

In the same vein, § 17 of the *Edict of Ammi-ṣaduqa* states that the *qīptum*-loan agreed by the innkeeper should not be repaid after the remission of debt proclaimed by the king:[35]

> The woman innkeeper who made a *qīptum*-loan of beer or barley may not collect anything that she has loaned out (after the remission of debt).

The point is that *qīptum* is usually understood as a form of commercial loan,[36] which in principle was not covered by the royal edict. But a comparison of this

---

32 Kraus 1984: 180–181; *sābitum u tamkārum ša i-na* [x x x *lā*] *kittim ... imât.*

33 Lion 2013: 395–396.

34 Kraus 1984: 178–179; *sabītum nawê ša kaspam šê sābûm ana ekallim išaqqalu aššum šarrum mīšaram ina matim iškunu ana ribbātišunu mušaddinu ul išassi.*

35 Kraus 1984: 178–179; *sabītum ša sikaram u še'am iqīpu mimma ša iqīpu ul ušaddan.* Translation from CAD *qâpu* A 97a.

36 Skaist 1994: 51.

provision with § 6 of the Edict[37] shows that the king declared a moratorium on all debts, including those deriving from a *qīptum*-loan, so that the content of § 17 echoes the dispositions of § 6.[38]

The bad reputation of the woman innkeeper is connected to the illegal activities mentioned in the *Code of Hammurabi* § 109, describing the tavern as a place visited by conspirators and criminals who have to be reported to the palace under penalty of death:[39]

> If there should be a woman innkeeper in whose house criminals congregate, and she does not seize those criminals and lead them off to the palace authorities, that woman innkeeper shall be killed.

But a Mari document shows that it could be also a rather decent place to stay, since witnesses apparently met there after an oath-taking to write down a tablet of ownership of a field:[40]

> (3) The sons of Šū-Dagan (5) made a claim (4) under the reign of Zimrī-Lîm about (1) 10 GAN$_2$ of field (2) belonging to Išar-Lîm the [...]. (6–7) They swore an oath of the god in front of Itûr-Mēr and proved the case. (8) They seized (the field). (9–10) A second time, in front of Itûr-Mēr, they have proved (the case). (11–41) In the temple, in front of Itûr-Mēr and Annunītum, (list of 18 witnesses). These men [were present] in [the ta]vern [for the drafting of this] tablet.

After all, innkeepers were thus involved not only in the production of beer, but also and maybe mainly in the practice of credit. Some Old Babylonian letters mention the alewife in connection with credit[41] but the odd thing is that to date, no loan contract featuring a *sabītum* as a creditor is known! A tentative explanation would be that she agreed preferably either short-term loans during lean periods, that did not require the writing of a tablet, or loans to outsiders (as mentioned in § 41 of the *Laws of Ešnunna*), who were not supposed to stay in town for too long and could have difficulty finding witnesses.

---

37 *Edict of Ammi-ṣaduqa* § 6: *qajipānum ana bīt Akkadî u Amurrî* [*ša iqīpušum*] *ul išasi i*[*šassīma*] *imâ*[*t*], "A creditor may not sue for payment against the household of any Akkadian or Amorite [to whom he had extended credit]; should he [sue for payment], he shall die". See Finkelstein 1969: 49–50 and Kraus 1984: 172–173.

38 Kraus 1984: 300–302.

39 Roth 1997: 101; *šumma sabītum sarrūtum ina bītiša ittarkasuma sarrūtim šunūti la iṣṣabtamma ana ekallim la irdiam sabītum šî iddâk.*

40 Charpin & Ziegler 2003: 250–252, no. 3.

41 See for instance AbB 6 178: 16–22 "I am sending a woman innkeeper to you, give her my silver or one shekel of my silver. They will bring me some barley, because I don't want to starve"; see also AbB 9 240 and YOS 13 315.

The personal status of these women is not clear.[42] It has been suggested that, given the bad reputation of the tavern, they were not married women; however, we have no information on this subject until the first millennium. In Achaemenid times, we hear of female slaves running taverns on behalf of the wealthy Egibi business men. F. Joannès has published two very illuminating documents on the subject.[43] Camb. 331 lists the goods entrusted to a slave-woman and states their total value (2 minas and 2 shekels of silver). The sum is said to belong to Itti-Marduk-balāṭu, who lends it to Isḫnunnatu. The interest is to be paid for a month and a half, and afterwards, the owner will probably receive a portion of the profits.[44] Thus, the contract is drafted like a loan. We know from another contract, written on the same day (Camb. 330) that the slave-woman took over the business of a former woman innkeeper, who performed it as an *u'iltu* "debt".[45]

It is difficult to say whether or not the innkeeper herself would be allowed to grant loans; her status of slave would certainly not hinder, since she had enough legal capacity to enter into a contract with her master. But despite

42 See Lion 2013: 397.

43 Joannès 1992a and 1992b. See recently Tolini 2013 who adds a third contract (OECT 10, 239) found at Kiš and in the Egibi archives from Babylon, featuring (the same?) Isḫunnatu.

44 Camb. 331: (1–8)1 mina of silver, price of 50 vats of fine beer with (their) *ḫaṣbattu*; 40 shekels of silver, price of 10 800 litres of dates, 22 shekels of silver, price of 2 bronze kettles weighing 7 minas 1/2, 7 bronze cups and 3 bronze bowls as well as 720 litres of *kasû* which are stored in the house, a total of 2 minas and 2 shekels belonging to Itti-Marduk-balāṭu, son of Nabû-aḫḫē-iddin, descendant of Egibi, are at the disposal of Ishunnatu, slave woman of Itti-Marduk-balāṭu. (9)Until the end of the month *ṭebētu* (x), she will pay an interest. (10–14)Not including: 5 beds, 10 chairs, 1 kettle, 1 vat, 1 stand lamp, 3 knifes, 1 iron hoe, 1 axe, 2 fermenting vats, 1 stand for fermenting vat, 1 vat of decantation, 2 *maššânu*. (14–17) Witnesses: Rēmūt, son of Aplaia, descendant of Arad-Nergal; Bēl-apla-iddin, son of Rēmūt, descendant of Paharu; Tukultī-Marduk, son of Iddin-Nabû, descendant of Šangû-parakki (17–18)And the scribe: Kalbaia, son of Ṣillaia, descendant of Nabaia (18–20)At Kiš, 11th day of *kislīmu* (ix), year 6th of Cambyses, king of Babylon, king of Lands. (Translation based on Tolini 2013).

45 Camb. 330: (1–2)Equipment which Marduk-iqīšanni will give to Ishunnatu, slave woman of Itti-Marduk-balāṭu: (3–7)5 beds, 10 chairs, 3 tables, 1 lamp stand, 3 knifes, 1 iron hoe, 1 axe, 1 fermenting vat, 1 vessel stand, 1 kettle, 1 vat?, 1 *maššânu*, 1 chest, 1 reed. (7–8)They own nothing jointly. (8)They will not renew litigation against each other. (9–10)Equipment which belongs to Ishunnatu, until the end of the month of *šabāṭu* (xi), Marduk-iqīšanni will not make it out. (11–12)Ishunnatu will pay the rent of the house by herself. (13–15)Witnesses: Rēmūt, son of Aplaia, descendant of Arad-Nergal; Bēl-apla-iddin, son of Rēmūt, descendant of Paharu; Tukultī-Marduk, son of Iddin-Nabû, descendant of Šangû-parakki (16–17)And the scribe: Kalbaia, son of Ṣillaia, descendant of Nabaia (17–19)At Kiš, 11th day of *kislīmu* (ix), year 6th of Cambyses, king of Babylon, king of Lands. (19–21) Marduk-iqīšanni will give the promissory note of fLillikanu to Ishunnatu. (Translation based on Tolini 2013).

this rather autonomous status in the management of her business, she was apparently under the permanent control of the Egibi house.[46] This Achaemenid picture does not match the documentation from the 2nd millennium, which is admittedly incomplete. Old Babylonian innkeepers also could have been slaves or servants attached to private households, but for the time being, we lack evidence in that direction.[47]

3 Wet-nurses

Another character mentioned in the law collections and in several contracts from the second millennium onward is the wet-nurse (*mušêniqtum*).[48]

The wet-nurse features in a difficult provision of the *Code of Hammurabi* (§ 194) that has been a matter of debate as to the nature of the offense she committed:[49]

> If a man gives his son to a wet-nurse and that child then dies while in the care of the wet-nurse, and the wet-nurse then contracts for another child without (the knowledge of) his father and mother, they shall charge and convict her, and, because she contracted for another child without (the consent of) his father and mother, they shall cut off her breast.

All the discussion revolves around the consecution or the simultaneity of the facts described in the case: a man gives his child to a wet-nurse; the child dies; the wet-nurse takes another child without informing the father and mother and incurs a punishment for that reason.

Whose parents were supposed to be informed: those of the first or of the second infant? It is usually understood that the wet-nurse has accepted a baby without advising its parents that a previous one had already died in her care; the possessive -*šu* would thus refer to the parents of the second child.[50] Alter-

46 Tolini 2013.
47 One of the few Old Babylonian examples of a tavern located in a city close to Larsa (AUCT 4 99; see Charpin 2005) involves a man of apparently free condition. Likewise, the tapster who witnesses a sale contract in a Neo-Sumerian document from Iri-Sagrig (Nisaba 15 279; see Owen 2013) was also a free woman.
48 About wet-nursing in the Ancient Near East, see Stol 2000: 181–190. Death of the mother in childbirth (Stol 2000: 140–141) was one reason for resorting to wet-nursing, but the sources rather point to other backgrounds such as adoption or unintended pregnancy (see below).
49 Roth 1997: 120; *šumma awīlum mārāšu ana mušêniqtum iddinma ṣiḫrum šû ina qāt mušêniqtim imtūt mušêniqtum balum abišu u ummišu ṣiḫram šaniamma irtakas ukannušima aššum balum abišu u ummišu ṣiḫram šaniam irkusu tulāša inakkisu.*
50 Scheil 1914; San Nicolò 1932; Driver and Miles 1956: 406; Szlechter 1977: 147–148.

natively, it has been suggested that the wet-nurse tried to deceive the parents by replacing the dead baby with another one,[51] just like in the famous Judgement of Solomon (I Kings 3: 16–28) where a mother suffocates her baby by sleeping on it and instead takes the one of her roommate. But the reaction of the cheated mother, who instantly realizes the substitution, makes this interpretation of the *Code of Hammurabi* very doubtful.

A third option would be that the wet-nurse contracted with two families at the same time,[52] so that this double suckling resulted in the death of one of the babies because of malnutrition. The Graeco-Aegyptian papyri contain clauses forbidding such practices, though they were probably rather common. To date, there is no similar prohibition in the Mesopotamian contracts, except maybe in one Neo-Babylonian document.[53] Admittedly, the case of two children suckled by the same woman is very rare too.[54] The "moonlighter"-scenario is also challenged by the grammar of the text: the accomplished form *iddin* "he gave" followed by the perfect *irtakas* "she has contracted" reflects the consecution of both acts (first a man gave his son who died, and then the wet-nurse contracted with another couple), in accordance with the chronological order usually followed in the description of a legal case.

So the law punishes the wet-nurse who has not informed her clients that a previous child had died while in her custody.[55] The text seems to allude to some sort of accident (just like in the Solomon case) rather than death by mistreatment or malnutrition[56]. Indeed, constant child supervision was one of the duties of the wet-nurse.[57] The careless wet-nurse of the Code is guilty of hiding her negligence for fear that the couple would not entrust the baby to her.

We know a bit more about the legal framework of the wet-nurse activities thanks to two additional legal provisions and several Old Babylonian contracts.

The *Code of Ur-Namma* (§ E2) and the *Laws of Ešnunna* (§ 32) both refer to the wages of the wet-nurse:

---

51 Johns 1903: 42–43; Kohler and Peiser 1904: 126–127; Eilers 1932: 64; Finet 2004: 110.

52 Cardascia 1982: 78–80.

53 Wunsch 2003–2004: 239 no. 21 (BM 94512): 10 ^{f}PN *pu-ut la ru-bu*$^{?}$-⸢*ú*⸣ "^{f}PN (the wet-nurse) stands for the non-rearing$^{?}$"; see also Wunsch 2003–2004: 213 and n. 190.

54 Wunsch 2003–2004: 213 and n. 191 refers to BM 82549 as a possible example for the Neo-Babylonian period.

55 San Nicolò 1932: 97.

56 But one cannot discard the possibility that the wet-nurse did not have enough milk, or transmitted a disease to the child through her milk.

57 See for the Old Assyrian period for instance, Michel 1997: 101.

> § E2 If someone nurses a man's child, her barley will be six **gur**, her wool thirty minas, and her oil thirty **sila**, for three years. It is part of the **nu-gig**-functions. The yearly fee of a hired nursemaid will be one shekel.[58]

> § 32 If a man gives his child for suckling and for rearing but does not give the food, oil, and clothing rations (to the caregiver) for three years, he shall weigh and deliver ten shekels of silver for the cost of the rearing of his child, and he shall take away his child.[59]

Both provisions show that the average duration of breastfeeding was three years, which is confirmed by the Old Babylonian deeds and the series *Ana ittišu*.[60] The *Code of Ur-Namma* adds another interesting aspect, which is reflected in the clauses of the Mesopotamian contracts. § E2 lists the ordinary rations in barley, wool and oil as a salary for what seems to be the suckling of a baby,[61] while the fee in silver pays the rearing of the child for an unspecified duration. The distinction between the **nu-gig** (*qadištum*) and the **um-me-da** (*tārītum*) refers to two different occupations, namely breastfeeding and rearing the child. The combination of the two wages covers the two successive stages of a full nursing process that could last several years. It is difficult to decide whether the two functions were carried out by the same woman or by two different persons. The use of two distinct words in § E2 tends to support the second view, but the wording of § 32 of the *Laws of Ešnunna*, where the baby is given *ana šūnuqim ana tarbītim*, "to suckle and to raise", favors the first option. The expression *ana mušêniqtim* in § 194 of the *Code of Hammurabi* could be a shorter version of the same phrase.

The double function mentioned in the law collections is found also in the Old Babylonian tablets where, along with regular allowances in kind, a fixed amount of silver could be paid to the woman. Such is the case in a document from Sippar (CT 47 46) where the mother – a *nadītum*-nun of Šamaš – gives to a couple four shekels in addition to (and not instead of)[62] the rations for three

---

58 Civil 2011: 251 (where **um-me-da** is translated "wet-nurse"), 281–284; **tukum-bi dumu lu$_2$-ra lu$_2$ ga i$_3$-ni-gu$_7$ mu-3-a še-ni 6 gur sik$_2$-ni 30 ma-na i$_3$-ni 30 sila$_3$ nig$_2$ nam-nu-gig-kam um-[me]-da hun-ga$_2$ mu-⸢a$_2$⸣-ni 1 gin$_2$-am$_3$.**

59 Roth 1997: 64, who reads 10 ⸢GIN$_2$ KU$_3$.BABBAR⸣ instead of 10 MA.NA, following a suggestion of Eichler 1987: 78 and n. 25; *šumma awīlum mārašu ana šūnuqim ana tarbītim iddinma epram piššatam lubuštam šalaš šanātim la iddin* 10 *šiqil kaspam tarbīt mārišu išaqqalma mārašu itarru.*

60 *Ana ittišu* tabl. 3: iii 47–50: **um-me-ga-la$_2$-a-ni-še$_3$** / *ana mušēniqtišu*, **mu 3-kam$_2$ še-ba i$_3$-ba** / 3 *šanāte ipra piššata*, **sik$_2$-ba tug$_2$-ba-bi** / *lubušta*, **in-na-ni-ib$_2$-kal** / *udannin* "For its (the child's) wet-nurse, for three years, barley, oil, wool rations he ensured for her".

61 About the **nu-gig** as a wet-nurse, see Civil 2011: 281–283.

62 See in this sense Finkelstein 1976: 190. Likewise, San Nicolò 1932: 97 thinks that silver and allowances are two alternate modes of payment.

years: based on the rate stated by the *Code of Ur-Namma*, one could surmise that the wet-nurse hired for three years was to keep the baby as a nursemaid during four more years. The child was thus intended to live in a foster home[63] for a rather long span of time (seven years), with the implied obligation for the foster parents to bring the girl to her mother regularly. Similar combinations of supplies and silver are attested in the Neo-Babylonian tablets.[64]

On the other hand, the ten shekels mentioned in § 32 of the *Laws of Ešnunna* appear as a fixed sum matching the whole duration of the contract and replacing the usual delivery of rations. Nothing is said about the separate amount of silver attested in the *Code of Ur-Namma* and in the Old Babylonian contracts. It seems to be included in the final payment defined as *tarbīt mārišu*, "(cost of) the rearing of the child": if the parents fail to pay the first stage of the contract, namely the allowances for the suckling, they can postpone the whole payment after the completion of the contract, once the child is reared. The law would thus offer a choice, at the discretion of the parents, between an advance or a final payment.[65] The last sentence ("and he shall take away his child") makes clear that the wet-nurse could retain the child until full delivery of her salary, or even keep it definitively. Such a situation is attested for instance in an Old Babylonian agreement (VS 7 10/11) whereby a *qadištum* received the baby boy she was feeding for default of payment by the mother. Here, the situation of the wet-nurse recalls that of the creditor who detains a pledge: withholding the infant could be a means of pressuring the parents to persuade them to repay their debt.

Other Old Babylonian contracts involving the wet-nurse and her husband were probably agreed in connection with an adoption,[66] although this background is not explicitly stated in the documents. The comparison with a Middle Babylonian example from Nuzi[67] supports this view: the adopters place the child into the care of the biological parents, provided that the latter would return him/her once he/she was grown. The payment of the wages was the undisputable sign of their new status of employees.[68] The attendance of the husband as a co-partner is unexpected in a context of wet-nursing but the

63 About fosterage (*tarbītum*) in the Ancient Near East, see Roth 1979: 177–184 and Démare-Lafont forthcoming.

64 Wunsch 2003–2004: 211–213.

65 Yaron 1988: 253 assumes that there is a punitive connotation in the total amount, but his opinion is based partly on the reading 10 minas instead of 10 shekels.

66 In addition to CT 47 46, see for instance CT 48 70, TCL 1 197, OECT 13 214

67 Fincke 1995: 6–7 no. 1. About the wet-nurses at Nuzi, see also Schneider-Ludorff 2009.

68 Fleishman 2001.

purpose of the documents was probably broader and included the rearing of the child, an occupation that was preferably entrusted to an already existing family rather than to a single woman.

Sometimes only the natural mother of the child was hired as a wet-nurse, especially in case of adoption[69] or of unintended pregnancy. Such a circumstance could explain for instance a Neo-Babylonian document[70] in which a man hired his daughter as a wet-nurse to feed a child until weaning. The contract was agreed on a one-year basis and was probably renewed every year until the term. The maiden was probably very young, since her father agreed the contract and her mother featured among the witnesses. Besides, she was required to stay in the family of the baby. These facts strongly suggest that the girl was the biological mother of the suckling, her employer being the father.[71]

It has been suggested that wet-nursing created a right to the child for the wet-nurse[72] but if it is assumed that in most cases she was the biological mother, then transferring the baby back to her would appear as a natural, or at least desirable issue. This would also explain why the formulation of the wet-nursing contracts differs from that of the service contracts and falls rather in the realm of family law: the participants to these deeds often had legal or biological ties with the infant. It is a pity that the sociology of this profession remains largely unclear to us. The scarcity of the sources on the subject tends to indicate that wet-nursing involved primarily slaves or domestic servants,[73] operating mostly outside any contract.

***

The final picture that emerges from this overview is full of gaps and questions. If we rely on the rather meagre material collected here, it seems that the Mesopotamian legal system was not concerned with women at work. This does not

69 San Nicolò 1932: 97. See for instance VS 8 127 (Old Babylonian), where a couple adopts a baby from a woman and her two children and gives her the suckling fees; see also TCL 1 146 (Old Babylonian), where a woman gives her daughter in adoption to a *qadištum* and receives allotments for breast feeding during three years.

70 San Nicolò 1935: 22–24; Stol 2000: 182; Wunsch 2003–2004: 211.

71 Joannès 2013. Stol 2000: 182 wonders if she could be a young widow; Wunsch 2003–2004: 211 notes that nothing is said about her own child, who could have died. The problem is solved if she is the mother of the infant.

72 Eichler 1987: 78.

73 See for instance an inheritance document quoted by Stol 2000: 182 n. 70 where the two named couples occurring among the items of a share are said to be given "for the rearing of the small ones" (*ana tarbît ṣeḫḫerūtim*).

mean of course that their economic activities were insignificant; but basically, the income that they could bring into the family was of no particular legal interest. The situation of the wife of the Assyrian merchants is very telling in this respect:[74] some accounting documents from their archives testify to a salary given by the husband to his wife as a payment for her contribution to the activities of the "house". Thus, legally speaking, she was considered a collaborating spouse, but her activity developed outside a contract. She was entitled to the products of her work, but she acted in a *de facto* situation.[75] A similar situation is depicted in the Neo-Babylonian sources, where food or textile production of the feminine workforce of the household was given out thanks to personal exchanges between women.[76]

This lack of "juridicity" is certainly the most salient feature of women's work in the ancient Near East.

Bibliography

Cardascia, Guillaume. 1982. La nourrice coupable. § 194 du Code de Hammurabi. Pp. 67–84 in *Mélanges à la mémoire de Marcel-Henri Prévost: droit biblique, interprétation rabbinique, communautés et sociétés*. Paris: PUF.

Cassin, Elena. 1961. Note sur le "commerce de carrefour" en Mésopotamie ancienne. *JESHO* 4: 164–167.

Charpin, Dominique. 2005. Le statut des cabaretiers à l'époque paléo-babylonienne. *NABU* 2005/2.

Charpin, Dominique and Nele Ziegler. 2003. *Mari et le Proche-Orient à l'époque amorrite. Essai d'histoire politique*. Florilegium marianum 5. Mémoires de NABU 6. Paris: SEPOA.

Civil, Miguel. 2011. The Law Collection of Ur-Namma. Pp. 221–310, in *Cuneiform Royal Inscriptions and Related Texts in the Schøyen Collection*, ed. Andrew R. George. CUSAS 17, Bethesda: CDL Press.

Démare-Lafont, Sophie. 2008. Quelques femmes d'affaires au Proche-Orient ancient. Pp. 25–36 in *Le droit, les affaires et l'argent. Célébration du bicentenaire du Code de commerce. Actes des Journées de la Société d'histoire du droit Dijon 2007*, ed. A. Girollet. Mémoires pour la Société d'Histoire du Droit et des institutions des anciens pays bourguignons, comtois et romands, 65. Dijon: SHDB.

Démare-Lafont, Sophie. Forthcoming. Adoption and Apprenticeship in Old Babylonian. To be published in *JEOL*.

Dombradi, Eva. 1996. *Die Darstellung des Rechtsaustrags in den altbabylonischen Prozessurkunden*. 2 volumes. FAOS 20. Stuttgart: Franz Steiner.

74 Michel 2006: 297–298; Thomason 2013.

75 Démare-Lafont 2008: 29.

76 Joannès 2013.

Driver, Godfrey R. and John C. Miles. 1956. *The Babylonian Laws* volume I. 2nd ed. Oxford: Clarendon Press.
Durand, Jean-Marie. 1997. *Les documents épistolaires du palais de Mari tome I*. Littératures anciennes du Proche-Orient, 16. Paris: Le Cerf.
Durand, Jean-Marie. 2000. *Les documents épistolaires du palais de Mari tome III*. Littératures anciennes du Proche-Orient, 18. Paris: Le Cerf.
Eichler, Barry L. 1987. Literary Structure in the Laws of Eshnunna. Pp. 71–84 in *Language, Literature, and History: Philological and Historical Studies Presented to Erica Reiner*, ed. Francesca Rochberg-Halton. American Oriental Series, 67. New Haven: American Oriental Society.
Eilers, Wilhelm. 1932. *Die Gesetzesstele Chammurabis*. Der Alte Orient 31 fasc. 3–4. Leipzig: J. C. Hinrichs.
Englund, Robert K. 1991. Hard Work-Where Will It Get You? Labor Management in Ur III Mesopotamia. *JNES* 50/4: 255–280.
Fincke, Jeannette. 1995. Beiträge zum Lexikon des Hurritischen von Nuzi. Pp. 5–21 in *Edith Porada Memorial Volume*, eds. Daniel I. Owen and Gernot Wilhelm. SCCNH 7. Bethesda: CDL Press.
Finet, André. 2004. *Le Code de Hammurapi*. 5th ed. Littératures anciennes du Proche-Orient, 6. Paris: Le Cerf.
Finkelstein, Jacob J. 1969. The Edict of Ammiṣaduqa: A New Text. *RA* 63: 45–64.
Finkelstein, Jacob J. 1976. *šilip rēmim* and Related Matters. Pp. 187–194 in *Kramer Anniversary Volume. Cuneiform Studies in Honor of Samuel Noah Kramer*, eds. Barry L. Eichler, Jane W. Heimerdinger, and Åke W. Sjöberg. AOAT 25. Neukirchen-Vluyn: Neukirchener Verlag.
Fleishman, Josef. 2001. Child Maintenance in the Laws of Eshnunna. *BZAR* 7: 374–384.
Joannès, Francis. 1992a. Inventaire d'un cabaret. *NABU* 1992/64.
Joannès, Francis. 1992b. Inventaire d'un cabaret (suite). *NABU* 1992/89.
Joannès, Francis. 2013. La place des femmes dans l'économie domestique néo-babylonienne. http://refema.hypotheses.org/202.
Johns, Claude Hermann Walter. 1903. *The Oldest Code of Laws in the World*. Edinburgh: T&T Clark.
Kohler, Josef and Felix E. Peiser. 1904. *Hammurabi's Gesetz* volume 1. Leipzig: Eduard Pfeiffer.
Kraus, Fritz Rudolf. 1984. *Königliche Verfügungen in altbabylonischer Zeit*. SD 11. Leiden: Brill.
Lafont, Bertrand. 2014. Women at Work and Women in the Economy during the Neo Sumerian (so called Ur III) Period, XXIst century BC. Pp. 57–77 in *Le rôle économique des femmes en Mésopotamie ancienne (REFEMA). Women's Role in the Economy of the Ancient Near East. Report: December 31, 2011–December 30, 2014*, eds. Francis Joannès and Fumi Karahashi. Tokyo.
Langlois, Anne-Isabelle. 2014. *Les archives de la princesse Iltani découvertes à Tell al-Rimah (XVIIIe siècle av. J.-C.)*. Thèse de l'Ecole Pratique des Hautes Etudes, Paris.
Lion, Brigitte. 2013. Les cabarets à l'époque paléo-babylonienne. *Cahier des thèmes transversaux ArScAn* 11: 393–400.
Lion, Brigitte. 2016. Male and female palace servants in the kingdom of Arrapḫe. *Orient* 51: 69–82.
Michalowski, Piotr and Christopher B. Walker. 1989. A New Sumerian "Law Code". Pp. 383–396 in *Dumu-E2-Dub-Ba-A: Studies in Honor of Åke W. Sjöberg*, eds. Hermann Behrens,

Darlene Loding, and Martha T. Roth. Occasional Publications of the Samuel Noah Kramer Fund, 11. Philadelphia: University of Pennsylvania Museum.
Michel, Cécile. 1997. Les enfants de marchands de Kaniš. *Ktèma* 22: 91–108.
Michel, Cécile. 2001. *Correspondance des marchands de Kanish*. Littératures anciennes du Proche-Orient, 19. Paris: Le Cerf.
Michel, Cécile. 2006. Femmes et production textile à Aššur au début du IIe millénaire avant J.-C. Pp. 281–297 in *Spécialisation des tâches et sociétés*, eds. A. Averbouh, P. Brun *et alii*. *Techniques & culture* 46 (http://halshs.archives-ouvertes.fr/halshs-00821277).
Nakata, Ichiro. 2014. *Nadītum*-women in the Field Lease Contracts from Sippar. http://refema.hypotheses.org/1067.
Owen, David I. 2013. *Cuneiform Texts Primarily from Iri-Sagrig / Āl-Šarrāki and the History of the Ur III Period*. 2 vol. Nisaba 15/1–2. Bethesda: CDL Press.
Owen, David I. and Rudolf H. Mayr. 2007. *The Garšana Archive*. CUSAS 3. Potomac: CDL Press.
Röllig, Wolfgang. 1970. *Das Bier im alten Mesopotamien*. Berlin: Blaschker.
Roth, Martha. 1979. *Scholastic Tradition and Mesopotamian Law: A Study of FLP 1287, a Prism in the Collection of the Free Library of Philadelphia*. PhD dissertation, Philadelphia: University of Pennsylvania.
Roth, Martha. 1997. *Law Collections from Mesopotamia and Asia Minor*, 2nd ed. Society of Biblical Literature Writings from the Ancient World, 6. Atlanta: Scholars Press.
San Nicolò, Mariano. 1932. Ammenvertrag. *RlA* 1: 96–97.
San Nicolò, Mariano. 1935. Parerga Babyloniaca XV–XVI. *ArOr* 7: 16–28.
Scheil, Vincent. 1914. Les nourrices en Babylonie et le § 194 du Code. *RA* 11: 180–182.
Schneider-Ludorff, Helga. 2009. Die Amme nach Texten aus Nuzi. Pp. 479–489 in *General Studies and Excavations at Nuzi* 11/2, ed. G. Wilhelm. SCCNH 18. Bethesda: CDL Press.
Skaist, Aaron. 1994. *The Old Babylonian Loan Contract. Its History and Geography*. Bar-Ilan: Bar-Ilan University Press.
Stol, Marten. 1998. The Care of the Elderly in Mesopotamia in the Old Babylonian Period. Pp. 59–117 in *The Care of the Elderly in the Ancient Near East*. eds. Marten Stol and Sveen P. Vleeming. Studies in the History and Culture of the Ancient Near East, 14. Leiden: Brill.
Stol, Marten. 2000. *Birth in Babylonia and the Bible. Its Mediterranean Setting*. Cuneiform Monographs, 14. Groningen: Styx.
Stol, Marten. 2004. Wirtschaft und Gesellschaft in altbabylonischer Zeit. Pp. 643–975 in *Mesopotamien. Die altbabylonische Zeit*, Dominique Charpin, Dietrich O. Edzard and Marten Stol. OBO 160/4. Fribourg–Göttingen: Universitätsverlag-Vandenhoeck & Ruprech.
Szlechter, Emile. 1977. *Codex Hammurapi*. Rome: Pontifica Universitas Lateranensis.
Thomason, Allison Karmel. 2013. Her Share of the Profits: Women, Agency and Textile Production at Kültepe/Kanesh in the Early Second Millennium BC. Pp. 93–112 in *Textile Production and Consumption in the Ancient Near East*, eds. Henriette Koefoed, Marie-Louise Nosch and Eva Andersson Strand. Ancient Textiles Series, 12. Oxford: Oxford Books.
Tolini, Gauthier. 2013. The Economic Activities of Isḫunnatu, a slave woman of the Egibi Family. http://refema.hypotheses.org/766.
Waetzoldt, Hartmut. 1988. Die Situation der Frauen und Kinder anhand ihrer Einkommensverhältnisse zur Zeit der III. Dynastie von Ur. *AoF* 15: 30–44.
Westbrook, Raymond. 1994. The Old Babylonian Term *napṭarum*. *JCS* 46: 41–46.

Westbrook, Raymond. 2003. Old Babylonian Period. Pp. 361–430 in *A History of Ancient Near Eastern Law. Volume One*, ed. Raymond Westbrook. HdO 72/1. Leiden: Brill.
Westbrook, Raymond and Richard Jasnow (eds.). 2001. *Security for Debt in Ancient Near Eastern Law*. CHANE 9. Leiden: Brill.
Wunsch, Cornelia. 2003–2004. Findelkinder und Adoption nach neubabylonischen Quellen. *AfO* 50: 174–244.
Yaron, Reuven. 1988. *The Laws of Eshnunna*. 2nd ed. Leiden: Brill.

Matteo Vigo

Sources for the Study of the Role of Women in the Hittite Administration

Mark W. Chavalas opens his anthological sourcebook on *Women in the Ancient Near East* stating: "Thus, we have made available in one volume selected documents concerning women, and thus filling a void in women's and in ancient Near Eastern historical studies. In this way, the student will be able to directly evaluate the primary source material. Because of the nature of the material, I have conscripted a group of scholars to contribute up-to-date translations and historical commentary on the documents in question. However, I emphasize that these have been selected based upon availability, and are thus not a comprehensive set of documents. In many respects, this work should be considered as a 'materials for the study of women in Ancient Near East'" (2014a: 3–4). The editor also stresses that: "Based upon these considerations, I have created a primary source textbook that has excerpts of Mesopotamian and other ancient Near Eastern (specifically Hittite) texts and other primary source materials, which further an understanding of women in the context of ancient Near Eastern history (...) However, there are many lacunae in terms of subject matter and region." (Chavalas 2014a: 5). All in all, Chavalas' book can really be considered a sourcebook in which texts (i.e. primary sources) from different periods and literary genres are offered in translation and commented upon with the main goal of providing some hints for the study of women in past times. Nevertheless, they present a very partial view of women in the Ancient Near East from an historical perspective; even less from a gender-oriented viewpoint. Some contributions seem concretely focused on the presentation of the Ancient Near Eastern women's "real life," so to say. This is the case, for instance, of the article by Harriet Crawford (even if it is very general) on women involved in professional activities in 3rd millennium BC Mesopotamia; by Martha Roth on the (alleged) predominantly passive role of women in law and by Cécile Michel on the very active involvement of Assyrian women in the textile trade in Cappadocia during the 18th century BC.[1] In other cases the picture of women sketched in this book can hardly reflect reality. In sum, they do not give us concrete clue towards understanding the role of women in Ancient

1 See Crawford 2014; Roth 2014; Michel 2014.

Matteo Vigo, Saxo Institute, University of Copenhagen; lbn956@ku.dk

Near Eastern societies because of the nature of the documentation (primarily literary texts). We cannot, however, absolutely blame the contributors for not having been able to provide interesting material in this respect, since the texts analyzed highlighted the very general role of women in society, with only few references to their work activities.

Tackling the objectives set for the conference where the present paper was delivered means actually trying to shed some light on different aspects of the administration and economy of ancient societies by answering illusory simple questions such as: what about a woman's work in past times? Can we identify through the analysis of texts the alleged "parallel universe" of women's activities in their own environments? Is it possible to delineate the relations between female and male worlds in light of the women's agency in men's *milieu*? Does the study of the hierarchy and professionalism of women only illustrate the world of "women of power"? Since it is generally accepted that we have no evidence of women's agency in Ancient Near East, or at least very little, because scholars are very selective in their fields of study, this contribution is also meant to reassess this matter as far as Hittite Anatolia is concerned.

As correctly pointed out by Harriet Crawford in the introduction of her paper: "Attempts to reconstruct and understand the past are, by the nature of the evidence, always incomplete;"[2] the study of the role of women in Hittite society is not defective in this respect. The documentation at our disposal is very meagre indeed. Additionally, no systematic study has yet been done on gender issues in the Hittite world. The holistic approach to it can then be reduced to few scholarly journal essays and book chapters on the role of women in ritual practice.[3] It is worth to mention a paper issued by Gary Beckman in the *Journal of Ancient Civilizations* (Beckman 1993), in which the author tries to stress the prominent role of women in specific rituals,[4] even if the possibility of distinguishing – for instance – in the so-called SISKUR(.SISKUR) rites between magical or medical approaches to human dysfunction and woe is complicated because of the nature of the documentation, and therefore becomes blurred upon closer examination. These problems also prevent us from distinguishing between female ritual practitioners, those actually carrying out the rites, and the more operative, professional role of women who practice healing by means of a "medical" approach. Trying to detect in rituals the difference between female magicians and female physicians would help us to compensate the (deceptive?) inequality between

2 Crawford 2014: 10.

3 Recently Collins 2014 and Bachvarova 2014.

4 According to the cursory survey of all Hittite rituals (also comprising rituals of foreign provenance), 53.5 % of ritual practitioners are indeed female. Beckman 1993: 36, with note 63.

female and male professionals in the Hittite society. As correctly already presented by Beckman (1993: 37–38), a case-study might be the definition of the role played by specific women in birth rituals. Those women are attested in Hittite sources with different names: ^{MUNUS}ŠU.GI (Hittite *hašauwa-*), the so-called "old woman;" ^{MUNUS}*haš(ša)nupalla-* (Sum. ^{MUNUS}ŠA$_3$.ZU), literally "bringer to birth," and ^{MUNUS}*harnauwaš*, to be rendered "woman of the birth-stool."[5] By examining the activities of these ritual practitioners, we find that their duties deal not only with recitation of incantations on behalf of the newborn, but also with actual physical tasks, so as to prepare the equipment necessary for the delivery, hence delivering the child (Beckman 1983: 235). If from an etymological point of view the aforementioned Hittite terms do not find convincing correspondence in any healing professions, it is quite obvious that these women can be considered real midwives.

1 Folk tales

Luckily, we do not need to extrapolate any specific connotations out of the Hittite ritual praxis in order to detect the role of women in work and society. It is a common opinion among Hittitologists that, according to the data available today, women in the Hittite society occupy a place distinctly inferior to that of men in many respects. Some passages of Hittite folk tales seem quite illustrative.[6]

The stories here presented were probably written down by the Hittite scribes from the fourteenth century BC,[7] on the basis of rhapsodic compositions.[8] These tales contain not only clear elements of Hurrian influence (names of holy cities, locations, deities belonging to the Hurrian pantheon), but *tòpoi* and literary patterns widespread in all the Ancient Near Eastern literature and properly re-elaborated together with indigenous elements. The main character of the first tale is named Appu, and the story is usually named after him. He

5 For a detailed discussion of these terms see Beckman 1983: 232–235.

6 We expressly used the term "Hittite" folk tale to indicate that these stories were apparently (re-)elaborated in the Hittite scribal environment as the result of different local and foreign folk tales, especially Hurrian. We also cautiously stay with Hoffner (1998: 85), who differentiates CTH 360 from CTH 363. For further discussion of these issues see among others Pecchioli Daddi and Polvani 1990: 164–166, 172–174.

7 At least the so-called *Tale of Appu* presents some features of the 14th century BC. See Siegelová 1971: 26–27.

8 See analogous considerations in Archi 2007: 198.

lives in prosperity with his wife, but they have no children, so they do not have the gods' favor. His wife quarrels with him about this issue and constantly complains about it with her maids. According to what it is stated in the preserved tablets of this story, Appu has never had sexual intercourse with his wife, and apparently there are no such intentions in his mind. Apparently it is painful for him, so we can suppose he is suffering from some sexual dysfunction, such as impotence. Before addressing the Sun god, who will guarantee him offspring, his wife complains to her maids:[9]

> "He has never had intercourse before.[10] You don't think he has now had success, do you?" The woman went and lay down with Appu with her clothes on.
>
> Appu awoke from his sleep, and his wife questioned him: "You have never had sex before. Have you now been successful?" When Appu heard this, he replied:
>
> "You are a woman and think like one: you know nothing at all!"

The second tale on focus denotes many features in common with the *Story of Appu*. The main divine character is, once again, the Sun god, who in the first tale is praised by Appu to help him in attaining fertility; in this second tale, often labeled by Hittitologists *The Sun god, the cow and the fisherman*, the Sun god himself impregnates a cow. A new born baby is the result of this union. Because the cow gets angry with the Sun god, the baby is sent by the deity to a hidden place until one day a fisherman finds him. Since the fisherman cannot have children he decides to take the baby home to his wife, considering the baby to be a gift from the Sun god. The tale proceeds as follows:

> The fisherman arrived at the city of Urma, went to his house, and sat down in a chair. The fisherman said to his wife: "Pay close attention to what I am about to say to you. Take this child, go into the bedroom, lie down on the bed, and wail. The whole city will hear and say: 'The fisherman's wife has borne a child!' And one will bring us bread, another will bring us beer, and still another will bring us fat.
>
> A woman's mind is clever, but she retains herself from commanding. She is (dependent)[11] from the gods' will. She stands in woman's subordination(?),[12] and she does not disobey the man's [wo]rd."[13]

9 § 6 (i 27–30) and § 6 (i 31–37); Hoffner 1998: 83.

10 For the sentence containing *katta ep-* Hoffner (1998: 83) proposes: "he has never had success(?) before. You don't think he has now had success(?), do you?".

11 Cf. CHD, L–N: 306b: [*kán*$^{?}$*-k*]*án-za*.

12 For the glossed *hapazuwalanni* of the text see CLL: 54.

13 § 16 (iv 42–52); Hoffner 1998: 87.

2 Defining the texts *corpus*

It is self-evident that these folk tales do not represent a reliable source to investigate the role of women in the Hittite world. Indeed, this view of women's social status has to be considered in light of the heterogenic context of the tales presented. It presumably reflects common beliefs about women diffused throughout the Ancient Near East, and thus is not specifically related to any notions of female gender among the Hittites. It also must be stressed that high-echoing sentences like those are necessary for the texts' framework and context. Anyway, Anthony Giddens in his book *Central in Social Theory: Action, Structure and Contradiction in Social Analysis* associates agency with power and autonomy, in contrast to powerlessness and dependency (Giddens 1979: 88–95). When we focus on the tale of the fisherman, we cannot disagree with Giddens' association, since powerlessness and dependency are clearly expressed in the words:

> A woman's mind is clever, but she retains herself from commanding. She is (dependent) from the gods' will. She stands in woman's subordination[(?)]...

In this paper we present evidence of women's agency within the Hittite administrative system, by considering agency according to the traditional definition in sociology: "the capacity of individuals to act independently and to make their own free choices," but also taking into account the definition subsequently developed by Saana Svärd for the Neo-Assyrian textual evidence, according to whom the women "agents" can be separated into two groups: the *explicit agents*, i.e., those who express their agency via *acting*, and the *implicit agents*, i.e., those who "actively" appear in social structures, even if they apparently *do not act* (Svärd 2007: 383). Their high position is even more appreciable in relation to cultic activities and worship, and certainly the "Hittite" rituals are the most productive text genre to testify the active role of women in specific structures. Nonetheless, we focus on the category of the Hittite documents labeled "*unica*;" that is texts that have never been copied by the Hittite scribes, at least as far as we have discovered until now. The subdivision of genres in "texts with duplicates" and "*unica*," on the basis of long term and short term records, fits quite comfortably with the "living character" of the latter source-type. Indeed, we are dealing with letters, palace and cult inventories, court depositions, and land deeds; in sum, all that kind of documents that were still in use (i.e., regularly checked), when the Hittite capital, Hattuša, and its archival spaces were abandoned by the Hittites at the beginning of the 12th century BC.[14] An exten-

---

14 For the texts subdivision, see especially van den Hout 2005. For different hypotheses on the last days of the Hittite capital Hattuša in light of the archival disposition of the tablets, see van den Hout 2007.

sive treatment of the administrative documentation in connection with the role of women would have required too extensive a study to be covered here. Hence, we limit our presentation to a general survey of the sources, both textual and archaeological, saving room for further, in depth investigation.[15] We specifically focus on:

1. Letters from the royal chancellery (generally in the queen's name) to royal counterparts;
2. Donations of lands granted by kings and queens to members of the royal family and palace officers;
3. Palace inventories (i.e., books accounting incoming luxury goods, or already stored in the royal treasuries).

The textual documentation is complemented, when possible, by the archaeological data, namely all those clay *bullae* that bear the impression of seals belonging to women involved in the palatial administration. We particularly refer to the seal impressions on clay lumps from the *Westbau* (i.e., a storehouse) in Hattuša. The sources for the study of the role of women in the Hittite administration are displayed in line with the division of women in the Neo-Assyrian records already proposed by Saana Svärd (2007):

1. Women of power (queens and royal family members);
2. Female administrators and household managers;
3. Women connected with the "palace", for which it is difficult to delineate the exact responsibilities.

The scanty reference to women's private life in literary works (anecdotes, myths, proverbs, etc.) does not represent real evidence to much extent; hence it will not be considered here.

3 Women of power (i.e. *explicit agency*)

The analysis of the corpus of administrative Hittite texts, even if somewhat fragmentary and scarcely exhaustive, highlights a prominent role of women of power, linked to the royal family, in different aspects of the Hittite administration (diplomatic affairs, household commitments, management of incoming goods,

15 For obvious reasons of time we cannot proceed with a detailed investigation of the trial court reports (*Gerichtsprotokolle*) in which a prominent role of the queen as "administrator of justice" is highlighted.

record keeping practices, etc.). We sporadically find glimpses of women's involvement in bureaucratic and administrative tasks in private and official letters. "In private, non-governmental correspondence, anyone might send or receive a letter. In official correspondence, letters are attested to and from kings, queens, princes, generals, and various grades of bureaucrats. The 'Royal letters' to or from kings, queens, princes, and princesses could cross international borders. Not just Hittite kings, but also their queens and children wrote and received letters from foreign courts. There was a kind of royal club, to which members of royal families in the Amarna Age belonged. And members of this club kept in regular contact with each other, sending greetings and gifts ... All the recovered Hittite letters are official in nature." (Hoffner 2009: 19–20)

The private contents of some "official" Hittite letters are pretty clear, as far as it can be inferred, for instance, from a fragmentary Middle Hittite letter found in Šapinuwa (modern Ortaköy, Turkey), written by an unnamed queen to her husband in which she complains about some physical discomforts:[16]

> "Say to His Majesty, my lord: Thus speaks the Queen, your maidservant: may all be well in the presence of Your Majesty, my lord! May the gods keep Your Majesty, my lord, alive and protect Your Majesty! Everything is well with me. I am still the same: my head and back hurt me. Please write to me how it is also with Your Majesty, my lord. And, Your Majesty, my lord, send (me your) greetings!"

Women in power, such as queens, were certainly involved in diplomatic affairs in the name of the kings. The most exhaustive evidence we have so far is the long letter written by the queen Puduhepa to the pharaoh of Egypt, presumably Ramses II:[17]

> [Thus speaks Puduhepa, Great Queen, Queen of the land of Hatti: Say to Reamašeša, Great King, King of the land of Egypt, my brother.]

The diplomatic issues treated in this letter are numerous. The dispatch opens with the standard blessing formula and the reciprocal ceremonial exchange of gifts:[18]

> Concerning the fact that you, my brother, wrote to me as follows: "At the time when your messengers came, they brought back to me gifts, and I rejoiced." When I heard that, I rejoiced likewise. The wife of your brother (i.e., Puduhepa, the wife of the Hittite king Hattušili III) enjoys full life. May the person of my brother likewise enjoy full life! Send

16 OrŠ. 90/800, 1–16; Hoffner 2009: 257–258.
17 KUB 21.38, Incipit restored; Hoffner 2009: 281–290.
18 KUB 21.38, 1′–6′; Hoffner 2009: 282.

> me [...] and may they be set with lapis lazuli! Furthermore, my lands enjoy full life. <May> your lands likewise <enjoy> full life! I have sent my greetings and my ornaments to my brother. With me all is well. May it be well with my brother likewise!

The prominent, active role played by the queen Puduhepa is expressed by means of ceremonious formulae constantly used in the correspondence between kings: the Hittite queen nicknames Ramses "my brother" (i.e. a person of the same rank). Her privileged status and position are also stressed by the confidence she has in addressing the pharaoh:[19]

> Does my brother have nothing at all? Only if the Son of the Sun God, the Son of the Storm God, and the Sea have nothing, do you have nothing! Yet, my brother, you want to enrich yourself at my expense! It (i.e., such behavior) is unworthy of name and lordly status.

Just after the blessing formula Puduhepa enters into negotiation with Ramses; the matter is an inter-dynastic marriage:[20]

> Concerning the fact that you, my brother, wrote to me as follows:
>
> "My sister wrote to me: 'I will give a daughter to you.' But you have withheld her from me. And now you are even angry with me! Why have you not now given her to me?" I will give you both my daughter and the dowry. And you will not disapprove of it (i.e., the dowry); you will approve of it. But at the moment I am not able to give her to you. (...)
>
> To whom should I compare the daughter of heaven and earth whom I will give to my brother? Should I compare her to the daughter of Babylonia, of Zulabi, or of Assyria?

Human reproduction is a core point of the letter because it metaphorically attests not only the independent and active role of the Hittite queens within the Hittite palatial system, but also the natural concern of the Hittites for the perpetuation of their society. This concern is clearly visible in the following passage:[21]

> When the Sun Goddess of Arinna (together with) the Storm God, Hebat, and Šawoška made <me> Queen, she joined me with your brother, and I produced sons and daughters, so that the people of Hatti often speak of my experience$^?$ and capacity for nurture$^?$. You, my brother, know this. Furthermore, when I entered the royal household, the princesses I found in the household also gave birth under my care. I raised them (i.e., their children), and I also raised those whom I found already born. I made them military officers [...] And may the gods likewise endow the daughter whom I will give to my brother with the Queen's experience$^?$ and capacity for nurture$^?$!

---

19 KUB 21.38, 15′–16′; Hoffner 2009: 283.

20 KUB 21.38, 7′–10′ and 12′–13′; Hoffner 2009: 288.

21 KUB 21.38, 56′–63′; Hoffner 2009: 287.

The ultimate promise of Puduhepa testifies to her parity in rank with the pharaoh himself and provides elements to evaluate the notion of women of power among the Hittites:[22]

> And now I know that Egypt and Hatti will become a single country. Even if for the land of Egypt [...] is not a treaty, the Queen knows thereby how you will conclude it out of consideration for my dignity. The deity who installed me in this place does not deny me anything. He/She has not denied me happiness. You, as son-in-law, will take my daughter in marriage.

Probably the same queen is the recipient of a fragmentary letter from the prince Tudhaliya (perhaps the fourth bearing this name). In this letter the prince seeks the intercession of his queen-mother in the apparent quarrel with the king of Hatti, his father. The prince seems to deeply trust the woman's support:[23]

> Say to the Queen, my lady: Thus speaks Tudhaliya: (regarding) my lord (*scil.* the Hittite king) whom I offended, if ever I$^{?}$ did not assuage his anger in the matter for which my lord dispatched me, did not my lord have officers? And to you [...] the one whom he dispatched there, should have spoken to me. Would I not have assuaged my lord's anger? Although I had elevated myself in the estimation of my lord, I have already offended that lord now. What grace$^{?}$ my lady has left in (her) hand, I would have acted in such a way.[...], I would have written to my kind$^{?}$ lady!

An interesting letter sent by the queen Puduhepa to his nephew-in-law, the prince Tattamaru,[24] sheds light on the relations between women and other members of the royal family, even if they are attached to it through political marriages, as in the case of Tattamaru himself, being the husband of the queen's niece:[25]

> You, Tattamaru, had taken the daughter of my sister in marriage. But Fate dealt you a grievous blow: she died on you! Why do they say: "A male in-law remains nevertheless fully an in-law, even if his wife dies?" You were my male in-law, but you do not recognize my family relationship (that binds you to me)[26]. You recognize none [...]. You were my [...] in-law and one day [...].

---

22 KUB 21.38, rev. 13–17; Hoffner 2009: 289.

23 KUB 19.23, 1–13; Hoffner 2009: 347.

24 For the discussions about the relationship between the sender and the recipient we refer to Hoffner 2009: 364, with previous bibliography cited there.

25 KUB 23.85, 5–13; Hoffner 2009: 365.

26 For the glossed term *purpurriyaman* see Hoffner 2009: 395, note 362.

During the Middle Hittite Kingdom, in particular the timeframe between the reign of Telipinu and that of Arnuwanda I (ca. 1525–1370 BC), the administrative processes, including the re-distribution, were steadily controlled by royal family members. They also encompassed the royal property transfer of real estates to families linked to the palace. A specific category of documents, labelled *Landschenkungsurkunden*, legitimated this kind of transfers by means of the royal sealing they bear.

In one of these land grant deeds the name (and the seal impression) of the queen Ašmunikal appears alongside that of his husband, the king Arnuwanda I:[27]

> Arnuwanda, the great king, Ašmunikal, the great queen and Tudhaliya, the son of the king, heir to the throne, they have decreed (it), so they gifted (it) to Kuwatalla, the female attendant (^{MUNUS}SUHUR.LA$_2$), their servant. In the future nobody shall sue her sons and nephews.
>
> The words of the Tabarna Arnuwanda, the great king, Ašmunikal, the great queen and Tudhaliya, the son of the king, heir to the throne, they are (made) of iron; (they) cannot be rejected, nor shattered; may the head (of whom) change them be cut off. This tablet was written by Inar, the scribe, in Hattuša, in the presence of Duwa, the chief of the palace officers.

During the eighties, two fundamental editions of the Hittite "palace inventories" were published (Košak 1982; Siegelová 1986). This *corpus* consists of hundreds, often fragmentary, cuneiform tablets in the form of lists and memoranda of terms indicating items, supplies and materials, containers and places of storage. Even if they are usually labeled "palace inventories", these texts actually report every step in the storage process of incoming luxury goods. It means that they give us precise information about how and where these activities were performed and by whom.

The queen appears in several "palace inventories", and according to the attestations, she plays a crucial role in the administration of the Hittite kingdom, by supervising all the record keeping activities.

A few examples may serve to describe these processes:

1. First step: Systematic inventories: the inventory IBoT 1.31 summarizes the procedures that take place in the storehouses, where presumably the administrators regularly check the temporary records of the incoming goods by comparing the invoices with the contents of the bags. In several passages the scribe annotates that the items are not yet inventoried (*nawi* [or *UL*] *hatiuitān* [or *hatiuitānzi*]) (IBoT 1.31, obv. 11; KUB 42.65, rev. 18, 24). Of particular importance for our brief investigation is the following note:

27 KUB 5.7, obv. 46–55; last edition by Rüster and Wilhelm 2012: 231–244.

The total amount of textiles is recorded on a wooden? tablet (GIŠ.HUR).[28] The queen states as follows: "As soon as I bring (it) (i.e., the bag or the provisional inventory) into the House of the Seal (E_2 ^{NA4}KIŠIB),[29] they (i.e., the scribes) will note it (i.e., the transfer) down on a (clay) tablet". (IBoT 1.31, obv. 13–15)

2. Second step?: Transfer to the "House of the Seal:" the existence of a "House of sealing" is proved by its attestation in the "palace inventories" and (probably) by archaeological evidence. We will return on the function of this structure later, by presenting the very archaeological data.
3. Final step?: Sealing process: she is indeed the administrator in charge of sealing the bags containing luxury goods and the attached lists of their contents.[30] It is her ultimate responsibility that the bags, once stored in the "House of the Seal," will be never opened without her authorization. (KBo 18.180, 3′–4′)
4. Inventory of personal items of royal family members: she is also listed in an inventory text as the recipient of jewels and precious stones. (KUB 42.75, obv. 11. Cf. Siegelová 1986: 63–67)
5. Regular inspection of stored goods: the queen is mentioned together with the king, within an inventory while she is checking precious garments already stored in the royal treasuries, on the occasion of a particular ceremony. (KUB 42.84, obv. 23–24)
6. Collecting goods from the storehouse for ceremonies and cultic activities: she supervises the procedures of collection of the treasured goods to be used during cultic activities or ceremonies.[31]

4 Female administrators and household managers

We have no attestations of female administrators in official letters, except for one fragmentary passage of a letter in which the officer based in a provincial centre sends a message to Hattuša in order that the daughter of a high female

28 For an in depth study of the material, layout and function of these devices, see the capital work by Marazzi 1994.
29 For a discussion on the process of hoarding of goods and its book accounting, we refer to Mora 2007.
30 See, for instance, KUB 42.66, obv. 4′: *IŠ-TU* ^{NA4}KIŠIB MUNUS.LU[GAL.
31 See for instance, KBo 9.91, left edge 1–3; KUB 26.66, iii 10–11.

officer, named Apaddā,[32] will be sent off the town of Ašušuha because of the pestilence (KBo 18.10, obv. 4′. Cf. Hagenbuchner 1989: 206). This fact is in itself not surprising, since Hittite private archives have never been found.

As we have seen afore, even a palace attendant (^{MUNUS}SUHUR.LA$_2$), often mislabeled *hierodule*, could be the beneficiary of a land donation.[33] A member of the royal family, namely Šahurunuwa, is the addressee of a particular royal decree in which the mother-queen Puduhepa and her son, the king Tudhaliya IV, confirm to him the exemptions from obligations already set by the king Hattušili III. Even the daughter of Šahurunuwa, namely Tarhuntamanawa, and her descendants appear as the beneficiaries of the exemption (Cf. Imparati 1974: 35–36).

> And what has been fixed in [th]ese tablets, even? the sons of Arumura concerning the deportees quoted in the tablet (lit. of the tablet) nobody to the sons of Tarhuntamanawa [...] and the properties of Tarhuntamanawa, Muwatalli, the great king, has been previously exempted from corvée or dues obligations (*šahhan* and *luzzi*). But when Hattušili, the great king, the hero {titles} and Puduhepa, the great queen, installed themselves in kingship, [on] that time the properties of Tarhuntamanawa from *šahhan*, *luzzi*, and *uppa*, {list of exemptions} were exempted ... (Excerptum § 11: KUB 26.43+, rev. 6–14)

Even if their presence within the so-called "palace inventories" represents a paltry percentage compared to the male functionaries (less than 7 %), the high ranking female administrators are involved in the record keeping activities at different levels.

A woman named Arumura, probably to be identified with her namesake in the aforementioned decree,[34] appears in a tablet belonging to a very interesting group of inventories in which the highest members of the Hittite royal family are listed as underwriters of the ultimate acquisitions of goods that are conveyed in Hattuša.[35] These texts present the same layout: indication of the material delivered (often luxury metal objects); the name of a community of people; the names of high officers followed by the Akkadogram *ĪDE*, literally "he/she (i.e., the officer) has seen (i.e. he/she knows);" probably to be understood as "he/she witnessed/he has checked (the hoarding of goods)."[36] In the same

32 For the possible identification of the homonym woman mentioned in a palace inventory see below.

33 Other women seem to appear as the beneficiaries of lands or household managers. See LSU Nrs. 15, 16, 22 in StBoT-Beiheft 4.

34 For a recent, brief prosopography of Arumura see Mora and Vigo 2012: 187.

35 KBo 16.83 + KBo 18.26, iii 10. For a re-evaluation of the category of the so-called *Ausgaben* see Mora and Vigo 2012: 185 ff.

36 For further interpretations see Mora 2007: 540; van den Hout 2007: 346; Mora 2010.

group of inventories we also find two other women who have the responsibility to supervise the activity of keeping record of luxury goods stored in the royal treasuries. The first is named Talya(-?) and she is checking an amount of raw metals, basically copper, in the presence of the prince Taki Šarruma, the high officers Zuzuli and Piha Tarhunta (KUB 40.95, rev. iii 11); the second is named Wattiya and she is in charge of the same duties together with the most prominent personalities of the last decades of the Hittite Empire: Walwaziti, the "Chief of the scribes," Tuttu, "the Chief of the storehouse," and the prince Ehli Šarruma. Jana Siegelová, the editor of the "palace inventory" KUB 42.51, has inserted this text in the category *Personliche Zuweisungen* (i.e., allotments *ad personam*) (Siegelová 1986: 344–345). Actually it reports a list of members of the royal family (the princes Ewri Šarruma; Nerikkaili, the heir to the throne and the queen) in connection with sets of ceremonial garments. Among the people listed we find a woman named Henti. Allegedly, the text could be a cult inventory of festive garments given to high-ranking palace functionaries on the occasion of ceremonies. Analogously, the "palace inventory" KUB 42.59 presents a very simple layout: the tablet is divided by a single-column separator; on the left are listed precious garments; on the right the names of women. Unfortunately, apart for the determinatives which identify gender, the lone name preserved is Apaddā. We wonder if we are dealing with the same person cited in the aforementioned letter. Siegelová classified this text among the *Zuweisungen für den persönlichen Gebrauch* (i.e., allotments for personal use) (Siegelová 1986: 336–343). The most important female administrator cited in the so-called "palace inventories" is Wašti. Her name is quoted in an accounting tablet in which luxury goods are listed. Each list is marked by a column divider and ends with the name of the administrator followed by the Hittite verb *dāš*, "he/she has taken." We cannot assure that the luxury goods listed were entrusted to the administrators, even if we cannot exclude this scenario because of the presence of other prominent members of the royal family, such as Talmi Teššob, probably to be identified with the homonymous king of Kargamiš (cf. Mora and Vigo 2012: 188).

5 Women connected with the "Palace" (i.e., *implicit agency*)

Among the women mentioned in the administrative texts, many of them seem to be carrying out unidentified tasks. Thus, we are not always able to detect their exact "active" role within the Hittite administration. The real estate granted by kings and queens to members of the royal family or palace officers comprises villages, towns, farms, lands as well as personnel. For the majority of workers, it is possible to reconstruct their duties also thanks to the professional titles they bear. Nonetheless, specifically considering women, we have no indications of profession. The general reference to their age (old women, women, maids, etc.) does not allow us to conclusively establish their professions. Here follows a list of women probably employed as labor force and quoted in the *Landschenkungsurkunden*. For different reasons we decided not to differentiate between women linked to the men-householders of the properties (E_2, literally "house") within an estate (allegedly householders themselves), and women evidently listed as workforce (often slaves); otherwise not necessarily employed as workers (e.g. the "Old Women" $^{MUNUS.MEŠ}$ŠU.GI). It must be stressed that the tablets are in general highly fragmentary. Hence, the number of women counted is obviously approximate.

Tab. 1: Women attested in the *Landschenkungsurkunden*.

Nr. LSU[37]	Nr. of women	PNs of women (very fragmentary names are not reported)
1	1	Zizzatta
15	113	
16	2	
21	3$^?$	
22	274$^?$	Hašiyarti, Mamalanni, Zuliyawiya, Annipazza, Muwalani, Miyanni, Aya, Annayati, Gullanda, Kuwiya, Dawatuwa, Marakuwanti, Hurmila
23	23	
25	8$^?$	
26	2	
31	5$^?$	
33	2	
40	29	Hillara, Pazza, Šašia, Allu, Pazšia, Uwawa
47	13$^?$	
48	4	Anuwaš[(...)], Tiwatawiya
52	1	Zinkuruwa
68	2	
69	1	Išpunā
74	1	Wāwā
82	2	
91	127	Anna, Annitti, Arhuwašši, Azziya, Hahharti, Huella, Huliyašuhani, Kapašananni, Kapurti, Mali, Mannā, Paškuwa, Pittiyanni, Puzzi, Šakkummilla, Šantawiya, Tešmu, Tiwatapara, Tuttuwani, Zamnawiya, Zidandu, Zithari

37 According to the numeration by Rüster and Wilhelm 2012. For the concordance between the old edition by Riemschneider and StBoT-Beiheft 4, see Rüster and Wilhelm 2012: 25–32.

The so-called "palace inventories" also list women for which it is not possible to delineate specific duties. In this case, the epithet "invisible women" also used by Svärd for similar women in Neo-Assyrian contexts fits quite comfortably (cf. Svärd 2007: 386). The inventories mention 22 women out of 160 administrators. It means the 14 % of the total. Twelve of the twenty-two women seem involved in the textile production.

The obverse and reverse of the indirect joined tablet KBo 18.199 (+) KBo 2.22 show a layout with two columns separated by a double column divider. On the left column are listed quantities (GIN_2, i.e., shekel[s]) of "white" wool (SIG_2 BABBAR) followed by the Hittite term *gaši(š)*; on the right column, names of women (cf. Siegelová 1986: 310–317). The meaning of *gaši* is not clear at all, but scholars suggest it could indicate a kind of color. This hypothesis might be supported by the fact that, at least in one case (KBo 18.199, rev. 2′), the word *gaši* is replaced by the term *ašara*, which is sometimes translated "white" in the Hittite dictionaries (cf. HEG, A: 79; HED, A: 206). If so, the Sumerogram BABBAR in the left column would indicate "raw," "unprocessed," rather than "white" wool. Unfortunately, according to its attestations the term *ašara* could designate the quality of wool more than its color.[38] In sum, we cannot infer any particular indications about which kind of activities are assigned to the women listed in these concise clay tablets. Other women seem involved in the allotment of textiles. In the *Inventurprotokolle* KUB 42.66 and KUB 42.102 is mentioned a woman named Anni. According to Siegelová, this group of inventories lists goods that are already provisionally stored in storerooms (Siegelová 1986: 90–95). Although the first text is very fragmentary, we can deduce that huge quantities of colored wool not yet recorded on wooden? tablets, but already sealed by the queen, are probably allotted to Anni (KUB 42.66, rev. 1′–8′). At the end of the text is specified that the colored wool is looped forming knots.[39] In the second text other quantities of colored wool containing impurities are presumably allotted to Anni. (KUB 42.102, 1′–11′). Due to the very fragmentary state of preservation of the tablets it is impossible to ascertain whether Anni takes charge of the finished products to be stored somewhere, or simply takes the bundles of wool in order to process them. At any rate it is quite clear that women are involved in the palace administration at different levels. Here follows the synoptic chart of the women quoted in the "palace inventories:"

38 See the detailed discussion in Mora and Vigo 2012: 177 ff.

39 KUB 42.66, rev. 10′. For this interpretation see Baccelli, Bellucci and Vigo 2014: 111.

Tab. 2: Women in Hittite Palace Inventories.

PN	Attestation	Duty	Cross reference (if applicable)
Anni	KUB 42.66, rev. 8′; KUB 42.102, 6″	Textiles allotment?	
Apaddā	KUB 42.59, rev. 18′	Book accounting of festive garments	KBo 16.34, obv. 8; KBo 18.10, obv. 4′
Apatti(ti?)	KBo 18.199, rev. 4′	Textile production?	NH 104
Arumura	KBo 16.83 + KBo 23.26, iii 10		NH 155
Ašpunawiya	IBoT 1.31, obv. 9	Gift (SUM) to the queen	NH 177
Elwattaru	KUB 42.65, obv. 4	Textile Production?	
Henti	KUB 42.51, obv.? 1	Allotment of cultic garments?	NH 363
Hepat-IR	KUB 42.49, obv. 9	Gift	
Hištayara	KUB 42.65, obv. 5	Textile production?	NH 376
Hurma	KBo 18.199, obv. 5′	Textile production?	(KBo 22.1, obv.? 8?)
Yarawiya	IBoT 1.31, obv. 21	Gift	NH 432
Kik(k)i?	KBo 18.199, rev. 3′	Textile production?	NH 569.2(KUB 50.64, rev. 1)
Kuwari	KUB 42.65, obv. 3′	Textile production?	
Malli[(-)	KBo 18.199, rev. 5′	Textile production?	NH 726
Parminza	KBo 18.199, obv. x+1′	Textile production?	
Pipi(-)	KBo 18.199, obv. 4′	Textile production?	
Talya-x[	KUB 40.95, rev. iii 11	Checking raw metals	NH 1223
Tawanti	KUB 42.65, obv. 2	Textile production?	
Ura-x[	KBo 18.199, obv. 3′	Textile production?	NH 1431?
Wašti	KUB 42.84, obv. 10	Record keeping of luxury goods	See the next chart
Wattiya	KUB 42.96 + Bo 1016, right col. 28	Record keeping of luxury goods	
Zapaten[-	KBo 18.199, Ro. 2′	Textile production?	

6 Archaeological evidence: the seal impressions form the *Westbau*

According to what can be inferred from the study of the fragmentary "palace inventories" the processes of storage of goods should consist of different stages:

1. The incoming goods are collected in storehouses next to the city walls of Hattuša and divided according to materials they are made of. A first selection also consists of a clear differentiation between tribute (*MANDATTU*)

and compulsory gift (IGI.DU$_8$.A). At this time the scribes draft on wooden$^?$ tablets a provisional list of the goods itemized. These tablets were probably attached to the bags or chests containing items.
2. Subsequently the bags are sealed after being checked by the queen, scribe-administrators and attendants.
3. The sealed bags are probably moved to the royal treasuries. There, the highest officers of the royal palace check the wooden$^?$ tablets and probably seal them. This operation, as well as the previous one, was recorded by scribes on clay tablets.
4. The scribes write on clay tablets the official and definitive inventories of the goods permanently stored in the treasuries.
5. All the clay tablets recording the different steps (those we basically call "palace inventories") were probably kept in the places in which all these operations were done.

Where were the treasuries located? Could the "House of the Seal" be considered the final destination of the goods?

From 1990 to 1991 the archaeologist Peter Neve has discovered in the *Westbau* storehouse of Nişantepe in Hattuša more than 3000 clay lumps and 28 badly preserved clay tablets. These tablets are what we now call *Landschenkungsurkunden*. According to the excavator the clay *bullae* were stored in the upper level of the building, filed in groups, which subsequently collapsed (cf. Herbordt 2005: 8). The hypothesis that the clay lumps found in the *Westbau* were attached to the land grants was quickly dismissed for two main reasons: the names of the witnesses listed in the land grants did not match those on the sealing of the clay lumps, and because the land grants of the *Westbau* are dated to the Middle Hittite period on the basis of the names of the kings on them, whereas most of the clay lumps of the *Westbau* rooms 1–3 bear sealing of the Hittite Empire kings, from Suppiluliuma I to Suppiluliuma II. It means that the land grant tablets were simply discharged before the capital was abandoned, while the majority of the clay lumps was not.

Out of 3402 *bullae*, 2062 were sealed with 1779 seal impressions of "Great Kings"; 313 with the simple title *Tabarna*, and 1286 with seal impressions of princes and functionaries.

Among the sealed clay lumps of functionaries, we find a very small amount (around 4 %) of seal impressions that bear the sealing of female administrators or members of the royal family. Here follows the synoptic chart of them (Mora and Vigo 2012: 192–193):

Tab. 3: Women attested on *bullae* from the *Westbau*.

Name	Title	Catalogue Nr. (Herbordt 2005)	Seals typology
Hatiya	REX.FEMINA	116–118 (one clay lump for each seal)	Round stamp seals
Muwati/Muwatti	REX.FEMINA	260–268 (28 clay lumps; the nr. 264 is impressed on 10 *bullae*)	Round stamp seals, except for nr. 267, (cylinder seal)
Ašmuhepa	REX.FILIA	11 (1 *bulla*)	Round stamp seal
(*Ku*-AVIS-*pi*-*tá*-*na*) Kupapitana?	REX.FILIA	165 (on 2 *bullae*)	Round stamp seal
Tiwatawizi (SOL-*wa*/*i*-*zi*/*a*)	REX.FILIA	464 (1 *bulla*)	Round stamp seal
DOMINA.OCULUS?	REX.FILIA	631 (1 *bulla*)	Round stamp seal
Muwati/Muwatti	REX.FILIA	269 (1 *bulla*), 270 (5 *bullae*)	269: round stamp seal; 270: ring stamp seal
Hwiya	BONUS$_2$.FEMINA	132 (1 *bulla*)	Round stamp seal
Lara	BONUS$_2$.SCRIBA FEMINA?	203 (1 *bulla*)	Round stamp seal
Maniya	FEMINA	231 (1 *bulla*)	Round stamp seal
Tarhuntamana (wa?)	BONUS$_2$.FEMINA	414 (2 *bullae*)	Round stamp seal
Wa/i-šu-á	BONUS$_2$.FEMINA	517 (1 *bulla*)	Round stamp seal
Wiyani (VITIS-*ní*)	BONUS$_2$.FEMINA	519 (1 *bulla*) 520 (1 *bulla*)	Round stamp seal

In light of the attestations some considerations must be taken.

None of the women attested in the seal impressions of the functionaries from the *Westbau* find specific correspondences with those of the "palace inventories." Nonetheless, their titles point to high status ranking women. Specifically, the titles REX.FEMINA and REX.FILIA should identify the daughter of the king, even if it is still difficult to demonstrate they are interchangeable.[40] The title BONUS$_2$.FEMINA should refer to a high ranking woman accredited to the royal family. This is the case of Tarhuntamanawa, tentatively identified with the daughter of Šahurunuwa, already mentioned in the royal decree presented above (cf. Mora and Vigo 2012: 194).

Two other important elements must be stressed:

a) None of the *bullae* bear multiple sealings. This could indicate that the women were in charge of the ultimate inspection of the items attached to

40 See the tentative identification of Muwat(t)i in Mora and Vigo 2012: 194.

the clay lumps. Nonetheless a single sealing for women vs. multiple sealings for men should not be underestimated in studying the involvement of women in administration.

b) Though the women from the *Westbau* are not attested in the "palace inventories," the majority of the names of male functionaries on the clay lumps from the *Westbau* are attested in the "palace inventories." It must also be stressed that the identifications proposed in the following chart are not unanimously accepted.[41]

Tab. 4: Synoptic Chart of Male Administrators in the documentation from Hattuša.

Name	Reference in the "palace inventories"	Catalogue Nr. (Herbordt 2005)	Title of the functionaries on the clay lumps from *Westbau*/Nişantepe
Akiya?	Aki-[xx: KBo 18.189, obv. 1	2	BONUS$_2$ SACERDOS$_2$ VIR$_2$, DOMUS.SIGILLUM VIR$_2$
Alalimi	KBo 16.83 + KBo 23.26, iii 12; KBo 9.94, obv.$^?$ 7	3	PITHOS.VIR.DOMINUS
		4	EUNUCHUS$_2$
		5	EUNUCHUS$_2$
		6	SCRIBA
		7	URCEUS
		8	BONUS$_2$ SCRIBA
		9	SCRIBA
Armapiya	KUB 31.65b, obv. 1; HT 50 (+) KBo 18.198, obv. right col. 5′	58	BONUS$_2$ SCRIBA
		59	BONUS$_2$ SCRIBA
		60	SCRIBA (?)
		61	BONUS$_2$ URCEUS
		62	BONUS$_2$ (?) VIR$_2$
		63$^{(?)}$	?
Atta	KUB 42.31, obv.$^?$ 10; KBo 18.181, rev. 10	76	BONUS$_2$ SCRIBA, L.414-DOMINUS+*MI*(?)
		77	BONUS$_2$ SCRIBA, L.414-DOMINUS+*MI*(?)
		78	SCRIBA
		79	SCRIBA
Ehli Šarruma	Ehli-LUGAL-ma: KUB 40.96 + Bo 1016, right col. 24	97	REX
		99	TONITRUS.PURUS.SOLIUM
		100	REX.FILIUS
			REX.FILIUS,

41 See for instance the discussion about Piha Tarhunta in Hawkins 2002: 224.

Tab. 4 (continued)

Name	Reference in the "palace inventories"	Catalogue Nr. (Herbordt 2005)	Title of the functionaries on the clay lumps from *Westbau*/Nişantepe
		101	MAGNUS.DOMUS.FILIUS REX.FILIUS,
		102	MAGNUS.DOMUS.FILIUS REX.FILIUS,
		103$^{(?)}$	MAGNUS.DOMUS.FILIUS REX.FILIUS
Ewri Šarruma	EN-LUGAL-ma: KUB 42.51, rev.$^{?}$ 5	133	REX.FILIUS
		134	REX.FILIUS, MAGNUS.DOMUS.FILIUS
		135 (Ibri-Teššup$^{!}$)	REX.FILIUS
Kaššu	KBo 18.153, rev. 12; KUB 26.66, iii 5	158	REX xx.REGIO
Kuwalana-^{D}LAMA	NBC 3842, obv. 15	194	BONUS$_2$ SCRIBA-la
Lullu$^{?}$	Lulluš ^{LÚ}patili-: KBo 18.153, rev. 16	206$^{?}$ Lulu[xxx]	BONUS$_2$ SCRIBA
Malala	KBo 18.197 (+) 197a (+) KBo 9.89+90 (+) KUB 42.44, ii 3	230 Mala[xxx]	SCRIBA
Mašamuwa	Masa-A.A: KUB 31.65, rev. 4	234	AURIGA
Nerikkaili	Nerik-[kaili$^{?}$: KUB 42.51, rev.$^{?}$ 5	TONITRUS. URBS+li	
		651	REGIO.DOMINUS
		652	REGIO.DOMINUS
		653	REX.FILIUS, REGIO.DOMINUS
		654	REGIO.DOMINUS, MAGNUS.PITHOS+ra/i, *NI*-*NI*-DOMINUS
		655	REGIO.DOMINUS, MAGNUS.PITHOS+ra/i, *NI*-*NI*-DOMINUS
		656	REX.FILIUS, *NI*-*NI*-DOMINUS, MAGNUS.PITHOS+ra/i
		657	REX.FILIUS, REGIO.DOMINUS, MAGNUS.PITHOS+ra/i
		658	REX.FILIUS, REGIO.DOMINUS,

Tab. 4 (continued)

Name	Reference in the "palace inventories"	Catalogue Nr. (Herbordt 2005)	Title of the functionaries on the clay lumps from *Westbau*/Nişantepe
			MAGNUS.PITHOS+ra/i
		659	$BONUS_2$ SCRIBA
Pallā	KBo 18.153(+)153a, obv. 5, 22; Bo 5166 + KUB 42.10, rev. B 11;	291	$BONUS_2$ SCRIBA
Pihamuwa	Piha-A.A: KUB 42.95, ii 4, 12	299	$EUNUCHUS_2$, PITHOS.VIR.DOMINUS
		300	URCEUS
		301(?)	?
		302	PITHOS
Pihaššamuwa	Pihašša-A.A: KUB 40.96 + Bo 1016, right col. 12	303	SCRIBA
Piha Tarhunta	Piha $^{D}U^{?}$ EN *UNŪTI*: KBo 16.83 + KBo 23.26, iii 1	305	$EUNUCHUS_2$
		306	$AVIS_3$+MAGNUS, $EUNUCHUS_2$, DOMINUS
		307	REX.FILIUS
Taki Šarruma	Taki LUGAL-ma: KUB 40.95, ii 4; Bo 6754, right col. 10; KBo 31.50, iii 1	391	$BONUS_2$ URCEUS(L.354)
		392	MAGNUS.SCRIBA
		393	REX.FILIUS
		394	REX.FILIUS, MAGNUS.SCRIBA
		395	REX.FILIUS, MAGNUS.SCRIBA
		396	REX.FILIUS, MAGNUS.SCRIBA
		397	REX.FILIUS, MAGNUS.SCRIBA
		398	REX.FILIUS, MAGNUS.SCRIBA
		399	REX.FILIUS, MAGNUS.SCRIBA
		400	REX.FILIUS, MAGNUS.SCRIBA
		401	REX.FILIUS, MAGNUS.SCRIBA
		402	REX.FILIUS, MAGNUS.SCRIBA
		403	REX.FILIUS, MAGNUS.SCRIBA
		Taki-Teššup$^{?}$	
		404	REX.FILIUS
Talmi Teššup	Talmi-^{D}[...] KUB 42.84, rev. 20	MAGNUS.TO NITRUS Ura-Tarhunta?	
		630	SCRIBA-la III, SCRIBA
		631	?
		625	?
		626	SCRIBA-la

Tab. 4 (continued)

Name	Reference in the "palace inventories"	Catalogue Nr. (Herbordt 2005)	Title of the functionaries on the clay lumps from *Westbau*/Nişantepe
		627	BONUS$_2$ SCRIBA
		628	BONUS$_2$ SCRIBA, L. 414-DOMINUS+*MI*(?)
		629	SCRIBA-la
Taprammi	KBo 18.161, rev. 17–18;	408	BONUS$_2$ SCRIBA
	KUB 42.80, obv. ? 4′–5′	409	EUNUCHUS$_2$
Tarhuntapiya	^{D}U.SUM-a:	418	BONUS$_2$ SCRIBA, BONUS$_2$ VIR$_2$
	KBo 16.83 +	419	MAGNUS.SCRIBA(?)
	KBo 23.26, iii 6;	Tarhuntapi[ya]	
	KUB 40.95, ii 10	420	?
Tudhaliya	KBo 16.83 +	468	MAGNUS.HASTARIUS
	KBo 23.26, iii 11;		
	KBo 18.197 (+) 197a (+)		
	KBo 9.89+90(+)		
	KUB 42.44, i 2;		
	KUB 42.42, iv 4?		
Walwaziti	UR.MAḪ.LU$_2$ GAL DUB.SAR^{MEŠ}:	515	BONUS$_2$ VIR$_2$
	KBo 18.153, rev. 15;		
	KUB 26.66, iii 9;		
	KUB 40.96+Bo 1016, right col. 16, 20		
Zuwa	KBo 18.197 (+) 197a (+)	68	SCRIBA
	KBo 9.89+90 (+)	536	AURIGA
	KUB 42.44, ii 6	537	BONUS$_2$ CRUX$_2$$^{(?)}$
		538	PITHOS, BONUS$_2$ VIR$_2$
		539	SCRIBA
		540	SCRIBA
Zuzu	KUB 50.95, ii 4, 9;iii 7′	549	L.135.2, CRUS(?)
Zuzul(l)i	IBoT 1.31, rev. 1;	551	BONUS$_2$ SACERDOS$_2$
	KBo 18.153 (+) 153a,	552	MAGNUS.URCEUS(L.354)
	obv. 5, 22,	553	MAGNUS.URCEUS(L.354)
	rev. 8$^{??}$, 10$^{??}$;	554	REX.FILIUS
	KUB 42.73,	555	REX.FILIUS
	obv. 16, 19$^{?}$, 21	556	REX.FILIUS

The names of male functionaries on the *bullae* from *Westbau* are chiefly attested in the category of the "palace inventories" labeled *Ausgaben* (i.e., outgoing goods). However, these texts probably report the final activities of book accounting by the highest palace officers and members of the royal family who double-check (Akkadogramm *ĪDE*) the ultimate storage of luxury goods in the royal treasuries (cf. Mora and Vigo 2012: 187–191). Moreover, one of the male functionaries attested both in the *bullae* from the *Westbau* and in the "palace inventories", namely Piha Tarhunta, is probably the owner of a high officer's cylinder seal from Emar (A75) and perhaps also the husband of a woman named Wašti (homonymous of one in the inventories), who bears the title of BONUS_2FEMINA on the same seal impression.[42] In conclusion, there is no way to ascertain that the "House of the Seal" mentioned several times in the "palace inventories" should be identified with the *Westbau* of Nişantepe in Hattuša, nor that it could be interpreted as a treasury. Indeed, we have no clear archaeological evidence of the location of the "House of Seal" in which the queen, male and female administrators used to check the stored goods. Nonetheless, it has been underlined several times that many of the clay lumps from the *Westbau* have traces of cords, wood and leather on their back (cf. Mora 2007: 543, with previous bibliography). It does not automatically imply that the traces should be associated with the bags or the wooden? tablets frequently mentioned in the "palace inventories."[43] Anyway, the very reference in the "palace inventories" to sealed documents and bags should not be underestimated.[44]

***

The evidence here briefly presented about the role of women in the Hittite administration deserves further investigation. We limited our study to displaying the sources which one should look at. In light of what we have shown so far, trying to answer the questions posed at the very beginning of this paper is not an easy task. However, it is clear that it is quite difficult to identify the alleged "parallel universe" of women's activities in their own environments. The sources we presented are always official; they were issued by the royal chancellery. As long as the private quarters and their archives are not archaeologically detectable in the Hittite centers, we will never be able to present con-

42 Cf. Mora and Vigo 2012: 195. *Contra* Hawkins 2002: 224.

43 For these matters see, above all, van den Hout 2007 and Marazzi 2007.

44 See, for instance, KUB 42.22, 9: 1 ^{GIŠ}*tuppaš* GAL *KÁNKU* GIŠ.ḪUR *parzakiš* NU.GÁL. We follow here the hypothesis of Košak (1982: 52, 231): *parzakiš* = *bulla*; corroborated by CHD "P": 202.

crete data. Even so, it would be difficult to sketch a precise scenario of women at work in their private environments.

Anyway, with this general investigation we tried to delineate the relations between female and male worlds in light of the women's agency in men's *milieu*. For what can be inferred from the fragmentary "palace inventories" as well as from the clay *bullae* from Nişantepe, it seems that women actively participated in the administration of the palace, even if the absence of *bullae* with the same names of the female administrators cited in the inventories remains obscure and the single sealing do represent a clear problem for interpretation. In addition, we have no elements to reconcile the picture of women as sketched in the folk tales with the evidence provided by the administrative texts. Anyway, it is noteworthy that, among the Hittites, women and men seem to operate side by side. We would cautiously suggest that, according to the little evidence we have, neither the male nor the female world was exclusive to one gender or another. In the management of the palace, and supposedly in the private sphere as well, men and women constantly cooperated. Finally, we must stress that the study of hierarchy and professionalism of women in the Hittite society illustrates only the world of "women of power."

Abbreviation

OrŠ Inventory number of the tablets unearthed in Ortaköy-Šapinuwa.

Bibliography

Archi, Alfonso. 2007. Transmission of Recitative Literature by the Hittites. *AoF* 34: 185–203.

Baccelli, Giulia, Benedetta Bellucci, and Matteo Vigo. 2014. Pp. 97–143. Elements for a comparative study on textile production and use in Hittite Anatolia and its Neighbours in *Prehistoric, Ancient Near Eastern and Aegean Textiles and Dress: An Interdisciplinary Anthology*, eds. Marie-Louise Nosch, Cécile Michel, and Mary Harlow. Ancient Textiles Series 17. Oxford: Oxbow Books.

Bachvarova, Mary. Hurro-Hittite stories and Hittite pregnancy and birth rituals. Pp. 272–306 in Chavalas 2014b.

Beckman, Gary. M. 1983. *Hittite Birth Rituals. Second Revised Edition*. StBoT 29. Wiesbaden: Harrassowitz.

Beckman, Gary M. 1993. From Cradle to Grave: Women's Role in Hittite Medicine and Magic. *JAC* 8: 25–39.

Chavalas, Mark. 2014a. Introduction. Pp. 1–9 in Chavalas 2014b.

Chavalas, Mark (ed.). 2014b. *Women in the Ancient Near East: A Sourcebook*. London: Routledge.

Collins, Billie Jean. Women in Hittite ritual. Pp. 246–271 in Chavalas 2014b.

Crawford, Harriet. 2014. An exploration of the world of women in third-millennium Mesopotamia. Pp. 10–27 in Chavalas 2014b.

Giddens, Anthony. 1979. *Central Problems in Social Theory: Action, Structure, and Contradiction in Social Analysis*. London: Macmillan Press.

Hagenbuchner, Albertine. 1989. *Die Briefe mit Transkription, Übersetzung und Kommentar*. Texte der Hethiter 16. Heidelberg: Winter Universitätsverlag.

Hawkins, J. David. 2002. Eunuchs Among the Hittites. Pp. 217–233 in *Sex and Gender in the Ancient Near East. Proceedings of the XLVIIe Rencontre Assyriologique Internationale, Helsinki, July 2–6, 2001*, eds. Simo Parpola, and Robert M. Whiting. Helsinki: Neo-Assyrian Texts Corpus Project.

Herbordt, Susanne. 2005. *Die Prinzen- und Beamtensiegel der hethitischen Grossreichszeit auf Tonbullen aus dem Nişantepe-Archiv in Hattusa – mit Kommentaren zu den Siegelinschriften und Hieroglyphen von J. David Hawkins*. Boğazköy-Ḫattuša 19. Mainz: Philip von Zabern.

Hoffner, Harry A. Jr. 1998. *Hittite Myths. 2nd edition*. SBL: Writings from the Ancient World 2. Atlanta: Scholars Press.

Hoffner, Harry A. Jr. 2009. *Letters from the Hittite Kingdom*. SBL: Writings from the Ancient World 15. Atlanta: Scholars Press.

van den Hout, Theo P. J. 2005. On the Nature of the Tablet Collections at Ḫattuša. *SMEA* 47: 277–289.

van den Hout, Theo P. J. 2007. Seals and Sealing Practices in Hatti-Land: Remarks à propos the Seal Impressions from the *Westbau* in Ḫattuša. *JAOS* 127: 339–348.

Imparati, Fiorella. 1974. Una concessione di terre da parte di Tudhaliya IV. *RHA* 32: 3–211.

Košak, Silvin. 1982. *Hittite Inventory Texts (CTH 241–250)*. Texte der Hethiter 10. Heidelberg: Winter Universitätsverlag.

Marazzi, Massimiliano. 1994. Ma gli ittiti scrivevano veramente su "legno"? Pp. 131–160 in *Miscellanea di studi linguistici in onore di W. Belardi. Linguistica indoeuropea e non indoeuropea*, eds. Palmira Cipriano, Paolo di Giovine, and Marco Mancini. Roma: Il Calamo.

Marazzi, Massimiliano. 2007. Sigilli, sigillature e tavolette di legno: alcune considerazioni alla luce di nuovi dati. Pp. 465–474 in *VITA – Festschrift in Honor of Belkıs Dinçol and Ali Dinçol*, eds. Metim Alparslan, Meltem Doğan-Alparslan, and Hasan Peker. Istanbul: Ege Yayinlan.

Michel, Cécile. 2014. Akkadian Texts – Women in Letters. Old Assyrian Kaniš. Pp. 205–212 in Chavalas 2014b.

Mora, Clelia. 2007. I testi d'inventario e gli "archivi" di cretule. Pp. 535–550. in *Tabularia Hethaeorum. Hethitologische Beiträge. Silvin Košak zum 65. Geburtstag*, eds. Detlev Groddek, and Marina Zorman. Dresdner Beiträge zur Hethitologie 25. Wiesbaden: Harrassowitz.

Mora, Clelia. 2010. Le sigillature multiple nell'archivio di Nişantepe (Ḫattuša, Città alta). Pp. 216–231 in *Studi di ittitologia in onore di Alfonso Archi*, eds. Rita Francia and Giulia Torri. *Or* 79/2.

Mora, Clelia and Matteo Vigo. 2012. Attività femminili a Ḫattuša. La testimonianza dei testi d'inventario e degli archivi di *cretulae*. Pp. 173–223 in *Centro Mediterraneo Preclassico. Studi e Ricerche III. Studi vari di egeistica, anatolistica e del mondo mediterraneo*, eds. Natalia Bolatti-Guzzo, Silvia Festuccia, and Massimiliano Marazzi. Serie Beni Culturali 20. Napoli: Suor Orsola Benincasa nell'Università.

Pecchioli Daddi, Franca, and Anna Maria Polvani. 1990. *La mitologia ittita*. Brescia: Paideia.
Roth, Martha T. 2014. Women and Law. Pp. 144–174 in Chavalas 2014b.
Rüster, Christel and Gernot Wilhelm. 2012. *Landschenkungsurkunden hethitischer Könige*. StBoT-Beiheft 4. Wiesbaden: Harrassowitz.
Siegelová, Jana. 1971. *Appu-Märchen und Ḫedammu-Mythus*. StBoT 14. Wiesbaden: Harrassowitz.
Siegelová, Jana. 1986. *Hethitische Verwaltungspraxis im Lichte der Wirtschafts- und Inventardokumente*. Praha: Národní Muzeum.
Svärd, Saana. 2007. Agency and the Neo-Assyrian Women of the Palace. *Studia Orientalia* 101: 381–420.

Brigitte Lion

Work and Gender in Nuzi Society

At the beginning of the 14th century BC, the kingdom of Arraphe was a small vassal state of the Mittani. It is well documented by ca. 5,000 tablets unearthed in one of its provincial towns, Nuzi.

The professions existing in this kingdom are mentioned in a variety of documents, which belong to the archives of both institutions and families. The administrative texts, produced mainly by the palace and the great households, include lists of workers as well as lists of the rations issued to these workers. A few contracts show that private individuals also hire shepherds or oxherds, weavers or wet-nurses.

After a short bibliographical overview, this paper will analyze the documentation related to professions within two sectors of activity which are usually considered to be an extension of the household chores of women, namely textile production and food processing: in Nuzi, both men and women are attested performing these tasks.

1 Bibliographical overview

The numerous profession names mentioned in the documentation from the Arraphe kingdom have been treated in two general studies.

The first one to pay attention to this topic was L. Oppenheim (1939). He noted: "les professions les plus fréquentes sont celles du pâtre (*rê'û*), du marchand (*tamkaru*) et du forgeron (*nappāḫu*)." After his study of these three professions, he remarked also those of the carpenter (*naggāru*), the gardener

Acknowledgements: I wish to thank my colleague Françoise Rougemont, CNRS, for the help she provided me with the translation of this contribution into English. I also thank warmly Philippe Abrahami: since we have been studying Nuzi material together for a long time, most of the refences given here derive from our common studies and he generously indicated to me some of them which escaped my attention. Moreover, some of the ideas developped here originate from our common discussions. Part 3, dealing briefly with professions linked to the food sector, is derived from his Habilitation Dissertation (Abrahami 2012), forthcoming: I thank him for his kind permission to use his data here. Of course, all errors that remain are mine.

Brigitte Lion, Université Lille 3 – UMR HALMA 8164; brigitte.lion@univ-lille3.fr

(LU_2.NU.GIŠ.SAR or *nukarribu*), or the weaver (LU_2.UŠ.BAR), as well as a few others still less well documented. This list contains mostly male professional designations, with a few exceptions: NIN.DINGIR, the priestesses, and, in JEN 507, *ušparātu ša qê*, the "tisserandes de fil" (female weavers of thread), a *sirāšû*, "c'est-à-dire d'une esclave qui prépare la boisson *siraš*" (a female brewer) and *ṭē'inētu*, "des esclaves qui moulent" (female millers).[1]

The second important study was written by W. Mayer. In his book, devoted to the Nuzi palace tablets, one half concerns functions and professions (1978: 104–207). A chapter deals with a mixed profession, "Musiker(innen) und Sänger(innen)". Another one, entitled "Frauenberufe," deals with 6 female professional designations: *mušēniqtu*, "wet-nurse," *iškihhuru*, "unguent maker," MUNUS.MEŠ *ša* ^{GIŠ}GADA, "women of the linen;" in addition, there are three trade names for which he does not suggest a translation: *hašartennu*, MUNUS.MEŠ *ša sà-aḫ-le-e* and MUNUS.MEŠ *uzzulika/irū*. Since 1978, some corrections have to be added. G. Wilhem (1992: 245–47 and n. 12) has shown that the *hašartennu* was in fact the "female perfume maker", and not the *iškihhuru* – a word whose translation is not known. And two professions, which W. Mayer considered to be female, are now also attested for males and should be removed from the list: there are mentions of LU_2.MEŠ *uzzalikarū* (Wilhelm 1995: 127), as well as LU_2 *sá-aḫ-lu* (singular) and LU_2 *ša sà-aḫ-le-e* (plural).[2] Some other professional designations appear in private archives, but are not mentioned in Mayer's book about the palace documents.

In a series of articles that deals with specific professions. C. Zaccagnini (1977) studied the merchants, their status and activities, including their links with the palace. M. A. Morrison (1981) gathered references related to shepherds and oxherds, who often practice the same trade as their fathers. P. Negri-Scafa (1998) also noted the transmission of the profession from father to son for doorkeepers (*abultannu*) in various towns of the Arraphe kingdom. She has also written several articles about the scribes (Negri-Scafa 1986, 1987, 1992, 1995, 1997, 1998, 1999a, 1999b, 2005, 2008). All these specialized studies deal with professions which, in the kingdom of Arraphe, are exclusively performed by men. J. Fincke (2015) has recently devoted an article to the tradition of professions within families, which also concerns the male professions of scribe, judge, and doorkeeper.

Female professions are not that well documented and have thus been less studied. An article by H. Schneider Ludorff (2009) concerns the activities of wet-nurses, which is the only female profession determined by sex and not by

1 Oppenheim 1939: 60–61.

2 HSS 16, 186: 14 and HSS 15, 42: 39. See Abrahami and Lion forthcoming.

gender. This study shows that the royal family, as well as rich families, hired wet-nurses.

Finally, the cult personnel was studied by P. Negri-Scafa (2013). Two papers deal with specific religious functions. The prophets are exclusively men in the kingdom of Arraphe, but there are in fact very few attestations (Lion 2000). On the contrary, the *ēntu*-priesthood is reserved for women and we do not know of any equivalent male function (Deller and Fadhil 1972).

These studies provide us with a better knowledge of these professions, some of which seem to be exclusively practiced by men, while others are reserved for women. However, it happens that some professions are performed by both. These are the cases I intend to study here. In the limited frame of this contribution, I will deal only with textile and food production, leaving aside the religious personnel, and other professions practiced by both men and women, such as musicians, *uzzulikarū* and MUNUS or LU_2 *ša šaḫlê*.

2 The textile production sector

This sector of activity includes, as a matter of fact, several professions which are practiced in different frames: the most numerous documents come from the palace of Nuzi, but private archives also provide us with texts dealing with these activities.

2.1 Palatial sources

2.1.1 Weavers and other male specialists

Weavers and other male textile specialists are very well attested in two different kinds of Nuzi tablets: lists of workers and lists of rations.

a) Lists of men working for the palace:
   - HSS 13, 46 (R 76)[3]: 6 young weavers (*ṣuḫārū* UŠ.BAR) are entrusted to Kelip-ukur.
   - HSS 13, 483[4] (R 76): total of "31 weavers (UŠ.BAR) and *kāṣirū*;" the very nature of this profession is still debated: perhaps a carpet maker, or a special kind of weaver?[5]

3 The reference of the tablet is followed by the room number in which it was excavated.

4 Partly transliterated in HSS 13, p. 103–104.

5 According to J. S. Smith (2013: 171–172), "if the occurrences of the word are taken on a case-by-case basis, the craft of the *kāṣiru* as one featuring assembly, especially one related to but

- HSS 14, 649 = HSS 16, 337[6] (R 76): list of 17 *ḫupšū*-weavers. This word designates free peasants or workers (Dassow 2008: 102–105 and 340–42).
- HSS 16, 350 (R 76): 13 young weavers are entrusted to Kelip-ukur. Some of them are also present in HSS 13, 46.
- HSS 16, 360 (L 27): 41 weavers, 25 of whom are IR_3 E_2.GAL, "palace slaves," and the other 16, *ḫupšū*. Some of these *ḫupšū* are also present in HSS 14, 649 = HSS 16, 337.

b) Lists of rations issued to craftsmen:
   - HSS 13, 33 (R 76): 16 or 17 weavers from Nuzi receive barley rations, 1 BAN_2 7 SILA_3 each.
   - HSS 13, 159 (R 76): 11 weavers receive barley rations, 1 SILA_3 each.
   - HSS 14, 593 (R 76): barley is distributed for one month to 83! LU_2.MEŠ IR_3 E_2.GAL, "palace slaves," who receive 2 BAN_2 per person. They are classified by professional groups: The most numerous is made up from 24 weavers (l. 1–14), followed by 4 *kāṣirū* (l. 15–17) and 4 *ašlākū*, "washers" (l. 18–20)[7].
   - HSS 16, 348 (R 76): barley is distributed to 14 weavers, 2 *kāṣirū*, 1 *elam-mihurri*, 1 coppersmith and 39 other men whose profession is not specified.

c) Uncertain: HSS 16, 384 (unknown provenance)[8] is fragmentary, so that it is not possible to classify it among lists of personal or lists of rations. Men are registered, sometimes with their patronyms, and with their profession. Weavers are listed in several places of the list, together with other workers such as bakers or shepherds.

Some of these men appear only once, but others are mentioned in several tablets, which are thus roughly contemporaneous. In fact, all these tablets seem

---

not creating the original woven portion of products, emerges." N. Postgate, studying Middle Assyrian documentation, considers the *kāṣiru* as "a craftsman who works with wool and 'knots', that is to say manufactures knotted carpets, as opposed to the weaver (*ušpār(t)u*) who presumably produced most woven textiles including kilims, and this pair of textile workers is occasionally listed together in contemporary Middle Babylonian texts too." (Postgate 2014: 407). He also notes that in Middle Assyrian texts, "in contrast to the weavers, there is no mention of a female 'knotter'" (Postgate 2014: 408).

6 The same tablet has been published twice: Klein 2002.

7 HSS 14, 620 shows that the *ašlāku* was in charge of washing textiles, cf. Mayer 1978: 175. See Jakob 2003: 428–429 for the Middle Assyrian data.

8 This tablet was probably found in the palace and is counted as such by Mayer (1978: 98, n° 596).

to belong to the same generation, except HSS 16, 384, which lists the names of weavers who are the sons or grandsons of those known by the other lists.[9] The presence of two or three generations of weavers in the lists shows that their craft was transmitted in the same families, from father to sons.

The Nuzi palace employed a numerous personnel, since more than 120 different names of weavers, and some *kāṣirū* and *ašlākū*, appear in these lists. At least 46 weavers are explicitly designated as dependents (IR_3 E_2.GAL), "slaves of the palace," whereas at least 26 are *ḫupšū*; the status of the others is unknown. Children as well as adults worked for the palace.

A tablet published by Wilhelm (1995), ERL 82+SMN 2963 (unknown provenance), records a great number of ^{GIŠ}BANŠUR, "tables" or "trays," associated with individuals or professional groups. The document comes from Nuzi, but we don't know its precise find spot; however, it can be brought together with the palace documents, since the same types of professional designations are mentioned. The craftsmen are not named, but considered as groups, such as the LU_2.MEŠ U[Š.BAR (?)] (l. 7) and the *ašl[āku]*.

The activities of weavers, *kāṣirū* and *ašlākū* thus appear as male professions. Moreover, several work assignments issued by the palace to make textiles are known, and they always involve men. Wool to make fabrics is always issued to men, as in HSS 13, 2 (L 14), HSS 13, 455 (R 76) and perhaps HSS 13, 288[10] (L 2). Craftsmen deliver finished products to the palace, for example in HSS 15, 172 (unknown provenance). The list HSS 15, 137 (L 32) deals with sewing work (*kubbû*) which has been done or not, a work entrusted to a man named Ar-Zizza. We do not find an equivalent documentation for women.

L. Sassmannshausen has made the same kind of observations based on the Middle Babylonian tablets from Nippur, which are slightly more recent than the Nuzi documents: he has shown that textile activities were "von Männern dominiert" (2001: 90), even if other tablets from Nippur show that women are also active in this sector (Tenney 2011: 99–100, 132, 136). L. Quillien (in this volume) has also noticed that, in Neo-Assyrian and Neo-Babylonian palaces and temples, the workforce was composed of men and women. From the Late Bronze Age on, the textile professions, at least in the institutional sector, seems to have been rather masculine, whereas in Early and Middle Bronze Age, mainly women were attested.

---

9 This means that most of these lists do not belong to the last generation attested at Nuzi, but to the previous generation at least.

10 Edited by Zaccagnini 1981: 356–357.

2.1.2 Women in the textile sector

However, women are not completely absent, even if they are less visible than men – exactly as in Middle Babylonian, Neo-Assyrian and Neo-Babylonian documentation.

A list of cereals issued for one month, HSS 14, 153 (unknown provenance), mentions, for the town of Al-ilāni, that is, the capital of the kingdom, Arraphe, 9 ANŠE 1 (PI) of barley "for the women and for the group of the weavers." The amount of rations corresponds to a group of 32 to 48 persons.[11] The reason for recording women and weavers together is not explained, but the possibility that these women also worked in the textile industry cannot be excluded. I would suggest that they might have been spinners. First, because the task of spinning, even if it is not referred to as such in Nuzi documentation, is usually assigned to women and we do not know of men performing it. Second, because of a Middle Babylonian text from Ur, dating to the 13th century, MBTU 1, in which a female spinner is associated with a male weaver;[12] the same division of work might have taken place in Nuzi.

Another ration list, HSS 14, 535 (R 76), starts with the names of 4 MUNUS.MEŠ *ša* GIŠGADA, "4 women of the flax/linen," before listing 25 other women, as well as 8 men, whose profession is not indicated. The first four women receive 2 $SILA_3$ of barley, whereas the other people recorded receive half this amount. Some of these women also appear on other tablets, HSS 14, 510 and 511 (both from R 76), but without a professional designation: thus it is possible that many women working for the palace had specialized professions, but that this fact was not systematically recorded. What is the job of these women? The writing GIŠGADA, with the determinative, could hint at the fact that the plant is concerned, and suggest a translation "women of the flax." But in Nuzi, the linen textiles may be qualified either as GADA, for example in HSS 14, 247 (L 27), HSS 15, 135B (unknown provenance), or as GIŠGADA, in HSS 14, 260 = 607 (M 79). Thus, it is not possible to choose between flax and linen. The same female profession is documented in the Idadda archive from Qaṭna, where 44 MUNUS-tu_4 *ša* GADA are mentioned (TT 14: 13, Richter and Lange 2012: 90–91).

11 G. Wilhelm (1980: 22) has shown that men belonging to the workforce of Šilwa-Teššub receive monthly about 3 BAN_2, and women 2 BAN_2. So that 9 ANŠE 1 PI = 96 BAN_2 of barley would approximately correspond to 32 men or 48 women. Since both men and women form the group mentioned in HSS 14, 153, this group should count between 32 and 48 persons.
12 According to MBTU 1, a woman is attributed to a male weaver *ana ṭāmûti*, "to spin." Then she is given back to her husband, but another woman is given to the weaver to replace her *ana ṭāmûti*.

It also appears in Nippur tablets, dating to the 13th century BC: in MUN 112 iii 6′–8′, two women who receive rations are qualified as LU$_2$ (sic!) GADA.MEŠ (Sassmannshausen 2001: 289–92 and pl. 35); for that reason, the mention of LU$_2$ GADA in MUN 173: 19′ might refer to either men or women (Sassmannshausen 2001: 322 and pl. 47). However, two male LU$_2$ *ša* GADA are known in the Old Babylonian period, in a Mari text recording the personnel of the house of Sammêtar (FM 6, 43 ii 27–29).[13]

The job of these persons is not known, but it might be suggested that they were in charge of making the thread, because the technology used to make linen thread from flax fiber is different from preparing wool thread.[14] In HSS 14, 639 (M 79), a man receives 5 minas of GADA.MEŠ *pilaḫu* belonging to the palace from the *šakin bīti* Elhip-Tilla, and has to give them back later. The word *pilaḫu* is an hapax and W. Mayer wondered whether it might be "eine Nebenform von *pilakku*, 'Spindel;'" he translated "5 Minen Flachs(?) und 2 *pilaḫau*."[15] In fact, there is no sign "2."[16] Should we translate "5 minas of flax and (1) spindle," or "5 minas of spun flax (Abrahami 2015: 181)?" In the latter case, the man receives linen yarn. But in the former, should we understand that he had to spin the flax – or to have it spun by somebody else?

In the archives produced by institutions, there is also an activity described as "making the wool." P. Abrahami (2014: 287–288) has gathered the attestations of this activity and has shown that both women and men are concerned. He suggested that it consisted in the preparation of wool before weaving: either spinning, or an activity performed earlier in the *chaîne opératoire*. The persons performing it are mentioned without reference to a profession.

2.2 In great households

In the house of Šilwa-Teššub, according to HSS 13, 193 (= AdŠ 498), 246 (= AdŠ 499), and 277 (= AdŠ 500), garments are to be made or have been made by men. These men could be weavers, but they are not qualified as such. One may also understand the verb *epēšu* as referring to other operations, such as repair-

13 van Koppen 2002: 352 translates: "2 men, linen weavers." They are mentioned among other male textile workers.
14 Breniquet 2008: 112.
15 Mayer 1978: 36 and n. 1.
16 The confusion probably derives from the number of the line given in the transliteration "[1]5 MA.NA GIŠ.QAT[meš] [2]bi-la-ḫa-ú ša ekalli[li]". There is no copy of the tablet, E. Lacheman gave only its transliteration. A photography taken by P. Abrahami confirms that there is no sign "2".

ing or washing clothes. Some women are mentioned, but their activities seem to concern dyeing rather than weaving.[17]

Textile production is also documented in the archives of the Tehip-Tilla family, which were found in a house north of the main tell (in the "Western Suburban Area"). Several hundreds of tablets were excavated in that area and allow us to follow the economic activities of the family during several generations. Some contracts involve textile workers.

JEN 572 ("house of Tehip-Tilla," room 16)[18] is an exceptional contract recording both an adoption and an apprenticeship convention. The little Naniya is handed by his biological father Hui-Tilla to a weaver, Tirwaya, slave of Enna-mati son of Tehip-Tilla, who adopts him. The adoptive father has to teach the boy his craft. If this condition is not respected, the adoption is cancelled. The combination of adoption and apprenticeship contract can be explained by the modalities of transmission of the professions from father to son[19] – which is clearly attested in the palace text HSS 16, 384, where two or three generations of weavers belonging to the same families are recorded. Weaving appears here, once more, as a male profession.

Enna-mati's nephew, Tarmi-Tilla, concludes with the weaver Zike the long-term contract JEN 314 ("house of Tehip-Tilla," room 13). He gives a precious *kusītu*-garment as model to Zike, who has to make five of these, one per year, over five years.

Another Zike, the brother of Tarmi-Tilla, hires two brothers as *ašlākū*, and pays them with wheat rations (SANTAG 4 20, unknown provenance.)[20] They declare that they are *aššābū* of Zike: this term refers to free people, "who were indeed residents or tenants of property owned by others, property that they cultivated on behalf of their landlords."[21]

However, another tablet, JEN 507 ("house of Tehip-Tilla," room 16), a list of people belonging to Enna-mati's household in Turša,[22] with professional

17 This point has been studied by Abrahami 2014: 298.

18 Transliteration and translation: Speiser 1963.

19 Fincke 2015: 565–566. In another adoption tablet, found in the temple, HSS 19, 44 (G 73), the adoptee, on the contrary, is the craftsman who has to teach weaving to the eldest son of the adopter.

20 Müller 1998: 70–73, collations by Maidman 2004: 308. An *ašlāku*, without name, is also mentioned in the ration list SANTAG 4 n° 36, a tablet which perhaps belongs to the archives of the same family.

21 Dassow 2008: 354–355, with previous bibliography.

22 Neither Enna-mati nor the town of Turša are mentioned in this tablet, but A. Fadhil (1983: 244–245) has established that the same persons are known from other tablets as belonging to Enna-mati's household in Turša.

designations, begins with 30 women defined as *ušparātu ša qê*, "weavers of the thread." This is a unique attestation. P. Abrahami (2014: 288–289) has discussed the meaning of this designation: we could think of spinners, because the thread is mentioned; the CAD translates by "thirty spinners of thread" and A. Fadhil (1983: 244) by "Spinnerinen." However, the term *ušparātu* refers to weaving; another possibility would be to think of women preparing the loom, perhaps warping.

Thus in the family of Tehip-Tilla, producing textiles was the matter of both men and women; but surprisingly, women may be this time recorded in great number – contrary to the palace tablets in which men are mainly attested.

2.3 Among private individuals

In other families, less rich than Enna-mati's, the household personnel was probably also less numerous. It is often assumed that textiles and garments were produced by women at home. For example, girls who receive land plots as their dowry, give to their father (or, in a particular case, their adoptive brother), a counter-dowry which might be partly made up from textiles (HSS 5, 76; HSS 19, 79; Gadd 31). We might suppose, in this case, that they had made these textiles themselves.[23]

Textiles could also be manufactured by specialized craftsmen, as attested by several work contracts.[24] HSS 5, 95[25] ("House of Zike," room A 34), is concluded between Ilanu and Puhi-šenni:

> "Puhi-šenni, son of Enšukru, received 14 minas of wool, belonging to Ilanu son of Tauki, *ana artartennūti*.[26] After the harvest, at the beginning of the month *kurilli* (iii), Puhi-šenni shall give back to Ilanu a *sasullu*-cloth of good quality, weighing 6 minas, 15 cubits its length, 5 cubits its width. If he does not give back the cloth in the month *kurilli*, he will add a *naḫlaptu*-coat weighing 2 minas. (Sealings)."

The difference of 8 minas (4 kg) between the weight of wool received and the weight of the textile item requested can be explained by two facts. Part of the wool might be lost while processing the raw material; and part of the wool also

23 Grosz 1981: 174; Justel and Lion 2014.

24 The textile work contracts of Nuzi have been discussed together with P. Abrahami in a common paper presented within the frame of the Nuzi session held at the 61st RAI in Geneva (june 2015).

25 Transliterated by Dosch 1976 n° 130 and by Zaccagnini 1981: 349.

26 The meaning of this word is uncertain, it is only attested in this text and in HSS 5, 36 (see below).

probably constituted the wages of the craftsman. If the textile is not provided within the time limit, the penalty will be to make another textile item, which will be, for Enšukru, an additional work, and will lessen his salary. One generation later, a very similar contract states that Ilima-ahi, the son of Ilanu, gives a textile also *ana artartennūti* to a craftsman, to be transformed into a "good" textile (HSS 5, 36,[27] A 34): the work involved is probably not weaving, but perhaps rather reparing an old fabric.

Two other tablets found in the same room A 34, HSS 13, 18[28] and HSS 5, 6,[29] concern loans of barley belonging to Pirazzana, to Tai-Tilla, who seems to be an impoverished craftsman. He agrees to work for Pirazzana for very low wages, and his work is probably to be considered as interest on the loan. There are still other examples of work contracts, and in all of them, weavers working for private persons are men.

3 The food sector

Another fundamental sector of the economy is the production of food. It is not much attested in the archives of private houses: we can suppose that the ladies of the house were in charge of most of the kitchen chores, so that it did not leave written documentation. However, preparation of food is, again, better documented in the palatial sector as well as for the great households. Among the numerous professions attested, some are documented for both men and women.

If we go back to the list HSS 14, 593 (R 76) found in the palace, which mentions barley rations for male slaves according to their profession, we find 4 bakers (*ēpû*), 1 brewer *sēbiu*, 1 person preparing groats (*ša mundu*), 2 *sirāšû*-brewers and one cook.

But at least two documents show that women also worked as brewers. In ERL 82+SMN 2963 (unknown provenance; Wilhelm 1995),[30] "tables" or "trays" are associated with professional groups, some of which are in charge of the preparation of food: male cooks, LU_2.MUHALDIM, but also *sirāsâtu*, female brewers, and *alaḫ̮ḫennātu*, "flour-processers," mentioned together as benefiting from the same "table." And at Enna-mati's house, the personnel list JEN

27 Transliterated by Dosch 1976 n° 137 and Zaccagnini 1981: 351, n° 7 and n. 9.

28 Transliterated by Dosch 1976 n° 73.

29 Transliterated by Dosch 1976 n° 72.

30 See above § 2.1.1.

507 (room 16) records two female cereal grinders, *ṭē'inētu* (l. 20–21) and a female brewer, whose name is partly broken (but the feminine determinative is preserved): ^{f}[...]-*ma-a-a sí-ra-sú-ú* (l. 19) Since the end of the line is broken, a last sign *sí-ra-sú-ú-*[*tù*] might be added to have here a feminine form.[31] But it is also possible that this professional designation is here written in the masculine form *sirāsû* (instead of *sirāšû*),[32] perhaps because it was mainly a male profession, at least during the second half of 2nd millennium.[33]

The association of the women preparing beer and flour on these two tablets is easy to explain, since both groups work with the same material, namely barley. The two different designations, *alaḫḫennātu* and *ṭē'inētu*, probably correspond to different specializations. According to N. Postgate, in the Middle Assyrian Offerings House archives from the Aššur temple, the *ṭē'inu* is actually the grinder who processes grain to produce flour; and the *alaḫḫenu* is the "preparer of farinaceous products" or "flour-processer" – this word is sometimes translated by "baker," which is not quite accurate.[34]

In Nuzi, male *alaḫḫennū* are also attested. In the archives of Šilwa-Teššub, son of the king, distributions of wool or textiles are made to 4 *alaḫḫennū* (HSS 13, 287 = AdŠ 45: 17–19; HSS 15, 211 = AdŠ 46: 25–28; HSS 16, 382 = AdŠ 47: 7–8. See Wilhem 1980: 158–59). The letter HSS 14, 31 (S 112), found in a private house, was sent by the *alaḫḫennu* of the Ṣilliyawe palace to the judges, and deals with a conflict about the irrigation of a field: so this *alaḫḫennu* is working for a palace. There was also perhaps a building or a house called *bīt alaḫ*[*ḫenni*], mentioned in HSS 14, 137 (L 2).

The term *ṭē'inu*, "grinder", masculine of *ṭē'intu*, is not attested at the moment in Nuzi. However, the activity was performed by both sexes: a tablet from the house of Tehip-Tilla, HSS 13, 66 (room 18) records four quantities of grain "to be ground" (*ana ṭêni*) which are handed to two men and two women, thus probably in charge of transforming it into flour.

31 This suggestion was made by W. von Soden in AHw: 1050a; see also Fadhil 1983: 244 and CAD S: 306b. Both dictionaries also give a reference to the (more correct) feminine form *sirāšītu* attested in Susa during the Old Babylonian Period (MDP 22 72: 24). CAD also records a MUNUS.ŠIM-*tum* in the Old Babylonian tablet CT 8 14c: 16, from Sippar, see Harris 1975: 283.

32 As underlined by G. Wilhelm (1995: 127).

33 See Breniquet 2009: 187 (referring to J.-J. Glassner): "en Mésopotamie aussi, la bière est une affaire de femmes, au moins jusqu'à l'époque paléo-babylonienne où l'activité sort de la sphère féminine et devient un véritable 'métier' aux mains des hommes." See also Michel 2009: 206–207 about female and male brewers during the first half of the 2nd millennium. On the contrary, in Middle Assyrian sources, only male brewers are attested, see Jakob 2003: 401–407.

34 Postgate 2013: 109–110. In a Middle Assyrian letter found in Dūr-katlimmu, two female *alaḫḫenātu* are also attested, perhaps as members of the household of the queen: Cancik-Kirschbaum 1996: 147–153, n° 10: 12.

In HSS 14, 97: 12 and HSS 14, 98: 13, two texts from unknown provenance but probably found in the Nuzi palace, men referred to as *kassiddaššu* receive bread. This profession is probably the equivalent of Middle Babylonian *kaṣṣiddakku* (Sassmannshausen 2001: 74–78); it has been translated as "Müller" in AHw: 458b and "miller" in CAD: 267b–268a, according to its Sumerian equivalent KA.ZID$_2$.DA or GAZ.ZID$_2$.DA, and it is probably another designation for people producing or processing flour. In Nippur tablets, *kaṣṣiddakkū* are, once more, associated with brewers (Deheselle 2004).[35] No woman performing this trade is (yet) attested, either in Nuzi, or in Middle Babylonian documentation.

In conclusion, even if male brewers, grinders and flour-processers seem predominant, women are also attested in these professions.

***

Both case studies examined, namely textile work and food production, are part of the most common activities: food had to be prepared daily, in every house, and most probably the same was true of textiles. According to Starr's excavation report, excavations in Nuzi have unearthed "hundreds of spindle whorls" as well as loom weights[36] (indicating that vertical warp weighted looms were used). Among these objects, very few were published; and among those which were published, the majority comes from private houses. This is the case, for example, of the two clay loom stands which were recovered in a house[37] (indicating that horizontal looms were also used). However, these finds give us no clue about the identity of the people working with these tools.

In order to answer that question, we have to look at the written documentation. The information available regarding work shows that, from the point of view of the organization, an opposition between the palace and the private

35 *Kaṣṣidakkū* operate as millers and bakers and are associated with brewers in Middle Babylonian documentation because both are working for temple offerings; I thank the anonymous referee for this information.

36 Starr 1939: 412–413 and 1937: pl. 116 S, T, perhaps V, and 127 FF (whorls), pl. 117 C–E and G (weights).

37 Two clay loom stands were recovered in the house called "Group 24," in room F 24 (but "below the floor of Stratum II"), and another one in room F 14, with "four bowls and a cup, as well as other vessel fragments;" this room was, according to Starr, "the center of considerable domestic activity." (Starr 1939: 218–219; Starr 1937: pl. 118 A and B, ancient loomstands, and 30 B, Arab loom).

individuals is not enough. We must take into account the great households, for which Nuzi offers two examples: the house of Tehip-Tilla and his son Enna-mati, and the house of Šilwa-Teššub son of the king. They are organized just as the palace, but at a reduced scale, with dozens of workers whereas the palace has hundreds, free or dependent. The palace of Nuzi, which is the best known, is only a provincial palace, so we must imagine a more developed and complex organization for Arraphe's palace.

Specialized workers, both men and women, are mostly known through the archives of the palace and these great households, since, due to their number, a special organization was developed, mostly for the distribution of food rations. The management of this workforce and its supplies left written evidence.

In these tablets, the specialization of workers is sometimes indicated by means of a professional designation. However, this is not systematic, which means that our information is far from being complete. We have seen the case of the women "of the linen," who are called that way only once, even though they appear in several tablets. We would not have known of their specialization if we did not have the single tablet mentioning it. Another example is to be found in the archives of the prince Šilwa-Teššub. Women worked in the process of dyeing the wool, and more generally, in the management of textiles. Their personal names are given without any indication of a profession.

We know of lists with several dozens of servants' names, both men and women, working for the palaces of different towns in the kingdom of Arraphe, but without any indication of specialization, even though there were probably many specialists among these workers.

In the private houses, we have very little information about professional skills, or work performed by non-professional workers, including the domestic work that must have been performed by women. We know of the hiring of specialists, but only when it is necessary to write a contract, which was rarely the case. We found several orders for textiles, and we have some other contracts with wet-nurses, shepherds, oxherds, and brick makers. However, a number of transactions with specialists were probably paid in cash and have left no written trace.

Lastly, indications of gender, when it comes to professions, differ according to places, time periods and maybe also the model for the organization of work. Sectors like textile working and food preparation are often viewed as "female," and may be so in the framework of the family. However, mentions of workers specialized in these fields of activities indicate that they were rather men, in the palaces and in the great households, and even craftsmen working for private individuals.

Abbreviations

FM	Florilegium marianum
MBTU	Gurney 1983.
MUN	Sassmannshausen 2001.
SANTAG 4	Müller 1998.

Bibliography

Abrahami, Philippe. 2012. *Les céréales dans les textes du palais de Nuzi (Yorghan Tepe – Iraq, 14ème s. av. J.-C.)*. Université François-Rabelais, Tours. Unpublished habilitation thesis.

Abrahami, Philippe. 2014. Wool in the Nuzi Texts. Pp. 278–304, in Breniquet and Michel 2014.

Abrahami, Philippe. 2015. L'intendant du palais (*šakin bīti*) à Nuzi. Pp. 177–192 in *Cahier des Thèmes transversaux ArScAn. Archéologies et Sciences de l'Antiquité – UMR 7041. Volume XII*, eds. Cécile Michel, Pierre-Marie Blanc, and Luc Bachelot. Nanterre: ArScAn (http://www.mae.u-paris10.fr/arscan/De-la-maison-a-la-ville-dans-l,1434.html).

Abrahami, Philippe and Lion, Brigitte. forthcoming. Workforce and Job Categories in the Nuzi Texts. In *What's in a name? Terminology related to work force and job categories in the ancient Near East*, ed. Agnès Garcia-Ventura. AOAT. Münster: Ugarit Verlag.

Breniquet, Catherine. 2008. *Essai sur le tissage en Mésopotamie, des premièes communautés sédentaires du milieu du IIIe millénaire avant J.-C.* Paris: De Boccard.

Breniquet, Catherine. 2009. Boire de la bière en Mésopotamie ... Pp. 183–196 in Faivre, Lion and Michel 2009.

Breniquet, Catherine, and Cécile Michel (eds.). 2014. *Wool Economy in the Ancient Near East and the Aegean: from the Beginnings of Sheep Husbandry to Institutional Textile Industry*. Ancient Textile Series 17. Oxford: Oxbow Books.

Cancik-Kirschbaum, Eva Christiane. 1996. *Die mittelassyrischen Briefen aus Tall Šēḫ Ḥamad*. Berichte der Ausgrabung Tall Šēḫ Ḥamad / Dūr-katlimmu 4. Berlin: Dietrich Reimer Verlag.

Dassow, Eva von. 2008. *State and Society in the Late Bronze Age. Alalaḫ under the Mittani Empire*. SCCNH 17. Bethesda: CDL Press.

Deheselle, Danielle. 2004. Meuniers et brasseurs kassites, travailleurs itinérants. Pp. 273–285 in *Nomades et sédentaires dans le Proche-Orient ancien. Compte rendu de la XLVIe Rencontre Assyriologique Internationale (Paris, 10–13 juillet 2000)*, ed. Christophe Nicolle. Amurru 3. Paris: Editions Recherche sur les Civilisations.

Deller, Karlheinz and Fadhil, Abdulillah. 1972. NIN.DINGIR.RA/*ēntu* in Texten aus Nuzi und Kurruhanni. *Mesopotamia* 7: 193–213.

Dosch, Gudrun. 1976. *Die Texte aus Room A 34 des Archivs von Nuzi*, Heidelberg. Unpublished Magister-Arbeit.

Fadhil, Abdulillah. 1983. *Studien zur Topographie und Prosopographie des Provinzstädte des Königreichs Arrapḫe*. Baghdader Forschungen 6. Mainz: Philipp von Zabern.

Faivre, Xavier, Brigitte Lion, and Cécile Michel (eds.). 2009. *Et il y eut un esprit dans l'homme. Jean Bottéro et la Mésopotamie*. Travaux de la Maison René-Ginouvès 6. Paris: De Boccard.

Fincke, Jeanette. 2015. The Tradition of Professions within Families at Nuzi. Pp. 555–566 in *Tradition and Innovation in the Ancient Near East. Proceedings of the 57th Rencontre Assyriologique Internationale at Rome 4–8 July 2011*, ed. Alfonso Archi. Winona Lake: Eisenbrauns.

Grosz, Katarzyna. 1981. Dowry and Brideprice in Nuzi. Pp. 161–182 in *Studies on the Civilization and Culture of Nuzi and the Hurrians in Honor of Ernest R. Lacheman*, eds. Martha M. Morrison and David I. Owen, Winona Lake: Eisenbrauns.

Gurney, Oliver R. 1983. *The Middle Babylonian Legal and Economic Texts from Ur*. London: British School of Archaeology in Iraq.

Harris, Rivkah. 1975. *Ancient Sippar. A Demographic Study of an Old-Babylonian City (1894–1595 B.C.)*. PIHANS 36. Leiden: Nederlands Historisch-Archaeologisch Instituut te Istanbul.

Jakob, Stefan. 2003. *Mittelassyrische Verwaltung und Sozialstruktur*. CM 29. Leiden–Boston: Brill & Styx.

Justel, Josué J. and Brigitte Lion. 2014. Real Estate Dowries and Counter-Dowries in the Kingdom of Arrapḫe. Pp. 39–41 in *Le rôle économique des femmes en Mésopotamie ancienne. Women's Role in the Economy if the Ancient Near East. Report: December 31, 2001–December 30, 2014*, eds. Francis Jaonnès and Fumi Karahashi. Tokyo.

Klein, Michael. 2002. Nuzi Note 66. HSS 14, 649 = HSS 16, 337. P. 166, in *General Studies and Excavations at Nuzi* 10/3, eds. David I. Owen and Gernot Wilhelm. SCCNH 12. Bethesda: CDL Press.

van Koppen, Frans. 2002. Seized by Royal Order. The households of Sammêtar and other magnates at Mari. Pp. 289–312 in *Recueil d'études à la mémoire d'André Parrot*, eds. Dominique Charpin and Jean-Marie Durand. Mémoires de N.A.B.U. 7. Florilegium marianum 6. Paris: SEPOA.

Lion, Brigitte. 2000. Les mentions de "prophètes" dans la seconde moitié du IIe millénaire av. J.-C. *RA* 94: 21–32.

Maidman, Maynard Paul. 2004. The British Museum Nuzi Tablets. *JAOS* 124: 305–314.

Mayer, Walter. 1978. *Nuzi-Studien I. Die Archive des Palastes und die Prosopographie der Berufe*, AOAT 205/1, Neukirchen-Vluyn: Verlag Butzon & Bercker Kevelaer.

Michel, Cécile. 2009. "Dis-moi ce que tu bois ...". Boissons et buveurs en Haute Mésopotamie et Anatolie au début du IIe millénaire av. J.-C. Pp. 197–220 in Faivre, Lion and Michel 2009.

Morrison, Martha A. 1981. Evidence for Herdsmen and Animal Husbandry in the Nuzi Documents. Pp. 257–296 in *Studies on the Civilization and Culture of Nuzi and the Hurrians in Honor of Ernest R. Lacheman*, eds. Martha A. Morrison and David I. Owen. Winona Lake: Eisenbrauns.

Müller, Gerfrid G. W. 1998. *Londoner Nuzi-Texte*. SANTAG 4 Wiesbaden: Harrassowitz.

Negri-Scafa, Paola. 1986. Gli scribi di Nuzi in funzione diverse da redattori di testi: osservazioni preliminari, *Mesopotamia* 21: 249–259.

Negri-Scafa, Paola. 1987. Criteri e Metodologie per uno Studio Degli Scribi di Nuzi. Pp. 215–223 in *General Studies and Excavations at Nuzi 9/1*, eds. David I. Owen and Martha A. Morrison. SCCNH 2. Winona Lake: Eisenbrauns.

Negri-Scafa, Paola. 1992. Scribes locaux et scribes itinérants dans le royaume d'Arrapha. Pp. 235–240 in *La circulation des biens, des personnes et des idées dans le Proche-Orient ancien (CRRAI 38, Paris, 1991)*, eds. Dominique Charpin and Francis Joannès. Paris: Editions Recherche sur les Civilisations.

Negri-Scafa, Paola. 1995. The Scribes of Nuzi and Their Activities Relative to Arms. Pp. 53–69 in *General Studies and Excavations at Nuzi 9/3*, ed. David I. Owen. SCCNH 5. Bethesda: CDL Press.

Negri-Scafa, Paola. 1997. Die "assyrischen" Schreiber des Königtums Arrapḫe. Pp. 123–132 in *Assyrien im Wandel der Zeiten. XXXIXe Rencontre Assyriologique Internationale, Heidelberg, 6.–10. Juli 1992*, eds. Hartmut Waetzoldt and Harald Hauptmann. HSAO 6. Heidelberg: Heidelberger Orientverlag.

Negri-Scafa, Paola. 1998. Gates in the Texts of the City of Nuzi. Pp. 139–162 in *General Studies and Excavations at Nuzi 10/1*, eds. David I. Owen and Gernot Wilhelm. SCCNH 9. Bethesda: CDL Press.

Negri-Scafa, Paola. 1999a. The Scribes of Nuzi. Pp. 63–80 in *Nuzi at Seventy-Five*, eds. David I. Owen and Gernot Wilhelm. SCCNH 10. Bethesda: CDL Press.

Negri-Scafa, Paola. 1999b. Confini geografici e orizzonti culturali: il caso degli scribi del regno di Arrapḫa. Pp. 153–158 in *Landscapes, Territories, Frontiers and Horizons in the Ancient Near East. Papers Presented to the XLIV Rencontre Assyriologique Internationale Venezia, 7–11 July, 1997*, eds. Lucio Milano, Stefano de Martino, Frederick Mario Fales, and Giovanni B. Lanfranchi. Padova: Sargon.

Negri-Scafa, Paola. 2005. Ethnical and cultural aspects related to personal names: the names of the scribes in the kingdom of Arrapha. Pp. 245–251 in *Ethnicity in Ancient Mesopotamia. Papers read at the 48th Rencontre Assyriologique Internationale, Leiden, July 1–4, 2002*, eds. Renée Kalvelagen and Dina Katz. Leiden: Nederlands Instituut voor het Nabije Oosten.

Negri-Scafa, Paola. 2008. The Scribes of Nuzi: Date Formulae and their Use in the Nuzi Corpus. Pp. 119–125 in *Proceedings of the 51st Rencontre Assyriologique Internationale, Held at the Oriental Institute of the University of Chicago, July 18–22, 2005*, eds. Robert D. Biggs, Jennie Myers, and Martha T. Roth. SAOC 62. Chicago: The Oriental Institute.

Negri-Scafa, Paola. 2013. L'ambito religioso a Nuzi. Questioni concernenti il personale cultuale. Pp. 451–460 in *Ritual, Religion and Reason. Studies in the Ancient World in Honour of Paolo Xella*, eds. Oswald Loretz, Sergio Ribichini, Wilfred G. E. Watson et José Ángel Zamora. AOAT 404. Münster: Ugarit Verlag.

Oppenheim, Leo. 1939. Métiers et professions à Nuzi. *Revue des Etudes Sémitiques*: 49–61.

Postgate, Nicholas. 2013. *Bronze Age Bureaucracy. Writing and the Practice of Government in Assyria*. Cambridge: Cambridge University Press.

Postgate, Nicholas. 2014. Wool, Hair and Textiles in Assyria. Pp. 401–427 in Breniquet and Michel 2014.

Richter, Thomas and Lange, Sarah. 2012. *Das Archiv des Idadda. Die Keilschrifttexte aus den deutsch-syrischen Ausgrabungen 2001–2003 im Königspalast von Qaṭna. Mit einem Beitrag von Peter Pfälzner*. Qatna-Studien 3, Ergebnisse der Ausgrabungen. Wiesbaden: Harrassowitz.

Sassmannshausen, Leonhard. 2001. *Beiträge zur Verwaltung und Gesellschaft Babyloniens in der Kassitenzeit*. BaF 21. Mainz: Philipp von Zabern.

Schneider Ludorff, Helga. 2009. Die Amme nach Texten aus Nuzi. Pp. 479–489 in *General Studies and Excavations at Nuzi* 11/2, ed. Gernot Wilhelm. SCCNH 18. Bethesda: CDL Press.

Smith, Joanna S. 2013. Tapestries in the Bronze and Early Iron Ages of the Ancient Near Earst. Pp. 161–188 in *Textile Production and Consumption in the Ancient Near East: Archaeology, Epigraphy, Iconography*, eds. Marie-Louise Nosch, Henriette Koefoed, and Eva Anderson Strand. Ancient Textile Series 12. Oxford: Oxbow Books.

Speiser, Ephraim. 1963. A Significant New Will from Nuzi. *JCS* 17: 68–70.
Starr, Richard F. S. 1937. *Nuzi, Volume 2, Plates and Plans*, Cambridge (Mass.): Harvard University Press.
Starr, Richard F. S. 1939. *Nuzi, Volume 1, Text*, Cambridge (Mass.): Harvard University Press.
Tenney, Jonathan S. 2011. *Life at the Bottom of Babylonian Society. Servile Laborers at Nippur in the 14th and 13th Centuries B.C.* Leiden and Boston: Brill.
Wilhelm, Gernot. 1980. *Das Archiv des Šilwa-Teššup Heft 2. Rationen Listen I.* Wiesbaden: Harrassowitz.
Wilhelm, Gernot. 1992. Notizen zum Hurritischen Wörterbuch. *SMEA* 29: 245–248.
Wilhelm, Gernot. 1995. *Bīt papāhi* in Nuzi. Pp. 121–128 in *Edith Porada Memorial Volume*, eds. David I. Owen and Gernot Wilhelm. SCCNH 7. Bethesda: CDL Press.
Zaccagnini, Carlo. 1977. The Merchant at Nuzi, *Actes de la XXIIIe R.A.I (1976), Iraq* 39: 171–189.
Zaccagnini, Carlo. 1981. A Note on Nuzi Textiles. Pp. 349–361 in *Studies on the Civilization and Culture of Nuzi and the Hurrians in Honor of Ernest R. Lacheman*, eds. Martha A. Morrison and David I. Owen. Winona Lake: Eisenbrauns.

Josué J. Justel

Women in Economic Agreements: Emarite sale contracts (Syria, 13th century BC)

Publication of the Emar cuneiform texts began in the 1970s, when the Emar archives were unearthed. The number currently stands at about a thousand documents of very different types. A large part of them are private legal texts; the greatest number is made up of sale contracts, which account for over one third of the texts; in second place comes a significant number of other financial deeds: loan contracts, donation agreements, etc.[1]

All that documentation is very useful when it comes to reconstructing some aspects of the society that produced it. For example, it is possible to establish the type of economy, the value of products, etc. It is also possible to focus on economic agents, i.e. people who carried out those transactions. Those agents included women in a variety of occupations.

In that regard, it has traditionally been highlighted that the cases attesting women as an active part of the deed were exceptions, since they are far fewer in number that those dealt with only by men (§ 2); those women were (almost) always widows and alone (§ 3); they were only able to manage their dowries, not any other family property (§ 4); and they mostly carried out those deeds in times of economic difficulty (§ 5). The intention of this contribution is to study the role of women in sales, and to show that those assertions are not correct, at least partially. The documentation chosen is due to the large number of testimonies and to its statistical richness. Loans, already dealt with in other *REFEMA* meetings,[2] have been left aside, as well as property exchanges, since no case has been attested in which women intervened actively.[3]

1 See the introductory assessments of Westbrook 2003 and Démare-Lafont 2010.

2 See the blog *hypothèse* Carnet de REFEMA: https://refema.hypotheses.org/.

3 Some twenty exchange contracts from the Late Bronze Age Syria have been published, but only Ugarit has produced four in which women intervened: RS 15.086 = PRU 3, p. 51, RS 16.158 = PRU 3, p. 62, RS 16.277 = PRU 3, p. 50 and RS 16.343 = PRU 3, p. 129 (see Justel 2008: 203).

Acknowledgements: This paper has been written thanks to a *Ramón y Cajal* contract (ref. 2013–13817), granted by the Spanish *Ministry of Economic Affairs and Competitiveness*.
I thank Brigitte Lion and Cécile Michel for their help and numerous suggestions.

Josué J. Justel, University of Alcalá, History and Philosophy Department (Section of Ancient History); josue.justel@uah.es

1 Emar Sale Contracts

A sale is the act of transferring a product or service, in return for money, an amount of silver, or other compensation.[4] Those economic agreements used to be consigned in a document. In the case of Emar, more than two hundred sale contracts have been published so far – but the specific number depends on the guidelines used to demarcate the corpus.[5] A characteristic of Emar documentation is that two scribal traditions can be recognised, which are commonly known as the "Syrian" [= S] and "Syro-Hittite" [= SH] traditions. Physical and formulaic differences exist between them, and it seems that two different legal conventions are reflected within the Emar scribal traditions. Most of the Emarite sales of property are recorded in documents of Syrian scribal tradition; a few sales of property and all sales of people are written down in documents of Syro-Hittite tradition (see e.g. Démare-Lafont 2010: 46–52 and Fijałkowska 2014).

To date, seventeen sale contracts have been published in which a woman sold property (four of the Syrian scribal tradition, the remaining of the Syro-Hittite one).[6] That number is far higher than those with the same features taken from other Late Bronze Age Syrian archives: two from Ugarit (RS 16.156 = PRU 3, p. 61, RS 17.022+ = Ugaritica 5: 3) and another one from Alalaḫ (AlT 70).

On the other hand, five sale contracts from Emar have been published in which a woman was the buyer.[7] That datum contrasts with the case of the neighboring city of Ugarit, where ten deeds document that same situation;[8] on the contrary, neither Alalaḫ nor Ekalte show documentary evidence of those circumstances.

4 See in general Cardascia 1976–80; Haase 1978–80; Hecker 1976–80; Kienast 1976–80; Krecher 1976–80; Petschow 1976–80; Wilcke 1976–80.

5 See a list of sale contracts in Justel 2008: 186 n. 6. For her part, Démare-Lafont (2010: 46, 49–50) establishes their number in ca. 190, as Fijałkowska (2014) does too. For sale contracts of landed property see Beckman 1997; Viano 2010, 2012; Fijałkowska 2014: 31–97; for the formulary see Di Filippo 2008; Démare-Lafont 2010: 46–52; Fijałkowska 2014: 31–34, 77–81; cf. also Skaist 2008.

6 *ASJ* 10, p. 165 [SH], *ASJ* 13, p. 276 [SH], *AulaOr.* 5, p. 225 [SH], AulaOr. Suppl. 1: 57 [S], AulaOr. Suppl. 1: 65 [SH], Emar VI 7 [SH], Emar VI 20 [S], Emar VI 35 [SH], Emar VI 80a [SH], Emar VI 82 [SH], Emar VI 89 [SH], Emar VI 113 [SH], Emar VI 114b [SH], Emar VI 130 [S], Emar VI 217 [SH], HANEM 2: 31 [S], HANEM 2: 68 [SH].

7 *ASJ* 12, p. 183 [SH], AulaOr. Suppl. 1: 81 [SH], Emar VI 111 [S], Emar VI 114a [SH], HANEM 2: 49 [S].

8 It is the case of RS 16.154a and b (= PRU 3, p. 127), RS 16.156 (= PRU 3, p. 61), RS 16.261+ (= PRU 3, p. 159), RS 17.086+ (= Ugaritica 5: 159), RS 17.102 (= Ugaritica 5: 160), RS 17.149 (= Ugaritica 5: 6), RS 17.231 (= PRU 4, p. 238), RS 17.325 (= Ugaritica 5: 161).

2 Women as sellers and buyers in ancient Mesopotamia

The first matter is that the amount of texts attesting women as active part of the sale seems scarce. In Emar, about 8 % of the persons who sold properties were women, and women represent 2.3 % of the buyers. In total, about five per cent of the people involved in sale contracts (i.e. sellers or buyers) were women. That low number may seem to indicate the limited legal capacity held by Emarite women. However, the data from Emar are not very different from those taken from other documentary sources – archives in which the sale contracts are sufficiently large in number, thus being representative:

a) In the Sargonic period, women were able to buy and sell properties,[9] sometimes on the margins of their husbands' activities.[10] Attestations for preceding periods are scarce, but they do exist.[11]
b) During the Ur III period, several cases of women sellers are known, whether acting alone or with their husbands;[12] at least one case of a woman buying properties is attested.[13]
c) Old Assyrian sources show many examples of women who intervene in those operations, almost always alone – although it may be a case of business carried out together with the husband – and on other occasions with the explicit presence of the husband in the deed.[14]
d) For its part, the huge amount of documentation from the Old Babylonian period centers on the *nadītum*-priestesses, which can lead to a misinterpretation of the statistics concerning the subject (see the contributions of Katrien de Graef and Ichiro Nakata in this volume). Other women could also intervene in those operations (see e.g. Diakonoff 1986: 225–26), but the examples of *nadītū* clearly outnumber the cases of women acting as buyers or sellers outside of the priestesshood.
e) Neo-Assyrian sources attest many cases of women buyers; Radner (1997: 318–37) lists more than thirty examples from Nineveh and Kalḫu. There are also cases of women selling properties.[15]

---

9 See e.g. Steinkeller 1982, esp. p. 367–368; Gelb, Steinkeller, and Whiting 1991: 17b; Sallaberger and Westenholz 1999: 70; Wilcke 2000: 362–364.

10 Foster 1982: 52 ff.; Gelb, Steinkeller, and Whiting 1991: 17b; Wilcke 2000: 363.

11 Bauer, Englund, and Krebernik 1998: 474.

12 Partially Wilcke 2000: 362–364.

13 Steinkeller 1989: 121; cf. also Waetzoldt 1988: 31; Gelb, Steinkeller, and Whiting 1991: 17b and recently Lafont 2014: 62.

14 Kienast 1984: 23; cf. also Michel 2010: 130 and 2014: 94, with further bibliography.

15 Petschow 1976–80: 520–521; Radner 2003: 894.

All those data give rise to percentages that are fairly similar to those found in Emar. In addition, there are other sets of documents and archives that are less prolific, but that enable us to see that it was usual for women to take part in sales, even if they were not in the majority. Based on some documents (e.g. KAJ 168), it is clear that Assyrian women could buy properties, or at least slaves, during the Late Bronze Age.[16] For that same period, in Southern Mesopotamia, "women appear in legal contexts most frequently as sellers of their children, but in these transactions they are almost always accompanied by men" (Slanski 2003: 498). Lastly, during the first millennium BC, it has been stated, for the South, that "women were able to conduct legal transactions: they could own and acquire property, conclude contracts, and enter into obligations even in the absence of their husbands" (Oelsner, Wells, and Wunsch 2003: 928).

3 Women acting alone or in concert with other people

The historiography has also highlighted the fact that, in general, the women involved in sale contracts were widows – or they held other special legal status.[17] In that regard, it is important to distinguish between their activities as sellers and as buyers.

3.1 Women as sellers

In Emar, a woman appears as the sole seller in ten of the seventeen contracts, most of them of Syro-Hittite scribal tradition.[18] In the remaining cases (and also in Ugarit and Alalaḫ), women acted in the sale in conjunction with other people.[19] The woman seller was mostly accompanied by men: her husband

16 See Démare-Lafont 2003: 533; in the example shown above, the sale is undertaken by a woman and a man, whose relationship is not known.

17 See Westbrook 2003: 39; Arnaud 1980: 256 (but cf. p. 258–259).

18 *ASJ* 10, p. 165 [SH], *ASJ* 13, p. 276 [SH], *AulaOr.* 5, p. 225 [SH], Emar VI 7 [SH], Emar VI 20 [S], Emar VI 35 [SH], Emar VI 82 [SH], Emar VI 113 [SH], Emar VI 114b [SH], HANEM 2: 68 [SH]. I understand – following Pruzsinszky (2003, CD p. 728) – that in *ASJ* 13, p. 276 [SH] the only seller is the woman named Šaggar-umarri.

19 In two cases, the relationship between those people and the woman is unknown: Emar VI 80a [SH] and Emar VI 89 [SH] (for the latter see Fijałkowska 2014: 198 n. 101).

(Emar VI 217 [SH], HANEM 2: 68 [SH], cf. RS 17.022+ from Ugarit), her brother (Emar VI 80a [SH], cf. RS 16.156 from Ugarit), or her son(s) (AulaOr. Suppl. 1: 57 [S], Emar VI 130 [S], HANEM 2: 31 [S]; cf. AulaOr. Suppl. 1: 65 [SH] below). Only four documents belong to the Syrian scribal tradition in this corpus: the three contracts (out of four) in which the woman acts with her son(s), and one in which she is alone in the sale (Emar VI 20 [S]).

A woman acted together with other women only in AulaOr. Suppl. 1: 65 [SH] (see Westbrook 2001: 23–31). The document states that a woman, together with her two daughters and two sons, sold "their father's house" (obv. l. 4: É-*tu*$_4$ *ša* ^{I}*a-bi-šu-nu*).[20] It is possible that the father was dead, leaving his widow to bear responsibility for the family property, or that, in reality, the widow was not the biological mother of the four children. In any case, the woman is listed first, and she appears to have carried some responsibility in the transaction. The subsequent clauses only mention the sons and daughters, but not the mother, for which reason it seems clear that the latter was merely managing the property on behalf of the descendants.

In that regard, in cases where the woman was accompanied by other people, we can wonder whether she was indeed selling her own property or merely managing other people's. That it was the woman's property is clear from two documents. In Emar VI 217 [SH], husband and wife alike sold a daughter; according to other related documents, we know that the woman, named Kuʾe, took part in the deeds concerning her children.[21] In addition, in Emar VI 80a [SH] (cf. Durand 1989: 188–189) two siblings (a man and a woman) sold a plot of land (*erṣetu*, see § 5.1) to a third sibling, a man. The logical suggestion is that the former two probably sold their share in the property to their brother.[22]

However, when the woman acted as seller together with her children, two variants could arise. In Emar VI 130 [S] and HANEM 2: 31 [S] (Durand 2013: 46–48), after the description of the property, the following clause appears:

> P *ša* PN *ištu* PN *u* PNF B ... *išâm*
> "The property P belongs to PN (= the son/sons); the buyer B has bought (it) from PN and PNF (= his/their mother)"

Meanwhile, in AulaOr. Suppl. 1: 57 [S], the formula is:

---

20 Cf. Fijałkowska 2014: 39 n. 50.

21 On this documentary set (Emar VI 216–220) see e.g. Cohen 2005.

22 A similar case is found in AulaOr. Suppl. 1: 81 [SH]: a man sold a plot of land to his sister. However, the formulary is different and we do not know if this plot was a family property.

P *ša* PN *u* PNF *ištu* PN *u* PNF B ... *išâm*
"The property P belongs to PN (= the son) and PNF (= his mother); the buyer B has bought (it) from PN and PNF"

In other words, the formulæ clearly show that in the first two cases, the property was owned by the child(ren), whereas in the latter case, it is explicitly stated that the property also belonged to the mother.[23]

That desire to record the true ownership of the property also seems apparent in the use of concrete formulæ within the operative section. In that sense, in Emar as in documents from other places, we found two general formulations for sale contracts, depending on the point of view of the wording:[24]

ex latere emptoris:
P *ištu/ša* S B *ana* X *šeqel kaspi ana šīmišu gamri išâm*
"The buyer B has bought from the seller S the property P for X shekel of silver, its full price"

ex latere venditoris:
P S *ana* B *ana* X *šeqel kaspi ana šīmišu gamri iddin/ittadin*
"The seller S has given the property P to the buyer B for X shekels of silver, its full price"

A formula *ex latere emptoris* is the most usual, since "sales of land at Emar are typically formulated from the buyer's point of view;"[25] formulæ *ex latere venditoris* were mostly saved for sales of slaves.[26] However those features were permeable, and there are several sales of property that express the purchase by using a formula *ex latere venditoris* – although no sale of slaves uses the habitual *ex latere emptoris* formula. In total, the proportion of *ex latere emptoris* to *ex latere venditoris* formulæ in Emar (only recognizable cases that are not totally fragmented) is ca. 80 % to 20 % (see below for Emar VI 35 [SH]).[27]

The data in respect to those seventeen Emar cases in which women acted as sellers change appreciably. *Ex latere emptoris* formulæ are used seven times.[28] Meanwhile expressions *ex latere venditoris* are more numerous, being

---

23 Cf. Fijałkowska 2007: 16 n. 8 and 2014: 197; but see also the conclusions in Fijałkowska 2014: 124 n. 79.

24 See in general Fijałkowska 2014.

25 Westbrook 2001: 25.

26 Démare-Lafont 2010: 51.

27 Note that the formulation of sales of immovable property during the first millennium is always *ex latere emptoris*, whereas that of movable is *ex latere venditoris* (Oelsner, Wells, and Wunsch 2003: 944–945).

28 *AulaOr.* 5, p. 225 [SH], AulaOr. Suppl. 1:57, Emar VI 20 [S], Emar VI 80a [SH], Emar VI 89 [SH], Emar VI 130 [S], HANEM 2: 31 [S].

present in up to eight cases,[29] perhaps nine if Emar VI 114b [SH] – partially broken – is counted. Those data appear to indicate that the proportion between the formulæ when the seller was a woman was ca. 45 % to 55 % (very far from the 80 % vs. 20 % indicated above).[30] That change is partially explained by the fact that women were more likely to sell slaves, a transaction in which an *ex latere venditoris* expression was always used. However, the same formulæ were used in sale contracts covering real estate sold by women.[31]

Worthy of note is the fact that, out of the five cases in which a woman acted in conjunction with someone else, four use *ex latere emptoris* expressions – which, as we see, are less common in the corpus of women sellers.[32] One explanation may be that given the very phraseology of the *ex latere emptoris* expression, there was a clear record of the nominal ownership of the property – and that the women had (or had not) simply acted as the children's guardians.

Also worthy of note is Emar VI 35 [SH], in which a woman (alone) sells a person, using an atypical expression; in fact, it is the sole example in the whole Emarite corpus. The formula is (obv. ll. 1–5): "The seller S has received X shekels of silver, the price of the property P, from the hand of the buyer B" (X *šeqel kaspi šīma ša* P *ištu qāti* B S *imḫur*). Specialists have not given this case any special attention.[33] The verb *maḫāru* in the context of sales is attested in Neo-Babylonian sources (CAD M/1: 57–58).

3.2 Women as buyers

As regards women who bought property, they acted alone in all cases. Some of them may have been of high status. If we examine the Ugaritic corpus of sale contracts, we find the same situation; in four documents, the buyer was the queen Ṯaryelli.[34]

29 *ASJ* 10, p. 165 [SH], *ASJ* 13, p. 276 [SH], AulaOr. Suppl. 1: 65 [SH], Emar VI 7 [SH], Emar VI 82 [SH], Emar VI 113 [SH], Emar VI 217 [SH], HANEM 2: 68 [SH].

30 Note that in Ugarit two deeds are attested, in which a woman sold a property (§ 2): both of them use a formula *ex latere venditoris*.

31 It is the case of AulaOr. Suppl. 1: 65 [SH], Emar VI 82 [SH], Emar VI 113 [SH], Emar VI 114b [SH], HANEM 2: 68 [SH].

32 The exception is Emar VI 217 [SH], the only case in which a person (the seller's daughter) was sold.

33 This document has been sometimes interpreted as a simple *memorandum* or economic record (Cohen 2011: 149 n. 24, Balza 2009: 25); however other authors indicate that it refers to a sale (e.g. Westenholz 2000: 49, 73).

34 RS 17.086+ (= Ugaritica 5: 159), RS 17.102 (= Ugaritica 5: 160, cf. Justel 2008: 197 n. 63), RS 17.231 (= PRU 4, p. 238, cf. Lackenbacher 2002: 294 n. 1059), RS 17.325 (= Ugaritica 5: 161).

In Emar, worthy of note is the case of HANEM 2: 49 [S]. The buyer's personal name is not given, just her category: she was a *qadištu* priestess.[35] It is the only case within the corpus under examination in which the seller of the property was the institution called "Ninurta and the Elders,"[36] only present in documents of the Syrian scribal tradition;[37] in the remaining cases, the seller was a *privatus*. Beckman (1996b: 68 n. 74) indicates that the *qadištu* priestess may have made the purchase in the institutional sense. However, that is not certain, since the field purchased bordered another that already belonged to the priestess: "On the second side (it is bordered by the property of) the *qadištu* (priestess)" (HANEM 2: 49 [S], obv. l. 7: SAG-KI 2-KAM-M[A] MUNUS-NU-GIG). In addition, we do not know the exact role of the *qašdātu* in Emarite society, or even if they were specifically organized. For those reasons, it is possible to consider that the purchase was carried out privately.[38]

In addition, it will be noted that in the transaction Emar VI 114a [SH], a woman bought an *erṣetu* (see § 4.1), which she later sold to someone else (Emar VI 114b [SH]). That may indicate that she acted as the intermediary in the sale.[39]

Were those buyer-women widows? The fact that the husband does not appear in the transaction does not necessarily mean that he had died; moreover, it is possible to assert that some of those women may never have been married. That appears to be the case in HANEM 2: 49 [S], in which the woman was a *qadištu* priestess. Moreover, only in Emar VI 111 [S] does the woman's name appear referenced using her husband's name[40] – in Emar VI 114a [SH], it appears referenced using first her father's name, then her husband's. In *ASJ* 12, p. 183 [SH], the woman's name appears referenced using only her father's name. Finally, in AulaOr. Suppl. 1: 81 [SH], there is no indication of parentage or of the husband's name, but that may be because the seller was her brother, and their father's name had already appeared in the text two lines before. Hence, it will be seen that nothing suggests definitively that those women were widows.

3.3 A variety of situations

Ultimately, the women who were directly involved in sale contracts may have found themselves alone (e.g. when buying properties) or not (generally, when

35 See Westbrook 2003: 664: "The *qadištu* (Sum. nu.gig) class of priestess may have been more independent (RE 49)."

36 Beckman 1997.

37 Démare-Lafont 2010: 47.

38 Such conclusion is also reached by Fijałkowska 2014: 207.

39 See however Fijałkowska 2014: 198 n. 99, 202.

40 See the possible implications in Fijałkowska 2014: 202.

they were selling them). In the latter case, it seems that the formulation of a number of elements gave a basis for establishing whether the properties actually belonged to the woman, or if she just acted in the transaction nominally, with the goods belonging to other people, i.e. her children. All cases show a multiplicity of family situations, indicating that the women were not necessarily widows, and that in some cases they do not appear to even have been married.

4 Properties bought and sold by women

Another important aspect is the type of properties that women sold or bought.[41] The key question is this: Did women have access only to their own dowries – whether or not they were already married – or could they operate with other family properties? To that end, it is important to know which properties were bought and sold (§ 4.1), and what type of dowry was given to women, i.e. daughters, in Emar (§ 4.2).

4.1 Movable and immovable property

The great majority of sale contracts from Emar cover property, be it a house, field, or other type of building or land.[42] On a secondary basis, there were about twenty sale contracts relating to slaves.[43] That same proportion between immovable assets and movable assets also appeared to exist in the neighboring city of Ekalte; however, Ugarit did not keep sale contracts relating to slaves, whilst Alalaḫ only kept deeds relating to slaves and animals.

Out of the seventeen cases in which the seller was a woman, the vast majority also dealt with real estate: they sold houses,[44] a vineyard (Emar VI 89 [SH]), an orchard (probably in Emar VI 82 [SH]), the plot of land called *erṣetu*[45] or that one called *tuguru*[46] (Emar VI 82 [SH]). On five occasions, a woman sold slaves.[47]

41 This part of my contribution has been much changed because of the suggestions of Sophie Démare-Lafont, whom I heartily thank for her input and comments.

42 See e.g. Lipiński 1990: 53–55; Beckman 1997; Viano 2010, 2012.

43 Démare-Lafont 2010: 50.

44 *AulaOr.* 5, p. 225 [SH], AulaOr. Suppl. 1: 57 [S], AulaOr. Suppl. 1: 65 [SH], Emar VI 20 [S], Emar VI 80a [SH], Emar VI 113 [SH]), (Emar VI 82 [SH].

45 Emar VI 114b [SH], Emar VI 130 [S], HANEM 2: 31 [S], HANEM 2: 68 [SH]. On the nature of the *erṣetu* see e.g. Pentiuc 2001: 99–102; Mori 2003: 49 or Fijałkowska 2014: 43–49.

46 See Pentiuc 2001: 46; Mori 2003: 65; Fijałkowska 2014: 41–42.

47 *ASJ* 10, p. 165 [SH], *ASJ* 13, p. 276 [SH], Emar VI 7 [SH], Emar VI 35 [SH], Emar VI 217 [SH].

Women bought houses (Emar VI 111 [S]), fields (HANEM 2: 49 [S]) or *erṣētu*.[48] That is to say, the properties bought by women appear always to have been immovable assets; that also occurs in Ugarit, with the exception of RS 17.231, where one learns that the queen Ṭaryelli bought a male slave for seventy shekels of silver.[49]

4.2 Dowries

It has traditionally been established that Ancient Near Eastern dowries were made up of a series of movable assets, domestic utensils, and slaves (Westbrook 1993–97). In the case of Emar, it appears that a dowry was also made up of movable goods, and may have included silver.[50]

During the meeting at which this study was presented, M. Yamada indicated that the archives of Emar have produced no dowry lists. It is certain that they are not extensive, as usual in the first-millennium sources,[51] but in my opinion, there are indeed indirect references in Emar to the make-up of the dowry:

a) As it has been asserted on a number of occasions,[52] the term *terḫatu* may refer in Emar and Ekalte to the dowry, as is always the case in Ugarit[53] and sometimes in first-millennium Mesopotamia (CAD T: 354a). With doubts, these cases may be Emar VI 112, AulaOr. Suppl. 1: 32, *ASJ* 13, p. 292–293, and in Ekalte WVDOG 102: 21 and 26 (Durand and Marti 2003b).
b) Other, more general references have been collected by Westbrook (2003b: 679) and Démare-Lafont (2010: 66): for example, references to "objects" (*unūte*) or other descriptions.[54]
c) Lastly, it is clear that HANEM 2: 6 contains a reference to a dowry – called in this case *nûpu* – and to its make-up (movable assets, domestic utensils,

---

48 *ASJ* 12, p. 183 [SH], AulaOr. Suppl. 1: 81 [SH], Emar VI 114a [SH].

49 However, note that Emarite women could also buy movable assets, as attested in some letters, e.g. Emar VI 25 (cf. Durand and Marti 2003a: 165–167) or Emar VI 260.

50 Justel 2008: 58–59.

51 See e.g. Roth 1989–90 and recently Joannès 2014: 26–27.

52 E.g. Arnaud 1980: 257 n. 64; Adamthwaite 1994: 20–21; Beckman 1996a: 69; Westenholz 2000: 11; Limet 2001: 2 n. 3; Durand and Marti 2003a: 176; Justel 2008: 48, 2014a: 68; Démare-Lafont 2010: 66.

53 See the bibliography presented in Justel 2008: 48 n. 59.

54 AulaOr. Suppl. 1: 23, AulaOr. Suppl. 1: 69, Emar VI 124, HANEM 2: 6, HANEM 2: 76.

jewels, etc.), according to the collations and suggestions by Durand (2013: 59,[55] cf. also Fijałkowska 2014: 198).

Westbrook (2003b: 679) proposes that some dowries could have contained immovable assets, but the specific examples provided by him may be simple donations or even belong to usual inheritance, not to a simple dowry. In that regard, we know that under different circumstances, it was possible for daughters to inherit properties of various types, i.e. immovable assets (Ben-Barak 2006: 152–173). However, that was a case of inheritance, not of dowry. It has been pointed out that: "Can one consider the dowry an advanced form of inheritance? Functionally, yes; legally, no, because a dowry as a voluntary gift is a favor and inheritance is a right."[56]

Ultimately, although it is a matter that appears to have occurred at other periods or areas,[57] Emarite women sold properties that did not necessarily come from their dowry.

5 Did women buy and sell in time of crisis?

A final aspect refers to the time of purchase, i.e., did women sell the properties in times of need? In that regard, Fijałkowska (2007: 15–17) has devoted a whole paragraph to the presence of women in those deeds:[58]

> Comme partout dans le Proche-Orient ancien, la majorité des immeubles appartenaient aux hommes, chefs de famille. Les femmes étaient parfois propriétaires, elles aussi, mais il paraît qu'elles pouvaient disposer de leurs biens moins librement que les hommes. Les textes syriens avec des femmes agissant comme propriétaires sont très rares, et les circonstances – toujours atypiques. La situation semble meilleure dans les documents syro-hittites, où les femmes apparaissent un peu plus souvent. Dans les documents des deux styles, les femmes achètent et vendent surtout des bâtiments – des maisons et des *kirṣitu* [sic], mais à cause du nombre limité de textes il est impossible de dire s'il s'agit ici d'un hasard.

---

55 This work contains other possible indirect references to dowries in Emar. See a parallel in Sigrist 1993, p. 176–177: 10; as well as the comments by Durand and Marti 2003a: 145–146.

56 Stol 1995: 134, see already Westbrook 1991: 157.

57 See e.g. Stol 1995: 136.

58 Cf. Viano 2012: 122. See also her comments in Fijałkowska 2014: 197–198, and 207: "Il semble donc que soit les femmes pouvaient disposer des immeubles moins librement que les hommes, soit les dispositions qu'elles effectuaient étaient *a priori* suspectes, peut-être parce qu'il était rare qu'une femme soit propriétaire d'un immeuble."

Fijałkowska (2007: 16 n. 8, 2014: 198, 201) implies that those "atypical circumstances" correspond, at least partially, to the fact that in some texts, it is stated that the female sellers carried out the transaction "during the year of famine and war." However, it has also been indicated that "in the contracts quoting the year of distress formula there is no evidence of an influence, on prices, of the economic difficulties of the sellers" (Viano 2012: 126).[59] As we see, the nature and implications of that expression are still contested. That issue has been partially covered (Justel 2014b: 33–35); I include the following data by way of summary.

It seems that by the middle of the thirteenth century BC, Emar (or its territory) was attacked by the Hurrian army; the attack would have taken place ca. 1250 BC. It is also evident that Emar was attacked on other occasions.[60] Those wars and other circumstances would have caused one or more deep economic crises. That phenomenon is explicitly stated in 42 documents from Emar by the reference to the "year of famine (and) war" (*a/ina šanat dannati nukurti*), with slightly different formulations. Those cases are distributed amongst the two scribal traditions present in the Emar archives.[61] In line with the above-mentioned episodes of war, some economic crises would have taken place in which the price of the food would have increased dramatically.[62] Only during the reign of Pilsu-Dagān, king of Emar, are sales of persons attested.[63]

In essence, those references are found in legal documents attesting two different financial transactions: transfers of landed property and of persons.[64] By the inclusion of this expression, it is therefore stated that the transaction took place at a difficult time for at least one of the parties involved. However, the exact implications of that formula remain unclear. For example, Zaccagnini (1995: 106) thinks that only in the case of the sale of persons would the actual cause have been the economic difficulties of those families. When landed property was involved, however, "these contracts do not seem to exhibit any distinctive feature that might be connected with war and famine." In those cases, he thinks that the reference to war and famine could be a "scribal mannerism." Adamthwaite (2001: 153, 168, 174) has calculated the prices of these transac-

59 However, note that Viano (2012: 122) also states: "Women mostly appear in the house sale contracts when they are forced to sell their properties due to economic difficulties as the quite low prices recorded in these texts seem to lead."

60 Zaccagnini 1995: 100; Vita 2002: 122.

61 Vita 2002: 116; Dêmare-Lafont 2010: 82.

62 Adamthwaite 2001: 171; Cavigneaux and Beyer 2006: 503 n. 26.

63 Divon 2008: 105.

64 Fijałkowska 2014: 167–69.

tions and pointed out that only the cases of sale of persons correspond to real economic difficulties.

It is unclear whether an economic crisis is to be posited only when the above-mentioned formula (*ina šanat dannati nukurti*) is employed. The formula probably does not reflect personal difficulties, but a generalized crisis in Emar (Zaccagnini 1995: 99; Adamthwaite 2001: 174). Démare-Lafont (2010: 81–82) points that "la clause paraît plutôt avoir une utilité juridique en ce qu'elle introduit une exception justifiant l'application de dispositions dérogatoires, qui diffèrent sensiblement selon qu'elles concernent la vente ou le prêt." In that case, it would be possible that the inclusion of the formula allowed the seller to buy this property again.

Among the seventeen cases of female sellers, in five it is stated that the transaction took place during a generalized crisis by the use of the formula "in the year of famine (and) war" (*ina šanat dannati nukurti*).[65] Another example, Emar VI 82 [SH], should be added. A woman seems to sell some landed property to a man; it is mentioned that this man therefore "has le[t her] children live" (obv. ll. 6–7: DUMU-MEŠ-[*ši*] *u*[*b*]$^{!}$-*te-li-iṭ*).[66] Later on (obv. l. 7 – rev. l. 1) a reference to the right of buying the property again seems to appear. Though there is no mention of the "famine and war" formula, it is evident that the woman experienced hardship. Out of the five sale contracts in which a woman was the buyer, just one (Emar VI 111 [S]) contains the expression "in the year of famine (and) war."

As is seen from all those data, it is inferred that there is no certainty over the implications of including the clause; there is also no pattern of use depending on whether the documents were of Syrian or Syro-Hittite scribal traditions. The expression was included in sale contracts with women participants, as well as in those with no women at all. The percentages of use compared with the total number of cases in which women intervene are normal.

Ultimately, the atypical circumstances of the cases under examination are not derived from the moment of the purchase, or from a situation that is – from an economic perspective – particularly harmful to women.

***

As we have seen, Emar sources form an ideal field of study for knowledge of the legal behavior of a range of groups, including women. Essentially, women

65 The cases are: *ASJ* 10, p. 165 [SH], AulaOr. Suppl. 1: 57 [S], AulaOr. Suppl. 1: 65 [SH], Emar VI 20 [S], HANEM 2: 31 [S]. See also Fijałkowska 2014: 197–198, 201.

66 See the comments of Fijałkowska 2014: 198 n. 99.

who were involved in sale transactions in Emar were not necessarily alone, and they do not exhibit signs of economic or legal weakness. It is true that there are not many cases, but in those identified so far, women acted with complete legal capacity.

Those sale contracts show some peculiarities, but only at a formulaic level, and that fact does not seem to indicate any disadvantages. Women managed large properties, not just the assets they received as a dowry. In some cases – but not always – they were perhaps widows, then acting as managers or representatives of their children, just as fathers did; but in other cases, the circumstances seem to have been completely different.

For that reason, it can be concluded that within the field of sale transactions, Emar women had full *de iure* capacity to act, as happened in other legal agreements. Note, however, that all those deeds are to be understood in the context of a patriarchal society, in which women intervened only sporadically.

Abbreviations

S Syrian tradition
SH Syro-Hittite tradition

Bibliography

Adamthwaite, Murray. 1994. Review of D. Arnaud, *Textes syriens de l'âge du Bronze Récent*, AulaOr. Suppl. 1, Sabadell: AUSA, 1991. *Abr-Nahrain* 32: 17–27.

Adamthwaite, Murray. 2001. *Late Hittite Emar: The Chronology, Synchronisms, and Socio-Political Aspects of a Late Bronze Age Fortress Town*. ANESS 8. Louvain: Peeters.

Arnaud, Daniel. 1980. Traditions urbaines et influences semi-nomades à Emar, à l'âge du Bronze Récent. Pp. 245–264 in *Le Moyen Euphrate. Zone de contacts et d'échanges*, ed. Jean-Claude Margueron. Travaux du Centre de Recherche sur le Proche-Orient et la Grèce antiques 5. Leiden: Brill.

Balza, Maria Elena. 2009. *Sigilli e modalità di sigillatura a Emar del tardo Bronzo (XIV–XIII sec. a.C.)*. StMed 21. Pavia: Iuculano.

Bauer, Josef, Robert K. Englund, and Manfred Krebernik. 1998. *Mesopotamien. Späturuk-Zeit und Frühdynastische Zeit*. OBO 160/1. Freiburg: Universitätsverlag and Göttingen: Vanderhoeck & Ruprecht.

Beckman, Gary. 1996a. Family Values on the Middle Euphrates in the Thirteenth Century B.C.E. Pp. 57–79 in *Emar: The History, Religion, and Culture of a Syrian Town in the Late Bronze Age*, eds. Mark W. Chavalas. Bethesda: CDL Press.

Beckman, Gary. 1996b. *Texts from the Vicinity of Emar in the Collection of Jonathan Rosen*. HANE/M 2. Padova: SARGON.

Beckman, Gary. 1997. Real Property Sales at Emar. Pp. 95–120 in *Crossing Boundaries and Linking Horizons. Studies in Honor of Michael C. Astour*, eds. Gordon D. Young, Mark W. Chavalas, and Richard E. Averbeck. Bethesda: CDL Press.

Ben-Barak, Zafrira. 2006. *Inheritance by Daughters in Israel and the Ancient Near East: A Social, Legal and Ideological Revolution*. Jaffa: Archaeological Center Publications.

Cardascia, Guillaume. 1976–80. Kauf. C. II. Mittelassyrisch. *RlA* 5: 514–520.

Cavigneaux, Antoine and Dominique Beyer. 2006. Une orpheline d'Emar. Pp. 497–503 in *Les espaces syro-mésopotamiens. Volume d'hommage offert à Jean-Claude Margueron*, eds. Pascal Butterlin, Marc Lebeau, Jean-Yves Monchambert, Juan Luis Montero Fenollós, and Béatrice Muller. Subartu 17. Bruxelles: Brepols.

Cohen, Yoram. 2005. Feet of Clay at Emar: A Happy End? *OrNS* 74: 165–170.

Cohen, Yoram. 2011. The Administration of Cult in Hittite Emar. *AoF* 38: 145–155.

D'Alfonso Lorenzo, Yoram Cohen, and Dietrich Sürenhagen (eds.). 2008. *The City of Emar among the Late Bronze Age Empires: History, Landscape, and Society. Proceedings of the Konstanz Emar Conference, 25–26. 04. 2006*, AOAT 349, Münster: Ugarit Verlag.

Démare-Lafont, Sophie. 2003. Middle Assyrian Period. Pp. 521–563 in Westbrook 2003a.

Démare-Lafont, Sophie. 2010. Éléments pour une diplomatique juridique des textes d'Émar. Pp. 43–84 in *Trois millénaires de formulaires juridiques*, eds. Sophie Démare-Lafont and André Lemaire. HEO 48, Genève: Droz.

Diakonoff, Igor Mikhailovich. 1986. Women in Old Babylonia not under Patriarchal Authority. *JESHO* 29: 225–238.

Di Filippo, Francesco. 2008. Gli atti di compravendita di Emar. Rapporto e conflitto tra due tradizioni giuridiche. Pp. 419–456 in *I diritti del mondo cuneiforme (Mesopotamia e regioni adiacenti, ca. 2500–500 a.C.)*, eds. Mario Liverani and Clelia Mora. Pavia: IUSS.

Divon, Shai Andre. 2008. A Survey of the Textual Evidence for "Food Shortage" from the Late Hittite Empire. Pp. 101–109 in D'Alfonso, Cohen and Sürenhagen 2008.

Durand, Jean-Marie. 1989. Review of D. Arnaud, *Recherches au pays d'Aštata: Emar VI*, Synthèse 18, Paris: Recherche sur les Civilisations, 1985–87 (Part 1). *RA* 83: 163–191.

Durand, Jean-Marie. 2013. Quelques textes sur le statut de la femme à Émar d'après des collations nouvelles. *Semitica* 55: 25–60.

Durand, Jean Marie and Lionel Marti. 2003a. Relecture de documents d'Ekalte, Émar et Tuttul. *RA* 97: 141–180.

Durand, Jean Marie and Lionel Marti. 2003b. Vue de dot elle est belle! *NABU* 2003/49: 56.

Fijałkowska, Lena. 2007. La propriété immobilière à Emar en Syrie, du XIVème au XIIème siècle av. J.-C. *RIDA* 54: 13–26.

Fijałkowska, Lena. 2014. *Le droit de la vente à Emar*. Philippika 64. Wiesbaden: Harrassowitz.

Foster, Benjamin R. 1982. *Umma in the Sargonic Period*. Memoirs of the Connecticut Academy of Arts and Sciences 20. Hamden: Academy.

Gelb, Ignace J., Piotr Steinkeller, and Robert M. Whiting, Jr. 1991. *Earliest Land Tenure Systems in the Near East: Ancient Kudurrus*. OIP 104. Chicago: The Oriental Institute of the University of Chicago.

Hecker, Karl. 1976–80. Kauf. C. I. Altassyrisch. *RlA* 5: 12–14.

Joannès, Francis. 2014. The Role of Women in the Economy of the Neo-Babylonian Period. Pp. 15–32 in Joannès and Karahashi 2014.

Joannès, Francis and Fumi Karahashi (eds.). 2014. *Women's Role in the Economy of the Ancient Near East. Report: December 31, 2011–December 30, 2014*. Tokyo: Japan Society for the Promotion of Science.

Justel, Josué J. 2008. *La posición jurídica de la mujer en Siria durante el Bronce Final. Estudio de las estrategias familiares y de la mujer como sujeto y objeto de derecho.* Serie Próximo Oriente Antiguo 4. Zaragoza: IEIOP.

Justel, Josué J. 2014a. Women and Family in the Legal Documentation of Emar (With Additional Data from Other Late Bronze Age Syrian Archives). *KASKAL* 11: 57–84.

Justel, Josué J. 2014b. Report 2011–2014. Pp. 33–38 in Joannès and Karahashi 2014.

Kienast, Burkhardt. 1984. *Das altassyrische Kaufvertragsrecht.* FAOS Beih. 1. Stuttgart: Franz Steiner.

Kienast, Burkhardt. 1976–80. Kauf. E. In Alalaḫ und Ugarit. *RlA* 5: 530–541.

Krecher, Joachim. 1976–80. Kauf. A. I. Nach sumerischen Quellen vor der Zeit der III. Dynastie von Ur. *RlA* 5: 490–498.

Lackenbacher, Sylvie. 2002. *Textes akkadiens d'Ugarit.* LAPO 20. Paris: Le Cerf.

Lafont, Bertrand. 2014. Women at Work and Women in the Economy during the Neo-Sumerian (so-called Ur III) Period, 21st century B.C. Pp. 57–77 in Joannès and Karahashi 2014.

Limet, Henri. 2001. Les femmes et le patrimoine dans le droit du IIe millénaire. Pp. 1–16 in *La femme dans les civilisations orientales et Miscellanea Aegyptologica. Christiane Desroches Noblecourt in honorem*, eds. Christian Cannuyer, Denise Fredericq-Homes, Francine Mawet, Julien Ries, Anton Schoors, and Jean-Marie Verpoorten. Acta Orientalia Belgica 15. Bruxelles, Louvain la Neuve and Leuven: Peeters.

Lipiński, Edward. 1990. Le marché immobilier à Ugarit et à Emar au XIIIe siècle av. n. è. Pp. 51–55 in *The Town as Regional Economic Centre in the Ancient Near East*, eds. Erik Aerts and Horst Klengel. Studies in Economic and Social History 20. Leuven: Leuven University Press.

Michel, Cécile. 2010. Women of Assur and Kanesh. Pp. 124–133 in *Anatolia's Prologue, Kültepe Kanesh Karum. Assyrians in Istanbul*, eds. Fikri Kulakoğlu, and Selmin Kangal. Kayseri Metropolitan Municipality Cultural Publication 78. Istanbul: Kayseri Metropolitan Municipality.

Michel, Cécile. 2014. The Economic Role of Women in the Old Assyrian Sources. Pp. 93–101 in Joannès and Karahashi 2014.

Mori, Lucia. 2003. *Reconstructing the Emar Landscape.* QGS 6. Roma: Casa editrice Università degli Studi di Roma.

Oelsner, Joachim, Bruce Wells, and Cornelia Wunsch. 2003. Neo-Babylonian Period. Pp. 911–974 in Westbrook 2003a.

Pentiuc, Eugene J. 2001. *West Semitic Vocabulary in the Akkadian Texts from Emar.* HSS 49. Winona Lake: Eisenbrauns.

Petschow, Herbert. 1976–80. Kauf. C. III. Neuassyrisch. *RlA* 5: 520–528.

Pruzsinszky, Regine. 2003. *Die Personennamen der Texte aus Emar.* SCCNH 13. Winona Lake: Eisenbrauns.

Radner, Karen. 1997. *Die neuassyrischen Privatrechtsurkunden als Quelle für Mensch und Umwelt.* SAAS 6. Helsinki: Helsinki University Press.

Radner, Karen. 2003. Neo-Assyrian Period. Pp. 883–910 in Westbrook 2003a.

Roth, Martha T. 1989–90. The Material Composition of the Neo-Babylonian Dowry. *AfO* 36/37: 1–55.

Sallaberger, Walter and Aage Westenholz. 1999. *Mesopotamien. Akkade-Zeit und Ur III-Zeit.* OBO 160/3. Freiburg: Universitätsverlag and Göttingen: Vanderhoeck & Ruprecht.

Sigrist, Marcel. 1993. Seven Emar Tablets. Pp. 165–187 in eds. A. F. Rainey *et al. kinattūtu ša dārâti. Raphael Kutscher Memorial Volume.* Tel Aviv OccPublSer 1.

Skaist, Aaron. 2008. Precursors of the Emar Conveyance Deeds. Pp. 219–229 in D'Alfonso, Cohen and Sürenhagen 2008.
Slanski, Kathryn. 2003. Middle Babylonian Period. Pp. 485–520 in Westbrook 2003a.
Steinkeller, Piotr. 1982. Two Sargonic Sale Documents concerning Women. *OrNS* 51: 355–368.
Steinkeller, Piotr. 1989. *Sale Documents of the Ur-III-Period.* FAOS 17. Stuttgart: Franz Steiner.
Stol, Marten. 1995. Women in Mesopotamia. *JESHO* 38: 123–144.
Viano, Maurizio. 2010. The Economy of Emar I. *AulaOr* 28: 259–283.
Viano, Maurizio. 2012. The Economy of Emar II – Real Estate Sale Contracts. *AulaOr* 30: 109–164.
Vita, Juan Pablo. 2002. Warfare and the Army at Emar. *AoF* 29: 113–127.
Waetzoldt, Harmut. 1988. Frauen und Kinder zur Zeit der III. Dynastie von Ur. *AoF* 15: 30–44.
Westbrook, Raymond. 1991. *Property and the Family in Biblical Law.* JSOT Suppl. 113. Sheffield: A&C Black.
Westbrook, Raymond. 1993–97. Mitgift. *RlA* 8: 273–283.
Westbrook, Raymond. 2001. Social Justice and Creative Jurisprudence in Late Bronze Age Syria. *JESHO* 44: 22–43.
Westbrook, Raymond. (ed.) 2003a. *A History of Ancient Near Eastern Law.* HdO 72. Leiden and Boston: Brill.
Westbrook, Raymond. 2003b. Emar and Vicinity. Pp. 657–691 in Westbrook 2003a.
Westenholz, Joan Goodnick. 2000. *Cuneiform Inscriptions in the Collection of the Bible Lands Museum Jerusalem: The Emar Tablets.* CM 13. Groningen: STYX.
Wilcke, Claus. 1976–80. Kauf. A.II. Nach Kaufurkunden der Zeit der III. Dynastie von Ur. *RlA* 5: 498–512.
Wilcke, Claus. 2000. Vom Verhältnis der Geschlechter im Alten Mesopotamien: *"Eine Frau mit eigenem Vermögen richtet das Haus zugrunde."* Pp. 351–381 in *Frauenforscherinnen stellen sich vor.* Leipziger Studien zur Frauen- und Geschlechterforschung A/6, ed. Ilse Nagleschmidt. Leipzig: Universität Leipzig.
Zaccagnini, Carlo. 1995. War and famine at Emar. *OrNS* 64: 92–109.

Masamichi Yamada

The *kubuddā'u*-Gift in the Emar Texts

The Emar texts[1] are from the period when Emar was a vassal kingdom of the Hittite empire after its conquest of Mittani in ca. 1325 BC. In those texts, mostly written in Akkadian, we can recognize two major scribal traditions, the so-called "Syrian" and "Syro-Hittite" types. These differ in various respects, such as paleography, orthography, terminology and phraseology, grammar, and format of legal contracts.[2] The Syrian type (= S) is regarded as the local scribal tradition of the land of Aštata, whose center was Emar, while the Syro-Hittite type (= SH) is thought to have been of foreign origin, probably in some way connected with the Hittites. In my opinion, in Emar, these two types of texts are concurrent, and date approximately to 1275–1175 BC.[3]

In this study, I would like to take up the issue of the means used to secure a woman's livelihood after the death of her husband. In the ancient Near East, it seems to have been the norm that when the head of a family died, his sons inherited all of his estate, accepting the task of caring for his wife. However, it is not difficult to imagine that the sons were not always loyal to her, particularly in the cases when there was no direct blood relation between them. We see in the texts that in principle, two strategies were used to secure a widow's livelihood.

The first one is where the head of a family designates his wife as the nominal *guardian* of all of the family estate while she is alive, prescribing that it be actually inherited by his sons after her death, on the condition that they care for her. In Emar this is done by designating the woman as "father and mother."[4] The second strategy is where the head of a family divides all of the

1 In the following discussion, references to the texts from Emar, as well as from the neighboring Ekalte, use the abbreviations appended below. I wish to express my gratitude to Josué Javier Justel and Sophie Démare-Lafont for their comments on an earlier version of this paper, read at the conference.

2 See Cohen 2013: 282–284 (with previous literature) for general remarks on the two scribal traditions; also Faist 2008; Démare-Lafont 2010; Cohen 2012: 33–38.

3 Yamada 2013; Yamada forthcoming. Cf. Cohen and d'Alfonso 2008; Cohen 2013.

4 For typical cases see *SMEA* 30-T 7 and TS 41; cf. also Emar VI 70, 112; *Iraq* 54-T 6; RE 37; *SMEA* 30-T 8; and TS 71 treated below. For a general treatment of this status in Emar, see Beckman 1996a: 60; Westbrook 2001: 38–40; Westbrook 2003: 681. Note that similar designations of the wife as the guardian are attested also elsewhere: "father and mother" in an Old Assyrian text (see Michel 2000), and "father" in the Nuzi texts (see Paradise 1972: 285–297).

Masamichi Yamada, Chuo University, Tokyo; masamuwa@gmail.com

family estate into two portions – one to be inherited by the sons immediately after his death, and the other given to his wife as a *dower*, which the sons who take care of her inherit only after her death. The subject of the present study, the *kubuddā'u*-gift in Emar, is to be evaluated in relation to this dower strategy.

1 The word *kubuddā'u*

The noun *kubuddā'u*, which is formed by the Akkadian *purussā'* pattern (GAG³, § 56o 34.IIβ),[5] literally means "becoming heavy or honored." This word is attested also in two texts of OB Mari with the meaning, "alourdissement" (Durand and Joannès 1990). In the Emar texts, however, it is generally accepted as referring to some kind of dower or gift (to the wife).[6] On its exact meaning or substance, however, scholars have not reached agreement. J.-M. Durand and F. Joannès think that *kubuddā'u* was "une part de l'héritage du père de famille ... dont la femme avait la jouissance en usufruit" (1990; see also Westbrook 2003: 680–681). According to M. R. Adamthwaite, "it could be argued that the *kubuddû* is in fact the bride-price," although at first glance it seems to be "some kind of marriage settlement, given to the wife ... at the husband's behest and disposal" (1994: 21–22), while G. Beckman describes *kubuddā'u* as a special bequest of the surviving wife's own which "was probably drawn from her own dowry" (1996a: 72). So in the following, I try to clarify what the *kubuddā'u*-gift actually was in Emar through a fresh analysis of the texts concerned.

The word *kubuddā'u* is found in eight Emar texts: two are of the Syrian type (*AuOr* 5-T 15, RE 8), five are of the Syro-Hittite type (BLMJE 14; Emar VI 112; *SMEA* 30-T 8; TS 22, 71), and one is a fragment whose type is unknown (Emar VI 198). Its attested spellings are as follows:

5 But lacking the expected shift *d* > *t* in the third radical after *b* (the second, in this case) in Akkadian (cf. GAG³, § 51d Nachtr.). Cf. Pentiuc 2001: 107–108, 267 (classified as "non-normative Akkadian").

6 As we see by various translations of this word: e.g., "douaire" (Arnaud 1986: 118; Arnaud 1991: 55), "bequest" (Beckman 1996b: 14), "*kubuddā'u*-gifts" (Westenholz 2000: 39), "bequest, dowry" (Pentiuc 2001: 107), and "~ honorific gift?" (CDA: 164b). Cf. also the following cognate nouns in Akkadian: *kubuttû* (SB), "abundance; abundant, rich gift" (CAD K: 490b–491a; also AHw: 498b); *kubuttatu* (Ugarit), "honoring gift" (see Huehnergard 2008: 135 [s.v. *kubuddatu*], 392; cf. *kubbuttu* [CAD K: 483b–484a; *AHw*: 497b]).

[*ku-bu*]-*ud-da-e*	Emar VI 198: 7′$^{?}$
ku-<bu>-ud-da-e	Emar VI 112: 14^{g} (see ll. 4^{a*}, 11^{a*})
ku-bu-da-e	*AuOr* 5-T 15: 13^{g}, 19^{g}, 25^{a*}; BLMJE 14: 13^{a*}, 19^{a*}, 22^{g}; RE 8: 17^{a*}
ku-bu-da-e.MEŠ	TS 71: 18^{g*}
ku-bu-da.MEŠ	*SMEA* 30-T 8: 19^{g*} (with [*ku*]-; cf. ll. 9^{a*}, 18^{a*}); TS 22: 2^{a*}

If this word is singular in the texts, it appears only in the genitive (= ^{g}) or accusative (= ^{a}). However, since several occurrences are apparently in the plural (= $\star$), it seems to me better to take all of them as plural oblique. Note also that there are some variations in the spelling. But the usual spelling seems to be the one without the doubling of *d*, which is attested in both Syrian- and Syro-Hittite-types of texts, and, if my interpretation is correct, with the final long vowel *ē* in the plural oblique form.

2 Texts: *kubuddā'u*-gift and Other Dowers

2.1 Texts concerning the *kubuddā'u*-gift

Below I present the relevant sections of the above texts, excluding the fragmentary Emar VI 198.[7] In each case, the head of a family gives a *kubuddā'u*-gift (lit. *kubuddā'us* = *ks*.) to his wife.

AuOr 5-T 15 (S): testament of Ya'eyanu

^{6} *a-nu-um-*[*ma*] 1 GIŠ.NA$_2$ *qa-du* NIG$_2$.BARAG$_2$.HA$_2$-*šu* ^{7} 1 URUDU.*dú-du* 1 *li-im* KI.LA$_2$.BI ^{8} 2 *nam-ḫa-rù* ZABAR ^{9} ^{mf}PN$_1$ *qa-du* DUMU.MEŠ-*ši* ^{10} 3 *ši-id-du*$_4$ *ša* IKU *i-na* GIŠ$^{?}$.KIRI$_6$.GEŠTIN ^{11} *a-na* ^{f}PN$_2$ ^{12} DAM-*ti-ia-ma*$^{!}$ ^{13} *a-na ku-bu-da-e-ši* ^{14} *ad-dì-in*

Now, I have given *the listed items* to my wife PN$_2$ as her *ks*. (Her four sons shall take care of her – any one of them who does not do so shall lose the right to the *ks*. – and when she dies, they shall divide her *ks*.)

BLMJE 14 (SH): statement of Abi'u

a-nu-ma ⌜*a*⌝-*na* ^{f}PN$_1$ DUMU.MUNUS$^{!}$ ^{m}PN$_2$ ^{f}PN$_3$ ^{3} GEME$_2$-*ia* 10 ⌜U$_8$⌝.MEŠ$_2$ 10 UZ$_3$.MEŠ$_2$ 1 ŠEN ZABAR 3 *me-at* KI.LA$_2$.BI ^{4} *ša* KASKAL-*ni-i*[*a*] 1 *a-sà-lu*$_4$ ZABAR 3

7 To facilitate a better understanding of the texts, however, in the translation I add summaries of the contents of the untransliterated parts within parentheses (e.g., *AuOr* 5-T 15: 15–26). For the untranslated items included in the *kubuddā'u*-gifts, see List 1 (appendix 1).

me-at KI.LA$_2$.BI ^{5} 1 *qà-bi-l[u]* ZABAR *ša šu-mi-ia i-na* ŠA$_3$*-šu ša-aṭ-ru* ^{6} 1 GAL ZAB[A]R *ša a-pa-pa-ri-ḫi* ^{7} 1 GAL *ša* x x(-)*ki-in-nu ša* HUR.SAG ^{8} 1 TUG$_2$ GIBIL 1 GIŠ.NA$_2$ GAL *ša* GIŠ.TUG$_2$ 1 TUG$_2$.*ma-qar-ru* GIBIL ^{9} 1 TUG$_2$.GUZ.ZA 1 *a-sà-lu*$_4$ ZABAR *ša* ŠU-*ti* ^{10} 1 *ut-ta-al-lu* ZABAR *ša šar-pá-aš-ši* 1 E$_2$ IZI ZABAR ^{11} 1 GIŠ.BANŠUR 1 GIŠ.GU.ZA 1 GIŠ.GIR$_3$.GUB ^{12} ⸢*a*⸣-[*n*]*a* E$_2$ *ur-*⸢*ši*⸣*-ša ma-am-ma la-a ir-ru-ub* ^{13} [*k*]*u-bu-da-e an-nu-ti a-na* ^{f}PN$_1$ DAM$^{!}$-*ia* ^{14} *at-ta-din*

Now, to (my wife) PN$_1$, daughter of PN$_2$: *listed items*. No one shall enter her retirement quarters. I have given these *ks*. to my wife PN$_1$. (My five sons shall take care of her, and any one of them who does so shall take her *ks*. If PN$_1$ remarries, she shall leave the household without taking anything and lose the right to her *ks*.)[8]

Emar VI 112 (SH): statement of Dagan-kabar

^{2} [*a-n*]*u-ma* ^{f}[PN$_1$ DUMU.MUNUS PN$_2$] DAM-*ia* ^{3} [*a-na*] *a-bi* [*ù* MUNUS.AMA *š*]*a* E$_2$-*ia aš-ku-un-*[*ši*] ^{4} ⸢*a*⸣*-nu-m*[*a ku-*(*bu-*)*ud-da-e š*]*a* ^{f}PN$_1$ DAM-[*ia*] ^{5} [*u*]*m-*[*te-ed-dì*] ⸢*ù*⸣ KU$_3$.BABBAR NIG$_2$.MUNUS.US$_2$.S[A (...)] ^{6} [*a-na ša-a-ši a*]*t-ta-din*

[N]ow, I have established my wife [PN$_1$, daughter of PN$_2$], as "father [and mother" o]f my household. No[w], I have [d]e[fined the *ks*. o]f [my] wife PN$_1$ and [g]iven [her] the silver of brideweal[th] (for marrying the sons). (*No list of items.* Her three sons shall take care of her, and when she dies, they shall divide her *ks*. Any one of them who does not do so shall lose the right to her *ks*., pay 20 shekels of silver, and leave the household without taking anything but his weapon.)[9]

RE 8 (S): statement of Abi-li'mu

^{5} *a-nu-um-ma* ^{mf}PN$_1$ DA[M-*t*]*i-ia* ^{6} *a-nu-um-ma* GIŠ.NA$_2$ *qa-du* TUG$_2$.NIG$_2$.BARAG$_2$-*šu* ^{7} TUG$_2$.MEŠ *na-ab/p-ša-ši* ^{8} ⸢10⸣ UDU.MUNUS GAL BABBAR 10 UZ$_3$.MUNUS GAL ^{9} 10 GIŠ.*zi-*⸢*zi*⸣ GIŠ.GEŠTIN 1 *qà-be-lu* ZABAR 70 KI.LA$_2$.BI ^{10} 1 UTUL$_2$ ZABAR 6 *me-at* KI.LA$_2$.BI ^{11} 1 *a-sà-lu*$_4$ ZABAR 5 *me-at* KI.LA$_2$.BI ^{12} 1 *a-sà-lu*$_4$ ZABAR 2 *me-at* KI.LA$_2$.BI ^{13} 1 *ut-ta-lu*$_4$ ZABAR 1 *me-at* KI.LA$_2$.BI ^{14} 1 UTUL$_2$ ZABAR TU[R] 50 ⸢KI⸣.LA$_2$.BI ^{15} 1 <*a*>*-sà-lu*$_4$ ZABAR 30 KI.LA$_2$.BI ^{16} ⸢50⸣ *PA* ŠE ^{mf}PN$_2$ ^{17} *ku-bu-da-e an-nu-*⸢*ti*⸣ ^{18} *a-na* $^{m⸢f⸣}$PN$_1$ DAM-*ti-ia ad-din-*[*š*]*i*

Now, PN$_1$ is my wi[f]e. Now, *listed items* – I have given these *ks*. to my wife PN$_1$. (List of the inheritance shares of the two sons. Now, my two sons shall

8 On l. 7 see Fleming 2002: 372. Cf. *ša k*[*a*$^{?}$*-a*]*t*$^{?}$*-ti*$_4$*-in-nu* (Westenholz 2000: 38); *ša kà-at-ti*$_4$*-in-nu* (Beckman 2001: 195). For the translation of *bīt urši* (l. 12) as "retirement quarters," see n. 30 below. Note that the phrase "without taking anything" in the summary is literally "she/he shall put her/his garment (TUG$_2$) on the footstool" (l. 21).

9 The restoration of the verb in l. 5 is based on *SMEA* 30-T 8: 9 and TS 22: 3.

divide all my estate according to the customary law of the city. If PN$_1$ remarries, she shall leave the household without taking anything.)[10]

SMEA 30-T 8 (SH): testament of [PN]

[^{f}PN$_1$ DUMU.MUNUS PN$_2$ D]AM-*ia* ⌜*a-na a*⌝-*bi ù* AMA ^{3} [*ša* E$_2$-*ti-ia aš-ku-un-ši* E$_2$-*ia gâb-ba mim-mu-i*]*a ad-din-na-aš-ši* ... /
^{9} [*a-nu-ma ku-bu-da*.MEŠ *ša* ^{f}]P[N$_1$ DA]M-*ia um-te-ed-dì* 1 ŠEN ZABAR 1 *li-im* KI.LA$_2$.BI ^{10} [x x x x x (x) KI].LA$_2$.BI <1> *ut*-[*ta-l*]*u* ZABA<R> *ša* SISKUR.MEŠ 1 *ut-ta-lu* ZABAR ^{11} [x x x x x x (x) *š*]*a*$^{?}$ KASKAL *a-du* ⌜*ú*⌝-*nu-te*.MEŠ-*šú ša* [*á*]*š*$^{!}$-*ša-aš-ḫi ra-ak-sú-ti* ^{12} [^{m}PN$_3$ *a-na* ... *la*]-*a i-qar-ri-ib* 2 D[UMU].MUNUS.NITA-*šú* ^{m}PN$_4$ SIPA ^{13} [*ù* ^{f}PN$_5$ ZA.LAM].GAR-*šú si-GAB-ti-šú* ⌜1 ME UDU⌝.HA$_2$ 2 ⌜GU$_4$.AB$_2$⌝ ^{14} [x x x x x x x (x)] x [x x x (x)]-*ši* GIŠ.KIRI$_6$.GEŠTIN-*ia* [*š*]*a* URU.⌜*da*$^{?}$⌝-[x] x [(...)] ^{15} [x x x x x x x x x x (x) *l*]*i-GIM-šú-nu*

[I have established] my [w]ife [PN$_1$, daughter of PN$_2$], as "father and mother" [of my household] and given her [my household and all m]y [possessions] (i.e., all my estate). (My three sons shall take care of her, and when she dies, they shall divide all my estate. Any one of them who does not do so shall lose the right to all my estate, and leave the household without taking anything.) / [Now], I have defined [the *ks.* of] my [wif]e P[N$_1$]: *listed items.* [...] ... (In the future, [...] they remained. My three sons shall take care of her, and when she dies, they shall divide her *ks.* Any one of them who does not do so shall lose the right to her *ks.*)[11]

TS 22 (SH): statement of Arwu

a-nu-ma ku-bu-da.MEŠ ^{3} *ša* ^{f}PN$_1$ DAM-*ia um-te-ed-dì* ^{4} 1 ŠEN ZABAR 5 ME KI.LA$_2$.BI ^{5} 1 *a-sà*-[*lu*$_4$ Z]ABAR 5 ME KI.LA$_2$.BI ^{6} 1 *ut-ta*-[*lu*$_4$] ZABAR 2 ME KI.LA$_2$.BI ^{7} 1 *a-zu-*

---

10 Durand reads l. 7 as TUG$_2$.MEŠ *na-ap-ša-lì*, "les voiles" (2013: 37). The reading 10 UZ$_3$.MUNUS in l. 8 follows Durand. Cf. 10 UZ$_3$$^{!?}$ (Beckman 1996b: 13). Note that "all the estate" (ll. 36–37) probably refers to the sum of the inheritance shares of the two sons (ll. 19–34). For the expressions denoting "all the (family) estate" used in the texts concerning the *kubuddā'u*-gift and other dowers dealt with in this study, see appendix 2.

11 On l. 9, cf. [*ku-bu-da*.MEŠ *ša* ^{f}]*Aš*- (Arnaud 1992: 207). The emendation in l. 11, [*á*]*š*$^{!}$- for [*p*]*a*-, is based on 1 *aš-ša-aš-ḫu ra-ak-sú*, "one packed *aššašḫu*-container" (BLMJE 23: 3). If this is correct, this line can be translated as: "[X fo]r traveling, together with its utensils in (lit. of) the packed *aššašḫus*." As for l. 12, I think that PN$_3$ is forbidden to approach the testator's wife (DAM-*ia*), or perhaps her retirement quarters (E$_2$ *ur-ši-ši*; cf. BLMJE 14: 12 and TS 22: 14–15 [but both with the verb *erēbu*]), whereas his two children (2 D[UMU].MUNUS.NITA-*šú*), one male (PN$_4$) and the other female (PN$_5$), are assigned to her (as her slaves). In l. 13, I suggest restoring PN$_3$'s tent (ZA.LAM.GAR; cf. BLMJE 20: 7–8) on the basis of the references to PN$_4$ as a shepherd (SIPA) above and to the livestock below (cf. also KASKAL, "road, trip," in l. 11). Note also on this line that in view of the handcopy (Arnaud 1992: 234), *si-GAB-ti-* seems preferable to *si-tab-bu-ti-* (Arnaud 1992: 207), although I cannot provide any word appropriate to this reading.

[*lu-u*]*š-ḫu* ZABAR 1 *ḫur-ti-ia-lu*$_4$ ZABAR [8] 1 *an-gu-ri-in-nu* [ZA]BAR 1 *qà-bi-lu*$_4$ 60 KI.LA$_2$.BI [9] 1 GAL ZABAR *ša pa-pa-ri-ḫi* 80 ⌜KI⌝.LA$_2$.BI [10] 3 GAL ZABAR 1 GIŠ.GU.ZA 1 GIŠ.GIR$_3$.>PAD<.GUB [11] 1 *a-sà-lu*$_4$ ZABAR 2 ME KI.LA$_2$.BI [12] 10 U$_8$.MEŠ$_2$ 5 UZ$_3$.MEŠ$_2$ 1 GIŠ.BANŠUR [13] mfPN$_2$ 40 GIŠ.*PA* ŠE.MEŠ [14] *i-na* E$_2$ *ur-ši-ša ma-am-ma* [15] *la-a ir-ru-ub*

Now, I have defined the *ks*. of my wife PN$_1$: *listed items*. No one shall enter her retirement quarters.[12]

TS 71 (SH): statement of Dagan-belu
a-nu-ma fPN$_1$ DAM-*ia*! [3] *a-na a-bi ù* AMA-*mi ša* E$_2$-*ia aš-ku-un-ši* [4] E$_2$-*ia gáb-bá mim-mu-ia a-na* fPN$_1$ DAM-*ia* [5] *at-t*[*a-din* ...] ... /
[16] *ù a-nu-ma* fPN$_2$ GEME$_2$-*ia* [17] 1 ŠEN ZABAR 4 ME KI.LA$_2$.BI [*a*]*n-nu-ti* [18] *a-na ku-bu-da-e*.MEŠ *ša* PN$_1$ DAM-*ia at-ta-din* /

Now, I have established my wife PN$_1$ as "father and mother" of my household, (and) gi[ven] my household and all my possessions (i.e., all my estate) to my wife PN$_1$. (My five sons shall take care of her, and when she dies, they shall divide all my estate. / But if any one of them claims his inheritance share while PN$_1$ is alive, he shall lose the right to all my estate and leave the household without taking anything.) /
Now, *listed items* – I have given [t]hese as the *ks*. of my wife PN$_1$. / (I have defined the houses of my sons: list of the inheritance shares of the five sons. /)[13]

2.2 Texts concerning other dowers

Besides the above texts, in four other Emar texts we find that the head of a family gives a dower to his wife. To these, I add Emar VI 31 and RE 57, where he gives a dower-like gift to his daughter designated "father and mother," as comparable cases.

Emar VI 70 (SH): statement of [...z]alu(?)
⌜*a*⌝-[*nu-ma*] [3] [f]PN [DAM-*ia a-na a-b*]*i* [4] *ù* AMA >X< *ša* E$_2$-[*ia aš-ku-u*]*n-šu-mi* [5] *a-nu-ma* 2 GIŠ.KIRI$_6$.GE[ŠTIN X G]U$_4$.MEŠ.HA$_2$ [6] 4 BANŠUR ⌜4? GIŠ⌝.[GU.ZA] [7] 2 *tu-pa-tu* ZAB[AR!] ⌜1⌝-*en ša* 4 *me-at* ⌜KI⌝.LA$_2$.⌜BI⌝ [8] 1-*en-ma ša* 2 *me-at* KI.LA$_2$.BI [9] *ù a-nu-*

12 The same scribal error GIŠ.GIR$_3$.PAD.DU/GUB (l. 10) for *kilzappu* is found in BLMJE 21: 13; 23: 14 (both SH). Cf. Fleming 2002: 373 (note on 23: 14).
13 For HA.LA.A (l. 12) as a variant of HA.LA, "inheritance share," see Yamada 1994/c. Cf. *ḫa-la-a*, "Renie-moi" (Arnaud 1991: 120 f.).

ma 2 DU[MU.MUNUS-*i*]*a i-na* E$_2$ *e-mi* 10 [*l*]*i-din-ma* KU$_3$.BABBAR ⌜NIG$_2$⌝.MU-NUS.US$_2$.MEŠ-*šu l*[*i-i*]*l-qè*

N[ow], I have [establi]shed [my wife] PN [as "fath]er and mother" of [my] household. Now, *listed items*. Now, she [sh]all marry (lit. give into the household of the father-in-law) [m]y two dau[ghters] and t[a]ke the silver of their(!) bridewealths. (Now, I have taken another wife with my own silver.)[14]

Emar VI 176 (S): testament of Dagan-mi-ilu
13 GIŠ.NA$_2$ *qa-du* NIG$_2$.BARAG$_2$.HA$_2$-*šu* 1 TUG$_2$.*ṣú-ba-tu* SIG 14 URUDU.ŠEN TUR *a-na* DUMU.MUNUS PN$_1$ DAM-*šu* 15 *id-di-in*

(List of the inheritance shares of Dagan-mi-ilu's five sons.) He has given *the listed items* to his wife, daughter of PN$_1$. (Her daughter PN$_2$ shall take care of her. If PN$_2$ rejects her, PN$_2$ shall give a female slave as her substitute and leave the household. If Dagan-mi-ilu's wife remarries, her possessions shall be given to her younger sons.)

***Iraq* 54-T 6 (S): testament(?) of Ḫinnu-Dagan**
6 *a-nu-um-ma* DUMU.MUNUS PN DAM-*ia* 7 *a-bu ù um-mu* 8 *ša* E$_2$-*ti-ia ši-it-ma* … 17 *a-nu-um-ma* GIŠ.NA$_2$ GADA *qa-d*[*u* NIG$_2$.BARAG$_2$] 18 [*š*]*a* DUMU.MUNUS PN [D]A[M$^?$-*ia*$^?$]

Now, my wife, daughter of PN, is the "father and mother" of my household. (My three sons shall take care of her. Any one of them who does not do so shall lose the right to his inheritance share. She shall slap his cheek and throw him into the street.) Now, *the listed items* [belo]ng to [my w]i[fe], daughter of PN. (Then poorly preserved.)[15]

RE 37 (S): testament of ^{d}IM-ili
18 1 *tu-di-it-tù* KU$_3$.BABBAR *ša*! 19 5 GIN$_2$ *qar-nu* ZU$_2$ AM.SI 20 *AN BI ID RU* 21 *ša* ^{f}PN 22 ^{f}PN *a-bu* 23 *ù um-mu*

(List of the inheritance shares of my three sons. If the second son complains about his share, he shall lose the right to the family estate in GN.) *The listed*

14 In view of the handcopy (Arnaud 1985: 747), there is no space for *-ti-* (so Arnaud 1986: 78) after E$_2$ in l. 4. The restoration of GIŠ.GU.ZA in l. 6 is based on BLMJE 14: 11. In l. 9 MUNUS is necessary (Durand 1989: 186), and so there is no space for MEŠ (cf. Arnaud 1986: 78; also Durand 1989: 186). Although Durand reads *-šu-n*[*u li*]*l-qì* in l. 10 (Durand 1989: 186), the sign LIL seems to be difficult according to the handcopy. At the beginning of l. 12, I suggest reading [*iš*]*-tu*, lit. "from," instead of [*qa-*]*dú* (Arnaud 1986: 78).

15 GIŠ.NA$_2$ GADA (l. 17) is attested also in RE 57: 9 below. Cf. GIŠ.NA$_2$ << GIŠ >> (Dalley and Teissier 1992: 103).

items belong to (my wife) PN. PN is the "father and mother." (My three sons shall take care of her. Any one of them who does not do so shall lose the right to all my estate.)[16]

Cf. Emar VI 31 (SH): contract made by Ḫaya in the presence of Šaḫurunuwa, king of Karkemiš

^{3} ^{f}PN$_1$ DUMU.MUNUS-*šu*$^{!}$ MUNUS.KAR.KID *a-na a-bu-ut-ti ù* AMA-*mi* ^{4} *ša* E$_2$-*ti-šu*$^{!}$ *e-pu-uš-ši* GIŠ.NA$_2$ *qa-du* TUG$_2$.NIG$_2$.URI.KI.MEŠ ^{5} TUG$_2$.HA$_2$: *na-ab/p-ša-ši ù ri-iš-tu*$_4$ ZABAR *ša* AN.MEŠ ⸢*kàt*⸣-*mu* ^{6} *ú-nu-te*.MEŠ *an-nu-ti* 2 GEME$_2$ ^{f}PN$_2$ *ù* ^{f}PN$_3$ ^{7} *a-na* ^{f}PN$_1$ DUMU.MUNUS-*ia at-ta-din*

I have made PN$_1$, my(!) daughter (and) the *ḫarimtu*-woman, the "father and mother" of my(!) household. *Listed items* – I have given these goods (and) two female slaves PN$_2$ and PN$_3$ to my daughter PN$_1$. (Now, I have made my other two daughters my sons. ... They shall take care of PN$_1$ – any one of them who does not do so shall lose the right to her inheritance share and leave the household without taking anything – and when she dies, they shall divide all my estate with each other. List of their inheritance shares. Then mostly broken.)[17]

Cf. RE 57 (S): testament of Iddi-ma

a-nu-um-ma ^{6} ^{f}PN$_1$ DUMU.MUNUS-*ia* <NU>.GIG ^{7} *a-bu ù um*$^{!}$-*mu ša* E$_2$-*ia* ^{8} *ši-it-ma a-nu-um-ma* ^{9} 1 GIŠ.NA$_2$ GADA 1 UTUL$_2$ ZABAR 4 *me-at* KI.LA$_2$.BE ^{10} 1 GIN$_2$ KU$_3$ 1 *a-sà-lu* 3 *me-at* KI.LA$_2$.BE ^{11} 1 AB$_2$ MU.3 *ú-nu-tu*$_4$ *an-nu-tu*$_4$ ^{12} *a-na* ^{f}PN$_1$ ^{13} DUMU.MUNUS-*ia* <NU>.GIG *id-din*

Now, PN$_1$, my daughter (and) the *qadištu*-woman, is the "father and mother" of my household. Now, *listed items* – I(!) have given these goods to PN$_1$, my daughter (and) the *qadištu*-woman. (PN$_1$ shall give these goods to her daughter PN$_2$. The brothers of PN$_2$ shall not claim them. As long as PN$_1$ is alive, there is no (claim on) the inheritance shares.)

---

16 It is difficult to understand actually how many dower items are mentioned in ll. 18–20. Beckman considers *tudittu* and *qarnu* as items and seems to regard *AN BI ID RU* (written on the erasure) as a category of property or gift (1996b: 59; cf. also Pentiuc 2001: 39). Against this interpretation, Durand recognizes only *tudittu* as an item (2013: 42, 43 n. 64). One could even suggest that the *AN BI ID RU* is a third item. So, I am inclined to leave open the possibility that there may be as many as three items.

17 E. J. Pentiuc translates the description of the GIŠ.NA$_2$ as: "A bed with Akkadian blanket, the *n.* and the bronze bedhead, which cover the 'sky' (of the bed)" (2001: 128).

2.3 General observations on the *kubuddā'u*-gift

Table 1 summarizes the contents of the above seven texts concerning the *kubuddā'u*-gift, while Table 2 does so for the texts concerning other dowers.

Glancing at Table 1, we immediately see that the situation concerning the *kubuddā'u*-gift is not always a simple dower strategy as outlined above. In four texts (*AuOr* 5-T 15, BLMJE 14, RE 8 and TS 22), the *kubuddā'u*-gift does seem to be such a dower; it appears to be only a part of the estate, and presumably the rest of the estate will be inherited by the sons at the time the head of the family dies. However, in the other three texts (Emar VI 112, *SMEA* 30-T 8 and TS 71), all of the Syro-Hittite type, at the time the head of the family defines his wife's *kubuddā'u*-gift, he also designates her as "father and mother," that is, guardian of all the estate. We see here a mixture of the guardian strategy and the dower strategy. Note also that surprisingly this mixed case can be seen in all the texts in List 2 (appendix 1) but Emar VI 176.

In any case, in *SMEA* 30-T 8 and TS 71 the *kubuddā'u*-gift is differentiated from "all the estate." Particularly in *SMEA* 30-T 8, methodically, both for the estate and for the *kubuddā'u*-gift, the sons are ordered to take care of the widow, their mother, in order to inherit that property. This raises several questions. Question 1: why is this distinction made? Question 2: how are the two kinds of property related? On the other hand, in Emar VI 112 the property

Tab. 1: Texts concerning the *kubuddā'u*-gift.

Text	*AuOr* 5-T 15	BLMJE 14	Emar VI 112
Text type	S	SH	SH
"Father & mother"			wife
Bequest to wife	*k.* list	*k.* list	*ks.* (= all); cf. *terḫatu*
Bequest to sons			
Caring by sons	+	+	+
Inheritance by sons	*ks.*	*ks.*	*ks.*
Losing by son	*ks.*		*ks.* & silver

Text	RE 8	*SMEA* 30-T 8		TS 22	TS 71	
Text type	S	SH		SH	SH	
"Father & mother"		wife			wife	
Bequest to wife	*k.* list	all	*k.* list	*k.* list	all	*k.* list
Bequest to sons	shares				shares	
Caring by sons		+	+		+	
Inheritance by sons	all	all	*ks.*		all	
Losing by son		all	*ks.*		all	

Tab. 2: Texts concerning other dowers.

Text	Emar VI 70	Emar VI 176	*Iraq* 54-T 6
Text type	SH	S	S
"Father & mother"	wife		wife
Bequest to wife	list & *terḫatu*	list	list
Bequest to sons		shares	
Caring by sons		+' (by daughter)	+
Inheritance by sons			
Inheritance by daughter			
Losing by son			share
Text	**RE 37**	**Emar VI 31**	**RE 57**
Text type	S	SH	S
"Father & mother"	wife	daughter	daughter
Bequest to wife	list	list	list
Bequest to sons	shares	shares?	
Caring by sons	+	+	
Inheritance by sons		all	
Inheritance by daughter			listed goods
Losing by son	all	share	

in the *kubuddā'u*-gift is not listed, and actually indicates "all the estate," since the text states that a son who does not take care of the widow shall lose the right to the *kubuddā'u*-gift and leave the household with only his own weapon at hand, that is, lose all of his inheritance share. This brings up Question 3: why is it necessary here to make all of the estate the *kubuddā'u*-gift? Keeping these questions in mind, let us examine the lists of the properties defined as *kubuddā'u*s.

3 *kubuddā'u* Lists

3.1 Categories

The items in the *kubuddā'u* lists are shown in List 1 (appendix 1).[18] When we compare it with List 2 (appendix 1), which gives the properties included in the other dower lists, we notice several points regarding property categories. Firstly, various categories of property are included. But List 1 does not include any

18 Note that Emar VI 112 is excluded, since it lacks a *kubuddā'u* list.

ornaments or cash (silver).[19] Secondly, there is no fixed order within the lists, such as furniture first and household utensils second, though there is a tendency for "bed" (GIŠ.NA$_2$), when it is mentioned, to appear first in the whole list.[20] Thirdly, generally speaking, the items in each category are grouped together.

When we look at the items in each category, firstly for real estate, in List 1 we find a portion of a vineyard or vines in two texts (*AuOr* 5-T 15: 10; RE 8: 9), and a vineyard in one text (*SMEA* 30-T 8: 14), and in List 2, one text refers to two vineyards (Emar VI 70: 5). But there is no mention of houses or agricultural fields. This point is a feature of property assigned to women in Emar, in contrast with that of men. When the inheritance shares of the sons are defined, they are listed in a house-centered way, as in RE 8.[21] Although references to fields are rare even in those male share-lists, we do find them, as for example, in RE 30.[22] On the other hand, even when all of the estate is given to a woman designated "father and mother," we seldom find any mention of fields.[23] This lack of reference to fields in property given to women is well illustrated in the

---

19 However, this would not necessarily mean that these could not be included in the *kubuddā'u*-gift. Their absence may have been circumstantial, particularly in the case of ornaments (cf. RE 37: 18–19; also l. 20?). Note that cash appears in List 2 (RE 57: 10), but though in Emar VI 112: 4–5 the widow is given silver, it is not part of the *kubuddā'u*-gift, but rather the bridewealth to be paid to outsiders in the future, so not given as the widow's property.

20 The only exception among the texts in Lists 1–2 is BLMJE 14 (l. 8).

21 "Now, the house o[f] the sons of PN$_1$ and the house of the son of PN$_2$; (the slaves) ^{m}PN$_3$ and ^{mf}PN$_4$, (as well as) ^{mf}PN$_5$, together with her son – (these are) the inheritance share of my son ^{m}PN$_6$" (ll. 28–34 [for ll. 29–30 see Durand 2013: 38]; see also ll. 19–27). We find one case where a daughter is given a house as her inheritance share from her father, as are her two brothers (Emar VI 177: 23′–25′, esp. 25′). However, in view of the fact that she and the eldest brother are called the "brothers" (ŠEŠ.MEŠ) of the second brother (l. 24′), I suspect that she had been designated as "man and woman," i.e., son. For this status, see my paper, "The Women Designated 'Man and Woman' in Emar and Ekalte," read at the fourth REFEMA workshop held at Chuo University, Tokyo, on May 26–27, 2014 (available at http://refema.hypotheses.org/1142); also Beckman 1996a: 60; Westbrook 2001: 36–38; Lion 2009: 12–22.

22 "Now, the main house, the small houses (for) dwelling (TUŠ), and the new house; (and) 55 (units) of field ... *ikû* (55 A.ŠA$_3$ IKU [x-*PI-d*]*u*$_4$) in Y[a...] – (these are) the inheritance share of [my son] P[N]" (ll. 15–19; see also ll. 8–14). Although Beckman reads IKU [*ši-id-d*]*u*$_4$ in l. 17 based on his reading IKU *š*[*i-i*]*d*$^!$-*du* in l. 11 (1996b: 50), this is doubtful according to the hand copy; the latter seems to be IKU x (x)-*PI-du*. On this problem, see Mori 2003: 108.

23 It is found in only two out of the twenty-five texts: "My houses, my fields (A.ŠA$_3$.HA$_2$-*ia*), (and) my properties" (RE 15: 7–8); and (for most of all the estate) "the main house, the field (A.ŠA$_3$), the vineyard, the properties, (and) the riches of my household" (TS 50: 9–11). Note also that similarly, even when a daughter is designated as "man and woman" and given all the estate of her father, "field" is normally not specified. It is mentioned only in *RA* 77-T 1 (= *ASJ* 13-T 25): 28 and RE 85: 25.

detailed description of "all the estate" in *ASJ* 13-T 23.[24] This may be because, unlike a vineyard, a field was difficult to divide by inheritance, since in all probability it was usually owned jointly by the head of the family and his brothers, and they divided its crops, not its area.

Furniture is usually included in the list. We may note here a contrast between mention of a bed with its "spread(s)," i.e., blanket(s), in the Syrian-type texts and mention of a table, chair and footstool in the Syro-Hittite-type texts, although there is a clear exception in Emar VI 31 (l. 4) in List 2. Since no life without both bed and table, etc., is conceivable, and, although only once, these four items are mentioned in BLMJE 14 – with the bed (l. 8) being separated from the other three (l. 11) – perhaps those references actually denoted the set of all four items in both types of text.[25]

Household utensils are commonly mentioned, though different items with different frequency. Most referents are vessels made of bronze;[26] note especially *ruqqu* (cauldron) and *uttallu*, as well as *asallu* and *qabbilu*. The weights of those vessels are frequently recorded; the heaviest are a bronze *ruqqu* (*SMEA* 30-T 8: 9) and a (copper) *dūdu* (*AuOr* 5-T 15: 7), both of 1,000 (shekels), while the lightest is a bronze *asallu* of 30 (shekels) in RE 8: 15.

Clothing / cloth is only occasionally mentioned (BLMJE 14: 8–9; cf. also Emar VI 176: 13 in List 2). This would not mean that the widows were usually not given garments, however. In this respect, note that the "garment" (TUG_2) given in the former text (l. 8) is specified as a "new" (GIBIL) one, while that ($^{\text{tug}_2}$*ṣubātu*) in the latter is a "thin (i.e., fine)" (SIG) one.[27] This suggests that the garments mentioned in the dower (including *kubuddā'u*) lists are only special ones, it being taken for granted that the others she had already were hers.

As for servants, most probably all slaves, it is interesting to note that a female servant is mentioned in all documents in List 1. She was probably need-

---

24 Given to the wife and her daughter, both designated "father and mother": "My houses (E_2.HA_2-*ia*), my garden, my oxen, my donkeys, my sheep, my properties, (and) my possessions (*mi*!-*im-mi-ia*), (as well as) my male slaves (and) my female slaves" (ll. 8–11).

25 It may be worth noting here that we find the set of a bed, table, chair and footstool in the "bedroom" (*bīt urši*) of the NIN.DINGIR of Ba'lu in his temple (Emar VI 369: 70–73; see Fleming 1992: 25–26, 57, also 116–117).

26 The only exception is "one (copper) *dūdu*" in *AuOr* 5-T 15: 7. Cf. also "a small (copper) *ruqqu*" in Emar VI 176: 14 in List 2. In this respect, it is interesting to note that when we check the household utensils included in the dower lists in the Ekalte texts (ca. 1400–1325 BC; see Werner 2004: 23–24), all of them are made of copper (Ekalte II 19: 10–11; 75: 14; 92 [= RE 69]: 8).

27 On TUG_2 (*ṣubātu*) meaning "garment" in the Emar texts, see n. 8 above. Although exactly what *maqarru* means is unclear, note that it also is described as "new" (BLMJE 14: 8).

ed for the personal support of the widow.[28] This feature is not shared by the texts in List 2 (attested only in Emar VI 31: 6).

Livestock are also frequently included in List 1, but not in List 2. Here, it is noteworthy that female animals are specified, ewes and she-goats (BLMJE 14: 3; RE 8: 8; TS 22: 12), and cows are mentioned once as well (*SMEA* 30-T 8: 13). Like the products of the vineyards above, their dairy products would have supplemented the widow's diet.

Provisions of barley are attested in RE 8: 16 and TS 22: 13. It should be noted that these are the only texts in which the sons are not specifically given the obligation to care for the widow. This indicates that feeding is the essential part of "caring." The volumes of barley given are 50 and 40 *parīsu* (ca. 2,500 or 2,000 l.). If this amount was provided to her each year (say, 360 days), it would mean ca. 6.9 or 5.6 l. per day. This is far more than one could consume. Even if it were for her and her servant, still the volume for one woman per day, ca. 3.5 or 2.8 l., may exceed what they could eat.[29] Perhaps this suggests that these provisions were for several years. In this case, however, it is not known how the sons were to provide them, whether at once or divided annually, and if in the latter case, for how many years.

3.2 Detailed lists vs. brief lists

When looking at the *kubuddā'u* lists (List 1 [appendix 1]), we see that there are both detailed lists and brief lists. The detailed lists are found in BLMJE 14, RE 8 and TS 22. Two points are noteworthy about these three texts. Firstly, in RE 8 and TS 22, we find the above-mentioned barley provisions in place of the caring duty. Secondly, BLMJE 14: 12 and TS 22: 14–15 state that no one is permit-

28 In this respect, it is interesting to note that when Mama defines the inheritance shares of his sons, he states: "I have giv[en] ^{f}PN$_1$, my female slave (GEME$_2$), a[s] / f[o]r the garment pin (⸢*a*⸣-[*n*]*a tu*-⸢*dì*⸣-*it-ti*) of my wife ^{f}PN$_2$" (RE 56: 21–22). Assigned to the widow, probably this slave is her personal maid, described as one who, like a garment pin, always attends her, or perhaps as who supports her by, for example, pinning up her garment.

29 Cf. M. Stol's note on the rations supplied to the adoptive parents in the OB adoption texts: "A reasonable minimum subsistence level was 2 litres of barley per day, which means 720 litres per year. This is, in fact, the figure that we find most often" (1998: 64). In the case of old women, however, its level may have been less than that, in view of the "standard ration" of 2 seah (ca. 20 l.) of barley per month, i.e., ca. 0.7 l. per day or 240 l. per year, for old women in the public sector workgroups in third millennium Mesopotamia (see Wilcke 1998: 26–34, esp. 27, 31).

ted to enter the widow's *bīt urši*, probably her "retirement quarters."[30] In these cases, since apparently it is expected that the widow would lead a more or less independent or isolated life, it is understandable that a detailed list of her properties would be required.

On the other hand, in *AuOr* 5-T 15, *SMEA* 30-T 8 and TS 71, the lists are brief,[31] and the sons are obliged to care for the widow. In these cases, since her life is dependent on the sons, and presumably at least one of them (I think, usually the eldest son) would live with her, a brief list is enough. As for the other items necessary for her daily life, particularly furniture and household utensils, she and her son(s) would both use the ones in the house that they share.

In two of the three texts with brief lists, in *AuOr* 5-T 15 (ll. 15–19) and *SMEA* 30-T 8 (ll. 16–19[32]), caring is the condition for inheriting the *kubuddā'u*-gift (see Table 1). This suggests that those sets of items were still attractive enough to

---

30 The term *uršu*, as well as *bīt urši*, is usually understood as "bedroom, personal quarters" within a house or building (CAD U and W: 251–252; also AHw: 1434a), and L. Marti (2007) showed that *bīt urši* is used in this meaning in Ekalte II 42: 9 and 12 (see also n. 25 above on the "bedroom" of the NIN.DINGIR in Emar). However, in my opinion, two cases of *bīt urši* in the Emar texts do denote "house," not a bedroom within it. Firstly, in RE 37 *bīt urši* (l. 7) obviously denotes a building (Marti 2007) used as a dwelling, whereas the simple *uršu* (l. 5) means a "bedroom" within a house. Secondly, note TS 67, where *bīt uršu*(sic) (l. 7) actually refers to a (smaller?) half space within one building, which was made separate by constructing an inner wall (l. 37) there, as again Marti clarified (2007). When we see that this part, not the physical building as a whole, is mentioned as an adjacent construction in the rear of the *tuggu-ru*-house of Aḫu-dannu, it is obvious that the *bīt uršu* was recognized as a distinct entity for dwelling, i.e., a "house" in legal terms (see E_2 in l. 37). Now, taking into account the prescription that no one (including the widow's sons) is permitted to enter her *bīt urši* in BLMJE 14 and TS 22, it seems that what is meant here by *bīt urši* is "retirement quarters" rather than a simple bedroom, whether it was a building within the same lot as the (main) house (cf. RE 37) or a separate space within that house (as in TS 67).

31 I should explain why I classify the list in *SMEA* 30-T 8 (ll. 9–14/15?), with as many as ten (and probably more) items, as "brief." Whereas the items in the "detailed" lists are distributed throughout many categories, with furniture and household utensils (i.e., the basic items for the widow's domestic life) as the main items, those in *SMEA* 30-T 8 are not; there is no mention of furniture, and only two kinds of household utensils are mentioned (see List 1 [appendix 1]). Although one might argue that these items were mentioned in the broken parts in ll. 10, 11(?), 14, 15(?), this cannot be verified, and the overall picture would not change drastically. Therefore, I regard the list in this text as "brief," in the meaning of, not like the other "detailed" lists.

32 I suggest reading: (When the widow dies) [18] [*ku-bu-da*.MEŠ-*ši li-zu-(uz-)zu m*]*a-an-nu-me-e* ⌜*i*⌝-*na* ŠA$_3$ 3 DUMU.M[EŠ-*ia*] [19] [DAM-*ia la-a i-pal-la-ḫu a-na ku*]-*bu-da*.MEŠ-*š*[*i* N]U TUK, "they (the three sons) [shall divide her *k*s. A]ny one of [my] three son[s who does not take care of my wife] shall [n]ot have (the right) [to] he[r] *k*s." Cf. Arnaud 1992: 208.

motivate the sons to care for her, although they look rather meager to us. However, in TS 71, where the *kubuddā'u*-gift consists of one cauldron and one female slave (ll. 16–17), the caring duty is not specifically linked to inheriting it. Probably, the head of the family felt he could hardly order his sons to take care of his wife in order to inherit only the two items, when in the previous section he had just ordered them to do so in order to inherit all of the estate (ll. 5–10), which he gave to his wife, designating her as "father and mother."

It is interesting to note that the same situation as in TS 71 can be assumed for the texts in List 2 (appendix 1), except for Emar VI 70 and 176.[33] In those texts (*Iraq* 54-T 6, RE 37; see also Emar VI 31, as well as RE 57), the sons are obliged to care for the widow (or their sister) designated "father and mother" in order to inherit all of the estate or their own inheritance shares (see Table 2),[34] and there is no reference to their inheriting the dower, which consists mostly of her personal goods. In TS 71, the slave and the cauldron of the *kubuddā'u*-gift are regarded as only a part of the estate properties located in the main(!) house, where she will live.[35] In a situation where she could use other items as noted above, why were they specifically chosen for the *kubuddā'u*-gift? I think, because she only had the right to full control on this part. In other words, the rest of the estate was substantially under the control of the sons.[36] If this is correct, the same can be said of the other dowers in List 2 (appendix 1).

---

33 Emar VI 70 was, in my interpretation, written when the head of the family married a second wife (ll. 11–12). He designated his first wife as "father and mother" and gave her the listed properties and the entitlement to the bridewealth of his two daughters to define her right *vis-à-vis* the second. Probably he intended to draw up another document later on the issues of caring for the first wife and the inheritance. In Emar VI 176 the widow's daughter is ordered to take care of her (ll. 15–17), most probably as a condition for inheriting the dower from her mother.

34 *Iraq* 54-T 6: 9–16; RE 37: 23–29; also Emar VI 31: 11–19. As for the remaining RE 57, the text states only that it is prohibited to divide the inheritance shares while the "father and mother" is alive (ll. 23–25). However, this seems to suppose implicitly the duty of caring for her by the sons of the head of the family, since it is difficult to think that a son who does not take care of her can inherit his share after her death.

35 In TS 71, the testator assigns the main house (E$_2$ GAL), where he is living, and another house to his four sons (ll. 20–22a), and the new house ([E$_2$-*tu*$_4$] GIBIL) to his eldest son ([DUMU-*ia* GAL]; ll. 22b–23). If this reading is correct, this suggests that the new house where the eldest son will live, most probably together with his mother (the testator's wife), will become the new main house after the father dies.

36 This is the key to answer Questions 1–2 above. Although all the estate is given to the wife designated "father and mother" in *SMEA* 30-T 8 and TS 71, she is the *nominal* guardian of those properties. The *kubuddā'u* list is necessary to define exactly which among them she actually owns. This is especially so when those items are included in the properties located in the house where she lives with her son(s).

3.3 *kubuddā'u*-gift and other dowers

Based on the above considerations, we may conclude that the *kubuddā'u*-gift and other dowers have in common the widow's right of full control over those properties while she is alive. But this was usufruct, as they were to be inherited by the sons after her death.

As TS 71 suggests, it is difficult to distinguish clearly the *kubuddā'u*-gift from other dowers. However, the following features can be pointed out for the *kubuddā'u*-gift.

Firstly, the range of the included properties is wide, from all the estate in Emar VI 112, to only two items in TS 71.

Secondly, as we can see from Table 1, its inheritors are restricted to sons. This point is no doubt applicable to RE 8 and TS 22, which specify supplying the provisions in place of caring; probably, the sons who actually supply the provisions will inherit the *kubuddā'u*-gift according to each one's ratio of contribution. On the other hand, in the texts summarized in Table 2, we find that the widow's daughter inherits the dower in RE 57 (ll. 14–17[37]) and probably also in Emar VI 176 (see n. 33 above).

Thirdly and most importantly, we can recognize the care in the provisions of the *kubuddā'u*-gift. Besides the above-mentioned provision of a female servant or slave in each case, we can note the close link between caring for the widow and the sons' inheriting it or losing it, or more accurately, their inheriting *and* losing it as found in three texts in Table 1 (*AuOr* 5-T 15 [ll. 20–26 and 17–19]; Emar VI 112 [ll. 9–12a and 12b–14], *SMEA* 30-T 8; cf. TS 71). This is especially so for *SMEA* 30-T 8, in which we see this link specified for inheriting all of the estate (ll. 5–6a and 6b–8) and also for inheriting the *kubuddā'u*-gift (ll. 17–18a and 18b–19). As for TS 71, it should be noted that although no such link is stated for the *kubuddā'u*-gift, we see here also the pairing of inheriting *and* losing of all of the estate in relation to caring (ll. 8–10 and 11–13). In the texts in Table 2, however, such a pairing relating to all of the estate or the individual shares is found only in Emar VI 31 (ll. 16–19 and 13–14). In the other two texts having a stipulation of caring by the sons, caring is connected with losing, but not with inheriting, that property (*Iraq* 54-T 6: 11–14; RE 37: 26–29).

---

37 I suggest reading the verb (l. 17) as *[t]i$_4$-id-din-aš-ši*, "she (daughter of the head of the family) shall give (the dower-like gift) to her (her daughter)." This *tiddin* (G pret. 3.f.sg.) is to be taken as jussive here. Cf. *[k]i id-din-* (Beckman 1996b: 75).

Taking into consideration this concern for his wife by the head of the family, it seems appropriate to take the word *kubuddā'u* as an "honorific gift," as CDA translates it (see n. 6 above).[38]

***

Although we find no clear distinction between the *kubuddā'u*-gift and other dowers, we may recognize in the former the especially strong wish of the head of the family to secure through it his wife's livelihood after his death. It covers a wide range of properties. Particularly Emar VI 112 shows that the whole estate can be given as *kubuddā'u*-gift. This means that the whole household is put under full control of the widow; her voice in this case must be heavier than in the cases of other "fathers and mothers."[39] Although houses and agricultural fields are never included in the *kubuddā'u* lists, household utensils and a female servant or slave appear in all, and basic furniture and livestock are frequently included. These properties are probably under her full control while she is alive, and are to be inherited only by the sons who take care of her.

Finally, let us touch on a remaining problem. Was the *kubuddā'u*-gift the dowry the wife brought when she married? Unfortunately, the Emar texts do not provide explicit dowry lists of brides,[40] although the dowry undoubtedly existed, as TS 23 shows. The text referring to Arwu's marrying his daughter reads:

> [4] *ù ú-nu-te*.MEŠ-*ši at-ta-din-mi* [5] *ù* KU$_3$.BABBAR.MEŠ NIG$_2$.MUNUS.US$_2$.MEŠ-*ši al-te-qè-mi*
>
> I have given her goods (as the dowry) and taken the silver of her bridewealth.

As for the contents of the dowry, we might acquire some hints from TS 28, which includes a list of the gifts a female head of the family gave to her husband when she divorced him:

---

38 Note that a cognate word for a religious ceremony in Emar seems to bear the same nuance: *kubadu*, which "should have something to do with the deriving meaning, 'honor' " (Fleming 1992: 169), or *ku/ibbadu*, "honoring (-ceremony)" (Pentiuc 2001: 106–107).

39 To answer Question 3, I think this is what her husband intended.

40 In my opinion, RE 6 includes a list of the gifts from the father-in-law to the daughter-in-law, not that of her dowry which she brought from her own family (so Beckman 1996b: 9–10; Durand 2013: 56–59). Furthermore, although several scholars argue that the word *terḫatu* can mean "dowry" as well as "bridewealth" in the Emar texts (e.g., Adamthwaite 1994: 21; Beckman 1996a: 69), this seems to me quite doubtful. I plan to discuss these issues elsewhere.

[19] 1 TUG$_2$ 1 ŠEN ZABAR 3 ME KI.LA$_2$.BI 10 GIN$_2$ KU$_3$.BABBAR.MEŠ [20] *na-qa-bu* ZABAR *a-gu-ri-in-nu* ZABAR

One garment, one bronze cauldron whose weight is 300 (shekels), 10 shekels of silver, a bronze hammer, and a bronze *angurinnu*.[41]

Presumably, the silver is the divorce money, and the other items, the dowry he brought when he entered her household (cf. Westbrook 2003: 670). Note that all these goods but the hammer are attested in the *kubuddā'u* lists. Furthermore, the items in the *kubuddā'u* lists fit in well with those in dowry lists in other texts, for example, those of the Old and Neo Babylonian periods (see Dalley 1980; Roth 1989–90).

At the same time, however, it should be noted that we occasionally find an item specified as belonging to the head of the family, such as "[f]PN, *my* female slave" (BLMJE 14: 2–3 and TS 71: 16), and one bronze *qabbilu*-vessel "on which *my* name is inscribed inside" (BLMJE 14: 5). Although it is of course possible that these are replacements for dowry items that were now dead, broken, sold, etc., this cannot be proved.

In conclusion, although it may be conceivable that at least a part of the *kubuddā'u*-gift consists of the wife's dowry,[42] this point remains to be demonstrated.

41 For *naqqabu*, "hammer," see Pentiuc 2001: 131–132. For *angurinnu*, see the Notes on Lists 1–2 [appendix 1].

42 Along this line of interpretation, one might argue that the *kubuddā'u*-gift is to be understood as "heavier gift," rather than "honorific gift," meaning the head of the family adds further items to those of her dowry. However, this seems unlikely. In the case of the *kubuddā'u*-gift in *TS* 71 consisting of only two items, although it is theoretically possible that one item is the dowry of the wife and the other is an additional gift from her husband, thus a heavier gift in total, note that the word *kubuddā'u* is used in the plural (see § 1 above). This means that the former item itself is recognized as a *kubuddā'u* here. On the nuance of "honorific" in the words deriving from **kbd* in Emar, see the above *kubadu* or *ku/ibbadu* (n. 38).

Appendix 1

List 1: *kubuddā'u*-gift.

Item (Akk. / Sum.)	English	*AuOr* 5-T 15 (S)	BLMJE 14 (SH)	RE 8 (S)	*SMEA* 30-T 8 (SH)	TS 22 (SH)	TS 71 (SH)
Real estate							
GIŠ.(KIRI$_6$.)GEŠTIN	vine(yard)	3 *šiddu*		10 ^{giš}*zizu*	(1)		
Furniture							
GIŠ.NA$_2$ (*eršu*), with	bed	1	1 boxwood	(1)			
(TUG$_2$.)NIG$_2$.BARAG$_2$	"spread"	pl.		(1) *n.*-cloth			
GIŠ.GIR$_3$.GUB(*kilzappu*)	footstool		1			1	
GIŠ.GU.ZA (*kussû*)	chair		1			1	
GIŠ.BANŠUR (*paššūru*)	table		1			1	
Household utensils							
angurinnu	?					1 bronze	
asallu	(vessel)		2 bronze	3 bronze		2 bronze	
azulušḫu	(vessel)					1 bronze	
E$_2$ IZI (*bīt išāti*)	brazier		1 bronze				
UTUL$_2$ (*diqāru*)	bowl			2 bronze			
^{urudu}*dūdu*	(vessel)	1 (copper)					
ḫurtiyalu	?					1 bronze	
GAL (*kāsu*)	cup		2 (bronze)			4 bronze	
namḫaru	vat	2 bronze					
qabbilu	(vessel)		1 bronze	1 bronze		1	
ŠEN (*ruqqu*)	cauldron		1 bronze		1 bronze	1 bronze	1 bronze
uttallu	(vessel)		1 bronze	1 bronze	2! (bronze)	1 bronze	
Clothing / cloth							
TUG$_2$.GUZ.ZA (*i'lu*)	(garment)		1				
^{tug2}*maqarru*	?		1				

(continued)

Item (Akk. / Sum.)	English	*AuOr* 5-T 15 (S)	BLMJE 14 (SH)	RE 8 (S)	*SMEA* 30-T 8 (SH)	TS 22 (SH)	TS 71 (SH)
TUG_2 (*ṣubātu*)	garment		1				
Servants (slaves)							
mPN	(male s.)				1 shepherd		
fPN	(female s.)	1+sons	1 slave	1	[1]	1	1 slave
Livestock							
UZ_3(.MUNUS) (*enzu*)	she-goat		10	10		5	
UDU (*immeru*)	sheep				100		
UDU.MUNUS (*immertu*)	ewe			10			
U_8 (*laḫru*)	ewe		10			10	
$GU_4.AB_2$ (*littu*)	cow				2		
Provisions							
ŠE (*še'u*)	barley			50 *parīsu*		40 *parīsu*	
Other							
ZA.LAM.GAR (*kuštāru*)	tent				(1)		
siGABtu (cf. *sitabbutu*)	?				(1)		
[... *š*]*a*? KASKAL	x for travel				(1)		

List 2: Other dowers.

Item (Akk. / Sum.)	English	Emar VI 70 (SH)	Emar VI 176 (S)	*Iraq* 54-T 6 (S)	RE 37 (S)	Emar VI 31 (SH)	RE 57 (S)
Real estate							
GIŠ.KIRI$_6$.GEŠTIN	vineyard	2					
Furniture							
GIŠ.NA$_2$ (*eršu*), with	bed		(1)	(1) linen		(1)	1 linen
NIG$_2$.BARAG$_2$	"spread"		pl.	[+]			
TUG$_2$.NIG$_2$.URI.KI	Akk. cloth					pl. *n*.-cloth	
GIŠ.GU.ZA (*kussû*)	chair	4?					
BANŠUR (*paššūru*)	table	4					
tuptu	footstool?	2 bronze					
Household utensils							
asallu	(vessel)						1
UTUL$_2$ (*diqāru*)	bowl						1 bronze
URUDU.ŠEN (*ruqqu*)	cauldron		(1 copper)				
Clothing / cloth							
^{tug2}*ṣubātu*	garment		1				
Servants (slaves)							
GEME$_2$ (*amtu*)	slave (f.)					2	
Livestock							
GU$_4$ (*alpu*)	ox	[x] (pl.)					
AB$_2$ (*littu*)	cow						1
Ornaments							
qarnu ZU$_2$ AM.SI	ivory horn				(1)		
tuditt	garment pin				1 silver		
Cash							
KU$_3$ (*kaspu*)	silver	cf. *terḫatu*					1 shekel
Other							
AN BI ID RU?	?				(1)		

Notes on Lists 1–2:

Real estate

GIŠ.(KIRI$_6$.)GEŠTIN – For discussions on the linear measure system in Emar, including *šiddu*, or more accurately *šiddu ša* IKU, "*š.* of *ikû*," used for the vineyard (GIŠ.KIRI$_6$.GEŠTIN = *kirî karāni*) in *AuOr* 5-T 15: 10, see Mori 2003: 104–105 (1 *šiddu* = 120 *ammatu*); Chambon 2008 (1 *šiddu* = 60 *ammatu*). On another measure *zizu*, used for vines (GIŠ.GEŠTIN = *karānu*) in RE 8: 9, see Durand 2012/b; Durand 2013: 35 and n. 36.

Furniture

eršu – The material is specified for only one item, "one large bed (made) of boxwood" (BLMJE 14: 8). On the other hand, GIŠ.NA$_2$ GADA, attested twice (*Iraq* 54-T 6: 17; RE 57: 9), should be understood as a "bed (whose surface is covered with) linen" (*ereš kitî*), or a "bed (and) a linen(-sheet)" (*eršu kitû*). As for the items associated with the bed, we find (TUG$_2$.)NIG$_2$.BARAG$_2$, *muṣû* / *uṣû* (see CAD M/2: 245b–246a; AHw: 679b; Durand 1990: 67) in three Syrian-type texts (*AuOr* 5-T 15: 6; RE 8: 6; Emar VI 176: 13; cf. *Iraq* 54-T 6: 17), and TUG$_2$.NIG$_2$.URI.KI, "Akkadian cloth," is in a Syro-Hittite-type text (Emar VI 31: 4). Here, it seems reasonable to think that both refer to substantially the same item (Durand 1989: 181), i.e., *a* "bedspread" (cf. verb *uṣṣû*). In this respect, the following passage in the text of the NIN.DINGIR installation is noteworthy. It describes the preparations for her spending the first night at the temple of Ba'lu (Emar VI 369 [Text A]; see Fleming 1992: 25–26, 44, 57):

> *i-na* ŠA$_3$ GIŠ.NA$_2$ [71] *ša-a-šu* TUG$_2$.NIG$_2$.URI *ša* E$_2$ x *ḫur-ši-ša* (cf. E$_2$ *ur-ši-ša* in Text D) KU$_3$.GA [72] *ù-ma-aṣ-ṣu-u*
>
> On that bed they will lay out one Akkadian blanket of her pure bedroom.

In this context, apparently the TUG$_2$.NIG$_2$.URI "serves as a spread or blanket for the bed" (Fleming 1992: 189 n. 348), and laying out a blanket would indicate the completion of the bedmaking. Furthermore, the fact that both TUG$_2$.NIG$_2$.BARAG$_2$ in RE 8 and TUG$_2$.NIG$_2$.URI.KI in Emar VI 31 are associated with a *nab/pšašu*-cloth (see Pentiuc 2001: 128–129) would support the above identification. According to Pentiuc (2001: 128), the description of the bed in RE 8: 6–7 is to be understood as: "A bed with its spread, the *n.*" (for Emar VI 31: 4–5 see n. 17 above). If this is correct, can we take the *nab/pšašu*-cloth as being in apposition to the preceding blanket (Pentiuc's "spread"), indicating its material? Or, if Durand is correct in that this cloth is to be understood as *napšalu*, "voile" (2013: 34, 35 n. 34, 37), can it be regarded as a paraphrase of the blanket? Finally, note that as with the TUG$_2$.NIG$_2$.URI.KI, in two cases

TUG$_2$.NIG$_2$.BARAG$_2$ is mentioned in the plural (*AuOr* 5-T 15: 6; Emar VI 176: 13). Possibly one of them was for spring-summer and the other for autumn-winter.
kussû and *paššūru*, as well as *kilzappu* – In the two texts (BLMJE 14: 11; TS 22: 10, 12) in List 1 these three items are in the singular in each case as one would expect, in Emar VI 70 (ll. 6–7) in List 2 they are plural: 4, 4?, and 2 (*tuptu* instead of *kilzappu*), respectively.
tuptu – See CAD T: 480a; AHw: 1372a. Their weights, no doubt in shekels as in the other cases below, are 400 and 200 (Emar VI 70: 7–8).

Household utensils

angurinnu – A metal household object. See CAD A/2: 118b–19a; AHw: 51a, 1543b; Pentiuc 2001: 25 (with other references in the Emar texts; add BLMJE 21: 8; 22: 8; 23: 6); Faist and Vita 2010.
asallu – See CAD A/2: 327b–28a; AHw: 73b; Westenholz 2000: 40 (for previous literature). In one case (BLMJE 14: 9), it has a "handle" (*ša qāti*). The weights are 300 (BLMJE 14: 4), 500, 200, 30 (RE 8: 11, 12, 15), 300 (RE 57: 10), 500 and 200 (TS 22: 5, 11). Note that except in one case (only 30), the weights are several hundred (shekels). It is attested also in Emar VI 22: 4; 186: 14 (cf. 187: 16′); BLMJE 21: 3; 22: 6; 23: 2. D. Arnaud also takes ASAL in Emar VI 187: 6′ (// 186: 7?; but cf. *a-sà-lu* in l. 14) as *asallu* (1986: 199, his translation of 186: 7).
azulušḫu – See Westenholz 2000: 56; Pentiuc 2001: 29–30 (with other references; add BLMJE 21: 5; 22: 10).
bīt išāti – See Westenholz 2000: 41 (with other references).
diqāru – See CAD D: 157b–59a; AHw: 172b–73a. The weights are 600, 50 (RE 8: 10, 14), and 400 (RE 57: 9). The one in RE 8: 14 is described as "small."
dūdu – See CAD D: 170; AHw: 174b. Its weight is 1,000 (*AuOr* 5-T 15: 7). Another reference (*dú-ú-du*) is found in Emar VI 283: 1 (Durand 1990: 81). The spellings *TU-du* (*AuOr* 5-T 15: 7) and *TU-ú-du* suggest that this word was pronounced as /tūdu/ (or /ṭūdu/) in Emar.
ḫurtiyalu – See Westenholz 2000: 56; Pentiuc 2001: 78 (with other references; add BLMJE 21: 5).
kāsu – In two cases (BLMJE 14: 6; TS 22: 9), one of the cups listed is decorated "with *papparḫû*-plants" (*ša* (*a*)*pappariḫî*). Another cup is described as "of X-*kinnu* of the mountain" (BLMJE 14: 7), but its meaning is not clear.
namḫaru – See CAD N/1: 227b–228; AHw: 727a (s.v. *namḫāru*[*m*]). Attested also in Emar VI 50: 1.
qabbilu – See Pentiuc 2001: 146–147 (with other references; add BLMJE 21: 6); cf. Arnaud 1986: 48; Westenholz 2000: 40. In one case (BLMJE 14: 5), the owner's name is inscribed inside (see above). The weights are 70 (RE 8: 9) and 60 (TS 22: 8).

ruqqu – The weights are 300 (BLMJE 14: 3–4), 1,000 (*SMEA* 30-T 8: 9), 500 (TS 22: 4), and 400 (TS 71: 17). Note that the first one, used "for travelling," is appropriately the lightest. There is also another one made of copper described as "small," whose weight is unknown (Emar VI 176: 14).
uttallu – See CAD U and W: 337b; AHw: 1401a (s.v. *udd/ttalû*); Westenholz 2000: 41; Pentiuc 2001: 191–192 (with other references; add BLMJE 15: 9; 21: 3; 29: 2). In one case (BLMJE 14: 10), it is "of cushion(-shape)" (see Huehnergard 1983: 25, 34, on *RA* 77-T 4 [= *ASJ* 13-T 27]: 20; also Pentiuc 2001: 171). Another one is used "for offering" (*SMEA* 30-T 8: 10). The weights are 100 (RE 8: 13) and 200 (TS 22: 6).

Clothing / cloth

i'lu – See CAD I and J: 90b; AHw: 373b; Westenholz 2000: 40–41. Attested also in BLMJE 23: 16.
maqarru – Meaning unclear. Attested only in Emar. See Westenholz 2000: 40 (for other references); cf. Pentiuc 2001: 121. For its feature see n. 27 above.
ṣubātu – For their features see above.

Livestock

The livestock are described as *enzu* – "large" (RE 8: 8); *immertu* – "large (and) white" (RE 8: 8); and *littu* – "three years old" (RE 57: 11).

Ornaments

qarnu ZU_2 AM.SI (*šinni pīrī*) – Although in my opinion, this horn (RE 37: 19) is a different dower item from the preceding silver *tudittu* (l. 18), its use might have been the same. Cf. 6 *tu-di-na-tum ša* ZÚ AM.SI, "six fibulas of ivory," in TLB 1 69: 12 (see CAD Š/3: 52a [s.v. *šinnu* A, mng. 2b–2′]).
tudittu – See CAD D: 168b–170a (s.v. *dudittu*); AHw: 1365b–1366a (s.v. *t/dudittu*[*m*]); Beckman 1996b: 59 (for previous literature); Durand 2013: 43 n. 61. Its weight is 5 shekels (RE 37: 18–19). This item is attested also in RE 56: 21; *TS* 69: 26. Durand is of the opinion that in RE 37: 18–20 the *tudittu* is the only dower item mentioned: "Le *tudittu* dont la valeur est de 5 sicles (consistant en) une défense en ivoire, (représentant une amulette de) Piṭru" (2013: 42).

Other

kuštāru – For other references, see n. 11 above.
[... *š*]*a*? KASKAL (*ḫarrāni*) – Cf. *ruqqu* (ŠEN) in BLMJE 14: 3–4, as another item specified as being for travel. For the attached containers *aššašḫu* (from Hurr. *ašhušhu*) in *SMEA* 30-T 8: 11, see CAD A/2: 428a (s.v. *ašḫaušsuḫu*); AHw: 86a, 1545b (s.v. *ašušḫu*); Westenholz 2000: 59 (for previous literature); Pruzsinszky 2000: 351. Note that *wa-aš-ḫa-aš-šu* (Tsukimoto 1991: 290) or *wa-*⸢*šu*⸣*-ḫa-aš-šu* (based on the handcopy in Huehnergard 1983: 22) in *RA* 77-T 4: 19 can be re-

garded as a variant (Tsukimoto 1991: 290). Although J. Goodnick Westenholz assumes this variant form for [x] x-*ḫa-aš-šu* in BLMJE 21: 4 (2000: 56), in view of the photograph and handcopy (Westenholz 2000: 170–171), the partly visible sign trace before *ḪA* would fit neither *AŠ* nor *ŠU*.

AN BI ID RU? – Although two lines of interpretation of this character string (RE 37: 20) have been proposed, neither one is fully convincing. Firstly, Pentiuc reads AN *bi-it-ru* without translation (2001: 39), though connecting it with the word *bitru*, "cutting, sluice; section, half." However, though the word is attested in the Emar texts, it is difficult to explain the first AN, as he admits (2001: 39–40), and the meaning of *bitru* does not seem to fit in the context. The second way of reading is to take it as the name of the goddess (representing her figurine or amulet): ^{d}*Pí-id-ru* (Tsukimoto 1998: 188) or ^{d}*pí-iṭ-ru* (Durand 2013: 42, 43 n. 64), both referring to the goddess *Pdry* (^{d}*pí-id-ra-i*) known in Ugarit. However, this association is rejected by Pentiuc because it disregards the final *y* (2001: 39). Note also that NA_4.*pí-it/ṭ-ru-um* in a list of goods (CT 48 41: r. 4), to which Durand refers, is understood as a stone vessel (CAD P: 442 [s.v. *pitru* D]) or a stone (AHw: 871b [s.v. *piṭru*(*m*), mng. 7]). But even if one takes the word in the dower list to refer to this vessel or stone, the AN still remains to be explained, as in Pentiuc's interpretation.

Appendix 2: Preliminary Remarks on the Expressions of "All the Estate" in the Emar Texts

The concept of "all the (family) estate" appears in the Emar texts using various expressions. Since there is not enough space to deal with all the data here, I limit myself to noting briefly those in the texts in Tables 1–2. When checking those thirteen texts, we find seven relevant occurrences in five texts, and they can be classified into four patterns as follows:

1. *bītu mimmû*[43]
   a) *bītu mimmû*, "house(hold) (and) possessions" (RE 37: 28 [S]; TS 71: 13 [SH])

43 E.g., ⌜E_2⌝-*ia mim-mu-ia*, "my household (and) my possessions" (TS 71: 13) for Pattern 1a. As can be observed in this document, there are cases in which *bītu* is mentioned in the singular in the expressions of Patterns 1–2, although the head of the family actually has plural houses (ll. 19–23 [see n. 35 above]). So I translate the former as "household," but when it is in the plural as in RE 8 (see the following footnote), as "houses."

   b) *bītu gabba mimmû*, "house(hold) (and) all the possessions" (*SMEA* 30-T 8: 7 [cf. also ll. 3, 6; SH]; TS 71: 4, 9 [SH])
2. *bītu* X *mimmû*[44]
   a) *bītu būšu bāšītu mimmû*, "house(hold), properties (and) possessions" (RE 8: 36–37 [S])
   b) *bītu kaspu mimmû*, "house(hold), silver[45] (and) possessions" (Emar VI 31: 17–18 [SH])

At a glance, it is obvious that Pattern 1a is the basic expression for "all the estate," since both the elements *bītu* and *mimmû* are common to all of these occurrences, and are well attested in the Emar texts of both the Syrian- and the Syro-Hittite types. Its variant Pattern 1b is frequently used in the latter type of the texts (e.g., Emar VI 30: 3). Pattern 2a (with its variants) is occasionally attested in the Syrian-type texts (e.g., *RA* 77-T 2 [= *ASJ* 13-T 26]: 13–15), though not restricted to them (e.g., *ASJ* 13-T 31: 4 [SH]). Pattern 2b is known only in Emar VI 31.

The expressions can be varied within the same text, as found in TS 71: Pattern 1b to Pattern 1a. Similar abbreviating can be observed in other texts as well: e.g., *ASJ* 13-T 31: 4 (Pattern 2a′), 11 (Pattern 1a), 15 (*bītu* only).

Abbreviations

ASJ 13-T	Tsukimoto 1991
AuOr 5-T	Arnaud 1987
BLMJE	Westenholz 2000
Ekalte II	Mayer 2001
Emar VI	Arnaud 1986
Iraq 54-T	Dalley and Teissier 1992
RA 77-T	Huehnergard 1983
RE	Beckman 1996b
SMEA 30-T	Arnaud 1992
TS	Arnaud 1991

44 E.g., E_2.HA_2-*ia bu-ši ba-ši-ti mim-mu-ia*, "my houses, (my) properties and my possessions" (RE 8: 36–37) for Pattern 2a. Note that since *būšu* and *bāšītu* always appear as a pair in the Emar texts, I take them as a kind of hendiadys. For the longest example of Pattern 2 (though a variant), that in *ASJ* 13-T 23, see n. 24 above.

45 Reading KU_3.BABBAR-*pí* (Durand 1989: 181). Cf. *gâb*$^!$-*bi* (Arnaud 1986: 44).

Bibliography

Adamthwaite, Murray R. 1994. New Bronze Age Texts from the Middle Euphrates: A Review Article. *Abr-Nahrain* 32: 17–27.

Arnaud, Daniel. 1985. *Recherches au pays d'Aštata: Emar*, VI.1–2. Paris: Éditions Recherches sur les Civilisations.

Arnaud, Daniel. 1986. *Recherches au pays d'Aštata: Emar*, VI.3. Paris: Éditions Recherches sur les Civilisations.

Arnaud, Daniel. 1987. La Syrie du moyen-Euphrate sous le protectorat hittite: contrats de droit privé. *AuOr* 5: 211–241.

Arnaud, Daniel. 1991. *Textes syriens de l'âge du Bronze récent.* AuOrS 1. Sabadell: Editorial AUSA.

Arnaud, Daniel. 1992. Tablettes de genres divers du moyen-Euphrate. *SMEA* 30: 195–245.

Beckman, Gary. 1996a. Family Values on the Middle Euphrates in the Thirteenth Century B.C.E. Pp. 57–79 in *Emar: The History, Religion, and Culture of a Syrian Town in the Late Bronze Age*, ed. Mark W. Chavalas. Bethesda. Maryland: CDL Press.

Beckman, Gary. 1996b. *Texts from the Vicinity of Emar in the Collection of Jonathan Rosen.* HANE/M II. Padova: Sargon.

Beckman, Gary. 2001. Review of Westenholz 2000. *BiOr* 58: 193–196.

Chambon, Grégory. 2008. L'écriture des mesures de longueur à Emar. Pp. 141–151 in d'Alfonso et al. (eds.) 2008.

Cohen, Yoram. 2012. An Overview of the Scripts of Late Bronze Age Emar. Pp. 33–45 in *Palaeography and Scribal Practices in Syro-Palestine and Anatolia in the Late Bronze Age*, ed. Elena Devecchi. PIHANS 119. Leiden: Nederlands Instituute voor het Nabije Oosten.

Cohen, Yoram. 2013. Problems in the History and Chronology of Emar. *Kaskal* 10: 281–294.

Cohen, Yoram and Lorenzo d'Alfonso. 2008. The Duration of the Emar Archives and the Relative and Absolute Chronology of the City. Pp. 3–25 in d'Alfonso et al. (eds.) 2008.

d'Alfonso, Lorenzo, Yoram Cohen, and Dietrich Sürenhagen (eds.). 2008. *The City of Emar among the Late Bronze Age Empires: History, Landscape, and Society.* AOAT 349. Münster: Ugarit-Verlag.

Dalley, Stephanie. 1980. Old Babylonian Dowries. *Iraq* 42: 53–74.

Dalley, Stephanie and Beatrice Teissier. 1992. Tablets from the Vicinity of Emar and Elsewhere. *Iraq* 54: 83–111, Pls. X–XIV.

Démare-Lafont, Sophie. 2010. Éléments pour une diplomatique juridique des textes d'Émar. Pp. 43–84 in *Trois millénaires de formulaires juridiques*, eds. Sophie Démare-Lafont and André Lemaire. HEO 48. Geneva: Librairie Droz.

Durand, Jean-Marie. 1989. Review of Arnaud 1986. *RA* 83: 163–191.

Durand, Jean-Marie. 1990. Review of Arnaud 1986 (cont.). *RA* 84: 49–85.

Durand, Jean-Marie. 2012. Mesures à Emar. *NABU* 2012/69.

Durand, Jean-Marie. 2013. Quelques textes sur le statut de la femme à Émar d'après des collations nouvelles. *Semitica* 55: 25–60.

Durand, Jean-Marie and Francis Joannès. 1990. *kubuddâ'u* à Mari et à Emâr. *NABU* 1990/70.

Faist, Betina. 2008. Scribal Traditions and Administration at Emar. Pp. 195–205 in d'Alfonso et al. (eds.) 2008.

Faist, Betina I. and Juan-Pablo Vita. 2010. angurinnu. *NABU* 2010/7.

Fleming, Daniel E. 1992. *The Installation of Baal's High Priestess at Emar.* HSS 42. Atlanta, Georgia: Scholars Press.

Fleming, Daniel E. 2002. Review of Westenholz 2000. *JESHO* 45: 365–376.

Huehnergard, John. 1983. Five Tablets from the Vicinity of Emar. *RA* 77: 11–43.

Huehnergard, John. 2008. *Ugaritic Vocabulary in Syllabic Transcription*. Rev. ed. HSS 32. Winona Lake: Eisenbrauns.

Lion, Brigitte. 2009. Sexe et genre (1): Des filles devenant fils dans les contrats de Nuzi et d'Emar. Pp. 9–25 in *Femmes, cultures et sociétés dans les civilisations méditerranéennes et proche-orientales de l'Antiquité*, eds. Françoise Briquel-Chatonnet, Saba Farès, Brigitte Lion, and Cécile Michel. Topoi Supplément, 10. Paris: De Boccard.

Marti, Lionel. 2007. Partage d'une maison à Munbâqa. *NABU* 2007/21.

Mayer, Walter. 2001. *Tall Munbāqa – Ekalte*, II: *Die Texte*. WVDOG 102. Saarbrücken: Saarbrücker Druckerei und Verlag.

Michel, Cécile. 2000. À propos d'un testament paléo-assyrien: une femme de marchand « père et mère » des capitaux. *RA* 94: 1–10.

Mori, Lucia. 2003. *Reconstructing the Emar Landscape*. Quaderni di Geografia Storica, 6. Rome: Università degli Studi di Roma "La Sapienza".

Paradise, Jonathan S. 1972. *Nuzi Inheritance Practices*. Ph.D. Dissertation, University of Pennsylvania.

Pentiuc, Eugen J. 2001. *West Semitic Vocabulary in the Akkadian Texts from Emar*. HSS 49. Winona Lake: Eisenbrauns.

Pruzsinszky, Regine. 2000. Review of Westenholz 2000. *WZKM* 90: 344–351.

Roth, Martha. 1989–90. The Material Composition of the Neo-Babylonian Dowry. *AfO* 36–37: 1–55.

Stol, Marten. 1998. The Care of the Elderly in Mesopotamia in the Old Babylonian Period. Pp. 59–117 in Stol and Vleeming (eds.) 1998.

Stol, Marten and Sven V. Vleeming (eds.). 1998. *The Care of the Elderly in the Ancient Near East*. Studies in the History and Culture of the Ancient Near East, 14. Leiden: Brill.

Tsukimoto, Akio. 1991. Akkadian Tablets in the Hirayama Collection (II). *ASJ* 13: 275–333.

Tsukimoto, Akio. 1998. Review of Beckman 1996b. *WdO* 29: 184–190.

Werner, Peter. 2004. *Tall Munbāqa – Ekalte*, III: *Die Glyptik*. WVDOG 108. Saarbrücken: Saarbrücker Druckerei und Verlag.

Westbrook, Raymond. 2001. Social Justice and Creative Jurisprudence in Late Bronze Age Syria. *JESHO* 44: 22–43.

Westbrook, Raymond. 2003. Emar and Vicinity. Pp. 657–691 in *A History of Ancient Near Eastern Law*, vol. 1, ed. Raymond Westbrook. HdO I-72/1. Leiden: Brill.

Westenholz, Joan Goodnick. 2000. *Cuneiform Inscriptions in the Collection of the Bible Lands Museum Jerusalem: The Emar Tablets*. CM 13. Groningen: Styx Publications.

Wilcke, Claus. 1998. Care of the Elderly in Mesopotamia in the Third Millennium B.C. Pp. 23–57 in Stol and Vleeming (eds.) 1998.

Yamada, Masamichi. 1994. Three Notes on Inheritance Transaction Texts from Emar. *NABU* 1994/2.

Yamada, Masamichi. 2013. The Chronology of the Emar Texts Reassessed. *Orient: Reports of the Society for Near Eastern Studies in Japan* 48: 125–156.

Yamada, Masamichi. forthcoming. How to Designate Women as Having Both Genders: A Note on the Scribal Traditions in the Land of Aštata. In *Cultures and Societies in the Middle Euphrates and Habur Areas in the Second Millennium BC*, vol. 1: *Scribal Education and Scribal Traditions*, eds. Daisuke Shibata and Shigeo Yamada. Wiesbaden: Harrasowitz Verlag.

Eiko Matsushima

Women in Elamite Royal Inscriptions: Some observations

For quite some time now, I have had the opportunity to study some of the cuneiform materials that are housed in the National Museum of Iran, Tehran. These materials were found during French-led excavations at Susa and Choga-Zanbil, as well as during American-led excavations at Tall-i Malyan. Many objects that were found at Susa and Choga-Zanbil were transported to the Louvre Museum in Paris, but some of them remain in Tehran.[1] I have been examining the materials in Tehran, and have published a portion of them, along with pictures (Matsushima, Teramura 2012). My colleagues and I continue to work on the texts in Tehran. In the course of my study on Elamite royal inscriptions, I have been especially interested in the fact that the personal names of royal women are often mentioned, especially during the time of Šutrukid Dynasty, that is, around the twelfth century BCE. Even before that period, a number of texts speak of a lineage of the "son of the sister of PN" (= a former king's name).

As far as I know, personal female names are rarely mentioned in Mesopotamian royal inscriptions, although there are occasional exceptions, especially in the Neo-Assyrian period.[2] Elamite inscriptions seem to be unusual, with repeated references to women. Therefore, I am going to present a set of references that I have collected concerning the women in Elamite royal inscriptions.

1 After initial publication in the MAD series, the texts from Susa and Choga-Zanbil have been revised and included in new publications, or in some cases, have been re-edited. Those housed in the Louvre Museum were entirely re-edited by Malbran-Labat 1995 (*IRS*). We also can take advantage of a website created by E. Quintata, www.um.es/ipoa/cuneiforme/elamita.

2 We know of several examples of royal women in the neo-Assyrian periods – such as Sammuramat and Naquia – who played a significant role as royal mothers. As for this topic, see especially Macgregor 2012, a lot of useful bibliographical data can be found on pp. 127–148. See also Svärd 2015. Only once was the expression "beloved wife" applied to Tašmetu-šarrat in an inscription of Sennacherib.

Acknowledgements: For the present study, I took advantage of the following grant-in-aids: Japan Society for the Promotion of Science (= JSPS), International Collaborations, Bilateral Joint Research Project with France (December 31, 2011–December 30, 2014), as well as JSPS KAKENNHI Grant no. 23251013 and Grant No. 24520866.

Eiko Matsushima, Hôsei University, Tokyo; eikoma@ttv.ne.jp

The epithets used to describe them, such as "beloved wife" or "my sister(s)," are impressive. Scholars have discussed matrilineal lineages in Elamite royal families. Some of them even speak of the possibility that brother-sister marriages took place. On the other hand, we know that there were a number of political interregional marriages between the Elamite kings/princes and princesses from Mesopotamian royal families, for example from Ur during the Neo-Sumerian period or from the Kassite Dynasty. Therefore, we can assume that royal women played an important role in Elamite Society.

Recently, Carter (2014) published an important article related to our concerns. Through a meticulous examination of works of art, Carter brings into relief a characteristic feature of Elamite iconography: that is, the frequent appearance of women in art from the late third millennium until the early first millennium BC. She discusses how these representations may reflect the position of Elamite women in society. I would like to discuss the women in royal inscriptions in order to establish some characteristic features of ancient Elam.

1 Examples

1.1 Early Dynasties

It is well known that we do not have enough evidence to reconstruct a history of the Elamite Kingdoms. The Elamites left few written sources and limited types of texts, so we often need to search for mentions or descriptions of them in other Mesopotamian sources, which are often presented from a specific angle. Moreover, we still have many questions relating to the understanding of their language. I do not discuss these difficulties in detail here: what I would like to say is that, in spite of these problems, scholars have tried to reconstruct their history.[3] Thus, we do know that the southwestern part of Iran was under the rule of the "*sukkalmaḫ* of Susa and Elam" from about the nineteenth to the sixteenth century BCE. The chronology of the *sukkalmaḫ*'s kingdom has not been precisely established, but at least thirteen of the tentative *sukkalmaḫ*s or

3 As far as I know, among the works published in the last twenty years, Potts 1999, with a comprehensive bibliography, is actually most useful for obtaining an overall view of the Elamite history and culture. In some other recent publications in the form of proceedings, for example, Álvarez-Mon and Garrison 2011, De Graef and Tavernier 2013, and Kozuh, Henkelman, Jones and Woods 2014, we can also find a lot of recent information. The "2nd Susa & Elam conference: History, language, Religion and Culture" took place in July 2015 at Leuven in Belgium.

*sukkal*s use the title "sister's son (*mār aḫātišu ša*/DUMU.NIN$_9$) of Šilhaha (or Silhaha)," who might have been the founder of the kingdom, or "sister's son of PN (= a former ruler or high-ranking official)."[4] Even some later *sukkalmaḫ*s, such as Kuk-našur III, Tan-Uli, and Temti-halki, used the term "sister's son of Šilhaha." The term then became a purely symbolic and honorific title in order to legitimate their rule. Therefore, even in the early period, the expression "son of the sister of a ruler" had already become very important, even indispensable, for authorizing the legitimacy of the actual ruler. I will not speak any more on this subject, because one of our colleagues in this colloquium has recently discussed it.[5]

1.2 Middle Elamite Dynasties (ca. 1500–1110 BC)

1.2.1 Igihalkid Dynasty (ca. 1400–1200 BC)

First, let me refer to a passage from *IRS* 21, in which Humban-numena (ca. 1350–1340 BCE) tries to legitimate his reign by pointing to his mother's lineage.

> "O Great god, Kiririsha and the (divine) protectors of the earth, (gods) of Liyan, I, Humban-numena, son of Attar-Kittah, I (am) the enlarger of the kingdom, the master (of the) Elamite land, the holder of the Elamite throne, the king of Anzan and Susa; on account of the continuity by (my) mother, (the) great god chose me and loved me; prosperity established (?), the crown restored (?), Inšušinak gave me kingship." (The English translation comes from Potts 1999: 209)

An agate stone object in circular form bears a nine-line inscription in Akkadian that reads as follows:

> "Humban-numena, son of Attar-Kittah, the king of Susa and Anšan, whose name, since (he was) in the womb of his mother, the great gods and Inšušinak, called. For his (own) life, he dedicated this (object)." (MDAI 53 no. 4)[6]

4 See Table 6.1 of Potts 1999: 164–165. Table 5.5 of the same book (p. 147) gives examples of the title "PN 1, 'son of the sister of PN 2 (= former ruler),'" used by Šimaškian kings attested during the Ur III and early Isin periods.

5 Katrien de Graef presented a paper relating to this topic during the 60th *Rencontre Assyriologique Internationale* in Warsaw, and during the conference *Ancient Iran: New Perspectives from Archaeology and Cuneiform Studies* held in Kyoto, Japan, December 6–7, 2014.

6 Stève 1987: 14, no. 4 (copy, transliteration, translation). This type of expression, "whom the gods created *ina* ŠÀ *ummišu*," is used by few kings of late period in Mesopotamia, especially by Assurbanipal. See *CAD* L 166b.

Therefore, Humban-numena occasionally mentions his mother in order to explain his legitimacy, but apart from him, none of the Igihalkids mentions his own mother, or the sister of a former ruler.[7]

The dynasty's most famous king is Untaš-Napiriša, a son of Humban-numena and the daughter of a Kassite king. Like his father, he married a Kassite princess. This princess could be identified with Napir-Asu, whose large bronze statue, with an inscription of her own name, is now in the Louvre Museum.[8] Untaš-Napiriša built many temples in Susa, a religious city, Choga-zanbil, and left a great number of inscribed bricks in which his building activities were recorded. In these bricks, he always refers to himself as "I, Untaš-Napiriša, son (*šak*) of Humban-numena, the king of Anšan and of Susa." As far as I know, he never mentions his mother or his sister.

1.2.2 Šutrukid Dynasty (ca. 1190–1110 BCE)

We have no clear idea of how the Igihalkid dynasty ended. However, the next historical figure to call himself "king of Anšan and Susa" was Šutruk-Nahhunte, the real founder of the Šutrukid dynasty.

Šutruk-Nahhunte (ca. 1190–1155 BCE)

Many bricks and fragments belonging to this king have been found at Susa and other Elamite sites. In these inscriptions, he always introduces himself as "I, Šutruk-Nahhunte, son (*šak*) of Halluduš-Inšušinak, king (*sunki*) of Anšan and Susa."

On the other hand, we have a letter in Akkadian that is now housed in Berlin. It was sent by an Elamite king to an unknown recipient, probably a king of Babylon. A broken part of the text prevents us from identifying the author, but it appears to be Šutruk-Nahhunte.[9] In this text, he meticulously traces his ancestry and lists the Kassite royal daughters married by Elamite kings and princes, his predecessors, and then states that he has the right to sit on the throne of the land of Babylonia because of his descent from the eldest daughter

7 Igi-halki, the founder of the dynasty, says in his inscription in Akkadian, found at Deh-e-Now, that the goddess Manzat-Ištar granted him kingship of Susa and Anšan (MDAI 53, no. 2, pp. 11–13), but does not mention any woman in the family. This may reflect the fact that he took his throne by a kind of *coup d'État* (see Potts 1999: 206–207).

8 Caubet 1994, first published as Harper, Aruz and Tallon 1992: 132–135. She states, in the inscription on her skirt, "I, Napir-asu, wife of Untaš-Napiriša, ..."

9 Potts 1999: 207 and 233; Goldberg 2004; Vallat 2006. Some specialists attribute authorship to Kutir-Nahhunte; see, for example Van Dijk 1986.

of the mighty King Kuligalzu.[10] We know that Šutruk-Nahhunte invaded Babylonia, overthrew the Kassite king in 1158 BCE, and brought an amount of booty back to Susa. This text may explain the background of this invasion. Anyway, it is well-known that, for an Elamite ruler to succeed to the throne as a legitimate heir, his maternal lineage was extremely important, even essential.

Kutir-Nahhunte (ca. 1155–1150 BCE)

The successor of Šutruk-Nahhunte, Kutir-Nahhunte refers to himself in the brick inscriptions as "I, Kutir-Nahhunte, son (*šak*) of Šutruk-Nahhunte, the king of Anšan and Susa."[11]

I would like to add one more reference here.

> "I, Kutir-Nahhunte, son (*šak*) of Šutruk-Nahhunte, king of Anšan and Susa. Humban-numena had built the temple of the goddess Kiririša (...) I (re)construct it. For my life, for the life of Nahhunte-Utu and (the life) of her descendant(s), with this intention I gave it to my goddess Kiririša." (*IRS 37*)

He mentions a woman's name, Nahhunte-Utu, without specifying her title. However, we understand that she must have both already had child(ren) and held a very special position, because the king offered a large gift to a great goddess for her life and for that of her descendant(s).[12]

Šilhak-Inšušinak (ca. 1150–1120 BC)

He succeeded the throne of his (elder) brother, Kutir-Nahhunte. In his inscriptions, he generally states "I, Šilhak-Inšušinak, son (*šak*) of Šutruk-Nahhunte, the king of Anšan and Susa."[13]

It is notable that, in certain inscriptions belonging to Šilhak-Inšušinak, royal women are also mentioned. For example:

> "(...) For my life, for the life of Nahhunte-Utu and (the life) of our descendants, with this intention I gave it (= a sanctuary) to my goddess Kiririša." (*IRS* 39, text 2)

Sometimes, he uses the following expression, without reference to his children:

> "(...) For my life, for the life of Nahhunte-Utu and (the life) of her descendants..." (*IRS* 43).

---

10 Van Dijk 1986.

11 *IRS* 35–37.

12 This reference to "her descendant(s)" rather to "our descendant(s)" makes us understand that she had at least one child before her union with Kutir-Nahhunte. See Stolper 1998: 85.

13 *IRS* 38–50. Sometimes, between his father's name and "king of Anšan and of Susa," he inserts the epithet "beloved servant of Inšušinak."

In some inscriptions, members of the royal family are listed (here, royal women are indicated in italics). There are two different ways in which they are listed.

> Type 1: "For my life, for the life of *Nahhunte-Utu*, for the life of Huteldus-Insusinak, for the life of Šilhina-hamru-lakamar, for the life of Kutir-Huban, for the life of *Išnikarab-huhun*, for the life of *Urutuk-El-halahu*, for the life of *Utu-ehihi-Pinigir* ..."(*IRS* 45)

Here, only Nahhunte-Utu's children by her former husband(s) are mentioned, first the boys, and then the girls.

> Type 2: "For my life, for the life of *Nahhunte-Utu*, my beloved spouse (*rutu hanik-uri*), for the life of Hutelduš-Inšušinak, for the life of *Išnikarab-huhun*, for the life of *Urutuk-El-halahu*, for the life of Šilhina-hamru-lakamar, for the life of Kutir-Humban, for the life of *Utu-ehihi-Pinigir*, for the life of Temti-tur-kataš, for the life of Lila-irtaš, for the life of *Bar-Uli*, my beloved daughter (*pak hanik-uri*) who represents my honor ..." (*IRS* 47, *IRS* 48A, *IRS* 48 B)

Here he mentions all the children of *Nahhunte-Utu*, including those born to her and her former husband(s) (from Hutelduš-Inšušinak to *Utu-ehihi-Pinigir*, six children) as well as those born to her and Šilhak-Inšušinak himself (from Temti-tur-kataš to *Bar-Uli*, three children), stressing his favoritism for his daughter *Bar-Uli*.[14]

In *IRS* 49, he says, "For my life, for the life of Nahhunte-Utu, my beloved spouse, for the life of our descendants," and in *IRS* 50, "for me and for *Nahhunte-Utu*, we who have established the lineage ..."[15]

Nahhunte-Utu's role in the royal family seems to have been particularly important, as she always takes the first position among the persons who are enumerated in the inscriptions written by two successive kings, Kutir-Nahhunte and Šilhak-Inšušinak.[16] Many scholars have assumed that the first husband was Kutir-Nahhunte, who could also have been her brother. Šilhak-Inšušinak declares that *Nahhunte-Utu* is his beloved wife. On the other hand, as we have just seen above, both Kutir-Nahhunte and Šilhak-Inšušinak use the title "son (*šak*) of Šutruk-Nahhunte;" that is to say, they are (half-)brothers. If we accept all of these assumptions, we can conjecture that she married two brothers successively.

---

14 We can find her image in a chalcedony pebble, given to her by his father: British Museum 113886. See Carter 2014: 41, n. 3, and 48, n. 76, as well as *IRS* p. 174.

15 In *IRS* 50, only the descendants of Nahhunte-Utu with former husbands are enumerated, not the children that she had with Šilhak-Inšušinak.

16 As for this extraordinary person, see especially Stolper 1998. See also Potts 1999: 237–238.

A number of scholars believe there were at least two brother-sister marriages here: between Kutir-Nahhunte and Nahhunte-Utu, then Šilhak-Inšušinak and Nahhunte-Utu. Some scholars also conjecture that she had been the partner of her presumed father Šutruk-Nahhunte, to whom she bore Huteldus-Inšušinak, the next king after Šilhak-Inšušinak; it has also been conjectured that she was later the partner of Huteldus-Inšušinak, her own son, to whom she bore a daughter.[17] For us, or for me at least, it seems strange that Nahhunte-Utu conceived nine children in her successive inner-family marriages. It may not be impossible, but would be quite extraordinary. In fact, we do not know her exact lineage. Even if Nahhunte-Utu was the sister of Šilhak-Inšušinak and Kutir-Nahhunte, there are many possible explanations as to why she is called "venerable mother (*amma haštuk*)" in one of the inscriptions of Huteldus-Inšušinak.[18] In any case, it is particularly difficult to reconstruct the family tree of the Šutrukids.[19] It is clear, however, that this woman, Nahhunte-Utu, was the key person in the succession of three consecutive rulers of the Šutrukid Dynasty.

Hutelduš-Inšušinak (ca. 1120–1110 BCE)

The next ruler, Hutelduš-Inšušinak, introduces himself in three ways:

> "beloved son of Kutir-Nahhunte and of Šilhak-Inšušinak" (*IRS* 51);
> "beloved son of Šutruk-Nahhunte, of Kutir-Nahhunte, and of Šilhak-Inšušinak" (*IRS* 52, *IRS* 53);[20]
> "legitimate descendant (*ruhu šak*) of Šilhaha" (Vallat 1978: 98).

He even refers to Šilhaha, the legendary ancestor of Elam, in order to legitimate his rule. On the other hand, he never uses the title *sunki,* which is usually translated as "king," but we will not discuss this problem here.[21] At least we understand, because of this expression, as well as the title of the two former

---

17 See Stolper 1998: 84–85 and the articles mentioned in the article. The conjecture that Hutelduš-Inšušinak's father was Šutruk-Nahhunte, is mainly based on the title of the former, used in some of his inscriptions, as we are going to see below.

18 König 1965, no. 65, l.6, who translates *amma haštuk* as "(meiner) 'Königin'-Mutter." In Hinz and Koch 1987, we see this expression, which is translated as "verehrte Mutter," often being applied to a goddess (pp. 51, 52, and 581). It seems to me that *amma* (= mother) in this expression does not necessarily mean the biological mother.

19 There are many debates among scholars about the Šutrukid family tree. As for the interrelationship of the Šutrukid family, see, other than Stolper 1998, for example, Vallat 1985; Glassner 1994; criticized by Vallat 1997, and *IRS* pp. 173–176. Most of these articles are mentioned in Stolper 1998, but each of their authors has different reasons.

20 In *IRS* 52, he adds after Šilhak-Inšušinak, "beloved brother of *Išunikarab-huhun.*"

21 See Anthonioz and Malbran-Labat 2013.

kings, that Kutir-Nahhunte and Shilhak-Inshushinak were brothers, or half-brothers, and that Huteldu-Inšušinak succeeded his stepfather, Šilhak-Inšušinak, because the latter had been husband to his mother.

In his inscriptions, Hutelduš-Inšušinak mentions his brothers and sisters (*igi šutu*), and occasionally a *ruhu šak* and a *ruhu pak*.[22] For example:

> "Hutelduš-Inšušinak, the enlarger of the kingdom, monarch of Elam and Susa. For my life, for the life of *Išnikarab-huhun*, for the life of *Urutuk-el-halahu*, for the life of Šilhana-hamru-Lakamar, for the life of Kutir-Huban, for the life of *Utu-ehihhi-Pinigir*, for the life of Temti-tur-kataš, for the life of Lili-irtaš, for the life of *Bar-Uli*, for the life of *Melir-Nahhunte*, my brothers and sisters (*igi šutu-upe*), for the life of *Utuk-Hutekašan*, descendant-daughter (*ruhu pak*) of Hutelduš-Inšušinak, for the life of Temti-bitet, descendant-son (*ruhu šak*) of Hutelduš-Inšušinak, for the sake of my family descendants, in Anšan, I renewed and constructed out of baked bricks the sanctuary of the Great God, of the Great Goddess, of Inšušinak and of Simut." (Lambert 1972)[23]

He enumerates all the members of his family here, both men and women. As for his brothers and sisters, he lists all the children of Nahhunte-Utu, including his half-brothers and half-sisters (at least, Temti-tur-kataš, Lili-irtaš, and *Bar-Uli*). The order in which they are listed must be simply from eldest to youngest, making no distinction between male and female. The fact that Hutelduš-Inšušinak does not mention his spouse, but mentions his descendant-daughter and descendant-son, leads us to think of several potential circumstances, as I have already mentioned above, but we do not have enough written materials to form a conclusion about this.

---

22 It is difficult to determine the meaning of *ruhu šak* (descendant-son) and *ruhu pak* (descendant-daughter). Hutelduš-Inšušinak himself once stated that he is a *ruhu šak* of Šilhaha, a legendary ancestor of old Elamite Dynasties. However, he also refers to a young woman and a young man as his *ruhu pak* and *ruhu šak* (in a text published Lambert 1972). Some scholars propose the meaning "nephew" and "niece," whereas others propose "legitimate descendants – male and female." See Vallat 1978: 100, note on l. 17; Vallat 1985 and 1997; Glassner 1994; and a comment of F. Malbran-Labat in *IRS* p. 173–176. See also Hinz and Koch 1987: 1004 (ru-hu), 1045 (ru-hu.pa-ak), and 1045–1046 (ru-hu.ša-ak).

23 The text was first published by Lambert 1972. Next year, Reiner 1973 concluded that it had come from Tall-i Malyan which was definitely identified with Anšan. Since then the text is called the Anšan brick: it was composed in order to commemorate the temple-building activities of Hutelduš-Inšušinak in that city. Previously, many scholars believed that he had died during the well-known expedition to the land of Elam, directed by Nebuchadnezzar I of the second Dynasty of Isin. Today, some of them object to this interpretation and believe that the Elamite king, having been defeated, retreated from Susa to Anšan, where he re-established his role and built the sanctuaries listed on the Anšan brick. See Vallat 1978: 104–105. As many small fragments of this inscription were found at Tall-i Malyan, I believe that Hutelduš-Inšušinak, after his loss of Susa, arrived at Anšan and there reset his rule to some degree, see Matsushima 2016.

2 Observations

We have looked at several royal inscriptions of Middle Elamite Dynasties. What can be inferred from them?

We notice that, in Elamite royal inscriptions, especially in the Šutrukid Dynasty, the names of royal women are frequently mentioned with other male members of the family, often without any gender hierarchy. In the order of enumeration, "beloved wife" takes the first place, and the children follow her from the eldest to the youngest. In some texts by Šilhak-Inšušinak, the boys are mentioned just after the beloved wife Nahhunte-Utu, and then the girls follow them, but in his other texts, there is no distinction between boys and girls. As for Huteldus-Inšušinak, he mentions all the family descendants in simple age order.

Among the royal women, Nahhunte-Utu, a (the) wife of Šilhak-Inšušinak, who already had children with her first husband(s), occupies a special position. We do not know whether she obtained political power. The main theme of Elamite royal inscriptions is the commemoration of a king's temple-building activities; they therefore seldom speak of political events. However, we can be sure that only the male heirs used the title *sunki*, to which we always give the equivalent word "king." No royal woman used this title, or its equivalent. However, this does not necessarily mean that only the male rulers held real political power. Whatever the situation was, the succession from one *sunki* to another was realized without exception. The order of the succession seems to be unique. Šutruk-Nahhunte to Kutir-Nahhunte was a succession from father to son; Kutir-Nahhunte to Šilhak Inšušinak was a succession from elder brother to younger brother; Šilhak-Inšušinak to Huteldus-Inšušinak was a succession from stepfather to stepson, who is actually the son of his wife and possibly his nephew. Maternal lines were important, but it was not a simple matrilineal system.

It is certain that the daughter(s) of a king played a significant role. We do not know exactly who the real parents of Nahhunte-Utu were. They were certainly high-ranking members of the royal family. On the other hand, Šilhak-Inšušinak speaks of a particular favoritism for his beloved daughter (*pak hanik*), Bar-Uli.[24] Huteldus-Inšušinak mentions Utuk-Hutekašan, his descendant-daughter, before his descendant-son. These facts indicate that a chosen daughter was a key person in the succession. Even though she does not sit on the throne, her position must be important: she is also a sister of an actual/future

---

24 See the discussion of Anthonioz and Malbran-Labat 2013: 421.

king. This reminds us of the traditional expression "son of a sister of Šilhaha (/of a former ruler)," which was frequently used in the *sukkalmah* period.

In her article, Carter (2014) discusses the frequent appearance of women in iconography that distinguishes Elamite art from contemporary Mesopotamian styles, then she adds one observation:

> "Women are absent in the Neo-Assyrian reliefs until the seventh century, and it even seems possible that the female images that appear late in the Neo-Assyrian period (the Assurbanipal banquet scene and the Esarhaddon bronze plaque) may reflect the increasing contact with Elam, both diplomatic and adversarial."[25]

Therefore, the remarkable presence of women can be seen in both written sources and works of art. This certainly reflects women's significant position in both family and society.

As I noted above, the succession hierarchy of power in Elam was not based on a simple patriarchal lineage, nor was it based on a simple matrilineal or simple brother-brother line.[26] A brother-sister relationship was also strong, firm, and important. We cannot find an exact term to categorize this order of succession. What is clear, however, is that daughters and sisters held an important position in Elamite society.

***

As we have just seen, the family system of the Elamite world was extremely complicated. It may seem too abrupt to refer here to the Tale of Genji, written by a court lady in eleventh-century Japan. Nevertheless, I would like to introduce a comparative viewpoint at the end of this article.

The relationships between heroes and heroines in this Tale are very complicated; for example, Prince Genji's youngest brother was in fact his own son with his stepmother, and as this young brother became the new emperor, Genji became the emperor's father.[27]

In the tale, we see that Genji behaved like the stepfather of a princess, whose mother had been one of his lovers in the youth, in order to marry her to the crown prince. He also chose his first wife, who had a very noble origin, to be the stepmother of his own daughter, whom he had conceived with a young woman from the provinces, so that his daughter achieved a high status

25 Carter 2014: 49.

26 Malbran-Labat 1995 gives some comments on this problem, especially in p. 173–176.

27 This episode is treated as a secret in the tale, but contemporaneous readers accepted and enjoyed it.

because of her stepmother and therefore was worthy of becoming the future spouse of the future crown prince.[28] We can find descriptions of half-brothers and half-sisters everywhere in the Tale, double or triple marriages – not only for men, but also for women – and adoptive daughters. I wonder if a similar kind of relationship – stepfather, stepmother, adoptive daughter, half-brother, half-sister, etc. – could have played an important role in the complex interrelationships of Elamite royal families. Thus, for example, if Nahhunte-Utu appears with nine "children" in royal inscriptions, it is not certain that they were all her own children. In addition, even if there were some inner-family marriages, the biological relationship between a male and a female might not be as close as we would assume after reading compact phrases in inscriptions.

We still know little about the Elamite history. However, as far as we understand it, from the second half of the third millennium onward, there were several political "centers" in the Lowlands and Highlands of what is now Iran – that is, the "Elamite Land." The relationships between different Elamite tribes, as well as the relationships between those tribes and certain powerful Mesopotamian city-states, were complicated. There had often been political inter-family marriages, both between different Elamite families and between Elamites and Mesopotamians. Royal women, whatever their origin may have been, might have played an important role, as they assured a biological line for the rulers, thus legitimizing the succession of political power. I suppose that this must be the background of the complicated inner-family relationships in the Elamite Dynasties.

The Tale of Genji shows us that, in spite of the complications among the high aristocrats, they all behaved in a friendly manner with each other and enjoyed a highly cultured life. Of course, we must be very careful when making such a comparison between two different and distant societies. However, I imagine that aristocratic Elamite families, although they maintained a complicated system of marriage and succession, took advantage of this complexity in order to consolidate their reigns.

Abbreviation

IRS see Malbran-Labat 1995.

28 It was very important for a nobleman to marry his daughters to (future) emperors. Once his daughter had a son, he would have the chance to become the grandfather of a future emperor, which would assure him enormous political power.

Bibliography

Álvarez-Mon, Javier and Mark B. Garrison (eds.). 2011. *Elam and Persia*. Winona Lake: Eisenbrauns.

Anthonioz, Stéphanie and Florence Malbran-Labat. 2013. Approche historique et philologique du titre royal 'likame/we riări'. Pp. 417–428 in *Susa and Elam. Archaeological, Philological, Historical and Geological Perspectives*, eds. Katrien D. Graef and Jan Tavernier. MDP 58. Leiden: Brill.

Carter, Elizabeth. 2014. Royal Women in Elamite Art. Pp. 41–61 in *Extraction & Control: Studies in Honor of Matthew W. Stolper*, eds. Michael Kozuh, Wouter F. M. Henkelman, Charles E. Jones, and Christopher Woods. SAOC 68, Chicago: The Oriental Institute, The University of Chicago.

Caubet, Annie (ed.). 1994. *La cité royale de Suse: trésors du Proche-Orient ancien au Louvre*. Paris: Edition de la Réunion des musées nationaux.

De Graef, Katrien and Jan Tavernier (eds.). 2013. *Susa and Elam. Archaeological, Philological, Historical and Geological Perspectives*. MDP 58. Leiden: Brill.

Glassner, Jean-Jacques. 1994. Ruhušak – mar ahatim: La transmission du pouvoir en Elam. *JA* 58: 219–236.

Goldberg, Jeremy. 2004. The Berlin Letter, Middle Elamite Chronology and Šutruk-Nahhunte I's Genealogy. *Iranica Antiqua* 39: 33–42.

Harper, Prudence O., Joan Aruz, and Françoise Tallon (eds.). 1992. *The Royal City of Susa. Ancient Near Eastern Treasures in the Louvre*. New York: The Metropolitan Museum of Arts.

Hinz, Walther and Heidemarie Koch. 1987. *Elamisches Wöterbuch*. Berlin: D. Reimer.

König, Friedrich Wilhelm. 1965. *Die elamischen Königsinschriften*. AfO Beiheft 16. Graz.

Kozuh, Michael, Wouter F. M. Henkelman, Charles E. Jones, and Christopher Woods (eds.). 2014. *Extraction & Control: Studies in Honor of Matthew W. Stolper*. SAOC 68, Chicago: The Oriental Institute, The University of Chicago.

Lambert, Maurice. 1972. Hutelutush-Insushnak et le pays d'Anzan. *RA* 66: 61–76.

Macgregor, Sherry Lou. 2012. *Beyond Hearth and Home; Women in the Public Sphere in Neo-Assyrian Society*, SAAS 21. Helsinki: The Neo-Assyrian Corpus Project.

Malbran-Labat, Florence. 1995. *Les inscriptions royales de Suse*. Paris: Réunion des Musées Nationaux.

Matsushima, Eiko and Hirofumi Teramura. 2012. *Brick Inscriptions of the National Museum of Iran. A Catalogue*. Ancient Text sources in the National Museum of Iran 1. Iran-Japan Project of Ancient Texts. Kyoto: Nakanishi Print.

Matsushima, Eiko. 2016. A Royal Inscription of Huteldush-Inshushinak from Tall-I Malyan. Pp. 93–99 in Ancient Iran, *New Perspectives from Archaeology and Cuneiform Studies*, ed. Kazuya Maekawa, Ancient Text Sources in the National Museum of Iran 2, Kyoto.

Potts, Daniel T. 1999. *The Archaeology of Elam: Formation and Transformation of an Ancient Iranian State*. Cambridge: Cambridge University Press.

Reiner, Erica. 1973. The Location of Anšan. *RA* 67: 57–62.

Stève, Marie-Joseph. 1987. *Nouveaux Mélanges épigraphiques. Inscriptions royales de Suse et de la Susiane*. MDAI 53. Nice: Serre.

Stolper, Matthew W. 1998. Nahhunte-Utu. *RlA* 9/1–2: 82–86.

Svärd, Sanaa. 2015. *Women and Power in Neo-Assyrian Palaces*, SAAS 23, Helsinki: The Neo-Assyrian Corpus Project.

Vallat, François. 1978. Une brique de Hutelutush-Insushnak. *Cahier de la DAFI* 8: 97–107.

Vallat, François. 1985. Hutelutuš-Inšušinak et la famille royale élamite. *RA* 79: 43–50.
Vallat, François. 1997. Nouveau problèmes de succession en Elam. *Iranica Antica* 32: 53–70.
Vallat, François. 2006. La chronologie méso-élamite et la lettre de Berlin. *Akkadica* 127: 123–136.
Van Dijk, Jan. 1986. Die dynastischen Heiraten zwischen Kassiten und Elamern: eine verhängnisvolle Politik. *Or* 55: 159–170.

Virginie Muller
Women and their Activities in Divinatory Texts

The topic of "women," from a gender-based perspective, is now reaching Assyriological studies.[1] Many papers have been published in this field in recent years, but very few deal with divinatory texts and especially omen collections.[2] Indeed, U. Koch-Westenholz (2001) was the only one to present a paper on this topic during the 47th *Rencontre Assyriologique Internationale* devoted to Sex and Gender in the Ancient Near East. In her contribution, "Everyday Life of Women According to First Millennium Omen Apodoses," she identified four general themes: marriage, childbirth, death and adultery. A. K. Guinan has also written about sexual behaviors mentioned in omens, and concerning women's sexual lives (incestuous relationships ...).[3] However, a detailed examination of this abundant documentation can provide more information on women. It generally dates from the first millennium BC, although it was known since the Old Babylonian period. Firstly, the place of women in family life can be developed (relationships with men, marriage, procreation, various family problems). Women can also be described as independent persons, in professional life as well as in social life. Finally, some remarks can be made about their representation and the multiple negative descriptions given of them.

1 Sources

1.1 Women in divinatory texts: A brief outline

The divinatory texts are very rich in data. They contain many omens about all kinds of subjects, which have been grouped in large thematic series. But this

1 See Lion 2007 for a definition of the notion of gender, its introduction in assyriological researches, and an overview on historical studies on women according to cuneiform texts.
2 See Maul 2003 for a general view of this kind of documentation.
3 Guinan 1997 and Guinan 2001 (mainly about *Šumma ālu* 103 and 104).

Virginie Muller, Archéorient, Maison de l'Orient et de la Méditerranée, Lyon; Virginie.Muller1@univ-lyon2.fr

corpus is of unequal value for the knowledge of women's lives in the Ancient Near East.

Most of the information comes from unsolicited divination, where the omens are derived from acts and events that are accidental, uncontrollable or from everyday life (habits ...). The collection *Šumma ālu*[4] gathers several tablets dealing with the circumstances of everyday life and also many allusions to women in different situations. The omen compendia *Šumma izbu*,[5] which is about births of malformed humans and animals, displays women in the protases but always in a procreative role. The *Šumma alamdimmû* group of texts[6] contains predictions from the physical aspect of people, and the sub-series *Šumma sinništu qaqqada rabât*, "When the head of a woman is big," is more particularly interesting. It focuses on women's physical appearance and offers some remarks on women's qualities and characteristics. Hemerologies and menologies, known by the series *Iqqur īpuš*, give the list of favorable and unfavorable days and months to do things, and more particularly information about when to get married.[7] Astrology, documented mainly by the collection *Enūma anu enlil* and by other planetary omens,[8] shows celestial signs usually pertaining to the king or the state; but omens from the movements of the planet Venus deal with women, mostly married or pregnant.[9] Finally, the *ziqīqu*-texts,[10] which deal with unsolicited signs revealed in dreams, give only very few and already well-known data.

Information from solicited omens, where the diviner examines a situation that he has voluntarily created, is also poor in details. The series *barûtu*,[11] dealing with the examination of sacrificed animals' organs, and especially the liver, gives various indications. Finally, the *tamītū*-texts are Neo-Assyrian questions addressed to the gods Šamaš and Adad, where the questioner wanted to know

4 See the general introduction by Maul (2003: 58–62). Freedman (1998 and 2006) gives a new edition of tablets 1 to 40. For others tablets of this compendium, see the old edition of Nötscher (1929 and 1930).

5 See Maul (2003: 62–64) for an introduction and Leichty 1970 for the edition of the text.

6 See the recent edition in Böck 2000, and see Maul (2003: 66–68) for a brief presentation.

7 See the edition in Labat 1939 and 1965.

8 See, for example, the edition by Virolleaud (1905–1912) and the four volumes of the BPO series.

9 BPO 3. See also Koch-Westenholz (2001: 307) for the link between Venus planet and childbirth.

10 See Maul (2003: 68–69) for a short introduction, and Oppenheim 2008 for the edition of the texts.

11 See for example the books of Koch-Westenholz (2000 and 2005), and some texts published in Heeßel 2007 and 2012.

whether something would occur or not.[12] It is mainly about military campaigns or people's safety (king, soldiers ...), but a few texts deal with the aspects of family life, notably mentioning pregnant or married women.

1.2 Women in protasis and apodosis: distribution of the mentions

Omen compendia are formulated in a casuistic structure: a protasis that recorded a hypothetical situation (or conditional clause: "If such-and-such is seen/ happens") followed by an apodosis that described the portended event in a declarative clause.[13] In the apodosis, mentions of women in various situations are common, as seen below.

However, the protases are usually concerned with men: "If a man does/ sees/...," "If something happens in the man's house ...," and women appear in the protasis only in a few situations. The absence of women in protases can perhaps be explained if we take the term NA or LU_2/*awīlum* with the meaning "someone, anybody," in a neutral gender. Thus, texts specify MUNUS/*sinništu* only in particular situations, as do the therapeutic texts. These latter references make use of the generic term NA or LU_2/*awīlum* to describe pathologies, while the term MUNUS/*sinništu* makes its appearance only in cases related specifically to female genital problems.[14]

In *Šumma izbu*, many omens begin with "If a woman is pregnant (BE MUNUS *arātma*)" or "If a woman gives birth (BE MUNUS U_3.TU)," but women's frequent presence is only in respect to their procreative role, and the apodosis could be about any kind of subject. However, one extract speaks with interesting precision and named the "woman of the king (MUNUS.LUGAL)," as in this example: "If a woman of the king gives birth to two identical boys – the woman will be happy."[15]

12 See, for example, the edition in Lambert 2007. To my knowledge, there are no specific mentions of women asking such a question.

13 This binary structure, protasis-apodosis, is peculiar to scientific compositions, as for example medical texts or law collections; see Fincke 2007 for the most developed and recent analysis of the similarities between omens and laws. Moreover, they share some topics, such as adultery ...; see also Guinan 2014 for a comparison on marriage and sexual relationship contained in both kinds of texts.

14 See for example the edition in Labat 1951.

15 BE MUNUS.LUGAL 2 UŠ.MEŠ *mitḫārtī* U_3.TU MUNUS DUG_3 ŠA_3 IGI-*mar* – *Šumma izbu* 4: 52. The "woman of the king" appears only in protasis from *Šumma izbu* 4: 47–61.

In some extracts of *Šumma ālu*, usually in tablets relating to actions of "soil animals" (snake, scorpion, lizard or gecko), women appear in the protasis.[16] They can do the action themselves, for instance "If a woman catches a snake,"[17] or they can be one of the elements of the action observed, as for example: "If a lizard carrying a snake is seen by a woman," or else: "If a lizard enters a woman's lap."[18] Other protases describe specific women: "If a lizard walks about on an unmarried young woman (KI.SIKIL)," or: "If a man divorces his first-ranking wife (NITLAM)."[19] Once again, the social status of women is highlighted. The woman's condition of pregnancy has a very important role too, as in these two examples: "If a snake falls onto a pregnant woman (*erīti*), her foetus [...]," and: "If a gecko climbs up onto a woman who is not pregnant (MUNUS NU $PEŠ_4$), that woman will become pregnant, give birth and be happy."[20] In the protasis, women also appear linked with one of their goods, as in these two examples: "If a snake climbs up and down the inner wall in a woman's house," and: "If a scorpion is seen in a woman's couch."[21] In each case, the apodosis affects the woman directly. It could be a good prediction: "that woman will be lucky" or "will have a good reputation,"[22] or else it could be a bad prediction: "she will go about unhappily," or: "that woman will die."[23]

---

16 On royal bowls from the Neo-Assyrian period, the names of female owners were replaced by the symbol of the scorpion. Thus, a scorpion was used to represent palace women (queens, ladies of the harem). Moreover, the scorpion was the symbol of Išhara whose role, linked to Ištar, has a great importance during weddings. See mainly Niederreiter (2008: 59–61), with previous bibliography on the role of scorpion in the Neo-Assyrian period (note 24). See the contribution of Otto in this volume.

17 DIŠ MUŠ MUNUS DIB-*su* – *Šumma ālu* 23: 104.

18 DIŠ EME.ŠID MUŠ *nāšîma* MUNUS IGI - *Šumma ālu* 32: 51′, and DIŠ EME DIR *ana* UR_2 MUNUS TU-*ub* – *Šumma ālu* 32: 9′ (Assur tradition). In this last example, the same text mentions the man's lap but also his neck, his leg ... which are not mentioned for the woman.

19 DIŠ EME.ŠID *ina* UGU KI.SIKIL DU.DU-*ak* – *Šumma ālu* 32: 64′, and DIŠ NA NITLAM-*šú īzib* – *Šumma ālu* 104: 44.

20 DIŠ MUŠ *ana muḫḫi erīti* ŠUB-*ut ša* $ŠA_3$-*ša* [...] – *Šumma ālu* 26: 8′, and DIŠ MUŠ.GIM.GURUN.NA *ana* UGU MUNUS NU $PEŠ_4$ E_{11} MUNUS BI $PEŠ_4$ U_3.TU-*ma* DUG_3 $ŠA_3$ BI – *Šumma ālu* 33: 37′.

21 *ina* E_2 MUNUS – *Šumma ālu* 23: 48, and *ina* KI.NA_2 MUNUS – *Šumma ālu* 30: 64′. In this last example, the text mentions the man's couch but also his table, his chair ... which are not mentioned for the woman.

22 MUNUS BI DINGIR TUK-*ši* – *Šumma ālu* 23: 104, and MUNUS BI MU MUNUS.SIG_5 TUK-*ši* – *Šumma ālu* 33: 38′.

23 *ina* $ŠA_3$. HUL DU.DU-*ak* – *Šumma ālu* 32: 120′, and MUNUS BI BA.UG_7 – *Šumma ālu* 32: 9′.

2 Women in the family sphere

2.1 A dependent person

Women appear mostly in regards to their relationship with men in many apodoses from various kinds of omens. The woman can be, very often, a "wife (DAM LU_2/NA)," with sometimes more precisely "of the owner of the house (EN E_2 BI DAM-*su*)," or else the "principal wife (MUNUS.UŠ.DAM/NITLAM)."[24] She can be a "daughter (DUMU.MUNUS)" or a "daughter-in-law (E_2.GI_4.A)," sometimes named "of the house (E_2)." More rarely, she is a "mother (AMA)"[25] or a "widow (munus*almānum*)."[26] She can also be a "woman loved by the prince (MUNUS *narāmat* NUN)"[27] and a "woman of the king (MUNUS.LUGAL),"[28] which usually means a concubine. So these terms, almost always used in the apodosis, describe the family status of women as a dependent person, namely, dependent on a male. In most cases, women are passive protagonists of the action and there is a prediction of death for them, rarely with such precision as "she will die in the middle of the year."[29]

2.2 Women as wives

Omens also give information about marriage, especially in two chapters of the series *Iqqur īpuš*, which deal with the best moment "to take a wife (DAM TUK-*ši*)," or "to make a wife enter in his house (DAM-*su ana* E_2-*šú* TU)."[30] It also concerns the kind of man a woman will take as her husband. For example, an extract mentions that a woman will marry the "husband of a friend (KI DAM TAB.BA)," and another says that she will marry "a prominent person (DU-GUD)."[31] The nature of the union is also described, as for example a second wedding mentioned in these extracts: "that man will marry another woman," and: "If a man divorces his first-ranking wife and then another (man) marries

24 *Šumma ālu* 104: 44 and K.3601: r. 28 (BPO 3).
25 *Šumma ālu* 19: 56′.
26 BPO 3: r. 2 and *Šumma sinništu qaqqada rabât*: 57, 71 and 135. For a study on widows, see for example Roth 1991–1993 for the Neo-Babylonian period.
27 *Multabiltu* 2: 32–33 (Koch-Westenholz 2000 no. 110).
28 *Šumma izbu* 4: 47–61, as seen above § 1.2. For concubines, see Parpola 2012.
29 DAM LU_2 *ina* $MURUB_4$ MU $UŠ_2$ – *Manzāzu* 6: 13 (Koch-Westenholz 2000).
30 *Iqqur īpuš* § 61 and § 62. On this topic, see also Koch-Westenholz 2001: 305.
31 *Šumma ālu* 32: 51′ and *Šumma ālu* 32: 64′.

her."[32] In these situations, women appear, again, only as potential brides or spouses.

Marital difficulties are also described in omens, as in this apodosis: "the man's wife will cause her spouse trouble,"[33] or in this one: "strife (will arise) between man and wife in the man's house"[34]. Living together can also be a problem, as written in this text: "men's wives will not live with their husband."[35] The texts never describe wrongs coming from the husband, so it seems that difficulties are always the wife's fault. But the many apodoses which deal with the dissolution of marriage, using the verb "divorce (TAG$_4$)"[36] or "separate (KUD)"[37] and sometimes both in the same sentence,[38] do not specify whether the divorce was requested by the wife or by the husband.

However, a menology from Emar, "[...] with his wife, his heart will be happy,"[39] and a passage from *Šumma ālu*, "his spouse will delight him,"[40] show that happy marriages can also exist, but according to omens this is not the standard situation.

2.3 Women as bad wives

2.3.1 Thieves and liars

Frequently, the qualifications and actions of women give a negative impression of them, especially when they are married. They are introduced as thieves several times in apodosis, as in these two examples. The first comes from an Old Babylonian haruspicy: "the wife of a priest will steal the *asakkum*; she will be

32 LU$_2$ BI *šanītamma iḫḫaz* – *Šumma ālu* 32: 52′, and DIŠ NA NITLAM-*šú īzibma šanûmma* TUK-*si* – *Šumma ālu* 104: 44.

33 DAM LU$_2$ DAM-*sa ušazzaq* – *Šumma ālu* 5: 75; *Iqqur īpuš* § 13: 7, § 17: 6 and § 21: 6; Emar VI.4 no. 611: 182′.

34 DU$_{14}$ DAM *u* DAM *ina* E$_2$ NA – *Šumma ālu* 37: 118.

35 LU$_2$ *ana* DAM.MEŠ-*ši-na* NU TUŠ.ME – BM 40111: 20′ (BPO 3).

36 For example: "If a snake falls onto a man and woman and separates them, the man and woman will divorce" (DIŠ MUŠ *ana* UGU NITA *u* MUNUS ŠUB-*ma uparrissunūti* NITA *u* MUNUS TAG$_4$.MEŠ – *Šumma ālu* 6: 79).

37 For instance: "If a snake falls onto a man and a woman, the man and the woman will separate" (DIŠ MUŠ *ana* UGU NITA *u* MUNUS ŠUB-*ut* NITA *u* MUNUS KUD.MEŠ – *Šumma ālu* 23: 114).

38 For example: "The man and women will separate; they will divorce" (NITA *u* MUNUS KUD.MEŠ TAG$_4$.MEŠ – *Šumma ālu* 23: 34). See also Guinan (2014: 108–110) for other examples of divorce in omens.

39 DAM-*su* ŠA$_3$.BI DU$_{10}$.GA – Emar VI.4 no. 615: 19′.

40 DAM-*su* ŠA$_3$-*šú* HUL.LA – *Šumma ālu* 6: 109.

burnt,"[41] and the second one from *Šumma ālu*: "a thieving woman of the house will remove the *lamassu*-figurines."[42] We should notice that priestesses are also described stealing the sacred property.[43]

A wife can also appropriate the goods of her husband, as in this text from *Iqqur īpuš*: "his goods will slip out (from him); they will fall in the hands of his wife,"[44] or else in this apodosis of *Šumma ālu*: "the wife of that man will take his goods."[45]

In another text, a man doesn't trust his wife so he asks the god in a *tamītu* whether she has told him the truth.[46] The lack of trust is sometimes justified, as in an apodosis of a liver omen predicting that "a man's wife will constantly betray secrets."[47] But this situation of treason happens for servants or nobles too.[48]

2.3.2 Adulterous and murderous women

Several times the omens predict adultery on the part of wives, as in these celestial omens of the planet Venus which indicate: "men's wives will commit adultery and run after men," and later in the same text: "men's wives will have adulterous relations; adultery will increase in the land."[49] An interesting example even specifies: "the man's wife has become pregnant by another man."[50] We can notice that, as in law collections, men committing adultery is never mentioned, because it is not important: men do not carry babies, so a man's adultery is without consequences.

---

41 *ênum asakkam ištanarriq iqallû-ši* – Bu 89-4-26: 11–13 (Nougayrol 1950: 29).

42 MUNUS E$_2$ BI *šāraqti* ^{d}LAMMA E$_3$ – *Šumma ālu* 16: 8. See also the stealing by Rachel of the *teraphim* of her father, the family figurines of ancestors in the Bible (Vita 2008). The domestic stealing by wives is well documented in law texts; see Démare-Lafont 1999: 291–300.

43 See below 3.1.2.

44 NIG$_2$.GA-*šú* ZAH$_3$ *ina* ŠU DAM-*šú* ŠUB – *Iqqur īpuš* § 31: 10.

45 DAM LU$_2$ BI NIG$_2$.ŠU-*šú* TI-*qí* – *Šumma ālu* 24: 56′. We also find in omen texts: "... the man's wife will die and he will take her property" (DAM NA UG$_7$-*ma* NIG$_2$.ŠU-*šá* TI-*qí* – *Šumma ālu* 26: r. 7′), but it might be justified by the death of the wife.

46 *tamīt* ^{munus}*annannītu*^{tu_4} *itti annanna* DAM-*šá* GI.NA.MEŠ *itammi* (Lambert 2007, *tamītū*-question no. 21: 1–9).

47 DAM LU$_2$ AD.HAL E$_3$.MEŠ – *pān takalti* 4: 9 (Koch-Westenholz 2000).

48 See for instance *pān takalti* 4: 36 (Koch-Westenholz 2000).

49 DAM LU$_2$.MEŠ *igarrušāma* EGIR NITA.MEŠ *idullā* – VAT 10218: 90, and DAM.MEŠ LU$_2$ *inakkū nīku ina* KUR *imaddū* – K.2226: 32 (BPO 3). See Koch-Westenholz (2001: 308) for others examples of adultery in omens.

50 DAM LU$_2$ *ana* MAN-*ma erāt* – *pān takalti* 15: r. 9′ (Koch-Westenholz 2000).

Another fault of the wife, "the man's wife will get her husband killed," appears few times in different apodoses of *Barûtu*-texts.[51] The use of the factitive verbal form *ušdāk* suggests again that women are only the instigators, and not the actors, of these murders. An apodosis concerning this situation is even more specific: "the man's wife will send (a letter) again and again about killing her husband: 'kill my husband and marry me!'"[52] Adultery leading to the murder of the husband is a male fear well known in law texts too.[53]

2.3.3 Witches and other negative women

The malevolent wife who does witchcraft is also well attested. In the sub-series *Šumma sinništu qaqqada rabât* especially, a woman is qualified as sorceress, *kaššāpat*, many times on account of her thick or pointed fingers described in the apodosis.[54] In an apodosis from *Šumma ālu*, the victim of the witchcraft is clearly identified: "the mistress of the house will cast a spell on her spouse."[55]

But sometimes it is not mentioned whether the witch is married or a single woman, as in this liver omen: "a witch (MUNUS.UŠ$_{11}$.ZU) will gather dust on which the feet of the man has walked, but she will be caught and killed."[56] In the same way, many apodoses from the sub-series *Šumma sinništu qaqqada rabât* introduce women, without any relevant details, as bad persons: "she is obscure," "she is a manipulator," or "she will bring ruin."[57]

2.4 Women as mothers

Divinatory texts largely focus on women in their reproductive function, as well as on the outcome of pregnancy. This is easily understandable in regards to

51 DAM LU$_2$ DAM-*sà ušdāk* – *Multābiltu* 2–3: 1 (Koch-Westenholz 2005); *Manzāzu* 6: 5 (Koch-Westenholz 2000); Heeßel 2012 no. 37: 25.

52 DAM LU$_2$ *ana* GAZ DAM-*šá* KIN.KIN DAM GAZ-*ma yâši aḫzani* – *Manzāzu* 6 (Koch-Westenholz 2000).

53 See Hammu-rabi's law § 153, for example, and the study of Démare-Lafont 1999: 397–405.

54 *Šumma sinništu qaqqada rabât*: 126, 131 and 133. For women and witchcraft, see Sefati and Klein 2001.

55 NIN E$_2$ DAM-*sà ukaššap* – *Šumma ālu* 38: 8. The variant "The man's wife (DAM LU$_2$) will cast a spell on her husband" also exists (*Multābiltu* 2–3: 4; Koch-Westenholz 2005).

56 SAHAR.HI.A *kibis* GIR$_3$ LU$_2$ MUNUS.UŠ$_{11}$.ZU TI.MEŠ-*ma* DIB-*ma* GAZ – *pān takalti* 3: 35 (Koch-Westenholz 2000).

57 Respectively: *eklet* – *Šumma sinništu qaqqada rabât*: 114, *eppešet* – *Šumma sinništu qaqqada rabât*: 221, 223, and *mulappinat* – *Šumma sinništu qaqqada rabât*: 137, 141 and 174.

the importance of offspring in Mesopotamian society, but also because pregnancy was associated with great anxiety. Pregnancy was an important and dangerous time, as the worries of questioners show in *tamītū*-texts. One man asks if his wife will survive her pregnancy, and another man worries about his wife who has complications in her pregnancy.[58] In omen collections, many different sentences predict the outcome of the pregnancy. It could be, for example, "she will have an easy childbirth."[59] But in many cases, it is about a problematic pregnancy and childbirth, expressed in different ways as she could "suffer pregnancy bleeding",[60] or she could "have troubles or difficulties giving birth."[61] More seriously, the prediction can be "she will die with the child in her womb," or, as in this Old Babylonian omen from Sippar: "The pregnant woman will die in labor."[62]

When apodoses are not about the pregnancy, they predict the sex of the unborn baby, almost always a boy (NITA): "she will give birth to a male,"[63] or: "what is inside that woman will be male."[64] The importance of having a boy is also shown by a *tamītū*-text where a man asks if his wife will only give him daughters.[65]

Omens also deal with family problems involving the relationship between mothers and their children. For example, a woman can banish her child in "barring her door to her daughter."[66] She can also get rid of her children by selling them: "the man's wife will be distracted and sell her children for money."[67] And some dramatic problems can lead to the murder of the mother: "The man's wife will be killed by her own sons."[68] As shown by these three exam-

---

58 Lambert 2007, *tamītū*-question no. 12: iii 1–17 and ii 4–14.

59 MUNUS.MEŠ *ina* U_3.TU SI.$ŠA_2$.MEŠ – K.2226: 20 and VAT 10218: 22 (BPO 3). See Couto-Ferreira (2014: 292–294) for a general approach to problems with childbirth and terminology.

60 GIG *naḫšātī* GIG-*at* – Heeßel 2012 no. 56: r. 12.

61 MUNUS.MEŠ *ina* U_3.TU NU SI.SA_3.MEŠ / *ušapšaqā* – K.8688: 19 and K.2226: 19 (BPO 3). See also the variant: "Women will give birth but will not do so easily" (MUNUS.MEŠ U_3.TU.MEŠ-*ma ul uštēšerā* – VAT 10218: 25).

62 MUNUS.ME *gadû šá* $ŠA_3$-*šina* UG_7.MEŠ – K.2226: 18 (BPO 3), and *erītum ina aladiša* BA.UG_x – Jeyes 1989 text 1: 6.

63 NITA *ullad*/U_3.TU – *Šumma ālu* 23: 23; *Šumma ālu* 24: 53′; *Šumma ālu* 26: r.8 and *Šumma ālu* 32: 63′.

64 MUNUS BI *šá* $ŠA_3$-*šá* NITA – *Šumma ālu* 33: 36′.

65 Lambert 2007, *tamītū*-question no. 12: i 11–17.

66 AMA UGU DUMU MUNUS-*šá* KA_2-*šá* TAB – VAT 10218: 193 (BPO 3).

67 DAM LU_2 IGI.MEŠ-*šá* GUR.MEŠ-*ma* DUMU.MEŠ-*šá ana* KU_3.BABBAR SUM-*in* – *Šumma ālu* 24: 1. See also the contribution of Justel (2013) on women as sellers of children during crisis in Emar (for instance text ASJ 10 E).

68 DAM LU_2 DUMU.MEŠ-*šá* GAZ.MEŠ-*ši* – *Multābiltu* 2–3, commentary 4: 40 (Koch-Westenholz 2005).

ples, as far as women are concerned inside the family sphere, divinatory texts seem to deal exclusively with difficult relationships: women appear as victims or as bad mothers.

3 Women in society

On the other hand, women are also described as independent persons who can act by themselves.

3.1 Activities and professions

3.1.1 Women's activities in the city

The most interesting and most detailed source which provides information about the activities and professions of women is the first tablet of the *Šumma ālu* series. Its protases list different kinds of men present in the city, and sometimes give their women equivalents, for the "female administrative officials (*šabrātu*)" and the "female ecstatics (MUNUS.GUB.BA.MEŠ)."[69] But this extract also introduces other activities for men, such as the "*kurgarrû*-performers (LU_2.KUR.GAR.RA.MEŠ)," the "porters (*pētû*.MEŠ)," the "mourners (*ēpiš* BA-LAG.DI)" or the "thieves (LU_2.NI_2.ZU.MEŠ)," without giving the female equivalents.[70] However, the lack of women professions here may not be significant, as female thieves are mentioned elsewhere in divinatory texts.[71] But on another hand, there are no words for female gatekeeper nor for female *kurgarrû*-performer in the rest of the cuneiform documentation,[72] which could mean that women cannot perform these jobs. But, this could also suggest that the two female activities named here were important enough in the political and religious life to be mentioned.

But this part of the text also quotes less expected categories of women: the "lame women (MUNUS.BA.AN.ZA.MEŠ)" and the "women with mental defects

69 *Šumma ālu* 1: 102 and 108.

70 *Šumma ālu* 1: 93, 97 and 106.

71 See above § 2.3.1. (stealing wife) and below § 3.1.2. (stealing priestess).

72 See for instances CAD P and CAD K (the MUNUS.KUR.GAR.RA existed but she is almost never mentioned).

(MUNUS.LIL.MEŠ)."[73] They are, in this extract, mentioned among other deficient persons: the "deaf men (U_2.HUB.MEŠ)," the "blind men (IGI.NU.TUK.MEŠ)" or the "cripples (KUD.KUD.MEŠ)," for example.

It does not seem that the presence of these kinds of female persons in a city was negative: indeed, the apodoses are the same as for men. Thus, the presence of idiot and lame people involves "that city will be happy (URU BI $ŠA_3$.BI DUG_3.GA)," and the presence in the city of numerous ecstatics and administrative officials brings respectively "troubles for the city (*nazaq* URU)" and "dispersal of the city (BIR URU)."[74]

3.1.2 Religious functions

The religious functions of consecrated women, nuns and priestesses (NIN DINGIR), are documented, briefly, as in a broken *Šumma ālu*'s protasis: "If a *nadītu* [...]."[75] It is also written in many apodoses of *Šumma sinništu qaqqada rabât* which mentions "She is a spouse of the god (DAM DINGIR/*ilānât*)." Moreover, a menology, "If in Elul month, an eclipse occurs at the dawn, Sîn wants a high-priestess,"[76] suggests that the nomination of the priestess could sometimes be decided by the god, as it was the case for the daughter of Nabonidus.[77] But most extracts with priestesses show them involved in forbidden sexual relations, as in this apodosis from haruspicy: "an **en**-priestess will have illegitimate sexual relations,"[78] or in an Old Babylonian haruspicy text: "a familiar of the temple will have sex with a high-priestess."[79]

In many apodoses of *Barûtu*-divination, the priestesses, like the dishonest wives, were also involved in thieving acts. For example, in this apodosis from

73 *Šumma ālu* 1: 87 and 88. The birth of a female idiot is also mentioned in *Šumma izbu* 1: 53. We find also other kinds of particular people, as with the birth of a female dwarf (MUNUS.NA.AN.ZA – *Šumma izbu* 1: 55) or of a woman with beard (MUNUS.MEŠ SU_6 *zaqnā* – *Šumma ālu* 1: 153).
74 *Šumma ālu* 1: 94, 95 and 98.
75 *Šumma ālu* 1: 139.
76 *Sîn* NIN DINGIR.RA APIN-*eš* – *Iqqur īpuš* § 73: 6. For the question relative to the nomination of the high-priestess, see Westenholz 2006.
77 See AO 6044, published in Dhorme 1914.
78 NIN.DINGIR *uštaḫḫa* – Heeßel 2012 no. 56: r. 14.
79 *muttallik* E_2 DINGIR EN *ittanīak* – Bu 89-4-26: 11–13 (Nougayrol 1950: 29). See Barberon (2012: 224) for the different aspects of the sexual life of the consecrated women.

a liver omen: "The *enu*-priestess will constantly steal the sacred property; she will be caught and killed."[80]

3.1.3 Other activities

In omen texts, a female domestic function is alluded to several times, through the NIN E_2. However, it is difficult to say if she is the "owner of the house" or a "simple housewife," or both. An omen from *Šumma izbu*, "The lady of the house will mourn,"[81] explains one of the domestic functions of this lady, as does the mother in this other extract: "The members of the family will be taken prisoners of war and their mother will mourn over them,"[82] or in this one: "The children of the house will be taken as booty and their mother will mourn for them."[83] A text from *Barûtu* mentions another domestic occupation, very briefly: "these female weavers (MUNUS.UŠ.BAR.MEŠ) will die in two months,"[84] without more information. As for the wife or the daughter, the prediction is usually negative: "she will die," "she will not prosper" or "hard times will afflict her."[85] We also find more positive, but less rife, predictions as "she will be happy" or "she will be lucky."[86]

3.1.4 Palace women

The term MUNUS E_2.GAL, contained in extracts from *Šumma izbu*, does not seem to mean the queen or a royal woman, but rather a concubine or a servant of the palace. Good things can happen to her, as in "If a woman of the palace

80 *enu* KU_3.AN *ištanarriq iṣṣabbatma iddâk* – *Manzāzu* 1: r. 4′, r. 5′ and r. 6′ (Koch-Westenholz 2000). See also above for wives as thieves.
81 NIN E_2 *idammum* – *Šumma izbu* 18: 6.
82 DUMUS.MEŠ E_2 NAM.RA TI-*ma* AMA-*šunu* UGU-*šunu idammum* – *Šumma izbu* 18: 5.
83 DUMU.MEŠ E_2 -*šallata* TI-*ma* AMA-*šunu* UGU-*šunu idammum* – *Šumma ālu* 41: 37′.
84 MUNUS.UŠ.BAR.MEŠ *šina ana* 2 ITI BA.$UŠ_2$.ME – Heeßel 2007 no. 14: ii 14–17. See for example Michel 2006 for Old Assyrian women who spend their days weaving, but are never referred to as "weavers."
85 Respectively $UŠ_2$ – *Šumma ālu* 19: 52′, NIN E_2 NU SI.SA_2 – *Šumma izbu* 4: 7, and NIN E_2 *dannatū* DIB-*sa* – *Šumma ālu* 37: 147.
86 Respectively DUG_3 $ŠA_3$ IGI-*mar* – *Šumma izbu* 4: 52, and NIN *šēda* TUK-*ši* – *Šumma izbu* 16: 11′.

gives birth to two identical boys – the woman will be happy,"[87] or, as it usually occurs, a fatal fate: "she will die violently."[88]

In these divinatory texts, we also find the NIN.KUR, which could designate the queen, as do the terms DAM LUGAL or NIN-*tu*,[89] and sometimes specifically "queen of the enemy land."[90] We also find the "prince's wife (DAM NUN)."[91] And, just as for ordinary women, death is also predicted for the queens and princesses. It should be noted that royal women are rarely mentioned. Even in astrological texts, which are directly related to the king, we do not find further mentions of royal female persons, in contrast to the prince, for example.[92]

3.2 Social rise and fall

Finally, the divinatory texts also document the social rise and positive changes in the women's condition. For example, a pregnant woman "will acquire fame,"[93] maybe in relation with her unborn child. Other occurrences deal with an unknown woman that "will become important,"[94] and a text coming from extispicy even specifies: she will be as "important as the king,"[95] suggesting a political context. On the other hand, a *Barûtu*-text from Sippar deals with the death of "a well-known woman (^{munus}*sinništum edûtum*),"[96] but doesn't specify how she had gained this fame. This social ascent is also possible for slaves or servants, as it is shown in this apodosis where one of them becomes "equal to her mistress,"[97] but only because she is loved by her master.

There are also attested examples where women are powerful, notably in this omen: "If a woman gives birth to a pig: a woman will seize the throne,"[98]

---

87 MUNUS DUG$_3$ ŠA$_3$ IGI-*mar* – *Šumma izbu* 4: 52.
88 MUNUS E$_2$.GAL *ina* ^{giš}TUKUL UG$_6$ – *Šumma izbu* 21: 52′. See also above § 1.2.
89 "The lady of the land will die" (NIN KUR UG$_6$ – *Šumma izbu* 5: 73); "the wife of the king will die" (DAM LUGAL UG$_6$ – *Šumma izbu* 14: 2); "the queen will die" (NIN-*tu* UŠ$_2$ – *Manzāzu* 2: 30; Koch-Westenholz 2000).
90 NIN-*tu šá* KUR KUR$_2$ – Heeßel 2007 no. 80–82: 8.
91 *Šumma ālu* 43: 34.
92 For the terms MUNUS E$_2$.GAL, DAM NUN ..., see Melville 2004.
93 MUNUS BI MU TUK-*si* – *Šumma ālu* 38: 90′.
94 MUNUS BI DUGUD – *Šumma ālu* 38: 89′.
95 UGU LUGAL DUGUD-*it* – Heeßel 2007 no. 80–82: 11.
96 BM 96962: 4′ (Jeyes 1989, text 1).
97 GEME$_2$ EN-*šá irâmšima mala* NIN-*šá imaṣṣi* – *Multābiltu* 1: 10–11 (Koch-Westenholz 2005).
98 BE MUNUS ŠAH U$_3$.TU MUNUS AŠ.TE DIB-*bat* – *Šumma izbu* 1: 8.

which can suggest either regency by the queen-mother, or an usurpation.[99] But it is worthwhile to note that this situation is correlated with an unrealizable omen, "giving birth to a pig" (unless this sentence means "giving birth to a fetus *which looks like* a pig"). Another omen could be interpreted as an attestation of female political participation: "If a snake falls into the middle of some women, those women will be eradicated."[100] The previous line of the compendium gives the same situation for an assembly (*puḫri*) of men (with a broken apodosis), so it is possible that this gathering of women was meant to have the same purpose as that of the males, but a bad fate befell them. Collective revolts of women are also documented in two celestial apodoses: "there will be a revolt of women in the land" and "women will kill men with weapons."[101]

If the social rise of women is attested, social fall and negative fates are too. It could be simply expressed as "downfall of the wife of the house,"[102] but the predictions are sometimes more specific, as in these two instances: "The man's wife will become a prostitute,"[103] or "she will be in prison,"[104] but texts do not specify why they deserve such a fate.

***

Some concluding remarks can be drawn from the few and scattered divinatory extracts which deal with the topic of women. There are even fewer divinatory extracts dealing with their activities.

These divinatory documents usually define women by their relationship to men, or by their procreative function, and thus in passive roles. Only a few texts deal with women as independent persons and describe their own activities or professional lives. We therefore mostly rely on other sources (epistolary, contracts and administrative texts) to document the roles of women and their various activities in the domestic, religious, institutional and working spheres.

---

99 The only example of a woman ruling an empire is Šammu-ramat, spouse of Šamšī-Adad V, who was regent of Assyria during few years until her son, Adad-nīrārī III, came of age (see RIMA 3 A.0.104.3).

100 DIŠ MUŠ *ana* MURU$_2$ MUNUS.MEŠ ŠUB-*ut* MUNUS.MEŠ *šinātu tappassasu* – *Šumma ālu* 26 iii: 12′.

101 DU-*iz* ZI-*ut* MUNUS.MEŠ *ina* KUR GAL$_2$ – K.229: 35, and NITA.MEŠ ^{giš}TUKUL *ušamqatū* – VAT 10218: 124 (BPO 3).

102 ŠUB DAM E$_2$ – *Šumma ālu* 37: 80.

103 DAM LU$_2$ *ana ḫarimuti* E$_3$ – *Multābiltu* 2–3: 2 (Koch-Westenholz 2005). For prostitution, see Cooper 2006.

104 *ina kīli iqatti* – *Šumma sinništu qaqqada rabât*: 232.

But an interesting point is that women are badly treated in omen collections. Indeed, most predictions are negative: "she will die," "she will bring ruin," "she will have no success"...[105] In the same way, women are also described in doubtful and difficult relationships with their husbands or with their children. They are depicted with evil behaviors too, committing negative actions such as witchcraft, theft or adultery, which, it seems, are intended to disturb their husbands and might even threaten the social order. So the description of women shown by divinatory texts is usually negative. Of course, positive predictions exist, such as "she will be happy, lucky, or honest,"[106] and we saw examples of important women, so it is not a completely negative picture. But these are rare, especially compared to predictions concerning men which, even if they can sometimes be negative, are more often positive in nature.

One might consider that this negative depiction of women could perhaps be linked to the fact that there are fewer mentions of women in omen collections than men, even in spontaneous divination which would normally represent events in daily life. If these documents were representative of real life, there should be more signs related to females. However, the lack of mention of women may be explained if we consider that these texts were written by and for men, like other kinds of texts.[107] Thus, omens take the man's, and more particularly the husband's, perspective, showing their vision and their fears. So, it is men who point to the bad aspects of women and describe them the way they see them, and not how they really are.

Abbreviations

BPO 3	Reiner 1998.
Emar VI.4	Arnaud 1987.
RIMA 3	Grayson 1996.
Iqqur īpuš	see Labat 1951.
Manzāzu	see Koch-Westenholz 2000.
Multābiltu	see Koch-Westenholz 2005.

105 Of course, men are also going to die according to omens, but less often and there are also for them indications of life expectancy, of gain ...

106 Respectively DUG_3 ŠA_3 BI – *Šumma izbu* 4: 52, *šēda* TUK-*ši* – *Šumma izbu* 16: 11′, and *išarat* – *Šumma sinništu qaqqada rabât*: 176–177, for example.

107 In the Ancient Near East, reading and writing were usually the prerogative of men, see Charpin 2008: 31–60. But see also Lion (2007: 54–57) for the few examples of documentation emanating from women.

Pān takalti see Koch-Westenholz 2000.
Šumma ālu see Freedman 1998 and 2006.
Šumma izbu see Leichty 1970.
Šumma sinništu qaqqada rabât see Böck 2000.

Bibliography

Arnaud, Daniel. 1987. *Recherches au pays d'Aštata, Emar VI tome 4, Textes de la bibliothèque, transcriptions et traductions.* Paris: Édition Recherche sur les Civilisations.

Barberon, Lucile. 2012. *Les religieuses et le culte de Marduk dans le royaume de Babylone.* Archibab 1. Mémoires de NABU 14. Paris: SEPOA.

Böck, Barbara. 2000. *Die Babylonisch-Assyrische Morphoskopie.* AfO Beiheft 27. Wien: Institut für Orientalistik der Universität Wien.

Charpin, Dominique. 2008. Lire et écrire à Babylone. Paris: PUF.

Cooper, Jerrold S. 2006. Prostitution. *RlA* 11: 12–22.

Couto-Ferreira, Maria Erica. 2014. She Will Give Birth Easily: therapeutic approaches to childbirth in 1st millennium BCE cuneiform sources. *Dynamis: Acta Hispanica ad Medicinae Scientiarumque Historiam Illustrandam* 34: 289–315.

Démare-Lafont, Sophie. 1999. *Femmes, droit et justice dans l'antiquité orientale. Contribution à l'étude du droit pénal au Proche-Orient ancien.* OBO 165. Fribourg: Academic Press and Göttingen: Vandenhoeck & Ruprecht

Dhorme, Édouard. 1914. La fille de Nabonide. *RA* 11: 105–117.

Fincke, Jeanette C. 2007. Omina, die göttlichen ‚Gesetze' der Divination. *JEOL* 40: 131–147.

Freedman, Sally. 1998. *If a City is set on a Height: the Akkadian Omen Series Šumma Alu ina Mēlê Šakin. vol. 1, Tablets 1–21.* Occasional Publications of the S. N. Kramer Fund 17. Philadelphia: University Museum.

Freedman, Sally. 2006. *If a City is set on a Height: the Akkadian Omen Series Šumma Alu ina Mēlê Šakin. vol. 2, Tablets 22–40.* Occasional Publications of the S. N. Kramer Fund 19. Philadelphia: University Museum.

Guinan, Ann Kessler. 1997. Auguries of Hegemony: the Sex Omens of Mesopotamia. *Gender and History* 9: 462–479.

Guinan, Ann Kessler. 2001. Erotomancy: Scripting the Erotic. Pp. 185–201 in Parpola and Whiting 2001.

Guinan, Ann Kessler. 2014. Laws and Omens: Obverse and Inverse. Pp. 105–121 in *Divination in the Ancient Near East: A Workshop on Divination Conducted during the 54th Rencontre Assyriologique Internationale at Würzburg, 20–25 July 2008*, ed. Jeanette C. Fincke. Winona Lake: Eisenbrauns.

Grayson, A. Kirk. 1996. *Assyrian Rulers of the Early First Millennium BC II (858–745 BC)*. The Royal Inscriptions of Mesopotamia: Assyrian Periods, 3. Toronto: University of Toronto Press.

Heeßel, Niels. 2007. *Divinatorische Texte I. Terrestrische, teratologische, physiognomische und oneiromantische Omina, Keilschrifttexte aus Assur literarischen Inhalts 1.* WVDOG 116. Wiesbaden: Harrassowitz.

Heeßel, Niels. 2012. *Divinatorische Texte II. Opferschau-Omina, Keilschrifttexte aus Assur literarischen Inhalts 5.* WVDOG 139. Wiesbaden: Harrassowitz.

Jeyes, Ulla. 1989. *Old Babylonian Extispicy: Omen Texts in the British Museum*. Leiden and Istanbul: Nederlands historisch-archaeologisch instituut te Istanbul.

Justel, Josué J. 2013. The Economic Role of Women during the Crisis in Emar (Syria). http://refema.hypotheses.org/175.

Koch-Westenholz, Ulla. 2000. *Babylonian Liver Omens: the chapters Manzāzu, Padānu, and Pān tākalti of the Babylonian extispicy series mainly from Aššurbanipal's Library*. Carsten Niebuhr Institute of Near Eastern Studies 25. Copenhagen: University of Copenhagen, Museum Tusculanum Press.

Koch-Westenholz, Ulla. 2001. Everyday Life of Women According to First Millennium Omen Apodoses. Pp. 301–309 in Parpola and Whiting 2001.

Koch-Westenholz, Ulla. 2005. *Secrets of Extispicy: the Chapter Multābiltu of the Babylonian Extispicy Series and Nisirti bārûti. Texts mainly from Aššurbanipal's Library*. AOAT 326. Münster: Ugarit Verlag.

Labat, René. 1939. *Hémérologie et ménologie d'Assur*. Paris: Librairie A. Maisonneuve.

Labat, René. 1951. *Traité akkadien de diagnostics et pronostics médicaux, transcription et traduction*. Leiden: Brill.

Labat, René. 1965. *Un calendrier babylonien des travaux, des signes et des mois*. Paris: Librairie Honoré Champion.

Lambert, Wilfred G. 2007. *Babylonian Oracle Questions*. Mesopotamian Civilizations 13. Winona Lake: Eisenbraun.

Leichty, Erle. 1970. *The Omen Series Šumma Izbu*, Texts from Cuneiform Sources 4. New York: J. J. Augustin Publisher.

Lion, Brigitte. 2007. La notion de genre en assyriologie. Pp. 51–64 in *Problèmes du genre en Grèce ancienne*, ed. Violaine Sebillotte-Cuchet and Nathalie Ernoult. Paris: Publications de la Sorbonne.

Maul, Stefan M. 2003. Omina und Orakel. A. Mesopotamien. *RlA* 10: 45–88.

Melville, Sarah. 2004. Neo-Assyrian Women and Male Identity: Status as a Social Tool. *JAOS* 124: 37–57.

Michel, Cécile. 2006. Femmes et production textile à Aššur au début du IIème millénaire avant J.-C. Pp. 281–297 in *Spécialisation des tâches et sociétés*, ed. Aline Averbouh *et al.*, *Techniques & Culture* 46. Nanterre.

Niederreiter, Zoltán. 2008. Le rôle des symboles figurés attribués aux membres de la cour de Sargon II. *Iraq* 70: 51–86.

Nötscher, Friedrich. 1929. Die Omen-Serie *šumma âlu ina mêlê šakin* (CT 38–40): I. *Or SP*: 39–42.

Nötscher, Friedrich. 1930. Die Omen-Serie *šumma âlu ina mêlê šakin* (CT 38–40): II. *Or SP*: 51–54.

Nougayrol, Jean. 1950. Textes hépatoscopiques d'époque ancienne conservés au Musée du Louvre (III). RA 44: 1–44.

Oppenheim, Leo A. 2008. *The Interpretation of Dreams in the Ancient Near East*. 2nd edition. Piscataway: Gorgias Press.

Parpola, Simo. 2012. The Neo-Assyrian Royal Harem. Pp. 613–626 in *Leggo! Studies Presented to Frederick Mario Fales on the Occasion of His 65th Birthday*, ed. Giovanni B. Lanfranchi, Daniele Morandi Bonacossi, and Cinzia Pappi. Wiesbaden: Harrassowitz.

Parpola, Simo and Robert Whiting (eds.). 2001. *Sex and Gender in the Ancient Near East. Proceedings of the 47th Rencontre Assyriolgique Internationale, Helsinki, July 2–6, 2001*, Helsinki: The Neo-Assyrian Corpus Project.

Reiner, Erica. 1998. *Babylonian Planetary Omens. Part three: Venus. In collaboration with D. Pingree.* Mesopotamian Civilizations 11. Winona Lake: Eisenbrauns.
Roth, Martha T. 1991–1993. The Neo-Babylonian Widow. JCS 43–45: 1–26.
Sefati, Yitschak and Jacob Klein. 2001. The Role of Women in Mesopotamian Witchcraft. Pp. 569–587 in Parpola and Whiting 2001.
Virolleaud, Charles. 1905–1912. *L'Astrologie Chaldéenne: le livre intitulé Enuma Anu-Il-Bel.* 14 fascicules. Paris: P. Geuthner.
Vita, Juan-Pablo. 2008. The Patriarchal Narratives and the Emar Texts. A new Look at Genesis 31. Pp. 231–241 in *The city of Emar among the Late Bronze Age empires*, ed. Lorenzo D'Alfonso, Yoram Cohen, and Dietrich Sürenhagen. AOAT 349. Münster: Ugarit-Verlag.
Westenholz, Joan Goodnick. 2006. Womenof religion in Mesopotamia: The high priestess in the temple. *Canadian Society of Mesopotamian Studies Journal* 1: 31–44.

Saana Svärd

Studying Gender: A Case study of female administrators in Neo-Assyrian palaces

The aim of this article is to propose a new methodological approach for the study of gender in Mesopotamia and make some preliminary suggestions as to how it could be used.[1] I will first outline the history of Assyriology and gender studies. In the second part of the paper I will outline a proposition on how women's work and gender could be researched. There I will introduce my case study of texts relating to *šakintu*s, the female administrators of the Neo-Assyrian palaces. Some preliminary remarks will be given on gender construction in the Neo-Assyrian Empire based on textual evidence concerning the *šakintu*s.

1 Assyriology, women and gender

Although Mesopotamian women have been an object of study for more than a hundred years,[2] most early publications treated women as an isolated category. "General" history was male history, where exceptional women occasionally intruded. In most of these studies the position of women was seen from an ethnocentric Western perspective.[3] Related to this are the "Orientalizing" tendencies of many of these early explorations on the status of women in Mesopotamia. In particular, the idea of "harem" in the ancient Near East was fascinating to both artists and scholars.[4] Furthermore, as part of "the eternal Orient," ancient Near Eastern women were often seen as if floating in their own bubble of otherness in a permanent ethnographic present.[5]

1 Some parts of the approach outlined here were briefly discussed in Svärd 2015: 14, 173.

2 Viktor Marx (Marx 1902) apparently being the first, or one of the first ones, although I have been unable to obtain a copy of his long article. For a comprehensive bibliography, now slightly outdated, see Asher-Greve 2002b.

3 See, e.g., Brooks 1922. For a critical overview of studies of Mesopotamian women, see Asher-Greve 2002b: 33–35.

4 The idea of "Orientalism" was originally presented by Edward Said (Said 1978). For Orientalism and Assyriology, see Holloway 2006b. See Solvang 2006; Asher-Greve 2006; and Van De Mieroop 1999: 145–152 on Orientalism and women in Assyriology.

5 As a specific example of this, even in the 1990s, see Beaulieu 1993: 13: "Due to particular circumstances some women could gain positions of influence but rarely of real power, and

Saana Svärd, Department of World Cultures / Assyriology, Helsinki; saana.svard@helsinki.fi

Ethnocentric and androcentric studies on women were challenged when studies relating to gender[6] emerged in the 1960s. The different approaches that developed under this rather large rubric can be described as "waves" of scholarship. These waves are more methodological than chronological, but the birth of the first wave can be placed in the 1960s. In a nutshell, the aim of this first wave was to write women "into" history. In historical research, the endeavors of men had been the most important object of study and this is what the first wave set out to change.[7]

Assyriology was mostly oblivious to these developments. Nonetheless, the 33rd *Rencontre Assyriologique Internationale* (1986) in Paris had "women" as its theme. The conference received justified criticism, but it did bring women's history into more mainstream Assyriology.[8] Before 1986, few works were dedicated to women, but in the years following the 33rd RAI, the number of articles and books concerned with women or gender markedly increased.[9] Here one should note, however, that the field of Assyriology is not uniform. In the case of Neo-Assyrian studies, much of the textual evidence became widely available only during the 1980s and 1990s. Thus, the first wave of gender scholarship in the field of Neo-Assyrian studies appeared later. There are several studies now, but most of them are recent.[10]

The second wave of feminist scholarship began in the late 1970s. No longer content to merely write women into history, many scholars now concentrated on studying the subordinate status of the female gender. This was done from two interconnected perspectives. Some assumed that women were always and

this often through the agency of their male relatives. In many respects the mentality which prevailed at that time has survived in the Near East until the modern era."

6 Labels like "women's studies" or "feminist studies" are often used for such research, sometimes interchangeably. Using "feminist studies" highlights the political commitment of these studies, whereas "women's studies," while seemingly neutral, highlights the exceptionality of women and implies the need to study half of population as a "special issue." Neither one seems quite right for the purposes of this article. Therefore, I use the general rubric "gender studies" – actually born much later – to refer to research which is intent on discovering more about women, men and gender.

7 See further Van De Mieroop 1999: 138–139 and Bahrani 2001: 14–15.

8 Papers of the conference are published in Durand 1987. For reviews of the conference, see Westenholz 1990 and Asher-Greve 2000: 2–4.

9 See the bibliography in Asher-Greve 2002b. Also noteworthy is Cameron and Kuhrt 1983, which predated the 33rd RAI.

10 One of the first to discuss the topic was Paul Garelli (Garelli 1998). Sarah Melville was the first to produce a book-length study (Melville 1999) as well as articles (Melville 2004, 2005). Macgregor 2012 is a recent monograph. An improved version of my PhD disseration (defended and published in 2012) was recently released (Svärd 2015).

everywhere a universally oppressed group. Other scholars believed that matriarchy was the historical reality of the ancient world and that patriarchy developed only in the late prehistoric and early historic periods. This view, of course, concentrated a great deal of attention on the study of the ancient Near East, where written history began. The weakness inherent in both perspectives is the idea of a uniform entity of patriarchy, which can be applied to or assumed for all of the ancient Near East. Defined as male power, patriarchy is not an unproblematic framework for understanding gender. It disregards other kinds of variables (age, class, specific location in time and place, etc.),[11] and it spreads like a blanket of snow across the vast geographical and chronological space of the ancient Near East, obstructing from view the myriad details and variations relating to gender.

One of the main achievements of the second wave was the development of the notion of gender, or the idea that biological sex is distinct from a socially constructed identity (gender). This influential idea was explicitly included in the title of the Helsinki *Rencontre* in 2001: "Sex and Gender in the Ancient Near East." This RAI was a similar landmark as the 33rd RAI in Paris. Although the aims of the Helsinki RAI were not theoretically ambitious,[12] it still marks the emergence of the second wave for Assyriology. Nonetheless, the impact of the second wave remained marginal. Although the number of books and articles steadily kept increasing, there are very few Assyriological studies that engage with oppression theory or matriarchy theory or use the strict dichotomy of sex/gender.[13] One could argue that in many ways, gender studies in Assyriology managed to skip the second wave altogether. The first-wave project of writing women into history was accepted as a worthwhile research goal at the Paris RAI, if not earlier, but it seems that it took so long for the ideas of gender research to reach the Assyriological community that most scholars who were interested in the topic skipped the second wave and proceeded directly to using the more sophisticated methodology of the third wave. This can also be seen in the journal *NIN: Journal of Gender Studies in Antiquity*, which was first published a year before the Helsinki RAI. Although short-lived (four issues, from 2000 to 2003), it reflected the growing interest in gender studies and its contents included contributions from all three waves.

11 Van De Mieroop 1999: 139–142; Bahrani 2001: 15–18; and Meyers 2014.

12 See Parpola 2002. Even at the Helsinki RAI, few scholars explicitly acknowledged the sex-gender division in their contributions (see papers of the conference published in Parpola and Whiting 2002).

13 Assyriological studies here meaning studies using primary sources in the original language. For an overview, see Van De Mieroop 1999: 141–142. For a recent overview on gender studies and archaeology, see Vogel 2012.

For the second wave, there were some books and articles that dealt with ancient Near Eastern women, but most of them were written by scholars from other fields of study. This meant that they were not really even noticed in Assyriology or, if they were, they were not considered important, because the authors lacked the first-hand experience with texts.[14]

The third wave of women studies began in the 1980s. Even more than the previous two waves, the third wave is a collection of myriad approaches, which are primarily connected to each other in their determination to deconstruct the basis of scientific knowledge production. Queer studies, masculinity studies, performativity, possible duality of gender structure and many other issues relating to the body and sexuality are all part of the third wave. The main point of agreement of the third wave relates to the nature of knowledge production. Instead of seeing the researcher as someone who is seeking to uncover the truth that is "out there," they advocate the framing of research as a project for making sense of different phenomena. This includes the knowledge that defines normative gender roles and sexuality. When knowledge production is seen in this way, as *production*, the traditional dichotomies of research – male and female, sex and gender, matriarchy and patriarchy, public and private, power and oppression – become suspect and the question arises, are these useful categories for producing knowledge? [15]

For the third wave, the dichotomy of sex and gender is problematic. It has been suggested that there is no biological sex outside of its social construction. This relates to the more philosophical discussion on the relationship between reality and language. We cannot talk about biological sex without talking about the meanings attached to it. Consequently, sex can never exist outside the norms of culture.[16]

Some studies on ancient Mesopotamian women employ these views or partially engage with them. There are studies relating to the importance of gender studies and analyses of how the field should proceed.[17] One also finds studies relating to the body and gender in iconographical evidence.[18] Furthermore, gender ambiguity and the possibilities of a third gender, as well as sexuality and its manifestations, have been researched.[19] A newly emerging area is the

14 Asher-Greve 2000: 3.

15 For an excellent overview of the third wave, see Bahrani 2001: 18–25.

16 For an overview of this discussion, see Bahrani 2001: 21–23.

17 Especially Westenholz 1990; Asher-Greve 1997; Van De Mieroop 1999: 137–159; Asher-Greve 2000; Bahrani 2001: 7–28; and Assante 2003 come to mind.

18 E.g., Winter 1996; Bahrani 2001; Asher-Greve and Sweeney 2006; and Assante 2006.

19 E.g., Guinan 1997; Nissinen 1998; McCaffrey 2002; Teppo 2008; Zsolnay 2013; and Peled 2014.

study of masculinity.[20] All in all, many of the third-wave studies have used iconographical and/or archaeological evidence as their main source material. For text-based research, traditionally understood as the core area of Assyriology, studies that engage with third-wave ideas are indeed few. Although the number of scholarly articles and books on gender in Mesopotamia has steadily increased, such research questions are still in the margins of Assyriological research. Concerns have been expressed about the lack of interest in issues of gender in the field of ancient Near Eastern studies.[21]

All in all, the discipline is mostly marked by first-wave studies, namely writing women into the history of ancient Mesopotamia. This is, of course, absolutely necessary. At the same time, however, first-wave studies have a number of problematic aspects. Essentialism is certainly one of them. Pursuits that have been seen by researchers as "essentially female," such as child-rearing or textile work, are often the focus of first-wave studies. For instance, child-rearing is an important topic of research, but researching child-rearing does not necessarily tell us anything about the construction of gender. Femininity and masculinity cannot be reduced to essentialist concepts, as masculinity and femininity are always cultural constructs. Therefore, cultural differences need to be properly acknowledged and grappled with.[22]

Thus, for good reason, third-wave research has shifted its focus from the study of women to the study of gender systems. The dynamic relationships of gender systems as part of other cultural and social systems form a challenging and fruitful new area of research. A methodological emphasis on intersectionality is based on the idea that women cannot be studied alone, because gender is part of all social relations.[23]

2 A new approach and the case study of *šakintus*

The problem of current research on Mesopotamian gender systems is twofold. On one hand, the naïve belief in objectivity in science has come to an end. On the other hand, modern methods and theories cannot be used indiscriminately on ancient material. Many of the more specifically third-wave approaches are

---

20 E.g., Zsolnay 2010 and Suter 2012.
21 Van de Mieroop 2013: 90.
22 Here I agree fully with Bahrani 2001: 8–10.
23 See also Garcia-Ventura in this volume.

not ideally suited for fragmented Mesopotamian material.[24] A case in point is the work of Judith Butler, which is at the center of many third-wave approaches. In second-wave studies, it was common to find an essential difference between "sex" (traditionally seen as referring to biological bodies) and "gender" (the meaning attributed to these bodies by society). Consequently, Butler's idea of gender as a repeated social performance and not as an expression of preexisting identity was groundbreaking in many ways.[25] It can be said to be the most significant contribution in recent decades of feminist studies. Butler's work has its roots in philosophy and is certainly thought-provoking, but it is difficult to grasp how it can be fruitfully applied to the meagre textual remains of Mesopotamia.

Since the aim of my research is to utilize primary sources for case studies, I have found the work of sociologists Candace West and Don H. Zimmerman to be more useful. In their now classic article "Doing Gender" (1987), West and Zimmerman write that "female" and "male" are not the binary, static, opposite categories that a rigid sex-gender division would imply. Rather, gender is "done" by individuals in social situations. It is portrayed through interaction, which produces it while at the same time naturalizing it.[26] In a nutshell, it is a process that transpires in all forms of human interaction.

The idea that gender does not exist independently of the actions creating it is especially valuable for the study of Mesopotamian women. Assyriologists have few texts at their disposal that would describe Mesopotamian views on masculinity or femininity. However, the texts and artifacts that remain from Mesopotamian cultures all provide information on social interactions. Following West and Zimmerman, I suggest that all of these actions produced gender.

Such an approach provides a new angle on research questions that touch on "complicated" gender situations. These include the position and gender of *ša rēši*, often translated as "eunuch,"[27] and the case of daughters adopted as sons in Nuzi and Emar.[28] Furthermore, interactions between people convey much more than just gender. On the basis of principles of intersectionality, it follows that by analyzing more closely the interactions between individuals we may gain a better understanding of the interplay of gender, ethnicity, class and so forth.

24 Asher-Greve 2000: 4–7; Bahrani 2001: 25–27.

25 Butler 1999: 11–18, 33–44.

26 West and Zimmerman 1987: 126–129, 132–140, 146. See also their follow-up article (West and Zimmerman 2009).

27 See Tadmor 2002; Siddall 2007; and Pirngruber 2011.

28 Lion 2009.

For this article I have chosen a case study from my own previous research to illuminate what I mean by gender construction and how it is useful for the study of women's work in the Neo-Assyrian palaces. I will examine how actions of individual *šakintu*s reproduce or reshape femininity. I originally wrote a paper on the role and duties of the Neo-Assyrian *šakintu* for my very first Assyriological conference in Verona in 2005. That workshop presentation eventually became an article,[29] which subsequently became a chapter in my PhD dissertation.[30] The next few paragraphs are based on the latest version of this work,[31] which presents the textual evidence that we have for the *šakintu* women. I determined the archival context of these documents (54 in number) and where the *šakintus* in question were most probably located. Documents concerning the *šakintu*s were found in five cities (Assur, Nineveh, Kalḫu, Tušḫan and Til-Barsip) and they name a total of 23 separate households (some of them within the same city) where *šakintu*s were working. By closely reading the available texts, I analyzed the functions of this administrative position and established that this high-ranking official worked for the queen. The *šakintu* was present in a number of cities, even far away from Assyria proper, and the title was used from 788 BCE until the end of the Neo-Assyrian Empire in 612 BCE.

There are some indications that the *šakintu*'s family life may have been unconventional. In a remarkable marriage document, the administrator Amat-Astarti marries off her daughter – a prerogative usually reserved for the male head of the family.[32] A son of a *šakintu* is also known,[33] but husbands are never mentioned in connection with a *šakintu*. She had a large staff; members of her staff appear in 13 documents. In the Old Palace of Kalḫu, she had a female official (*laḫḫennutu*). In the Review Palace (Fort Shalmaneser) of Kalḫu, the *šakintu* had at her disposal the female scribe of the queen and a female deputy. In addition, her household included a cook, a man who was apparently "in charge of sacks" and *ša rēši* officials.[34]

The texts show very clearly that the *šakintu* was mainly engaged in financial matters; approximately half of the texts mention this. She often bought slaves (both male and female, as well as children) and/or land. Her other finan-

---

29 Teppo 2007.

30 Svärd 2012: 140–157.

31 An improved version of the dissertation is published in the State Archives of Assyria Studies (Svärd 2015: 70–71, 91–105, 232–239).

32 Postgate 1976, text no. 14.

33 Ahmad and Postgate 2007, text no. 6.

34 Svärd 2015: 98–99, 232–239.

cial activities included lending and borrowing, releasing people from servitude, receiving provisions and giving gifts.[35]

The *šakintu* had regular contact with men and women, and there is no evidence of her being confined within the palace. In fact, there is neither archaeological nor textual evidence which would be sufficient to suggest seclusion of elite women in Neo-Assyrian palaces. The perennial myth of "Oriental harems" should finally be dispensed with.[36]

In order to avoid repeating my previous work too much, I merely underline here that the evidence indicates that in many Neo-Assyrian palaces there were households of the queen which were headed by a *šakintu* and employed hundreds of people, probably in textile production. My suggestion is that the *šakintu*s were key agents in managing the immense fortune and vast household of the queen.

On the whole, I am still of the opinion that the original article and the subsequent chapter were not a total waste of paper, but that the work did manage to make a contribution to our knowledge of the Neo-Assyrian Empire. However, when I now place this research in the context of gender studies, it is very clear that it is typically first-wave research. I have taken a group of women, examined the textual evidence on them and written them into history, describing the way that they worked in the administration of Neo-Assyrian palaces. This needed to be done, but with my current understanding I see that I failed in not taking things further and asking new questions of the material. Next I will take the same textual evidence and demonstrate a third-wave approach, as outlined above.

In this new approach, where femininity is seen as a cultural construct and gender is treated as constructed by individuals in their everyday actions, what types of gender are *šakintu*s' actions constructing? What we find here is a female individual who is actively engaged in financial actions. We have someone who is ordering her staff around, someone who is clearly an important and high-ranking figure in the court. In one case, she is even marrying off her daughter, an action commonly performed by males. At first it would seem that her actions are creating active femininity, making "female" into a

35 Svärd 2015: 99.

36 A recent article by Simo Parpola (2012) advocates the existence of the Neo-Assyrian harem in somewhat "Orientalist" terms. Furthermore, the article does not take fully into account all relevant textual and archaeological evidence. For a full discussion of women in Neo-Assyrian palaces, see Svärd 2015 (pp. 109–120 for evidence of seclusion) and Kertai 2014: 196–198. For Orientalism and Assyriology, see Holloway 2006a; for the Mesopotamian "harem," see Solvang's article therein.

powerful actor in the everyday social reality. However, the image changes when we examine her actions from a more comprehensive social perspective. In that social reality, the majority of people that acted in the way that *šakintu*s acted were male. Thus, one could even say that the *šakintu* occupied a male gender role.

Yet this interpretation is not sophisticated enough, since it assumes that femininity and masculinity are static constructions. From an intersectional point of view, it is clear that we cannot talk about static Neo-Assyrian femininity and Neo-Assyrian masculinity as if all biological males and biological females had the same experience. Rather, we need to evaluate the *šakintu*'s actions in light of other factors. Theoretically there are many such factors, but in the case of *šakintu*s, status seems to be the most obvious point of analysis. Thus, the actions of the *šakintu*s – through interactions with other individuals – created a specifically *elite* feminine gender identity.

Finally, the actions of the *šakintu* have to be viewed within a larger, gendered cultural matrix. Although little research has been done on how Mesopotamians themselves viewed masculinity and femininity, some portrayals of gender have been identified. In these portrayals, which of course are almost exclusively written by men, women are described as being meek and silent.[37] Thus, there is an interesting discrepancy between imagined reality and what actually took place in the Neo-Assyrian court. *Quantitatively* speaking, arenas relating to writing were masculine spheres of action – and the majority of persons appearing in the texts are men. However, there is little *qualitative* difference in the ways in which elite women and elite men acted in the palace administration. Although femininity has been *perceived* as silent and subservient, when we look at the evidence from the palaces this is not the image we see. It seems that social rank influenced a person's responsibilities more than gender. In other words, rules were different for elite women.

When we compare this situation to the construction of masculinity, the situation is quite different. The imagined masculine gender and the portrayal of maleness are militant and vocal.[38] This is well-represented in the texts. The majority of evidence relates to activities of individuals grammatically identified as male. They formed the bulk of office holders, were the sole holders of the highest administrative positions, and dominated military affairs. Thus, there seems to be a fairly close match between how masculinity was portrayed and how male individuals actually engaged in social interactions. However, it

37 Asher-Greve 2002a. See also the contributions of Matuszak and Muller in this volume.
38 Zsolnay 2010.

would be interesting to examine if the masculinity of men from lower social classes (without social, political or economical power) differed from the masculinity of elite men.

Bibliography

Ahmad, Ali and John Nicholas Postgate. 2007. *Archives from the Domestic Wing of the North-West Palace at Kalhu/Nimrud*. Edubba, 10. London: Nabu Publications.

Asher-Greve, Julia. 1997. Feminist Research and Ancient Mesopotamia: Problems and Prospects. Pp. 218–237 in *A Feminist Companion to Reading the Bible: Approaches, Methods and Strategies*, eds. Athalya Brenner and Carole Fontaine. Sheffield: Sheffield Academic Press.

Asher-Greve, Julia. 2000. Stepping into the Maelstrom: Women, Gender and Ancient Near Eastern Scholarship. *NIN* 1: 1–22.

Asher-Greve, Julia. 2002a. Decisive Sex, Essential Gender. Pp. 11–26 in Parpola and Whiting 2002.

Asher-Greve, Julia. 2002b. Women and Gender in Ancient Near Eastern Cultures: Bibliography 1885 to 2001 AD. *NIN* 3: 33–114.

Asher-Greve, Julia. 2006. From 'Semiramis of Babylon' to 'Semiramis of Hammersmith'? Pp. 322–373 in Holloway 2006a.

Asher-Greve, Julia and Deborah Sweeney. 2006. On Nakedness, Nudity, and Gender in Egyptian and Mesopotamian Art. Pp. 125–176 in Schroer 2006.

Assante, Julia. 2003. From Whores to Hierodules: The Historiographic Invention of Mesopotamian Female Sex Professionals. Pp. 13–47 in *Ancient Art and Its Historiography*, eds. A. Donohue and Mark Fullerton. New York: Cambridge University Press.

Assante, Julia. 2006. Undressing the Nude: Problems in Analyzing Nudity in Ancient Art, with an Old Babylonian Case Study. Pp. 177–207 in Schroer 2006.

Bahrani, Zainab. 2001. *Women of Babylon: Gender and Representation in Mesopotamia*. London: Routledge.

Beaulieu, Paul-Alain. 1993. Women in Neo-Babylonian Society. *The Canadian Society for Mesopotamian Studies Bulletin* 26: 7–14.

Brooks, Beatrice. 1922. Some Observations Concerning Ancient Mesopotamian Women. *AJSL* 39: 187–194.

Butler, Judith. 1999. *Gender Trouble: Feminism and the Subversion of Identity*. London: Routledge.

Cameron, Averil and Amélie Kuhrt (eds.). 1983. *Images of Women in Antiquity*. London: Croom Helm.

Durand, Jean-Marie (ed.). 1987. *La femme dans le Proche-Orient antique: XXXIIIe Rencontre Assyriologique Internationale (Paris, 7–10 juillet 1986)*. Paris: Edition Recherche sur les Civilisations.

Garelli, Paul. 1998. Les dames de l'empire assyrien. Pp. 175–181 in *Intellectual Life of the Ancient Near East: Papers Presented at the 43rd Rencontre assyriologique internationale Prague, July 1–5, 1996*, ed. Jiri Prosecký. Prague: Oriental Institute.

Guinan, Ann Kessler. 1997. Auguries of Hegemony: The Sex Omens of Mesopotamia. *Gender & History* 9: 462–479.

Holloway, Steven (ed.). 2006a. *Orientalism, Assyriology and the Bible*. Hebrew Bible Monographs, 10. Sheffield: Sheffield Phoenix Press.
Holloway, Steven (ed.). 2006b. Introduction: Orientalism, Assyriology and the Bible. Pp. 1–41 in Holloway 2006a.
Kertai, David. 2014. From *bābānu* to *bētānu*, Looking for Spaces in Late Assyrian Palaces. Pp. 189–202 in *The Fabric of Cities: Aspects of Urbanism, Urban Topography and Society in Mesopotamia, Greece and Rome*, ed. Natalie Naomi May et al. Leiden: Brill.
Lion, Brigitte. 2009. Sexe et genre (1). Des filles devenant fils dans les contrats de Nuzi et d'Emar. Pp. 9–25 in *Femmes, cultures et sociétés dans les civilisations méditerranéennes et proche-orientales de l'Antiquité*, ed. Françoise Briquel-Chatonnet Topoi Supplément, 10. Lyon: De Boccard.
Macgregor, Sherry Lou. 2012. *Beyond Hearth and Home: Women in the Public Sphere in Neo-Assyrian Society*. SAAS 21. Helsinki: The Neo-Assyrian Text Corpus Project.
Marx, Victor. 1902. Die Stellung der Frau in Babylonien gemäss den Kontrakten aus der Zeit von Nebukadnezar bis Darius (604–485). *Beiträge zur Assyriologie und Semitischen Sprachwissenschaft* 4: 1–77.
McCaffrey, Kathleen. 2002. Reconsidering Gender Ambiguity in Mesopotamia: Is a Beard Just a Beard? Pp. 379–391 in Parpola and Whiting 2002.
Melville, Sarah. 1999. *The Role of Naqia/Zakutu in Sargonid Politics*. SAAS 9. Helsinki: Neo-Assyrian Text Corpus Project.
Melville, Sarah. 2004. Neo-Assyrian Royal Women and Male Identity: Status as a Social Tool. *JAOS* 124: 37–57.
Melville, Sarah. 2005. Royal Women and the Exercise of Power in the Ancient Near East. Pp. 219–228 in *Companion to the Ancient Near East*, ed. Daniel Snell. Oxford: Blackwell.
Meyers, Carol. 2014. Was Ancient Israel a Patriarchal Society? *JBL* 133: 8–27.
Nissinen, Martti. 1998. *Homoeroticism in the Biblical World: A Historical Perspective*. Minneapolis, Minnesota: Augsburg Fortress.
Parpola, Simo. 2002. Introduction. Pp. xiii–xv in Parpola and Whiting 2002.
Parpola, Simo. 2012. The Neo-Assyrian Royal Harem. Pp. 613–626 in *Leggo! Studies Presented to Frederick Mario Fales on the Occasion of His 65th Birthday*, ed. Giovanni Lanfranchi. Leipziger Orientalische Studien, 2. Wiesbaden: Harrassowitz.
Parpola, Simo and Robert Whiting (eds.). 2002. *Sex and Gender in the Ancient Near East: Proceedings of the XLVIIe Rencontre Assyriologique Internationale, Helsinki, July 2–6, 2001*. Helsinki: The Neo-Assyrian Text Corpus Project.
Peled, Ilan. 2014. *Assinnu* and *kurgarrû* Revisited. *JNES* 73: 283–297.
Pirngruber, Reinhard. 2011. Eunuchen am Königshof: Ktesias und die altorientalische Evidenz. Pp. 279–312 in *Die Welt des Ktesias: Ctesias' World*, ed. Josef Wiesehöfer. Classica et Orientalia, 1. Wiesbaden: Harrassowitz.
Postgate, J. Nicholas. 1976. *Fifty Neo-Assyrian Legal Documents*. Warminster: Aris & Phillips Ltd.
Said, Edward. 1978. *Orientalism*. New York: Vintage.
Schroer, Silvia (ed.). 2006. *Images and Gender: Contributions to the Hermeneutics of Reading Ancient Art*. Orbis Biblicus et Orientalis, 220. Freiburg: Universitätsverlag and Göttingen: Vandenhoeck & Ruprecht.
Siddall, Luis. 2007. A Re-examination of the Title *ša reši* in the Neo-Assyrian Period. Pp. 225–240 in *Gilgameš and the World of Assyria: Proceedings of the Conference Held at the Mandelbaum House, the University of Sydney, 21–23 July, 2004*, eds. Joseph Azize and Noel Weeks. ANESS, 21. Leuven: Peeters.

Solvang, Elna. 2006. Another Look 'Inside': Harems and the Interpretation of Women. Pp. 374–398 in Holloway 2006a.

Suter, Claudia. 2012. The Royal Body and Masculinity in Early Mesopotamia. Pp. 433–458 in *Menschenbilder und Körperkonzepte im Alten Israel, in Ägypten und im Alten Orient*, ed. Angelika Berlejung. Tübingen: Mohr Siebeck.

Svärd (Teppo), Saana. 2012. *Power and Women in the Neo-Assyrian Palaces*. Helsinki: University of Helsinki.

Svärd (Teppo), Saana. 2015. *Women and Power in Neo-Assyrian Palaces*. SAAS 23. Helsinki: The Neo-Assyrian Text Corpus Project.

Tadmor, Hayim. 2002. The Role of the Chief Eunuch and the Place of Eunuchs in the Assyrian Empire. Pp. 603–611 in Parpola and Whiting 2002.

Teppo (see also Svärd), Saana. 2007. The Role and Duties of the Neo-Assyrian *šakintu* in the Light of Archival Evidence. *SAAB* 16: 257–272.

Teppo (see also Svärd), Saana. 2008. Sacred Marriage and the Devotees of Ištar. Pp. 75–92 in *Sacred Marriages: the divine-human sexual metaphor from Sumer to early Christianity*, eds. Martti Nissinen and Risto Uro. Winona Lake, Indiana: Eisenbrauns.

Van De Mieroop, Marc. 1999. *Cuneiform Texts and the Writing of History*. London: Routledge.

Van De Mieroop, Marc. 2013. Recent Trends in the Study of Ancient Near Eastern History: Some Reflections. *Journal of Ancient History* 1: 83–98.

Vogel, Helga. 2012. Das Konzept "Gender" in der Vorderasiatischen Archäologie. Pp. 121–137 in *Zwischenbestimmungen. Identität und Geschlecht jenseits der Fixierbarkeit?*, eds. Marita Günther-Saeed and Esther Hornung. Würzburg: Königshausen & Neumann.

West, Candace and Don H. Zimmerman. 1987. Doing Gender. *Gender and Society* 1: 125–151.

West, Candace and Don H. Zimmerman. 2009. Accounting for Doing Gender. *Gender and Society* 23(1): 112–122.

Westenholz, Joan Goodnick. 1990. Towards a New Conceptualization of the Female Role in Mesopotamian Society. *JAOS* 110: 510–521.

Winter, Irene. 1996. Sex, Rhetoric and the Public Monument: The Alluring Body of Naram-Sin of Agade. Pp. 11–26 in *Sexuality in Ancient Art*, ed. Natalie Kampen. Cambridge: Cambridge University Press.

Zsolnay, Ilona. 2010. Ištar, "Goddess of War, Pacifier of Kings": An Analysis of Ištar's Martial Role in the Maledictory Sections of the Assyrian Royal Inscriptions. Pp. 389–402 in *Proceedings of the 53e Rencontre Assyriologique Internationale Vol. 1: Language in the Ancient Near East*, ed. Leonid Kogan. Winona Lake, Indiana: Eisenbrauns.

Zsolnay, Ilona. 2013. The Misconstrued Role of the Assinnu in Ancient Near Eastern Prophecy. Pp. 81–99 in *Prophets Male and Female: Gender and Prophecy in the Hebrew Bible, the Eastern Mediterranean, and the Ancient Near East*, eds. Jonathan Stökl and Corrine L. Carvalho. Ancient Israel and Its Literature, 15. Atlanta: Society of Biblical Literature.

Francis Joannès

Historiography on Studies Dedicated to Women and Economy during the Neo-Babylonian Period

This paper aims to present an overall appraisal of what has been produced within the REFEMA project and what has been done on the historiography of the Neo-Babylonian period these last few years, in particular linked to women and their role in the economy of Mesopotamia.

By surveying the analyses of S. Svärd[1] and B. Lion[2], we can distinguish three series of studies on women in the ancient Near Eastern context: in the sixties and seventies, what was initially needed was to gather references concerning women in Near Eastern textual documentation; a second wave, typical of the seventies and eighties, made the notion of *gender* emerge, that is the social construction of female identity, and exploited different types of textual documentation. Finally, during the eighties and nineties, a third wave sought to connect the concept of gender with certain social practices. As is quite rightly underlined by the authors of these analyses, we must bear in mind that these three waves coexisted and did not follow each other, one replacing the other.

In parallel, a research on the socio-economic aspects of Babylonia during the "long Sixth century BC" was developed, based on Neo-Babylonian textual documentation, a study *a priori* separated from the notion of gender but which met the concept several times in a more or less deliberate manner: while some family archives[3] were revisited or large institutions[4] were studied, bringing out the role of certain women, pioneer work that gathered textual data on the situation of women and marriage were undertaken by S. Démare-Lafont[5] and by M. Roth, after her work on Neo-Babylonian marriage[6] and numerous subse-

1 Svärd 2005.
2 Lion 2007. See also the contributions of S. Svärd and B. Lion in this volume.
3 Abraham 2004; Baker 2004; Beaulieu 1993; Joannès 1989; Kessler 1991; Stolper 1985, 1990, 1992, 1998, 1999; Waerzeggers 1999, 2001, 2002; Wunsch 1993; 1995, 2000.
4 Jursa 1995; Bongenaar 1997; Kleber 2008.
5 Demare-Lafont 1999.
6 Roth 1987, 1989a and 1989b.

Francis Joannès, Université Paris 1 Panthéon – Sorbonne, Archéologies et Sciences de l'Antiquité, Nanterre; francis.joannes@mae.u-paris10.fr

quent studies, while M. Dandamaiev's work on slavery[7] provided essential information on the situation of women servants within a domestic or institutional context. Parallel works on the social structure and the economic management of large temples[8] also illustrated women's role in the economy. Finally, the projects of the research team gathered in Vienna under M. Jursa's direction since 2004 allowed the undertaking of extremely well documented studies on the functioning of the economy in Babylonia during the long Sixth century BC and the following periods (Achaemenid and early Hellenistic).[9] We should also note that as early as 1994, the economic aspects of the Neo-Babylonian woman's life provided material for a very useful analysis by M. Weszeli, entitled "Frauen im Wirtschaftsleben Mesopotamiens (7.–5. Jahrhundert v. Christus)."[10]

Therefore, the considerable amount of data generated, as well as new proposals for the interpretation of social, economic and legal facts turned "Neo-Babylonian Studies" into one of the most active fields of Assyriological research these past twenty-five years. And we only speak here of elements directly concerning the social construction of female identity and studies related to the economy, leaving aside philological studies dedicated to the epistolary corpus, or political, cultural or religious areas.

It is in this context that the French-Japanese project REFEMA was simultaneously launched in Tokyo and Paris, and developed between 2012 and 2014, with the aim of studying the role and status of women in the economy of ancient Mesopotamia over a very long period (3rd–1st millennium). Several of its participants (L. Cousin, F. Joannès, E. Matsushima, G. Tolini, Y. Watai) have explored the Babylonian textual corpus of the 1st millennium. It is on this previously listed and accepted methodology that this research is based, and the aim of this presentation is not to draw up an exhaustive appraisal of this project but to put forth certain conclusions reached in relation with works on the economy and on Babylonian society during the Neo-Babylonian period.

The project itself is aimed at observing the relationship between the social construction of female identity and the data on the economy at our disposal. This was looked at in terms of mechanisms of production, constitution and transmission of assets, and the various means of women's intervention in the economic sphere. Sources used for the Neo-Babylonian period are contracts and the administrative texts of large institutions: they therefore concern private individuals, thanks to archives that provide a rather homogeneous sam-

7 Dandamaiev 1984.

8 Joannès 2008; Payne 2007; Ragen 2006; Waerzeggers 2010; Zawadzki 2006, 2013a and 2013b.

9 Baker and Jursa 2005; Jursa 2010.

10 Weszeli 1994.

ple, from slaves to notable's daughters, via women employed by temples with oblate status, and the female population of the palace, even if this particular is more difficult to grasp than for the Neo-Assyrian period[11]. But we must acknowledge that a large part of the daily activities of women escapes us because they left no written trace and because the archaeological evidence is uncommunicative regarding distinctions of sex.

I will here attempt to link up certain conclusions obtained, even provisional ones, with older studies, to try to demonstrate what can be considered as granted, what still gives rise to debate, and what calls for the creation of new research tools.

This study will focus on family structure and its determining role, the autonomy of women's economic actions and their conditions, and the legal status of dependent women.

1 Family structure

The best attested structure, in texts from the Neo-Babylonian period, is not the nuclear family, but the extended family. It is apparently the most widespread economic mode of operation for the family. As a result, beyond the simple man/woman relationship within a family, we find several internal hierarchies that establish statuses based on different situations: male/female, but also direct descent/kinship by marriage, married/single (that is a person not yet married, but also a person who finds herself or himself alone because of widowhood), free/domestic, etc. We can therefore propose an internal female hierarchy that isn't frozen but is likely to evolve through time, such as a person who entered a family as daughter-in-law will then find herself the wife of the head of the family, to perhaps later become an isolated widow.

This collective aspect of the family's mode of operation was first brought to light by studies on Babylonian society for other periods. We can cite the standard works of I. Diakonoff, in particular his 1996 study dedicated to the 2nd millennium, as well as the communications by D. Charpin or E. Stone, published in the proceedings of the 40th *RAI* in Leiden.[12]

If we heed D. Charpin's remarks, we must separate what concerns the mode of residence, by distinct family units, and what concerns family asset

11 This wealth of material has resulted in the project on Neo-Babylonian female prosopography conducted by Yoko Watai; see the contribution of Y. Watai in this volume.
12 Diakonoff 1996; Charpin 1996; Stone 1996.

management including activities linked to production. From this point of view, it appears that in a household there is a collective economic mode of operation, even if the different generations do not live in a space that is entirely a shared one. This supposes the re-evaluation of what C. Castel has called the "lived-in space" ("*l'espace vécu*") within the "built-in space" ("*l'espace bâti*") of urban houses:[13] in the Neo-Babylonian period, a part of the house could be used for shared activities (reception room, courtyard and spaces for food production), while other parts were occupied in a more individual manner by each of the households making up the home. Rather than a distribution of space of the type "family members" space *versus* "domestic staff space" ("*espace des membres de la famille/espace des domestiques*") that C. Castel had justly criticized, we should think in terms of households within a partially shared space, especially for activities that are economic in nature, including storage spaces that involved centralized management. All this is worthy of being developed in future studies, including archaeological and textual data when possible.

Elsewhere, it is of course the legal and socio-economic consequences of marriage on family life that have held the attention of researchers these past thirty years, as they were presented by S. Démare-Lafont in a recent synthetic analysis.[14] From this point of view, the foundational works for the "Neo-Babylonian period" remain those of M. Roth and have continued to be so since 1987,[15] while other studies concentrate on endogamous phenomenon[16] or economic activities developed within these family sets.[17] We can otherwise note the important aspects of C. Wunsch's or J. Hackl's approach when they highlight certain characteristics of female onomastics in family or institutional context.[18]

The study of textual data, especially those derived from private archives, therefore leads to reviewing the *a priori* idea we had about the family structure in Babylonia during the 1st millennium. In fact, there is a rather natural tendency to see the nuclear family of the Occidental type as the norm, when, as regards to its mode of operation and even, it seems, its habitat, it is family groups that emerge. The Neo-Babylonian urban household can be divided into several distinct, and even independent, family units, but what concerns its "economic

13 Castel 1992.
14 Démare-Lafont 2013.
15 Roth 1987, 1989a, 1989b, 1991, 1993, 1994, 2000.
16 Joannès 1989; Waerzeggers 2002.
17 Kuhrt 1989.
18 Wunsch 2006; Hackl 2013.

mode of production" (mainly food and cloth production) often appears as being globalized.[19]

One of the reasons for this situation could be a form of optimization of the relationship between resources available to the family and the expenses it must bear, which have often lead to a joint ownership among heirs of property or commercial asset management.

This family cohesion and the joint ownership that goes with it are not necessarily permanent: the study of the Egibi family's activities in Babylon – thanks to C. Wunsch who organized the archive – demonstrates that this family shows solidarity in order to constitute a large urban residence in the center of Babylon towards the end of the 6th century. But later, under the reign of Darius I, they proceed to a division as inheritance of various urban properties located in Babylon, Kiš and Borsippa, and of domestic staff.[20]

A point we could also underline is the apparent contradiction between this mode of collective management and the much more individualized treatment that legal texts suggest when they talk about family, whether they are Neo-Babylonian or, already in the *Code of Hammurabi*, of which an important part was still in use during the Neo-Babylonian period. It is from the representation found in legal texts that we have extracted the idea of a structure type more nuclear in nature (in particular with regard to marriages: articles often only envisage the link between spouses, or parents and children). But this individualized presentation of the law does not necessarily mirror a real society. It reflects the concern of the legislator's authority who takes into account individual situations to redress or prevent injustices committed against certain individuals. It also reflects without a doubt the way in which law is made, which precisely begins from individual cases and develops general norms from them.

We also see, when looking at clauses in property acquisition contracts from the 1st millennium in Babylonia, that to guarantee the buyer's right, such collective family structures as *kimtu*, *sallatu* or *nesūtu* are mentioned, and this implies broader forms of groupings. This social model, founded on the family's collective economic mode of production, is the one that written sources on daily life supply us with. It is mainly centered on notable urban families who own assets, and probably begins to vary as soon as we draw close to cases of

---

19 See for exemple Tappašar's case in the Nappāḫu archive and the records of expenses of the Egibi family, as set out in F. Joannès' contribution to the first REFEMA workshop in 2012 (http://www.refema.hypotheses.org/202: "La place des femmes dans l'économie domestique néo-babylonienne").

20 Watai 2012.

rural tenant families, whose status is that of free individuals, but who make use of lands that they don't own. However, the rural society that the Murašu archives document in Nippur during the 5th century is also complex and multiform, and the principle of military tenures that associate the exploitation of a domain and the provision of a soldier also rests on the principle of families that are larger than the simple nuclear family.

Once we accept this, that is to say when we acknowledge an organization based on family groups rather than on nuclear families that are geographically separated, the conclusions to be drawn concerning the status of women inside the family are of consequence. There is, recurrently so, a concentration of women's activities of an economic nature inside the occupied house, but they are not undertaken in an undifferentiated or interchangeable manner, and there exists a hierarchy between the different women of the household. It is this second point that emerged during this study: the management of resources is carried out by the female equivalent of the family chief and it implies that this person possesses a certain degree of personal agency.

2 The importance of *household* hierarchy

During the Neo-Babylonian period, a woman who manages the household doesn't bear a specific title, but she exercises a right of management on the income and expenditure of resources and an authority over domestics. Furthermore, she can legally act on her own assets, that is, on what comes from her *nudunnu*, commonly translated by "dowry."

We therefore find the domestic workers under her orders and the female members of the family under her authority. This latter group includes her unmarried daughters and her sons' wives who live in the house, but the hierarchy that exists between them remains unknown to us. It is probable that relationships between daughters-in-law and mothers-in-law were not exempt from conflicts of priority, especially if the daughter-in-law's social status was high.

Aside from this, we must not assume that the lady of the house is the oldest woman. She is the one who has the most extensive right of management. We thus see a parallel problem emerge: within what we call the social construction of an identity, not only relations between sexes but also between social levels are at play. To evaluate a Babylonian woman's degree of autonomy, at least from an economic point of view, we must not only consider the aspect of gender, but also the social aspect. This is of course no discovery, but the study of numerous individual cases, made possible by private Neo-Babylonian archives, has shown the importance of this double approach.

There is indeed an assignation of specific tasks to women in the economy of the "Neo-Babylonian household," but the social level is a parameter that must be taken into account. It was shown that several women's tasks could be externalized, as in a laundry or bakery. We even find women at a certain level of notability who enjoy a quasi-independence of management. Specific research should be undertaken over the entire range of female activities displaying "agency." This is the aim of the project undertaken by Y. Watai based on data provided by female prosopography.

We see that some women can give their daughters in marriage, can be creditors, and can by their own volition sell property or assets and make property acquisitions. We must therefore try to gather a set, as specific as possible, of these various cases and see where they are placed on the social scale.[21] Moreover, within Neo-Babylonian society, women cannot exercise certain functions. From this point of view, the religious sphere has been the most explored area, but we can naturally also say the same about political responsibilities. However, even there, women can play a role in the execution of certain functions: we know of cases where women are nominal owners of prebends in large Neo-Babylonian sanctuaries. But we can also note the case of a prebender whose mother must prove his descent is legitimate, and, as C. Waerzeggers and M. Jursa have rightly shown, with regard to text OIP 122 nr. 36,[22] rather than ritual purity, family legitimacy is the biggest concern here.

3 The characteristics of the status of dependent women

If we go down the social hierarchy and look at women employed in large organizations, two interesting conclusions emerge:

---

21 Cf. the case of Ina-Esagil-ramat, studied par L. Cousin: "Dowry management in the neo-babylonian period: A case study" (http://refema.hypotheses.org/223).

22 Waerzeggers 2008. The text OIP 122 nr. 36 says: "[PN], your son, is to be consecrated for service before the Lady of Uruk. Now, shouldn't there definitely be a *zibu*-ornament on (his) neck? If there has been any claim of impurity raised against you, tell us so in the assembly." Inqāya said as follows: "Ištar-nādin-apli has taken me for his wife as a virgin, but my father and my mother have not placed *zību*-ornament on my neck." Later, (four men) who had made enquiries regarding Inqāya, the wife of Ištar-nādin-apli, and Ilatā, the daughter of Pir'u of the Iddin-Papsukkal family, the first wife of Ištar-nādin-apli, swore an oath by Bēl and Nabū (and) by the Lady of Uruk and Nanāya: "Certainly nothing special has been given to her as a share, (and) we definitely have not seen, heard, come to know nor heard rumours about a query

First, it is obvious that the temple plays a social role in 6th century Babylonia as the place where dependent elderly individuals finish their lives. The numerous donation contracts mentioned in the archives of the Eanna of Uruk often stipulate that domestic slaves come to join the temple as oblates (*širku*) after their owners' death. We can also suppose that after the donor's death, the family who inherited the estate wasn't really interested in retaining a female slave (often advanced in age) who will no longer have children and whose capacity for work has decreased. The temple, in welcoming her, plays a social role and prevents her from a miserable end to her life.[23] The problem remains to determine what real benefit the temple stands to gain from this donation practice.

Continuing on with one's life as an elderly individual was probably a problem that occurred more often for women than for men: E. Gehlken's study[24] shows an average male life expectancy of around 40, excluding the impact of infant mortality. M. Jursa had already presented identical conclusions in 2004,[25] but insisted on the lack of information for corpus statistics for women. We can reasonably put forward the hypothesis that women used as domestic workers did not have a life expectancy much higher than that of men. To plan for a female slave to join the temple as an oblate through a *post mortem* gift after around 25 years of service in a private family is to expect the length of her life as an oblate in "full service" to range from 5 to 10 years maximum.

The work carried out by women in temples was studied in detail by K. Kleber[26] and concerns mainly milling and textile production.[27] Maintenance rations provided by the temple were not generous in general, and more often than not we find men or women oblates trying to become private slaves, not the opposite. It seems that we should interpret this fact as a sign that belonging

---

(regarding), or impurity pertaining to, Inqāya, daughter of Mušalli-Marduk, wife of Ištar-nādin-apli. She is definitely a *sallūḫatu*-woman."

23 This explanation was first proposed by M. Dandamaiev (1984: 472–487); then by G. van Driel (1998: 178–179); M. Jursa (2005: 15); and R. Magdalene and C. Wunsch (2014). G. van Driel wrote: "For our subject, it is of some significance that the temple could function as a kind of repository, or rather dump, for people, i.e. slaves, no longer required by their owners. (...) In practice this means that the slaves are transferred to the temple when they are old and worn. Also for declassed free persons the temple could be a last resort. (...). Within limits, the temple's social role must however, be accepted."

24 Gehlken 2005.

25 Jursa 2005: 56.

26 Kleber 2008.

27 See also the contribution of L. Quillien in this volume.

to the temple's domestic personnel did not mean a restful life. But at least people stayed there until their deaths, and the temple fulfilled an obvious social role.

The records concerning the embezzlements of Gimillu the oblate, which the temple of Uruk discovered on several occasions,[28] show that people who left mainstream society's framework, voluntarily or not, led their lives mainly outside the city. A study that remains to be concluded on urban criminality in Babylonia seems to indicate there was a strict control of movement and activities of the temple's personnel for a sanctuary like the Eanna inside Uruk. We can hypothesize that the temple taking care of individuals (where the number of women was no doubt important) who were not integrated in a stable family structure not only meant their material care, but also their constant surveillance.

The female personnel that the temple looked after were composed of oblates (*širkitu*) among whom some were called *zakîtu*. These women's legal status remained the subject of discussions for a long time, and thanks to the studies of K. Kleber on the one hand and of R. Magdalene and C. Wunsch on the other, the situation is now much clearer[29]: K. Kleber has demonstrated that oblation is not a servitude from a legal point of view; and as I indicated in my presentation during the REFEMA's third workshop:

> "Contrary to a private slave whose master is the owner, an oblate is not a sanctuary "possession;" he or she enjoys no autonomy vis-à-vis the sanctuary, even though during the process of the donation to the temple, the master first frees his or her slave[30]. We must therefore take into account the notion that C. Wunsch and R. Magdalene call *potestas*, defined as the customary legal right that a natural authority (paternal, religious, royal) has over its subordinates, within a family or within an institution. (...) C. Wunsch and R. Magdalene thus propose to interpret the *širkūtu* as a socio-legal category in which an individual finds himself or herself subject to the *potestas* of the divinity represented by the temple administration, just as the *mār banūtu* is the category in which an individual finds himself or herself subject to the family's authority."

We must also not forget the role of women who are wives and daughters of farmers, which is little attested in texts but still essential, or of agricultural tenants dependent of the temple. Textile production in the context of temples is a good example of this, and is treated by L. Quillien in this volume. We must add to it, within a non-institutional context like this one, the cases of the Mu-

28 Last synthesis in Jursa 2004.
29 Kleber 2011; Magdalene and Wunsch 2014.
30 Text OIP 122 nr. 38 was especially debated from this point of view: see Roth 1989c; Weisberg 2000 and Westbrook 2004.

rašu dependents' wives studied by G. Tolini who freed their husbands by providing an economic guarantee.[31] We also find in Neo-Babylonian documents examples of women paying certain taxes on behalf of their absent husbands.

***

What conclusions can we draw from all of this? The historiography of these last thirty years dedicated to the economy of Babylonia in the 1st millennium BC, and to the situation of women in Mesopotamia during the same period, was used as the basis of studies undertaken within the context of the REFEMA project. We clearly see certain major factors emerge. At the bottom of the social scale (slaves, oblates, dependents) there are women and men who carry out activities differentiated by their area of competence and deemed specific to each: hard labor and work performed outside by men, and domestic tasks and work linked to food and textile production by women. Like in previous periods, this division of labor does not preclude the undifferentiated use of a servile or dependent female workforce when institutions have a pressing need for them, like in public construction projects, large infrastructure work, etc.

When we climb up the social scale, two logics coexist: one is founded on the same "functional" bi-partition that associates women more often with the household's internal economy and introduces an internal female hierarchy within a family environment that is often collective in nature. This hierarchy supposes various degrees of autonomy in decision-making and in the management of the family's resources.

The other logic arises out of the social situation from the role that women play in asset ownership and transmission in notable urban families. The autonomy of management that women can use with regard to their own assets depends on their social status and can lead to relative independence.

We thus finally end up with a complex subject of research that must be approached as a system. The established relationships between the constituent parts of this system are as important for understanding it as the constituent parts themselves, if not more important. There is not one model of family structure, but several; there is not one basic system of economic production in Neo-Babylonian households, but several, coordinated by one person who possesses internal management 'authority.' This system is therefore marked by diversity and interacts continuously.

31 Tolini 2013.

Bibliography

Abraham, Kathleen. 2004. *Business and politics under the Persian Empire: the financial dealings of Marduk-nāṣir-apli of the House of Egibi (521–487 B.C.E.)*. Bethesda: CDL Press.

Baker, Heather. 2004. *The Archive of the Nappāḫu Family*. AfO Beiheft 30. Vienne: Institut für Orientalistik.

Baker, Heather and Michael Jursa. 2005. *Approaching the Babylonian Economy Proceedings of the START Project Symposium Held in Vienna, 1–3 July 2004. Veröffentlichungen zur Wirtschaftsgeschichte im 1. Jahrtausend v. Chr.* Band 2. AOAT 330. Münster: Ugarit-Verlag.

Beaulieu, Paul-Alain. 1993. Women in Neo-Babylonian Society. *The Canadian Society for Mesopotamian Studies Bulletin* 26: 7–14.

Bongenaar, Hermann C. 1997. *The Neo-Babylonian Ebabbar Temple at Sippar: Its Administration and its Prosopography*. PIHANS 80. Leiden: Nederlands Historisch-Archaeologisch Instituut te Istanbul.

Castel, Corinne. 1992. *Habitat urbain néo-assyrien et néo-babylonien; de l'espace bâti à l'espace vécu*. Bibliothèque archéologique et historique (B.A.H.) n° CXLIII. Paris: IFAPO.

Charpin, Dominique. 1996. Maisons et maisonnées en Babylonie ancienne de Sippar à Ur. Remarques sur les grandes demeures des notables paleo-babyloniens. Pp. 221–228 in Veenhof 1996.

Dandamaiev, Igor M. 1984. *Slavery in Babylonia from Nabopolassar to Alexander the Great (626–331 B.C.)* (nouvelle édition). DeKalb: Northern Illinois University Press.

Démare-Lafont, Sophie. 1999. *Femmes, droit et justice dans l'antiquité orientale. Contribution à l'étude du droit pénal au Proche-Orient ancien*. OBO 165. Fribourg: Editions Universitaires and Göttingen: Vandenhoeck & Ruprecht.

Démare-Lafont, Sophie. 2013. Le mariage babylonien – Une approche historiographique, *ZABR* 18: 175–190.

Diakonoff, Igor. 1996. Extended Family Households in Mesopotamia (III-II Millenia BC). Pp. 55–60 in Veenhof 1996.

Gehlken, Erlend. 2005. Childhood and Youth, Work and Old Age in Babylonia – A Statistical Analysis. Pp. 89–120, in *Approaching the Babylonian Economy: Proceedings of the START Project Symposium held in Vienna, 1–3 July 2004*, eds. Heather D. Baker and Michael Jursa, AOAT 330, Münster: Ugarit-Verlag.

Hackl, Johannes. 2013. Frau Weintraube, Frau Heuschrecke und Frau Gut – Untersuchungen zu den babylonischen Namen von Sklavinnen in neubabylonischer und persischer Zeit. *WZKM* 103: 121–187.

Joannès, Francis. 1989. *Archives de Borsippa: La famille Ea-ilûta-bâni. Etude d'un lot d'archives familiales en Babylonie du VIIe au Ve siècle av. J.-C.*, Genève: Droz.

Joannès, Francis. 2008. Place et rôle des femmes dans le personnel des grands organismes néo-babyloniens. Pp. 465–480 in *L'archive des Fortifications de Persépolis: État des questions et perspectives de recherches*, eds Pierre Briant, Wouter Henkelman, and Matthew W. Stolper. Persika 12. Paris: De Boccard.

Jursa, Michael. 1995. *Die Landwirtschaft in Sippar in neubabylonischer Zeit*. AfO Beiheft 25. Wien: Institut für Orientalistik.

Jursa, Michael. 2004. Auftragsmord, Veruntreuung und Falschaussagen: Neues von Gimillu. *WZKM* 94: 109–132.

Jursa, Michael. 2005. *Neo-Babylonian Legal and Administrative Documents: Typology. Content and Archives*, GMTR 1, Münster: Ugarit Verlag.

Jursa, Michael. 2010. *Aspects of the Economic History of Babylonia in the First Millennium BC. Veröffentlichungen zur Wirtschaftsgeschichte im 1. Jahrtausend v. Chr.* Band 4. AOAT 377. Münster: Ugarit-Verlag.

Kessler, Karlheinz. 1991. *Uruk. Urkunden aus Privathäusern in Uruk. Die Wohnhäusern westlich des Eannatempelbereichs. Teil I. Die Archive der Söhne des Bēl-ušallim, des Nabu-ušallim und des Bēl-supê-muḫur*. AUWE 8. Mayence: P. Von Zabern.

Kleber, Kristin. 2008. *Tempel und Palast. Die Beziehungen zwischen dem König und dem Eanna-Tempel im spätbabylonischen Uruk. Veröffentlichungen zur Wirtschaftsgeschichte im 1. Jahrtausend v. Chr.* Band 3. AOAT 358. Münster: Ugarit-Verlag.

Kleber, Kristin. 2011. Neither Slaves nor truly free: the Status of the Dependents of Babylonian Temple Households. Pp. 101–112 in *Slaves and Households in the Near East, Papers from the Oriental Institute Seminar, University of Chicago 5–6 March 2010*, ed. Laura Culbertson. Oriental Institute Seminars 7. Chicago: The Oriental Institute of the University of Chicago.

Kuhrt, Amelie. 1989. Non-Royal Women in the Late Babylonian Period: A survey. Pp. 215–243 in *Women's Earliest Records from Ancient Egypt and Western Asia*, ed. Barbara Lesko, Atlanta: Scholars Press.

Lion, Brigitte. 2007. La notion de genre en assyriologie. Pp. 51–64 in *Problèmes du genre en Grèce ancienne*, eds. Violaine Sebillotte Cuchet and Nathalie Ernoult. Paris: Publications de la Sorbonne.

Magdalene, Rachel and Cornelia Wunsch. 2014. Freedom and Dependency: Neo-Babylonian Manumission Documents with Oblation and Service Obligation. Pp. 337–346, in *Extraction and Control: Studies in Honor of Matthew W. Stolper*, eds. Michael Kozuh, with Wouter Henkelman, Charles E. Jones, and Christopher Woods, SAOC 68. Chicago: Oriental Institute.

Payne, Elizabeth. 2007. *The Craftsmen of the Neo-Babylonian Period: A Study of the Textile and Metal Workers of the Eanna Temple*. Unpublished PhD thesis.

Ragen, Asher. 2006. *The Shirku of Babylonia A Study of Ancient Near Eastern "Temple Slavery"*. Unpublished PhD thesis.

Roth, Martha T. 1987. Age at Marriage and the Household. A Study of Neo-Babylonian and Neo-Assyrian Forms. *Comparative Studies in Society and History* 29: 715–747.

Roth, Martha T. 1989a. *Babylonian marriage agreements: 7th–3rd centuries B.C.* AOAT 222. Kevelaer: Butzon & Bercker and Neukirchen-Vluyn: Neukirchener Verlag.

Roth, Martha T. 1989b. The Material Composition of the Neo-Babylonian Dowry. *AfO* 36–37: 1–55.

Roth, Martha T. 1989c. A case of contested Status. Pp. 481–489 in *DUMU-E_2-DUB-BA-A: Studies in Honor of W. Sjöberg*, eds. Hermann Behrends *et alii*, Occasional Publications of the Samuel Noah Kramer Fund 11. Philadelphia: University Museum.

Roth, Martha T. 1991. The Dowries of the Women in the Itti-Marduk-balaṭu Family. *JAOS* 111: 19–37.

Roth, Martha T. 1993. The Neo-Babylonian Widow. *JCS* 43–45: 1–26.

Roth, Martha T. 1994. The Neo-Babylonian Family and Household. *Bulletin of the Canadian Society of Mesopotamian Studies* 28: 19–29.

Roth, Martha T. 2000. Tašmêtu-damqat and Daughters. Pp. 387–400 in *Assyriologica et Semitica: Festschrift für Joachim Oelsner anläßlich seines 65. Geburtstages am*

18. Februar 1997, eds. Joachim Marzahn and Hans Neumann. AOAT 252. Münster: Ugarit-Verlag.
Stolper, Matthew W. 1985. *Entrepreneurs and Empire. The Murašû Archive, the Murašû Firm, and Persian Rule in Babylonia,* PIHANS 54. Istanbul-Leiden: Nederlands Instituut voor het Nabije Oosten/Netherlands Institute for the Near East.
Stolper, Matthew W. 1990. Late Achaemenid Legal Texts from Uruk and Larsa, *Baghdader Mitteilungen* 21: 559–623.
Stolper, Matthew W. 1992. The Estate of Mardonius. *Aula Orientalis* 10: 211–221.
Stolper, Matthew W. 1998. Inscribed in Egyptian. Pp. 133–143 in *Studies in Persian History: Essays in Memory of David Lewis*, eds. Maria Brosius and Amelie Kuhrt. Achaemenid History 11. Leiden: The Netherlands Institute for the Near East.
Stolper, Matthew W. 1999. Lurindu the Maiden, Bêl-ittannu the Dreamer, and Artaritassu the King. Pp. 591–598 in *Munuscula Mesopotamica. Festschrift für Johannes Renger*, eds. Barbara Böck, Eva Cancik-Kirschbaum, and Thomas Richter. AOAT 267. Münster: Ugarit-Verlag.
Stone, Elizabeth C. 1996. Houses, households and neighbourhoods in the Old Babylonian period: the role of extended families. Pp. 229–235 in Veenhof 1996.
Svärd, Saana. 2005. *Women and their Agency in the neo-assyrian Empire.* Unpublished PhD thesis.
Tolini, Gauthier. 2013. Women and Family Solidarities in the Murašû Archive (Nippur – Fifth century B.C.), http://refema.hypotheses.org/227.
van Driel, Govert. 1998. Care on the Elderly: The Neo-Babylonian period. Pp. 161–197 in *The Care of the Elderly in the Ancient Near East*, eds. Marten Stol and Sven P. Vleeming, Studies in the History and Culture of the Ancient Near East 14. Leiden: Brill.
Veenhof, Klaas R. 1996. *Houses and Households in Ancient Mesopotamia. Papers read at the 40th Rencontre Assyriologique Internationale, Leiden, July 5–8, 1993.* PIHANS 78. Leiden: Nederlands Historisch-Archaeologisch Instituut te Istanbul.
Waerzeggers, Caroline. 1999. The Records of Insabtu from the Naggaru Family. *AfO* 46/47: 183–200.
Waerzeggers, Caroline. 2001. A Note on the Marriage Gift Biblu in the Neo-Babylonian Period. *Akkadica* 122: 65–70.
Waerzeggers, Caroline. 2002. Endogamy In Mesopotamia In the First Millennium BC. Pp. 319–342 in *Mining the Archives. Festschrift for Christopher Walker on the Occasion of his 60th Birthday*, ed. Cornelia Wunsch. Dresden: ISLET.
Waerzeggers, Caroline. 2008. On the Initiation of Babylonian Priests (With a contribution by Michael Jursa), *Zeitschrift für Altorientalische und Biblische Rechtsgeschichte* 14: 1–38.
Waerzeggers, Caroline. 2010. *The Ezida Temple of Borsippa. Priesthood, Cult, Archives.* Achaemenid History 15. Leiden: The Netherlands Institute for the Near East.
Watai, Yoko. 2012. *Les maisons néo-babyloniennes d'après la documentation textuelle.* Unpublished PhD thesis.
Weisberg, David B. 2000. *Neo-Babylonian Texts in the Oriental Institute Collection, University of Chicago*, OIP 122, Chicago.
Westbrook, Raymond. 2004. The quality of Freedom in Neo-Babylonian Manumissions, *RA* 98: 101–108.
Weszeli, Michaela. 1994. Frauen im Wirtschaftsleben Mesopotamien (7.–5. Jahrhundert v. Chr.). Pp. 111–142 in *Frauenreichtum. Die Frau als Wirtschaftsfaktor im Altertum*, ed. Edith Specht. Wien: Wiener Frauenverlag.

Wunsch, Cornelia. 1993. *Die Urkunden des babylonischen Geschäftsmannes Iddin-Marduk. Zum Handel mit Naturalien im 6. Jahrhundert v. Chr.*, Cuneiform Monographs 3a and b. Groningen: STYX.

Wunsch, Cornelia. 1995. Die Frauen der Familie Egibi, *AfO* 42/43, 33–63.

Wunsch, Cornelia. 2000. *Das Egibi-Archiv. I. Die Felder und Gärten*. Cuneiform Monographs 20a and b. Groningen: STYX.

Wunsch, Cornelia. 2006. "Metronymika in Babylonien. Frauen als Ahnherrin der Familie". Pp. 459–469 in *šapal tibnim mû ilakkū. Studies Presented to Joaquín Sanmartin on the Occasion of his 65th Birthday*, eds Gregorio del Olmo Lete, Lluis Feliu, and Adelina Milet-Alba. Aula Orientalis Supplementa. Barcelona: Sabadell.

Zawadzki, Stefan. 2006. *Garments of the Gods. Studies on the Textile Industry and the Pantheon of Sippar according to the Texts from the Ebabbar Archive.* Vol. 1. OBO 218. Fribourg: Academic Press and Göttingen: Vandenhoeck & Ruprecht.

Zawadzki, Stefan. 2013a. *Garments of the Gods.* Vol. 2. OBO 260. Fribourg: Academic Press and Göttingen: Vandenhoeck & Ruprecht.

Zawadzki, Stefan. 2013b. *Neo-Babylonian documents from Sippar pertaining to the Cult.* Poznan: Instytut Historii Uniwersytetu im. Adama Mickiewicza.

Louise Quillien

Invisible Workers: The role of women in textile production during the 1st millennium BC

In the Sumerian myth of Enki, the god of crafts, weaving is called "the woman's art".[1] However, according to cuneiform sources on textile production in Mesopotamia during the 1st millennium BC, almost exclusively men performed textile work. It is not surprising that the representations conveyed by the literary texts are different from the picture conveyed by the study of the records of daily life. But even these records are biased because they only document part of the reality. Indeed, the majority of these texts are produced by the institutions – temples and palaces – and they concern the manufacturing of precious textiles in most cases. Examining the rare attestations of women involved in textile work in 1st millennium BC, we can wonder if behind this over-representation of men in the texts, a much higher number of women are hidden.

The expression "invisible workers" refers to the situation of the near absence of women compared to men in the texts dealing with textile work for the Neo-Babylonian period.[2] Specialists in gender studies have shown that the under-representation of women in the texts is a common phenomenon in history and does not reflect reality. For instance, Françoise Thébaud (1998: 72) proposed to: "Lire les sources en creux, pour faire surgir, par le regard qu'on leur porte, les femmes."

---

1 This story tells how Enki, the god of crafts, distributed the different crafts amongst the gods. He gives weaving to the goddess Uttu: "He wove the *mug*-cloth, guided the *te*, Enki perfected the woman's art. For Enki, the people [...] the [...]-garment. The one who is the dignity of the palace, the decorum of the king, Uttu, the unfailing woman of silence, Enki placed in charge of them;" translation of Kramer and Maier (1989: 53). See also Bottéro and Kramer (1989: 178) and Vanstiphout (1990a and 1990b).

2 The expression has been invented for other periods of History; I borrow the phrase from Bridenthal, Koons and Stuard (1987).

Acknowledgements: I deeply thank Cécile Michel, Brigitte Lion and Kristin Kleber for their careful review of this writing. I thank also Michael Jursa and Kristin Kleber for having provided me transcriptions of unpublished texts dealing with women and textile work, and Saana Svärd-Teppo for having sent me her unpublished dissertation about women in Neo-Assyrian palaces. Any errors are my own.

Louise Quillien, Université Paris 1 Panthéon – Sorbonne; louise.quillien@wanadoo.fr

Indeed, the documentation is not homogeneous within the 1st millennium BC. For the Neo-Assyrian period (8th century–610 BC), the cuneiform archives mainly come from the royal palaces, and they do not concern the textile workshops directly. But some female weavers appear sporadically in texts dealing with other subjects. For the Neo-Babylonian and Achaemenid period (610–334 BC), the texts come from the temple's archives and they document the production of garments for the cult or for the temple's staff. Even though the temples' craftsmen were all men, some exceptions show that women were also active in textile work for the temples. Private letters sometimes mention domestic textile production in the hands of women, but this is poorly documented. Lastly, the marriage contracts list the clothes pertaining to a woman's dowry and may reflect the products of domestic work.

In spite of these scarce sources, it is possible to restore the real place of women in textile work during the 1st millennium BC. But we have to be careful not to emphasize the role of women just because of the presupposition that textile production is "a women's work".[3] Indeed, the idea that this task is natural for women because it is compatible with the care of children has been criticized by specialists of gender history. Marie Louise Stig Sørensen (2000: 67–68) asks about that type of statement, where the generalization ends and where the stereotype begins.[4] For Mesopotamia, D. T. Potts (1997: 92–93) warns about the assumption of a gender-based division of textile labor, and J. G. Westenholz (1990: 511) about the presuppositions based on our own culture.[5] Even though women are more numerous in textile production, especially in the industrial workshops of Ur III, Lagaš, and Mari, men are sometimes present, for example in Nuzi and in Middle Babylonian archives.[6] The 1st millennium male weavers of the temples of Uruk and Sippar are not an exception.

---

3 About the idea that the manufacturing of textile is mostly a women's work see Barber (1994: 29–30), who quotes Brown (1970: 1073–1078).

4 Stig Sørensen (2000: 67–68). See also the workshop "Gender, methodology and the Ancient Near East," held in Helsinki, October 27–28, 2014.

5 About the collection of the wool, which is sometimes a man's task and sometimes a woman's task in Mesopotamia, D. T. Potts (1997: 92–93) writes: "It is difficult to say just what the significance of the change in gender roles from the Ur III period signifies, and why the activity of fleece plucking should have been, apparently, such a gender-specific occupation in each period. To adequately understand the problem, however, would undoubtedly require a much broader look at gender roles across a range of professions in ancient Mesopotamia through time." Westenholz (1990: 511) writes that, "at this time, there is great emphasis in gender study on the development of the awareness of the unconscious culture-specific assumptions that give a distorting bias in reconstructing society."

6 Waetzoldt (1972), for Ur III; Lambert (1961), for Lagaš; Ziegler in the present volume, for Mari; Cassin (1962), Mayer 1978: 169–175, Justel and Lion (2014: 41) and Lion in this volume for Nuzi; Tenney (2011) for the Middle Babylonian documentation.

Above all, this reflection leads us to observe the respective roles of women and men in textile production without basing the argument on the texts *a priori*, and interpreting them in the framework of other studies about the society and economy of 1st millennium Mesopotamia. In this way, we can wonder what the place of women in textile production is in 1st millennium BC Mesopotamia, and what the economic consequences of their work for their families are.

1 What was the place of women in the textile production in the palaces?

1.1 In search for the female weavers in the Neo-Assyrian palaces.

The Neo-Assyrian documentation is mainly palatial. But the archives of palace's textile workshops, if they ever existed, have not been discovered. The archives of the ladies of the palace record their economic transactions (purchase of lands and personnel, loans contracts, debts ...), but not much of their involvement in textile production.[7] However, some letters and administrative documents mention textile workers, including women as well as men.

First of all, spinning is a woman's task according to the Neo-Assyrian representations. In the Vassal-Treaties of Esarhaddon, a clause warns the person who would break the agreement in this way: "May all the gods who are called by name in this treaty tablet spin you around like a spindle-whorl, may they make you like a woman before your enemy," SAA 2, 6: 616a–617. Here the spinning is associated with women. But the idea that only women did the spinning work cannot be confirmed or invalidated by the archives because no names of spinning workers are recorded.

The situation is different for weaving. The texts indicate that many weavers, both men and women, worked for the different services of the palace. For example, in the letter, SAA 1, 33: obv. 19–24 (dated approximately 710–705 BC), Sennacherib, crowned prince, asks his father Sargon II if the "female weavers of the king" have to do the selection of the red wool due from the Commageneans as war tribute.

An example of the archives of Nineveh, dated from 721 to 612 BC, illustrates the complexity of the textile production in the palace, which is performed in various places by various actors, both men and women. The text SAA 7, 115 re-

7 Villard (2009).

cording the delivery of linen and dyes in the palace shows the great diversity of recipients: places (the Central City, the palace of Nineveh, the palace of Kalhu, cities), institutions and workshops (the house of the queen, the domestic quarters, the house of the tailors, the temple of Ištar), officials (the treasurer, the gate overseers ...), and specialists (the weavers of scarves, the clothing dealers). We can suppose that at least in the house of the queen and in the domestic quarter which were specific living places of women in the palace of Nineveh, the weavers were women. Indeed, Saana Svärd-Teppo has demonstrated that in the households of the female *šakintu* officers of the queen, female weavers were working under their direction. She remarked for instance that in the text quoted above, the palaces where the flax was distributed were part of *šakintu*'s household.[8] On the other hand, the weavers working in the palaces were not always women, as other administrative documents mention male weavers in the domestic quarter,[9] and even in the queen's palace.[10] The king's wife had a large number of personnel, including women and men performing textile work.[11] Thus, the situation is not uniform and it is difficult to quantify the number and the repartition of female staff in comparison to the males.

In addition to the Assyrian female weavers, the palace employed foreign specialists brought to Assyria as war captives. In particular, some Egyptian women were recognized as experts of textile work, and our sources show that they were listed according to their profession.[12] Therefore, they were probably assigned to do specialized textile work in the Assyrian palaces.

The Assyrian palaces employed men and women to perform textile work. Even if the palatial archives in the Neo-Babylonian period are almost completely lost, one text indicates that the textile workers there were of both genders, too.

1.2 The women textile weavers of the Neo-Babylonian palaces

Neo-Babylonian cuneiform documents from the palaces are scarce. Most of the texts come from temples' archives. But one text, PTS 2121, edited by Kristin

8 Svärd-Teppo (2007: 266–267).

9 "Two house gowns, the front red, of the part, from Ibbiya, in the domestic quarters, care of Aššur-killanni," 658 BC, Nineveh, SAA 7, 93.

10 "Šamaš-na'id, weaver of the palace of the queen," Nineveh, SAA 11, 222.

11 Melville (2004: 48).

12 SAA 11, 169, Nineveh, record of Egyptian deportees: "[...] the woman Ešarṭe[šu], total 4 female weavers." There is no representation of weavers on the bas-reliefs picturing female captives according to Albenda (1987: 17–21).

Kleber (2008: 247) gives a glimpse into the palatial textile economy. The textile workers appear to be both men and women. The women, in particular, had a leading position in textile production.

The text is associated with the Eanna archive and is dated from the reign of Nabonidus. It is a long list of deliveries of wool and goat hair over two years to "the *šakintu* and the weavers." An extract of the text reads:

> "31 talents ^{f}Banāt-Esagil, the overseer (*šakintu*); two talents Zababa-šar-uṣur, weaver; one talent 10 minas Nanaia-iddin, weaver; one talent 18 minas Tudadi, linen bleacher; 10 talents ^{f}Ēṭirtu of the *bīt redūti*; one talent Arad-Nabû. Total: 46 talents 28 minas of wool for the *šakintu* women and the weavers. The 5th year, Nabonidus king of Babylon."[13]

Kristin Kleber (2008: 247–248) demonstrates that this document is a list of expenses of a minor royal palace or several small royal institutions outside Babylon. An amount of wool coming from the Eanna temple had been given to a royal officer, and was then distributed to the staff of several palaces: the *šakintu* and weavers. Kristin Kleber proposed that they were in charge of supervising teams of workers.

Indeed, the amount of wool they received here is between one and 31 talents (30 kg–930 kg). As a comparison, one talent of wool is the quantity necessary to make twelve standard garments called ^{TUG2}KUR.RA of 2.5 kg each, and one ^{TUG2}KUR.RA is the expected production of a woman in one year, according to the administrative archives of the temples in Neo-Babylonian period.[14] Banāt-Esagil received 930 kilograms of wool, enough to make 372 ^{TUG2}KUR-RA. This points to the existence of workshops in the palaces, supervised by female overseers (*šakintu*s). Even if we do not know which type of textile the weavers had to make, the amount of wool is large enough for numerous craftsmen and -women during one year.

The presence of female overseers (*šakintu*s) in this text is interesting because it is the only Neo-Babylonian text that mentions them. During the Neo-Assyrian period, the *šakintu*s were important women managing palatial households, and they also controlled textile production.[15] During the Neo-Babylonian period, several titles of court officials are similar to Neo-Assyrian ones.[16]

---

13 PTS 2121: 27–34: 31 GU$_2$ ^{f}*ba-na-a-tú*-E$_2$.SAG.IL$_2$ ^{f}GAR-*ti* 2 GU$_2$ ^{Id}*za-ba$_4$-ba$_4$*-LUGAL.URI$_3$ ^{LU2}UŠ.BAR 1 GU$_2$ 10 MA.NA ^{Id}*na-na-a*-MU ^{LU2}UŠ.BAR 1 GU$_2$ 18 MA.NA ^{I}*tu-da-di* ^{LU2}*pu-ṣa-a-a* 10 GU$_2$ ^{f}*e-ṭir-ti šá* E$_2$ *re-du-tu* 1 GU$_2$ ^{I}IR$_3$.^{d}NA$_3$ PAP 46 GU$_2$ 28 MA.NA SIG$_2$.HI.A *a-na* ^{f}GAR.MEŠ *ù* ^{LU2}UŠ.BAR.MEŠ MU 5 KAM ^{d}NÀ.NÍ.TUK LUGAL TIN.TIR^{KI}.

14 See 2.2 of this contribution.

15 Svärd-Teppo (2007).

16 Jursa (2014: 121–148).

One can suppose that the *šakintu*s had the same role in Babylonia as their counterparts in Assyria.

This involvement of women in textile work for the palace may be confirmed by the letter TCL 9, 116 from Uruk, where the vice-governor of the Sealand asked the *šatammu* of the Eanna to weigh and give wool to his messengers because the women were lacking material for their work: "there is no more wool of the temple, and (the) women are idle without wool."[17] The civil authorities from Neo-Babylonian palaces were buying large quantities of wool from the temples. Here the women are not called "weavers" and we do not know what their tasks were.[18] The claimed amount of two talents of wool was enough to make 24 $^{\text{TUG2}}$KUR-RA. In Neo-Babylonian palaces, as in Neo-Assyrian ones, the textile workers were both men and women.

As a comparison, the Persepolis fortification tablets show that in the Persian palaces, during the Achaemenid period, the workforce of textile production was feminine, working in teams specialized in certain tasks according to the quality of the fabric they had to produce.[19]

The sources about the textile work of women in palaces in Neo-Assyrian and Neo-Babylonian periods are scarce, but they give clues of women's presence and importance, along with men, within the palatial textile economy. In the Neo-Babylonian temples, the women were also involved in textile production even if they are almost invisible in the sources.

2 Women textile workers of the temples

2.1 Were women excluded from manufacturing the garments of the gods?

One of the major bodies of cuneiform sources of 1st millennium Babylonia is the temples archives. In particular, the important administrative records of the temples of Sippar and Uruk contain hundreds of texts about the manufacture of the garments regularly offered to the god's statues during religious ceremonies. Most textile workers, weavers, washers, and menders were men with a few exceptions.

17 TCL 9, 116: 5–8, see Kleber (2008: 252): SÍG.HI.A *ina* E_2 *ia-a-a-nu* MUNUS.MEŠ *il-la* SÍG.HI.A *baṭ-la-a'*.

18 Kleber (2008: 152).

19 Briant (1996: 445). Inside the group of the weavers, who include a minority of men for a majority of women, the rations are divided in three groups according to the fineness of the produced fabric.

Tab. 1: The texts mentioning Muranātu.

No. of text	Date	Type of text	Place of Muranātu
Cyr 326	Cyr 08-ii-08	Delivery of linen garments by linen weavers as their labor assignment *iškaru*	Muranātu is responsible for the manufacturing of one garment as the other workers, but this garment is delivered by Šulaia.
GG II, 345 (BM 72810)	–	List of linen garments delivered by linen weavers	She made six minas of linen thread while the other workers are delivering garments. She appears in last position in the list of 14 workers.
CT 56, 684	–	Delivery of garments by linen weavers	The front of the tablet lists 11 linen weavers. Muranātu is the last in the list. She delivers 4 garments like the other workers (the amount is broken but can be deduced from the total).
CT 55, 327	[...]-viii-[...]	Ration list	The front of the tablet lists 15? linen weavers. Muranātu is the last in the list. The quantity she received is broken.
CT 56, 685	–	Ration list	The front of the tablet lists eight linen weavers. Muranātu is the last in the list and receives two GUR (of barley) while others receive four.
CT 56, 734	–	Ration list	The front of the tablet lists eight? linen weavers. Muranātu is the last in the list and receives four GUR (of barley) like the others.
GG II, 639	[Cyr] 04	Delivery of flour to linen weavers and menders employed for the building of a channel.	Muranātu is the last in the list of 15 linen weavers.
BM 62063	–	Broken text	Muranātu is the last in the list of linen weavers.

One of these exceptions is Muranātu, the only woman who was involved in the manufacturing of cultic garments at Sippar. She appears in eight texts dated from the reign of Cyrus in Babylonia, 539–530 BC (see Table 1 above). She is mentioned without her patronymic. She had the profession of "linen weaver."[20] She was integrated in a team directed by Šulaia, a linen weaver often mentioned

20 At Nuzi, women called linen workers are also attested, see Lion in this volume.

in the archives.[21] In the lists of food rations for the workers, she occupied the last position and received sometimes the same, sometimes half the rations of a man. She participated in the chore of digging a canal like the other craftsmen. In the text Cyr 326, she performed the same work as her colleagues: weaving a garment for the gods. But, according to the disposition of the document, it seems that the linen garment she made was actually delivered by the headmaster of the team, Šulaia. According to the text CT 56, 684, she made the same amount of garments as her colleagues. According to GG II, 345, she delivered linen thread, while the other craftsmen were delivering linen woven clothes.

Muranātu seems to have enjoyed the same status as other weavers and seems to have performed the same work, maybe with a specialization in spinning. Her situation was exceptional but it shows that women were not excluded from the manufacturing of sacred garments, even though they never occupied the highest status of prebendary weaver.

Murānātu produced three kilograms of linen thread by year according to GG II, 345, which was not sufficient to cover all the spinning work necessary to manufacture all the linen garments for the gods.[22] Maybe the linen thread she delivered here was a special kind of thread for sewing or stitching.

In 1st millennium Babylonian ritual texts, as for older periods, spinning was associated with women. For example, in order to keep away the evil goddess Lamaštu from a new born baby, the mothers had to give her feminine objects: beauty accessories (mirror, pins) and tools for processing wool (comb, distaff and spindle).[23] In the incantation to help the mother who is in travail, the male baby is represented by a weapon, and the female one by a spindle.[24] But, in the special case of the making of the god's garments, one does not know if the linen weavers were doing the spinning work with the raw linen they received, or if they were using a female workforce not recorded in the documentation, with the exception of Murānātu.

One single document from Sippar attests the presence of women working at the manufacturing of religious paraphernalia: the text CT 55, 867 dated from Nabonidus' reign. According to this text, ten shekels of blue-purple wool are brought to "the women" for a *pišannu*-bag.[25] These bags were part of the cultic paraphernalia; they were made with linen fabrics, colored wool, and used to

---

21 Bongenaar (1997: 351–352); Quillien (2015: 279).

22 In the same text, 13 *salḫu* are delivered, and one *salḫu* can weight from 1.4 to 5 kg (estimations calculated from BM 64591 and Nbn 164).

23 Farber (2014: 150–151 and 298–299).

24 Michel (2004); Stol (1995: 124); Cassin (1964).

25 CT 55, 867: obv. 1–3: 10 GIN$_2$ ^{SIG2}ZA.GÌN.KUR.RA *a-na pi-šá-an-nu a-na* MUNUS.MEŠ *šu-bu-ul*.

store precious objects. The task of the women was probably to decorate them, making braids or embroideries. But the attestation of a female staff member is unique in the Sippar archives. These women were making paraphernalia, not garments for the gods.

As a comparison, the textile workers of the Eanna temple in Uruk were also all men, with one exception, Hipāia. She appears in one text, where she receives garments of the gods made of linen and wool to work on them.[26] Her task is specified and differs from the usual job of the craftsmen at Uruk (weaving, mending, washing). She was asked to sew or patch a garment (verb *kubbû*).[27]

According to the temple archives, women did not participate in the making of the garments of the gods with a few exceptions or by performing subsidiary tasks. Even though large textile workshops employing a lot of women are not attested in the 1st millennium BC, women were involved in the production of the garments worn by the temples' staff.[28]

2.2 The invisible female weavers of the temples

A file of several texts coming from the temple archives shows how women took charge of the manufacturing of the standard garments worn by the temple's workers and soldiers, the TUG2KUR.RA.[29]

The temples distributed raw wool to female workers in exchange for the production of garments. The documentation consists of simple lists, not formal contracts with witnesses. This practice already existed early in the 1st millennium in Babylonia. Indeed, according to the text BRM 1, 5, dated from Nabonassar's reign (747–734), probably coming from Uruk, amounts of dyed wool are given to male and female workers. The two women, Damgāt and Ba'ianu, are responsible for manufacturing two TUG2KUR.RA. In the same context, the text

26 Text Eames R 27, Payne (2007: 119–120).

27 The verb "*kubbû*" or "*ḫubbû*" means "to patch, to sew" according to the CAD K: 482 and the AHw, p. 497 "benäht," or "to burnish, to attach," according to the CAD H: 214. This word is also used in relation with the golden appliqués added on the garments (GCCI II, 69: "172 rosette and *tenšu*-sequin have been taken of the *muṣiptu*-garment to be "*kubbû*"). Here this verb could mean "polish, repair."

28 About the implication of women in large textile workshops in Mesopotamia, see Cassin (1964: 977).

29 The "TUG2KUR.RA" is a generic term meaning a garment given to workers and soldiers of the temples. It is an outer garment suitable for working, which can have different configurations and uses. See Zawadzki (2010: 413–414).

BRM 1, 7 attests to the presence of a feminine workforce in charge of textile work for the temples: eight talents of combed wool are given to the "women weavers", but we do not know what kind of textile they had to produce.

Later during the Neo-Babylonian period, the text CT 55, 783, undated, from Sippar, lists nine women who receive standardized amounts of wool for making either one or two $^{\text{TUG2}}$KUR.RA for the temple. Some of them worked in pairs. They usually receive three kilograms of wool for making one cloth:

> "[12$^{?}$ minas of wool] for two $^{\text{TUG2}}$KUR.RA: Arnabi and her daughters; six minas for one $^{\text{TUG2}}$KUR.RA: Didītu; six minas for one $^{\text{TUG2}}$KUR.RA: Iāti, Zēr-Ebabbar; six minas for one $^{\text{TUG2}}$KUR.RA: Ištar-dannat (and) Nūptaia; six minas for one $^{\text{TUG2}}$KUR.RA: Busasa; [...] minas for one $^{\text{TUG2}}$KUR.RA: [...]-ninni and Lū'ahassu, [...] Bazītu, [x mi]nas of wool; four minas: Qari'; six minas: Diditu, daughter of Iqīša[ia]".[30]

The same system existed at Uruk. According to the Neo-Babylonian text NBC 4920, various amounts of wool were given to freedwomen (*zakītu*) to make $^{\text{TUG2}}$KUR.RA.[31] The *zakītu* were single women among the oblates of the temple[32]. Here we see that they could have a specialization in textile production. The garments weighed from 2 to 2.5 kilograms each.

The delivery of wool to women by the temples could also be more formally recorded with an acknowledgement of debt. In the text Jursa 1997, n° 13, from Uruk, dated from Nebuchadnezzar's reign, a woman named Tuqnaia owes 10 minas of wool equivalent of a woven garment of 2.5 kilograms ($^{\text{TUG2}}$*mīḫṣi*) that she has to deliver to the Eanna temple.

Some other texts show the supply of woven garments by women to the temples according to *iškaru* contract. The term *iškaru* meant "labor assignment."[33] These contracts, in presence of witnesses, obliged the person to deliver the product of his/her work, made with materials given by the temple, with-

---

30 CT 55, 783:1–17: [12$^{?}$ MA.NA SIG$_2$].HI.A *a-na* 2 $^{\text{TUG2}}$KUR.⌜RA⌝.MEŠ, ^{f}*ar-na-bi u* DUMU.⌜MUNUS⌝.MEŠ-*šú*, ⌜6⌝ MA.NA *a-na* 1+EN $^{\text{TUG2}}$KUR.RA, ^{f}*di-*⌜*di*⌝*-i-tu*$_4$, 6 MA.NA *a-na* 1 $^{\text{TUG2}}$KUR.RA, ^{f}*ia-a-ti* ^{f}NUMUN.E$_2$.BABBAR.RI, 6 MA.NA *a-na* 1 $^{\text{TUG2}}$KUR.RA, ^{fd}*iš-šar-dan-*⌜*at*⌝ $^{\text{[f]}}$⌜*nu*⌝*-up-ta-a*, 6 MA.NA *a-na* 1 $^{\text{TUG2}}$KUR.RA, ^{f}*bu-*⌜*sa-sa*⌝, [x] MA.NA *a-na* 1 $^{\text{TUG2}}$KUR.RA, [^{f}]⌜x⌝*-nin-ni u* ^{f}*lu-ú-a-*⌜*ḫat*⌝-[*su*], [.......]^{f}*ba-zi-tu*$_4$, [x MA].⌜NA⌝ SIG$_2$.HI.A, ⌜4$^{?}$⌝ MA.NA ^{f}*qa-ri-i'*, 6 MA.NA ^{f}*di-di-i-tu*$_4$, DUMU.MUNUS-*su šá* ^{I}BA-⌜*sa*⌝-[*a*].

31 Thanks to Kristin Kleber for providing me the transcription of this text.

32 According to Joannès (2014: 23), the *zakītu* was a single woman, she couldn't marry a private individual without the temple's consent but she could have children who became oblates too. Several weavers of the Eanna temple were called "sons of *zakītu*" according to Payne (2007: 60–62).

33 Bongenaar (1997: 360–361) and Postgate (1974).

in a determined period of time. Several contracts of this type are known for Uruk, Borsippa and Sippar.

For instance, in the contract BM 114480 of Uruk, dated from Cyrus' reign, a woman named Aška'ītu-ṭābat, an oblate, had to make in one year a ^{TUG2}KUR.RA weighing 2.5 kilograms (five minas), which had to be delivered to the temple of Uruk by her husband. The contract reads as follows:[34]

> "Since the 1st day of the month Ṭebētu of the ninth year of Cyrus, king of Babylon, king of the lands, yearly, one TUG$_2$-KUR-RA weighing five minas, will be the working assignment of Aška'ītu-ṭābat, oblate of the Lady of Uruk, wife of Ana-bītišu. Ana-bītišu son of Arrabi, oblate of the Lady of Uruk, will deliver it to the Eanna's treasure. Iddin-Nanaia, son of Arrabi, oblate of the Lady of Uruk, assure the guaranty for his brother Ana-bītišu. Witnesses: Iddin-Nabû son of Marduk-šum-ibni descendant of Egibi, Ina-tešī-ēṭir son of Nabû-apla-uṣur descendant of the [doorkeeper] Šamaš-ibni son of [PN descendant de PN], Gimillu the scribe, [son of Innin-zēr-iddin], Uruk, [month Ṭebētu, 1st day], 9th year, [Cyrus king] of Babylon, king of the lands."

Other contracts of this type are known. At Babylon, during the reign of one Artaxerxes, the women of the Atkuppu family had to deliver three kilograms of textile production by year according to the text BM 95530. At Sippar, widows were sometimes obliged to make textiles for the temple. In a contract dating from the reign of Darius, the temple of Sippar asks three of them to make one *gulēnu*-garment, as their yearly "labor assignment": "among (them), Imattu, Mistaia and Bazītu will deliver themselves three *gulēnu*-coats yearly, as their working assignment, to Šamaš."[35] They cannot take another husband, their children cannot be adopted and they cannot leave the city where they are settled. This city, named Bīrtu-ša-Kīnaia, is a locality under the dependency of Sippar.[36] This shows that the women employed by the temple to make gar-

---

34 BM 114480: Ob. *ul-⸢tu⸣* U$_4$ 1 KAM *šá* ITI AB MU 9 KAM, ^{I}*kur-áš* LUGAL TIN.TIR^{KI} LUGAL KUR.KUR *šá* MU.AN.NA, 1 ^{TUG2}KUR.RA *šá* 5 MA.NA KI.LÁ-*šú iš-ka-ri*, *šá* ^{fd}*áš-ka-a-a-i-tu$_4$-ṭa-bat* MUNUS RIG$_7$-*tu$_4$*, *šá* ^{d}GAŠAN *šá* UNUG^{KI} DAM ^{I}*a-na*-E$_2$-*šú*, ^{I}*a-na*-E$_2$-*šú* DUMU-*šú šá* ^{I}*ar-ra-bi*, ^{LU2}RIG$_7$ ^{d}INNIN-*šá*-UNUG^{KI} *a-na*, NÍG⸣.GA É.AN.NA *i-nam-di*, (lo.e.) ^{I}MU-^{d}*na-na-a* DUMU-*šú šá*, ^{I}*ar-ra-bi* ^{LU2}RIG$_7$ ^{d}INNIN-*šá*-UNUG^{KI}, (rev.) *pu-ut* ^{I}*a-na*-E$_2$-*šú* ŠEŠ-*šú na-ši*, ^{LU2}*mu-kin-nu* ^{I}MU.^{d}NA$_3$ DUMU-*šú šá* ^{Id}AMAR.UTU.MU.DU$_3$, DUMU ^{I}*e-gi-bi* ^{I}*ina*-GISSU.DINGIR.DUR.DIM, DUMU-*šú šá* ^{Id}NA$_3$.DU$_3$.ŠEŠ DUMU [^{LU2}I$_3$.DU$_8$] (restored from Beaulieu 2003: 359), ^{Id}UTU-*ib-ni* DUMU-*šú šá* [PN DUMU PN], ^{LU2}UMBISAG ^{I}*gi-mil-lu* [DUMU-*šú šá* ^{Id}INNIN.NUMUN.MU] (restored from YOS 7 p. 22), UNUG^{KI} [ITI AB U$_4$ 1 KAM], MU 9 KAM ^{I}[*kur-áš* LUGAL], TIN.TIR^{KI} LUGAL KUR.KUR. I thank the Trustees of the British Museum for the permission to publish this text.

35 Dar 43: 5–7: *ina lìb-bi* ^{f}*i-mat-tu$_4$* ^{f}*mi-is-ta-a u* ^{f}*ba-zi-tu$_4$ ina* MU.AN.NA 3 ^{TUG2}*gu-li-en iš-ka-ri a-na* ^{d}UTU TA *ra-man-ši-na i-nam-din-na-'*. See: Achemenet; Kohler and Peiser (1898: 16); Bongenaar (1997: 307); Ragen (2006: 218–221); Joannès (2008); Dandamaev (2009: 410, 513, 521, 532, 554).

36 Zadok (1985: 77) and Jursa (1995).

ments did not work in workshops in the temple but could be settled in the countryside. Francis Joannès has proposed that these women were former slaves given by private families to the temples.[37]

Indeed, even if the status of these women working for the temples is not always specified we can suppose that they were oblates.[38] In the *iškaru* contracts, the remuneration of these women is not mentioned. They could have received rations, wool, or silver. In a text of Sippar, Cyr 287, dating from Cyrus' reign, some women received silver for their *iškaru* in a long list of workers including men and women.

The *iškaru* contracts allowed the women to work at home, in the city or in the countryside.[39] The temples ordered their female dependents to produce textiles and gave them the raw material. One question is how much is the small number of contracts recovered representative of the total production of these women. They may have been numerous enough to supply the demand of the temples, which gave garments to its soldiers and travelers. Maybe the administration only wrote a formal contract in exceptional situations, or, more likely, we only possess the contracts for the tasks which were not successfully completed. But the temples, more often, preferred to give wool as a ration to its workers rather than garments. The workers had to transform the wool into garments themselves. In this case, the work may have been done by women in their families.

Sometimes, the temples leased their female workforce to others in exchange for a rent to be paid in woven textiles. In the contract NCBT 176, a woman and her daughter are placed at the disposal of two men in exchange of a yearly delivery of two ^{TUG2}KUR.RA to the temple, in the presence of the *qīpu* (high official) of the temple of Uruk. The text, dated from Kandalanu's reign (647–627 BC), reads:

> "^{f}Ilat, daughter of Eanna-ibni, is at the disposal of Iqīšaia, son of Marduk-šarranni, and Ṣillaia, son of Eanna-ibni. Yearly, Iqīšaia and Ṣillaia will deliver two ^{TUG2}KUR.RA for Ištar of Uruk and Nanaia, in the presence of Šamaš-ilaia, the *qīpu* of Uruk and the Eanna. (Witnesses, scribe, date)".[40]

---

37 Joannès (2014: 22).

38 See Beaulieu (1993: 7–14); Joannès (2008); Joannès (2014: 21–25) for studies of women status in Neo-Babylonian temples.

39 This is comparable to the "domestic system" in the European countryside during the 16th century.

40 NCBT 176: 1–9: "^{f}*i-lat* [erasure *u*] DUMU.MUNUS-*su* <*šá*> ^{I}E$_2$.AN.NA-*ib-ni ina pa-an* ^{I}BA-*šá-a* A-*šú šá* ^{Id}AMAR.UTU.LUGAL-*an-ni ù* ^{I}*ṣil-la-a* A-*šú šá* ^{I}E$_2$.AN.NA.DU$_3$ MU-*an-na* 2 TUG$_2$.KUR.RA.MEŠ *a-na* ^{D}INNIN UNUG^{KI} *u* ^{d}*na-na-a* ^{I}BA-*šá-a u* ^{I}*ṣil-la-a i-nam-din-nu ina* GUB-*zu šá* ^{Id}UTU.DINGIR-*a-a* ^{lú}*qí-i-pi šá* UNUG^{KI} *u* E$_2$.AN.NA", Ellis (1984: 43 no. 7).

The two women were probably temple oblates. As in the *iškaru* contracts, the expected yearly payment for one woman is one $^{\text{TUG2}}$KUR.RA. But here the woven cloth had to be delivered by the men. We do not know if the garments were produced by the women, because these garments are only a substitute payment for the women. They could have employed the women to do different tasks. However, it is probable that they were actually making the garments, and that they had to work on top of that for their new masters. At least, this text indicates a woman's yearly working capacity in weaving could exceed the making of one garment, for otherwise it would not be worthwhile for the men to hire them at this price. It is also possible that these women were relatives of these men who wanted to bring them back home to do the domestic work.

In a similar text from Uruk, PTS 2443, dated from the reign of Cambyses, an oblate of the Eanna temple was put at the disposal of another woman, in exchange for the yearly delivery of one $^{\text{TUG2}}$KUR.RA weighing 2.5 kilograms (5 minas).[41] It is a formal contract, with witnesses, very similar to the previous one, even if the *qīpu* was not present. With this system, the temple of Uruk outsourced the production of the $^{\text{TUG2}}$KUR.RA, entrusting women to private persons. These persons were intermediaries between the temple and the workforce in charge of manufacturing garments.

The $^{\text{TUG2}}$KUR.RA was a standardized garment weighing between four and six minas (two and three kilograms). It was a woolen outer garment given to soldiers and workers, not a fine piece of cloth.[42]

This file of texts shows that the temples during the Neo-Babylonian period did not have specialized workshops with a female workforce. The women employed by the temple to make garments were working at home. Thus, it is probable that the usual clothes worn by the personnel of the temples, counting several hundred people, were made by female workers. The poor documentation of their work is due to the fact that they were mainly working at home, in contrast to the textile workers who produced the garments of the gods, who worked in workshops and who, furthermore, used precious materials.[43] Indeed, the temples also bought TÚG-KUR-RA from men, as in the text BM 66261.[44] But we do not know who made these garments; perhaps they had been woven by women in their families.

---

41 Thanks to M. Jursa for providing me the transcription of this text.

42 The textiles traded by the Assyrian merchants from Aššur in the 2nd millennium BC, for instance, were lighter, see Veenhof (1972); Michel (2006).

43 CT 2: 2 mentions workshops of the textile craftsmen of the temple. See Joannès (1992). The text CT 55, 222 mentions a *bīt meḫṣi*, see Joannès (2013: note 15). About the precious garments of the gods: Zawadzki (2006) and Beaulieu (2003).

44 BM 66261 is edited by Jursa 2004: 190–192.

The temple archives indirectly document the domestic production of women. But women were also working for themselves and their family, not only for the temple.

3 The feminine domestic textile production

3.1 The textiles woven at home

Women weaving for their family were certainly numerous, but they rarely appear in our texts. The only women mentioned as specialists of textile work in the texts are slaves. Some texts mention slaves purchased for their knowledge in this field. In the *kudurru* BBSt 9: iv a 11, dating from the reign of Nabû-mukīn-apli (979–944 BC), Buruša gave a slave, a female weaver, as part of a field's purchase price. The value of the woman was 60 shekels of silver.

The letter CT 22, 201 (Hackl, Jursa and Schmidl 2014: 252), coming from the Sippar archives, and dating to the 6th century BC, mentions a female weaver (*išparti*) valued at half a mina of silver (250 grams). The author of the letter sent this weaver as a gift to his lord. The specialized experience of these slaves in textile work was a valuable asset. The text PTS 2324 (Kleber forthcoming no. 95) mentions a slave woman bringing 2.5 kilograms of wool "for the house." Here the slave has no specialized profession. According to Kristin Kleber the small quantity of wool in this text was probably used for the domestic textile production.

Another Neo-Babylonian example, Nbn 340, records the lease of a slave whose profession was "linen bleacher" (*puṣa'itu*). It is a debt note for half a mina of silver. The work of the slave serves as interest for the time of the duration of the loan, one month. As the interest for half a mina of silver was half a shekel, the value of the work of the bleacher during one month was assessed at this price. This text gives the only attestation of a woman linen bleacher in the archives. This is a sign that the women were more numerous in every-day textile work than the picture suggested by their few attestations in the documentation. Some of them practiced a specialized profession. But most of the women attested with a qualifier of profession are slaves. They worked in the domestic context and not in private associations of several peoples receiving money for their work, according to the texts at our disposal. These enterprises existed for the laundry at Borsippa and other cities, as Caroline Waerzeggers (2006: 83–96) has demonstrated, but the workers there were men.[45] In the elite

45 Waerzeggers (2006).

urban families, the specialized slaves in private houses must have helped in domestic textile production, or they released the other (free) women from certain specialized tasks.[46]

3.2 The economic value of the feminine textile work

The domestic work of women is documented only indirectly. In the marriage contracts recording the dowries brought by the bride into her husband's house textiles are sometimes mentioned. Most often, the textiles are not listed but mentioned by the generic term of *muṣiptu*, meaning: "garment." In some texts more details are given, such as wearable clothes and textiles for furniture. A part of these textiles was surely made by the bride or the women of her family, a text mentions a $^{\text{TUG2}}$*kirku ša ina bīti maḫṣu*, a fabric roll which has been woven at home.[47] The work of women participated in increasing the family's patrimony. Another part of these clothes may have been bought. Indeed, the texts giving the value in silver of garments attest the existence of a market.[48]

Women appear in several documents in the position of owning a garment. The text JCS 28: 42 lists possessions of several men and women, including garments: *muṣiptu*, $^{\text{TUG2}}$KUR.RA, and *šir'am*. In the text AJSL 16: 16, from Darius's reign, a woman named Šipaia issued a debt-note for a very fine *šir'am* – a jerkin worn by soldiers – owned by a man: "one outer *šir'am*, fine, of very good quality, belonging to Šamaš-iddin son of Bēl-ušallim, is owed by Šipaia, *sagittu*$^{(?)}$, daughter of Qariḫia. She will deliver this fine *šir'am*, a single one, of good quality, in the month Šabāṭu."[49] It is an order for a *šir'am* in form of a debt-note, and not an actual loan of a garment. This text indicates that outside the temples, women could also take orders to manufacture garments for private persons. This means that they could make profit with their production. According to George A. Barton (1990: 73) who edited the text, it is part of several documents referring to the transactions of a woman, the daughter of a slave, who managed provisions in the city of Šibtu. She also contracted with farmers and loaned silver.

---

46 Joannès (2014: 16–18).

47 TBER p. 93, Roth (1989: no. 34).

48 For instance: GCCI I, 290.

49 Barton 1990: 73 no. 2: 1–8: [1-*et* $^{\text{TUG2}}$]*šir-a-am e-le-ni-tu*$_4$ *mu-ru-qu-ut-tu*$_4$ *bab-ba-ni-tu*$_4$ *šá* ^{Id}UTU.MU DUMU *šá* $^{\text{Id!}}$EN.GI$^!$ *ina muḫ-ḫi* ^{f}*šip-pa-a* MUNUS$^!$ *sa*$^!$*-gi-tu*$_4$ DUMU.MUNUS-*su šá* ^{I}*qa-ri-hi-a*(sic) *ina* ITI ZÍZ 1 *šir-a-am* A$_4$ 1-*et*$^!$ *mu-ru-qu-ut-tu*$_4$ *bab-ba-ni-tu*$_4$ *ta-nam-di*.

In another text, BM 114603, Esagil-ah-ibni declared in the presence of the local notabilities (*mār banî*) that she was the owner of the *šir'am* she delivered to another woman.

Some texts give a glimpse inside the daily routine in textile work of women. In a letter from Sippar, written by a woman, Qutnānu, to another woman, Inṣabtu, Qutnānu is sending to her "sister" four minas of wool.[50] She asks her to weigh it. The exact nature of the work she has to do with this wool is lost because of a break in the tablet. Nevertheless, this text shows how the women managed the stocks of wool and their use by themselves. The similar text PTS 3015 from Uruk, Nabonidus' reign is an acknowledgement of a debt. A woman has to pay to the Eanna temple 5 shekels of silver, the value of the 30 minas of wool she bought. We do not know if the wool was bought for processing by her or in order to be traded. But it is the only sale of wool on credit from the Eanna archive where a woman is the debtor, and thus it cannot be taken as a rule.[51] Usually men were usually in charge of the wool trade and loans in 1st millennium Mesopotamia.

One important question is which part of the domestic textile production was traded in the 1st millennium BC. Several models of textile trade are known for Mesopotamian history, such as the trade inside and outside Mesopotamia during the Sargonic period, the Old Assyrian textile production of women in Assur that was sold in Anatolia, or on the trade of the surplus from domestic production on the local market at Nuzi.[52]

In an Uruk letter, Ṣillaia asked his wife Kalbaia to sew and pack a *šabattu*-garment from the clean garments and to send it to him by a messenger.[53] The woman here was doing the finishing work on a textile. The use of the garment by the husband is not specified (for sale, gift, or personal use), but it proves that a part of the domestic production did not stay in the house. At Uruk again, a letter belonging to the Ṣāhit-ginê B archive shows Ninurta-ahu-uṣur's wife employing a slave to work for her. Michael Jursa (2010: 221) has supposed that

50 NBB 226 = CT 22, 226, edition Ebeling (1949: 122).

51 Kleber (2015 185: no. 132)

52 About Sargonic period: Foster (1977: 31–43). He quotes the example of Quradum, merchant from Sippar trading clothes but also metals, cattle, foodstuff in Mesopotamia. About Old Assyrian trade Veenhof (1972) and Michel (2006). About Nuzi: Justel and Lion (2013): "we can hypothesize that besides an institutional or professional textile production, a domestic sector also produced surpluses which could be exchanged between private individuals."

53 BIN 1, 6, edition Hackl, Jursa and Schmidl (2014: 351–352). The "*šabattu*" meant a white cloth during the Mari period according to Durand (2009: 114). But the word appears only in the present text for the Neo-Babylonian period. The term is preceded by the determinative for the garments, TUG_2, and its qualities are not described.

this text refers to the traded textile production made in domestic contexts.[54] According to Caroline Waerzeggers (2014: 54 and 84), Ninurta-aḫ-uṣur was a trader working with Marduk-rēmanni. She supposed that the textile production of his wife was organized as a "cottage industry" for the purpose of trading. As spinning takes a lot more time than weaving, it is in the interest of the lady to employ a slave to do this work, and it should have increased the productivity of the house. In Egypt, the production of garments by women in the household was also an important source of wealth for the family.[55]

The archives of Sîn-uballiṭ, discovered at Ur, attest to the local trade in textiles. Sîn-uballiṭ was a member of the urban elite. His archive, found in his private house at Ur, date from Nabopolassar's reign. They document his economic activities in Northern Mesopotamia. Sîn-uballiṭ was probably employed by the royal administration to recover taxes and to participate in the military conscription.[56] In a letter to his wife Iṣṣurtu, Sîn-uballiṭ reprimanded her for not having completed the work with the wool he gave her: "You caused troubles with the wool! [See]: since I gave you the wool, you did not achieve [the wo]rk!"[57] His wife was thus in charge of a domestic textile production. In another letter, whose recipient is not named but may be also Iṣṣurtu, Sîn-uballiṭ asks a duplicate of the tablet concerning a purification's ceremony,[58] and requests the preparation of 40 jerkins *šir'am*: "See: the purification's ceremony tablet concerning linen which is before you, establish its duplicate. Write to your brother. Get 40 *šir'am* from the stockroom and write to me in what condition (they are)."[59] The amount of garments here shows that, either the familial production was organized at a large scale, or Sîn-uballiṭ was also buying garments. The important presence of the *šir'am* in the texts dealing with private cloth production may have been linked with the royal demand to provide

54 "In NBC 6189 from the Ṣāhit-ginê B archive, one reads of a female worker's spinning duties which are supervised by the wife of one of the archive's chief protagonists, Ninurta-ahu-uṣur. This must refer to work for the family's trading business which was done by women weaving and spinning from their home. Since the temple archives also refer to women weaving and spinning in their homes, one can assume that this was a typical arrangement rather than an exceptional one." Jursa (2010: 221).

55 See the study of J. Eyre (1998).

56 Jursa (2005: 135–137).

57 UET 4, 183: obv. 5–7: [... *te-i*]*q-ti ina* SIG$_2$.HI.A *tal-ta-kan-na* [*a-mur*] *a-ga-a ul-tu* SIG$_2$.HI.A *ad-dak-ka* [*ši-ip*]*-ra ul tu-qa-ta-a'*. Edition Ebeling (1949: 172–173).

58 The rich families sometimes delegated the washing of the garments to professional bleachers, according to Neo-Babylonian archives, see Waerzeggers (2006).

59 UET 4, 182: rev. 14–19: *a-mur tup-pi šá te-lil-ti šá a-na muḫ-ḫi* [*ki*?]-⸢*tu*⸣-*ú ina pa-ni-ka gab-ri-šú su-dir-ma a-na* ŠEŠ-⸢*ka*⸣ *šup-ri-i* 40 ^{TUG2}*šir-a-am ul-tu lìb-bi šu-li-i ki-ki-e u šup-riš*. Ebeling (1949: 171–172).

equipment for soldiers. This could have encouraged a specialization of some families in their production and trade. In a letter to his associate Dannia, Sîn-uballiṭ complained that Dannia was claiming a garment that he already gave to him.

> "When I wrote to you 'go and keep watch for my fresh dates, bring a garment, give it to me', you brought nothing at all! And when you came, you claimed for a garment!"[60]

This file of texts shows that the domestic textile production of women was not only used in the familial context but also used in business.

***

The cuneiform documentation of the 1st millennium BC dealing with textile production shows the importance of the economic role of women in textile production, even though they have only left few traces in the texts. In the Neo-Assyrian and Neo-Babylonian palaces, women and men were involved in textile production, according to the sources at our disposal. In the temples, women did not participate much in the production of garments of the gods, but they were responsible for the manufacture of clothes woven by the temple dependents. The temples used the "domestic system" of the *iškaru* contract to secure the annual production of standard garments by women working at home. Female domestic production is also visible in the dowries. A part of this production may have been traded, but the texts do not yet allow an evaluation of the economic importance of this phenomenon.

By performing textile work, women had a crucial role in the economy as producers of wealth. In institutional context, their production was used in the cult or the court. In domestic context, it increased the family's patrimony, and supplied stock for private trade.

Abbreviation

GG II Zawadzki (2013).

---

60 UET 4, 187: obv. 2–8: *ki-i áš-pu-ru-ka um-ma a-lik-ma* U$_2$.HI.NI-*ia a-mur u mu-ṣip-ti i-šá-am-ma i-bi in-nu mím-ma ul taš-šá-am-ma ul ta-ad-di-nu ù ki-i tal-li-ka a-gan-ni mu-ṣip-ti te-ri-šá-an-ni*. Ebeling (1949: 176–177).

Bibliography

Albenda, Pauline. 1987. Woman, Child, and Family: their Imagery in Assyrian Art. Pp. 17–21 in *La Femme dans le Proche-Orient Antique. Compte rendu de la XXXIIIe Rencontre Assyriologique Internationale*, ed. Jean-Marie Durand. Paris: Recherche sur les Civilisations.

Barber, Elizabeth. 1994. *Women's Work, the First 20,000 Years, Women, Clothes and Society in Early Times*. New-York: Norton & Company.

Barton, George A. 1990. Some contracts of the Persian Period from the KH^2 Collection of the University of Pennsylvania. *AJSL* 16: 65–82.

Beaulieu, Paul-Alain. 1993. Women in Neo-Babylonian Society. *The Canadian Society for Mesopotamian Studies, Bulletin* 26: 7–14.

Beaulieu, Paul-Alain. 2003. *The Pantheon of Uruk During the Neo-Babylonian Period*. CM 23. Leiden–Boston: Brill – Styx.

Bongenaar, Arminius V. C. M. 1997. *The Neo-Babylonian Ebabbar Temple at Sippar: Its Administration and its Prosopography*, PIHANS 80. Leiden: Nederlands Historisch-Archaeologisch Instituut te Istanbul.

Bottéro, Jean and Samuel Noah Kramer. 1989. *Lorsque les dieux faisaient l'homme, mythologie mésopotamienne*. Paris: Gallimard.

Briant, Pierre. 1996. *Histoire de l'empire perse*, Paris: Fayard.

Bridenthal, Renate, Claudia Koons, and Susan Stuard. 1987. *Becoming Visible. Women in European History*. Boston: Houghton Mifflin.

Brown, Judith. 1970. Note on the Division of Labour by Sex. *American Anthropologist* 72: 1073–1078.

Cassin, Elena. 1962. L'influence babylonienne à Nuzi. *JESHO* 5: 113–138.

Cassin, Elena. 1964. Tissage. P. 976 in *Dictionnaire archéologique des techniques II*, Paris: Editions de l'Accueil.

Dandamaev, Muhammad. 2009. *Slavery in Babylonia: from Nebopolassar to Alexander the great (626–331 B. C.)* translated by Victoria A. Powell and David B. Weisberg; revised edition. Chicago: Northern Illinois University Press.

Durand, Jean-Marie. 2009. *La nomenclature des habits et des textiles dans les textes de Mari*. ARM 30. Paris : CNRS Editions.

Ebeling, Erich. 1949. *Neubabylonische Briefe*. München: Verlag der Bayerischen Akademie der Wissenschaften.

Ellis, Maria DeJong. 1984. Neo-Babylonian Texts at Yale. *JCS* 36: 1–67.

Eyre, Christopher. 1998. The Market Women of Pharaonic Egypt. Pp. 173–191 in *Le commerce en Égypte*, eds. Nicolas Grimal and Bernadette Menu. IFAO Bibliothèque d'étude 121. Cairo: IFAO.

Farber, Walter. 2014. *An Edition of the Canonical Series of Lamaštu Incantations and Rituals and Related Texts from the Second and First Millennia B.C.* Winona Lake: Eisenbraun.

Foster, Benjamin R. 1977. Commercial activities in Sargonic Mesopotamia. *Iraq* 39: 31–43.

Hackl, Johannes, Michael Jursa, and Martina Schmidl (eds.). 2014. *Spätbabylonische Privatbriefe, Late Babylonian Private Letters, band. 1.* AOAT 414/1. Münster: Ugarit-Verlag.

Joannès, Francis. 1992. Les temples de Sippar et leurs trésors à l'époque Néo-Babylonienne. *RA* 86: 159–184.

Joannès, Francis. 2008. Place et rôle des femmes dans le personnel des grands organismes néo-babyloniens. *Persika* 12: 465–480.

Joannès, Francis. 2014. The Role of women in the Economy of the Neo-Babylonian Period. Pp. 15–32 in Joannès and Karahashi 2014.
Joannès, Francis and Fumi Karahashi (eds.). 2014. *Le rôle économique des femmes en Mésopotamie ancienne (REFEMA). Women's Role in the Economy of the Ancient Near East. Report: December 31, 2011-December 30, 2014*. Tokyo.
Justel, Josué and Brigitte Lion. 2013. Real Estate Dowries and Counter-Dowries in the Kingdom of Arrapḫe. Website refema.hypotheses.org/524.
Justel, Josué and Brigitte Lion. 2014. Real Estate Dowries and Counter-Dowries in the Kingdom of Arrapḫe. Pp. 39–41 in Joannès and Karahashi 2014.
Jursa, Michael. 1995. *Die Landwirtschaft in Sippar in Neubabylonischer Zeit*. AfO Beih. 25. Vienna: Institut für Orientalistik der Universität Wien.
Jursa, Michael. 2004. Accounting in Neo-Babylonian Institutional Archives: Structure, Usage, Implications. Pp. 145–198 in *Creating an Economic Order-Record-Keeping, Standardization, and the Development of Accounting in the Ancient Near East*, eds. Michael Hudson and Cornelia Wunsch. Bethesda, MD: CDL Press.
Jursa, Michael. 2005. *Neo-BabylonianLegal and Administrative Documents: Typology, Contents, and Archives*. Münster: Ugarit-Verlag.
Jursa, Michael. 2010. *Aspects of the Economic History of Babylonia in the first millennium BC. Economic Geography, Economic Mentalities, Agriculture, the Use of Money and the Problem of Economic Growth*. AOAT 337. Münster: Ugarit Verlag.
Jursa, Michael. 2014. The Neo-Babylonian empire. Pp. 121–148 in *Imperien und Reiche in der Weltgeschichte*, eds. Michael Gehler and Robert Rollinger. Wiesbaden: Harrassowitz.
Kleber, Kristin. 2008. *Tempel und Palast Die Beziehungen zwischen dem König und dem Eanna-Tempel im spätbabylonischen Uruk*. AOAT 358. Münster: Ugarit-Verlag.
Kleber, Kristin. forthcoming. *Spätbabylonische Texte zum lokalen und regionalen Handel sowie zum Fernhandel aus dem Eanna-Archiv*. Dresden: ISLET Verlag.
Kohler, Joseph and Felix Ernst Peiser. 1898. *Babylonischen Rechtsleben*, Band. 4. Leipzig: Eduard Pfeiffer.
Kramer, Samuel Noah and John R. Maier. 1990. *Myths of Enki, The Crafty God*. Oxford: Oxford University Press.
Lambert, Maurice. 1961. Recherches sur la vie ouvrière, les ateliers du tissage de Lagaš. *ArOr* 29: 422–443.
Mayer, Walter. 1978. *Nuzi-Studien I. Die Archive des Palastes und die Prosopographie der Berufe*. AOAT 205/1. Neukirchen-Vluyn: Butzon & Bercker.
Melville, Sarah C. 2004. Neo-Assyrian Royal Women and Male Identity: Status as a Social Tool. *JAOS* 124: 37–57.
Michel, Cécile. 2004. Deux incantations paléo-assyriennes. Une nouvelle incantation pour faciliter la naissance. Pp. 395–420 in *Assyria and Beyond: Studies Presented to Mogens Trolle Larsen*, ed. Jan Gerrit Dercksen. PIHANS 100. Leiden: Nederlands Instituut voor het Nabije Osten.
Michel, Cécile. 2006. Femmes et production textile à Aššur au début du IIe millénaire av. JC. *Techniques et culture* 46: 281–297.
Payne, Elizabeth. 2007. *The Craftsmen of the Neo-Babylonian Period: A Study of the Textile and metal Workers of the Eanna Temple*, PhD Dissertation presented to the Faculty of Graduate School of Yale University.
Postgate, John Nicholas. 1974. *Taxation and conscription in the Assyrian empire*. Rome: Biblical Institute Press.

Potts, Daniel T. 1997. *Mesopotamian Civilization, The Material Foundations.* London: the Athlone Press.

Quillien, Louise. 2015. Flax and linen in the 1st Millennium Babylonia BC: the Origins, Craft Industry and Uses of a Remarkable Textile. Pp. 271–296 in *Prehistoric, Ancient Near East and Aegean Textiles and Dresses, an Interdisciplinary Anthology*, eds Mary Harlow, Cécile Michel, and Marie-Louise Nosch. ATS 18. Oxford: Oxbow Books.

Ragen, Ascher. 2006. *The Neo-Babylonian Širkatu. A Social History.* PhD Dissertation. Harvard University.

Roth, Martha. 1989. *Babylonian Marriage Agreements 7th–3rd Centuries BC*, AOAT 222, Kevelaer: Butzon und Bercker.

Stig Sørensen, Marie Louise. 2000. *Gender Archaeology.* Cambridge: Polity Press.

Stol, Martin. 1995. Women in Mesopotamia. *JESHO* 38: 123–144.

Svärd-Teppo, Saana. 2007. The Role and Duties of the Neo-Assyrian šakintu in the Light of Archival Evidences. *SAAB* 16: 257–272.

Tenney, Jonathan. 2011. *Servile Laborers at Nippur in the 14th and 13th Centuries B.C.* Leiden: Brill.

Thébaud, Françoise. 1998. *Ecrire l'histoire des femmes et du genre.* Fontenay-Saint-Cloud: ENS Editions.

Vanstiphout, Herman L. J. 1990a. A Double Entendre Concerning Uttu. *NABU* 1990/57.

Vanstiphout, Herman L. J. 1990b. Once Again: Sex and Weaving. *NABU* 1990/60.

Veenhof, Klaas. 1972. *Aspects of Old Assyrian Trade and its Terminology*, Studia et documenta vol X, Leiden: Brill.

Villard, Pierre. 2009. Les femmes et l'écrit à l'époque Néo-Assyrienne. Pp. 306–319 in *Femmes, cultures et sociétés dans les civilisations méditerranéennes et proche-orientales de l'Antiquité*, eds. Françoise Briquel-Chatonnet, Saba Fares-Drapeau, Brigitte Lion and Cécile Michel. TOPOI, Suppl. 10. Lyon: Maison de L'Orient Méditerranéen Jean Pouilloux.

Waerzeggers, Caroline. 2006. Neo-Babylonian Laundry, *RA* 100: 83–96.

Waerzeggers, Caroline. 2014. *Marduk-remanni. Local Networks and Imperial Politics in Achaemenid Babylonia.* OLA 223. Leuven: Peeters.

Waetzoldt, Hartmut. 1972. *Untersuchungen zur neusumerischen Textilindustrie.* Roma: Inst. per l'Oriente.

Westenholz, Joan Goodnick. 1990. Toward a new conceptualization of the female role in Mesopotamian society. *JAOS* 110: 510–521.

Zadok, Ran. 1985. *Geographical Names According to New- and Late-Babylonian Texts.* Répertoire Géographique des Textes Cunéiformes 8. Wiesbaden: Reichert Verlag.

Zawadzki, Stefan. 2006. *Garments of the Gods. Studies on the Textile Industry and the Pantheon of Sippar according to the Texts from the Ebabbar Archive.* OBO 218. Fribourg und Göttingen: Academic Press

Zawadzki, Stefan. 2010. Garments in non-cultic context. Pp. 409–429 in *Textile Terminologies in the Ancient Near East and Mediterranean from the Third to the First Millennia BC*, eds. Cécile Michel and Marie-Louise Nosch. Oxford: Oxbow Books.

Zawadzki, Stefan. 2013. *Garments of the Gods. Vol. 2: Texts.* OBO 260. Fribourg und Göttingen: Academic Press.

Yoko Watai

Economic Activities of Women in 1st Millennium Babylonia

Within the framework of the REFEMA project, my research project has been the compilation of a prosopographical database of women in the Neo-Babylonian period and the Achaemenid period (from the end of the 8th century BC to the end of the 4th century BC, especially the "long sixth century"[1]), paying particular attention to economic aspects. The objective of my research is to present a complete overview of women's economic activities.

It was not just a few women who participated in various economic activities, according to the Neo-Babylonian documentation, though the number of women involved in these activities is indeed much smaller than that of men. Many preceding archival studies show that women, especially those who belonged to the families of urban notables, took part in economic activities in the familial framework.[2]

In order to outline Neo-Babylonian women's economic role and activities, I have collected data of women's activities from documents published, edited, and translated in these archival studies and integrated them into a database. I have classified these activities into two groups: "active" and "passive."[3]

It must be noticed that these two categories are not antithetical. As we will discuss below, it is difficult to distinguish them clearly. Women acting as agents of contracts apparently did not always participate in activities through their own initiative; their actions were often integrated into the economy of their households. In that case, women could act as agents, but we cannot consider them as having true autonomy. Meanwhile, we find, for example, a slave woman who managed the business of her master, as we will see below.[4] She can be also situated in the buffer zone between "passive women" and "active women." Moreover, we suppose that the degree of the economic autonomy of women was different according to their condition: age, social strata, etc.

---

1 Jursa 2010: 4–5.

2 Joannès 1989; Wunsch 1995 and 2005; Waerzeggers 1999; Roth 2000; Baker 2004; Cousin forthcoming, etc. See also 2003b.

3 The subject of "women as agents" in the Neo-Assyrian period has been discussed in Teppo 2007.

4 Joannès 1992a and b; Tolini 2012.

Yoko Watai, Research Fellow of Japan Society for the Promotion of Science, Tsukuba University; wataiyoko@gmail.com

Despite the difficulty of defining this classification, I believe that the study of "passive women" and "active women" illustrates roughly the range of activities in which women participated and their degree of economic autonomy. The existence of tens of thousands of tablets that have survived from the Neo-Babylonian period makes this study possible, though obviously not all texts pertain to women's activities.

This paper will investigate two types of women's positions, passive and active, in the economic sphere (see Section 2), and will examine whether elements that determine women's economic autonomy exist (see Section 3).

It should be noted that the compilation of the database will continue for my future research; this paper is therefore considered to be a preliminary study.

1 Corpus of texts

The research source material for this study is predominantly based upon socio-economic documentation found in private and familial archives.[5] Neo-Babylonian contracts of this type have been edited, published, and discussed within several archival studies over the last thirty years. I have mainly collected data from across these archival studies. For now, the study is based on 622 women: 92 belong to the archives of the Egibi family of Babylon (not only family members but also slave women and those who did transactions with the family; see Roth 1991b; Wunsch 1995 and 2000; and Abraham 2004); 49 belong to the Nappāḫu family of Babylon (Baker 2004); 18 belong to the Iddin-Marduk archives of Borsippa (Wunsch 1993); 55 belong to the Ea-ilûta-bāni family of Borsippa (Joannès 1989); 18 belong to the archives of Kuta (Jursa 2003); 16 belong to the Bēl-rēmanni archives (Jursa 1999); 24 belong to the Murašû family, and 3 royal women will be mentioned below (Stolper 1985; Donbaz and Stolper 1997; Tolini 2013); 13 belong to the Gallābu family;[6] 10 belong to the Šangû-Ninurta family;[7] and 327 belong to others.[8] Apart from them, 9 women belong

5 Administrative documents in the temple archives, especially those of Uruk, will be integrated in the future. Bénédicte Cuperly discussed women in Uruk in her Master's thesis (Cuperly 2003). Concerning the oblates of the *Eanna*, see Joannès 2013b.

6 Olga Popova, PhD student at Paris 1 University, gave me this information. Information on the other women who appear in the archives of the Gallābu family will be integrated into the database in future.

7 Wunsch 2005b; Cousin forthcoming.

8 Joannès 1982 and 1994; Stolper 1990; Roth 1991a and 2000; Wunsch 1997, 2003a, and 2005; Waerzeggers 1999; Watai 2012, etc.

to the royal families: Ba'u-asītu, Kaššaia and Innin-eṭirat, daughters of Nebuchadnezzar II;[9] Adad-guppi, mother of Nabonidus, and En-nigaldi-Nanna, his daughter,[10] who appear in inscriptions of Nabonidus; Gigītu, daughter of Neriglissar; Amisiri' (Amestris), queen of Xerxes I and queen-mother of Artaxerxes I; Purušatu/iš (Parysatis), queen of Darius II; and Madumitu, a court woman, who appears in the Murašû archives. Apart from the royal women, 477 women are free women and 145 are slave women.

2 Women's activities

The majority of women participate in only one or two activities, but some women appear in five to ten documents and more. The most "active" woman is Ina-Esagil-ramât, wife of Iddin-Nabû of the Nappāḫu family, who appears in 46 texts in our corpus.

As mentioned above, I classified women's activities into two groups: "passive" and "active," in order to investigate the degree of women's autonomy in the economic sphere. Active women are defined as those who act as the agents of the transactions treated in the texts; for example, as creditors, debtors, sellers, or those who file lawsuits, etc. They own properties and can manage them independently. Meanwhile, passive women[11] signify those who are quoted in the texts, but do not act through their own initiative; examples include young brides who are given dowries (not for themselves but rather for their grooms), and especially slave women who appear as the objects of sales or exchange contracts, among others. According to this classification, we find 263 women acting as agents at least in one text, and 260 women mentioned only as objects.

2.1 Women as active agents

This category includes women who appear independently or with their family members, such as a husband, sister(s), son(s), and daughter(s), as agents. As Table 1 shows, the most frequent activities of women are as creditors, debtors, and sellers. In the family sphere, there were much fewer active women than

9 Joannès 1980; Beaulieu 1998.
10 Dhorme 1914; Beaulieu 1989 (especially pp. 121–122, and pp. 127–131).
11 Teppo 2007 uses the term "invisible women."

Tab. 1: Women as active agents.[12]

(1) Business activities			
Creditor		48 persons[13]	
Debtor		50	
Seller	Slaves	19	43
	Houses	10	
	Agricultural lands	12	
	Prebend	2	
Buyer	Slaves	6	16
	Houses	4	
	Agricultural lands	5	
	Prebend	1	
House or Field rent	Owners	13	22
	Tenants	9[14]	
Land management			16
Exchange of properties			5
Guarantors of the debt			6
Receiving silver instead of family members (husband or son)			2
(2) Familial activities			
Adopting a child			7
Put her child up for adoption			8
Transfer	to children, grandchildren, mother or the second husband		17
Division	with sisters, sons, or other members of the family		6
Marriage	Receiving and accepting a proposal of marriage		2
	Giving her daughter/sister in marriage		12
	Asking the parents of the girl to marry her son		1
Entrusting her child to a wet-nurse			2
Changing the heir			2
Finding (and adopting) a child			2

12 If a woman participates in the same type of activity in several texts, we count her as one person for that activity. Meanwhile, when a woman participates in more the one activity, we count her as one person for each one.
13 A slave woman is included.
14 A slave woman is included.

Tab. 1 (continued)

(3) Job			
Wet-nurses[15]		4	10
Tenant farmers (charged an estimated yield *imittu*)		6	
Management of a tavern		1[16]	
(4) Legal activities			
Party in a lawsuit		10	63
Witness	*ana mukinnūtu ina libbi/ ṭuppi ašbat*	2	
	ina ašābi[17]	44	
	ina ṭuppi … ašib/ušešab	2	
	ina kanak ṭuppi … ašbāta[18]		
	ana šībūti (ina libbi) ušešib/attašab	2	
	mukinnu	1[19]	

passive women. Women were not excluded from the judicial domain, although their position was much more restricted than that of men. They could file a lawsuit, and be present as witnesses, but only in contracts in which they or their relatives were concerned. We find few varieties of women's jobs.

---

15 We find two types of documents concerning wet nurses: contracts and receipts (Zawadzki & Latowski 2008). Wet-nurses contracts are characterized by the verb *enēqu* Š ("suckle"). For example: PN *ina ḫūd libbīšu ana* PN_2 *taqbi umma* PN_3 *mārāka adi* 3 *šanāti* <*lū*>*šenniqu*, "PN said voluntarily to PN_2 as follows: 'I will suckle PN_3, your son, for 3 years'" (BM 74330 = Wunsch 2003, No. 19: 1–5); PN *ana mušēniqūtu ana* 2.ta *šanāti mārtu ša* PN_2 *tušēšab* "PN will settle the daughter of PN_2 for suckling, for two years" (BM 33978 = Wunsch 2003, No. 20: 1–4), etc. In an adoption contract (BM 59804 = Wunsch 2003, No. 5), a single mother gives her son for adoption to a man, and receives the silver and a garment for him. The mother was likely employed as wet-nurse (see Wunsch 2003: 211–214).

16 It is a slave woman who managed a tavern for the benefit of her master but with her own authority to a great degree.

17 Introduced by the clause *ina ašābi ša* ^{f}PN, placed after the list of witnesses.

18 This phrase is contained in a house sale contract (TuM 2/3, 8: 38–39). The woman presenting at the draft of the sealed document received 3 shekels of silver. We do not know her relationship to the contract, but she must be the spouse or mother of the seller. We find several documents in which witnesses receive a gift or a payment of a small sum of silver. See San Nicolò 1947: 290–302.

19 It is a slave woman (BM 77461 = Wunsch 2005a, No. 4: 8 and BM 59804 = Wunsch 2005a, No. 5: 12).

The "active" women can be classified into two subcategories: women with "true" autonomy and women with autonomy for the family's benefit.[20]

2.1.1 Women with true(?) autonomy

The first subcategory includes women who participate in economic activities independently and truly for their own interests.

We take the example of Lūrindu of the Ilûta-bāni family, as studied by Joannès 1989. After her marriage, she preserved and managed at least a part of her dowry properties; according to the text TuM 2/3 2 = Joannès 1989: 166, she rented a house belonging to her dowry.

Another woman called Ṭābatu, daughter of Nabû-aḫḫē-iddin, descendant of Sîn-tabni, appears in two texts of our database. In the first document (VS 5 70 + 71 = Baker 2004, No. 188), she is apparently a creditor of a certain Nidintu-Bēl and Kabtaia, his mother. They sold a slave to Itti-Nabû-balāṭu, spouse of Ṭābatu. Itti-Nabû-balāṭu paid the debt to his wife in place of two debtors. Ṭābatu was present as *ina ašābi*-witness. Two years later, Itti-Nabû-balāṭu sold the slave, who he had bought from Nidintu-Bēl and Kabtaia, to Ina-Esagil-ramât of the Nappāḫu family (VS 5 73 = Baker 2004, No. 189). Ṭābatu again was present as *ina ašābi*-witness in this contract; therefore, she could have held certain rights to the slave. The payment to Ṭābatu by Itti-Nabû-balāṭu was maybe just on paper; nevertheless, the texts convey the impression that Ṭābatu and her husband had a business relationship and acted independently of each other. It is, therefore, possible to presume that Ṭābatu was economically autonomous.

However, it is difficult to distinguish women with the complete economic independence from others. Ina-Esagil-ramât, the spouse of Iddin-Nabû of the Nappāḫu family, is mentioned in 46 texts, and seems to act with true economic autonomy. For example, she manages and exploits the fields given by her father as her dowry in her own name. Her situation can be explained through the condition of her marriage; she was born into the wealthy Egibi family,[21] and thus her marriage and dowry brought especially valuable real estate to her husband's family (Baker 2004: 26; see also Cousin 2012). However, she always shared the properties either with Nabû-tabni-uṣur, her brother, or with Amat-

20 Teppo 2007 expresses the former as "explicit agents," and the latter as "implicit agents."

21 However, she did not belong to the best-known line of the Egibi family from Babylon studied in Wunsch 2000.

Mulissu (or Gigītu), her sister. She did not, therefore, strictly speaking, enjoy complete economic independence; in reality, she could be independent of her husband, but not of her parental family.

2.1.2 Women with autonomy for the family's benefit

Other women are mentioned as independent agents, but their activities are considered as a part of the economy of the household. Women of this type are certainly more numerous than those who participated in economic activities through their own initiative.

For example, we consulted a series of documents, which have been studied by Martha M. Roth, Cornelia Wunsch, and Caroline Waerzeggers, concerning the property of Amat-Bāba, wife of Marduk-nāṣir-apli, chief of the Egibi family.[22] Fifteen years after the transfer of her dowry (BM 34241, dupl. BM 35492 = Wunsch 1995, No. 4), Amat-Bāba was given one lot of field and nine slaves from her husband, Marduk-nāṣir-apli, in exchange for the dowry, which was composed of thirty minas of silver, two minas of gold, five minas of silver jewelry, and two slaves (BOR 2, 3; dupl. Wunsch 1995, No. 5). This contract meant that the husband "wishes to utilize the dowry silver, or has already done so," and therefore "he may be compelled to substitute some other commodity of comparable value for that silver" (Roth 1989a: 5). Three months later, she sold the seven slaves for twenty-four minas of silver, but this contract was cancelled "by wish of Amat-Bāba (*ana ṣibûti ša Amat-Bāba*)" (Dar. 429). Following the cancellation of the sale of these slaves, Amat-Bāba transferred them to her three daughters (BM 33997 = Wunsch 1995 No. 8). However, the transfer was finally cancelled "by wish of Marduk-nāṣir-apli." The daughters then no longer had a share (DT 233 = Wunsch 1995, No. 9). According to C. Waerzeggers, the first sale contract must have been drafted by Marduk-nāṣir-apli, in his wife's name (see Waerzeggers 1999: 195). However, Amat-Bāba did not agree to the selling of her slaves; she cancelled the sale contract, and transferred them to her daughters. Amat-Bāba "tried to do all she could to keep the slaves in the family while Marduk-nāṣir-apli wanted to sell them" (Waerzeggers 1999: 196). Ultimately, probably because of his wife's death, Marduk-nāṣir-apli succeeded in selling the slaves. If this explanation is correct, the position of Amat-Bāba was completely dependent, though she appears as agent, except for the fact that she rejected and cancelled the sale of her slaves against her husband's wishes.

---

22 See Roth 1989a and 1991: 27–29; Wunsch 1995; and Waerzeggers 1999: 194–196.

Another example is Bū'ītu, wife of Kidin-Maduk of the Šangû-Gula family. She was a co-debtor with her husband and his brother (DT 225 = Wunsch 2000, No. 122). She sold her field, and in the same contract, her son, the mother of her husband, and his brother sold their own lands simultaneously (Cyr 161(+) = Wunsch 2000, No. 125). The property that she sold was apparently her own property. She had bought it from her brother. We can probably consider that she participated in the purchase contract of the property herself, although the more detailed context is unknown. Concerning the contract referred to in the second text, however, she clearly sold her properties in order to pay the debt of her husband's family. Bū'ītu therefore assumes a double position: at one time an agent with economic autonomy, and at another time an agent without true autonomy, acting in the framework of the household, in another time. In fact, most of the active women seem to hold this double position; the question is the degree of control that the household allowed over their activities. This question will be analyzed further in next papers.

2.1.3 Women as witnesses

It should be noted that I have included women appearing as witnesses in the "active agents" category. In contracts accompanied by the transfer of property or possessions, such as the purchase contracts of real estate (including fields and urban houses) or slaves, and marriage contracts with the transfer of dowries, women belonging to the families that give possession of the property, for example the wife of the seller of fields or the mother of the bride, are often presented as witnesses, introduced by the phrase "*ina ašābi* (in the presence of)," and the like. Unlike men, women are only present in contracts related to their family members.[23] Their presence is considered in this case to signify their approval for selling or otherwise disposing of the properties.[24]

However, we also find women as sellers with their husbands or sons. In these cases, we consider that the properties were part of their dowries, though this is not always mentioned in the contracts. Compared with these women, those present in contracts seem to be rather passive. We notice again that it is difficult to distinguish between the "active women" and the "passive women."

23 One exception is the case of BM 77461 = Wunsch 2005a, No. 4: 8 and BM 59804 = Wunsch 2005a No. 5: 12, in which a slave woman is present in a list of a *mukinnu* witnesses of the adoption contract. Apparently, she did not have any family relationship with the woman who gave her child for adoption.

24 Concerning the *ina ašābi*-witness, see San Nicolò 1947; Roth 1989b: 20–23; von Dassow 1999.

Tab. 2: Women as passive

(1) Business activities			
Paying the debt of family members			3
Confined to prison by their husbands' creditors			7
Owners (by themselves but without management, or mentioned as neighbors)	Lands, houses, slaves, etc.		39
(2) Familial activities			
Object of marriage (often accompanied by the transfer of dowries to husbands)			68
Receipt of properties (by herself)	from husbands from parents (fathers and/or mothers), brothers, sons	10 18	28
Receipt of a subsistence allowance			3
Adopted			7
Foundlings			1
Her child is adopted by her second husband			1
(3) Slave women			
Sold and purchased			37
Objects of transfer or division among the family members			54
Mortgaged, guarantee for their masters' debt, or confined to prison by creditors of their masters			32
Object of exchange			3
Transferred for the *ḫarrānu*			6
Object of lawsuits			4
Released			1
Fugitives			3
Hired out by a third person[25]			6

25 M. A. Dandamayev regards the case of Amtia (or Amat-Mullissu), a slave girl of Itti-Marduk-balāṭu of the Egibi family (Nbn. 679 = Wunsch 1997, No. 17; Nbn. 682 = Wunsch 1997, No. 18), as "the hire of slave women for use in Brothels" (see Dandamayev 1984: 132–136); but this interpretation is doubtful when we accept the translation of line 5 of the text Nbn. 679 by C. Wunsch (see Wunsch 1997: 87).

2.2 Passive women

"Passive women," or "invisible women" according to the expression of Teppo 2007, includes two categories. The first is women appearing as objects in the texts: for example, daughters given by their fathers or brothers to future husbands in marriage contracts, women with transferred gifts, adopted daughters, etc. The second category is women whose names are mentioned in the texts who do not have any connection with the contracts: for example, neighbors of the real estate dealt with in the contracts, owners of the fields that other people controlled, etc. Some royal women who appear as landowners belong to this category, as well as slave women.[26]

3 Decisive factors for determining women's autonomy

As we have seen above, the economic situations of women were seemingly diverse. Can we find, however, any factor that determines their autonomy in the economic sphere? We will examine if two aspects, age and social status, were possible factors.

3.1 Age

3.1.1 Children and young girls (daughters)

Children and young girls did not have any autonomy, as guardians generally controlled young girls. These authority roles were normally played by a girl's parents, whether only a father or both father and mother; or the elder brother if the father is deceased; or only the mother, if the father is dead and the family lacks an adult brother.

A group of texts from Nippur, during a period of siege in the 7th century that was studied by Oppenheim 1955, presents such subordinate situations of girls. Nine texts belonging to the archives of a Ninurta-uballiṭ concern the sales of small children, caused by a huge rise in the price of barley under the special circumstances of siege by Šîn-šar-iškun. All of the children sold were girls be-

26 A very small number of slave women act apparently as agents (see above).

tween infancy and puberty, with only one exception. This fact permits us to consider that girls were sent away from their families more frequently than boys were.

Under normal conditions, girls were made to marry in their teens. The girl's future husband requested the marriage from her guardian, and the latter gave the dowry to the groom. Girls did not have any freedom to choose their husband by themselves.

One text (Cyr. 307) shows that a daughter who wants to marry a man without the agreement of her parents suffers the risk of exclusion from her family, and the risk of becoming a slave:

> (Cyr. 307: 1–9 and 17b–18) The day when Ṭābatu-Iššar, daughter of Yaše'iama will be seen with Kulû, son of Kalbaia, or when he will take her away with false words without her preventing it, or if she does not say to the head of the family: "Write to Kalbaia, father of Kulû," Ṭābatu-Iššar will receive a slave-mark." (...) In the presence of Halâ, mother of Ṭābatu-Iššar.

Joannès 1994 proposed two possible explanations: first, Ṭābatu-Iššar continued having frequent assignations with her boyfriend, and her family forbade her to see him in order to defend the reputation of the girl and her family; second, the girl eloped with Kulû, or perhaps she was abducted. If Ṭābatu-Iššar were to ask the head of her family to write a letter demanding permission from Kulû's father for her marriage to Kulû, Ṭābatu-Iššar and Kulû could be married. Otherwise, if she does not do so, she must be punished by the family and become a slave. In this text, it is interesting to note that her father (with a Judean name) maintains the right of deciding on the marriage. In other words, the daughter could marry the lover (?) if she first asks for the approval of her father. It suggests that, generally, young girls certainly did not have autonomy to decide their own marriages.

Generally, women had no right to inherit family property, except when they had already received property as a dowry. We find, however, the example of young girls as landowners. Amat-Nanaia (the mother of Lūrindu, who was mentioned above) and her sister Amat-Sutīti of the Ilûta-bāni family appear to be co-owners who manage an orchard with their uncle Širiktu, and then, following his death, with his son Bēl-uballiṭ. Širiktu was originally the co-owner of the orchard with his brother Nādin, the father of the two girls, and they had not divided it. When Nādin died after the 17th year of Nabonidus, Širiktu married his brother's widow Kabtaia, the mother of Amat-Nanaia and Amat-Sutīti. The two girls therefore seem to appear as successors of their father Nādin (see Joannès 1989: 50–56). Amat-Nanaia and Amat-Sutīti appear to be co-owners of the orchard between the 3rd year of Cyrus (536 BC) (TCL 12–13, 128) and the 10th year of Darius (512 BC) (TuM 2/3, 167) for twenty-four years (see Joannès

1989: 83–84). Six texts exist from this period concerning the management of the orchard, and they mention Širiktu (or his son Bēl-uballiṭ), Amat-Nanaia and Amat-Sutīti. It is clear that the two young girls did not manage the orchard in practice, because they were undoubtedly very young at that time. The marriage contract between Kabtaia and Nādin was dated to the 6th year of Nabonidus (550 BC, TuM 2/3 1); moreover, Nādin must have died during 539–538 BC. Hence, their daughters, Amat-Sutīti and Amat-Nanaia, must have been between thirteen and three years old when they inherited their portions of the property. The question that must be asked is whether this inheritance is the same thing as the two girls' dowries. While this cannot be ascertained, we can at least say that this property did not come from their mother's dowry nor did it constitute the dowry of Lūrindu, the daughter of Amat-Sutīti. Thus, the daughters seem to have received a portion of the inheritance in addition to their dowries in this case, although this fact does not imply their active participation in the management of the property.

3.1.2 Married women (wives)

Married women could participate in economic activities according to the social and economic situation of the family, for themselves or for their household.

We recall women who are presented as *ina ašābi*-witnesses discussed above. These women are not strictly agents, but their agreement must have been necessary for the transfer of the property. Moreover, in sale contracts of real estate, "the lady of the house (*bēlet bīti*)," namely the wives or mothers of sellers, were often given a *lubāru*-garment by the buyer. The gift of the *lubāru*-garment can be considered something pertaining to a social relationship, and given in order to gain the consent of the housekeeper concerning the transfer of the property. "The lady of the house" was not unconnected to the transfer of familial property, though she did not have the legal right of ownership of the properties. The "lady of the house" could, as housekeeper, obtain social respect.

3.1.3 Aged women (widows and mothers)[27]

The situation of widows was different; some continued to live in their husband's house and manage their properties, while others remarried.

27 See van Driel 1998 and Tonietti 2006.

In principle, women could not inherit familial properties. The husband, however, donated the property to his wife during his lifetime, or put his son(s) under a duty to support his wife.

We find some women who were co-debtors with their sons, and who would return the debts of their sons. According to one document (BM 32174 = Wunsch 1997, No. 20), a creditor declared that he had not lent silver to a person without the agreement of the latter's mother.

> (BM 32174 = Wunsch 1997, No. 20: 1′–8′) [PN] declared in front of Sîn-erība, the chief judge, and judges of Nabonidus, king of Babylon, as follows: "Arad-Marduk said to me, in the second year of Nabonidus, the following: '[...] Lend me the silver. I will give you my field and my house as security.' I did not pay the silver to him without the agreement of Busasa, his mother."

The mother and the sister of Arad-Marduk were guarantors of his debt. The context is no longer clear, but the text shows that, in all likelihood, the mother's financial power was important for her son's economic activities.

In the case of remarriage, women could choose their second husband (Neo-Babylonian Laws § 13, see Roth 1997). Women could be agents of their own marriage contract. Ḫubbuṣītu of the Ilī-bāni family, for example, gave half of her dowry to her child, that is the first husband's child, and the other half to her second husband (TCL 12–13, 174 = Joannès 1989, 317).

Nevertheless, not all widows and aged women, of course, had financial power. The text Nbk. 101 mentions a mother (Ḫammaia) who married her daughter (Lā-tubāšinni) to a man and received a financial help from him.

> (Nbk. 101: 1–9) Dāgil-ilī said to Ḫammaia the following: "Give me Lā-tubāšinni, your daughter. She will be my wife." Ḫammaia heard him and gave him Lā-tubāšinni for a spouse. Dāgil-ilī voluntarily gave Ana-muḫḫi-bēl-amur, a slave man, whom he bought with a half mina of silver, and a half mina of silver to Ḫammaia.

The agent of the marriage contract of Lā-tubāšinni was her mother, as her father must have been dead and she had no adult brother. Ḫammaia, mother of the bride, received the silver and a slave. However, in reality, Dāgil-ilī was a slave, and Lā-tubāšinni herself became a slave after the marriage, according to another document drafted thirty-two years later.[28] When that document was drafted, Lā-tubašinni had been liberated from slavery. She filed a lawsuit, probably against the master of her husband, because he had sold her children as slaves. As a result of the examination by judges, it was determined that her

28 Cornelia Wunsch explained that Lā-tubāšinni was a girl whom Ḫammaia had found on the street and raised (Wunsch 1997: 65).

children were born before Lā-tubāšinni's release from slavery; the conclusion was that the sale of her children as slaves was valid.

Thus, while some old women seem to have enjoyed economic authority, the lives of others were difficult, as many texts demonstrate. A certain number of widows and older slaves depended on temples and acted as oblates.

3.2 Social status of the family

3.2.1 Women of high rank

We have only a few documents relating to women belonging to royal families or who were high priestesses.

En-nigaldi-nanna, daughter of Nabonidus, was appointed as the *entu*-priestess of Sîn at Ur by her father. Before this appointment, Nabonidus had "probably installed his own daughter in Eanna (in Uruk) in the position formerly held by Kaššaya," the daughter of Nebuchadnezzar, according to P. A. Beaulieu 1989: 122. However, when he had ordered that "the rations of the king's daughter be integrated into the king's box" (YOS VI 10: 22) in the Eanna temple (28-i-Nbn 1), "the allotment of rations to the king's daughter was cancelled, on which basis one may infer that the king had plans for her transfer to a new office outside Uruk" (Beaulieu 1989: 119). En-nigaldi-Nanna was then consecrated as *entu*-priestess of Ur during the same period that her father claimed to restore the *gipāru* of the temple of Ur for her residence:

> "I installed my daughter as a high priestess and called her name, En-nigaldi-Nanna. I made her enter the *gipāru*" (E'igikamma cylinder inscription, lines 13–14).[29]

En-nigaldi-nanna's situation is apparently passive, as this appointment does not reflect her personal decision. However, she lived in her own residence and must have enjoyed actual economic autonomy, in terms of the management of her revenues from the cashbox (*quppu*). We must then inquire whether she held autonomy in this situation. This question is difficult to answer, because the royal inscriptions written by Nabonidus indicate only that he had reinstalled the post of *entu*-priestess and restored the residence of the priesthood for his daughter, but do not explain her actual situation.

29 Schaudig 2001: 366–367, 369. See also Dhorme 1914.

3.2.2 Women of urban families

In rich urban families, it remains evident that, on the one hand, the dowries of daughters and wives of the Egibi family, for example, were managed by the heads of the family. On the other hand, Ina-Esagil-ramât, who married into the Nappāḫu family, enjoyed a certain degree of autonomy, and several women belonging to other families seemed to manage their own properties. The situation of Ina-Esagil-ramât could indeed be considered an exceptional case, as other women of the Nappāḫu family did not receive such favorable treatment in contracts. However, in the Egibi family, for example, the men who were heads of families always controlled the family properties, and they would never have permitted this type of situation. We can therefore presume that wealth and prestige were not decisive factors for the economic autonomy of women.

3.2.3 Women of the lower class

Women from the lower class were mainly slaves, who submitted passively to their situations as objects of sale, transfer, or mortgage, or as oblates. However, certain slave women were engaged in some economic activities.

The most famous example is Isḫunnātu, slave of the Egibi family, who managed a tavern. According to Gautier Tolini, her management of the tavern was entirely under the instructions of her master, Itti-Marduk-balāṭu; however, she seems to have wielded considerable autonomy in running the business.[30]

In the text BM 30544 = Wunsch 1993, No. 196, a slave woman called Maḫutu, the slave of a certain Esagil-ramât, was the creditor of thirty shekels of silver received by a slave man serving another person. Both slaves probably acted under the orders of their master or mistress, but this is not indicated in the text.

The other documents (Nbk. 439 = Wunsch 2005a, No. 4, BM 59804 Wunsch 2005a, No. 5) describe a slave woman of the chief priest (*šangû*) of Sippar, who appears as a witness. This text refers to the list of witnesses used in an adoption contract, in which an unmarried woman gave her two-year-old son for adoption.[31] Muhammad Dandamayev remarks: “the fact that a slave woman is mentioned as a witness is of great interest since free Babylonian women, regardless of their privileged status, could not, as a rule, appear as witnesses” (Dandamayev 1984: 398). Certainly, we do not find any free woman mentioned

30 Tolini 2012. See also Joannès 1992a and 1992b.

31 For the discussion of the texts, see Wunsch 2005b: 178–182.

on a list of *mukinnu*, although she could be present as a witness in the contract concerning her own rights. This case is therefore considered to be an exceptional situation. The mother of the adopted child was single, undoubtedly had no relatives, and was probably an oblate. For that reason, the witnesses of these contracts are those who work in the temple of Šamaš, such as a seal engraver, a leather worker, a gatekeeper, and two slaves man belonging to the chief-priest of Sippar. Notwithstanding this exceptional situation, this example provides enough evidence to suggest that women or slave women were not excluded from acting as witnesses.

***

The Neo-Babylonian society does not seem to have been favorable for promoting the economic authority of women. There were few jobs for women, except in roles as wet-nurses, farm workers, and certain positions for slaves and oblates. This fact indicates that for the majority of women, especially in the case of urban families, a "woman's domain" remained primarily the domestic household. In the domestic area, women seem to have obtained a certain social respect as "the lady of the house," though their situation seems to have been rather passive in the familial activities. However, women were not excluded from business. They could participate in various situations and activities to manage their properties. In most cases, their activities were more or less influenced by the household, and they had a "double situation," active-passive. But we also find some women who may have been economically independent. Indeed, the degree of authority exerted by women in economic spheres was influenced by their ages or their social status, but these criteria were not definitive. It depended rather on unsystematic and personal factors.

This analysis must be continued in greater detail in order to better understand women's activities amidst the complete picture of Neo-Babylonian economic activities, including those of men.

Bibliography

Abraham, Kathleen. 2004. *Business and Politics under the Persian Empire: the financial dealings of Marduk-nāṣir-apli of the House of Egibi (521–487 B.C.E.)*. Bethesda: CDL Press.

Baker, Heather, D. 2004. *The Archive of the Nappāhu Family*. AfO Beiheft 30. Wien: Institut für Orientalistik der Universität Wien.

Beaulieu, Paul-Alain. 1989. *The Reign of Nabonidus, King of Babylon 556–539 B.C.* Yale Near Eastern Researches 10. New Haven, London: Yale University Press.

Beaulieu, Paul-Alain. 1998. Ba'u-asītu and Kaššaya, Daughters of Nebuchadnezzar II. *Orientalia* 67: 173–201.

Cousin, Laura. 2012. Dowry Management in the Neo-Babylonian Period: A Case Study. http://refema.hypotheses.org/223.

Cuperly, Bénédicte. 2013. *Le rôle économique des femmes à Uruk à l'époque néo-babylonienne: étude prosopographique.* Mémoire de M1, Université Paris 1. Panthéon-Sorbonne.

Dandamayev, Muhammad A. 1984. *Slavery in Babylonia.* DeKalb, Illinois: Northern Illinois University Press.

Dassow, Eva von. 1999. Introducing the Witnesses in Neo-Babylonian Documents. Pp. 2–22 in *Ki Baruch Hu: Ancient Near Eastern, Biblical, and Judaic Studies in Honor of Baruch A. Levine*, eds. Robert Chazan, William W. Hallo, and Lawrence H. Shiffman. Winona Lake, Indiana: Eisenberauns.

Dhorme, Paul. 1914. La fille de Nabonide. *RA* 11: 105–107.

Donbaz, Veysel and Matthew W. Stolper. 1997. *Istanbul Murašû Texts*, PIHANS 79, Istanbul: Nederlands Historisch-Archaeologisch Instituut te Istanbul.

Driel, Govet van. 1998. Care of the Elderly: the Neo-Babylonian Period. Pp. 161–179 in *Care of the Elderly in the Ancient Near East*, eds. Marten Stol and Sven P. Vleeming. Leiden: Brill.

Joannès, Francis. 1980. Kaššaia, fille de Nabuchodonosor II. *RA* 74: 183–184.

Joannès, Francis. 1982. *Textes Économiques de la Babylonie Récente (Étude des textes de TBER – Cahier n° 6).* Études Assyriologiques. Paris: Éditions Recherche sur les civilisations.

Joannès, Francis. 1989. *Archives de Borsippa. La famille Ea-ilûta-bâni. Étude d'un lot d'archives familiales en Babylonie du VIIIe au Ve siècle av. J.-C.* Genève: Droz.

Joannès, Francis. 1992a. Inventaires d'un cabaret. *NABU* 1992/64.

Joannès, Francis. 1992b. Inventaires d'un cabaret (suite). *NABU* 1992/89.

Joannès, Francis. 1994. Amour contrarié. *NABU* 1994/72.

Joannès, Francis. 2013. The Economic Role of Women in Neo-Babylonian Temples. http://refema.hypotheses.org/745.

Jursa, Michael. 1999. *Das Archiv des Bēl-rēmanni.* PIHANS 86, Leiden: Nederlands Historisch-Archaeologisch Instituut te Istanbul.

Jursa, Michael. 2003. Spätachämenideische texte aus Kutha. *RA* 97: 43–140.

Jursa, Michael. 2010. *Aspects of the Economic History of Babylonia in the First Millennium BC*, AOAT 377, Münster: Ugarit-Verlag.

Oppenheim, A. Leo. 1955. Siege document from Nippur. *Iraq* 17: 68–89.

Pinches, Theophilus G. 1887. *A Babylonian Dower-Contract.* BOR 2 (1887): 1–8.

Roth, Martha T. 1987. Age at Marriage and the Household: A Study of Neo-Babylonian and Neo-Assyrian Forms. *Comparative Studies in Society and History* 29: 715–747.

Roth, Martha T. 1989a. The Material Composition of the Neo-Babylonian Dowry. *AfO* 36/37: 1–55.

Roth, Martha T. 1989b. Babylonian Marriage Agreements 7th–3rd Centuries B.C. AOAT 222. Kevelaer: Verlag Butzon & Bercker; Neukirchen-Vluyn: Neukirchener Verlag.

Roth, Martha T. 1991a. The Neo-Babylonian Widow. *JCS* 43–45: 1–26.

Roth, Martha T. 1991b. The Dowries of the Women of the Itti-Marduk-balāṭu Family. *JAOS* 111/1: 19–37.

Roth, Martha T. 1997. *Law Collections from Mesopotamia and Asia Monor*, 2nd edition. Atlanta: Scholars Press.

Roth, Martha T. 2000. Tašmētu-damqat and Daughters. Pp. 387–400 in *Assyriologica et Semitica. Festschrift für Joachim Oelsner*, eds. Joachim Marzahn et Hans Neumann. AOAT 252. Münster: Ugarit Verlag.

San Nicolo, Mariano. 1947. Zum atru und anderen Nebenleistungen des Käufers bein neubabylonischen Immobilarkauf. *Orientalia* 16: 273–302.

Schaudig, Hanspeter. 2001. *Die Inschriften Nabonids von Babylon und Kyros' des Großen.* AOAT 256. Münster: Ugarit-Verlag.

Stolper, Matthew W. 1985. *Entrepreneurs and Empire: The Murašu Archive, the Murašû Firm and Persian Rule in Babylonia*, PIHANS 54, Istanbul: Nederlands Historisch-Archaeologisch Instituut te Istanbul.

Stolper, Matthew W. 1990. *Late Achaemenid Legal Texts from Uruk and Larsa* (Taf. 49–51). *BaM* 21: 559–624.

Teppo, Saana. 2007. Agency and the Neo-Assyrian Women of the Palace. *StOr* 101: 381–420.

Tolini, Gauthier. 2012. The Economic Activities of Isḫunnatu, a Slave Woman of the Egibi Family. http://refema.hypotheses.org/766.

Tolini, Gauthier. 2013. Women and Family Solidarities in the Murašû Archive (Nippur – Fifth Century B.C.), http://refema.hypotheses.org/227.

Tonietti, Maria Vittoria. 2006. "Ho stabilito mia moglie come Padre e Madre della Mia Casa." Invecchiamento e Diritte delle Donne nell'Antica Mesopotamica. *Storia delle Donne* 2: 115–139.

Waerzeggers, Caroline. 1999. The Records of Inṣabtu From the Naggaru Family. *AfO* 46/47: 183–200.

Watai, Yoko. 2012. *Les maisons néo-babyloniennes d'après la documentation textuelle*, thèse de doctorat, Université Paris 1 – Panthéon Sorbonne, Paris.

Wunsch, Cornelia. 1993. *Die Urkunden des babylonischen Geschäftsmannes Iddin-Marduk: zum Handel mit Naturalien im 6. Jahrhundert v. Chr. Cuneiform monographs.* Groningen: STYX Publications.

Wunsch, Cornelia. 1995. Die Frauen der Familie Egibi. *AfO* 42/43: 33–63.

Wunsch, Cornelia. 1997. Und die Richter berieten ... Streitfälle in Babylon aus der Zeit Neriglissars und Nabonids. *AfO* 44/45: 59–100.

Wunsch, Cornelia. 2000. *Das Egibi Archive I. Die Felder und Gärten*, 2 tomes, Groningen: STYX Publications.

Wunsch, Cornelia. 2003. *Urkunden zum Ehe-, Vermögens- und Erbrecht aus verschiedenen neubabylonischen Archiven.* Babylonische Archive 2. Dresden: ISLET.

Wunsch, Cornelia. 2005a. The Šangû-Ninurta Archive. Pp. 365–379 in *Approaching the Neo-Babylonian Economy. Proceedings of the START Project Symposium Held in Vienna, 1–3 July 2004*, eds. Heather D. Baker and Michael Jursa. AOAT 330. Münster: Ugarit Verlag.

Wunsch, Cornelia. 2005b. Findelkinder und Adoption nach neubabylonischen Quellen. *AfO* 50: 174–244.

Zawadzki, Stefan and Karol Latowski. 2008. A new Neo-Babylonian text concerning the wet nurse. *NABU* 2008/12.

Laura Cousin

Beauty Experts: Female perfume-makers in the 1st millennium BC

> "*Why not just dwell on this high plane tree,*
> *or this pine, as it is permitted us ?*
> *Why not drink, our grey hair scented by fragrant rose petals,*
> *and anointed with Assyrian perfumes ?*".
> Horace (*Ode* II, 11, 13–17)

> "*I have no mother here,*
> *To clasp my relics to her widowed breast;*
> *No sister, to pour forth with hallowing tear*
> *Assyrian perfume where my ashes rest*".
> Tibullus (*Elegy* I, 3, 5–9)

The question of perfume, or even more generally of body care, remains a problem poorly dealt with in Assyriology. The most famous work dealing with perfume is *Parfümrezepte und Kultische Texte aus Aššur* (Ebeling 1950), and shows very well that the interest in this matter is archeo-botanic in nature, its purpose being to find again the scents of ancient near-eastern antiquity. Other studies appeared also on this olfactory research (Jursa 2004, and 2009 on Neo-Babylonian perfume recipes; or more recently Middeke-Conlin 2014 for the Old Babylonian period).[1] The other problem, which has been well explored, focuses on techniques used to prepare perfumes (Joannès 1993). Mesopotamian perfumes differ very much from those known today, of course, and came mostly in the form of perfumed oil. Last, it is quite difficult to determine the real nature of these perfumes. Although we have many recipes, they mainly deal with the procedures that must be performed, not with the proportions, making reconstitutions difficult, as with culinary recipes.[2]

1 Middeke-Conlin 2014: 1–53. The author discusses trade with aromatic products, fabrication of perfumes, and their introduction in the local economy of Larsa.
2 Bottéro 1995.

Acknowledgements: I am very grateful to Denis Bouder and Baptiste Fiette for their kindful help during all the preparation of this article. I wish also to express my thanks to Maria Giovanna Biga, Adelheid Otto, Julie Patrier and Mustapha Djabellaoui for their remarks and references.

Laura Cousin, Université Paris 1 Panthéon-Sorbonne, Archéologies et Sciences de l'Antiquité, Nanterre; laura.cousin2@wanadoo.fr

People who prepared these products, who can be called "perfumers," receive little attention from scholars and the studies about them are confined to general considerations, not relying on concrete testimony.[3] The term perfumer and his female equivalent are translated in Akkadian with *muraqqû* and *muraqqītu* in the 1st millennium,[4] and come from the verb *ruqqû* "to make perfume." Of course, the profession of perfumer had to be a polyvalent function, combining cooking,[5] medicine[6] and bodily care in Ancient Mesopotamia. Female perfume-makers *muraqqītu* specifically appear in the documentation of the 1st millennium BC in a palatial context, so those women's occupations and their potential origins are particularly interesting to study. The profession of perfume-maker is also an example of integration of women into the palaces' production circuit.

1 Perfume professions in 2nd millennium palaces

1.1 In the Mari documentation

In the rich documentation of the Royal Archives of Mari, only one female perfume-maker is known up to now. In ARM 10, 86, Inbatum, who is presumably the wife of Ḫimdiya, a vassal of Zimrî-Līm, asks her husband for a cook or a female perfume-maker (*luraqqītum*).[7] These two professions share many similarities. However, apparently only male perfume-makers work in the king's service. Inside the fabrication circuit, people devoted to oil production differ from those dealing with perfumes. Several craftsmen are in charge of the perfumery; among these, Nūr-ilī is referred to as *raqqû*, "perfumer" in the Old Babylonian period.

Nūr-ilī belongs to the *bīt raqqî*, the perfume makers' bureau in Mari, as well as the other eight perfumers, all men.[8] He received filtered oil that he had to transform into aromatic oil. Furthermore, Nūr-ilī was likely responsible for managing the inventory of the products:[9]

3 See Forbes 1955: 5.

4 Several terms are known for perfumer: *luraqqû* (Old Babylonian period), *muraqqû* (Middle Assyrian, Neo-Assyrian and Neo-Babylonian periods), or *raqqû* (Old Akkadian, Old Babylonian and Middle Babylonian periods).

5 This aspect is reflected for example in some translations of *murraqītu*, like "spice-bread baker" by Fales and Parpola in SAA 7: 24 rev. 8.

6 See for instance Limet 1978: 147–159.

7 ARM 10: 86 rev. 7′.

8 See Joannès 1993: 263. The perfumers are Aham-arši, Balū-Eštar, Bēlī-muštâl, Nabî-Eštar, Qīšti-Mamma, Yahatti-Ēl, Yarham-Ēl, and Zurunân.

9 About Nūr-ili, see ARM 9: 277; ARM 21: 107–109 and 111–116; ARM 23: 469–475, 477–480, 483–488, 491.

- ARM 23: 488 (25-vi-ZL 16): "90 *qû* (± 90 liters) of vegetal oil, from the storehouse of fine oil; received by Nūr-ilī."[10]
- ARM 23: 491 (?-?-ZL 16): "[x] cypress oil, opoponax oil[11], *tamrīrum*-oil;[12] received from Nūr-ilī."[13]

The perfumer workshops, though not excavated, should be located inside the royal palace, according to the epigraphic documentation. It appears through the letter B.287 (= A.4446), from Il-asûm sent to Yasmaḫ-Addu, king of Mari, that the palace in Šubat-Enlil used to produce perfumed oils in a shop dedicated to that function:

> "To my Lord, so speaks Il-asûm, your servant. We made high-quality oil in the workshops of Šubat-Enlil, but it lacks woods for its maceration. Now I sent one of my servants to my Lord. May my Lord send to Šubat-Enlil [x liters] of cypress, [x] + 50 liters of myrtle, [x] + 50 liters of boxwood, [x] + 50 liters of reed."[14]

Perfume seems to be a product reserved for the elite. In Mari, the king received juniper and cypress oil, and re-allocated part of it to his female entourage and part of it to the great officials of the Court.[15]

1.2 The donation tablets from Boğazköy

Among the donation tablets discovered at Boğazköy in 1990 and 1991, Bo 90/732, the largest (71 lines) and best preserved tablet from *Westbau*, is an inter-

---

10 Transliteration in ARM 23: 488: 0,1.3. I$_3$.GIŠ *a-na* E$_2$ *ra-qí-im i-na na-kam-tim ša* E$_2$ I$_3$ DU$_{10}$.GA *šu-ti-ia nu-úr-ì-lí.*

11 Opoponax is a kind of balm obtained from the resin of a herbaceous plant.

12 According to CAD T: 146, *tamrīrum* comes from the verb *marārum*, "to be bitter," and it is an adjective meaning "bitter." *AHw*: 1316 mentions "ein Körperpflege-Öl."

13 Transliteration in ARM 23: 491: [x x x] I$_3$.GIŠ *šu-úr-mìn* sag [x x x] I$_3$.GIŠ.GIG [x x x] I$_3$.GIŠ *šu-úr-mìn* US$_2$ [x x x I$_3$.GIŠ] *šu-úr-m*[*ìn* 3] x [x x] I$_3$ *ma-ri-tu*[*m*] [x x x I$_3$] *tam-ri-tum* 80 40 ŠU.NIGIN$_2$ 8 GUR x [x] *nu-úr-ì-lí am-ḫu-ur.*

14 Transliteration and translation Joannès, with collation of Durand. See Joannès 1993: 260, n. 36: *a-na be-lí-ia qí-bí-ma um-ma* AN-*a-sú* IR$_3$-*ka-a-ma* I$_3$ DU$_{10}$.GA *i-na ḫu-ur-še-e ša šu-ba-at-*^{d}EN.LIL$_2^{KI}$ *i-pu-úš ù* GIŠ.HA$_2$ *a-na ru-mu-ki-šu i-na qa-ti-ia ma-ṭu-ú i-na-an-na* 1 LU$_2$ DUMU-*ri* [*a*]-*na ṣe-ri be-lí-ia* [*aṭ-ṭa*]-*ar-da-a*[*m*] [x] ^{GIŠ}*šu*$^{!}$-*ur-mi-na* [x+] 0,0.5 ^{GIŠ}*a-su* [x+] 0,0.5 *ši-me-ša-lu-ú* [x+] 0,0.5 GI DU$_{10}$.GA *be-lí a-na šu-bat-*^{d}EN.LIL$_2^{KI}$ *li-ša-bi-lam na-ši* GIŠ.HA$_2$ *šu-nu-ti be-lí a-di šu-bat-* ^{d}EN.LIL$_2^{KI}$ *la* <*i*>-*ka-al-la.*

15 About redistribution of perfumes in Mari, see ARM 7: 401; ARM 22: 53–54; Charpin 1984: 43.

esting example of the importance of the profession of perfumer.[16] It belongs late in the reign of Telipinu or early in that of Alluwamna,[17] and 400 persons were registered on the tablet, but the place where they lived cannot be precisely determined.[18] Bo 90/732 gives useful information about demography in the Hittite Land and registers houses and their population (how many men, women, children, babies, old people, and slaves lived in the houses), because donation tablets are interested in the labor force. Bo 90/732 lists 17 households, whose heads may own several houses and have quite different professions. The list includes ploughmen (^{LU2}APIN.LA$_2$), administrators (^{LU2}*hilammi*), potter (^{LU2}BAHAR$_2$), gardener (^{LU2}NU.^{GIŠ}KIRI$_6$), *paštu*[19] and two perfume-makers (^{LU2}I$_3$.RA$_2$.RA$_2$), named Zuliya and Āllī.[20] There are 26 persons, two male slaves and one female slave in the house of Zuliya (it is the second largest household of the tablet Bo 90/732, after that of the administrator Mišeni with 39 persons and 86 slaves), and 17 persons and two slaves (one male and one female) in the house of Āllī, his colleague. A perfumer appears also in KBo 10: 10 ii 23′, a large list of women given to the palace.[21]

1.3 Several elements in Middle Assyrian documentation

Middle Assyrian documentation sheds more light on the function of perfume-maker (see Ebeling 1950 and Jakob 2003). Female perfume-makers are mentioned in the following five texts:

- MARV II: 22, 23–24 (ingredients list): "Total 1 *emār* 3 ½ *qû* (± 103.5 liters) of oil at the disposal of Tukultī-ša-šāmê, female perfume-maker."[22]
- KAR 220: rev. iv 8′–9′ (ingredients list intended for the king's perfume): "Perfume preparation for 2 *sūtu qû* (± 20 liters) of fine oil from the upper part of reeds for the use of the king, entrusted to Tappūtī-Bēlet-ekalle, female perfume-maker, that was extracted."[23]

16 Wilhem 2009: 226.

17 Wilhem 2009: 227, "The tablet was written by the scribe Išpunnuma who also wrote the tablet of Alluwamna KBo 32.136 found in Temple 7."

18 Wilhem 2009: 228. The author proposes that they lived in the "land of Tapikka, which is to be located in the region of present-day Maşat."

19 *paštu* is an unknown profession and probably a *hapax* (see CAD P: 265–267).

20 For the details of this list, see Wilhem 2009: 231–232.

21 Pecchioli Daddi 1982: 402: [*ša* E$_2$] ^{I}*mu-u-wa ša* ^{LU2}I$_3$.RA$_2$.R[A$_2$] [*i-na* ^{URU}X] X-*ni*.

22 Transliteration and translation in Jakob 2003: 102–103: ŠU.[NGIN$_2$] 1 ANŠE 3 ½ SÌLA I$_3$ *ša* ŠU ^{fGIŠ}TUKUL-*ti-šá*-AN-*e mu-ra-qi-te*.

23 Transliteration and translation in Jakob 2003: 483: *tar-qi-tu ša* 2 BAN$_2$ I$_3$.MEŠ ^{GIŠ}GI *e-le-e* DU$_{10}$.GA *šá* UGU LUGAL *ina pi-i* ^{f}*tap-pu-ti*-^{d}NIN.E$_2$.GAL-*lim* MUNUS *mu-raq-qi-te na-ás-ha*.

- MARV III: 1 rev. vi 11′ (list of courtiers) mentions "one female perfume-maker."[24]
- Letters MARV III: 64, 47 and KAV 194, 9 both mention several "female perfume-makers."[25]

Overseer female perfume-makers are also mentioned in:
- The list of courtiers MARV III: 1 rev. vi 13′. She receives [x] *qû* of oil from the palace.[26]
- MARV I: 51 rev. 7′–8′ (mission order from the palace): [x] *emār* 2 *sūtu* 5 ½ *qû* (at least ± 125.5 liters) and 3 *kāsu*-cups are at the disposal of three overseers of female perfume-makers.[27]

Among these documents, two are particularly interesting. First, KAR 220 is a long list of ingredients intended for the king's perfume, above all myrtle-based. The task of preparing the sovereign's perfume is entrusted to Tappūtī-Bēlet-ekalle (KAR 220 rev. iv 9), a female perfume-maker who practiced under Tukultī-Ninurta I (eponym Šunu-qardū). Her name, meaning "The assistant of the Lady of the Palace," reports probably an onomastic of function. The other document, MARV 51, tells about Samnuha-ašarēd, steward in the palace of Aššur (**agrig** in Sumerian, *abarakku* in Akkadian), entrusting oil to a group of three *rab muraqqīte* to transform it into perfume. In this text appears Tukultī-ša-šamê, who bears the title of *rab muraqqīte* and practiced under Ninurta-apil-Ekur (from the eponym of Adad-mušabši to the eponym of Ragiššanu, from 1191 to 1179).

2 Origins of female perfume-makers in the 1st millennium BC

From the available documentation, only four tablets from the 1st millennium BC, from both the Neo-Assyrian and Neo-Babylonian periods, refer to female perfume-makers in a palatial context: SAA 7: 24 from the South-West Palace of Nineveh, Bab 28122, Bab 28186, and Bab 28232 from the Southern Palace in Babylon.[28]

---

24 Jakob 2003: 477.

25 Jakob 2003: 484–485.

26 MARV III:1 rev. vi 13′, [x] SILA$_3$ GAL *mu-ra-qi-a-t*[*u*].

27 Transliteration and translation in Jakob 2003: 478: [X A]NŠE 2 BAN$_2$ 5½ SILA$_3$ 3 *ka-sa-tu ša* ŠU 3 GAL.MEŠ [*mu-ra*]-⸢*qi*!-*a*⸣-*te*^{MEŠ}.

28 See Weidner 1939: texts A, C and D.

These data present the female perfume-makers in a particular context: they are connected with workers of foreign origins, often coming from the west of the Ancient Near East. But are these cases isolated? Or, is it possible to find other attestations of this phenomenon?

2.1 Sources

2.1.1 The Neo-Assyrian tablet SAA 7: 24

SAA 7: 24, dated to the reign of Esarhaddon,[29] belongs to a group of four similar tablets (SAA 7: 23–26) which are lists that record the palace female staff. SAA 7: 24 is divided into three parts. In the first part, the text lists 140 women: 94 court women and 46 of their maids, according to their region or city of origin, situated mostly in the West (among them Arameans, Koushites, Hittites, Tyrians, and women from the cities of Arpad, Ašdod). This first part ends with the sum: "total, of the father of the crown prince, in all, 140" (PAP$^{!}$ *ša* AD-*šú šá* A.MAN PAP 1 ME 40), re-establishing these women in a palatial context.

In the second part, the names of two of them are mentioned. The first woman bears an Akkadian-sounding name, Šīti-tabni, and the other bears an Egyptian one, Amat-emūni. These are the only women named, certainly because of their importance. They are accompanied by two and three maids respectively.

In the last part, SAA 7: 24 presents 94 women and their 52 maids. Among them, 33 occupy skilled professions. In its last lines the list mentions a *gallābtu* (female hairdresser) and a female perfume-maker *muraqqītu* escorted by two servants.[30] One might reasonably wonder about the association between a perfumer and a hairdresser, and even consider it to be a coincidence. If perfume can be considered as "olfactory beauty,"[31] it is often associated with hairdressing, as shown in a very famous piece in the Sacred Marriage, when the female lover preparation consists in several phases: bathing, anointing with perfumed oils, applying cosmetics and hairdressing.[32]

29 Parpola 2012: 618–619.

30 SAA 7: 24 rev. 7–10: 1 MUNUS.ŠU$^{!}$.I PAP 33 PAP 1 ME 94 [x] 52$^{?}$ $GEME_2$.MEŠ 1$^{!}$ MUNUS *mu-raq*$^{!}$-*qí-tú* 2 $GEME_2$.MEŠ-*šá* PAP 1 ME 56$^{!}$ [x x x].

31 Michel 2007: 58.

32 Kramer 1983: 118.

2.1.2 Neo-Babylonian sources: tablets from the N1 archive

This Neo-Assyrian list may be completed by three texts found in the Southern Palace of Babylon. The N1 archive,[33] to which these texts belong, was found next to the *Osthof* of the Southern Palace of Babylon, precisely in a corner called *Gewölbebau* where R. Koldewey believed the Hanging Gardens to be located (Fig. 1).

On tablet Bab 28122, a list of oil rations, six female perfume-makers appear twice:

- obv. 9: "to the 6 female perfume-makers 2 *qû* (± 2 liters) entrusted to Nabû-dūr-makî."[34]
- rev. 11: we find the same attestation.

The tablet can be dated from the 13th year of Nebuchadnezzar II, that is 593/592,[35] and lists the quantity of sesame oil allotted either to individuals or to groups of people, for the months of *Nisânu* on the obverse and *Ayyaru* on the reverse. This text is remarkable on several grounds. It mentions Joiakin, king of Juda, exiled to Babylon by Nebuchadnezzar II, who receives a ration of oil for himself and his family (obv. 29: *a-na* ^{I}*ia-'-ú-gin* LUGAL *šá* KUR *ia-ú-du*). There are also mentioned princes and eight people native of the kingdom of Juda, like Ur-milki (rev. 13), Gadi-ilu (obv. 18), Šalam-yama the gardener (rev. 22) or Samaku-yama (obv. 28).

The other two tablets are less preserved:

- Bab 28186 rev. 5: "[to the x] female perfume-makers 1 *qû* (± 1 liter) entrusted to Nabû-dūr-makî."[36]
- Bab 28232, 6: "[to the x] female perfume-makers 1 *qû* (± 1 liter) [entrusted to PN]."[37]

We do notice a difference in that on the first tablet, Bab 28122, the six female perfume-makers receive 2 *qû* of oil (2 liters), and only 1 *qû* according to the others, but the reason for these quantities remains unclear. Then, in at least 3 out of 4 references, female perfume-makers receive their rations through a man named Nabû-dūr-makî, who is also supposed to be present on the last tablet. This Nabû-dūr-makî, if the name is right (there are parallels in Neo-Assyrian

33 Pedersén 2005a: 110–127.

34 *šá* 6 MUNUS *mu-raq-qé-e-tú* 2 $SILA_3$ a_4 *ina* $ŠU^{II}$ $^{Id}NA_3.BAD_3$-*ma*-[*ki*$^?$-*i*$^?$] (Weidner 1939: Pl. 1. and Pl. 2).

35 Pedersén 2005b: 268.

36 [x] *mu-raq-qé-e-tu*$_4$ 1 $SILA_3$ a_4 *ina* $ŠU^{II}$ $^{Id}NA_3.BAD_3$-*ma-ki*$^?$-*i*$^?$ (Weidner 1939: Pl. 4).

37 [x *mu*]-*raq-qé-e-tú* 1 $SILA_3$ a_4 [*ina* $ŠU^{II}$ ^{I}PN] (Weidner 1939: Pl. 5).

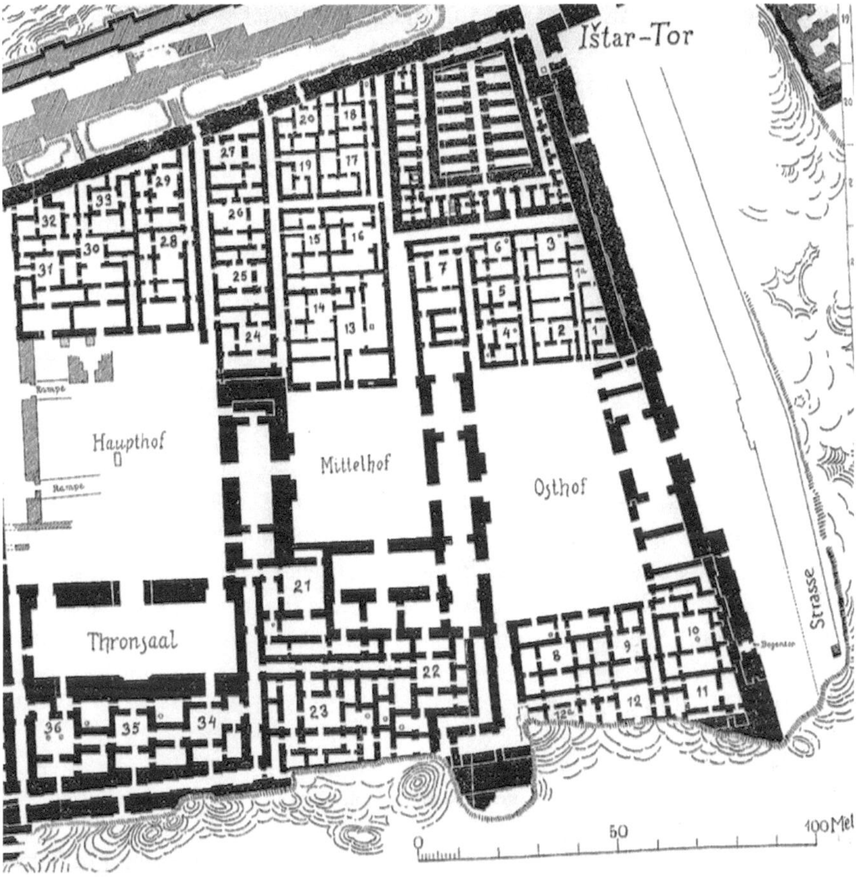

Fig. 1: *Osthof* and *Gewölbebau* in the Southern Palace of Babylon, R. Koldewey, the Southern Palace of Babylon (Koldewey 1931: Pl. 2).

onomastic and it means Nabû-is-the-protective-wall-of-the-frail),[38] appears in another part of Bab 28122 obv. 25–26:

> "For Marma' the Lydian, 3 *qû*, and 2 *qû* for his men, from the *bīt qīpūtu*, entrusted to Nabû-dūr-makî."[39]

Furthermore, Marma' seems to be an important man, considering the quantity of oil he gets. According to M. Jursa, all these tablets come from the *bīt qīpūti*,

38 Baker 2001: 823.

39 [x] ^{I}*mar-ma-'* ^{LU_2}*lu-da-a-a* 3 SILA$_3$ 3 ERIN$_2$ 2 SILA$_3$ *a*$_4$ *a-na* E$_2$ *qí-pu-*⌜*tú*⌝ *šá ina* TIN.TIR^{KI} *ina* ŠU^{II} ^{Id}NA$_3$.BAD$_3$-*m*[*a*$^?$-*ki*$^?$-*i*$^?$] (Weidner 1939: Pl. 1 rev. 25–26).

the palace administrative wing, in the area of the *Osthof*.[40] We therefore stand in the administrative part of the palace, and the fact that the female perfume-makers appear in this context shows that they have close ties with the Crown. In the *bīt qīpūti* sphere of influence we find specialized craftsmen such as beer brewers, sesame oil-pressers, craftsmen specialized in reed (*atkuppu*), builders (*itinnu*), cleaners, water carriers, gardeners and grooms, some of them of foreign descent. One of the most interesting aspects of this corpus of three texts issued from the Southern Palace is the mention of a majority of non-Babylonian individuals, coming from the West (Lydia, Caria, Syro-Palestinian coast) and the East (Media, Elam) who work in the palace or for the palace. The female perfume-makers are also therefore linked with the palace bureaucracy, which leads to the question of their position in those lists with a large number of foreign individuals.

In the Southern Palace, the team of archaeologists led by R. Koldewey excavated fragmentary alabasters in the North and South of the *Osthof*, where a royal alabastron atelier probably stood.[41] However R. Koldewey does not specify where exactly this material was found. Nevertheless, it is very interesting to remark that the atelier and the tablets mentioning the female perfume-makers are located in the same area around the *Osthof*. Another alabastron with the name of king Nebuchadnezzar II was found in Susa by J. de Morgan. The object bears the following inscription:

> "1 *qû* and 8 *ninda*. Palace of Nebuchadnezzar, king of Babylon, who acts with the confidence of the gods Nabû and Marduk, his Lords; son of Nabopolassar, king of Babylon".[42]

Other alabastra inscribed with the name of Amēl-Marduk were found in Babylon and also Susa.[43] Like the alabastron with the name of Nebuchadnezzar, these are little objects and their capacity varies between 0.27 liter and 1.45 liter, while their height is around 15 cm. The alabastra were used to contain perfumes or other precious liquids, and considering their small size, they could travel easily.

40 Jursa 2010: 71.

41 Koldewey 1925: 72: "Es scheint, daß hier eine königliche Flaschenfabrik betriben wurde; eine sehr große Anzahl von Stücken dieser schöngeformten Gefäße, die in der griechischen Kunst Alabastra heißen, fand sich gerade in diesen Raümen, namentlich solche Stücke, die bei der Fabrikation abfallen."

42 Transliteration and translation from the photograph of André-Salvini 2008: 214, n° 157: 1 SILA$_3$ 8 NINDA E$_2$.GAL ^{d}PA.NIG$_2$.DU.URU$_3$ LUGAL TIN.T[IR^{KI}] *šá ina* KU-*ti* ^{d}PA *u* ^{d}AM[AR.UTU] EN.MEŠ-*šú* DU.DU-*ku* A ^{d}PA.A. URU$_3$ LUGAL TIN.TIR[^{KI}].

43 Da Riva 2013: 107 (V1 The Babylon vase) and 109–110 (V4 The Susa vase 3).

2.2 Leads of reflections on female perfume-makers

2.2.1 The perfume-industry at Pyrgos, Cyprus

In ancient times, perfume is often connected with beauty and seduction, like the Homeric hymn 5 (55–65) to Aphrodite shows us:

> "Therefore, when laughter-loving Aphrodite saw [Anchises], she loved him, and terribly desire seized her in her heart. She went to Cyprus, to Paphos, where her precinct is and fragrant altar, and passed into her sweet-smelling temple. There she went in and put to the glittering doors, and there the Graces bathed her with heavenly oil such as blooms upon the bodies of the eternal gods – oil divinely sweet, which she had by her, filled with fragrance."[44]

Italian archaeologists led by Maria Rosaria Belgiorno discovered a perfume workshop at Pyrgos, on the island of Cyprus, situated 90 kilometers South-East of Nicosia.[45] The factory was destroyed around 1850 BC during an earthquake and measured 300 square meters. Archaeologists excavated perfume bottles, funnels, mixing jugs and stills, and the team succeeded in identifying 14 fragrances used in perfume production (among them: cinnamon, myrtle, laurel, anise, pine, coriander, citrus bergamot, almond, lavender, rosemary and parsley) and also four recipes.

In Pyrgos, M. R. Belgiorno's team found large amounts of pottery and stone tools in the eastern wing of the olive press-room.[46] The discovery enables the identification of three methods used to extract the aromatic substances: the boiling of barks, distillation and the maceration in warm water or olive oil – so quite the same techniques used in Mari in the 2nd millennium BC[47] – and the atelier could produce essential oils and scented waters.

2.2.2 Products used in perfumery

If we assume the hypothesis that female perfume-makers who appear in the Neo-Assyrian and Neo-Babylonian documents are foreigners, could their origin

44 Translation of H. G. Evelyn-White is available on the website perseus.tufts.edu. data.perseus.org/citations/urn:cts:greekLit:tlg0013.tlg005.perseus-eng1: 33–74.

45 See the website http://www.pyrgos-mavroraki.eu/pyrgos-mavroraki_000015.htm.

46 The factory was the subject of six exhibitions: two in Cyprus in 2004 and 2005, and four in Italy in 2006, 2007, 2008 and 2009.

47 Joannès 1993.

be related to the products used in perfumery? The great capitals are the points of arrival of essences from the West (cedar trees from Lebanon, aromatic plants such as cypress, Aleppo pines, juniper from Phoenicia), coming from a vast international trade with the Mediterranean coast, and of tributes sent to Babylon or Nineveh, to manufacture those luxury products.[48]

2.2.3 Another perfumer in SAA 14: 161

Neo-Assyrian document SAA 14: 161 gives a complementary insight on perfume-makers in the 1st millennium BC. It is a contract drafted in Nineveh in 623, and it describes the following situation: Nihti-Eša-rau, mother of Ṣi-hû, bought a woman called Mullissu-hāṣinat, daughter of Nabû-rēhtu-uṣur, for her son, presumably to be his wife.[49] The document goes on with the usual selling clauses,[50] and a perfumer ($^{\text{LU2}}$I$_3$.RA$_2$.RA$_2$) named Sa-hpi-māu appears amongst the three guarantors "against a fine, stolen property, and debts."[51] SAA 14: 161 is particularly interesting because it presents three people with Egyptian theophoric names: the mother and buyer Nihti-Eša-rau ("Isis is strong against them"), her son Ṣi-hû ("The face of DN has said") and the perfumer Sa-hpi-māu ("May Apis seize him") pointing out their non-Mesopotamian origin, and thus shows a concrete example of a perfume-maker of foreign origin living in Assyria.

2.2.4 Female perfume-makers in the Book of Samuel

Finally, a noteworthy mention appears in the Bible, in 1 Sm 8: 11–13:

> "This will be the name of who will reign over you! He will take your sons and appoint them for himself, for his chariots, and to be his horsemen: they will run in front. He will also appoint them as overseers of thousand and overseers of fifty, to plough his plough and harvest his harvest, to make his weapons and prepare his vehicles. And your daughters, he will take them as female perfume-makers, cooks, bakers." [52]

---

48 Graslin-Thomé 2009: 215–231.
49 SAA 14: 161 obv. 8–13. $^{\text{f.d}}$NIN.LIL$_2$-*ḫa-ṣi-na* DUMU.MUNUS-*su šá* ^{Id}PA.KAD$_3$.PAP *tu-piš-ma* $^{\text{f.}}$*ni-iḫ-ti-e-šá-ra-u ina lìb-bi* 18 GIN$_2$.MEŠ KU$_3$.BABBAR *a-na* ^{I}*ṣi-ḫa-a* DUMU-*sá a-na* MUNUS-*ú-ti-šú tal-qi*.
50 SAA 14: 161 obv. 16–rev. 5.
51 SAA 14: 161 rev. 9–14.
52 This citation has been highlighted in Ziegler 1999: 2.

In this extract, Samuel warns the Elders of Israel who are tempted by monarchy. It is interesting to notice that these young girls from Israel are referred to and characterized as female perfume-makers, or at least could become female perfume-makers.

***

The question of the origin of female perfume-makers is difficult to solve because of the scarcity of sources and of their equivocal nature. Nevertheless, it should be noted that they always appear in the documentation of the 1st millennium BC alongside people of foreign origins, from the west of the Ancient Near East.

Although only women are mentioned as working as perfume-makers in the 1st millennium palaces, we can not yet conclude that a feminization of this profession in this specific context has taken place.

Perfumes and preparation of perfumes are often depicted in Antiquity:

- In Egypt, a relief from the reign of Psammetichus II (595–589 BC) issued from the tomb of Païrkep shows female perfume-makers at work with lily or lotus flowers.
- In Assyria in the "Garden Party" relief (the oldest scene we know of a lounging banquet) showing Assurbanipal and his queen Libbali-šarrat after the royal campaign of the Assyrian king in Elam. The fact that the queen is present is rather rare and therefore notable, and in this garden where the royal couple clearly takes refreshments, we observe two perfume-burners that seem to keep them apart from the other human beings present.
- The "Scene of an Audience with the Great King" which was visible in the Apadana of Persepolis, represents king Xerxes I and behind him the crown prince Darius, cut off from other mortals by two perfume-burners.
- In Roman Empire, the very well known "Fresco Fragment with Cupids and Psyche Making Perfume" of the Villa Getty, and those of the House of the Vettii in Pompeii are the most famous testimonies about making perfume in Antiquity.

Bibliography

André-Salvini, Béatrice (ed.). 2008. *Babylone*. Paris: Hazan, Musée du Louvre éditions.

Baker, Heather (ed.). 2001. *The Prosopography of Neo-Assyrian Empire. Vol. 2, part II, L–N*. Helsinki: the Neo-Assyrian Text Corpus Project.

Bottéro Jean. 1995. *Textes culinaires mésopotamiens*. Mesopotamian Civilizations 6. Winona Lake: Eisenbrauns.

Charpin, Dominique. 1984. Inscriptions votives d'époque assyrienne, MARI 3: 41–81.

Da Riva, Rocío. 2013. *The Inscriptions of Nabopolassar, Amēl-Marduk and Neriglissar*. Studies in Ancient Near Eastern Records 3. Boston-Berlin: De Gruyter.

Ebeling, Erich. 1950. *Parfümrezepte und kultische Texte aus Assur*. Scripta Pontificii instituti biblici 101. Rome: Pontificium Institutum Biblicum.

Forbes, Robert James. 1955. *Studies in Ancient Technology III*. Leiden: Brill.

Graslin-Thomé, Laetitia. 2009. *Les échanges à longue distance en Mésopotamie au Ier millénaire: une approche économique*. Orient et Méditerranée 5. Paris: De Boccard.

Jakob, Stefan. 2003. *Mittelassyrische Verwaltung und Sozialstruktur*. Cuneiform Monographs 29. Leiden–Boston: Brill.

Joannès, Francis. 1993. La culture matérielle à Mari (v): les parfums. Pp. 251–270 in *Mari. Annales de Recherches Interdisciplinaires* 7. Paris: Editions Recherche sur les Civilisations.

Jursa, Michael. 2004. Parfüm(rezepte). A. In Mesopotamien. *RlA* 10 5/6: 335–336.

Jursa, Michael. 2009. Die Kralle des Meeres und andere Aromata. Pp. 147–180 in *Philologisches und Historisches zwischen Anatolien und Sokotra. Analecta Semitica In Memoriam Alexander Sima*, ed. Werner Arnold Wiesbaden: Harrassowitz.

Jursa, Michael. 2010. Der neubabylonische Hof. Pp. 67–106 in *Der Achämenidenhof. Akten des 2. Internationalen Kolloquiums zum Thema « Vorderasien im Spannungsfeld klassischer und altorientalischer Überlieferungen ». Landgut Castelen bei Basel, 23.–25. Mai 2007*, ed. Bruno Jacobs. Classica et Orientalia 2. Wiesbaden: Harrassowitz.

Koldewey, Robert. 1925. *Das wieder erstehende Babylon: die bisherigen Ergebnisse der deutschen Ausgrabungen*. Sendschrifts der Deutschen Orient-Gesellschaft 6. Leipzig: Hinrichs.

Koldewey, Robert. 1931. *Die Königsburgen von Babylon*. WVDOG 54. Leipzig: Hinrichs.

Kramer, Samuel Noah. 1983. *Le mariage sacré à Sumer et à Babylone*. Paris: Berg International.

Limet, Henri. 1978. Pharmacopée et parfumeries sumériennes. *Revue d'histoire de la pharmacie* 238: 147–159.

Michel, Cécile. 2007. La production, la transformation et l'usage des parfums en Mésopotamie ancienne. Pp. 57–59 in *Des origines à nos jours. Une histoire mondiale du parfum*, ed. Marie-Christine Grasse. Paris: Somogy editions d'art.

Middeke-Conlin, Robert. 2014. The Scents of Larsa: A Study of the Aromatics Industry in an Old Babylonian Kingdom. *CDLJ* 2014/1: 1–53.

Parpola, Simo. 2012. The Neo-Assyrian Royal Harem. Pp 613–626 in *Leggo! Studies Presented to Frederick Mario Fales on the Occasion of His 65th Birthday*, ed. Giovanni B. Lanfranchi *et al.* Leipziger Altorientalistische Studien 2. Wiesbaden: Harrassowitz.

Pecchioli Daddi, Franca. 1982. *Mestieri, professioni e dignita' nell'Anatolia ittita*. Incunabula Graeca 79. Rome: Edizioni Dell'Ateneo.

Pedersén, Olof. 2005a. *Archive und Bibliotheken in Babylon. Die Tontafeln der Grabung Robert Koldeweys 1899–1917.* Abhandlungen der deutschen Orient-Gesellschaft 25. Saarbrücken: Saarländische Druckerei und Verlag.

Pedersén, Olof. 2005b. Foreign Professionals in Babylon: Evidence from the Archive in the Palace of Nebuchadnezzar II. Pp. 267–272 in *Ethnicity in Ancient Mesopotamia. Papers Read at the 48th Rencontre Assyriologique Internationale Leiden, 1–4 July 2002*, ed. Wilfred H. van Soldt. Leiden: Nederlands Instituut voor het Nabije Oosten.

Weidner, Ernest Friedrich. 1939. Jojachin, König von Juda, in babylonischen Keilschrifttexten. Pp. 923–935 in *Mélanges Syriens offerts à Monsieur René Dussaud II*, ed. Académie des Inscriptions et Belles-Lettres. Bibliothèque Archéologique et Historique 30. Paris: Geuthner.

Wilhem, Gernot. 2009. Demographic Data from Hittite Land Donation Tablets. Pp. 223–233 in *Central-North Anatolia in the Hittite Period. New Perspectives in Light of Recent Research. Acts of the International Conference Held at the University of Florence (7–9 February 2007)*, ed. Franca Pecchioli Daddi *et al.* Studia Asiana 5. Rome: Herder.

Ziegler, Nele. 1999. Le harem du vaincu. *RA* 93: 1–26.

Websites

www.perseus.tufts.edu
www.pyrgos-mavroraki.eu

Julien Monerie

Women and Prebends in Seleucid Uruk

Our knowledge of the last centuries of history of the age-old Mesopotamian prebendary system derives almost exclusively from the documentation of the ancient city of Uruk, in Southern Babylonia, where more than two hundred cuneiform tablets concerning the prebendary system of the local city temples have been unearthed by archaeologists and illegal excavators since the mid-19th century. These documents are, for the most part, legal contracts dated to the Seleucid period (305–141 BC) recording sales of prebend shares entitling their owners to perform a cultic activity for a certain time in exchange for regular revenues, which usually derived from leftovers of the ritual offerings presented to the divine statues during their service.[1] The analysis of this corpus allows a detailed reconstruction of the organization of the local prebend system, especially when studied in light of the much richer sources from the Neo-Babylonian and Early Achaemenid period, three centuries earlier. This does not mean, however, that the Mesopotamian prebend system remained unchanged over the whole 1st millennium BC, and the corpus from Seleucid Uruk also displays some original features in regard to the earlier documentation. One of the most striking of these features is undoubtedly the active involvement of women of local notability in the prebend system.[2]

Although women were already allowed to be in possession of prebend shares in the Neo-Babylonian and Early Achaemenid period, female prebend ownership only remained exceptional at the time. Women were legally forbidden to purchase prebend entitlements on their own, and they could only acquire them by means of endowment from male relatives, who usually seem to have done so in situations of familial crisis, when they had no adult male offspring to bequeath them to.[3] The cuneiform documentation from Seleucid Uruk, on the contrary, provide numerous examples of rich women of the local elite selling and purchasing prebend shares without any interference from their

1 On the Mesopotamian prebend system during the 1st millennium BC, see e.g. van Driel 2002: 31–151; Corò 2005a; Démare-Lafont 2010; Jursa 2010: 155–168; Waerzeggers 2010 and Monerie forthcoming.

2 As already noticed by McEwan 1981: 118–120 and Waerzeggers 2010: 93.

3 On these matters, see e.g. Waerzeggers 2010: 92–94.

Julien Monerie, Paris 1 Panthéon-Sorbonne; julienmonerie@gmail.com

male relatives.[4] This apparently active involvement in the prebend system is actually not unproblematic, since the performance of the prebendary cultic service was rigorously restricted to initiate male members of the local priestly elite.[5] In other words, women from Seleucid Uruk who happened to own a prebend share were not allowed to perform the cultic activities corresponding to their entitlement but were compelled to hire a substitute among the authorized personnel, who performed the service in their stead in exchange for a part of their prebendary income.[6]

Concurrently, one can detect other developments in the prebend system between the first and the second half of the 1st millennium BC, such as the rise of multi-prebend holding,[7] the apparent dissolution of the links that formerly tied certain families to given types of prebendary cultic activities,[8] or the state of extreme fragmentation of the shares of cultic service attested by the Seleucid Uruk sales.[9] The conjunction of these evolutions has led some scholars to conclude that the traditional prebend system had undergone a process of decay in the course of its long history, evolving from a strictly personal assignment in the 3rd millennium BC to a fully alienable property in the end of the 1st millennium BC by means of a gradual disconnection between the entitlement property and the actual performance of ritual activities, ultimately leading to the emergence of a "prebendary leisure-class" exclusively interested in their regular earnings.[10] This statement has been recently criticized for the Neo-Babyloni-

4 For a comprehensive catalogue of these attestations, see appendix below.

5 On these matters, which are well attested by the Neo-Babylonian and Early Achaemenid sources, see Jursa and Waerzeggers 2008 as well as Waerzeggers 2011. There is no reason to assume that these ritual restrictions were no longer observed in the Seleucid period.

6 See Corò 2005a: 48–58.

7 This expression designates the gathering of various types of prebends within the hands of a single individual who could obviously not have performed them all in person. For a study of multi-prebend holding in the Seleucid period, see e.g. Corò 2005a: 86–99 and Corò 2005b.

8 Only a few professions requiring highly technical scholarly knowledge remained tied to given families in Seleucid Uruk, such as the lamentation priests (*kalû*) with the Sîn-lēqe-unninni family (see Beaulieu 2000) or the exorcists (*āšipu*) with the Ekur-zākir family (see Corò 2009).

9 As R. Pirngruber already noticed, this impression of fragmentation is partly due to a shift in the mode of expression of the size of cultic service concerned by these sales from an annual basis in the Neo-Babylonian period to a monthly basis in the Seleucid Period (Pirngruber and Waerzeggers 2011: 113–114). Nonetheless, the fragmentation of the prebendary service in Seleucid Uruk remains impressive. See for example Corò 2005a txt. BM 105196, which records the sale of 1/60th of a day of monthly service of "temple enterer" (*ērib bīti*) in 197 BC, or BiMes 24 10, concerning a sale of 1/20th plus 1/720th of a day of monthly service of brewer, in 171–170 BC.

10 See most notably Funck 1984: 86–87 and 269–277, as well as Démare-Lafont 2010: 9. For an introduction on the prebendary system before the 1st millennium BC, see van Driel 2003–2005.

an and Early Achaemenid period by M. Jursa, who insisted on the cultic and financial obligations incumbent on the prebend owners.[11] A study of the involvement of women in the prebend system of Seleucid Uruk allows us to test the validity of this statement for the second half of the 1st millennium BC.

Over the ca. 200 prebendary transactions recorded in our corpus, thirty-one feature women as one of the principals, for a total of twenty-five different female prebend owners i.e. almost 20 % of the total number of prebend owners attested in Seleucid Uruk.[12] The economic role played by women in the system was therefore far from being marginal, especially when compared to the earlier periods. The cultic service involved by these transactions covers the whole spectrum of prebendary activities attested in Uruk, from the "ritualists" (tempel-enterers, exorcists) to the "purveying trades" (bakers, butchers, brewers, oil pressers) and "auxiliaries" (goldsmiths of the cultic paraphernalia, temple attendants, preparers of offering tables), and involve not only the cult of the major city temples, the Bīt Rēš and the Irigal, but also secondary shrines such as the Egalmah or the Edursaggani.[13]

As far as we can infer from our sources, these women seem to have acquired their prebends either by endowment from close male relatives or by purchase. The former was probably not much more frequent under the Seleucids than in the Neo-Babylonian and Early Achaemenid period, for only one undisputable example is known for the Seleucid period, which obviously records an exceptional situation. It is a *donatio mortis causa* (YOS 20, 20) written in 270 BC in the otherwise unattested city of Antioch-on-the-Ištar-canal, which was probably not far from Uruk: Anu-zēr-iddin, son of Nanaya-iddin, belonging to the Ekur-zākir family and father of the well-known multi-prebend holder Lābāši, bequeaths various properties – among which an unspecified prebend share is mentioned – to his wife Nidintu on the condition that after her death, these properties would go to his sons, who were most probably not Nidintu's.[14] In other words, these properties were only conveyed to Nidintu as

11 See Jursa 2010: 161.

12 In almost all the cases, the counterparts of these women are male members of the local priestly elite, with only one exception, a prebend sale dated to 197–196 BC featuring women as both principals (YOS 20, 54, see below). On the designation of women in the cuneiform sources from Seleucid Uruk, see recently Corò 2014.

13 The Egalmah was a small temple dedicated to the goddess Bēlet-balāṭi (George 1993 no. 321). Our sources describe this building as "attached to the Eanna" (*ša itti Eanna ṭepû*, see e.g. BRM 2, 36: 6). The Edursaggani was situated in the Urukean countryside and dedicated to the goddess Bēlet-ṣēri.

14 On this document, see McEwan 1984: 211–212. On Lābāši, son of Anu-zēr-iddin, see Corò 2005a: 87–94 and Corò 2005b.

means of sustenance during her widowhood, but she had no power of disposition over them since they were bound to return to the sons of her late husband after her death.

Apart from this exceptional document, it remains difficult to determine whether the practice of giving prebend shares to female relatives as endowments existed at all.[15] The few cuneiform documents known for the Hellenistic period listing the content of dowries never mention prebends, and one would be inclined to think that a male prebend owner would have generally preferred to bequeath his entitlements to his sons if he could do so, but the lack of relevant sources hampers any final conclusion.[16]

The examples of women purchasing prebend shares, on the other hand, are quite numerous in Seleucid Uruk and clearly stand out as a novelty when compared to Neo-Babylonian and Early Achaemenid period. The first attestations of this practice actually predate the Seleucid period, as can be seen from a document pertaining to the Gallābu archive from Ur and dated to the very end of the Persian period (UET 4, 25): it records the purchase of a prebend of doorkeeper by a certain Nikkal-tarībi, daughter of Kuṣur-Ea, from two individuals who may have been her cousins in April 331 BC, six months before the Macedonian conquest.[17]

As for Uruk, an interesting evolution of the identity of the individuals selling of prebend shares to women can be detected over the Seleucid Period. The earliest occurrence of purchase of a prebend share by a woman is dated to the beginning of the 3rd century BC[18], but one can reasonably assume on the grounds of the earlier evidence from Ur that this practice already existed in the 4th century BC, before the relevant sources became abundant again in Uruk. In the first half of the 3rd century BC, all the known female buyers appear to

15 Another possible example can be found in OECT 9, 38, a quitclaim written in Uruk in 214–213 BC, by which another Anu-zēr-iddin gives up claim over various properties among which we find prebend shares in favour of his stepmother Ēṭirtu and her sons. According to G. McEwan (1995: 24), Ēṭirtu and her sons could have received these properties from Anu-ab-utīr, the late husband of Ēṭirtu, who was also the father of Anu-zēr-iddin.

16 The dowry documents from Seleucid Uruk exclusively concern slaves (see BRM 2, 5, OECT 9, 4, OECT 9, 12 // OECT 9, 13, OECT 9, 17, OECT 9, 66). For the Hellenistic marriage contracts from other Babylonian cities mentioning dowries, see Roth 1989: 114–131.

17 On this tablet, see van Driel 1987: 164–165 and Joannès 2006: 128. Another document from the same archive (IM 17281, published in Oelsner 2006) records the lease of a prebend of doorkeeper in the main city temple by a certain Sîn-ahhē-bulliṭ (who could be a brother of Nikkal-tarībi) to a woman called Matuqtu, in 325 BC.

18 The earliest evidence is dated to 276 BC (BRM 2, 08) and records the sale of a share of brewer's prebend by a certain Anu-ahhē-iddin, son of Anu-uballiṭ and member of the Sîn-lēqe-unninni clan, to his wife Dannatu.

have been directly related to the seller by blood or by marriage. This was, for instance, the case of Ana-rabût-Nanaya and her sister Nupētu, who bought a prebend share of temple attendant (*gerseqqû*) from their grandfather Anu-iqī-šanni around 266–262 BC for ten shekels of silver (*BM 109936), before selling it for the same price to the multi-prebend holder Lābāši, son of Anu-zēr-iddin and descendant of Ekur-zākir less than four years later (Corò 2005a: txt. BM 105203).

After ca. 240 BC, on the contrary, women buying prebend shares outside the inner circle of their family become attested.[19] Over the following decades, these transactions tend to replace purchases from close relatives, which disappear almost completely after 200 BC.[20] In other words, while the sources of acquisition of prebend entitlements for women appear to have been restricted to close relatives before 240 BC, these women seem to have been able to purchase prebends freely after this date, provided they were related to one of the local priestly families by blood or marriage. This last restriction is particularly conspicuous in the case of Antiochis, who is attested during the 190's BC as purchaser of two different prebend shares of "temple enterer" (*ērib bīti*), including one from another woman.[21] Antiochis was most probably of Hellenic descent and therefore excluded *a priori* from the prebend system. However, she was also married to Anu-uballiṭ~Kephalôn, who not only belonged to one of the local priestly families (the Ah'ûtu clan) but was also the *rab ša rēš āli* of Uruk and the *šatammu* of the city temples – in other words, one of the most powerful Urukeans of his time.[22] There can be little doubt that it was these connections which enabled Antiochis to purchase prebends in the city temples.

The role played by women of the local priestly elite in the prebend system of Uruk therefore seems to have gained importance in the course of the 3rd

19 The earliest attestation of purchase of a prebend by a woman sharing no familial bond with the seller is dated to 239 BC (OECT 9, 15), which records the purchase of a share of baker's prebend by a certain Ēṭirtu, who was the daughter of a certain Anu-uballiṭ and the wife of a member of the Hunzû clan, from two individuals named Kidin-Anu and Balāṭu, belonging to the Luštammar-Adad clan.

20 No woman purchasing prebends from a kin appear to be attested after 216 BC at the latest (VS 15, 28), with only one exception dated to ca. 186–174 BC (OECT 9, 51).

21 This transaction is recorded by the tablet YOS 20, 54, a sale of prebend of *ērib bīti* before Anu and other gods dated to 197–196 BC: the seller is Ana-rabûtišu, daughter of Šamaš-iddin and descendant of Hunzû. The other transaction, which is dated to 191 BC, is a sale of prebend of *ērib bīti* before Enlil and other gods by a man called Lābāši, son of Ina-qibīt-Anu (BiMes 24, 6 // VS 15, 7).

22 On Anu-uballiṭ~Kephalôn and his family, see Monerie 2012: 333–343. The previously unknown title of *šatammu ša bītāti ilāni ša Uruk* is now attested by a tablet from the Louvre (AO 6498, on which see Clancier and Monerie 2014: 236–237).

century BC, as they became entitled to buy prebend shares outside the inner circle of their family from ca. 240 BC onwards. This does not mean, however, that any woman willing to purchase prebend shares would have been able to do so. No outsider, male or female, seems to have been authorized to acquire prebend entitlements, which remained the prerogative of the families of the local priestly elite. Moreover, this partial opening of the internal barriers of the system does not seem to have led to the emergence of a "prebendary leisure-class", since most of the female prebend owners from Seleucid Uruk are known to have possessed only one prebend type.

Two exceptions, however, are attested in our corpus. The first is Bēlessunu, whose father Anu-ab-uṣur was a nephew of the aforementioned multi-prebend holder Lābāši.[23] She is attested as purchaser in no less than eight transactions between 206 and 197 BC, implying nine different prebend types and worth more than four minas of silver in total.[24] The second is Rubuttu, who belonged to the Ah'ûtu clan and bought a cluster of prebends of various types for one mina of silver under the reign of Demetrius I (161–151 BC).[25] These instances, however, remain exceptional, and it seems probable that most of the women attested in our corpus could not live solely on their prebendary income.

Moreover, we have seen above that all these female prebend owners were compelled to hire a substitute among the authorized personnel in order to perform their cultic duties. Interestingly, the preserved hiring contracts from Seleucid Uruk show an evolution of the clauses of engagement between the prebend owners and their substitutes that appears to be almost exactly contemporary with the opening of the purchase for women outside their familial inner circle. While in the first half of the 3rd century BC, the lessee simply committed himself to fulfill his duties faithfully without causing interruption in the deliverance of the cultic offerings[26], from the 230's BC onwards, the hiring periods tend to get longer[27] and a new clause makes its appearance in

---

23 On Bēlessunu, see Corò 2005a: 99–100.

24 Almost half of this sum was disbursed for a single transaction dated to 199 BC (Corò 2005a: txt. BM 105188 // *BM 109943), by which Bēlessunu acquired shares of seven different prebend types from a certain Nidintu-Anu, son of Šamaš-ēṭir.

25 *Doc. Jur.* 5. The seller, Anu-zēr-iddin, was a descendant of Ekur-zākir.

26 See e.g. OECT 9, 9: 15–16. On these clauses, see conveniently Corò 2005a: 55–58.

27 In the first half of the 3rd century BC, the hiring periods go from three years (OECT 9, 9) to five years (*BM 105204, TCL 13, 238). After ca. 240 BC, most of the contracts stretch out to ten years (OECT 9, 16, Corò 2005a: txt. BM 105191, OECT 9, 36, Corò 2005a: txt. BM 116692, OECT 9, 62, BRM2, 47) with some exceptions at five (YOS 20, 69) and eight years (OECT 9, 37) until ca. 150 BC, after which the hiring period extends again up to twenty years (*BM 114420, VDI 1955/4, txt. 8). The exact meaning and implications of this evolution remain to be thoroughly assessed.

the contracts, by virtue of which both contractors are bound to respect their engagement until the end of the term, under penalty of having to give twenty shekels of silver to their counterpart.[28]

Although one cannot absolutely rule out the possibility that the apparent simultaneity of these evolutions – the enablement of women to purchase prebend entitlements outside the inner circle of their family on the one hand and the tightening of the control exerted over hiring practices of substitutes for prebendary service on the other – was merely fortuitous, we can be sure that none of these would have occurred without the consent of the temple authorities. This simultaneity tantalizingly suggests the existence of a concerted wish of the Urukean temple board to open prebend property to new prebend owners, provided they would belong to the local priestly community and with a corresponding increase of the control exerted over the hiring practices of prebendary substitutes in order to avoid any disturbance in the cult.

***

These seemingly concurrent evolutions of the Urukean prebend system during the third quarter of the 3rd century BC naturally raise the question of the motives that could have led the temple authorities to allow this internal opening of the otherwise tightly closed prebend system. Although the cuneiform sources from Seleucid Uruk do not provide any explicit answer to this question, one would be tempted to link these changes with contemporary developments of the local temple economy. I have tried elsewhere to demonstrate on the grounds of the evolution of the prebend prices that the Urukean prebend owners had to contribute financially to the building works of their city temples during the Hellenistic period.[29] The two visible drops in the prebend prices in 260–240 BC and 220–200 BC (cf. Fig. 1) could then have been caused by a corresponding drop in the demand for prebends, in consideration of the major building works undertaken at the initiative of the governor (*šaknu*) Anu-uballiṭ~Nikarchos and the *rab ša rēš āli* Anu-uballiṭ~Kephalôn and completed in 244 BC and ca. 202 BC respectively, which would have led to major costs for the local prebend owners.[30] If this assumption is correct, one might be tempted to interpret the ability for women of the local priestly elite to purchase outside

28 This clause is first attested in a hiring contract dated to 235–234 BC (Corò 2005a: txt. BM 105191: 17–21; see also OECT 9, 36: 24–26 and OECT 9, 37: 23–25).
29 These financial contributions are explicitly attested for the 6th century BC by the documentation from Borsippa (see Waerzeggers 2010: 342–344).
30 On these questions, see Monerie forthcoming.

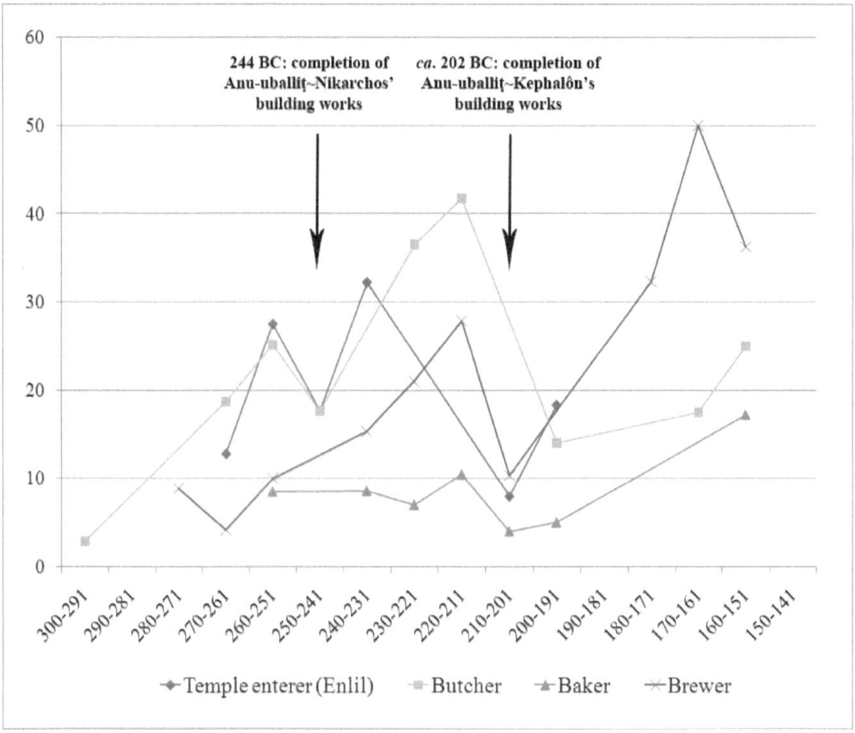

Fig. 1: Evolution of the mean price of several types of Urukean prebends over the Seleucid period, in shekels per day of monthly service.

their inner family circle after ca. 240 BC as an attempt to interest new solvent individuals in the financial sustenance of the local prebend system in exchange for the corresponding prebendary revenues.

This reconstruction must naturally remain hypothetical for the time being, since much work remains to be done on the economic evolution of temples during the second half of the 1st millennium BC. We still lack crucial information for most of the Achaemenid period, between the beginning of the 5th century BC and the Macedonian conquest,[31] and our scarce information from other cities seems to suggest that the evolution of the prebend system was not identical in all the temples of Babylonia over the Seleucid period.[32] However, despite

31 However, see recently Hackl 2013.

32 See e.g. the tablets from Nippur dated to the reign of Demetrius I (161–151 BC) and published by R. van der Spek (1992: 250–260), which display much shorter periods of engagement for prebendary substitutes: three years in van der Spek 1992 txt. 2, at a time when the Uruk material usually records engagements of twenty years.

these uncertainties, it appears quite clearly that the role played by women in the Urukean prebend system cannot be taken as a proof of the decay of the prebend system, which seems to have undergone constant adaptations in order to fit the needs of the local temple economy.

Appendix: Prebendary transactions involving women in Seleucid Uruk

The following table summarizes the available data concerning women in connection with the prebend system of Seleucid Uruk. The abbreviations used are the following:

B	buyer
d.	descendant
dr.	daughter
gdr.	granddaughter
ggs.	great-grandson
gs.	grandson
H	holder
ND	unkonwn
S	seller
s.	son
*	approximative date estimated on prosopographical grounds

Women	Transaction	Date (BC)	Prebend type	Role	Other contractor	Relationship w/other contractor	Price in shekels
f**Dannatu** (dr. Anu-ahhē-iddin), wife of Anu-ahhē-iddin (s. Anu-uballiṭ, d. Sîn-lēqe-unninni)	BRM 2, 08	276	Brewer	**B**	Anu-ahhē-iddin (s. Anu-uballiṭ, d. Sîn-lēqe-unninni)	husband	13
f**Taddin-Ištar** (dr. Lābāši, d. Kurî), wife of Anu-bēlšunu (s. Mukīn-apli, d. Kuri)	Corò 2005a txt. BM 109954 // *ibid.* txt. BM 109985	275	Preparer of the offering tables (*mubannû*)	**B**	Anu-bēlšunu (s. Mukīn-apli, d. Kurî)	husband	20
f**Nidintu** (dr. Anu-ab-uṣur), wife of Anu-zēr-iddin (s. Nanaya-iddin, d. Ekur-zākir)	YOS 20, 20	270	ND	**H**	Anu-zēr-iddin (s. Nanaya-iddin, d. Ekur-zākir)	husband	
f**Nupētu** and f**Ana-rabût-Nanaya** (drs. Anu-balāssu-iqbi, gdrs. Anu-iqīšanni, d. Kurî)	*BM 109936	ca. 266–262*	Temple attendant	**B**	Anu-iqīšanni (s. Ina-qibīt-Anu, d. Kurî)	grandfather	10
f**Nupētu** and f**Ana- rabût -Nanaya** (drs. Anu-balāssu-iqbi, gdrs. Anu-iqišanni, d. Kurî)	Corò 2005a txt. BM 105203	262	Temple attendant	**S**	Lābāši (s. Anu-zēr-iddin, d. Ekur-zākir)		10
f**Ana-rabûtišu** (dr. Anu-ah-utīr, gdr. Anu-zēr-lišir), along with Anu-balāssu-iqbi (s. Anu-uballiṭ)	BRM 2, 16	Before 255	Exorcist	**S**	Nidintu-Anu (s. Kidin-Anu, d. Ekur-zākir)		ND
f**Ēṭirtu** (dr. Anu-uballiṭ), wife of Kidin-Anu (s. Anu-ahhē-iddin, gs. Nanaya-iddin, d. Hunzû)	OECT 9, 15	239	Baker	**B**	Kidin-Anu and Balāṭu (ss. Anu-mār-ittannu, gss. Nidintu-Anu, d. Kurî)		20

^{f}**Ana-rabûtišu** (dr. Mukīn-apli), wife of Tanittu-Anu (s. Anu-bēlšunu, d. Ah'ûtu)	VS 15, 11	229	Temple-enterer (before ND deities)	**B**	Anu-bēlšunu (s. Tanittu-Anu)	Father-in-law$^{?}$	110
^{f}**Nidintu** (dr. Ubar), wife of Anu-uballiṭ (s. Nanaya-iddin, d. Hunzû)	VS 15, 28	ca. 222–216?*	Oil Presser	**B**	Dumqi-Anu (s. Anu-uballiṭ, gs. Nanaya-iddin, d. Hunzû)	Son-in-law$^{?}$	13
^{f}**Ēṭirtu** (dr. Ina-qibīt-Anu, d. Kurî), wife of Murašû	OECT 9, 28	ca. 222–216?*	Baker	**S**	Kidin-Anu (s. Anu-ahhē-iddin, d. Ḫunzû)		22 or 32$^{?}$
^{f}**Dannatu** (dr. Anu-ab-uṣur, gdr. Nidintu-Anu, d. Hunzû), wife of Lābāši (s. Anu-zēr-iddin, d. Ekur-zākir)	YOS 20, 84	ca. 216*	Exorcist	**B**	Ina-qibīt-Anu (s. Anu-uballiṭ, gs. Ina-qibīt-Anu, d. Ekur-zākir)		17
^{f}**Eṭirtu** (dr. Anu-ahhē-iddin), wife of Anu-ab-utīr (s. Nanaya-iddin, d. Luštammar-Adad)	OECT 9, 38	214–213	ND	**H**	Anu-zēr-iddin (s. Anu-ab-utīr, gs. Nanaya-iddin, d. Luštammar-Adad)	Stepson	
^{f}**Bēlessunu** (dr. Anu-ab-uṣur, gdr. Nidintu-Anu, d. Hunzû), wife of Anu-uballiṭ (s. Anu-zēr-iddin, gs. Lābāši, d. Ekur-zākir)	Corò 2005a txt. BM 105186	209–203*	Temple-enterer (before Anu)	**B**	Nidintu-Anu, Lābāši, Anu-ittannu and Lābāši-Anu (ss. Tattannu, d. Ekur-zākir)		15

Women	Transaction	Date (BC)	Prebend type	Role	Other contractor	Relationship w/other contractor	Price in shekels
^{f}**Bēlessunu** (dr. Anu-ab-uṣur, gdr. Nidintu-Anu, d. Hunzû), wife of Anu-uballiṭ (s. Anu-zēr-iddin, gs. Lābāši, d. Ekur-zākir)	Corò 2005a txt. BM 109949	ca. 209–192*	Temple-enterer (before Anu)	**B**	Anu-balassu-iqbi (s. Šamaš-ēṭir, gs. Kidin-Anu, d. Luštammar-Adad)		55
^{f}**Bēlessunu** (dr. Anu-ab-uṣur, gdr. Nidintu-Anu, d. Hunzû), wife of Anu-uballiṭ (s. Anu-zēr-iddin, gs. Lābāši, d. Ekur-zākir)	YOS 20, 58	ca. 209–192*	Baker	**B**	Tattannu (s. Nanaya-iddin, gs. Anu-uballiṭ, d. Hunzû)		5
^{f}**Bēlessunu** (dr. Anu-uballiṭ~Kephalôn, gdr. Anu-balāssu-iqbi, d. Ah'ûtu), wife of Anu-ah-ittannu (d. Ah'ûtu)	NCTU 23	ca. 209–175*	Service in the Edursaggani	**B**	Anu-uballiṭ (s. Rihat-Anu) ?		ND
^{f}**Bēlessunu** (dr. Anu-ab-uṣur, gdr. Nidintu-Anu, d. Hunzû), wife of Anu-uballiṭ (s. Anu-zēr-iddin, gs. Lābāši, d. Ekur-zākir)	YOS 20, 49	206	Butcher	**B**	Balāṭu (s. Šamaš-ēṭir, gs. Kidin-Anu, d. Luštammar-Adad)		25
^{f}**Bēlessunu** (dr. Tanittu-Anu)	OECT 9, 67	ca. 205–203*	Baker	**S**	Ubar (s. Anu-uballiṭ, gs. Ubar)		150

f**Bēlessunu** (dr. Anu-ab-uṣur, gdr. Nidintu-Anu, d. Hunzû), wife of Anu-uballiṭ (s. Anu-zēr-iddin, gs. Lābāši, d. Ekur-zākir)	Corò 2005a txt. BM 105174	ca. 205–197*	Butcher	**B**	Ubar (s. Ina-qibīt-Anu, gs. Dumqi-Anu, d. Hunzû)	17
f**Bēlessunu** (dr. Anu-ab-uṣur, gdr. Nidintu-Anu, d. Hunzû), wife of Anu-uballiṭ (s. Anu-zēr-iddin, gs. Lābāši, d. Ekur-zākir)	RIAA² 294	204	Temple-enterer (before Enlil)	**B**	Anu-mār-ittannu (s. Anu-ušallim, gs. Kidin-Anu, d. Luštammar-Adad)	8
f**Bēlessunu** (dr. Kidin-Anu), wife of Anu-ah-ittannu (s. Ša-Anu-iššû, gs. Tanittu-Anu, d. Hunzû)	YOS 20, 50	204–203	Baker	**B**	Ina-qibīt-Anu (s. Kidin-Anu, gs. Lābāši, d. Kurî)	20
f**Amat-bānītu** (dr. Anu-mukīn-apli, gdr. Anu-uballiṭ), wife of Anu-ah-iddin (s. Anu-balāssu-iqbi)[33]	OECT 9, 57	ca. 202–192*	Goldsmith of the cultic paraphernalia	**S**	Idāt-Anu (s. Illut-Anu, gs. Dannat-Bēlti, d. Luštammar-Adad)	20
f**Antu-banat** (dr. Illut-Anu, gdr. Ana-rabût-Anu), wife of Illut-Anu (s. Anu-uballiṭ, d. Kurî)	CM 12, 05	201	Oil Presser	**B**	Tattannu (s. Nanaya-iddin, gs. Anu-uballiṭ, d. Hunzû)	6

33 The names of Amat-bānītu's relatives are attested in OECT 9, 54 // OECT 9, 55: 15–16.

Women	Transaction	Date (BC)	Prebend type	Role	Other contractor	Relationship w/other contractor	Price in shekels
^f^**Bēlessunu** (dr. Anu-ab-uṣur, gdr. Nidintu-Anu, d. Hunzû), wife of Anu-uballiṭ (s. Anu-zēr-iddin, gs. Lābāši, d. Ekur-zākir)	Corò 2005a txt. BM 105188 // *BM 109943	199	Temple-enterer (Anu, Enlil), baker, butcher, temple attendant, service in Egalmah and Edursaggani	**B**	Nidintu-Anu (s. Šamaš-ēṭir, gs. Kidin-Anu)		120
^f^**Ana-rabûtišu** (dr. Šamaš-iddin, gdr. Nidintu-Anu, d. Hunzû), wife of Lābāši-Anu (s. Tattannu, d. Ekur-zākir)	YOS 20, 54	197–196	Temple-enterer (before Anu)	**S**	^f^Antiochis (dr. Diophantos), wife of Anu-uballiṭ~Keph-alôn (s. Anu-balāssu-iqbi)		15,5
^f^**Antiochis** (dr. Diophantos), wife of Anu-uballiṭ~Kephalôn (s. Anu-balāssu-iqbi, d. Ah'ûtu	YOS 20, 54	197–196	Temple-enterer (before Anu)	**B**	^f^Ana-rabûtišu (dr. Šamaš-iddin, gdr. Nidintu-Anu, d. Hunzû)		15,5
^f^**Bēlessunu** (dr. Anu-ab-uṣur, gdr. Nidintu-Anu, d. Hunzû), wife of Anu-uballiṭ (s. Anu-zēr-iddin, gs. Lābāši, d. Ekur-zākir)	Corò 2005a txt. BM 105196 // YOS 20, 85	197	Temple-enterer (before Anu)	**B**	Anu-uballiṭ (s. Lābāši, gs. Tattannu, d. Ekur-zākir)		5
^f^**Antiochis** (dr. Diophantos), wife of Anu-uballiṭ~Kephalôn (s. Anu-balāssu-iqbi, d. Ah'ûtu	BiMes 24, 06 // VS 15, 7	191	Temple-enterer (before Enlil)	**B**	Lābâši (s. Ina-qibīt-Anu)		55

[f]**Linakušu~Kua** (dr. Anu-uballiṭ, gdr. Kidin-Anu, d. Luštammar-Adad), wife of Nanaya-iddin (s. Anu-ab-uṭīr, d. Luštammar-Adad)	OECT 9, 51	ca. 186–174*	Goldsmith of the cultic parapher-nalia, temple attendant + *bīt qāti*	B	Anu-uballiṭ (s. Nanaya-iddin, gs. Anu-ab-utīr, d. Luštammar-Adad)	son	240
[f]**Rubuttu** (dr. Anu-uballiṭ, gdr. Nidintu-Anu, d. Ah'ûtu), wife of Anu-ah-ittannu (s. Antipatros, d. Ah'utu)	*Doc. Jur.* 5	ca. 161–151*	Temple-enterer (Anu, Enlil), temple-enterer and butcher (Egalmah), meat portions	S	Anu-zēr-iddin (s. Anu-uballiṭ, gs. Anu-zēr-iddin, d. Ekur-zākir)		60
[f]**Antu-banat~Ereštu-Nanaya** (dr. Anu-balāssu-iqbi, gdr. Šamaš-ēṭir, d. Luštammar-Adad), wife of Antiochos (s. Ina-qibīt-Anu, gs. Anu-balāssu-iqbi, d. Ah'ûtu)	NCTU 2 // NCTU 16	156	Butcher	S	Idāt-Anu (s. Dumqi-Anu, gs. Arad-Rēš) member of the *kiništu* of the Bīt Rēš		50
[f]**Ēṭirtu** (dr. Anu-mār-ittannu, gdr. Nanaya-iddin, d. Hunzû), wife of Kidin-Anu (s. Illut-Anu, gs. Kidin-Anu, d. Hunzû)	RIAA² 297	152	Baker	B	Ana-rabût-Anu (d. Hunzû)		15
[f]**Ereštu-Nanaya** (dr. Tanittu-Anu), wife of Anu-bēlšunu (s. Anu-ah-ittannu, gs. Anu-bēlšunu, d. Ah'ûtu)	*Iraq* 59, 38 // *BM 114406	150	Various meat portions	B	Lābāši (s. Anu-ah-ittannu, gs. Anu-bēlšunu, ggs. Anu-uballiṭ~Nikarchos, d. Ah'ûtu)		7

Bibliography

Beaulieu, Paul-Alain. 2000. The Descendants of Sîn-lēqi-unninni. Pp. 1–16 in *Assyriologica et Semitica: Festschrift für Joachim Oelsner anlässlich sein 65. Geburtstages am 18. Februar 1997*, eds. Joachim Marzahn and Hans Neumann. AOAT 252. Münster: Ugarit-Verlag.

Clancier, Philippe and Julien Monerie. 2014. Les sanctuaires babyloniens à l'époque hellénistique: évolution d'un relais de pouvoir. *TOPOI* 19: 181–237.

Corò, Paola. 2005a. *Prebende Templari in età seleucide*. History of the Ancient Near East Monographs 8. Padova: S.A.R.G.O.N.

Corò, Paola. 2005b. Business profiles of "multi-prebend holders" in Seleucid Uruk. Reconsidering the dossier of Labashi/Anu-zer-iddin//Ekur-zakir. Pp. 75–88 in *Approaching the Babylonian Economy*. ed. Heather Baker and Michael Jursa. AOAT 330. Münster: Ugarit-Verlag.

Corò, Paola. 2009. Esorcisti e prebende dell'esorcista nella Babilonia di I millennio: il caso di Uruk. *Studi Classici e Orientali* 51: 11–24.

Corò, Paola. 2014. Identifying Women in Hellenistic Uruk: a matter of perspective? *KASKAL* 11: 183–192.

Démare-Lafont, Sophie. 2010. Les prébendes dans la Mésopotamie du Ier millénaire av. J.-C. Pp. 3–17 in *L'organisation matérielle des cultes dans l'Antiquité*. ed. Barbara Anagnostou-Canas. Paris: Cybèle.

Funck, Bernd. 1984. *Uruk zur Seleukidenzeit: eine Untersuchung zu den Spätbabylonischen Pfründentexten als Quelle für die Erforschung der sozialökonomischen Entwicklung der hellenistischen Stadt*. Schriften zur Geschichte und Kultur des Alten Orients 16. Berlin: Akademie Verlag.

George, Andrew. 1993. *House Most High. The temples of Ancient Mesopotamia*. Winona Lake: Eisenbrauns.

Hackl, Johannes. 2013. *Materialen zur Urkundenlehre und Archivkunde der spätzeitlichen Texte aus Nordbabylonien* (2 vol.), Diss. Universität Wien.

Joannès, Francis. 2006. La Babylonie méridionale: continuité, déclin ou rupture ? Pp. 101–134 in La transition entre l'empire achéménide et les royaumes hellénistiques (vers 350–300 av. J.-C.). eds. Pierre Briant and Francis Joannès. Persika 9. Paris: De Boccard.

Jursa, Michael (ed.). 2010. *Aspects of the Economic History of Babylonia in the First Millennium BC*. AOAT 377. Münster: Ugarit-Verlag.

Jursa, Michael and Caroline Waerzeggers. 2008. On the initiation of Babylonian Priests. *Zeitschrift für Altorientalische und Biblische Rechtsgeschichte* 14: 1–38.

McEwan, Gilbert. 1981. *Priest and Temple in Hellenistic Babylonia*. Freiburger Altorientalische Studien 4, Wiesbaden: Franz Steiner Verlag.

McEwan, Gilbert. 1984. Inheritance in Seleucid Babylonia. *Bulletin of the School of Oriental and African Studies* 47: 211–227.

McEwan, Gilbert. 1995. Family Law in Hellenistic Babylonia. Pp. 20–36 in *Legal documents of the Hellenistic World*. eds. Markham Geller and Herwig Maehler. London: The Warburg Institute.

Monerie, Julien. 2012. Notabilité urbaine et administration locale en Babylonie du sud aux époques séleucide et parthe. Pp. 327–352 in *Communautés locales et pouvoir central dans l'Orient hellénistique et romain*. ed. Christophe Feyel *et al.* Études Anciennes 47. Nancy: A.D.R.A.

Monerie, Julien. forthcoming. *Aspects de l'économie de la Babylonie à l'époque hellénistique (IVe s.–IIe s. av. J.-C.)*, Studies in Ancient Near Eastern Records. Berlin / New York: De Gruyter.

Oelsner, Joachim. 2006. Zu spätbabylonischen Urkunden aus Ur und dem Archiv der Familie Gallabu 'Barbier'. Pp. 75–87 in *Recht gestern und heute. Festschrift zum 85. Geburtstag von Richard Haase*, eds. Joachim Hengstl and Ulrich Sick. Philippika 13, Wiesbaden: Harrassowitz Verlag.

Pirngruber, Reinhard and Caroline Waerzeggers. 2011. Prebend Prices in First-Millennium BC Babylonia. *JCS* 63: 111–144.

Roth, Martha. 1989. *Babylonian Marriage Agreements 7th–3rd Centuries* BC. AOAT 222. Neukirchen: Verlag Butzin & Bercker Kevelaer / Neukirchener Verlag.

van der Spek, Robartus. 1992. Nippur, Sippar and Larsa in the Hellenistic Period. Pp. 235–259 in *Nippur at the Centennial.Papers read at the 35th Rencontre Assyriologique Internationale, Philadelphia, 1988*, ed. Maria DeJ. Ellis. Philadelphia: S. N. Kramer Fund.

van Driel, Govert. 1987. Continuity or Decay in the Late Achaemenid Period: Evidence from Southern Mesopotamia. *Achaemenid History* 1: 159–181.

van Driel, Govert. 2002. *Elusive Silver*. Publications de l'Institut Historique et Archéologique Néerlandais à Stamboul 95. Leiden: Nederlands Instituut voor het Nabije Oosten.

van Driel, Govert. 2003–2005. Pfründe. *Reallexikon der Assyriologie* 10: 518–524.

Waerzeggers, Caroline. 2010. *The Ezida Temple of Borsippa, Priesthood, Cult, Archives.* Achaemenid History 15. Leiden: Nederlands Instituut voor het Nabije Oosten.

Waerzeggers, Caroline. 2011. The Babylonian Priesthood in the Long Sixth Century BC. *Bulletin of the Institute of Classical Studies* 54: 59–70.

Violaine Sebillotte Cuchet

Women and the Economic History of the Ancient Greek World: Still a challenge for gender studies

The history of women and gender, considered as an academic field, has progressed a lot since the year 2000, even in France. Therefore, every reader would expect to be enlightened on the methodological and theoretical positions assumed by the author of this paper. Working on the cultural context of ancient Greece and engaged in the specific scholarship background of French historiography (anthropological history renewed by feminism), my purpose is to develop the meaning of "women" for scholars like myself who study individuals (male and female) in the *era* of gender studies (part 1). My second point is about the economic approach: working on the history of women in the field of economics is, from my point of view, a great challenge. Economic and gender scholarship have never really merged and this volume is very interesting and innovative on this point (part 2). For this reason, joining gender and economic studies in Antiquity sounds very promising, even in Greek and classical studies. In engaging scholars in collecting various types of documents, textual as well as archeological, the act of joining gender and economic studies also provides several specific kinds of insight into ancient society and its various ways of speaking of individuals. Some documents underline the distinction between male and female, while others do not (part 3).

1 What benefit do women's studies gain from gender studies?

Women's studies are a broad academic field. When gender studies started in the sixties, it led to theoretical and political divisions among American feminists. Consider the French version, many years later, of this great divide be-

Acknowledgements: I would like to thank Lillian Doherty who did the revision of my English text.

Violaine Sebillotte Cuchet, Université Paris 1 Panthéon-Sorbonne, Anthropologie et Histoire des Mondes Antiques, Paris; Violaine.Sebillotte@univ-paris1.fr

tween women's and gender studies. In 2002, a conference was held in Paris by a feminist academic association and the main point was to discuss whether or not gender was a useful concept for women's history (Fougeyrollas-Schwebel et al. 2003). The main arguments against gender were that 1. gender was a new word (an English one) that French people wouldn't accept (the French language can use "rapports sociaux de sexe," "sexe," "hommes et femmes," etc.); 2. gender was a way to avoid women and to speak of social constructions without paying as much attention to real ancient people as one should; 3. gender was politically neutral and couldn't support a feminist cause. Gender's academic "success" was interpreted as proof of its lack of political weight.

It is quite funny to recall this argument since gender has become the highly controversial and political concept we know today. From that conference of 2002 in France to the present, gender has been largely adopted by International Organizations, scholars, even the media. Nevertheless, even in 2015, no one can say that it has become a politically neutral concept. In France, 2014 was a very bad year for gender studies: the French government, facing an "anti-genre" coalition, finally choose to retreat and to erase gender from its vocabulary, as Zancarini-Fournel pointed out (2014). In this context, writing the history of women without gender could appear either "out of date" or politically marked. The point is not to discuss these connotations or quick judgments but to shed light upon what is at stake when using gender in the field of history: what is the scientific gain, if any?

Gender, in its normal English usage, means the social aspect of being a man or a woman. In the sixties and in a culturalist perspective (Scott 1986), *gender* was a better word than *women* as gender meant the social interpretation of bodies whereas *women* referred to bodies themselves. In contrast to French, *sex* could not be used as it would have mostly meant sexuality.[1] In the international context, the word *gender* was adopted into many other languages, even in French where the word "genre" – in France, most people often ignored it – was a good equivalent. From the 13th century, "genre," translating the latin *genus*, has been used not only as a grammatical category but also as a sexual category (see Chevalier and Planté 2014 and Offen 2006). French feminists were unlikely to accept the word (either *gender* or *genre*) as it blurred bodies and sexual difference. But, at once, they did. In a way, the word allowed new ques-

1 In an important article about women's agency, Lin Foxhall (1989: 24) makes the distinction very clear, using either gender, or sex: "In the course of even one lifetime roles, statuses, economic resources and even personnel change. Sex does not change, though gender roles may."

tions. More important, it led to a decisive change in the scientific paradigm of women's history.

Gender was used as a category of analysis (according to Joan Scott), that is to say, a scientific tool (recently and in a French context, see Scott 2012). Setting bodies and sex in the cultural sphere, considering gender as a category (as Greeks said the ἀνθρώπων γένος or the γυναικῶν γένος), led to a new question: what do people do with sexual difference? Do they ignore it? Or does it make sense to them? If it does, why and how? Thus, sexual difference became a question in itself (Sebillotte Cuchet 2012).

Gender studies have also proved that the naturalization of sexual difference is an historical process. As Thomas Laqueur wrote in 1990, in the past, men and women could differ by what he called temperament or gender. In this organization of differences, various bodies were signs of various temperaments. From the modern medical point of view that has been developed since the middle of the 18th century, female and male bodies were as different as apples and oranges (Laqueur 1990; Steinberg 2008: 198). Laqueur's thesis has long been discussed and criticized (recently King 2013: 1–27 and 31–48). Today, gender studies are more sensitive to the different forms of discourses about sex and body, and scholars (as Holmes 2011) are more sensitive to emphasize either gender fluidity (individuals could be perceived as feminine or masculine in different contexts) or gender fixity (one cannot be female *and* male, one can never change one's sex – at least in Antiquity).

Therefore, the aim of gender studies, from my point of view, is to not describe women as a group of people sharing the same experience, by definition different from that of the group of men. What is at stake, rather, is to analyze the contexts, actions and functions that gave meaning to sexual difference (in other words, the contexts that construct gender). Sexual difference, in this perspective, is a relative notion. What is the difference between being a priest or a priestess? A god or a goddess? A king or a queen? A salesman or a saleswoman? A female or a male prostitute? etc. Examining that difference is the necessary precondition to being able to say what *women* means, in each context. In other words, comparing women and men when engaged in the same function is a good method to understand how various societies, activities, and documentary contexts differentiate (or not) women from men (on this method, see Boehringer and Sebillotte Cuchet 2011: 13–34). With the gender approach, the question of the place of women in history is definitely not the same as it was 40 years ago: we still use the category of women as *our* modern category but we actually are in search of what that category meant for the Ancient Greeks. Are we right to translate *gunē* (γυνή) by "woman" or does *gunē* meant wife? Or mother? Or is it just a word for a female body?

In analyzing the meaning given by the Ancients to sexual difference, the benefits are not only for women's studies but also for history as a whole. Actually, it is quite the rule that in Ancient societies the distinctions between individuals lay mostly in social status rather than in sexual status. Incidentally, we are not even certain of what "social status" and "individual" meant in Ancient Greece, as Boehringer pointed out in an anthropological perspective (Boehringer 2013). As individualization is an historical process and ancient Greece is characterized by the agency of the divine, we should also ask whether, when a man's actions are directed by a female divinity, such as Aphrodite, he is entirely a "man" i.e., someone with a psychological and personal identity that makes him different from a "woman." Ancient gender characteristics should be put together in a more complex manner than in our modern use of the term gender.

Thanks to gender studies, "women" are now in question. In the eighties, Black feminism underlined the historical and cultural gap between White women and Black women in the United States (Davies 1982). Actually, women as a homogeneous group do not exist. Therefore, what is of historical interest is to notice what makes women exist as a group. At this point I would insist how far gender radically transformed the questions usually asked about women and our ability to answer them. In this regard, women's studies are definitely not the same today as they were previously. Women's studies have gained from gender studies. We should not forget this and should keep this point in mind: it helps to put women (back) in the question.

2 Economic and gender scholarship never really merge

Working on women's history in the field of economics is a great challenge as economic and gender scholarship never really merge. Today, one main trend in economic studies is to propose and examine models of economic development, more or less ignoring the actors (for example, see Archibald, Davies, and Gabrielsen 2011). In *The Cambridge Economic History of the Graeco-Roman World*, edited by Ian Morris and Richard P. Saller in 2007, where space is made for sociological approaches, only one chapter out of 28 concerns women in the ancient economy: This is the chapter devoted to "Household and gender" that includes women with children (15 pages out of 770 pages). It seems that women could not exist without children and outside the domestic sphere of the house. In the recent *Companion to Women in the Ancient World*, edited by Sharon

L. James and Sheila Dillon, no more room is reserved for the question of women in economics.[2] Although described from a feminist perspective, women's work within the house (*oikos*–οἶκος) and feminine patronage are, as usual, the only way to deal with women in economics.

Yet it should be recalled that since the beginning of the eighties, feminist sociologists, even in France, have been leading a strand of scholarship that seriously contested the stereotypical picture of women at home they resumed by the phrase: "Seules les femmes sont inscrites dans une famille, seuls les hommes sont à leur place dans le monde du travail: des femmes inactives et des hommes sans famille" (Barrère-Maurisson 1984: 8). What was challenging in the early eighties of the last century is still challenging at the beginning of the 21st century.

The fact is that this very traditional representation of men (at work) and women (at home) is still taken for granted by most scholars, as I have tried to show with the two examples quoted above. Still today, it seems natural to assume that, in Antiquity, women were consumers (obviously only consumers) and men producers (obviously never consumers).[3]

Three points present valuable alternatives to escape from this stereotypical opposition:

1. Taking into account the bias of the vocabulary. Pieter Herfst, in a classic and still valuable book published in 1922, listed the feminine Ancient

---

2 In James and Dillon 2012, the main topics are historiography, medicine, law, and religion. Another trend is to discuss women's agency and women's representation (iconography, sculptures, portraits). Only a few pages are devoted to women in the economy (p. 325–326 based upon the papyri documentation and p. 478–490 in Emily A. Hemelrijk's paper about the occidental part of the Roman Empire).

3 See, for exemple, Julien Zurbach's comment on *Works and Days* 376–380 ("Puisses-tu n'avoir qu'un fils pour nourrir le bien paternel – ainsi la richesse croît dans les maisons – et mourir vieux en laissant ton fils à ta place. Mais, à plusieurs enfants, Zeus peut aisément aussi donner une immense fortune: plusieurs font plus d'ouvrage, plus grand est le produit"): "Hésiode parle de mariage à plusieurs reprises et aussi du nombre de fils. Ce qui est important dans ce passage n'est sans doute pas tant le nombre de fils que le fait même que ce soient des fils, plutôt que des filles ou des petits-enfants en bas âge. Cela signifie qu'ils peuvent travailler avec leur père, c'est-à-dire que le grand nombre de fils installe à l'intérieur de la famille une proportion favorable entre ceux qui travaillent la terre et ceux qui ne la travaillent pas. On comprend mieux dès lors ce jugement sur le nombre de fils, qui est assez important pour entrer en conflit dans ce passage avec la grande méfiance d'Hésiode envers les héritages par division, qui incitent au contraire à réduire leur nombre. On touche ici à la question de l'équilibre entre besoins et travail, qui est fonction de la relation entre nombre de producteurs et nombre de consommateurs au sein d'une cellule domestique qui apparaît clairement comme le principal, sinon le seul, horizon économique d'Hésiode" (Zurbach 2009: 16).

Greek words used for female trades (Herfst 1979; Savalli 1983: 81–89). Maria Cecilia D'Ercole, in a recent paper, stressed that only one out of five of the Ancient Greek merchants' terms listed by Pieter Herfst existed in a feminine form (D'Ercole 2013: 55). What does that mean? Were women less involved in commercial activities, as D'Ercole suggests? I think one should be very cautious with such an interpretation. One the one hand, we must keep in mind that the near-invisibility of female workers is often due, even in modern languages, to the male oriented vocabulary (masculine forms are used for generic forms, what we call masculine epicenes).[4] The question is a methodological one that influenced the understanding of entire societies. A few years ago, Cynthia Patterson noticed that *politai* (πολίται) – usually translated as "citizens" and, in French, "citoyens" (only male) – was used in epic and tragedy to describe the inhabitants of the *polis*, drawing water from the well or watching the war behind the walls of Troy (Patterson 1987: 49–67). From this activity and the context, one could affirm that those *politai* (πολίται) were mostly female citizens. In an economic context, think of the word *talasiourgos* (ταλασιουργός) that means "wool-worker" but can be used for both male and female workers. In the inscriptions of the *phialai exeleutherikai* (φιάλαι ἐξελευθερικαί), attesting to the manumission of 375 slaves in Athens at the end of the 4th century, the word qualifies women, not men (Todd 1997: 120–123, Wrenhaven 2009: 367–386). Inscriptions mentioned the price paid for manumissions and sometimes the names and occupations of the persons manumitted. On the 63 women mentioned with their occupations, 51 (or 81 %) are designated as *talasiourgoi* (ταλασιουργοί).

2. Keeping in mind that the male distribution of civic (public) functions does not mean that women were outside of the economy. We can guess that very

4 Still rare are the papers assuming the question of gender and of language. It is noteworthy that, in 1898 (1st ed.), the *Recueil des Inscriptions Juridiques Grecques*, did mention this discrepancy between lexical and grammatical gender and individuals involved in Epicteta's will (circa 200 BCE): "L'objet du testament est la création d'une corporation ou communauté perpétuelle, comprenant tous les parents mâles de la testatrice, présents et à venir; les présents sont dénommés, au nombre de vingt-cinq, en tête le gendre et le frère adoptif d'Epictéta. Cependant quoique la communauté soit expressément qualifiée de corporation masculine (ἀνδρεῖος, II, 29 et suiv.), la testatrice, par une disposition supplémentaire (§ 9), décide qu'on y admettra également: 1. les femmes des premiers membres et leurs filles tant qu'elles seront en puissance de leurs pères; 2. les descendantes (sans doute seulement par les mâles) des membres originaires, tant qu'elles remplissent la même condition; 3. les épiclères avec leurs maris et leurs enfants; 4. à titre exceptionnel, huit femmes (avec leurs maris et leurs enfants), dont l'une est la fille épiclère de la testatrice, deux les soeurs de son gendre, trois les filles ou soeurs de membres du κοινόν." (Dareste, Haussoullier, and Reinach 1965: 106–107).

often, only the man had that function, but the female members of the family were also at work. As C. Chandezon has recently noticed in regard to Xenophon's *Oeconomicus*: "the responsibility for bookkeeping in the estate falls not on the overseer but on the mistress of the house, Ischomachos' wife, who plays the role of the *tamias*, the treasurer. She has to receive the harvests, calculate and organize the expenditures, assess the amount of reserves to be kept and 'make sure she does not spend in one month the expenses planned for one year'." (Xen. *Oec.* 7.36, Chandezon 2011: 108). Female workers were almost invisible because of texts oriented by androcentric organization and shaped by masculine forms of language. In this case, deductive reasoning could help to right the balance. For example: even if textile production is not well known due to the lack of archeological data, we know Greek people considered this work as a women's role, and it was probably so (iconography, archeology, epigraphy, and textual tradition repeatedly stressed what can be understood as a common assumption). Various elements otherwise allowed C. Chandezon to affirm that textile production was of great importance in Ionia: a special breed of sheep was used to produce a highly famous variety of wool from the 6th century to the Hellenistic period (Chandezon 2003: 200–201). Working at home or in collective workshops, women must have played a central role in the production of this regional wealth, as it is hardly probable that there were only male workers.

3. Taking into account all the data concerning women at work or engaged in economic transactions and not only the textual documentation transmitted by the manuscript tradition. *Works and Days*, the Hesiodic poem written to advise Perses against departing from *dikē*, good behavior, sets up the figure of the peasant living in the 7th century. The social environment is full of ill-behaved people and the weather not that good. The poor peasant trying to escape the fate of poverty and slavery should be moved by the good *eris*, the good struggle, not the bad one. The good *eris* engages him to work in his fields in order to make his home prosperous (*Works and Days* 17–23). The vivid description is rooted in the present of the poet and his audience: the Iron Race must struggle and work for livelihood. This situation is explained by the poet as a consequence of Prometheus's *mētis*: the grain has been held by Zeus under the earth, evil and sickness have spread, hard labor has become necessary to live, and sexual union imposed on the new Race, the Iron Race, has made each one mortal. Beside its misogynistic and even misanthropic tone, the poem – didactic in producing an ethic of the good life – does not tell us anything about women in the economy except incidentally. One can read that the ideal is to keep

> the young girl at home in winter, with her mother, spinning the wool. We could infer that working the wool is a women's ideal task.[5] The main purpose of the landowner is to keep his property free and transmit it to his children. Thus, the social reference of the narrative is that of the *oikos* in its patrimonial aspect: coming from the father and transmitted to son(s). In this picture, the wife couldn't be anything other than a sexual partner whose function is giving birth to the potential heirs. In this narrative, and because of the narrative choice of *WD*, nothing else is expected of her.

It is true that this ideal of a complementary opposition between men and women's roles is repeated, even in a different form, in one of the most important pieces of written evidence for the Classical period, Xenophon's *Oeconomicus*: husband and wife are presented as complementary managers, each one organizing his or her own sphere, the indoors and the outdoors, independently. This oppositional organization is based on an interpretation of their bodies: the male one is as tough as the female is soft (*Oec.* VII, 18, 22–28). This didactic treatise is correctly understood by commentators as an ideal for a valuable citizen life: getting married and taking care of the estate to transmit it to heirs. Once more, the narrative choice led to the oppositional and complementary depiction of the spouses.

Archaeological data have confirmed these narrative codes: funerary steles and vases displayed images of women in domestic activities or managing domestic staff. The stereotypical opposition of the spindle and distaff for spinning wool and the hoplite panoply is very well known even as a literary *topos*.[6] This norm is highly political: it applied to the world of landowners, a world of female and male citizens in Classical Athens. But even in the world of citizens, these political norms cannot be considered as reflecting any social or economic reality. François Lissarrague demonstrated in 1990 how far images of women at the loom diverged from actual labor. Vases often show women in brilliant dress, with garlands, jewelry and sometime heroic names such as Clytemnestra, Iphigenia, or Cassandra. For the people looking at the images, could it be anything other than an idealistic world where work is done without sweat (Lissarrague 1991: 229–231)?

5 Pandora, the first wife (γυνή), is described as skilled in weaving (v. 64), an ambivalent attribute (v. 373, 375). Nevertheless, even the poor ploughman must weave (*WD* 538: μηρύομαι), by himself, to cover his body and protect it against the cold winter (see West 1978: 294). So, if women are mainly engaged in textile tasks, it is unlikely that only women were doing textile work: sewing, weaving, spinning and carding. See the recent bibliographic survey in Brøns 2014: 85–89.

6 Herodotus IV 162; IX 109; Aristophanes, *Lysistrata* 530–538; Polyen, *Strategemata* VIII, 53.

I would like to emphasize, at this point, how far the economic functional division between men and women, as producers and consumers, is derived from textual tradition and from this very specific point of view of the household and its claim to transmission through male generation. To proceed further, I need to present the archaeological data that lead to a very contrasting opinion about women at work. In other words, the archeological data help to understand how diverse were the situations of women (and men) and how far women could act, in social life, as economic partners.

3 Women's place in the Ancient Greek economy: stakeholders, individual agency and documentary norms

Textual tradition, often repetitive, tells us a lot about civic attitudes, social and political concerns, and ethical behaviors, but not about everyday life. By contrast, the archaeological data is diverse, heterogeneous and usually not in conformity with the civic norm we find in texts. Historians are, therefore, always confronted with the question of the general, or, inversely, the question of the unique. What is at stake is the representativeness of each document and the representativeness of each woman. As we still don't have, and probably never will have, the exhaustive database that could allow us to produce statistics, we are actually trying to examine each assertion and generalization in order to find out both the purpose of the author/producer of the document and/or the documentary conventions that imposes particular formula or *mises en scène*. In other words, the variety of acts displayed by archeological data also had to conform to norms. Some vases, for example, could repeat textual norms when those vases are intended to promote an idealized vision of men or women. But they could, by contrast, convey different meanings, particularly when they are meant to make people laugh (Lissarrague 2013). At a minimum, archeological data displayed various performances of life.

3.1 Women's involvement in economic transactions: Thespiae and Tenos

Ten years ago, Isabelle Pernin, analyzed various *stelai* found in Thespiae (Beotia), dated from the second half of the 3rd century BC (Colin 1897; Pernin 2004; Roesch 2009; and now Pernin 2014). Those inscriptions are lease contracts (μισθῶσεις) on behalf of the city, which was the landowner of public estates. The most complete is inscribed with an irregular and unclear script on a limestone stele (about 0.77 cm in height × 0.50 cm in length) presently in the museum of Thespiae. Its context of discovery is unclear, coming from a citadel (φρούριον) located above the modern village of Erimocastro. On this stele, 25 plots (γύαι) are rented. Previous renters had priority to renew their previous agreement unless they had misbehaved. Nine plots changed renters. The 25 plots involved not 25 persons but only 16 (as one single individual can rent more than one plot) including two male children (Thumias and Rhodios) and three women (in fact, one among them might have been a child). The women in each case are involved as new renters, like the two "boys" and also a man, named Poleas (plot 22). All the new renters invoked a parentage with the previous one: the children, Thumias and Rhodios are the *paides* (παῖδες) of Pouthodotos; Poleas is the brother of Pherekleios, Zopoura the daughter of Dionysios, Dinophila the daughter of Ismeinodoros. Phrounicha, the last woman mentioned, declares herself to be the closest relative to Wimmpidas whom she succeeded in taking the location of two plots.

In those transactions women, less numerous than men (3 out of 16), acted on their own. The formula is the same for men and women: name of the previous renter (if any), name of the renter, parentage with the previous one, verb (ὑπογράψασθαι), price, guarantor(s). The plots seem to be of the same value (we don't have all the information) whether they are rented by men or women. The women produced guarantor(s) (προστάτας) sometimes called φίλοι (close relations), like all the men. But, unlike men, women also needed to present a witness that Isabelle Pernin called an assistant (the Greeks used the word παρεῖαν that indicates the witness's presence along with the woman). Zopoura, daughter of Dionysos, rented a plot, previously rented by her brother Dionysodoros. She presented two witnesses, Poleas son of Archias and Saosias son of Sosipolis, and three close relations (φίλοι) came along with her (παρεῖαν Ζωπύρη τῶν φίλων ...) when she entered into the contract: the two witnesses whose names are repeated and Dionysios son of Dionysios. For that one, no husband is mentioned, thus Zopoura might have been either a single person or a child. Dinophila, daughter of Ismeinodoros, presented two witnesses and produced her husband Archias (without patronymic) as an "assistant." The husband is presented in a subordinate form (Dinophila's man): παρεῖς Διvοφίλη Ἀρχίας ὁ ἀνείρ. The focalization is that of the one, whether male or female, who acts as the renter.

Another piece of evidence for women's involvement in economic transactions is the stele of sales from Tenos. It is the most important document attesting sale contracts and no documents of this nature have been found in Attica.

The stele noted 47 agreements listed in chronological order and covering a period of one and half years. The stele might have been erected in a public space and the dating is from the archontat of Ameinolas at the end of the 4th century BC or the beginning of the 3rd.[7]

Roland Etienne, who analyzed the stele, noticed that women were involved in 30 agreements out of 47, and in 5 out of the 8 most important (in financial terms). We can observe that the formula is the same for men and women: name of the buyer, patronymic, name of the tribe; name of the seller, patronymic and name of his tribe; verb; description of the property. From the end of the 19th century, the stele has been commented upon from a juridical point of view. Different types of sales have been noticed in these agreements (new sales, results and developments of previous transactions, parts of familial economic strategies; see Etienne 1990: 52–67 and Game 2008: 105). The question of the economic agency of the women quoted in the inscription has never been precisely considered except by Claude Vial and Anne-Marie Vérilhac who emphasized it (Vial and Vérilhac 1998: 125–207). Otherwise the debate is over simplified by considerations about the so-called "freedom" of "Tenian women" compared to "Athenian women" (Etienne 1985: 61–70).

What are the main conclusions of this scholarship?

1. As in the Thespian agreements, when a woman is involved in Tenos, she acts like a man. The verb is exactly the same as for a man (ἐπρίατο). The plot might be described with mention of the neighbors – men or women (Petale: § 35). Sometimes, the land is noted to have been in the possession of a previous owner who could have been a woman, thus Timothea (§ 28) and Archestrate (§ 30). Thus, it is clear that some women were landowners.[8] Those women could participate in exchanges of property as men did and were, thereby, involved in financial transactions (usually mortgage, other attestations in Vial and Vérilhac 1998: 179–195).
2. Some women could possess lands that were not part of a dowry but personal estates. Thus Pheido, daughter of Chabyssios, owned a plot given by her maternal grandfather, and participated in a joint ownership (joint-stock company?) that also belonged to her mother Iphikrite and her brother

7 *CIG* II, 2338; *IJG* I: 64–87; *IG* XII 5.2, 872 (new ed. of the text); Etienne 1990: 51–84; Game 2008: 173–190 (text and translation). Image: British Museum 1818,0110.4. I use the numbering of the agreements followed, since *IJG*, by Etienne 1990 and Game 2008, from § 1 to § 47.
8 Foxhall 1989. Vial and Vérilhac 1998: 152 and 187–91 for other examples and the conclusion: "La majorité des historiens et des juristes ont sous-estimé la place tenue dans les dots par les biens immobiliers. Les exemples dont nous disposons sont nombreux et viennent de régions diverses."

Chairelas II. Iphikrite, herself, a daughter without a brother, possessed properties coming from her own father, Chairelas I. The women's properties do not come only from dowries (§ 33, § 36, § 38, § 39, § 40, § 41; Vial and Vérilhac 1998: 156 and 167).

3. Sometimes, previous ownership is mentioned, and among these landowners, a few are women: Timothea (§ 28) and Archistrate (§ 30). Etienne considers that when previous landowners are mentioned that means that the real property is still theirs and that the transaction is purely a loan, not a sale (Etienne 1990: 54–55). Without discussing the conclusion of the argument, we notice that the presence of women mentioned as previous landowners of the plot "for sale" clearly indicate that women were considered as "real" landowners. The same could be deduced from the mention of female neighbors: thus Petale (§ 35).
4. Actually, on some occasions, the consent of a woman is asked for. This makes sense if we consider, as it is usual, that the land the man wants to "sell" is part of the mortgage on the wife's dowry (for the "general mortgage" on the husband properties, see Vial and Vérilhac 1998: 195–197 and 202–203). Thus, Thespieus son of Thespieus, Aristonas son of Aristolochos and the community of Theoxeniastes bought from Artumachos son of Aristarchos some estates that have been previously their own property before they sold them to Aristarchos with the participation and consent of Manto (συνχωρούσης καὶ συνεπαινούσης Μαντῶς), daughter of Demokrines and present with her *kurios* (μετὰ κυρίου) Artumachos himself (§ 45). In other words, the *kurios* is here interpreted as the husband. But, in another agreement, we can read that two men give their consent, and in quite the same way as Manto does: "Kalliphon son of Kteton, Heraclides, bought from Phokos son of Phokion, Thruesios, the house that was previously owned by Kteton, his father, the neighbors being Simias and Kallikrates, for 1700 silver drachmas, with the consent of Phokos and Kteton, father of Kalliphon (συνεπαινοῦντος)" (§ 16). The consent is given by the father of the buyer and by the seller, who previously bought the house from the father of the buyer. The sale looks like a loan mortgaged on a house. No woman is involved in the transaction. Nevertheless, the same formula of consent applied here for men.

The interpretation of the sale as a *prasis epi lusei*[9] has often be taken as an argument that it was only to allow their husband or sons to get money or to

9 Jean Game makes the point very clearly and emphasizes the specificity (in our documentation) of Tenos: Game 2008: 167.

protect their dowries that women were involved in financial agreements. But, it is very difficult to evaluate the distinction between a sale and a loan – the *prasis epi lusei* is only known, by that name, in Athens (Finley 1952, Game 2008: 168) – and interpretations are often based on the interpreters' preconceived ideas about what might be the right place of women in society.[10]

Instead of reasoning only in terms of dowries and mortgages,[11] which implies putting women in a different economy (as passive partners), I suggest that it would be useful to reason in term of individuals (even rooted in collective networks such as the household, kinship and political associations) because, as I noted at the beginning of this paper, feminist historiography – even in the rare studies devoted to female agency in economics – have persistently understood gender as a cognitive system based on two complementary and oppositional poles, a polarity that led to an impasse.

3.2 Gender and individuals' agency

One very influential paper on the subject of women's agency in economics was that of Lin Foxhall, who argued against the traditional view of passive women that has been widespread in scholarship since David Schaps' book published in 1979. In 1989, Lin Foxhall described her method in the field of gender studies: Lloyd's description of polarity and analogy in Greek culture (Lloyd 1966) prompted her to affirm that "in ancient Greek culture, broadly speaking, it can be argued that pairs of complementary oppositions are a fundamental aspect of cognition, intruding into every corner of social interaction from μέν and δέ to men and women" (Foxhall 1989: 23). She added that "the most usual contexts for gender are provided by the poles of another complementary opposition: the private world of the household and the public world of the communi-

10 Etienne 1985: 64, "Sous les termes d'achat et de vente se cache une simple circulation d'hypothèques sous la forme de *prasis epi lusei* (vente à pacte de rachat), bien connues par la documentation de l'Attique. Dans ce mouvement des créances qui passent de main en main un seul point reste obscur. "L'ancien propriétaire", Eurykratès, conserve-t-il des droits de propriété, ou le bien a-t-il été acquis par Amphylis en pleine propriété ? *Il est difficile de trancher*, mais dans ce type de contrats *je penserais volontiers* que l'expression "biens qui appartenaient auparavant à ..." ne sert pas de référence supplémentaire pour désigner l'objet du contrat, venant s'ajouter à la mention des voisins, mais doit établir ou rappeler les droits réels de la personne nommée. *J'entends donc* qu'Eutykratès reste propriétaire – et peut-être même occupant – d'une moitié de ferme sur laquelle une hypothèque a circulé, passant deux fois dans les mains d'Amphylis." Emphases are mine. The author alludes to Tenos § 12.

11 The beginning of the inscription does not help the understanding: "About lands, sales of houses and constitution of dowries," *IJG* I: 64. l.1.

ty" (*ibidem*). The major point she made was to make scholars fully aware of the implicit content of texts (Athenian documentation from the 4th century), of the solidarity of the household (including males and females) and of the distinction between legal and social descriptions.[12] Social relations could not be confused with legal formulations.[13] Nevertheless, her use of gender (as a metaphor of social roles that could change within the household depending on age, place in the family, or accidents of life, etc.) and sex (being a female or a male) was not so easy to understand. Actually, gender, presented as "the most vigorous expression of meaning available to ancient Greek culture" in her analysis (Foxhall 1989: 23), overlaps with the male/female opposition (unified in the ideal context of the household).

Less than ten years after Lin Foxhall's paper, Christiane Sourvinou-Inwood published another influential article in 1995 that stresses once more the organization of Ancient Greek society, divided between a private and a public sphere, a male and a female sphere. As Sourvinou-Inwood demonstrated: "it is not the case that in Classical Athens women were excluded from the public sphere; they played an active role in public life in religion, as priestesses and other cult personnel as well as worshippers; that is, they played an active role in central part of polis activity, in which women were complementary and equal to men" (Sourvinou-Inwood 1995: 112). In addition, and *contra* Foxhall, she emphasized how subordinated women were in the *oikos*.

None of these studies, produced in the eighties or the nineties, used gender as I do when I consider the concept as a scientific tool to interrogate the division between men and women in Antiquity (Scott 1986; Schmitt Pantel 2009). It is useful to put this new question at the fore and to take the step made by

---

12 For this last point, Foxhall distanced herself from the juridical approach of D. Schaps who concludes in 1979 on the existence, in Greece, of "the status of women" (Foxhall 1989: 98). The point is clearly made in Foxhall 2013: 44 and 158: "And yet, it is clear that although gender may present itself most clearly as a dichotomy of male and female, the lived reality was far more complex, not least because of its intersections with other socio-cultural and political factors (age, class, status, wealth, etc.)", with reference to what sociologists call insectionality.

13 See on this point the anthropological analysis of the society of Karpathos in the 20th century "Dans cette société, marquée par ailleurs par le tabou des relations sexuelles avant le mariage ainsi que par une très forte séparation entre les sexes, les enfants de chaque sexe sont en effet condamnés, notamment par suite des exigences parentales, à se préoccuper sans cesse et depuis le plus jeune âge du sort, des intérêts et des désirs des enfants de l'autre sexe avec qui ils sont engagés dans un courant d'échanges particulièrement intensifs: constitution des dots sororales avec ce que cela peut impliquer de sacrifice, accompagnement au bal, aide dans la recherche d'un mari et protection d'un côté, avec comme contrepartie de l'autre, reconnaissance, admiration, respect, dons symboliques (louanges) et services domestiques divers" (Vernier 1985: 22–23).

gender studies from a description of complementary oppositions (male/female; men/women) to the question of the meaning and the relevance of such an opposition.

The main point of the previous discussion concerns the ability of women to act by themselves, that is to say, the conditions of their ownership, or in other words, their right to dispose of property.[14] It is in terms of degree of freedom or subordination that R. Etienne introduced his article about women, real property and money in Tenos published in 1985: Would Cycladic women have been more emancipated than "their Athenian sisters" (Etienne 1985: 61)? According to R. Etienne, the direct involvement of women in the sales contracts of Tenos should not be interpreted as a sign of more freedom for them. The main argument against their agency was the presence, along with them, of their *kurios*.[15]

Roland Etienne was right to point to the fact that women in Tenos were engaged in transactions with the constant guardianship of their husbands (or brothers or other male relatives). Actually, the only difference between men and women involved in transactions in the Tenos' stele is that women are identified not only by the grammatical form of their name but also by the presence of a *kurios* (κύριος), introduced with the coordination "καί" or "μετά" or the relative pronoun "ἧς." In any case, we could not infer the function of the *kurios* from the term and we can be sure that, even done "with" a *kurios*, or with the attendance of men – as is the case in Thespiae – the act is the woman's. We never get the formula that the *kurios* bought, sold or consented on behalf of a woman.

Lin Foxhall thus suggested that we read the economic transactions at the intersection of the household and the public spheres. Because the transaction concerning wealth of the household needed to "operate in the legal/political sphere, it had to be represented by a household member capable of acting in this sphere: an adult male, normally the head of household. The consequence is that the holder of this key position also becomes highly visible in the documents" (Foxhall 1989: 43). Two different agencies are at stake, the one in the household (male or female) and the one in the legal/political sphere (male).

---

14 Foxhall 1989: 24–27. The discussion goes back to Schaps 1979, who himself summarizes the previous scholarship in his preface (p. v–vi) and discusses – very briefly – the notion of property (Schaps 1979: 2).

15 "L'intervention des femmes dans les contrats ne doit pas pourtant laisser croire qu'elles jouissaient d'une plus grande "liberté" qu'à Athènes. La présence d'un *kyrios* est toujours requise pour que leur action soit juridiquement valable. Les formules sont donc exactement les mêmes que lorsqu'il s'agit de mineurs: en ce sens, les principes du droit à Ténos sont bien les mêmes qu'à Athènes. L'émancipation de la femme, qui progresse à l'époque hellénistique en dehors du cadre de la cité, ne passe certainement pas par Ténos." (Etienne 1985: 62).

Nevertheless, the male legal sphere should not be equated with the public sphere. The women acting in these agreements were highly visible for their contemporaries, and this visibility is yet a step passed in the political/public sphere.[16]

At Tenos, the stela was erected in a public place and the engraving was done under the control of magistrates, the *astunomoi*, equally naming women and men. It is, I presume, a strong argument to say that women were part of economic exchanges, whether those exchanges were of land or money. Women could control wealth without shame either for them or for their male relatives. The public visibility of these women gave them social recognition. In Olynthus, an inscription recording the transaction between Xenon and Euboulides named two guarantors (βεβαιωταί), Pytheeas, Pythion's son, and Philaina, Heron's daughter. Philaina does not need a *kurios* to act as a guarantor (Game 2008: 62). This inscription, from 350 BC, has been found *in situ*, in the ruins of a house near the North-East angle of the Agora. Located by the entrance, the stone was visible to everyone coming into the house. Everyone could read the name of Philaina and she must have incurred of the social esteem of all (Game 2008: 171–172).

It is correct that female citizens in well-known Greek cities needed a tutor, the *kurios*, for certain public acts they were engaged in.[17] But, it is also important to note that recent works have tended to put in perspective the influence of the *kurieia*, stressing its formal nature. For example, comparing Greek women and Egyptian women involved in loan contracts preserved on Egyptian papyri from the 3rd to the 2nd century BC, Damien Agut and Anne-Emmanuelle Veïsse pointed out that the *kurioi* mentioned in those contracts had no influence on the decisions (Agut-Labordère and Veïsse 2014). Indeed, Egyptian and Greek women act in the same way, whether they have a *kurios* or not. The mention of the *kurios*, always present in agreements made by Greek women, seems to be used as a formal clause and linked to only very specific legal acts, in other words, to documentary traditions (Veïsse 2011).

To summarize, the legal sphere where the *kurios* intervenes is not homogeneous, neither in the Greek world nor in all periods of Greek history, and probably not even inside the same city. The legal sphere is not synonymous with "public sphere," as visibility of women is very well attested in various

---

16 For a recent discussion about these categories, see now Azoulay 2014.

17 Not all acts, if we think of the well-known example of the loan made by 223 BC by Nikareta from Thespiae to the city of Orchomenos: Migeotte 1999. Her husband, present as a *kurios*, is mentioned on only one occasion, when Nikareta made the Orchomenians acknowledge their debt.

aspects of public life, such as religious practices (Sourvinou-Inwood 1995: 114–118). The economic transactions involving women impinge on legal practices (written agreements) and political practices (magistrates record the contract) as well as social ones (households interactions): women could not be said to be confined in another world that would be the household and the domestic sphere. Actually, the women mentioned in the sale or loan contracts are rich women, with high social status. Is it fair to consider them as "women", apart from "men", or do we have to compare rich men and women, as opposed to poor men and women?

On this point, the question meets with the lack of documentation. We know from the Attic orators about Athenian female citizens who became so poor that they needed to work: some were nannies, others street vendors, others grape pickers and others farm workers (Scheidel 1995: 207–210, 1996; D'Ercole 2013: 64–65). Plato is even more explicit when he says, in *Laws* 805 d–e, that in Thracia and in many other places, women were harvesting – an unusual occupation for women in Athens, Plato added. Roger Brock, in an important paper published in 1994, suggested that textual documents, reflecting the highly normative ideology of the complementarity of the inside and the outside, downplayed that fact (Brock 1994). Actually, even in the very didactic Hesiodic *Works and Days*, one can read: "First build a house (οἶκον) and get an ox for the plow (βοῦν τ'ἀροτῆρα), and a woman (γυναῖκα) for a price (κτητήν) – no formal wedding (οὐ γαμετήν) – to follow your oxen (βουσὶν ἕποιτο)" (*WD*: 405–406). A woman bought for a price meant that nobody could claim any kind of ownership over her body and children (unlike the spouse in a formal wedding), except the one who bought her. She did not get any dowry to manifest her own property and wealth (deriving from her family's) against her husband's. The high vulnerability of poor women was a *topos* in Athenian comedy: one poor Megarian citizen tried to sell his daughters, wife and mother, because of hunger (*Acharnians*, 729–775 and 811–817). Women, in this case, were not far away from slavery (Jameson 1977/78: 137–138, Foxhall 2013: 96). The glorious Eurykleia, wet-nurse of Odysseus, is this kind of woman, both free and slave, doing all the work a female slave would do, including sexual work (Scheid 2015).[18]

***

18 Scheid 2015. The question of prostitution as sexual work should be considered as part of economic transactions. Schaps excluded this activity from his study because he focused on the "ordinary free Greek woman" (Schaps 1979: 2). The point is that we do not know what makes a free Greek woman that "ordinary."

To conclude, one can say that there were, in Ancient Greek societies, as many situations for women as for men. The gap between archaeological data and textual tradition is huge. The bias of textual tradition is not only androcentric (because of the language that use masculine forms for generic purposes) but also ideological: texts tended to focus on "*ho boulomenos*," the *homopoliticus*' type. And, even if archeological data exist and are increasingly published and taken into account, the work is actually in its infancy for understanding how far the fact of being born a girl influenced one's adult role in the economy and society. I have tried to demonstrate that to answer that question, it is important not to think that women were all considered in the same way, as female, or that their story is a different story, apart from political, economic, and social characterizations. The legal dispositions that made for the differences between male and female, only concerned men and women of citizen status and social importance. In this group, women – always less represented than men – did have economic and financial capacities, which depended on the composition of their native households and their involvement in strategies of acquisition. The goal for historians is less to evaluate a global subordination of women to men, private to public, or Ancients to Moderns than to understand the conditions (social, political, generic) that construct the different forms of subordination.

Abbreviations

CIG Böckh, August, Curtius, Ernst, Kirchhoff, Adolf, Franz, Johannes, Röhl, Hermann, (eds). *Corpus Inscriptionum Graecarum*. 4 vol. 1825–1877. Berlin: Preussische Akademie der Wissenschaften.

IG Dittenberger, Wilhelm, Hiller von Gaertringen, Friedrich, Kirchner, Johann (eds). *Inscriptiones Graecae*. 14 vol. 1890–1939. Berlin: Preussische Akademie der Wissenschaften.

IJG Dareste, Rodolphe and Haussoullier, Bernard. *Recueil des inscriptions juridiques grecques: texte, traduction, commentaire*. 1965. Roma: "L'erma" di Bretschneider

Bibliography

Agut-Labordère, Damien and Anne-Emmanuelle Veïsse. 2014. Grecques et Egyptiennes dans les contrats de prêt aux IIIe et IIe siècles av. J.-C. Pp. 415–423 in *Le myrte & la rose. Mélanges offerts à Françoise Dunand par ses élèves, collègues et amis*, 2, eds. Gaëlle Tallet and Christiane Zivie-Coche. Montpellier: CENiM 9.

Archibald, Zobia H., John K. Davies, and Vincent Gabrielsen. 2011. *The Economies of Hellenistic Societies. Third to First Century BC.* Oxford: Oxford University Press.

Azoulay, Vincent. 2014. Repenser le politique en Grèce ancienne. *Annales HSS* 69: 605–626.
Barrère-Maurisson, Marie-Agnès (ed.). 1984. *Le Sexe du travail*. Grenoble: Presses universitaires de Grenoble.
Boehringer, Sandra. 2013. Vingt ans de réflexion. *Mètis* et le genre (1992–2012). Pp. 5–18 in Boehringer and Sebillotte 2013.
Boehringer, Sandra and Violaine Sebillotte Cuchet (eds.). 2011. *Hommes et femmes dans l'Antiquité grecque et romaine. Le genre: méthode et documents*. Paris: Armand Colin.
Boehringer, Sandra and Violaine Sebillotte Cuchet (eds.). 2013. *Des femmes en action. L'individu et la fonction en Grèce antique. Mètis* hors série n° 1. Paris–Athènes: Éditions de l'EHESS-Daedalus.
Brock, Roger. 1994. The Labour of Women in classical Athens. *Classical Quaterly* 44 (ii): 336–346.
Brøns, Cecilie. 2014. *Gods and Garments. Textiles in Greek Sanctuaries in the 7th–1st Centuries BC*. PhD diss. University of Copenhagen: SAXO Institute.
Chandezon, Christophe. 2003. Les campagnes de l'Ouest de l'Asie Mineure à l'époque hellénistique. Pp. 193–217 in *L'Orient méditerranéen, colloque de la SOPHAU 2003*, ed. Francis Prost. Rennes: Presses Universitaires de Rennes.
Chandezon, Christophe. 2011. Some aspects of large estate management. Pp. 97–121 in Archibald, Davies, and Gabrielsen 2011.
Chevalier, Yannick and Christine Planté. 2014. Ce que le genre doit à la grammaire. Pp. 13–31 in *Qu'est-ce que le genre* ? eds. Laurie Laufer and Florence Rochefort. Paris: Payot.
Colin, Gaston. 1897. Inscriptions de Thespies. *BCH* 21: 551–571.
Dareste, Rodolphe, Bernard Haussoullier, and Théodore Reinach. 1965. *Recueil des Inscriptions Juridiques Grecques*. II. 2nd ed. Roma: L'Erma di Bretschneider.
Davies, Angela. 1982. *Women*, Race *and* Class. London: The Women's Press Ltd.
D'Ercole, Maria Cecilia. 2013. Marchands et marchandes dans la société grecque classique. Pp. 53–71 in Boehringer and Sebillotte 2013.
Etienne, Roland. 1985. Les femmes, la terre et l'argent à Ténos à l'époque hellénistique. Pp. 61–70 in *La femme dans le monde méditerranéen* 1. Lyon: Maison de l'Orient.
Etienne, Roland. 1990. *Ténos II, Ténos et les Cyclades du milieu du IVe siècle av. J.-C. au milieu du IIe siècle après J.-C.* Athènes, Paris: ÉFA, De Boccard.
Finley, Moses I. 1952. *Studies in land and credit in ancient Athens*, 500–200 b. c.: *the Horos-Inscriptions*. New York: Columbia University Press.
Fougeyrollas-Schwebel, Dominique, Christine Planté, Michèle Riot-Sarcey, and Claude Zaidman. 2003. *Le Genre comme catégorie d'analyse. Sociologie, histoire, littérature*. Paris: L'Harmattan.
Foxhall, Lin. 1989. Household, Gender and Property in Classical Athens. *The Classical Quaterly* 39/1: 22–44.
Foxhall, Lin. 2013. *Studying Gender in Classical Antiquity*. Cambridge: Cambridge University Press.
Game, Jean. 2008. *Actes de vente dans le monde grec. Témoignages épigraphiques des ventes immobilières*. Lyon: Maison de l'Orient Méditerranéen.
Herfst, Pieter. 1979. *Le travail de la femme dans la Grèce ancienne*. 2nd ed. Utrecht: Arno Press.
Holmes, Brooke. 2011. *Gender: Antiquity and Its Legacy (Ancients & Moderns)*. Oxford: I. B. Tauris, Oxford University Press.
James, Sharon L. and Sheila Dillon. 2012. *A Companion to Women in the Ancient World*. Malden, MA, Oxford, Chichester: Wiley-Blackwell.

Jameson, Michael H. 1977/78. Agriculture and Slavery in Classical Athens. *The Classical Journal* 73/2: 122–145.
King, Helen. 2013. *The One-Sex Body on Trial: Using the Classical and Early Modern Evidence*. Ashgate: Farnham.
Laqueur, Thomas. 1990. *Making Sex. Body and Gender from the Greeks to Freud*. Cambridge, London: Harvard University Press.
Lissarrague, François. 1991. Femmes au figuré. Pp. 159–251 in *L'Histoire des femmes en Occident*, eds. Georges Duby et Michelle Perrot. Vol. 1. *L'Antiquité*, ed. Pauline Schmitt Pantel. Paris: Plon.
Lissarrague, François. 2013. *La cité des satyres. Une anthropologie ludique (Athènes, VIe–Ve siècle avant J.-C.)*. Paris: Éditions de l'EHESS.
Lloyd, Geoffrey E. R. 1966. *Polarity and Analogy. Two Types of Argumentation in Early Greek Thought*. Cambridge: Cambridge University Press.
Migeotte, Léopold. 1999. Affairisme féminin à la haute période hellénistique. *Saitabi. Revista de la Facultat de geografia i Historia* 49: 247–257.
Offen, Karen. 2006. Le *gender* est-il une invention américaine ? *Clio. Histoire, Femmes et Sociétés* 24: 291–304.
Patterson, Cynthia. 1987. Hai Attikai: The other Athenians. *Rescuing Creusa: new methodological approaches in antiquity*, *Helios* 13: 49–67.
Pernin, Isabelle. 2004. Les baux de Thespies (Béotie). Pp. 221–232 in *Les hommes et la terre dans la Méditerranée gréco-romaine*. *Pallas* 64. Toulouse: Presses Universitaires du Mirail.
Pernin, Isabelle. 2014. *Les baux ruraux en Grèce ancienne. Corpus épigraphique et étude*. Lyon: Maison de l'Orient et de la Méditerranée.
Roesch, Paul. 2009. *Inscriptions de Thespies, II, 44–87 (Baux. Fondations. Bornes. Listes de magistrats)*. http://www.hisoma.mom.fr/production-scientifique/les-inscriptions-de-thespies
Savalli, Ivana. 1983. *La donna nella società della Grecia antica*. Bologna: Pàtron.
Schaps, David M. 1979. *Economic Rights of Women in Ancient Greece*. New York: Columbia University Press.
Scheid, Evelyne. 2015. Eurykleia, une vie, un nom. *Pallas* 99: 21–30.
Scheidel, Walter. 1995. The Most Silent Women in Greece and Rome: Rural Labour and Woman's Life in the Ancient World (I). *Greece & Rome*. 2 ser. 42: 202–217.
Scheidel, Walter. 1996. The Most Silent Women in Greece and Rome: Rural Labour and Woman's Life in the Ancient World (II). *Greece & Rome*. 2 ser. 43: 1–10.
Schmitt Pantel, Pauline. 2009. *Aithra et Pandora. Femmes, genre et cité dans la Grèce antique*. Paris: L'Harmattan.
Scott, Joan W. 1986. Gender: A Useful Category of Analysis. *The American Historical Review* 91: 1053–1075.
Scott, Joan W. 2012. *De l'utilité du genre*. Paris: Fayard.
Sebillotte Cuchet, Violaine. 2012. Régimes de genre et Antiquité grecque classique. *Annales HSS* 67/3: 573–603.
Sourvinou-Inwood, Christiane. 1995. Male and female, public and private, ancient and modern. Pp. 111–120 in *Pandora*, ed. Ellen D. Reeder. Baltimore: Trustees of the Walters Art Gallery in association with Princeton University Press.
Steinberg, Sylvie. 2008. Sexe et genre au XVIIIe siècle. Quelques remarques sur l'hypothèse d'une fabrique du sexe. Pp. 197–212 in *Ce que le Genre fait aux personnes*, eds. Irène Théry and Pascale Bonnemère. Paris: Éditions de l'EHESS.

Todd, Stephen C. 1997. Status and Gender in Athenian Public Records. Pp. 113–124 in *Symposion* 1995. *Vorträge zur griechischen und hellenistischen Rechtsgeschichte*, eds. Gerhard Thür and Julie Vélissaropoulos. Köln: Böhlau Verlag.

Veïsse, Anne-Emmanuelle. 2011. Grecques et Égyptiennes en Égypte au temps des Ptolémées. *Clio. Femmes, Genre, Histoire* 33: 125–137.

Vernier, Bernard. 1985. Stratégies matrimoniales et choix d'objet incestueux (Dot, diplôme, liberté sexuelle, prénom). *Actes de la recherche en sciences sociales* 57–58: 3–27.

Vial, Claude and Anne-Marie Vérilhac. 1998. *Le mariage grec. Du VIe siècle av. J.-C. à l'époque d'Auguste*. *BCH* suppl. 32. Athènes, Paris: ÉFA, De Boccard.

West, Martin L. 1978. *Hesiod. Works & Days*. Oxford: Clarendon Press.

Wrenhaven, Kelly N. 2009. The identity of the "whool-workers" in the Attic manumissions. *Hesperia* 78: 367–386.

Zancarini-Fournel, Michelle. 2014. Les mouvements socio-politiques en France contre la "théorie du genre". Fondements, effets et ripostes. *Genesis* XIII: 201–208.

Zurbach, Julien. 2009. Paysanneries de la Grèce archaïque. *Histoire et sociétés rurales* 31: 9–44.

Index of professions and activities

English

Acrobat 140; 218 n.18
- female acrobat 83
administrator 302–303; 337; 344; 350
- female administrator 2; 131; 151; 250; 297; 333 and n. 15; 338–340; 342; 344; 351; 447–458
- male administrator 51; 59; 63 and n. 16–17; 67; 99; 211 n. 4; 346; 515
agricultural activities
- farmer, farming, farm work 2; 14; 17–18; 102; 212; 341; 367; 387; 498; 509; 551
- grape picker (female) 559
- harvesting 102; 313; 362; 522; 549; 559
- peasant 357; 549
- ploughing 21; 204; 515; 522; 550
animal husbandry 13–14; 18; 99 n. 23; 150–151; 153; 157; 196; 243 n. 56; 296
- milking 18
- oxherd 354–355; 366
- shepherd 102; 197; 354–355; 357; 366; 392 n. 11; 407
- swineherd 160; 204; 234 n. 20
artisan see craftspeople
attendant 117; 120; 339; 344
- female attendant 44; 50; 121; 142; 337
- male attendant 528; 530; 535; 539–540

baker 198; 357; 363–364; 365 n. 35; 528; 530 n. 19; 525–540
- female baker 465; 522
- spice-bread baker 513 n. 5
banker 197
barber
- female barber 39; 517
- male barber 51; 198
boat hauler or tower 3; 154–155; 157; 160–161; 169
borrowing 63; 166; 169; 454
braider 68; 157; 159
brewing activities
- alewife, female innkeeper/tavern keeper 1 n. 2; 41; 52 n. 109; 155 n. 19; 204; 214–215; 218 and n. 17; 223 n. 26; 224; 311–319; 498 and n. 16; 508
- male innkeeper/tavern keeper 214; 218 n. 17; 313 n. 17
- brewer 313 n. 17; 363–365
- female brewer 3; 16; 20; 32; 39; 132 and n. 36; 133; 142; 151; 157; 218; 355; 364
- male brewer 3; 52; 132 n. 36; 157; 520; 527–529; 535
- maltster 160
building work 169
- female building work 151
- male building work 479; 520; 532
butcher (male) 51; 132; 136 n. 46; 528; 537–540
buyer, buying 169; 286; 463; 478; 553–554;
- female buyer 63; 166–167; 202 n. 17; 203; 238; 272–273; 275; 280 n. 13; 288; 291 and n. 37; 293; 372–374; 377–378; 380 n. 49; 380–383; 497; 505; 522; 529–531; 535–540
- male buyer 105; 375–377; 489

carpenter (male) 58 n. 7; 67; 95; 157; 160; 197; 354
chief herald (male) 117
chief of the assembly 117
chief of the storehouse 340
childrearing 177; 451
churning 8; 14–18; 20–22
cleaner (male), washer 198; 357 n. 7; 361; 481; 489 n. 58; 520
cloistered woman 24; 255–295
comedian 128
cook 157; 194; 513
- chief cook 132

– female cook 39; 83–85; 234; 236 and n. 26; 238; 239 n. 41; 250; 302; 522
– male cook 3; 42; 50–51; 154; 160 197; 363; 453; 513
cosmetic producer 39
court people, courtier 120; 126; 516
craftspeople, artisan 15; 39; 50–51; 67
– reed craftsman 157
creditor 63; 277; 289; 311
– female creditor 63; 202; 218; 272; 276; 289–291; 314 and n. 22, n. 24; 317 and n. 37; 322; 465; 496–497; 499; 502; 568
– male creditor 506
cult personnel, cultic personnel 31; 34 and n. 23; 36–39; 42; 49–52; 299; 356; 556
– female cult personnel 52 n. 109
cupbearer (male) 51; 83–84; 114
– female cupbearer 83 n. 39

dancer
– female dancer 83 and n. 36–37; 121; 126–128; 142
– male dancer 218 n. 18
debtor 276; 289; 311
female debtor 80; 202; 272; 276–277; 488; 496–497; 499; 501; 506
– male debtor 314 n. 24
diviner 49
– female diviner 47; 50; 198; 204
– male diviner 39 n. 54; 49; 115 n. 4; 301; 430
– dream diviner/interpreter, oneiromancer 42
– female dream interpreter 39 and n. 54; 47; 49; 136; 138; 198; 204
– necromancer (female) 47 and n. 91; 50–51
doctor *see* physician
domestic labor 180; 464–466
donkey driver 197
doorkeeper 154
– female doorkeeper, porter 40 and n. 67; 157
– male doorkeeper, porter 40 n. 67; 156–157; 159–160; 187; 197; 355; 438; 483; 529 and n. 17

ecstatic 439
– female ecstatic 41; 47; 49; 438
emissary 221 n. 22
entertainer (female) 223
estate manager 118 n. 10
– female estate administrator 131
exorcist
– female exorcist 40
– male exorcist 527 n. 8; 528; 535–536

female deputy 453
fisherman 331–332
food production 197; 356; 365; 462
foreman 117; 184; 186–187
– forewoman 164; 184; 185 n. 23; 186
freighter 197
functionary 81; 184 n. 22

gardening, gardener 14; 18
– female gardener 20; 151
– male gardener 10; 160–161; 165; 197; 354; 515; 518; 520
goldsmith (male) 157; 528; 538; 540
governor 97 and n. 17; 99; 150; 152; 167; 184; 213; 478; 532
grinding 210–211; 233
– female grinder 154; 179; 197 and n. 5; 204; 234; 235 and n. 22; 236–239; 241–242; 246; 364
– male grinder 237; 364–365
groom (male) 520

hairdresser
– female hairdresser 39
– male hairdresser 51
hierodule 339
horseman 522
housewife 153; 199; 228–254; 440
household manager (female) 333; 338; 339 n. 32

inspector (male) 184 n. 22
itinerant artist (female) 143

judge (male) 198; 222; 230 n. 4; 314 n. 24; 355; 364; 506
juggler 128

kitchen personnel (female) 132–133; 142

laborer, worker 1; 3; 5; 80; 93 n. 9; 94 n. 12; 95–96; 103 n. 25; 104; 109; 156; 159–164; 179; 184–185; 211; 231; 238; 241–242; 251; 310; 312 n. 13; 341; 354; 356; 357 and n. 5; 366; 481 and n. 29; 484–485; 517; 548
- female laborer 4–5; 23; 32; 39; 46; 50; 71; 73; 81; 84–85; 93 and n. 9; 94; 102; 104; 105 n. 27; 106; 109; 151; 155–156; 159; 162; 169; 183; 184 and n. 21; 186–187; 311; 313; 481; 485; 489; 548–549
- male laborer 51; 101; 186–187; 239; 549
lady-in-waiting 74
lady's attendant 44; 50
leasing (female) 1; 256–267; 275–276; 285; 291;
leather worker (male) 151; 157; 160; 509
lending 166; 285; 291–293; 300; 454
lessee
- female lessee 272; 274–275
- male lessee 288; 531
lessor 274–275
- female lessor 255–257; 260 and n. 22; 261; 272; 275; 288; 293
- male lessor 288

magician (female) 52 n. 109; 329
magistrate 558–559
maid 80–82; 151; 323; 331; 334; 341; 400 n. 28; 517
mason 126 n. 25; 160
- stonemason 126 n. 25
merchant, trader (male) 1; 82; 107–108; 193–197; 203; 280; 314–316; 324; 355; 485 n. 42; 488 n. 52; 498; 548
- street vendor 559
metal worker
- coppersmith (male) 357
- goldsmith (male) 157; 528; 538; 540
- female metal worker 4 and n. 7
- male metal worker 67; 95; 157; 197
midwife 31; 33; 41; 50; 59; 63; 65–67; 135–138; 141–142; 155; 194; 198
military personnel, soldier (male) 4; 24; 51; 78 n. 21; 108 n. 37; 211; 213; 335; 431; 464; 481 and n. 29; 484–485; 487; 490
miller 157
- female miller 3; 85; 154–156; 158; 160–162; 169; 186; 234 n. 14; 355; 365
- male miller 153; 365 n. 35; 160 (overseer of)
mourner (female) 45; 84; 438
musician/singer 43; 45 and n. 85–86; 51; 62–63; 117; 127; 155; 219–221; 356
- female musician/singer 45; 49; 51; 83; 105; 119; 121; 126–129; 142; 158; 221; 297; 300 n. 14; 302; 304–305; 307
- male musician/singer 128; 220; 251

nurse, nursemaid 3; 31; 44 n. 81; 48–50; 68; 131; 198; 204; 321–322

officer
- female officer 476
- male officer 74; 333; 337–340; 344; 350; 477
official
- female official 438; 453
- male official 24; 29–30; 57; 64; 150; 184; 196–197; 213; 221; 297; 299–301; 305; 418; 439; 453; 476; 484; 514
oil peddler 197
oil-presser 160; 520
- female oil-presser 39; 154–158; 161–163; 169; 234; 239
oblate 80–81; 461; 466–468; 482–485; 495; 507–509
overseer 65; 67–68; 160; 185–186; 280; 313; 476–477; 516; 522; 549

perfumer, perfume professions 355; 512–525
physician, doctor 4
- female physician, doctor 4 n. 6; 40; 44; 82–83; 135; 143 n. 51; 155; 300; 304; 329;
- male physician, doctor 135; 155
- women in the healing practice 3; 329–330
poet 123; 549
polisher (female) 39–40

porter *see* doorkeeper
potting 14–17; 20; 22; 24
– potter 157; 160; 197; 515
prebend owner/holder 5; 465; 480; 497; 526–542
preparer of offering table 528; 535
priest 10; 12–13; 25; 32; 37 and n. 36, 39; 42; 51; 64; 97 and n. 17; 116–117; 196; 198; 299 n. 11; 434; 508–509; 527–528; 530–532; 545
– dirge singer, lamentation priest 51; 271
– priestess 30–44; 49–52; 62; 72; 79–81; 115–116; 118; 120–126; 134; 142; 211 n. 4; 252; 270; 278–279; 355–356; 373; 378; 435; 438–440; 507; 545; 556
– head priestess 37
– high priestess 37–38; 300; 439 and n. 76; 507
– incantation priestess 35
– purification priest 155
prophet 356
prostitute (female) 32; 40; 43–44; 49–52; 59; 128–129; 142–143; 149–150; 209–227; 233; 311; 312 n. 8; 442
– male prostitute 545

reed craftsman, mat maker 157; 160
– reed-mat weaver 168
rider 39
– female rider 39–40
ritual practitioner 329–330
– female ritual practitioner 329
rope-maker 168
royal household personnel 40; 64

salesman 545
– saleswoman 545
scribe 37 n. 38; 71; 78; 98; 104; 160; 195; 251–252; 300; 330; 332; 337–338; 344; 355;
– chief scribe, chief of the scribes on wooden tablets 59; 61; 67; 340
– female scribe 4; 40 n. 68; 44 n. 81; 52; 155; 453
– male scribe 4; 40; 59; 155; 198; 251; 318 n. 44; 355; 483–484; 515 n. 17
– scribe-administrator 344
seller, selling 63, 107; 166–167; 210; 213; 264–266; 272–273; 280 n. 13; 286; 315; 373–379; 382–383; 437 n. 67; 496–499; 501–502; 505; 522; 526; 529–531; 534; 553–554
servant 80; 82; 118; 152; 199; 231; 238; 240–241; 300; 305; 311; 319; 366; 399; 407–408; 420; 435; 441
– female servant 32; 50; 57; 59; 64–68; 73; 76; 121; 130; 134; 301–302; 323; 334; 337; 399–400; 403–404; 440; 460
– male servant 33; 80; 122–124; 126; 514; 517
– palace servant 297
soldier *see* military personnel
slave 4–5; 25 and n. 51; 150–152; 161; 163; 165–166; 310; 374; 376–377; 379–381; 454; 468; 499–502; 507; 515; 548; 559
– female slave 52 n. 109; 197 n. 5; 200; 212; 218; 223–224; 234 n. 14; 240–242; 249; 307; 311–315; 318–319; 323; 341; 394–395; 399 and n. 24; 400 n. 28; 404–405; 407–408; 441; 461; 466–467; 484; 486–489; 494–498; 502–504; 507–509; 559
– male slave 33; 240; 357–358; 361; 363; 399 n. 24; 402; 407; 466–467; 506; 509
sorcerer 48 and n. 95
– sorceress 40; 48; 50–52; 436
– mother sorceress 40 n. 66
steward
– female steward 5; 31
– male steward 32; 516
supervisor 92–108; 160; 164; 184; 192–195
sweeper 154
– female sweeper 39; 154; 157

temple personnel v; 25; 154; 156; 196; 209; 223; 358; 364; 365 n. 35; 461; 466–467; 474; 476; 478–486; 490; 507; 530; 536–540
– oblate 80–81; 461; 466–468; 482–485; 495; 507–509
– temple attendant 528; 530; 535

– temple administrator 63 n. 16; 198; 211 n. 4; 467
– temple musician 223
textile work 3; 14; 18–20; 23; 25; 45–46; 50–51; 65; 67–68; 84; 90–109; 154; 156–159; 161; 164; 174–189; 195; 198–204; 209; 216 n. 16; 219; 234 n. 14; 242; 246–247; 250; 297; 300; 302–303; 305; 311 n. 5; 313; 324; 342–343; 354; 356–363; 365–366; 454; 463; 466–468; 473–493; 549–550
– carding 550 n. 5
– comb wool, wool comber 46 and n. 87; 201; 246–247; 480
– dyeing 84; 361; 366; 476; 481
– female dyer 84; 361; 366; 481
– female apprentice dyer 84
– female textile worker 3; 14; 18–20; 23; 25; 45–46; 50–51; 84; 97–109; 133–134; 142; 158; 161; 174–189; 195; 199–204; 209; 219; 234 n. 14; 242; 246–247; 250; 297; 300; 302–303; 311 n. 5; 324; 342–343; 354–355; 358–362; 366; 451; 467–468; 473–493; 549–550
– finishing textiles 198; 200; 488
– flax worker 18–19; 94; 104; 154; 157; 159; 359–360; 476
– fuller 58 n. 7; 67; 95; 100; 154; 157; 159
– making the thread 200; 246; 355; 360; 362; 479–480
– making the wool 22; 106; 360
– male textile worker 3; 51; 175; 198; 305; 356–358; 360–363; 366; 473–479; 481; 485 and n. 43
– overseer, supervisor of textile workers 65; 67–68; 92–108; 164; 184–186; 313
– plucking wool 46; 241; 246; 474 n. 5
– repairing an old fabric 103–104; 360–361; 481 and n. 27
– sewing 358; 480–481; 488; 550 n. 5
– spinning, spinning women 18–23; 46; 50; 94; 106; 133; 138; 154–155; 157; 159; 200–201; 204; 243; 246–248; 359–360; 362; 365; 375; 480; 489 and n. 54; 550
– warping 18; 362
– washing, cleaning the wool 200–201; 312
– weaver, weaving 194; 201;
– male weaver 51; 153; 157–158; 160; 186–187; 198; 200; 354–361; 363; 474–482; 550 n. 5
– female weaver 3; 14; 18–25; 33 n. 22; 65; 84; 91–111; 134; 151; 153–164; 169; 186; 199–200; 204; 234 n. 14; 246–247; 297; 303; 307; 311 n. 5; 312–313; 355; 357 n. 5; 362; 440 and n. 84; 473–493; 550 n. 5
thief 243 n. 55; 434; 438; 440 n. 80
trader *see* merchant
transporter 3; 197
traveler 202; 211; 484
treasurer 476; 549

vizier 71–79; 135

wailing/weeping woman 84
water carrier 297; 305–307; 520
wet-nurse 1 n. 2; 3; 68; 72; 74; 82; 85; 129–132; 142; 198; 204; 311–312; 319–324; 354–356; 368; 497–498; 509; 559
witch 53 n. 109; 436
woman producing wine 81 n. 44

Sumerian

abgal, abgal$_2$ priest: 42 n. 74–75
abrig cultic functionary 42 n. 74
ad-kup$_4$, ad-KID reed craftsman, mat maker 68; 157; 160
aga$_3$-us$_2$ soldier 51
agrig steward 32; 67; 516
– munus agrig female steward 31–32
munus al-e$_3$-de$_3$ ecstatic woman 47
munus al-nu-nu spinner 46 and n. 87; 50
ama-e-he-a$_2$-e$_3$ 49
ama-lul-la ecstatic woman 47

amalu (AMA.^{d}INANNA) priestess 31–32; 34; 41
^{lu2}apin.la$_2$ ploughman 515
arad$_2$ male slave, worker 33–34; 51; 152; 162; 312 n. 13
ar$_3$-ra grinder 154
ar$_3$-tu munus female royal household personnel 57; 59–60; 64–67
ašgab leather worker 58 n. 7; 63; 67; 157; 160
azlag$_2$, azlag$_3$ cleaner, fuller 36 and n. 35; 39 n. 58; 58 n. 7; 67; 154; 157; 159
– geme$_2$ azlag$_2$ 154
a-zu diviner 49
a-zu physician 155
– munus-a-zu, azu-munus female physician 5 n. 6; 40; 155

bahar$_2$ potter 157: 160; 515
munus bar-šu-gal$_2$ hairdresser, cosmetic producer? 39

dam-dingir priestess (wife of a god) 31; 34; 79 and n. 25
dam/dumu-munus-gun$_3$ female dyer 84
dam IGI a weeping woman 84
dam me member of the cultic personnel 31
dam/dumu-munus tug$_2$-nu-tag female textile worker 84
dam NE-ra woman responsible for fire 85
dub-sar scribe 60–61; 155; 160; 251 n. 88
– munus dub-sar female scribe 40; 155; 164
– dub-sar mar-sa scribe of the arsenal 160

egi$_2$-zi high priestess 37–38; 42
– egi$_2$-zi an-na priestess of An 38 and n. 43; 42
eme-bal wailing woman 84
emeda, eme$_2$-da nursemaid 31–32; 34; 41; 44 n. 81; 130
en priest, priestess 37; 41–42; 121–123; 439
munus en-nu-un nursemaid 48; 50
engar farmer 35; 51
engiz temple cook 37 n. 39; 42 and n. 74–75
enkum treasurer 42 and n. 76
ensi dream interpreter 37 n. 39; 39 and n. 54; 42 and n. 74–75; 49
– munus ensi female diviner, dream interpreter 39; 47; 49
ensi$_2$ governor 59–61; 97 and n. 17; 107 n. 35; 114; 115 n. 4; 152; 184
ereš-dingir, ereš-dingir-ra high priestess 31–32; 34; 37–38; 42; 44; 62–63; 124 and n. 21
munus eš$_3$-ta-la$_2$ female musician 45

munus ga-an-za-za 40
lu$_2$ gada flax/linen worker 360
munus *ša* ^{giš}gada woman of the flax 355; 359
ga-du$_8$ wet-nurse 74; 82
munus ga$_2$-ga$_2$ lady's attendant 44
gala lamentator 51; 62; 284
– gala-mah chief lamentator 31 n. 17
munus ga-rig$_2$-ak-a wool comber 46
munus gar-u-u female stone borer 4 n. 7
geme$_2$ female worker, female slave, servant 32–34; 39; 46 n. 87; 73; 76 n. 18; 80; 93–94; 96 n. 16; 97–98; 152–157; 159–164; 183–184; 186–187; 231; 240–242; 312–313; 391; 393; 395; 400 n. 28; 408; 441 n. 97; 517 n. 30
lu$_2$-geštin cupbearer responsible for wine 84
– munus-geštin woman producing wine 44 n. 81
munus-lu$_2$-geštin innkeeper 313 n. 18
gir$_2$-la$_2$ butcher 51
giš-kin-ti artisan group 67
gu, lu$_2$-gu flax worker 157; 159
– geme$_2$-gu flax worker, spinner 93–94; 154
munus lu$_2$-gub-ba female ecstatic 41
gudu$_4$ purification priest 49; 155
munus-gudu$_4$ female purification priest 155

guruš young man 36 n. 35; 41
guruš male worker 51; 152–153; 154 n. 17; 157; 159–160; 163–164; 186–187; 312 n. 13

hub_2-ki acrobat 83

i_3-du_8 doorkeeper 154; 156–157; 159–160; 187
– dumu i_3-du_8 apprentice doorkeeper 40 n. 67
– $geme_2$ i_3-du_8 female doorkeeper 154; 157
– munus i_3-du_8 female doorkeeper 40
$^{lu2}i_3$-ra_2-ra_2 perfume-maker 515 and n. 21; 522
i_3-sur, $^{geš}i_3$-sur oil-presser 43; 157–158; 160
$geme_2$ i_3-sur, $geme_2$ $^{geš}i_3$-sur female oil-presser 39; 154–156
munus i_3-sur emale oil-presser 39; 43; 51
igi-nu-du_8, igi-nu-tuku blind workers 64; 93 n. 5
munus IGI.ŠID-e_{11}-e-de_3 female necromancer 47; 50
ir_3 servant 357–358
ir_{11} servant 80

munus ka-pirig exorcist 40
kar-kid, kar-kid_3, kar-ke_4 prostitute? 40 and n. 65; 43; 48–49; 59; 61; 63; 66 and n. 25, 214; 231 n. 4; 233
– $geme_2$-kar-kid, $geme_2$-kar-kid_3, $geme_2$-$karkid_x^{kar\text{-}kid3}$ 32 and n. 20; 66; 150
– kar-kid-mu-gub 40 n. 65
– kar-kid-$šuhub_2$-si 40 n. 65
– kar-kid-gi-te-te 40 n. 65
– kar-a-[kid?] 40 n. 65
kaš-a gub-ba beer producer 157
– munus lu_2-kaš-$kurun_2$ female beer merchant 41
munus ke-ze_2-er-ak prostitute? 40; 43
$kikken_2$ miller 156–157; 160
– $geme_2$-$kikken_2$ female miller 154–156; 158
kisal-luh (courtyard) sweeper 154; 157
– $geme_2$ kisal-luh female courtyard sweeper 154
– munus kisal-luh female courtyard sweeper 39
kinda hairdresser 51
ku_3-dim_2 goldsmith 157
lu_2 kur-gar-ra 438
– munus kur-gar-ra 438 n. 72

lu_2-ma female diviner 47
lukur priestess 31–32; 37; 39; 41; 43–44; 49 n. 102; 62 and n. 12; 117; 124; 257; 278 and n. 8
– ama-lukur-ra 39
– lukur-gal chief lukur 39 and n. 51
lunga, lu_2-lunga brewer 51; 156; 160
– $geme_2$ $lunga_3$ female brewer 32–33
– munus lu_2-lunga female brewer 39; 51

ma_2-gid_2 boat tower 160
maš-šu-gid_2-gid_2, $maš_2$-šu-gid_2-gid_2 diviner 39 n. 54; 49
mu-zuh *see* lu_2-zuh
muhaldim cook 51; 154; 156–157; 160; 234; 236; 363
– $geme_2$ muhaldim female cook 154
– munus muhaldim, muhaldim-munus female cook 39; 51; 83; 154
$munu_4$-mu_2 masltster 160
mur-ra-aš female diviner 47
$murub_2$ (SAL.LAGAR) priestess 34–35; 37–38; 42

nagar carpenter 58–59 n. 7; 67; 157; 160
nar singer, musician 51; 155; 158; 221 n. 22
– $geme_2$-nar female musician 155
– munus nar, nar-munus female musician 45; 83; 155
– munus NAR-BALAG *tigi*-player 45
NE.DI-munus female dancer 83
munus ni_2-su-ub ecstatic woman 47
nin-dingir priestess 259 n. 20; 278; 355; 399 n. 25; 401; 409; 439 and n. 78
ninkum priestess 30; 42 and n. 76
nu-bar priestess 44; 49 and n. 102
nu-$banda_3$ overseer 51; 60
nu-$eš_3$ dignitary (cultic personnel) 49
nu-gig priestess 31 and n. 18; 33; 39; 44; 49 and n. 102; 378

nu-gig midwife 31 and n. 18; 33; 44 n. 81; 49 and n. 102; 59–60; 63; 65–66; 159 n. 19
lu_2 nu-^{giš}kiri$_6$ gardener 515
^{nu}nunuz$_x$(?)-MUŠ×PA(lahšu) incantation priestess? 35
nunuz$_x$-zi, nunuzzi priestess 34–35; 37–38; 42

pa$_4$-šeš priest 116–117
pa$_4$-šeš servant 82
– dam/dumu-munus pa$_4$-šeš maid 81–82

ra-gaba rider 39
– munus ra-gaba female rider 39–40

sa$_{12}$-du$_5$ land recorder? 51
sag-rig$_9$ type of personnel 33–34
– munus sag-rig$_7$-ga, munus sag-rig$_9$ 32–33; 50
sagi cup-bearer 51
SAL.LAGAR *see* murub$_2$
sanga priest 63 n. 16; 97 and n. 17; 286
ki-siki (female) textile worker, weaver 33 n. 22; 67; 92–99; 101–102; 104–105; 107
– munus siki peš$_5$-ak-a female wool plucker 46
simug metalworker/smith 67; 157
– munus simug female smith 4 n. 7
sipa shepherd 51; 392 n. 11
– sipa šah$_2$ swineherd 160
munus suhur-la$_2$ prostitute? 40; 43 and n. 78
munus suhur-la$_2$ female attendant 337; 339

ša$_3$-gu$_4$ 51
ša$_3$-tam official 51
ša$_3$-zu, munus ša$_3$-zu midwife 31 and n. 17; 48; 50; 66; 82; 330
šagina, šakkan$_6$ general 56; 152
šar$_2$-ra-ab-du official 184
lu$_2$-ŠE+TIN cupbearer 83
šennu priest of Nanše 38; 42
šitim mason 160
šita priest 32

šu-i barber 51
– munus šu-i female barber, hairdresser 39

munus tigi *tigi*-player 45
munus lu$_2$-tilla$_2$ 41
tug$_2$-du$_8$ rope-maker, braider 68; 157; 159
munus tug$_2$-tug$_2$-bal (textile) worker 46 and n. 87

u$_2$-hub$_2$ “deaf”, a function 36 n. 35
munus u$_2$-še$_3$-la$_2$ female singer 45
munus u$_2$/u$_3$-li-li mourner 45
ugula foreman, forewoman, overseer 51; 67; 93–95; 97; 101; 160; 164; 184–185; 187; 313
ugula geme$_2$ uš-bar supervisor of female weavers 93 n. 9; 313
ugula kikken$_2$ supervisor of millers 160
ugula ki-siki supervisor of weavers 67; 93–95; 97; 101
ugula uš-bar supervisor of weavers 93 and n. 9; 164; 184
munus uh$_2$-zu sorceress 48; 50
ukurrim priest of Inanna 38; 42
um-me-ga-la$_2$ wetnurse 49; 321 n. 60
un-IL$_2$ menial 159–160; 162
– geme$_2$ un-IL$_2$ female menial 162–163
lu$_2$-ur$_3$-ra polisher 39 n. 58; 43
– munus lu$_2$-ur$_3$-ra female polisher 39–40; 43
uš-bar, guruš uš-bar, lu$_2$ uš-bar weaver 51; 93 and n. 5, n. 9; 103; 106; 107 n. 33; 153; 156–160; 164; 184–186
– geme$_2$ uš-bar female weaver 93 and n. 9; 153–156; 159; 187; 312
– munus uš-bar female weaver 440 and n. 84
uš$_7$-zu sorcer 43
– ama uš$_7$-zu mother sorceress 40 n. 66
– munus uš$_7$-zu, munus uš$_{11}$-zu witch, sorceress 40; 43; 436 and n. 56

zirru priestess of Nanna 37–38; 42
lu$_2$-zuh, ni$_2$-zuh thief 243 n. 55

Akkadian

abarakku(m) steward 516
abultannu(m) doorkeepers 355
ašlāku(m) cleaner (of textiles), washer 36, n. 35; 39, n. 58; 198; 357 n. 7; 358; 361, n. 20
aštalû(m) musician 45, n. 85
- *aštalītu(m)* female musician 45, n. 85
atkuppu(m) craftsman specialized in reed 483 (PN); 520

bārû(m) diviner 49
- *bārītu(m)* female diviner 198

dayyānu(m) judge 198

ēmiqtu(m) nurse 198
ēnu(m) priest, priestess 37; 42; 435 n. 41; 440 and n. 80
- *ēntu(m)* high priestess 38; 44; 134; 211; 356; 507
ēpiš BALAG.DI mourner 438
ēpu(m) baker 363
eštalitu(m) female musician 46 n. 86

gallabu(m) barber 198
- *gallābtu(m)* female barber 517
gubabtu(m) consecrated woman 198

ḫabbištu(m) (textile) worker 46 n. 88; 51
ḫābêt mē water carrier 305
ḫaleštu(m) wool comber 46
ḫarimtu(m) prostitute 211 and n. 5; 213; 220–221; 223; 311; 395
ḫašartennu(m) female perfume maker 355
ḫuppû(m) acrobat 218 n. 18

igiṣītu(m) high priestess 38; 44
išparu(m), *išpartu(m)* see *ušparu(m)*, *ušpartu(m)*
itinnu(m) bricklayer, builder 197; 520

kakardinnu(m) confectioner 197
kassiddaššu(m) flour producer 365
kāṣiru(m) knotted carpet maker 356–358
kaššāptu(m) witch, sorceress 51
kezertu(m) priestess 40 n. 62–63; 43 n. 78; 220 and n. 20; 223
kisalluḫatu(m) courtyard sweeper 40 n. 63
kulmašītu(m) priestess 44; 49 n. 102; 278–279
kumru(m) priest 198

laḫḫennutu(m) female official 453
lukurgallu(m) chief lukur 39 n. 51
luraqqû(m) perfume maker 513 n. 4
- *luraqqītu(m)* female perfume maker 513

muḫḫūtu(m) female ecstatic 41; 47
marraqu(m) polisher? 39 n. 58
munabbītu(m) wailing woman 84
muraqqû(m) perfume maker 513 and n. 4
- *muraqqītu(m)* female perfume maker 513; 517
- *rab muraqqīte* 516
muṣappirtu(m) lady's attendant 44
mupištu(m) sorceress 48
murabbītu(m) 49
mušēlitu(m) female necromancer 51
mušēniqtu(m) wet-nurse 49; 198; 311; 319 and n. 49; 355
muwālitu(m) midwife 82

nadītu(m) priestess 4–5; 37; 44; 49 n. 102; 222 n. 24; 255–295; 310 n. 3; 321; 373; 439;
naggāru(m) carpenter 197; 355;
nāpištu(m) female wool plucker 46 n. 88; 51
nappāhu(m) metallurgist 197; 355; 463 n. 19;
nāru(m) musician 45 n. 85;
- *nārtu(m)* female musician 45 n. 85;
nuḫa/ittimu(m) cook 197; 234
nuka/iribbu(m) gardener 197

paḫḫāru(m) potter 197
parkullu(m) seal engraver 197
pāsiru(m) ša šamni(m) oil peddler 197
pētu(m) porter 438

qadištu(m) consecrated woman, priestess 39; 44; 198; 279 n. 12; 289; 321–322; 323 n. 69; 378; 395

rab ša rēš āli 530; 532
rābiṣu(m) attorney 198
raqqû(m) perfumer 513 and n. 4
rāzimtu(m) wailing woman 84
rē'u(m) shepherd 197; 354

sābû, sābiu(m) male innkeeper/tavern keeper 197; 214; 216; 219; 234 n. 17; 316 n. 34
– *sabītu(m)* female innkeeper/tavern keeper, alewife 41; 197; 214; 216; 218–219; 224; 311; 313–318
sangû(m) temple administrator 198; 318 n. 44; 508
sēbiu(m) brewer 363
sekertu(m) 40 n. 63
sirās/šu(m), sirāsâtu brewer (male, female?) 355; 363–364

ṣāḫittu(m) female oil-presser 39 n. 56
ṣuhāru(m) employee, worker 356
– *ṣuhārtu(m)* female employee 311 and n. 5

šabrātu(m) female administrative official 438
šabsūtu(m), šabšūtu(m) midwife 48; 198
šakintu(m) female administrator 4; 447; 451; 453–455; 476–478
šaknu(m) governor 280 n. 13; 532
šā'iltu(m) female dream diviner 198
ša mundu the one preparing groats 363
šasinnu(m) bow maker 197
ša šahlê 356
ša šamni(m) oil trader 197
ša ṭābti(m) salt trader 197
šipru(m) messenger 197
širku(m) oblate 466–467

tamkāru(m) merchant 314–316; 354
tārītu(m) nursemaid 321
tegitu(m), tigiatu(m) tigi player 45–46
tē'ittu(m) flour grinder 197

ṭāmētu(m) spinner 46; 50
ṭupšarru(m) scribe 197–198

ugbabtu(m) priestess 38; 44; 278 and n. 10
ušparu(m) weaver, textile worker 51; 198
– *ušpartu(m)* female weaver 93; 311 n. 5
– *ušpartu(m) ša qê* female weaver of thread 355; 362

wakil tigiāti(m) 46 n. 86

zabbatu(m) ecstatic woman 47
zammeru(m) singer 45 n. 85
– *zammertu(m)* female singer 45 n. 85

Hittite

munus*harnauwaš* woman of the birth-stool 330
munus*haš(ša)nupalla* midwife 330

Hurrian

alaḫḫennu flour-processor 364
elammihurri 357
iškihhuru unguent maker 355
uzzulikarû 356

www.ingramcontent.com/pod-product-compliance
Lightning Source LLC
Chambersburg PA
CBHW020602300426
44113CB00007B/476

* 9 7 8 1 5 0 1 5 1 7 0 1 3 *